AF574953

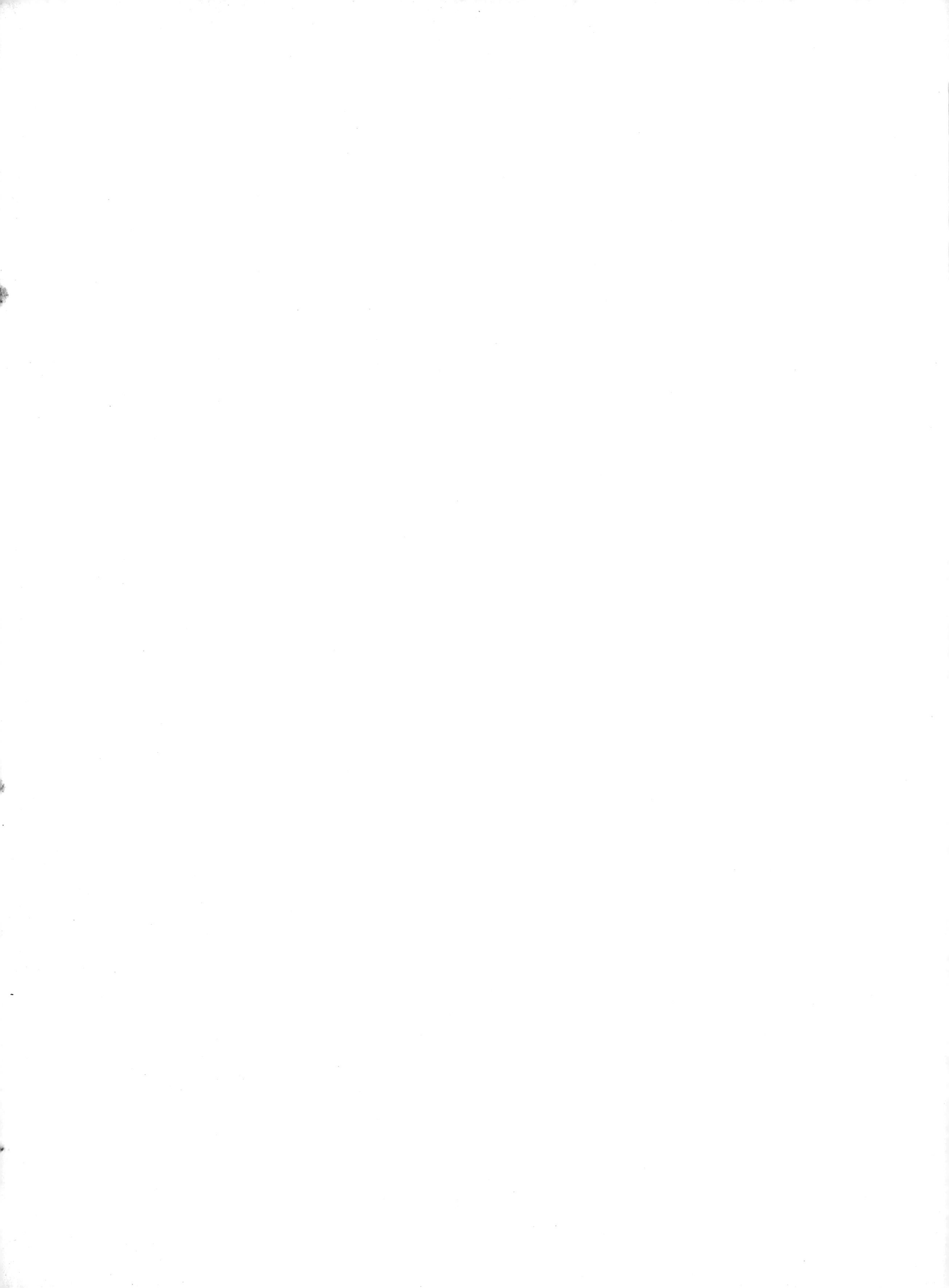

SCHOOL OF

DRAWING

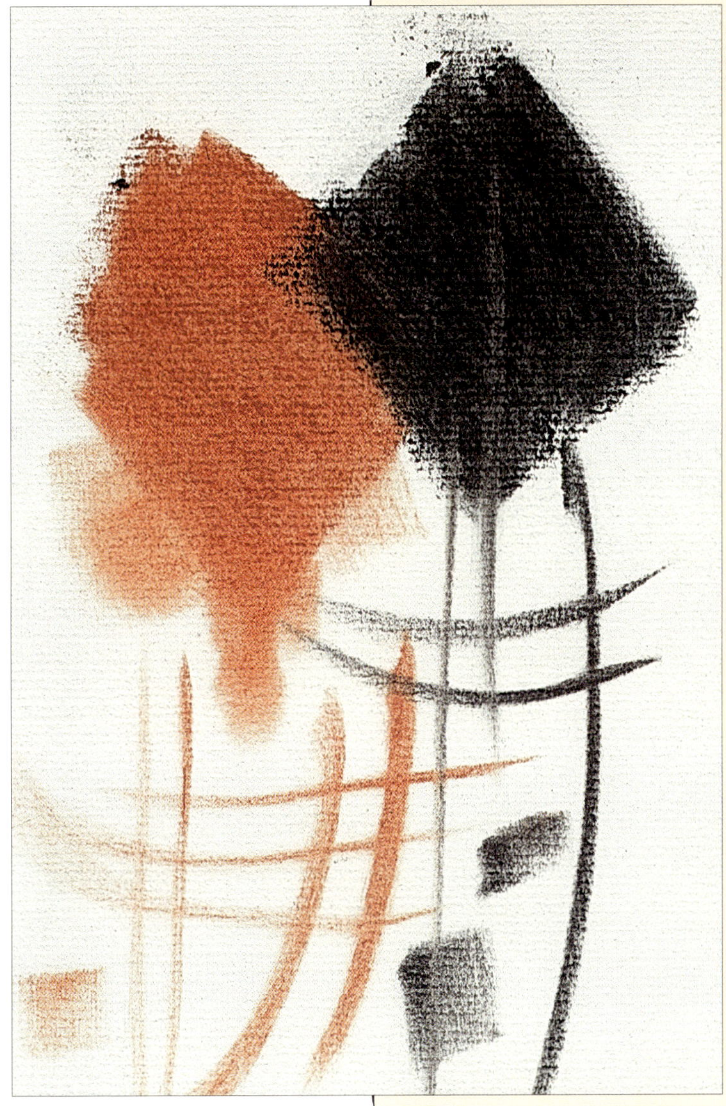

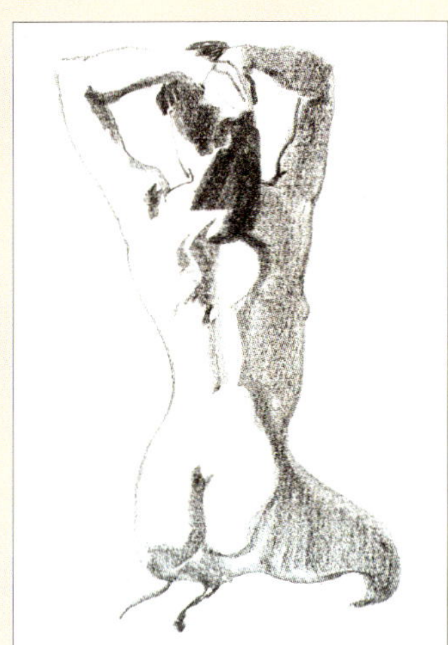

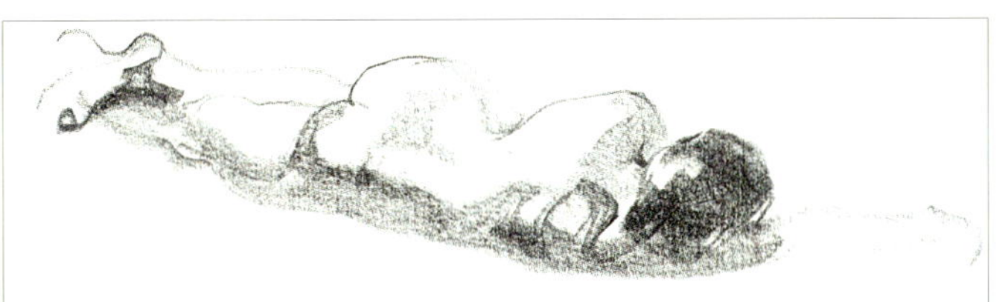

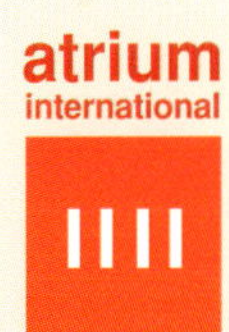

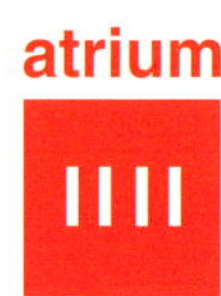

Author: Arco Editorial Team
Editor: Francisco Asensio Cerver
Publishing Director: Nacho Asensio
Graphic Design & Layout: David Mataró
Translation: Harry Paul

c/ Ganduxer, 115, 4º
08022 Barcelona, Spain
Tel.: 34-93 418 49 10
Fax: 34-93 211 81 39
E-mail: arcoedit@ibernet.com

ISBN: 84-8185-228-7
Dep. Legal: B.11779-2000
Printed in Spain
Cayfosa-Quebecor
Sta Perpetua de la Mogoda
(Barcelona)

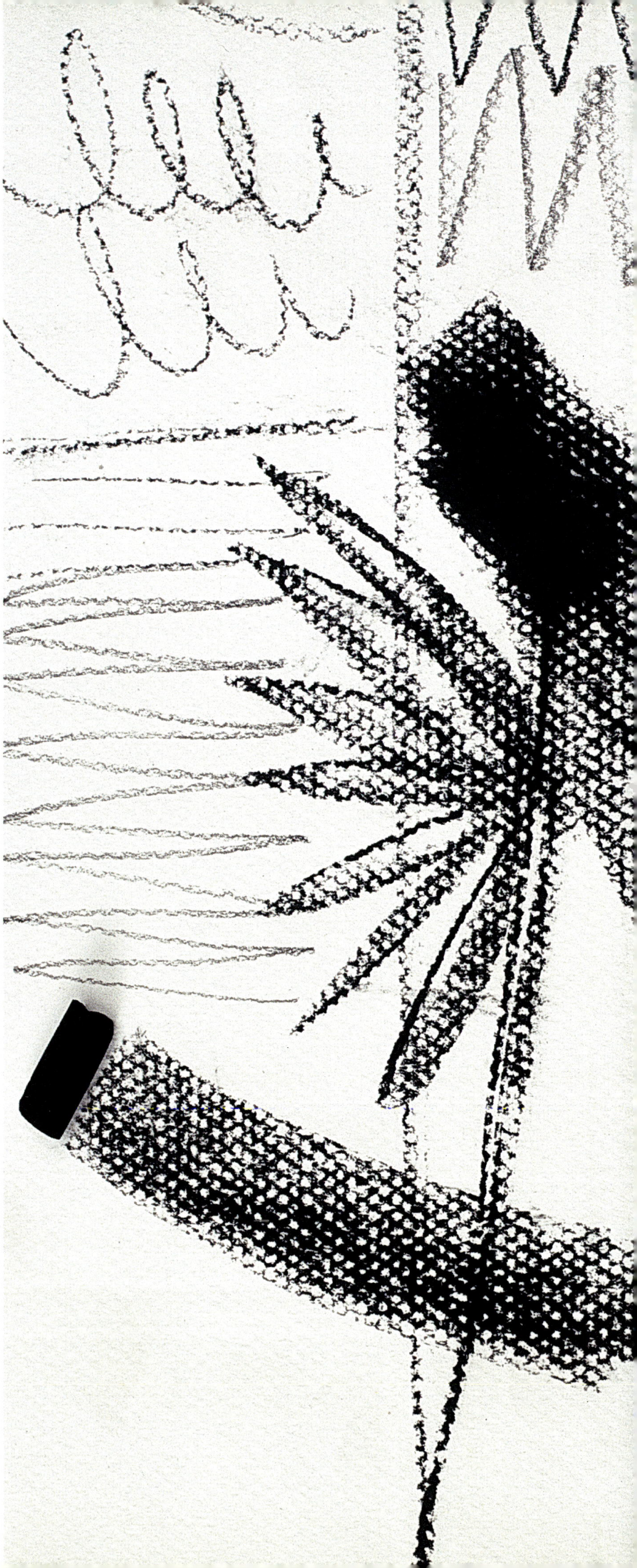

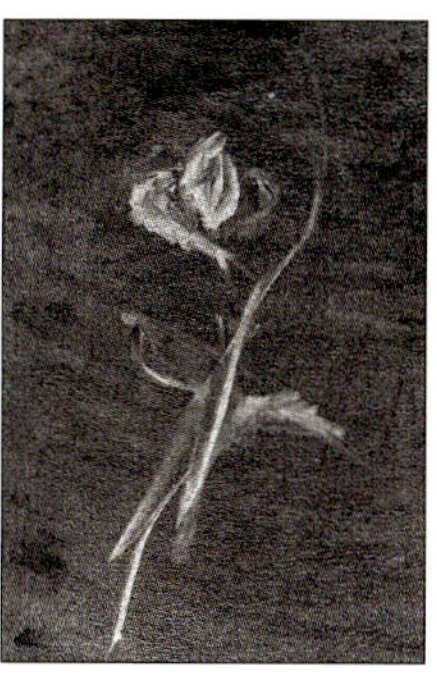

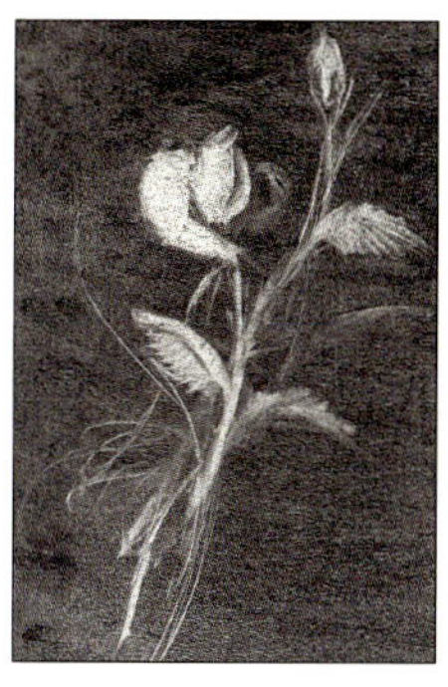

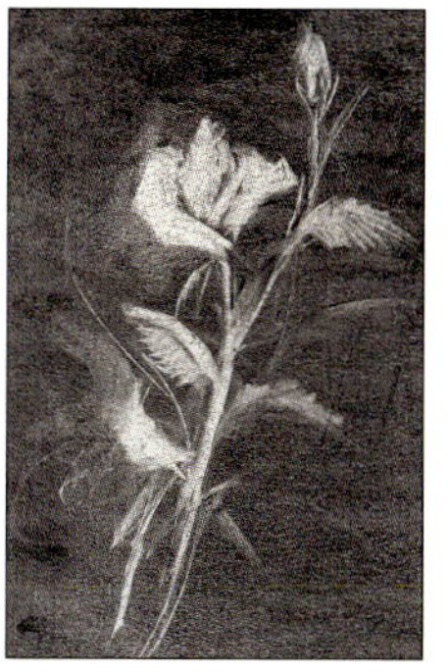

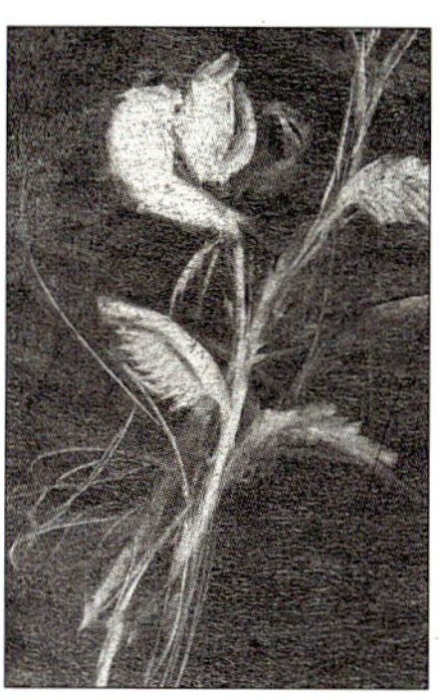

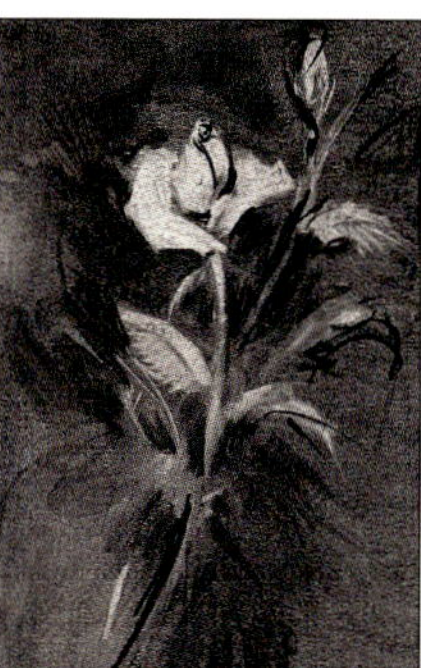

THE DRAWING is the structure upon which any plastic creation is built up. Imagine, for example, starting to build a house with the windows. It would be impossible for all buildings need a ground plan drawing, a framework, beams, pillars, etc. In the same way, to construct a painting we will need, at least, a basic knowledge of the fundamentals of drawing.

Getting familiar with these will be a sacrifice for some people at the beginning, but in a not very long run your patience and perseverance will be paid off. When a picture, be it a landscape, a still life or a figure composition is contemplated, it is not always easy to catch basic forms. Therefore, if you learn how to observe it will be so much easier to progress in this fascinating artistic creation.

A drawing can be a work of art in its own right or it may just be a probing sketch, later converted into a more elaborated piece. Whatever the case, a drawing always retains the magnetism of the first impression and spontaneous expression of the artistís intention. The purpose of a drawing is determinant in deciding its size, the mediums used and the cost of the support.

Always bear in mind that a drawing is the linear rendition of objects, an apple, a landscape, or concepts, on the carrier, which is normally paper. How these lines are arranged will determine the success of the artistís intention.
Organizing these lines and shadings creates what we call a plastic representation, and to do this we will use all the techniques and materials that have come into play in the History of Art, already practiced by the great artists who have bequeathed us their masterpieces.

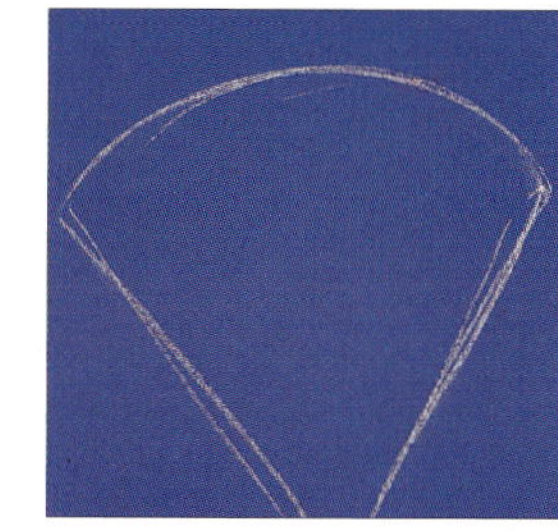

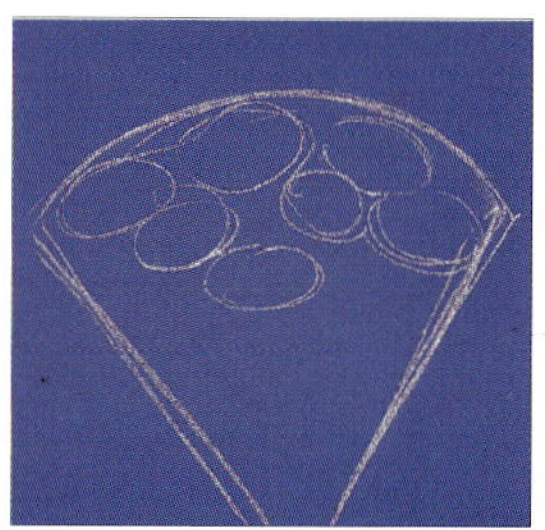

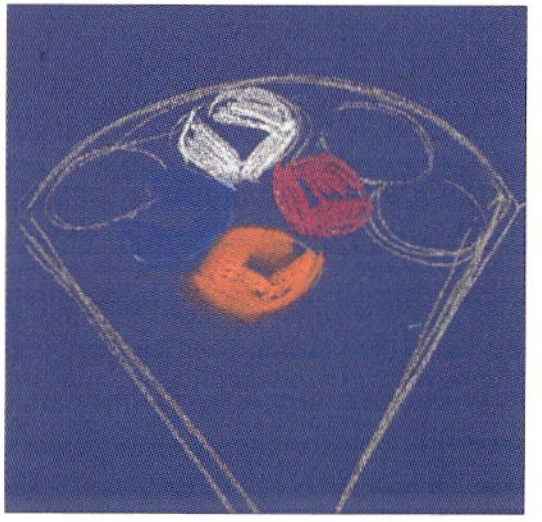

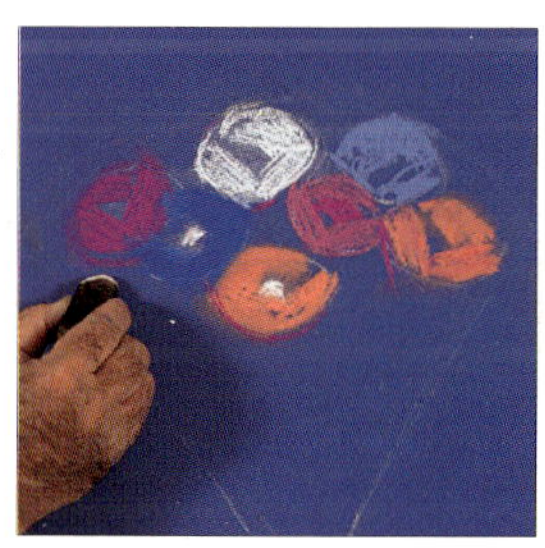

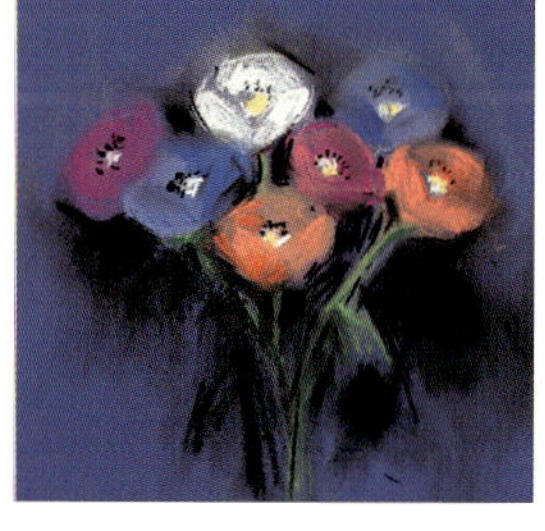

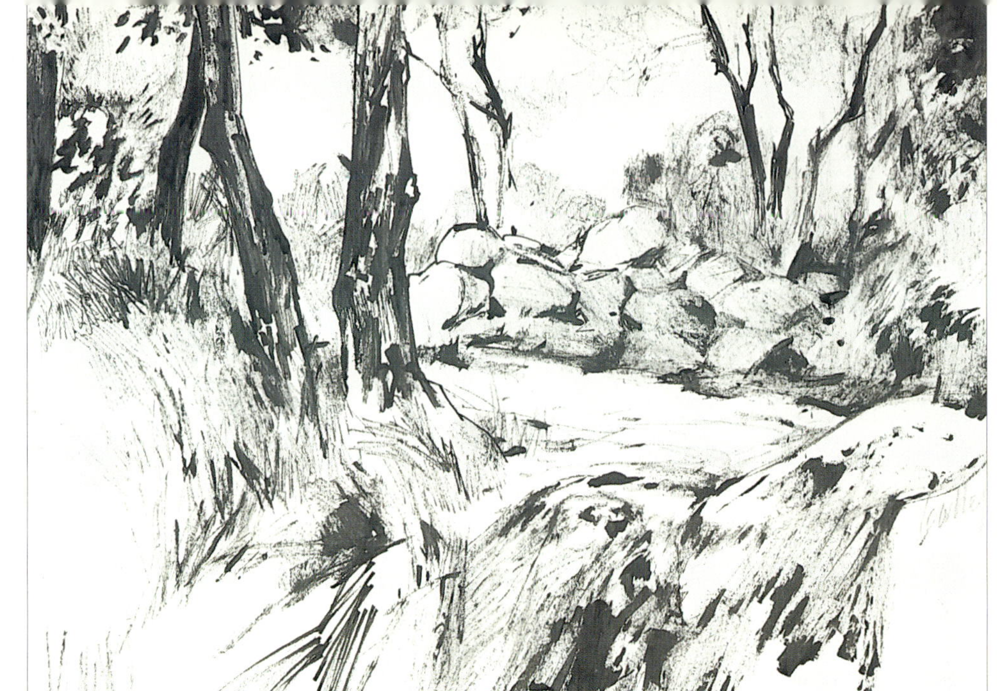

INDEX

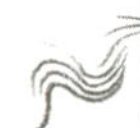

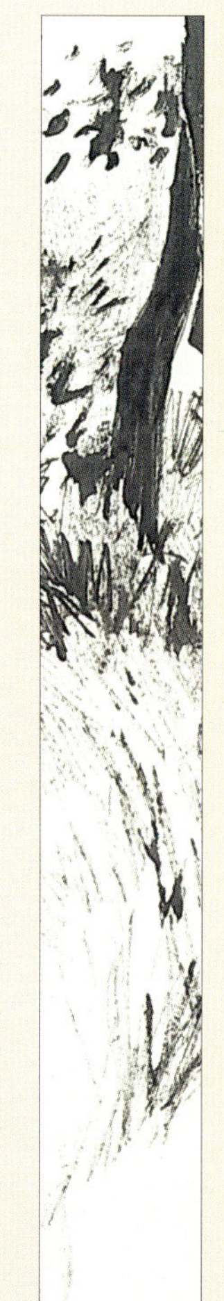

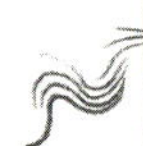

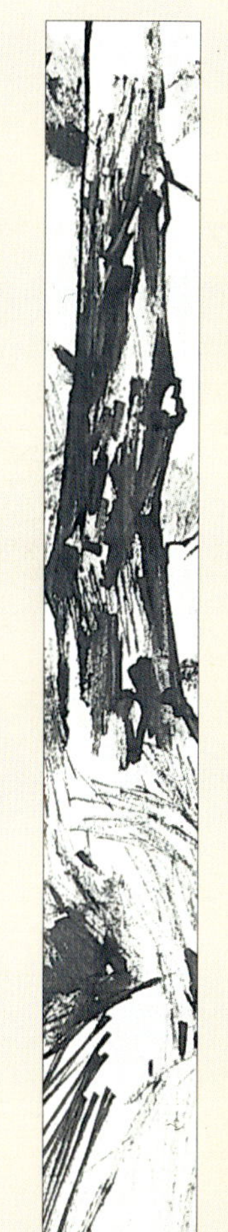

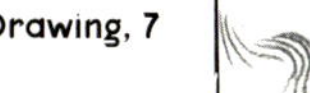

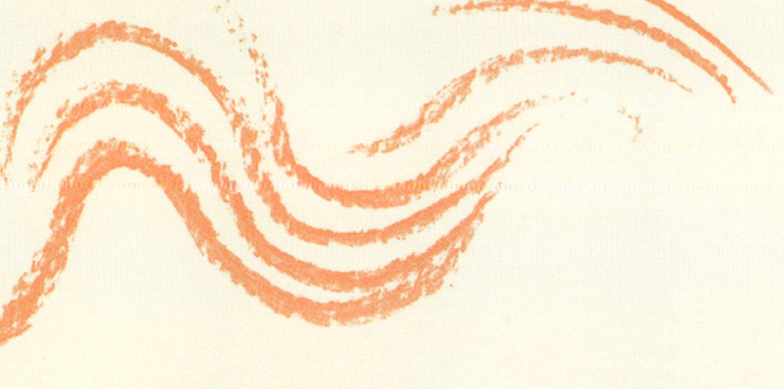

DRAWiNG MATERiALS

CONCEPTS STUDiED

- Get to know the drawing materials and tools.
- How to choose them correctly.
- Recommended material.

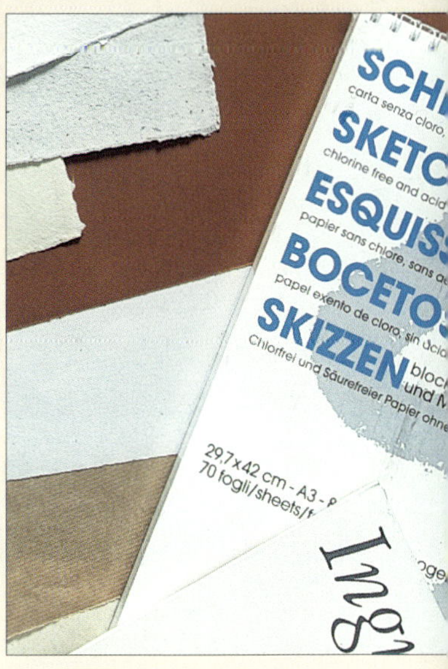

In this section we are going to explain what you need to know about the necessary materials to start drawing. It is not too expensive because you can draw on almost any surface and even a piece of charcoal can give surprisingly good results. A wide range of products are available in the market, some of them are mentioned at the beginning of the relevant exercises.

Different types of paper used for drawing.

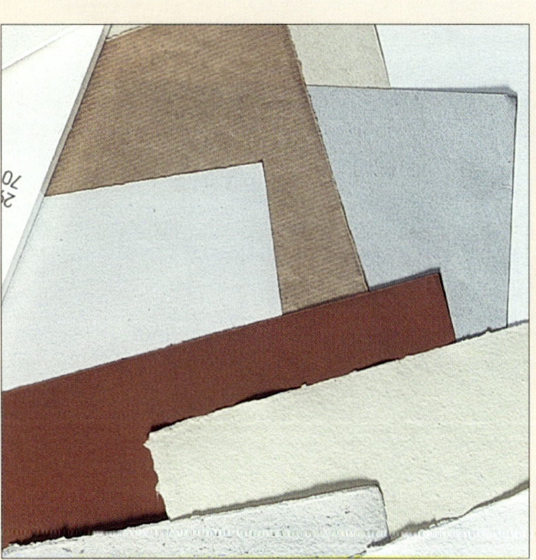

THE SUPPORT

The most common support for drawing is paper. Curiously, if we go back into the distant past, the forerunner of paper was called papyrus. Five thousand years ago it was used for drawing and writing. Then parchment came onto the scene, pushing aside papyrus. Paper was first used in China in the second century. Its use then spread to Japan a little later and reached the Arabs by the eighth century. From then onwards it was manufactured all over Europe. The first European paper factory is believed to have been in the Italian town of Fabriano. After 900 AD paper was an everyday work material in the workshops of European painters.

Today there are many brands and types of papers, all of them suitable for drawing with charcoal, provided that the surface has some ëtoothí. The paper, acting like sandpaper, wears away the charcoal as it is passed over. Every type of paper has different characteristics, not necessarily related to the price. True works of art have been done on wrapping paper. All types of paper can be used, and, in fact, you will learn by trying them out.

Certain papers, like Ingres and Canson, are especially suitable for charcoal drawing. Their toothed, textured surface favors the charcoal marks. Good quality papers have a watermark and are available in the shops in a variety of presentations, loose leaf, blocks, note-books or small, multi-sized folders. Loose sheets normally measure 65 by 50 cm. Sometimes the size is revealed by the DIN system, the measurements of which increase by a factor of two. The smallest is DIN A-5, 210 by 148 mm, and the biggest is DIN A-1, 841 by 591 mm.

The grain establishes its weight per square meter. Thick, hand-made papers are 600g and sheets of writing paper are 85g per square meter. Papers come in a wide variety of colors, something which you can learn to put to good use.

In this photo we show some of the papers used for drawing, ranging from those that compete on price, through to high quality, hand-made ones. For unparalleled excellence they cannot be beaten.

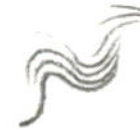

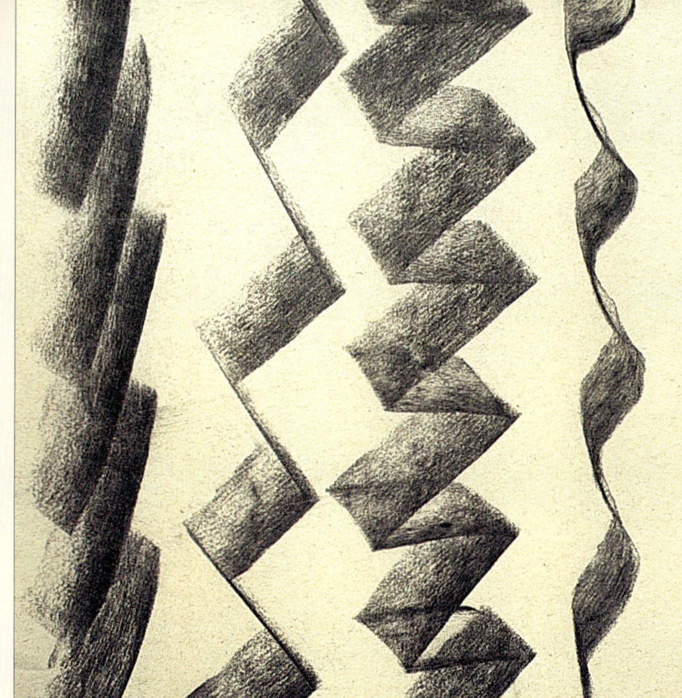

Different charcoal strokes.

OILED CHARCOAL

Oiled charcoal is sold in short bars. Its hardness is indicated by the letters H or B, the former being the hardest: the higher the preceding number is, the harder it is. The opposite is true of the B crayons: the higher the number, the softer the crayon is. So, for example, a 4B is softer than a 2B, which is not so hard as a 2H.

Oiled charcoal is darker than normal charcoal, and is therefore useful for getting deep blacks and bringing out the contrast in a drawing. However, it is difficult to rub out, so be careful using it.

THE TOOLS.

To draw well it is indispensable to have the basic tools. We will now explain the "kit".

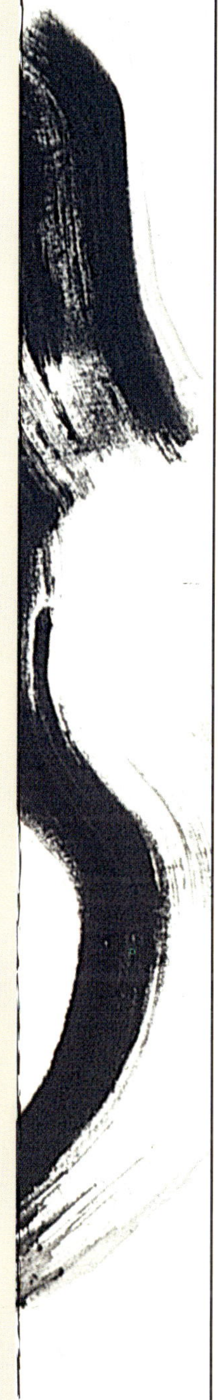

CHARCOAL

To draw with charcoal we use branches or twigs of carbonized wood. Different trees provide this "raw material", willow, walnut trees, etc. The crayon can vary in thickness and hardness. Charcoal is good for shading as it is easy to handle and can cover wide areas. In Fine Arts shops the bigger sticks or crayons are normally sold loose, while the thinner ones come in cases of five or six. Thin crayons give fine lines and thick chunks are ideal for shading wide spaces.

Charcoal is easy to rub off, or "retrieve", with a cloth or eraser. Its lack of adhesiveness also means that it is easily knocked off, inadvertently, so it must be fixed with a varnish. This is normally sold as an aerosol which sprays on an even layer. Putting it on with a brush would be tricky and would probable smudge the drawing.

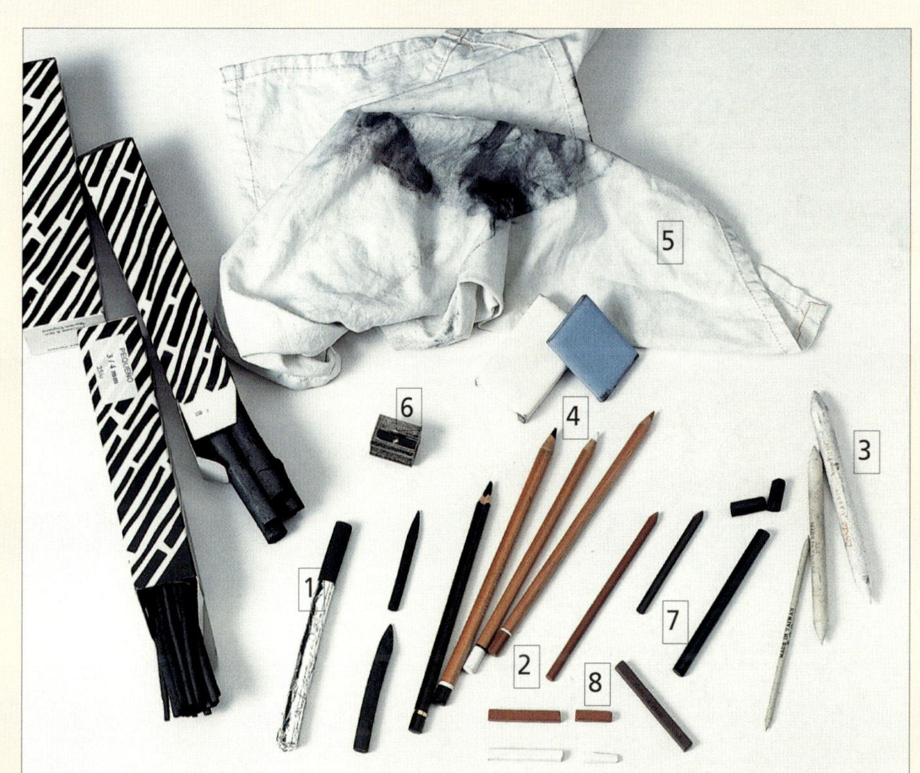

Different types of charcoal and other implements: charcoal stick (1), charcoal pencil (2), stumps (3), putty eraser (4), cotton cloth (5), pencil sharpener (6), different colored chalks, white, sanguine and sepia (7 and 8).

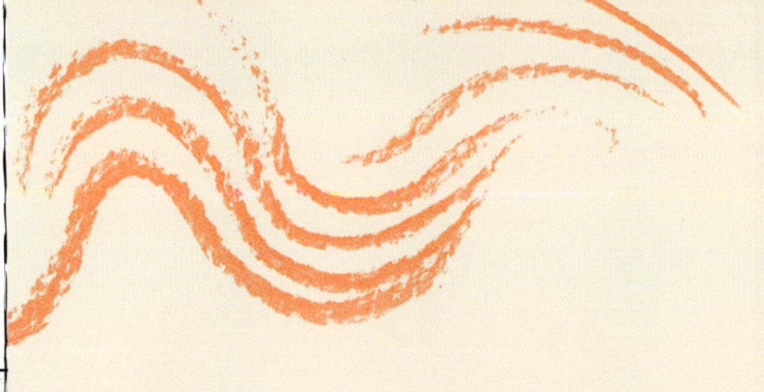

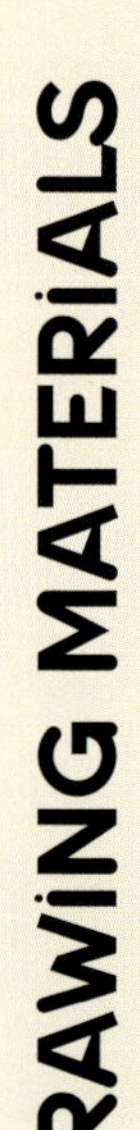

CHALKS

Chalks come in bars, like oiled charcoal, made of inert pigments. The colors vary as they are mixed with colored earth materials like sanguine, a dark red color, or sepia, which is a dark brown dyestuff of animal origin. White chalk is also sold and is very useful for drawing on tinted paper (also called colored paper) and for resolving highlights, the spots of greatest illumination. Chalks were used by the classic painters of the Renaissance to do beautiful works. When combined with charcoal interesting effects are achieved.

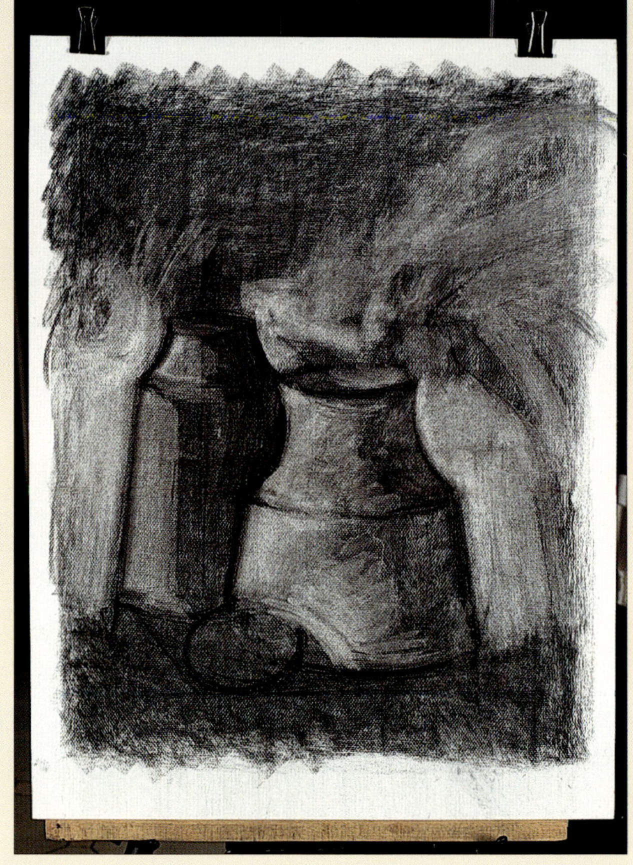

Style life written with oiled charcoal and charcoal crayon.

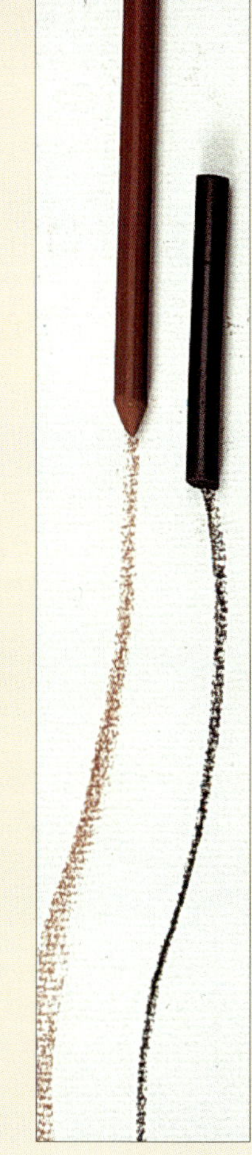

Different chalks and different strokes on paper.

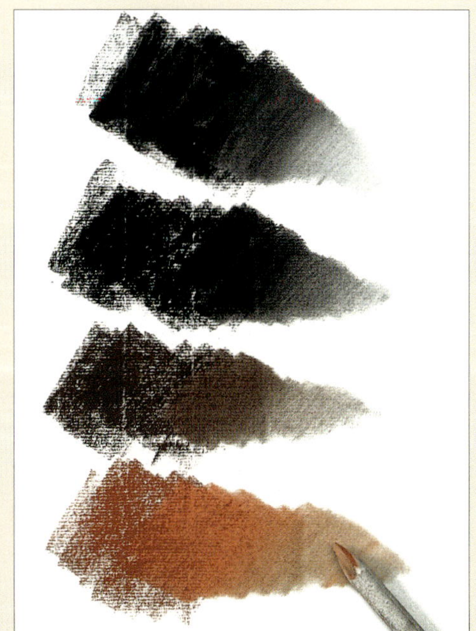

Different charcoal and chalk shadings stumped.

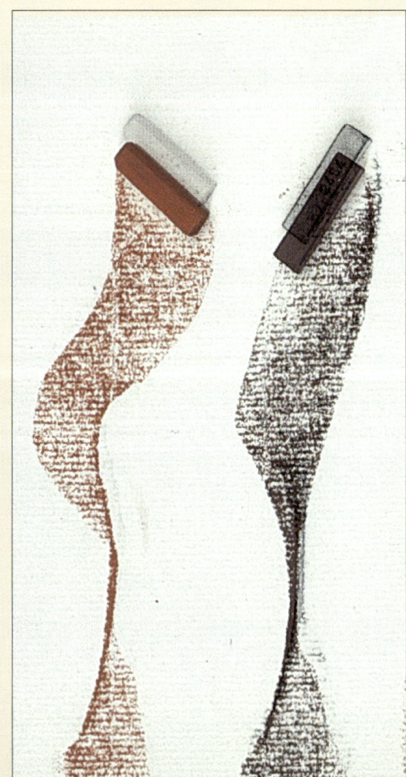

Different strokes done with oiled charcoal.

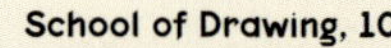

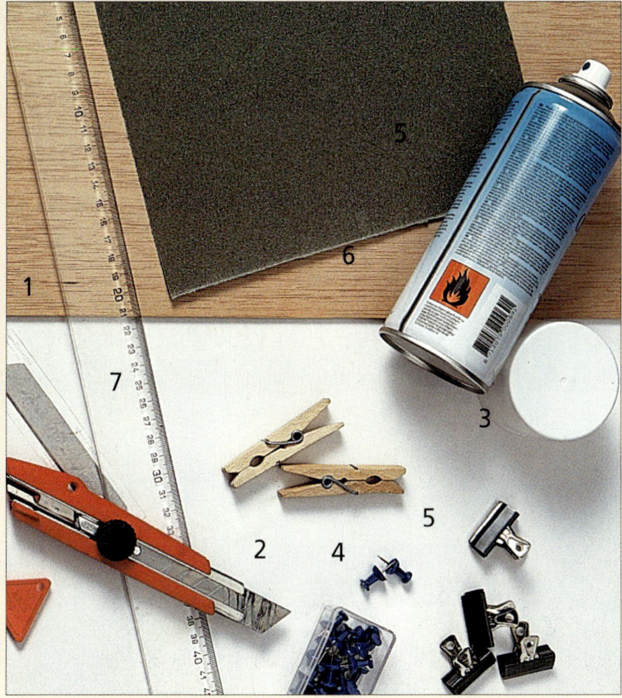

A board (1), cutter (2), spray fixer (3), drawing pins (4), pegs (5), sandpaper (6), a ruler (7).

AN ERASER

The putty eraser rubs out but it also can be used as a constructive drawing implement. As we will see later, it can draw lines in negative. This sticky rubber picks up the charcoal particles and cleans the desired zone, either removing the error or opening up an illuminated zone. Synthetic erasers have hard edges, something which can produce interesting effects.

White chalk, a sanguine crayon, a white pencil and different strokes.

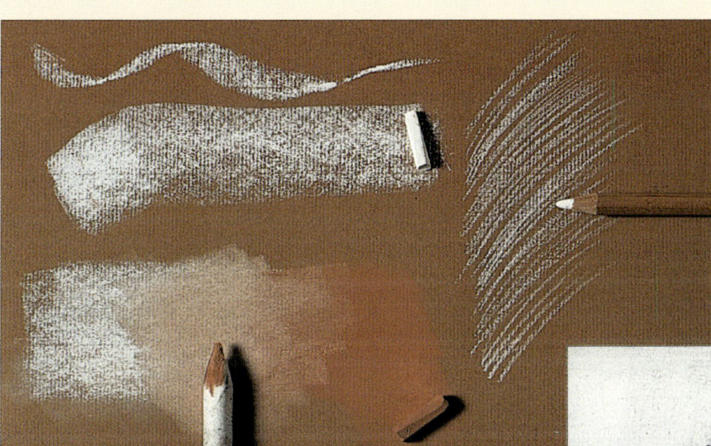

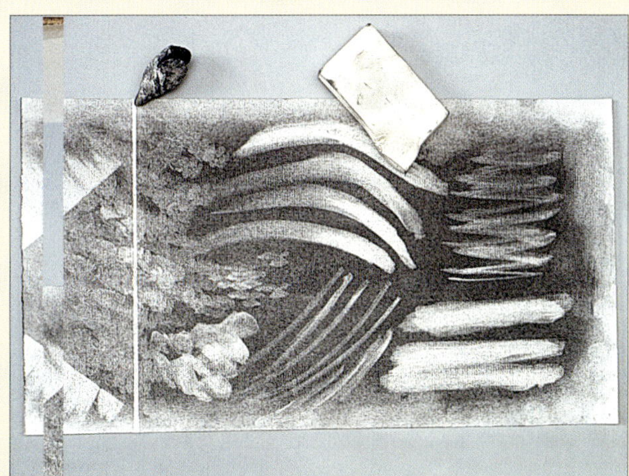

Various charcoal and chalk shadings gone over with the eraser.

THE CLOTH

A cotton cloth is indispensable when drawing with charcoal. It can spread or erase the charcoal in different gradations, working as a stump.

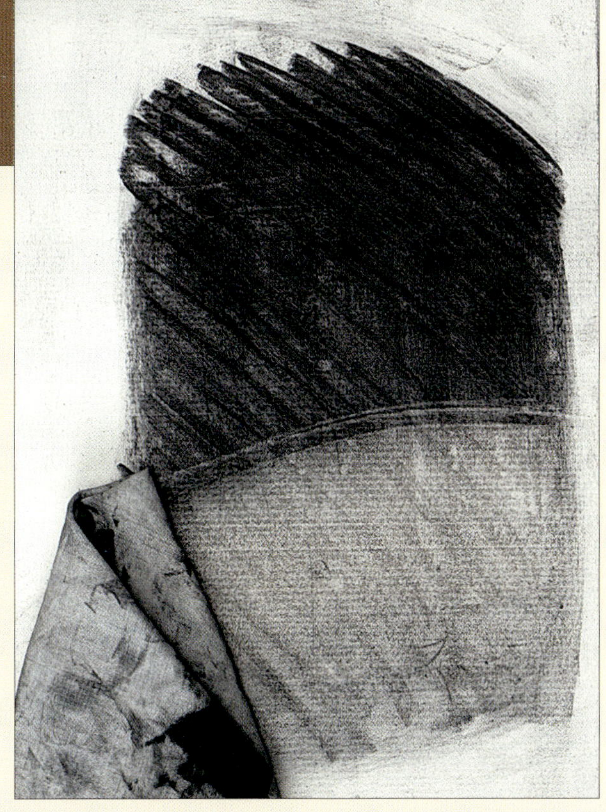

The cloth allows the strokes to be rubbed like this.

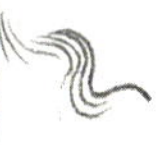

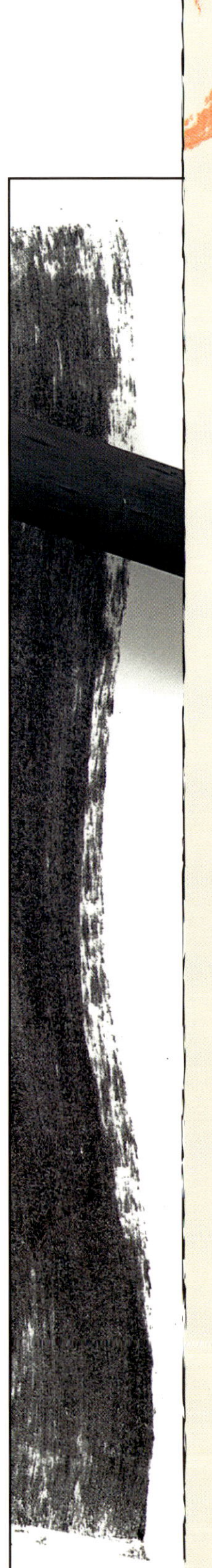

Clips and pegs (1), a board (2), spray fixative (3), charcoal (4), and cloth (5).

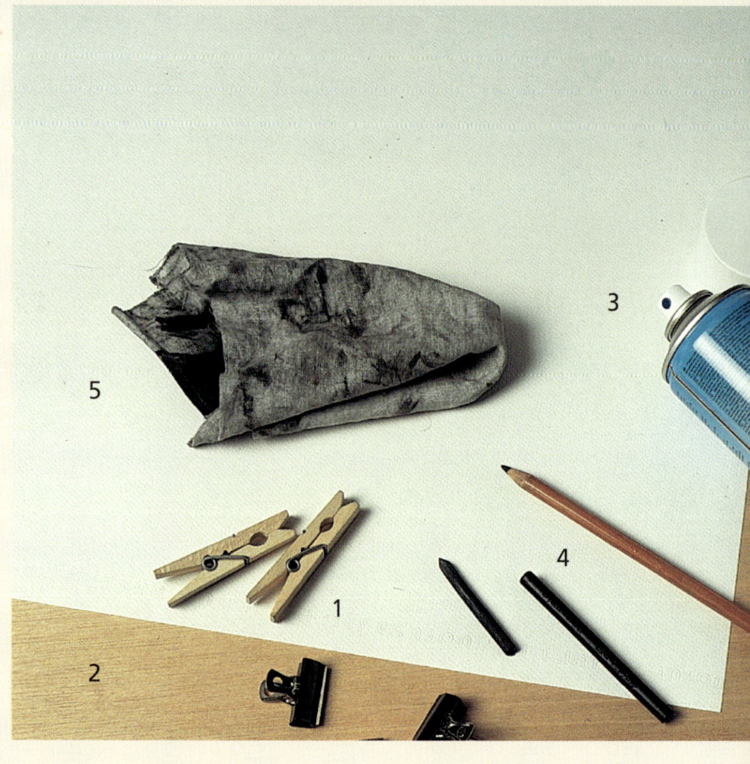

THE STUMP

A stump is normally a cylindrical piece of paper rolled up into a point, the diameter of which can vary. They can be used as cleaners, too, but they are especially useful for doing soft gradations from one tone to another, substituting the fingers. A stump is good for getting medium tones, softening outlines and for sizing. The material remains that stick to the stump can be used to do lines and shadings characterized by their softness.

PEGS OR CLIPS

Any shop for artists will have clips for holding the paper to the board in stock. They come in different sizes and in different materials, metal ones being the most common. Even clothes pegs or drawing pins will do if you have nothing else. Just stick them into the board.

THE BOARD

A board is necessary because the paper must be held firmly to a solid support. Any plywood at least 5mm thick is good enough. Chipboard can also be used but normally it is thicker, heavier and, therefore, more cumbersome. A folder can be leant on but the paper still has to be held down.

Sanguine and charcoal strokes realized with a stump.

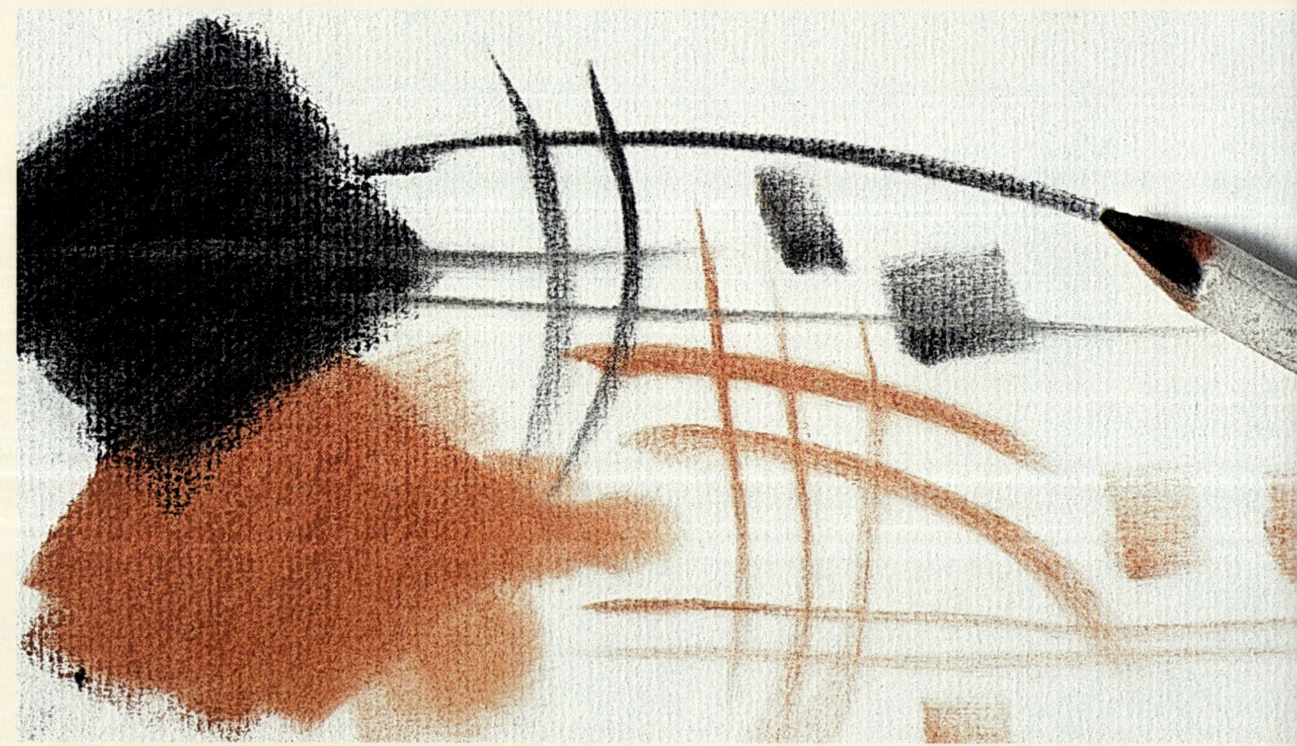

SPRAY FIXATIVE

As charcoal lacks adhesiveness it needs to be preserved by spraying an aerosol varnish on to it. Try to spread the varnish uniformly over all the drawing surface, being careful not to get too near. The recommended distance will be on the side of the can. It is better to do several thin layers instead of one thick one. Do not overuse it.

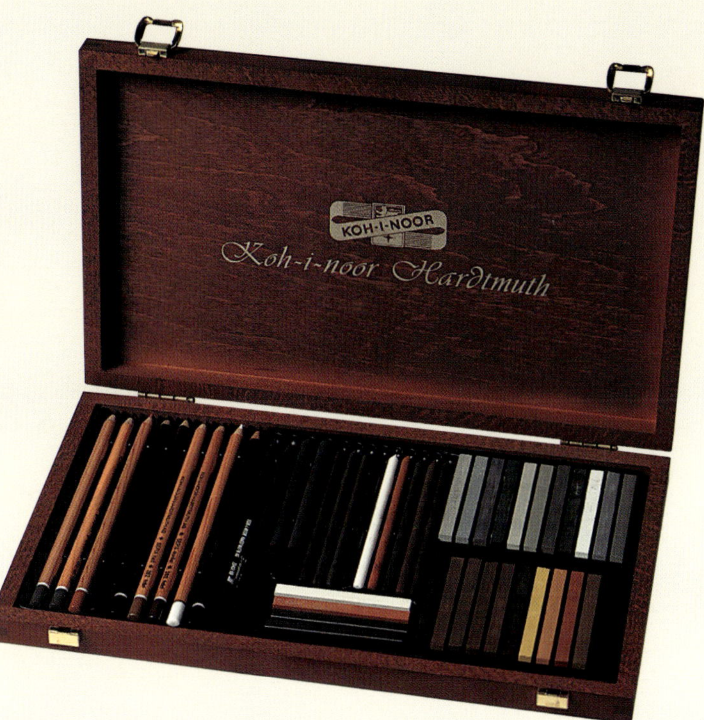

A box of white chalks and charcoal crayons.

A range of pencils varying in hardness

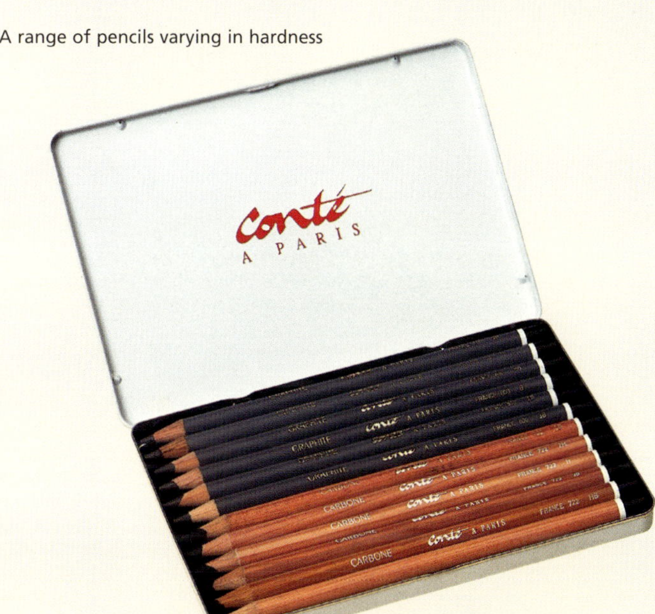

Charcoal sticks, sharpened with sandpaper, and putty erasers.

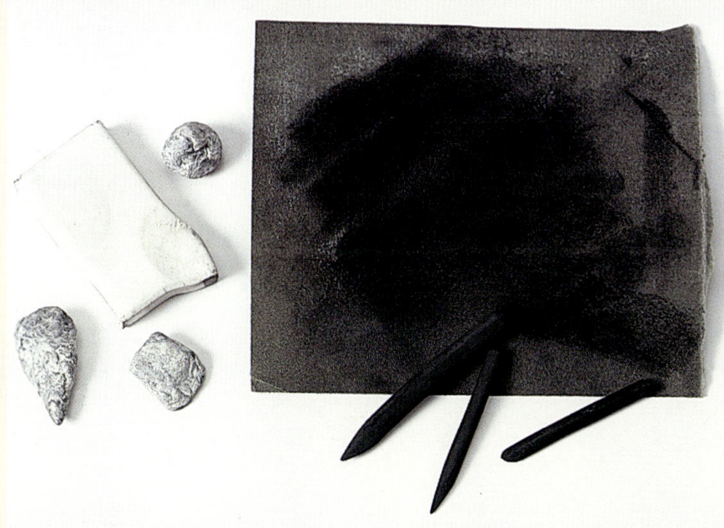

OTHER MATERIALS

Other recommendable materials are a cutter, sandpaper for sharpening charcoal, and, of course, an easel for supporting and holding the board.

The materials you need depend on what and how you are drawing. Look after your implements well but do not let this get in the way of getting the most out of them. They must adapt to your needs.

All the materials can be acquired separately. However, there are cases or boxes available which make up working kits. In these every crayon or pencil has its own place so they are easy to keep tidy and in good condition.

It is always worthwhile trying out the materials before going on to complex themes or compositions. In the exercises throughout this book we are going to use different materials in different combinations. Our aim is not to do important works of art but simply to pick up experience and learn how to get different effects.

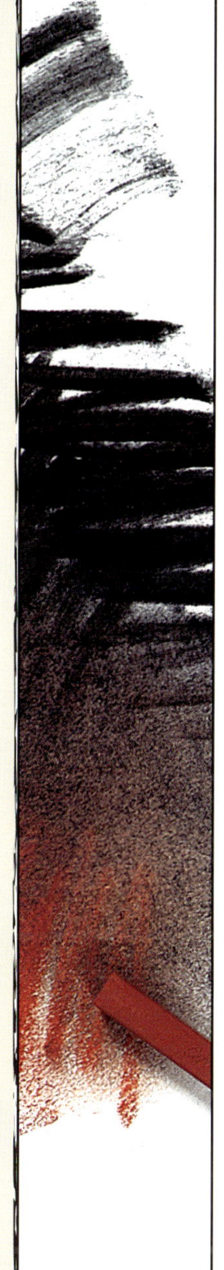

CHARCOAL. THE FIRST STROKES.

1

Charcoal, the easiest drawing medium to use, is applied intuitively, picking up a feel for it as you go along. As a drawing tool it is almost like an extension of the fingers. Another characteristic is that its softness means errors are easy to correct.

In this first chapter on charcoal we will set forth the basic notions which will enable the learner to become familiar with this drawing medium. We will explain the materials necessary to start drawing and some techniques vital for getting the most out of charcoal drawing.

MATERIALS NECESSARY TO DRAW IN CHARCOAL

The materials necessary to start drawing in charcoal are the following:

-Charcoal crayons
-Paper
-A soft eraser
-A cloth
-Drawing pins or pegs
-A support board
-Spray fixer

Charcoals are available in boxes or as individual sticks. As they are quickly used up it is advisable to buy several at the same time.

The same commentary can be made of the paper, too. It need not be high quality when you begin or when you are doing tests. Some paper manufacturers sell paper by the weight, which works out much cheaper.

In the market there are a wide range of charcoal erasers. However, the best ones are the softest and most malleable.

The following complementary elements are necessary: a cloth to shake off the charcoal and to clean up, a stiff folder or a board for supporting the paper, and drawing pins or pegs to hold the paper in place.

CHARCOAL OR A CHARCOAL PENCIL?

Charcoal comes in two different forms, in a pencil or in a stick, also called a crayon. The latter gives a great variety of strokes, from thick to thin. You can even paint with it or draw using all its length. The pencil offers less possibilities because you are limited to the tip. Moreover, a charcoal pencil is very fragile: if it falls to the ground the lead will probably break.

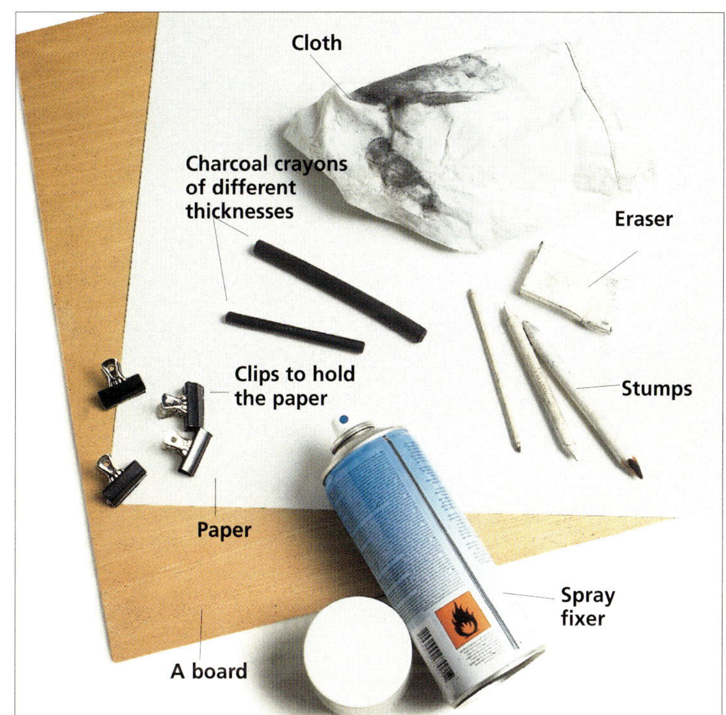

Basic material necessary to draw with charcoal.

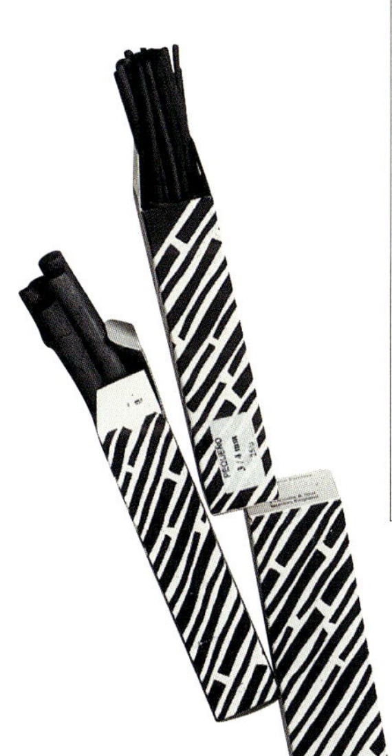

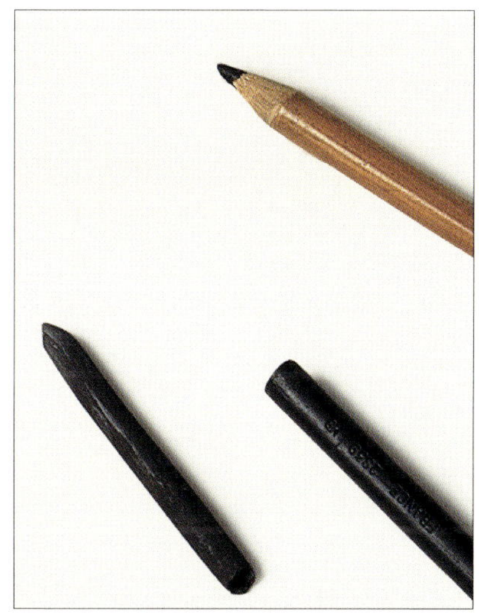

A charcoal pencil does not allow you to draw with all the surface. This is one advantage of a charcoal crayon.

THE THICKNESS OF THE CHARCOAL.

In the Fine Arts shops charcoal crayons come in a wide range of thicknesses. The thicker the better for even thick crayons can realize fine strokes, just like the thin sticks. However, only the latter do not offer the possibility of doing thick lines.

CHARCOAL. THE FIRST STROKES.

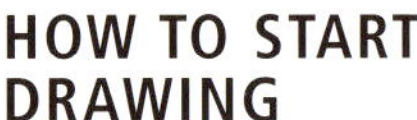

THE CHARCOAL STROKE.

Charcoal offers immense drawing possibilities. A stroke is no more than the mark of the charcoal on the paper. The shapes formed come from flat strokes, precise ones, or long drawn-out movements. In this illustration by **T.A. Steinlen (1859-1923), "A woman resting"**, you can clearly see how he took advantage of the strokes. The background was done with flat strokes, while the body was realized with the point of the charcoal.

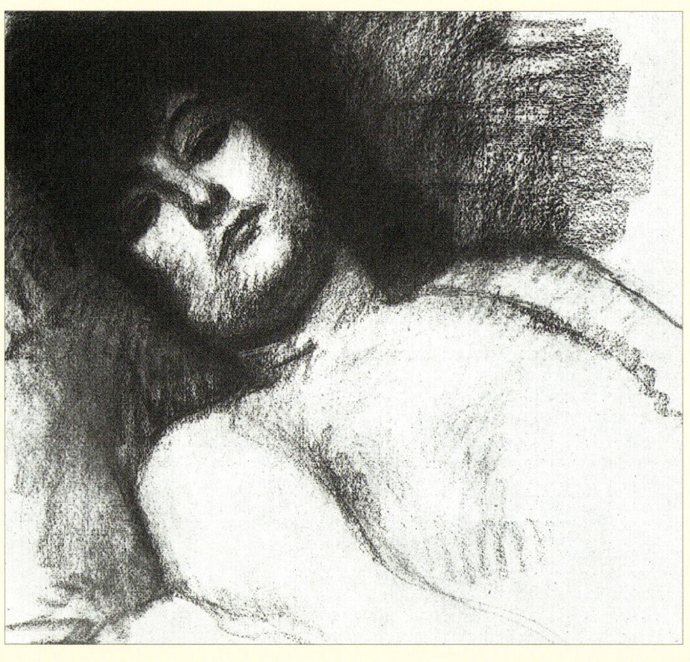

HOW TO START DRAWING

The way you approach the drawing medium is fundamental if you want to go on to master it. This is why it is important to follow the steps laid out in the following pages. Read the explanatory texts and use the drawings as models.

BREAKING THE CRAYON

The crayon you bought in the shop is certainly too long and awkward to draw with. The first thing you must do before starting to draw is to break it into comfortable chunks which snugly fit into your hand.

Do not be afraid to break the charcoal into chunks four or five centimeters long.

The bar snaps easily as charcoal is extremely brittle. Just press it a little to obtain the chunks necessary for drawing, neither too short nor too long. Depending on the type of drawing you are going to do, four or five centimeter fragments will give good results.

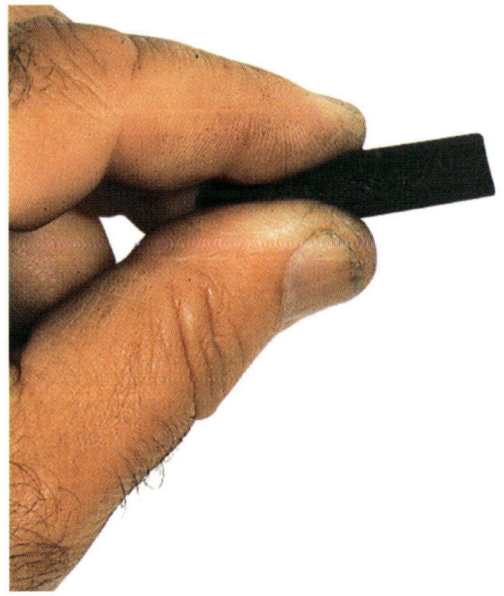

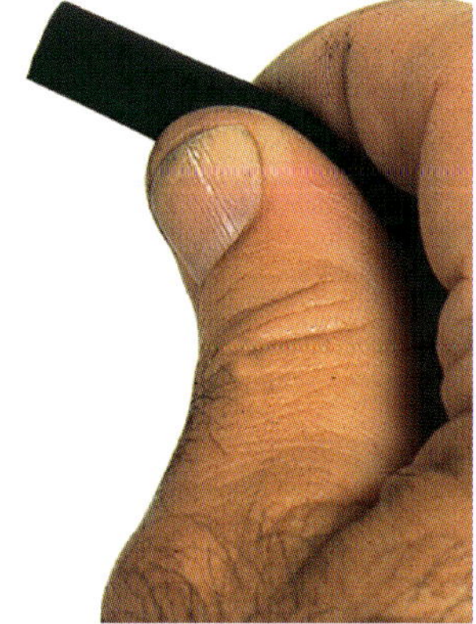

Break the charcoal stick freely into fragments four or five centimeters long.

HOW TO HOLD THE CRAYON

All the surface of the crayon is usable for drawing and painting. It will shade the paper widthwise or lengthwise, and, of course, the tip can also be used. So the way you grip the charcoal is very important.

THE CHARCOAL TIP

Holding the crayon vertical and using the tip gives precise, very controlled lines. By pressing hard you can draw dense lines. However, drawing with the charcoal point makes it difficult to totally dominate the line because everything depends on a very small surface: the charcoal tip.

FLAT AND VERTICAL CHARCOAL STROKES

Using the charcoal flat and vertical on the paper, you will be sure to do straight lines. As all the length of the crayon draws the line, the stroke will not be shaky. However, it is not possible to draw curves this way.

THE CHARCOAL FLAT AND SIDEWAYS

Once again place the crayon flat on the paper, but this time horizontally. This stroke will use all the width of the charcoal crayon and is especially suitable for covering large areas.

HOW TO HOLD THE CRAYON.

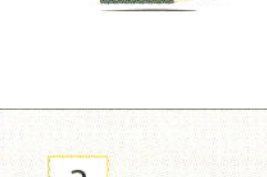

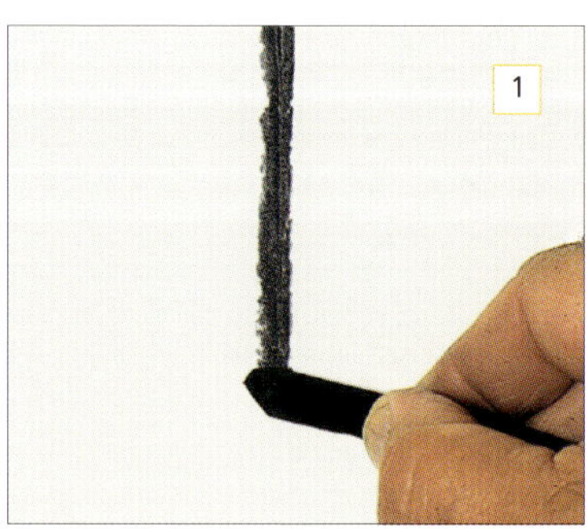

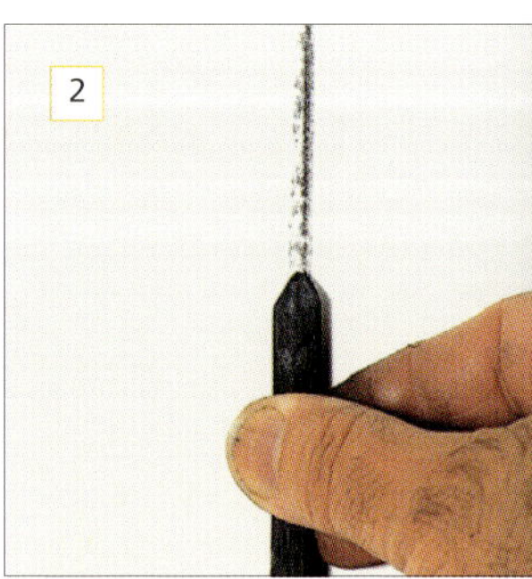

1· The charcoal point.

2· The charcoal flat and vertical.

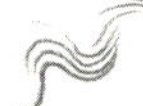

SCRAPING THE PAPER

There is no better way of starting to draw than by making marks on the paper. Do not be afraid of the drawing tools: with time and practice you will pick up the habit intuitively and naturally.

Start by doing some loose strokes on the paper. Take note of the way the tip can be used. The stroke is made applying medium pressure, without breaking the bar. To draw these lines the hand gesture must be accompanied by the wrist. This first exercise is important to learn how to master the stroke.

DOING LINES

To get the effect you are looking for from the stroke, many types of lines have to be tried out so start experimenting freely. Although it is not a highly entertaining exercise it will enable you to develop your control of the drawing. In fact, all the exercises done in charcoal will give you confidence when drawing with the other media.

First of all draw a vertical line, holding the charcoal as if it were a pencil. As the chunk here is small, it fits nicely into the palm of the hand. Next to the vertical line, do another one as parallel as you can make it. After doing a series of lines like this, draw some lines that curve to the right at the end. Repeat this exercise as many times as is necessary.

To start off the process do some free strokes on the paper. This will help you to master the drawing tool.

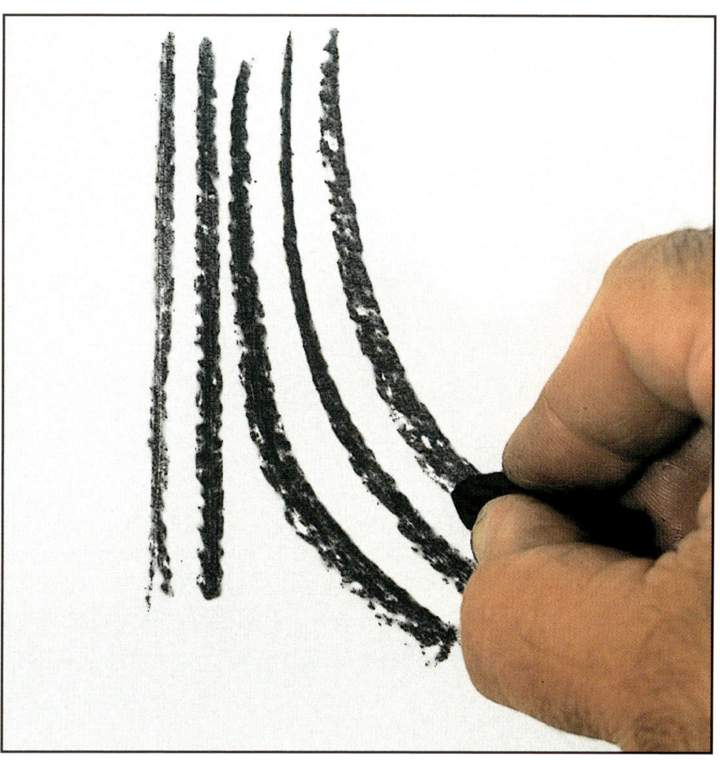

Draw vertical and curved lines holding the charcoal as if it were a pencil. Repeat the exercise until you perfectly master the stroke.

DRAWING AS IF IT WERE A PENCIL

At some time everyone has done doodlings with a pencil or a pen. Now you must do the same but with the charcoal tip. You can do strokes by guiding the crayon with the wrist or with the fingers.

Take a chunk of charcoal between the index and ring fingers and the thumb. Doing a test with the crayon vertical gives a short but controlled line when the index finger is pulled towards the palm.

On the paper different types of curves can be made by contracting the fingers inwards. If you add wrist movements you will be able to realize curves like those shown on the left.

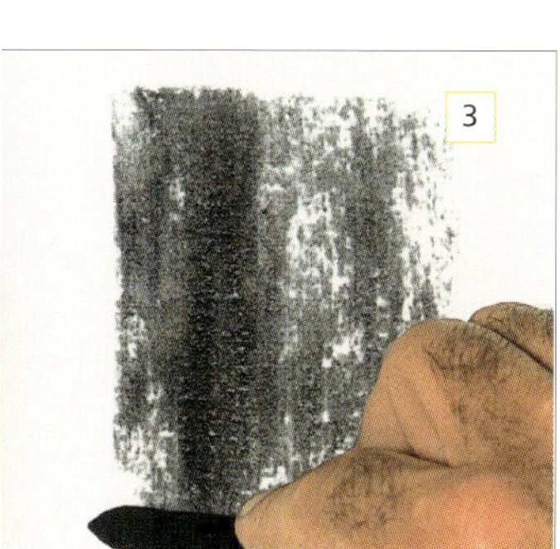

3· The charcoal flat and horizontal.

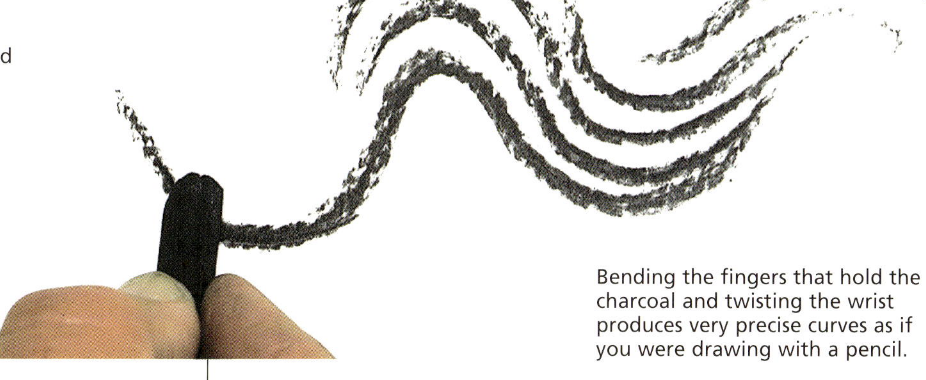

Bending the fingers that hold the charcoal and twisting the wrist produces very precise curves as if you were drawing with a pencil.

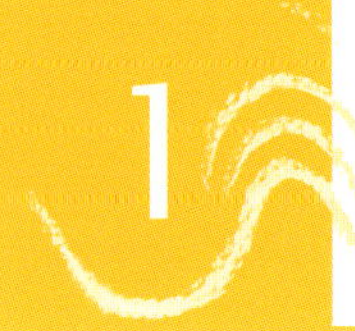

1 CHARCOAL. THE FIRST STROKES.

RUBBING THE CRAYON OVER THE PAPER

Rubbing the charcoal crayon over the paper gives different effects in the strokes. The crayon does not have to draw with the point: it can be held flat to produce different and interesting results.
The thickness of the stroke depends on the chunk width. Sometimes you will have to cover a wide surface and at other times you will concentrate on small areas.
There is another factor to be considered: charcoal does not always draw in the same way. The chunk becomes worn away as it is used, and this happens much more quickly when the charcoal is held flat. To overcome this wearing away you continuously have to vary the edge of the crayon used.
Two types of marks can be left on the paper by the charcoal. The first is linear and follows the hand"s path. The second is aimed at covering an extensive surface in gray.
Very varied strokes can be made with abrupt changes of direction.

VARIED STROKES

Holding the charcoal flat allows a stroke to be modified when the crayon is turned on the paper. First do strokes with the chunk flat. This will allow you to do soft waves without affecting the stroke. When you do a brusque change of direction, switching to a lengthwise stroke, the change will be noticeable.

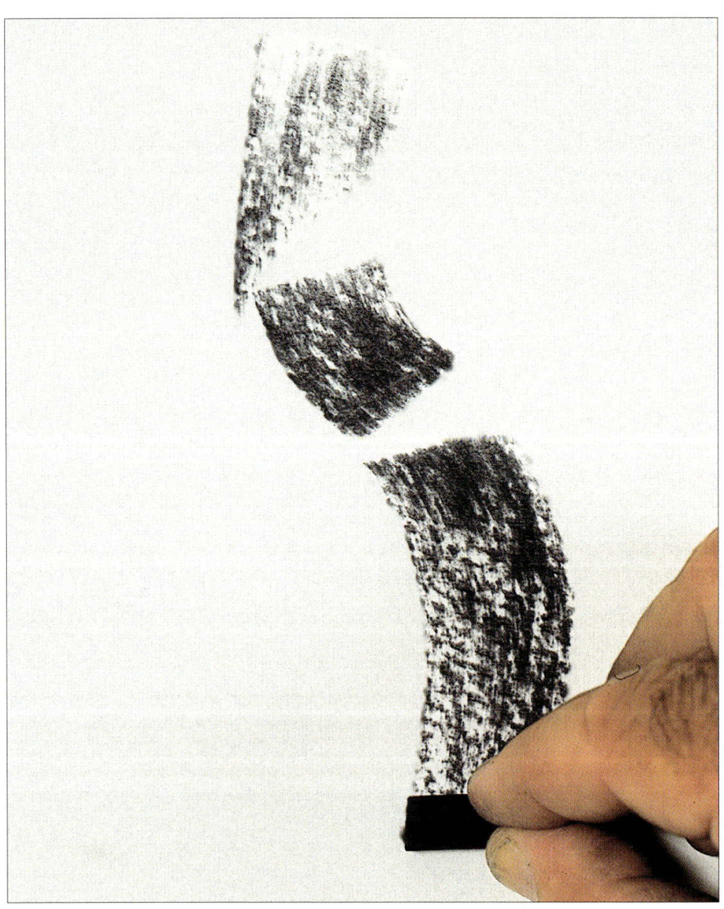

Use the charcoal flat to produce different strokes varying the downward force.

Rapidly changing the direction of the charcoal will give interesting strokes.

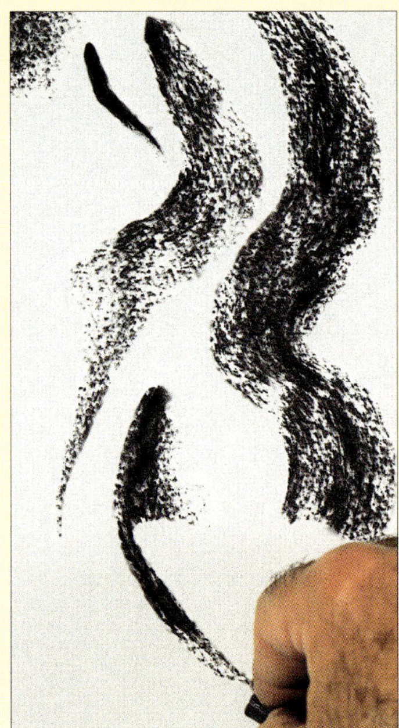

SMUDGE THE LINES

As was said before, charcoal has only slight adhesiveness, merely touching it is enough to "make it run" as it sticks to the finger or palm and thus spreads out. This can be put to good use by the draftsman to create smudges from the strokes for textures and very alluring effects.
Smudging involves spreading the charcoal mark on the paper with the finger or the palm. It is different to stumping, which is controlling the expansion of the charcoal stroke by softly rubbing with a finger or a stump.

When smudging do not press too hard to avoid that the charcoal, or rather the charcoal powder, becomes encrusted in the pores of the paper.
Normally the smudging is done with the fingertips and, therefore, the area covered can be controlled substantially. Passing the hand or the fingers over lightly gives the desired effects on the chosen strokes.

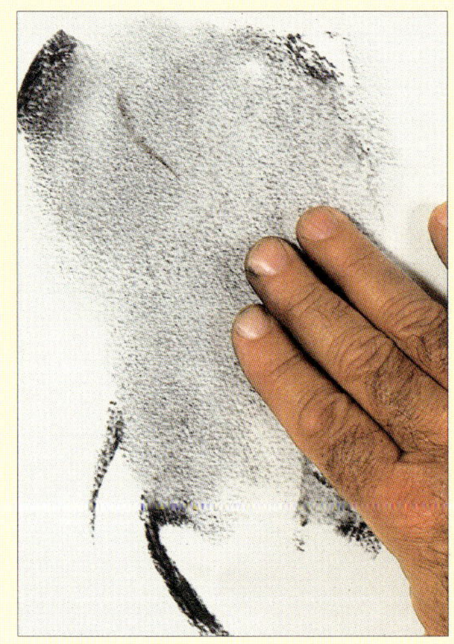

Pass the palm of the hand or the fingertips over the strokes on the paper, forming soft circles that rub the charcoal and spread it over all the area. A smudge will be formed.

A DIRTY HAND

Every time you touch the charcoal your hand becomes dirty. This is part of drawing and need not worry you during the session. In fact, grimy hands, used in the right place, are an important tool for smudging, stumping and shaking the paper (but be careful with the last one). On many occasions a finger stained by charcoal will be an excellent means with which to obtain different effects on the paper, or to resolve various aspects of the work, like shading, gradations and stumpings.
Charcoal impregnated on the hands is easily cleaned off by rubbing with a cloth or washing them in water.

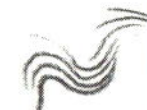

ERASING CHARCOAL

As we said before, charcoal is very unstable and does not stick firmly to the paper, offering us many advantages which permit not only the rubbing out of strokes and lines to get different effects, but also the easy correction of mistakes. We can erase where we went wrong.
Indeed, erasing can be used as part of the creative process, shaping lighter spaces or even opening up whites in the compositions. Charcoal can be rubbed out with a finger, a cloth or an eraser, depending on the effect we are seeking. Also you can rub out with a stump. However, this implement will never produce a perfect white.

ERASING WITH A CLOTH

Just rubbing a cloth over, or flicking with it, will suffice to rub out a zone. However, as is the case when erasing with the fingers, slight gray traces remain on the paper. Perhaps this is the effect you were after, but if not you will have to use an eraser.

RUBBING OUT WITH AN ERASER

If you want to rub out without leaving any trace of charcoal on the paper it is best to use an eraser. In this way not only do you eliminate all charcoal marks, allowing you to correct and redraw, but also you can introduce lines or white spaces into the drawing.

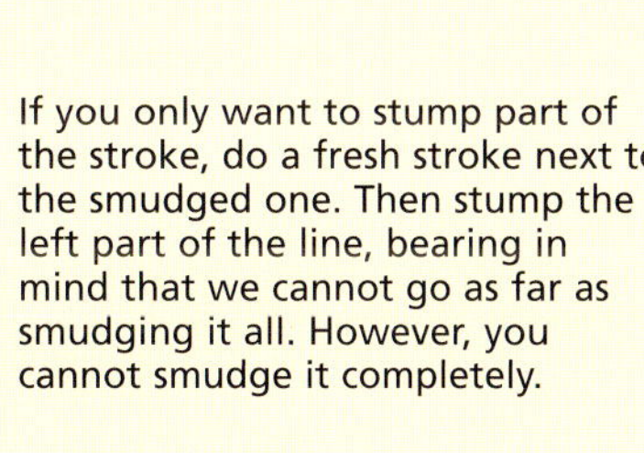

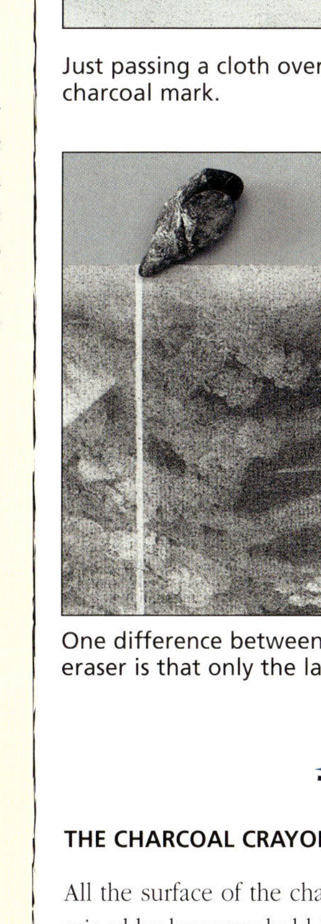

If you only want to stump part of the stroke, do a fresh stroke next to the smudged one. Then stump the left part of the line, bearing in mind that we cannot go as far as smudging it all. However, you cannot smudge it completely.

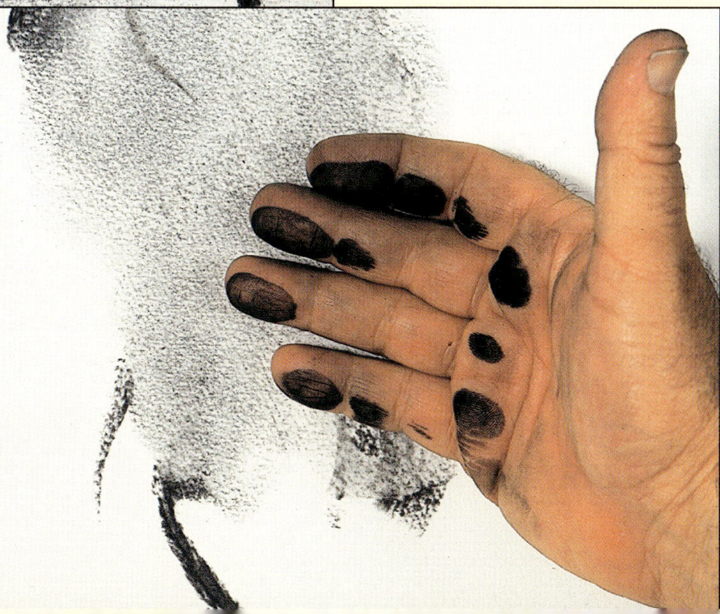

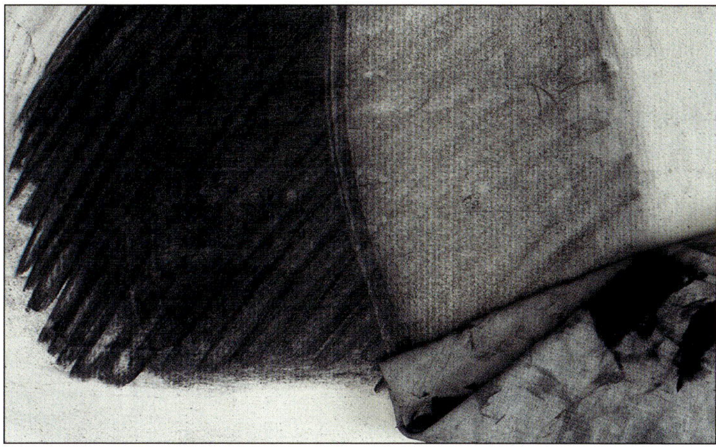

Just passing a cloth over is enough to remove a charcoal mark.

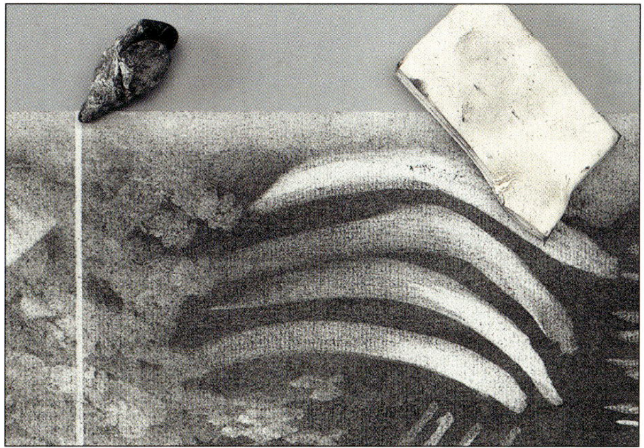

One difference between erasing with a cloth and with an eraser is that only the latter removes all charcoal traces.

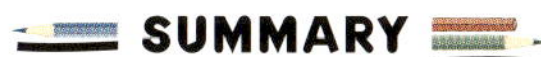

SUMMARY

THE CHARCOAL CRAYON.

All the surface of the charcoal will mark the paper. The stroke will be determined by how you hold it.

HOW TO HOLD THE CHARCOAL.

The charcoal crayon can be held flat, upright or at an angle.

STROKES.

Quite straight strokes can be drawn using the crayon vertical and flat. If it is placed horizontally, the stroke will be as wide as the crayon.

SMUDGING STROKES.

The precariousness of charcoal means that any stroke can be smudged by passing a finger over it.

ERASING CHARCOAL.

Charcoal can be rubbed out with the fingers or with a cloth, leaving a slight gray mark. If an eraser is used the stroke is completely eliminated.
If an eraser is used all traces of charcoal are removed from the paper, something that does not happen with a cloth.

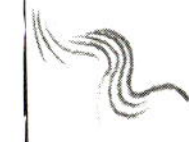

1 Exercices *Step by step*

The objective of this exercise is to understand the importance of what has been explained up until now, and to learn how to apply it. The model to be tried out is very complicated, but it permits the practice of simple recourses like crossed strokes or rubbing out. Do not worry about achieving a great likeness to the model. Its purpose is to be a reference point for your practice.

In this exercise we have selected a fragment of the head from a drawing by **Andrea del Sarto** so that we can try out loose and crossed strokes. All the drawing has to be done with the same piece of charcoal, which as it wears out must be turned in your hand before continuing with another edge.

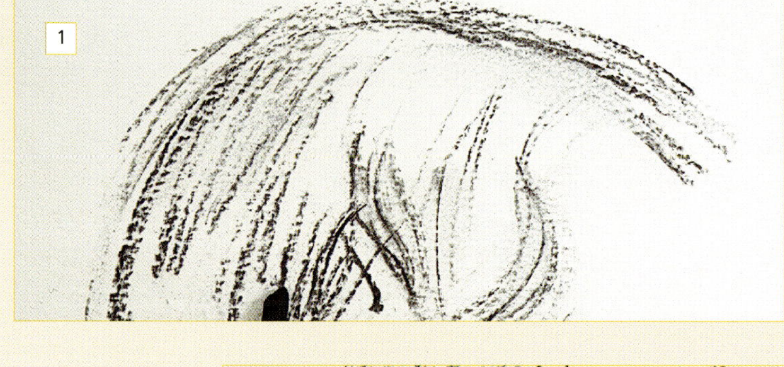

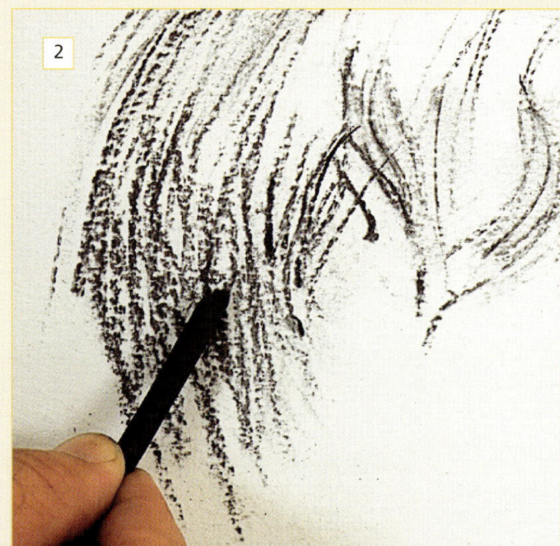

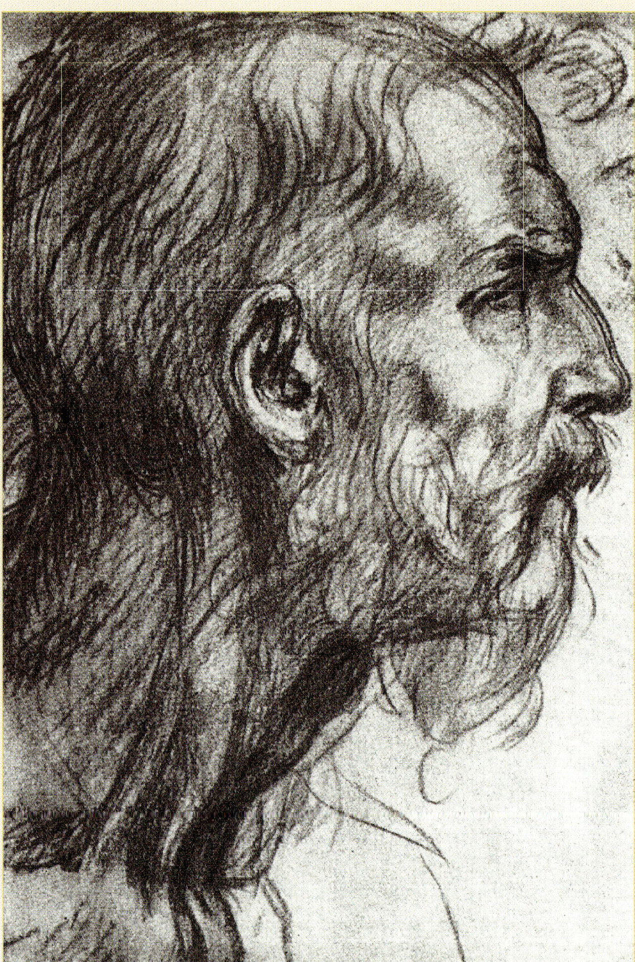

Andrea del Sarto (Florence 1486-1530). Head of an old man, charcoal drawing. Galerìa degli Uffizi, Florence.

1· DRAW A CURVED line to outline the upper part of the head.

2· STARTING FROM THIS CURVE, going downwards, draw two types of strokes: "s" shaped strokes and straight, crossed strokes. This is done using the point of the charcoal, without pressing too hard.

USE YOUR FINGERTIPS TO SMUDGE the strokes you have already put down. However, do not rub them out.

ON TOP OF THE SAME ZONE, do crossed, sloping parallel lines.

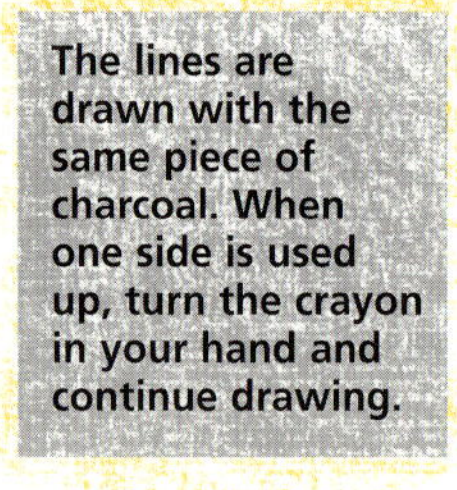

The lines are drawn with the same piece of charcoal. When one side is used up, turn the crayon in your hand and continue drawing.

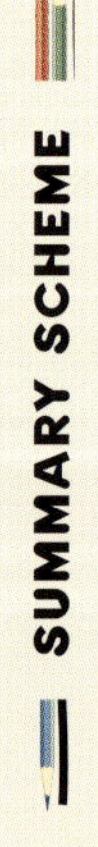

Loose, sloping strokes done with the charcoal point and brusque wrist movements. The pressure on the charcoal must be soft.

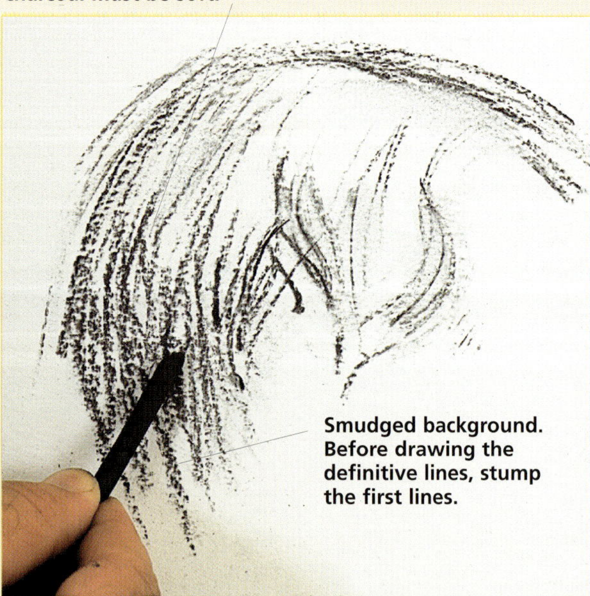

Smudged background. Before drawing the definitive lines, stump the first lines.

Loose strokes and crossed strokes

1

This illustration by Tiziano which is going to be used for the exercise is a complex drawing that contains all types of stroke recourses. However, if you look at the practice zone you will see that there are only crossed strokes. It is, therefore, a good example with which to learn to master this technique in charcoal. Hatching can be defined in the following way: many parallel lines are drawn in one direction, and then, on top of these, other lines are drawn to form criss-crossing. The closer together the lines are, the darker they will be.

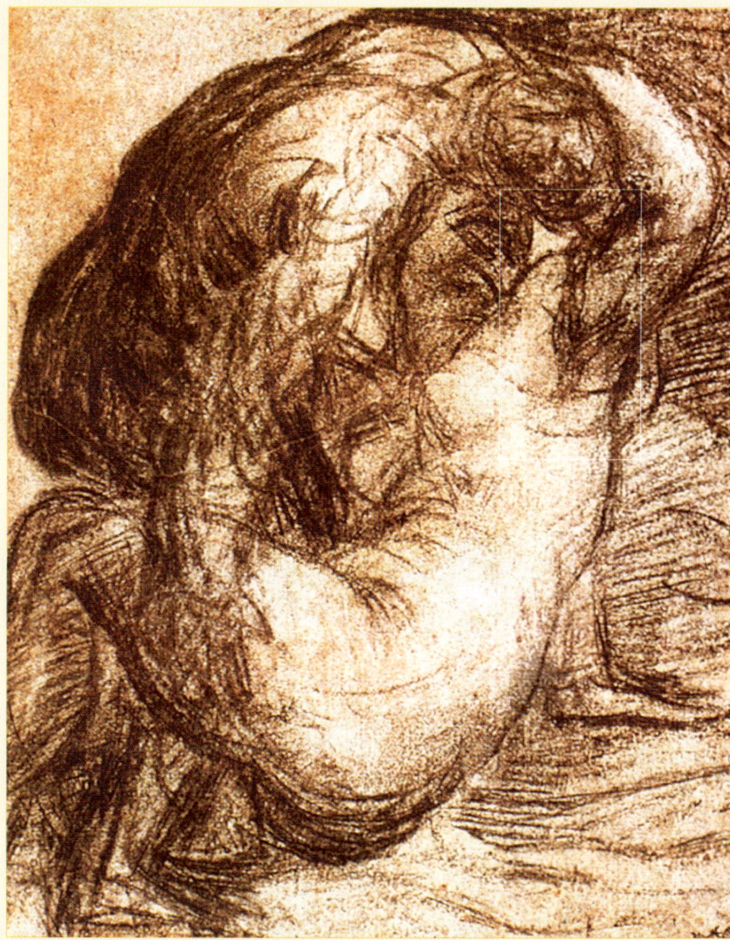

Tiziano (Pieve di Cadore 1488/89- Venice 1576), "Jupiter and I", drawing in charcoal. Fitzwilliam Museum, Cambridge.

1·DRAW THE LINES of the figure's bent arm.

STARTING FROM THESE SIMPLE STROKES, start to draw long, parallel lines, very close together but never actually touching. The parallel lines should be done with rapid, loose strokes.

2· DO THE CROSSED STROKES in the same way as you did the previous ones, but this time sloping them to the right and cutting the lines drawn in the first step. The lines must follow the drawing scheme of the arm.

THE LINE IS FINISHED WITH QUICK, FREE STROKES. Allow the wrist to dominate when rubbing the charcoal over the paper.

SUMMARY SCHEME

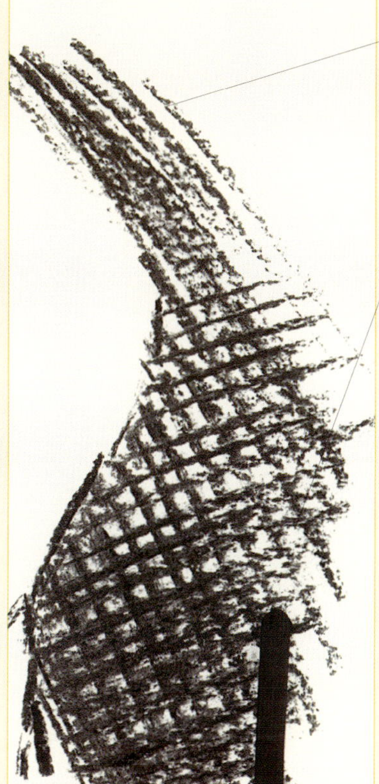

The limit of the drawing is where the line is started. The first lines were done very gently.

Crossed strokes. The strokes have been done with a very firm wrist movement

Drag the charcoal rapidly with the fingers until just turning the wrist would scuff up the paper.

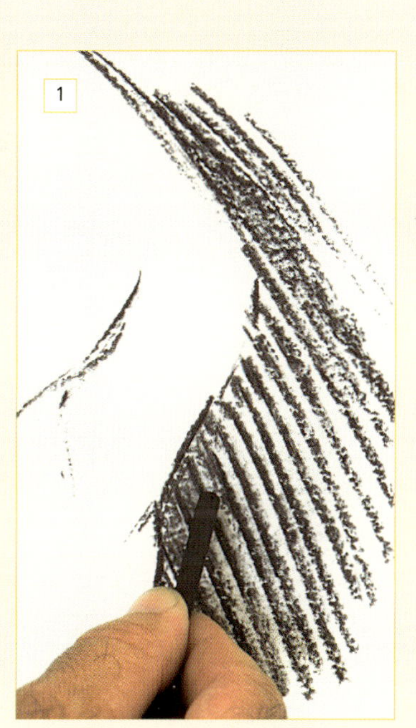

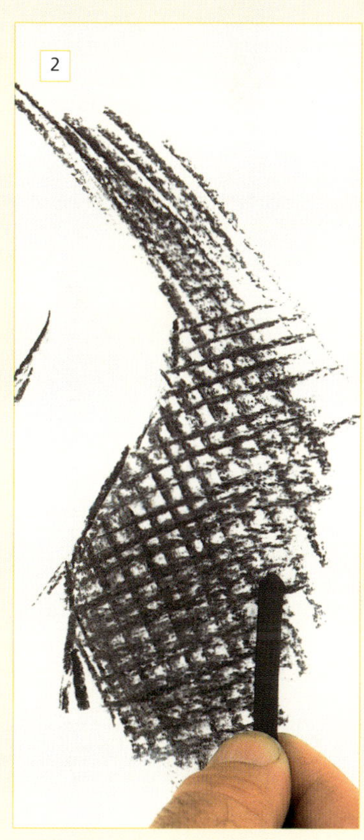

1 Exercices *Step by step*

CHARCOAL. THE FIRST STROKES.

Part of a drawing by **Federico Barocci** can be used to practice this stumping exercise. We are to draw the cheek zone that appears in the illustration and the technique is straightforward: softly stump the specifically done charcoal strokes.

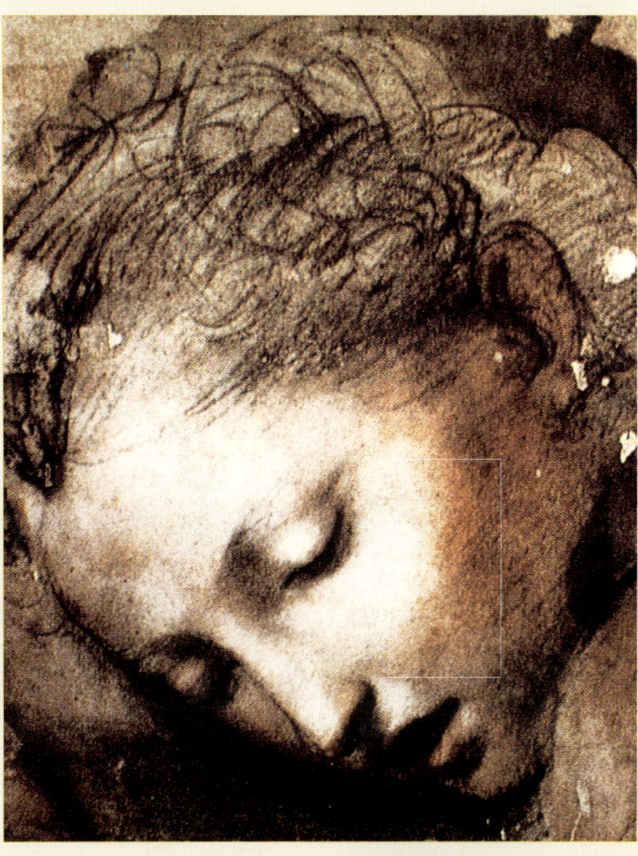

When doing intense strokes with the charcoal, the chunk used has to be short, otherwise the pressure applied would break it.

Federico Barocci (Urbino, 1535–1612), "The virgin's face", drawing in charcoal. The Museum of Fine Arts and Archaeology, Besançon.

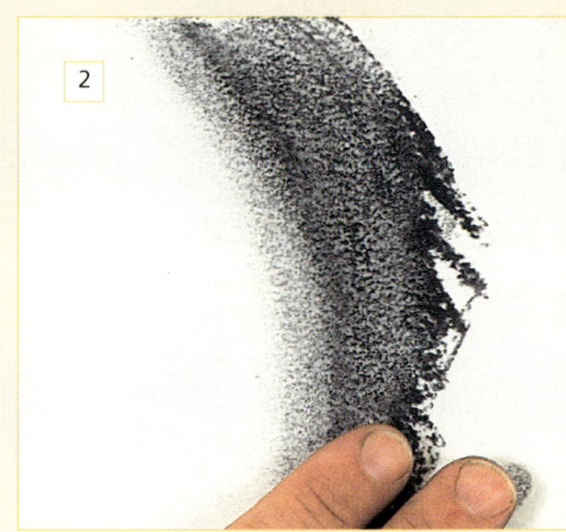

2· USE YOUR INDEX FINGER to softly smudge the left side of the stroke. Rub part of the charcoal outline towards the white part of the paper. Pass the finger over several times in a curved line.

AFTERWARDS, smudge the inside part to tone down the stroke.

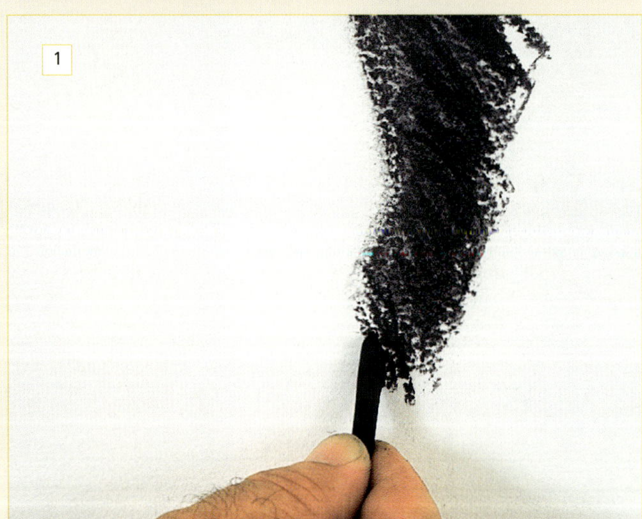

1· DO INTENSE STROKES sloping to the right. Whenever you start intense strokes, the pressure at first must be soft. As you continue to rub the charcoal over, increase the pressure, but without interrupting the movement. In this example the stroke follows a very tight zigzag path.

THE CHARCOAL should not be lifted from the paper to start a parallel stroke when you finish the previous one.

SUMMARY SCHEME

This part is softly stumped. Use the finger to softly smudge the charcoal.

Zone where the smudging is started. In this zone, do strong strokes before beginning to smudge.

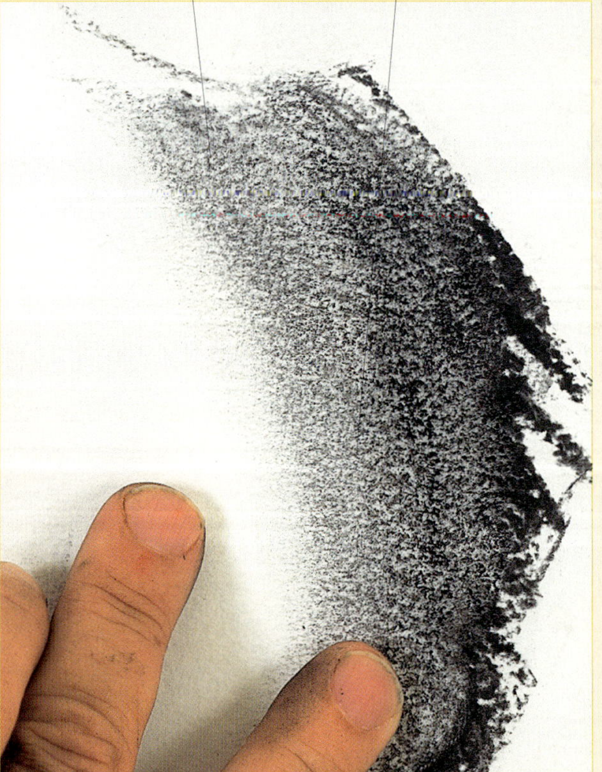

Stumping

Once again, part of another splendid drawing, this time by **Michelangelo**, will be used to practice what has been learnt so far. The aim is to do a stumping starting from a defined line.

The figure"s shoulder is ideal for doing the exercise. Remember that it is not necessary to achieve a great likeness: the model is only a reference.

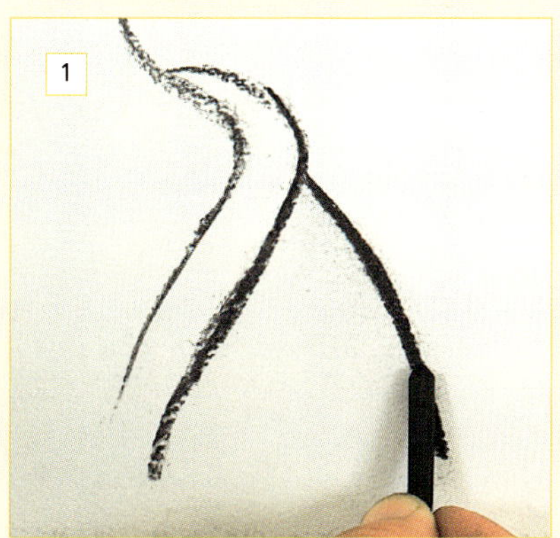

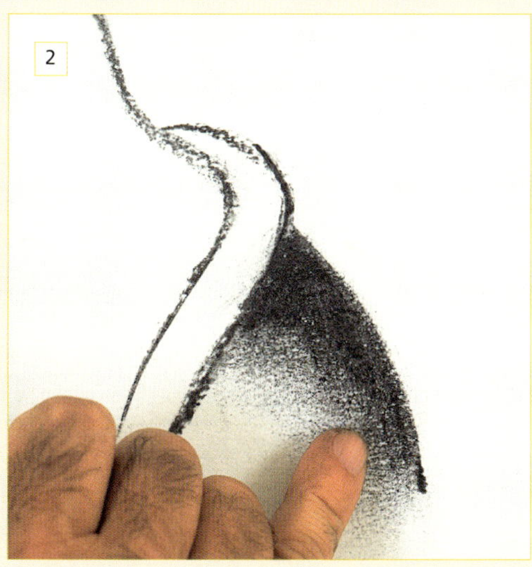

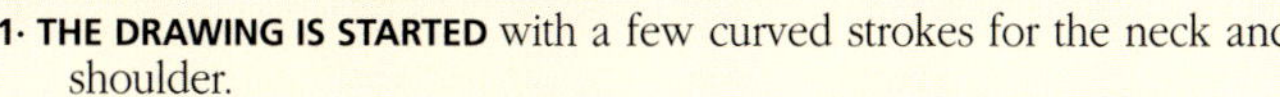

1· THE DRAWING IS STARTED with a few curved strokes for the neck and shoulder.

AFTER DOING the first upper curved line, do parallel curved lines.

THE STROKE THAT DEFINES THE SHOULDER line is a straightforward curve and must be done with considerable pressure.

2· STARTING FROM THE DARKEST LINE, rub part of the charcoal towards the white zone of the paper using the little finger. Be careful to only shade the drawing as necessary: do not go too far.

THE FINGER PRESSURE most gradually decrease. At the end the rubbing finger will hardly touch the paper.

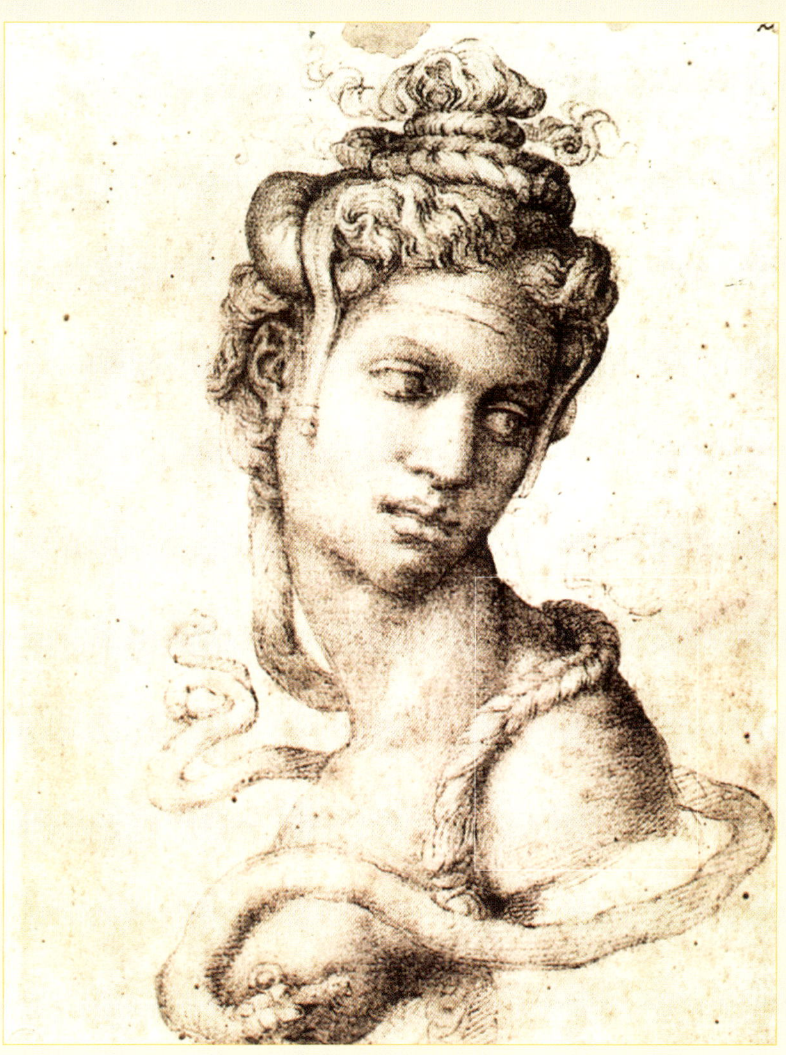

Michelangelo (Caprese, 1475- Rome, 1564)
Cleopatra, drawing in charcoal. Buonarroti Galllery, Florence.

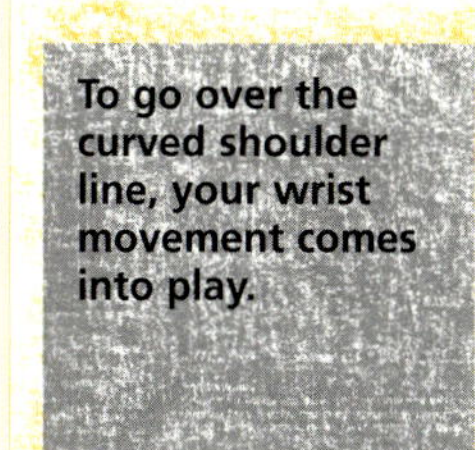

SUMMARY SCHEME

Zone where the line starts. Draw the line softly at the beginning, and increase the pressure as you go over the stroke.

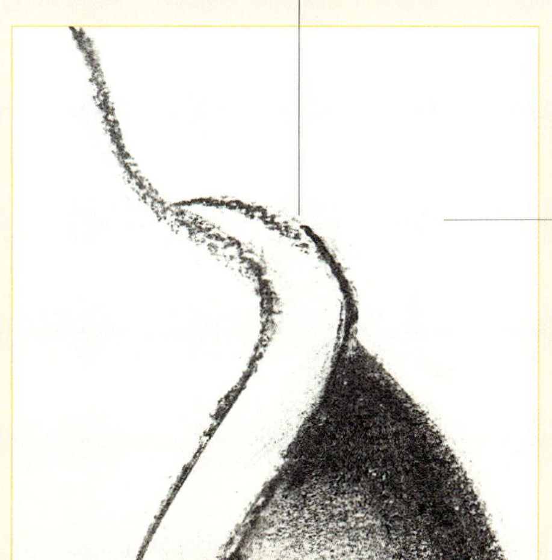

Tone dragged by the finger. After doing a charcoal stroke, go over it with the finger to drag the tone.

CHARCOAL. STUDYING THE STROKE.

The ideas explained in this chapter will help the learner to master different types of strokes that can be made in charcoal. At the same time we will go into the multiple possibilities that erasing offers to this drawing medium, either using an eraser, the hand or a cloth.

THE STROKE

The stroke is the basic "building block" that composes the drawing, which, however complicated it may be, can always be reduced to simple lines. The lines can join together or can leave white spaces between each other. The result, the drawing, is the visual perception that these lines create.

In the last chapter we have already dealt with strokes and the basic related concepts, but as they are the essence of drawing we must study them more deeply.

As we have seen, many very varied lines and strokes can be realized with charcoal, right from soft, fine lines through to thick ones. Charcoal is the best medium with which to practice strokes because it acts almost like a continuation of the hand.

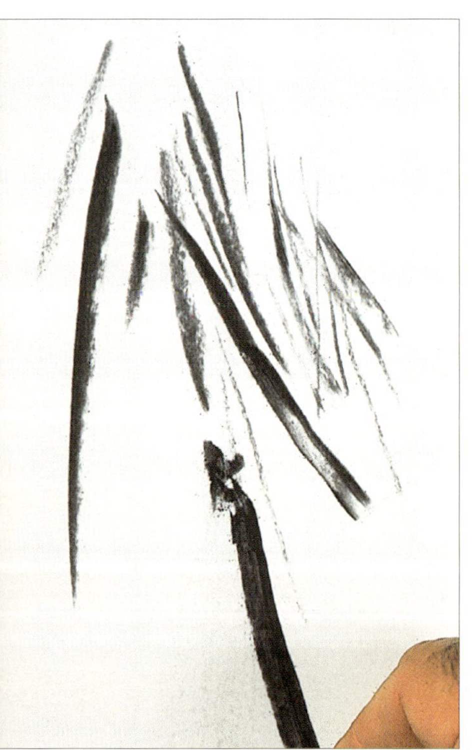

The main type of strokes which can be obtained from charcoal.

PRESSURE AND THICKNESS OF THE STROKE

Charcoal is so brittle that when it is pressed strongly against the paper it crunches and then crumbles into powder. This brittleness means that the more pressure applied, the blacker and denser the stroke will be. Of course, different pressures can be applied in the same stroke, or the pressure can be constant throughout the stroke.

Strokes varying the pressure. In the first case, hold the charcoal flat between the fingers. Do a straight line with the crayon perpendicular to the stroke direction. The start of the stroke is done with very little pressure, but as the line is developed, press the charcoal more firmly against the paper. This gives a gradation from light gray to dark gray.

Strokes with constant pressure. A second trial consists of doing two curves with the charcoal crayon. Firstly, do a stroke with a fair amount of constant pressure on the paper.

THE PRESSURE OF THE STROKE.

The stroke will look the same along its length if a constant pressure is applied. Applying different pressures along the stroke will produce gradations.

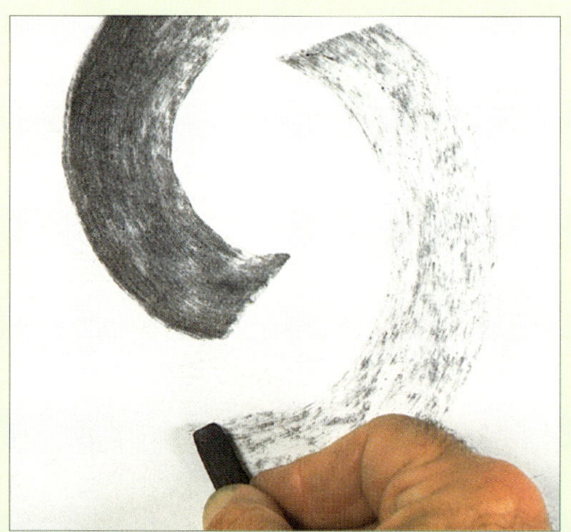

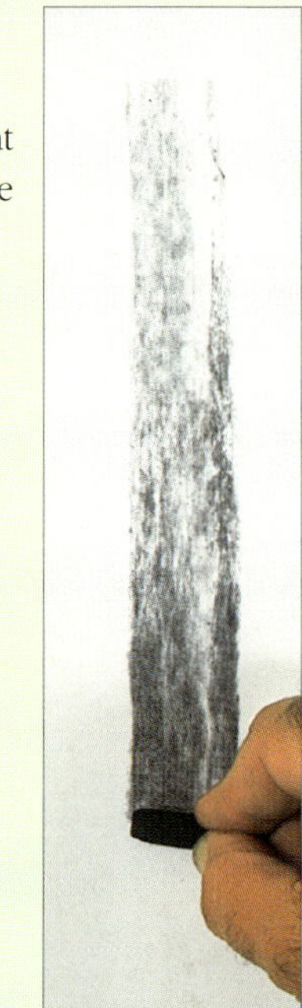

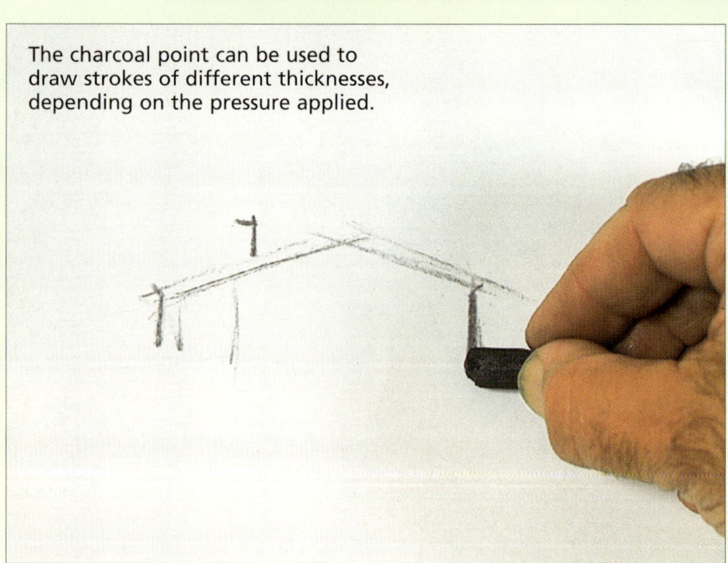

The charcoal point can be used to draw strokes of different thicknesses, depending on the pressure applied.

STROKES WITH THE CHARCOAL POINT

Working with the point enables you to do strokes of different widths. If you want to do a fine and continuous stroke, you have to twist the crayon so that you are always drawing with a sharp edge. Alternatively, if you draw with the same side of the charcoal, the stroke will gradually become thicker.

The thickness of the stroke obtained from the charcoal point also depends on the pressure applied when drawing: the greater the pressure, the thicker, darker and denser the stroke will be. Another way of getting a thicker stroke is to go over the lines several times until they are firmer.

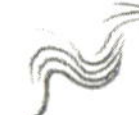

Charcoal, sanguine and pencil can be dragged over the surface of the paper, or make a much more compact mark. When they are dragged they leave behind them a trace or a mark called a stroke.

2

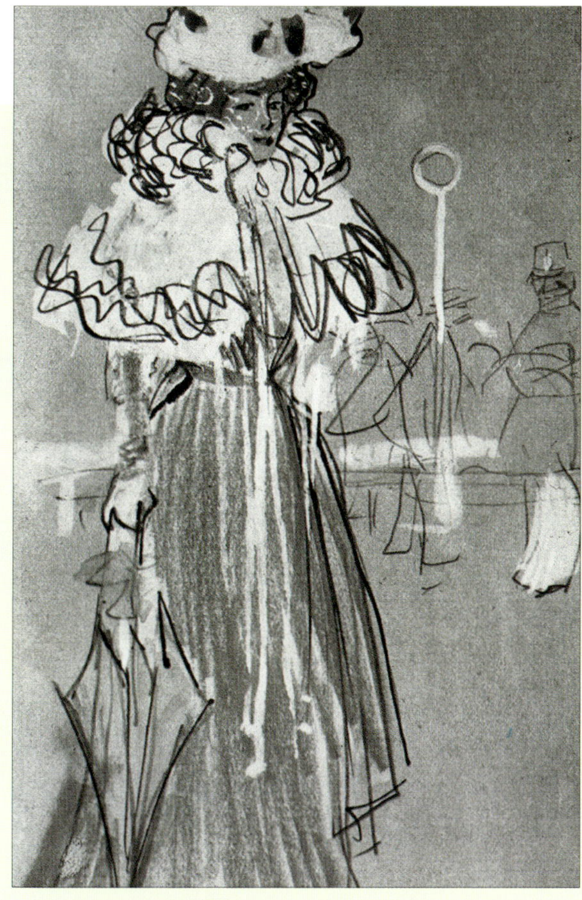

STROKES AND THEIR SIGNIFICANCE.

A stroke alone represents nothing: it is the adding together of the lines and marks that forms a particular shape. In this charcoal drawing by RamÛn Casas (1866-1932) "Parisian woman with an umbrella" you can observe how the strokes work together to form the drawing. Although the piece is perfectly defined, if you look close up, the strokes taken on their own appear meaningless and out of control. Despite this they complement each other to form the picture.

STRAIGHT LINES, CURVES AND THICKNESSES

The play of the fingers, the wrist and arm are fundamental to control the charcoal drawing. The movements of all three when drawing will enable you to do straight and curved strokes of varying thickness and intensity.

If you are drawing with the charcoal point, the way the fingers are tensed and relaxed will give little, controlled curves with different pressures. If you draw with all the length of the charcoal crayon, wrist movements will give you very precise, varied strokes. However, when drawing straight lines the wrist must not twist; rather the arm must guide the movement, the fingers controlling the pressure on the paper.

STRAIGHT LINES

To achieve very precise straight lines, hold the charcoal flat between the fingers and draw lengthwise with all its surface. The charcoal will guide all the line. If you slide the charcoal without varying the pressure during the movement, the stroke will not suffer. According to the pressure applied, the stroke will be fine or thick and dense.

CURVES AND SHADES OF GRAY

If curved strokes are realized on top of each other, the two shades of charcoal are added together. Depending on the pressure applied different gradations of gray can be carried out.

DRAWING IN ZIGZAG

To obtain a zigzagged drawing, do a fine vertical line with the charcoal flat between the fingers, and then move the crayon sideways, and back up and down again.

STRAIGHT AND CURVED STROKES

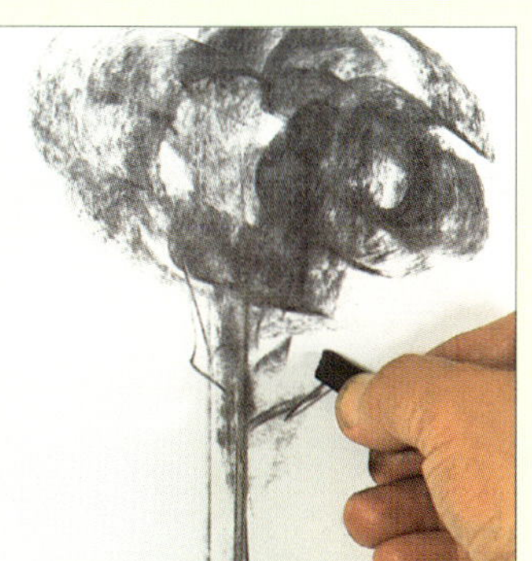

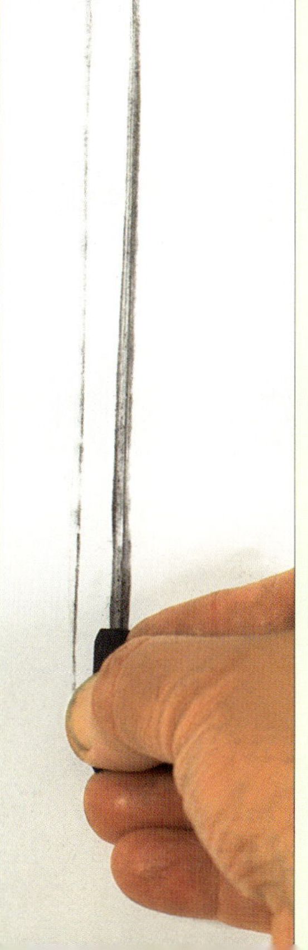

To do straight lines, place the charcoal flat and lengthwise against the paper.

Gray gradations are obtained by superimposing on top of each other curved strokes done with different pressures.

The zigzag effect is achieved by alternating flat, vertical strokes with dragging the charcoal sideways.

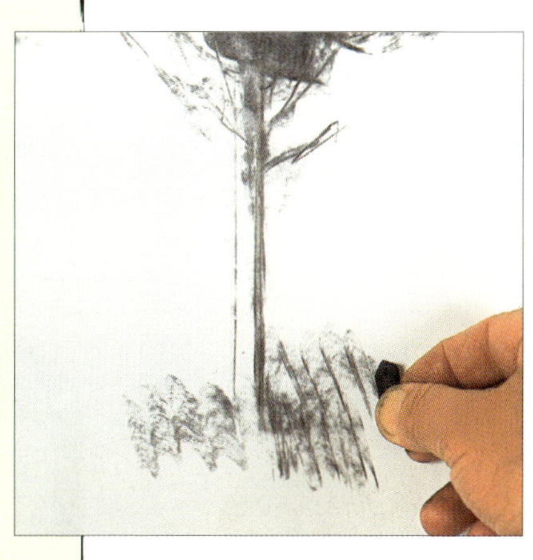

HOW TO ERASE

As we have seen in the last chapter, erasing is fundamental in charcoal drawing, both because it allows corrections to be made and because it can be used to smudge strokes and lines, and to open up white spaces.

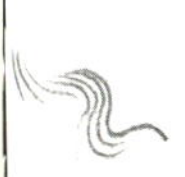

CHARCOAL. STUDYING THE STROKE.

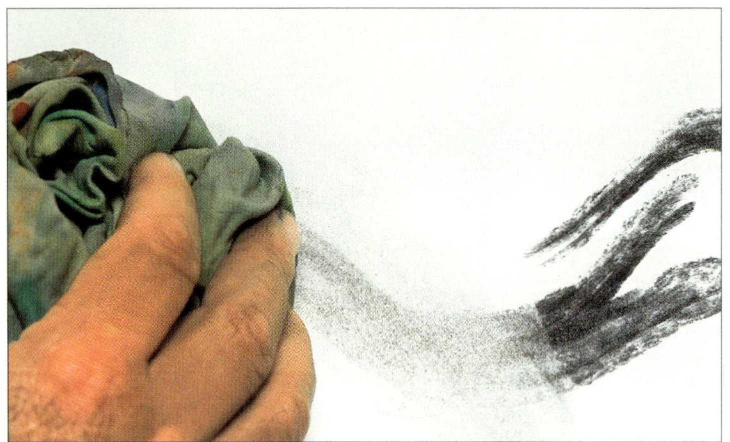

A cloth can be used to clean almost completely any charcoal trace.

HOW TO USE THE CLOTH

We have already commented that when working with charcoal it is necessary to have a cloth handy to remove any unwanted stain quickly. The most suitable cloths are cotton ones. Absorbent kitchen paper can also be used. However, the latter is not reusable, whereas a cloth can be washed and used again.

ERASING WITH THE HAND

You can use your hand to remove charcoal: it is an accurate implement for cleaning up a large area. One of its advantages over a cloth is that as well as eliminating the charcoal from the surface

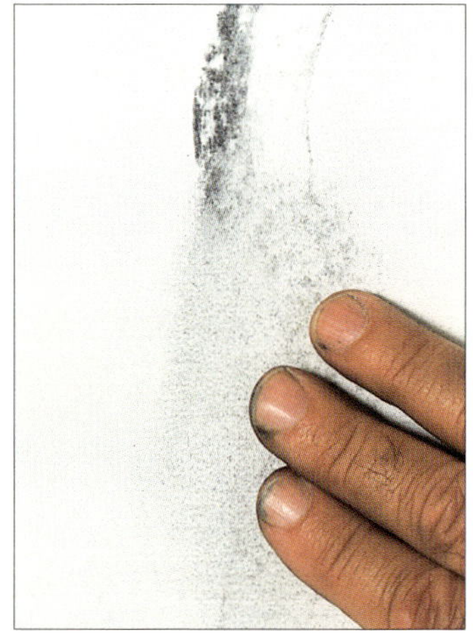

The hand allows you to stump and to do soft gradations, or to get rid of a charcoal line.

USING THE ERASER

The eraser is one of the draftsman"s most multipurpose tools. It can hide away errors, clean up big zones giving the paper back its original whiteness, or even "draw" on areas which have previously been stained by charcoal or pencil.

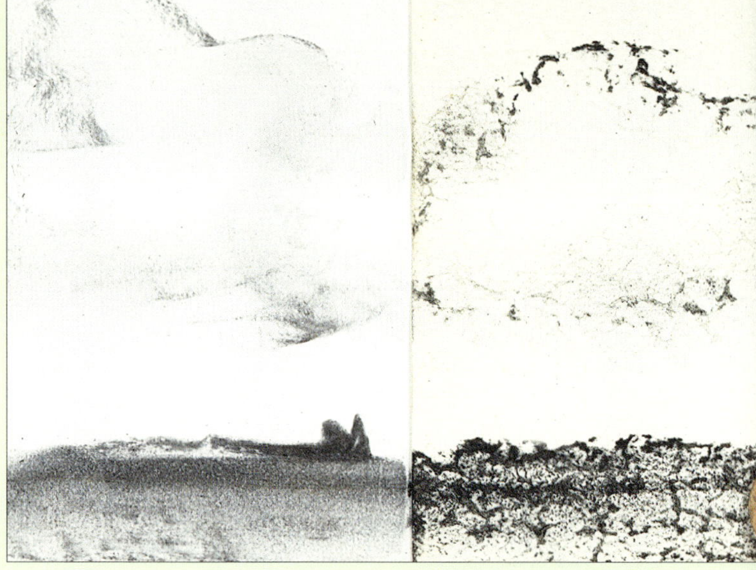

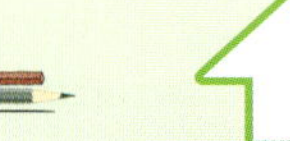

THE STROKE AND THE PAPER

To get a good stroke the paper has to be chosen carefully for not all of them have the same texture. Some are rough while others are smooth. To make sure you choose correctly, test out the papers and observe how the charcoal responds in each case.

A good trial method is to join together two papers with different grains as if they were one sheet. Practices strokes and smudging on them. We can see that the paper on the left has hardly any grain, while the one on the right is medium grained. On the first paper the charcoal barely leaves a mark, and it is difficult to obtain deep black. In contrast, on the paper on the right the tone is much darker and denser.

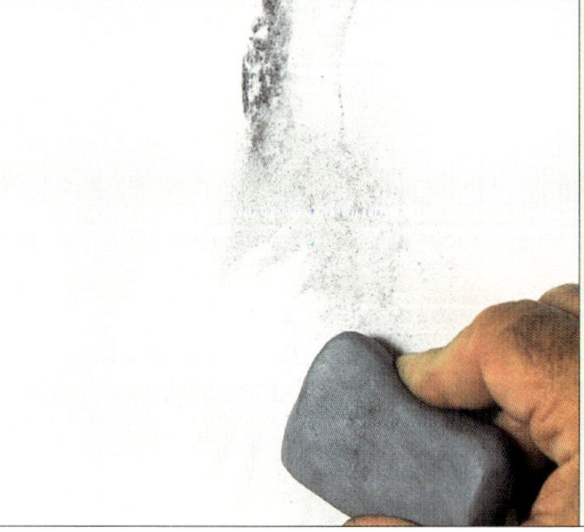

The eraser allows you to eliminate all traces of charcoal, giving the paper back its original color.

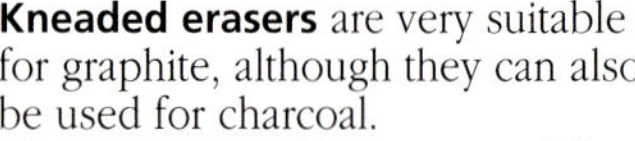

ERASERS

There are many different types of erasers.

Hard erasers are used on papers that have been inked. They are abrasive and quickly deteriorate the surface of the paper.

Kneaded erasers are very suitable for graphite, although they can also be used for charcoal.

Plastic erasers. They are good for eliminating graphite as well as charcoal.

Putty erasers. These are especially useful for charcoal, being so soft that the can go into any shape and perfectly absorb the charcoal, leaving the paper completely white again.

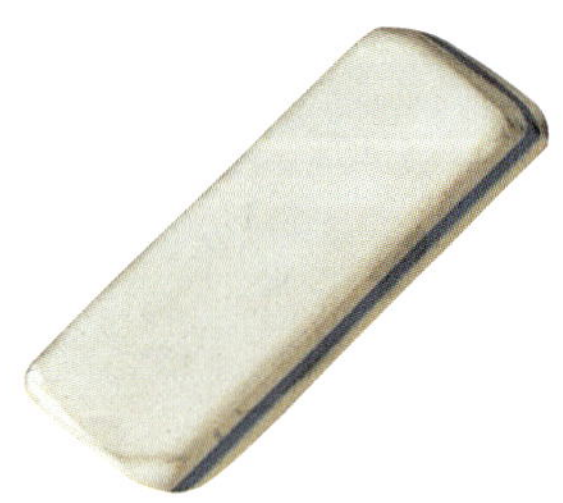

Hard eraser

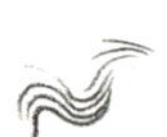

COMBINING THE ERASER, A CLOTH AND CHARCOAL

If you want to learn how to use an eraser and a cotton cloth properly, and to discover their artistic possibilities, try the following simple exercise which combines using both of them together with charcoal. The aim is to practice creating a landscape by erasing in a constructive manner.

Firstly, color all the paper for the exercise holding the charcoal flat. Make the strokes carefully to avoid scratching the paper.

Having done this, open up a white space in the lower half of the paper with a cloth. This corresponds to the floor. Just passing the cloth over softly will suffice to get rid of the excess charcoal.

Thirdly, use an eraser to open up several whites. In the sky, very luminous whites must be opened up which will give form to the clouds. In the lower section, straight lines will depict the waves in the field. As can be appreciated, the stumping of the charcoal is combined with whites opened up using the eraser.

Finally, to finish off, use charcoal to draw the contrasts and the forms of the landscape. These strokes must be simple shadings rather than exact and detailed shapes.

SUMMARY

THE PRESSURE ON THE CHARCOAL.

The stroke can be realized with different pressures depending on the degree of darkness that you want to obtain. To draw with charcoal it is better to start out with soft strokes and increase the pressure gradually.

STRAIGHT LINES.

Draw accurate straight lines by holding the charcoal flat between the fingers and making lengthwise movements.

THE PAPER AND THE STROKE.

When drawing with charcoal, not very smooth paper must be used to obtain strongly contrasted black tones.

ERASING WITH THE HAND.

When erasing charcoal with the hand, very precise stumpings can be realized.

THE MOST SUITABLE ERASER.

The putty eraser has a texture especially suitable for absorbing charcoal totally and leaving the paper completely white.

AN ERASER, A CLOTH, AND CHARCOAL.

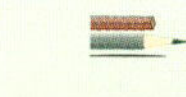

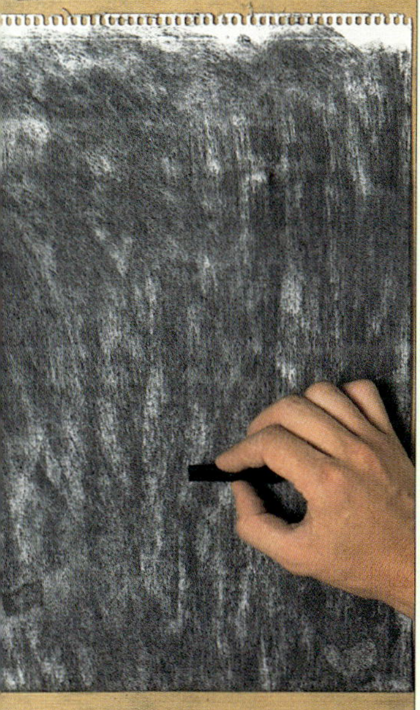

Cover the entire paper surface using the charcoal flat.

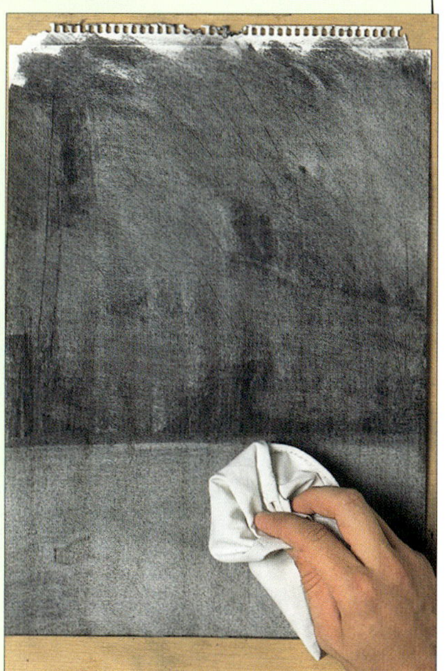

Clean the lower part of the drawing with a cloth.

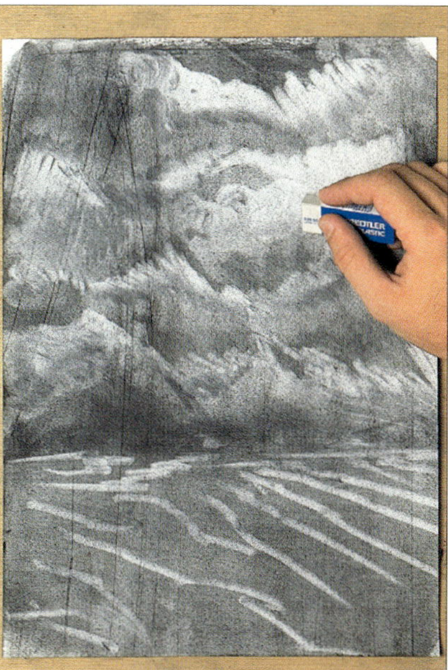

Use the eraser to open up whites with straight and circular strokes.

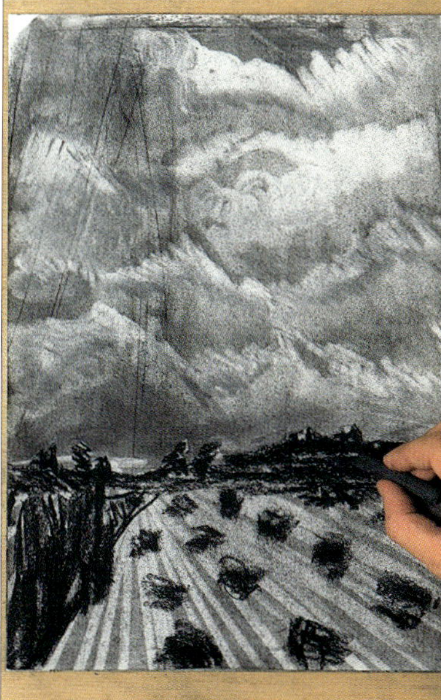

Use charcoal to draw the shapes of the landscape.

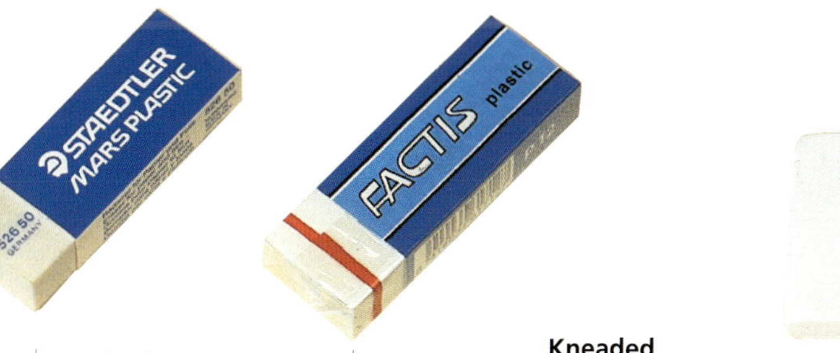

Plastic erasers

Kneaded eraser

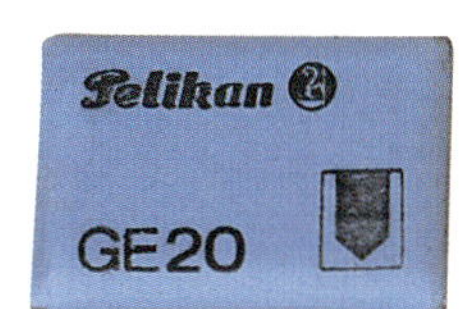

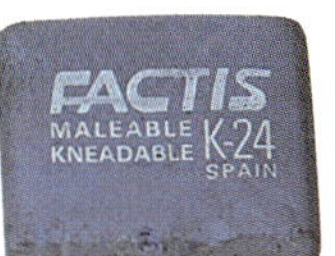

Putty erasers

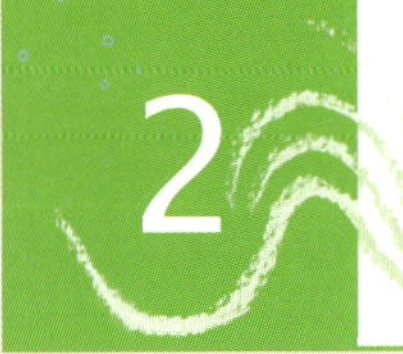

2 Exercices *Step by step*

Drawing need not be complicated. A few well chosen and carefully placed strokes can give you optimum results right from day one.
In the next exercise, we are going to put into practice the guidelines we have examined in this chapter to realize this landscape in charcoal. Before actually starting the drawing it is recommendable to pay attention to the steps involved, and to read the accompanying explanations.

NECESSARY MATERiAL

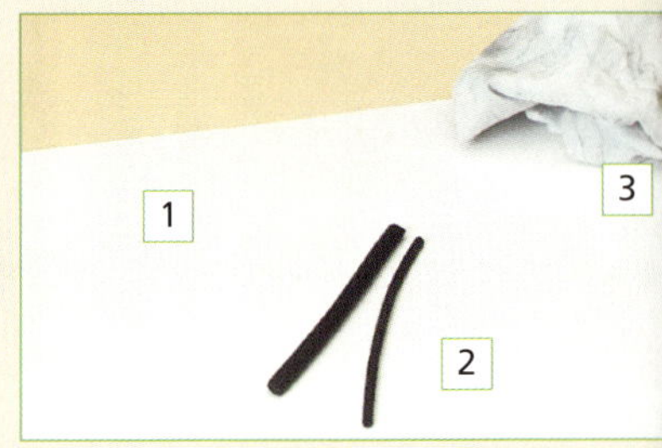

Drawing paper (1), charcoal crayons (2), and a cleaning cloth (3).

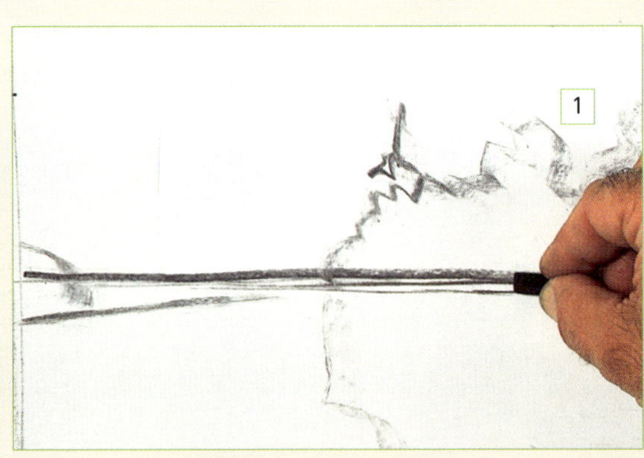

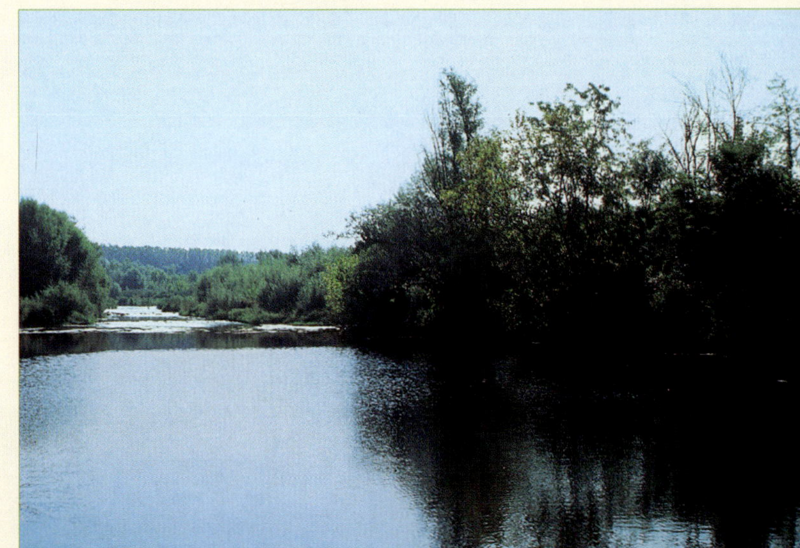

1· HOLD THE CHARCOAL CRAYON crosswise between the fingers and start to do vertical strokes in the upper zone.

2· DO NOT APPLY TOO MUCH PRESSURE on the paper because the aim is only to shade the sky background.

3· USE THE FINGERTIPS TO SOFTLY RUB THE BACKGROUND, removing the stroke like appearance and spreading the charcoal to form a gray mist.

DO NOT INSIST TOO MUCH when using the eraser on the charcoal. There are two risks: making it too light, or, leaving grease on the paper so that permanent charcoal shadings are formed.

DO A LAYOUT OF THE ZONE where you are going to draw. This rectangle, done with the charcoal flat to control the stroke more fully, will allow you to outline the drawing precisely.

A LITTLE ABOVE THE HALFWAY LINE of the rectangle, draw the line that will be the horizon. On top of it, use the charcoal point to draw the outline of the trees freehand.

USE THE CHARCOAL flat and broadwise between the fingers, pressing only lightly, to draw the reflection in the water. The horizon line is drawn pressing down more to make it stand out.

4· IN THE LOWER ZONE DO NEW STROKES, exactly the same as in the sky. This time the charcoal is pressed harder to get a darker black.

DO THE STROKE HOLDING THE CHARCOAL FLAT. This means that the black tone will not be as dark as if you were drawing with the charcoal point.

AS YOU ARE USING THE CHARCOAL BROADWISE, the texture of the paper comes through in the lightest points for the pore is not completely covered.

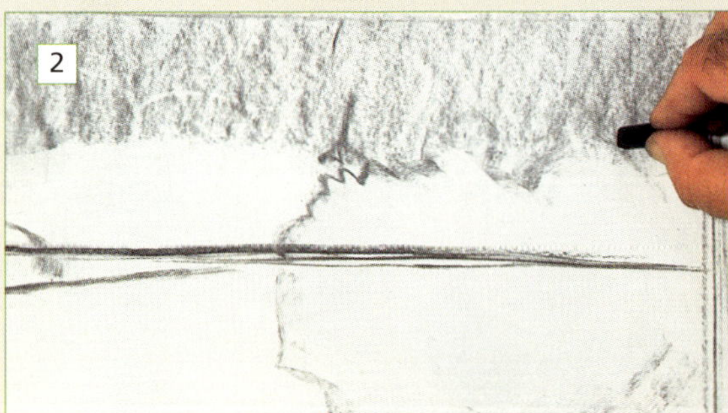

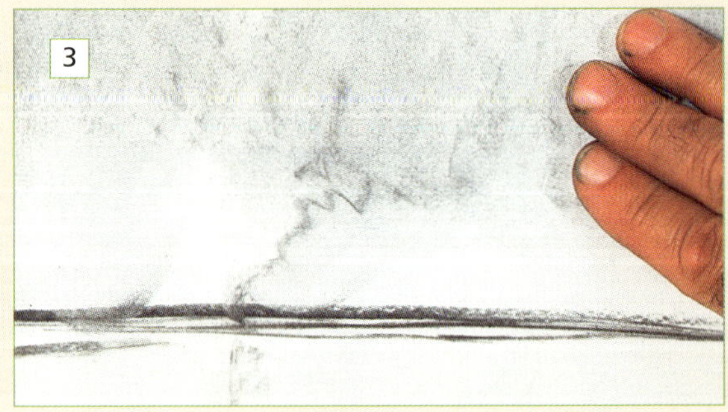

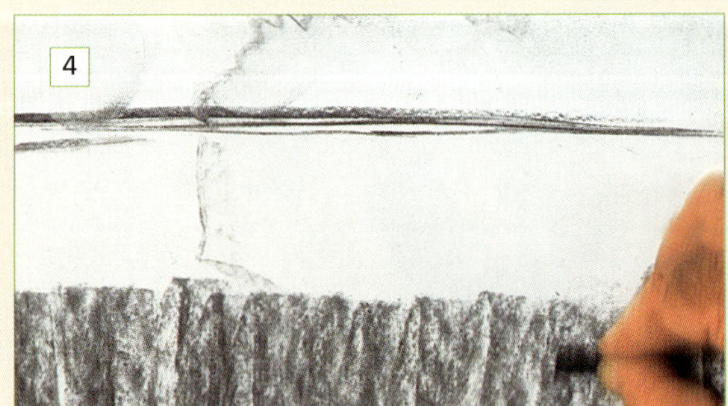

A simple landscape to practice strokes

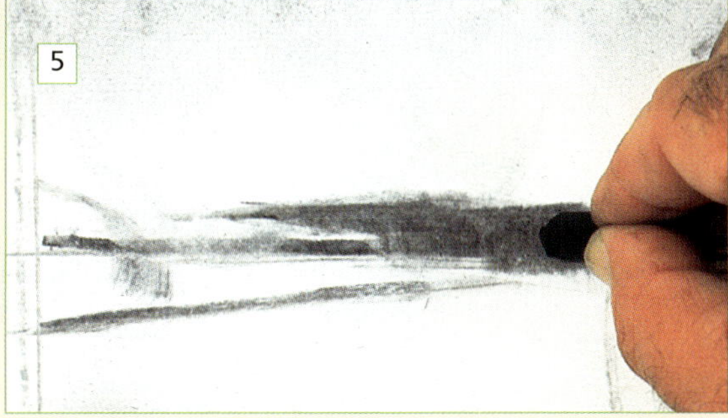

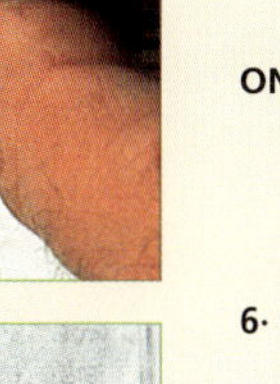

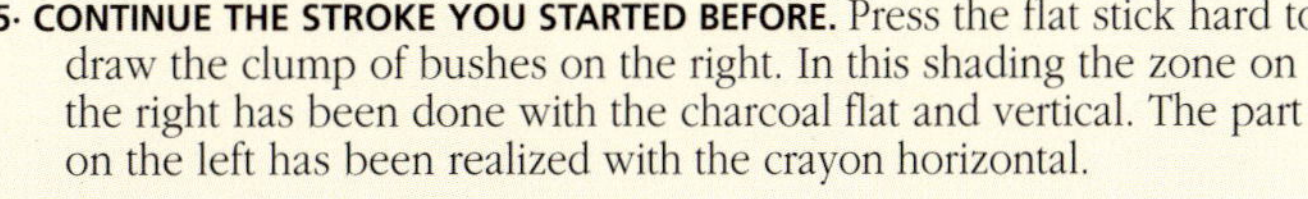

5· CONTINUE THE STROKE YOU STARTED BEFORE. Press the flat stick hard to draw the clump of bushes on the right. In this shading the zone on the right has been done with the charcoal flat and vertical. The part on the left has been realized with the crayon horizontal.

ONCE AGAIN USING THE CRAYON flat and horizontal, but this time pressing more softly, do the reflection in the water. The upper zone is drawn with very close together vertical strokes. The lower part is done zigzagging.

To modify and, correct the charcoal, just rubbing it gently with a hand or a cloth is sufficient.

6· CONTINUE TO DRAW THE REFLECTION in the water in the lower part, until a much darker and denser tone is obtained. The stroke style is the same.

DARKEN THE LEFT zone intensely with a flat, vertical stroke.

HOLD THE CHARCOAL BETWEEN the fingers as if it were a pencil to draw the loose shapes of the trees. The stroke style can be alternated provided that it is always free and spontaneous.

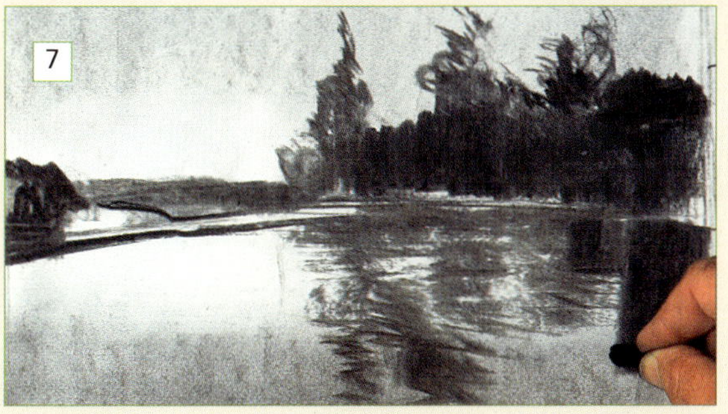

7· SMUDGE THE LAST STROKES with the fingertips. This time the gray is much darker than the first stumping. The charcoal density has also increased.

WHEN YOU PASSED YOUR HAND over the paper, part of the drawing of the trees and their reflection in the water were also rubbed away, or perhaps completely eliminated. Restore them with a very soft stroke.

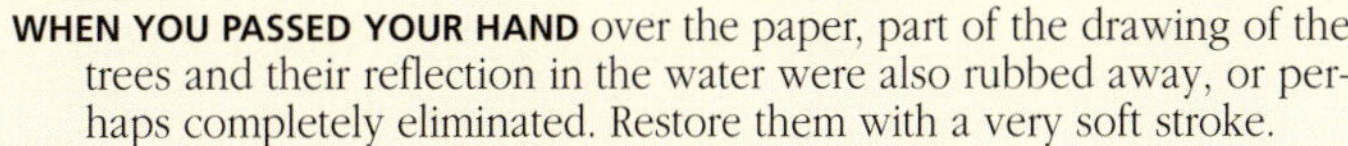

8· ABOVE THE HORIZON LINE, start on the dark areas of the background using the point to obtain an intense stroke.

THE REFLECTION IN THE WATER is finished off with a strong zigzag stroke using the charcoal point. At the reflection's edge do a few free, zigzag strokes. The bank of the lake is reinforced with a much darker fresh stroke.

THIS WILL FINISH OFF THIS CHARCOAL LANDSCAPE. If you go back over what you have done you will see that all the zones are just strokes working together to create an effect. Everything will fall into place to give unity.

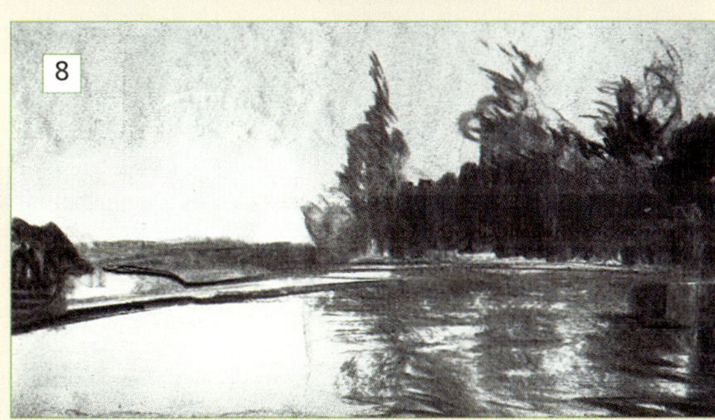

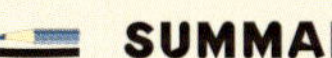

SUMMARY SCHEME

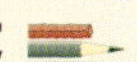

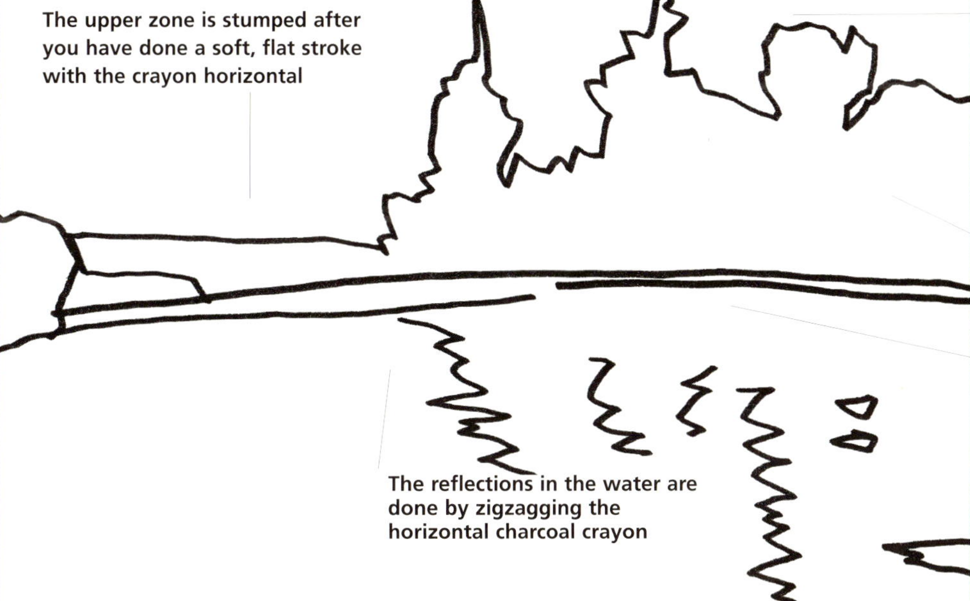

The top of the trees are drawn with generous freehand strokes

The tree area is drawn precisely, combining vertical strokes with horizontal ones

The bank is marked with an intense freehand stroke

3 THE OUTLINE. THE FIRST STEPS

THE TRIANGLE

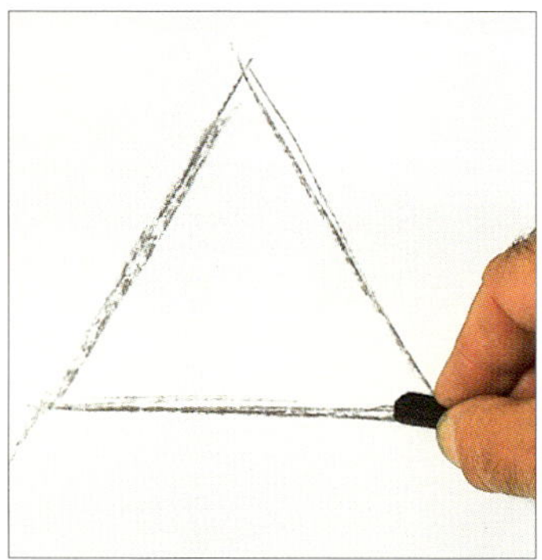

Drawing a triangle is straightforward. Just make sure you do not deform it.

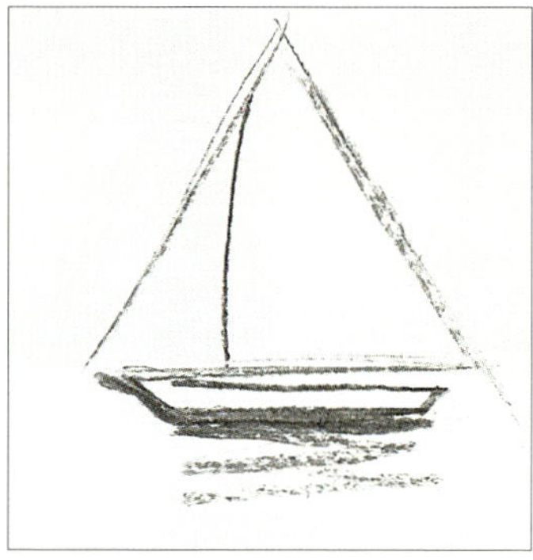

Starting from the triangle, draw a trapezium just below it. Darken it with a second stroke. Afterwards do a freehand zigzag stroke to represent this plain sailing boat"s reflection in the water.

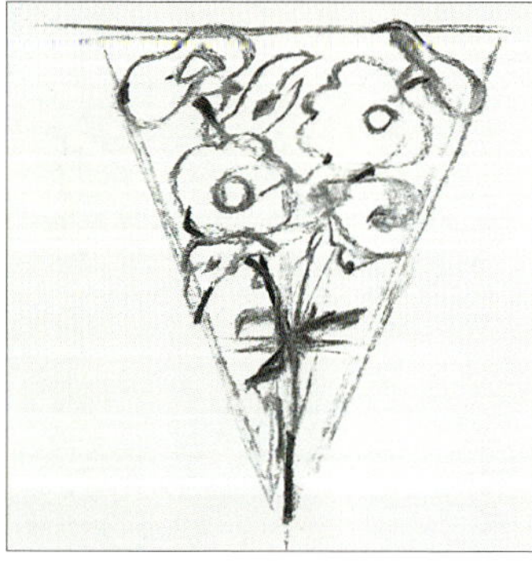

An upside-down triangle can also be drawn and a great variety of objects fitted into it, like this bunch of flowers. The shapes are complicated but the outline limits are simple.

A straight line, the simplest to draw, is realized holding the charcoal flat and vertical between the fingers. As everybody knows, when three straight lines are joined together, a triangle is formed, four make a square or a rectangle, and a complete 360° curve makes a circle. These three figures are enormously important in drawing for with them any shape can be drawn, however complex it may be.

THE OUTLINE

If an object is placed in a made to measure box, the object is held tight even though not all of its edges touch the "wrapping". If you want to do a drawing, which is easier to draw, the box or the object? The box, of course, because its forms are more straightforward. You give a drawing a solid base when you start it by outlining the elemental external forms, as if we were introducing the object to be represented into a tightly holding box.

ELEMENTAL FORMS

Doing an outline of the drawing means that more complex shapes can be fitted into simpler ones. When a drawing is started by doing

THE TRIANGLE.

Everyone knows the shape of a triangle and how to draw one on paper. The correct process is to use the charcoal flat between the fingers to do a preliminary outline. Straight lined shapes are drawn with vertical strokes and no shakiness. Afterwards, use the charcoal point to go over the stroke. If any line has to be rubbed out, a mere touch with the hand or the cloth is enough.

Remember that building on this straightforward form it is possible to draw more complicated ones inside. The trickiness of a drawing is increased if you do not start out with a preliminary basic scheme: fit the complex forms into simpler ones.

THE CIRCLE.

A circle is more complicated to represent than any straight lined object. The difference is that it has to be drawn freehand. Hold the charcoal crayon flat and horizontal between the fingers and do a complete curve. The smaller the chunk is, the less likelihood there is of shape deformation. If it does not turn out as round as it could be, you can always use a glass, or a saucer, as a guideline. However, it is worth persevering until you reach an acceptable level.

Just like the triangle, a circle is an elemental shape that can be the basis for more complicated drawings. So, for example, when drawing an orange if you do not draw a circle beforehand it may turn out deformed or squashed.

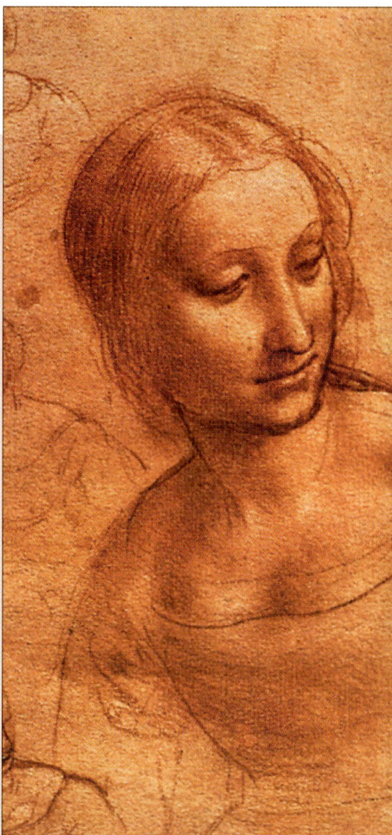

"A young woman" by Leonardo da Vinci (1452-1519). In the drawing it can be noted that all the forms can be reduced to simpler ones. This is especially true for the head, which is based on a circle.

THE CIRCLE

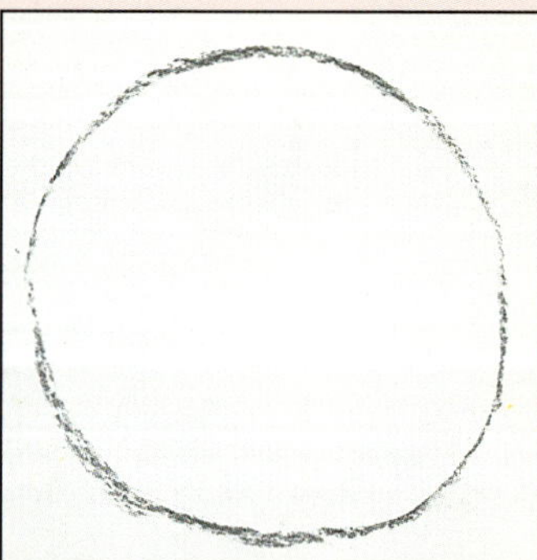

A circle is the basis for complicated outlines. Drawing it correctly requires a certain amount of practice and great mastery of charcoal.

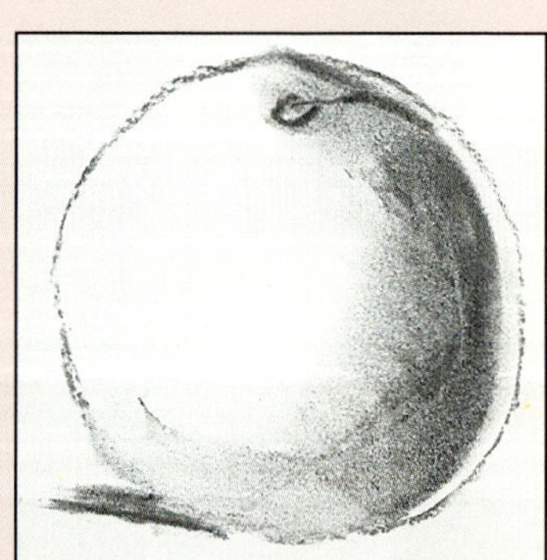

Here is another example of the usefulness of a circle: outlining a orange. As you can see, an object is much more manageable to draw an object if it is outlined in simpler forms.

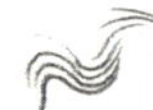

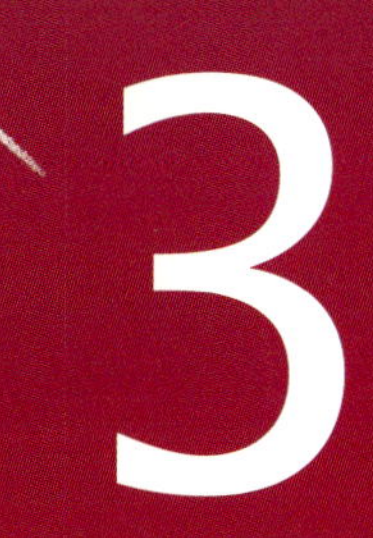

Up until now we have studied drawing by analyzing flat, straight, curved and zig-zagged strokes. The next step is to join these strokes to form triangles, squares and circles, the basic shapes into which the drawing fits.

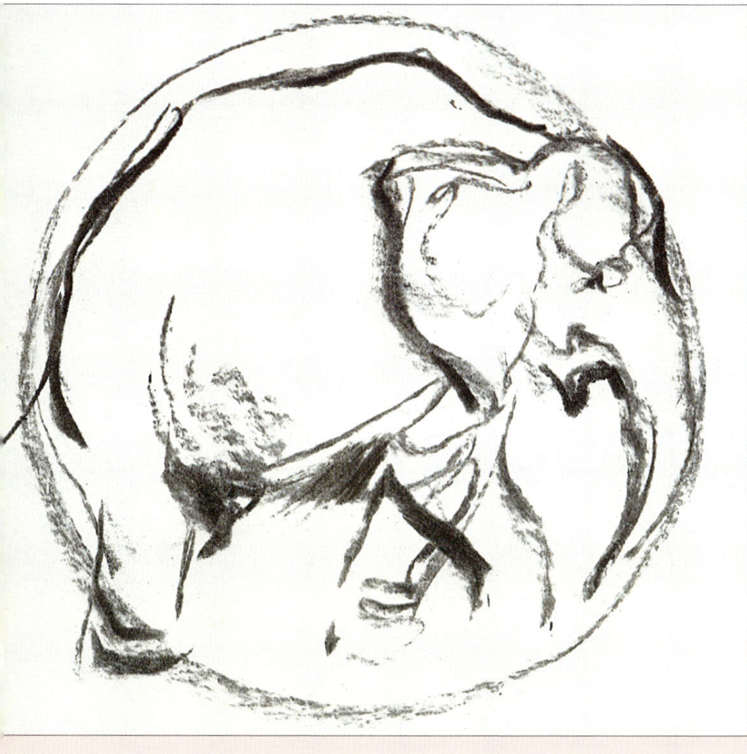

This drawing of an elephant started out as a circle. The drawing process was thus greatly simplified.

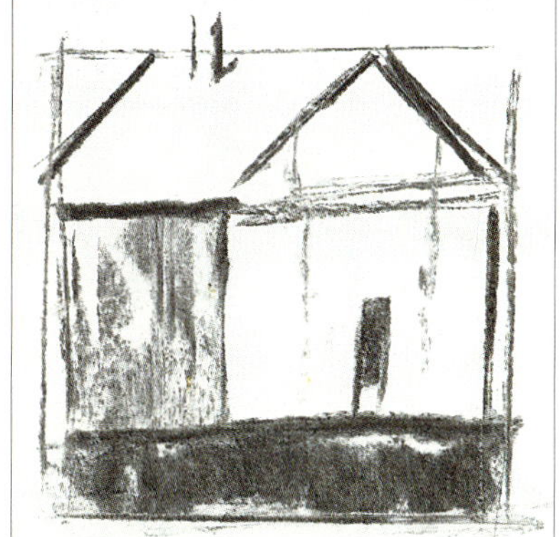

To do this drawing, start with a square into which the elemental forms of the house are placed. All the complex forms can be broken down into simpler ones.

THE SQUARE

Squares and rectangles are easier to draw. Often, inside of them more complicated forms, consisting of triangles and circles, are fitted.
Squares and rectangles are drawn in the same way as a triangle: slide the side of the charcoal over the paper to produce firm lines. The shape of a rectangle enables you to do the outline for all the picture or to distribute the individual elements that make up the drawing.

Draw an orange starting from a circle. Shade the right side with the crayon flat and use the fingers to spread the charcoal and to tone down the stroke-like appearance. Afterwards, use the charcoal point to do some freehand lines that come together at the top. Do a little shadow on the lower part.

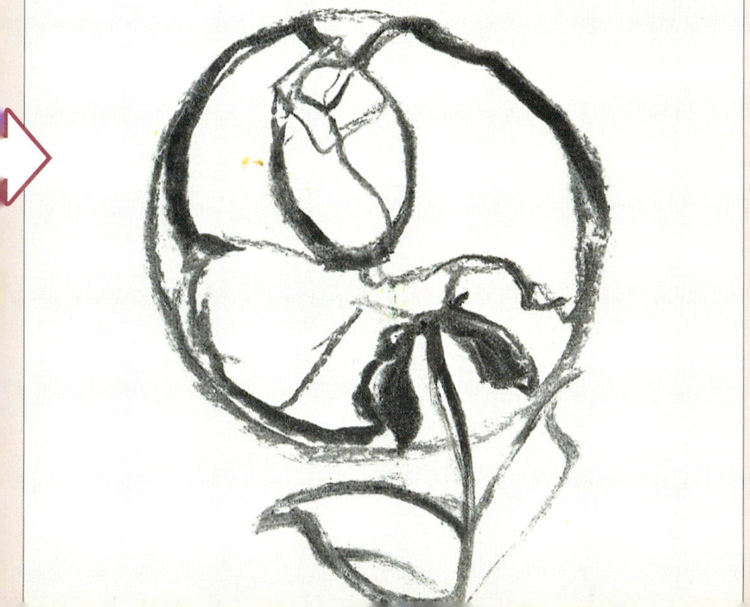

SIMPLE FORMS FOR COMPLICATED PICTURES

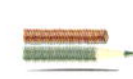

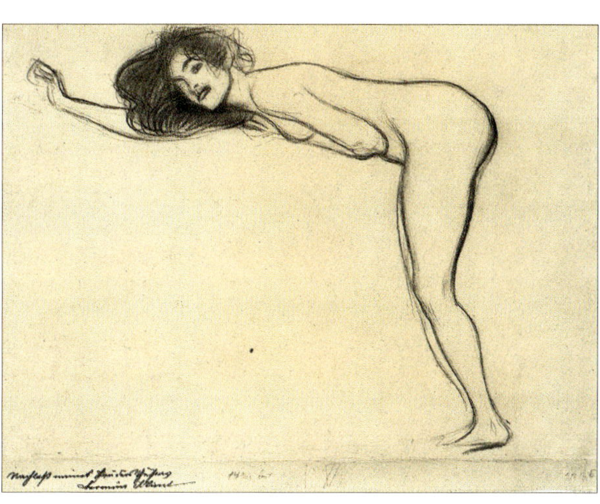

One of the most positive exercises that can be done to understand the internal forms of an object, and its outline, consists in taking a picture and trying to find how the outline was done by superimposing lines on top. This exercise can be done with all types of pictures, models or works of art. You can examine masterpieces to find out how the artists have been able to get down to concrete details starting from simple geometric forms.
As you can see in the drawing **"Nude leaning forwards"** in black pastel by **Gustav Klimt (1862-1918)** the process started from a triangle outline. Within this triangle there is another one, identical but smaller, which outlines the figure.

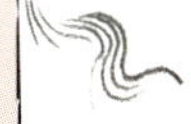

3 THE OUTLINE. THE FIRST STEPS

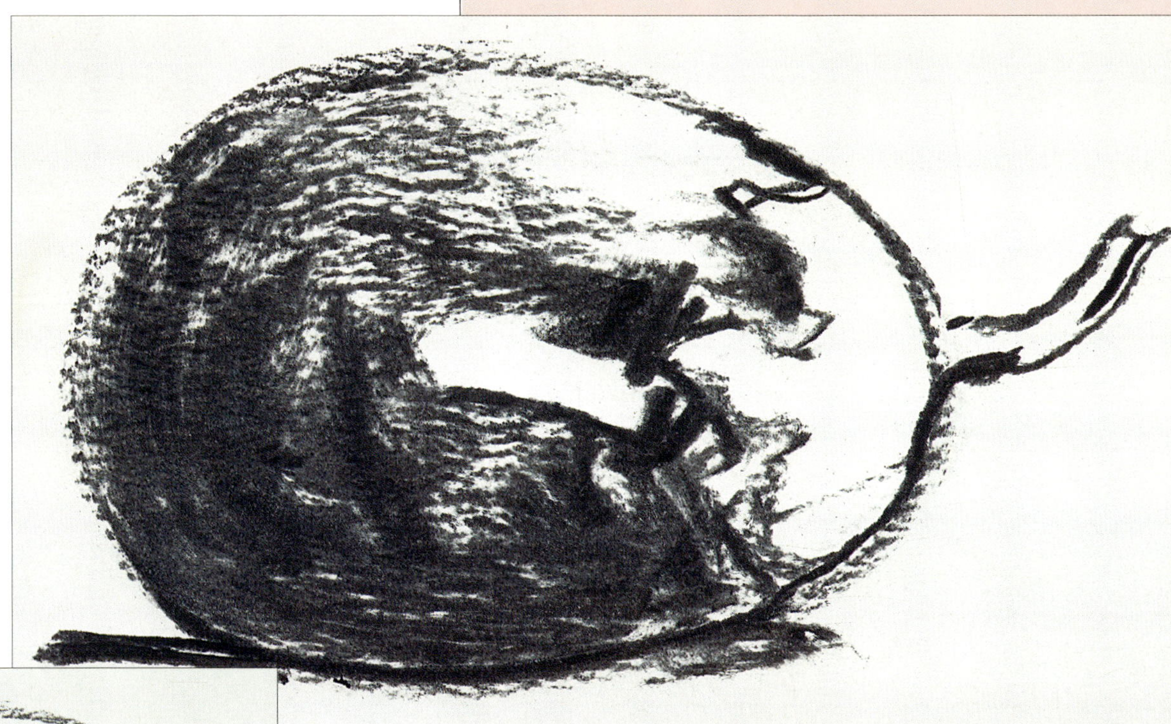

This eggplant has been fitted into an oval shape drawn beforehand.

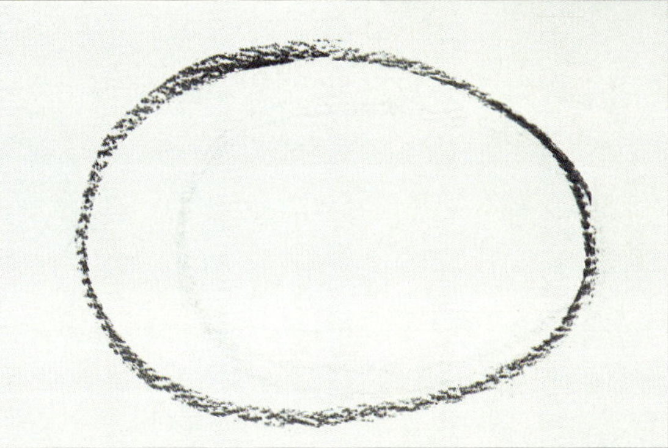

An oval is one of the most complicated geometric forms that exists.

COMPLEX FORMS

Besides the triangle, the circle and the square, there are other geometric forms that are complicated, especially those that require you to draw freehand curves. Unless you are an experienced draftsman you will probably have to do continuous corrections until you get it right. This is the advantage of charcoal: it is easily rubbed out. When a shape is not good enough just flick it off and start again, guided by the faint trace left before.

COMBINING FORMS TOGETHER

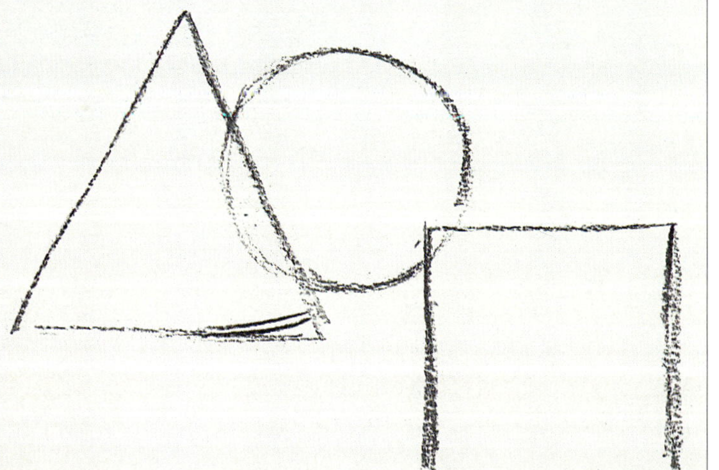

This triangle, circle and square, combined together are the basis for this drawing, the definitive objects of which do not yet appear but will be fitted into these geometric shapes.

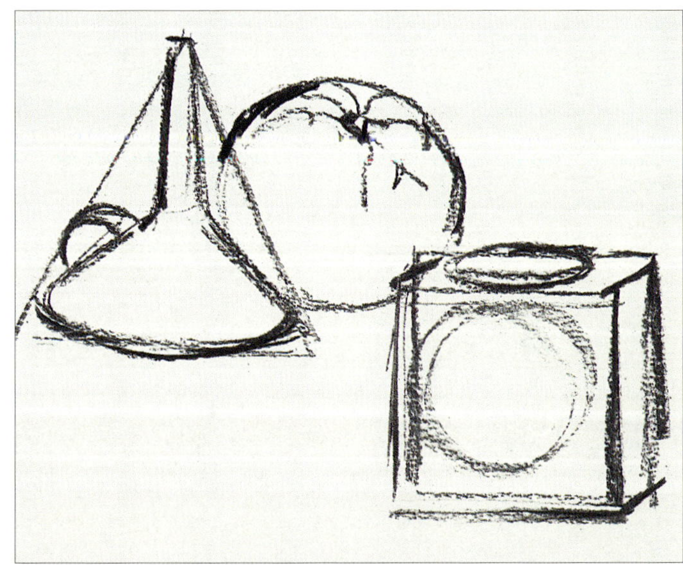

Starting from these shapes above, it is easy to complete the drawing fitting in the objects. The superfluous lines, once they have been used for the outline, can be erased.

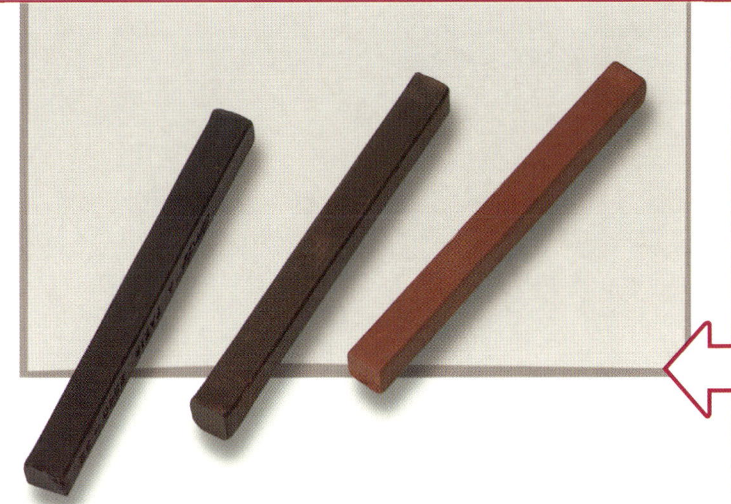

DRAWING WITH DRY MEDIA

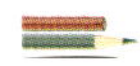

Drawing uses many media, among which the so-called dry media stand out. They do not need any moistness to be applied, nor do they require a brush. One example is the combination of sanguine and sepia colored chalk. Other colored chalks can also be used.

Sanguine -which is available in the market in square bars- offers the possibility of obtaining earth red tones very different to those possible with charcoal. Chalk bars come in different tones and colors, and, like sanguine, they are very brittle. The technique for these two dry media is identical to charcoal. Another very similar drawing medium, oiled charcoal, produces very dense blacks and is more stable than normal charcoal. Its appearance is very similar to sanguine.

THE OVAL.

The oval, like the circle, is another geometric shape that requires certain mastery. Its unique shape means that many varied elements can be fitted inside it, elements that would only fit into other simple shapes with difficulty, for example, avocados, eggs or any round thing drawn in perspective.

A good way of drawing an oval is to fit it inside a rectangle. This will help you to get the proportions right.

COMBINING FORMS

Having analyzed how to fit diverse elements into simple forms, we can go onto another question: how to combine these forms together to get more complicated groups of elements.

Often in a drawing, especially in a still life, there are several different objects which have their own outline. Combining them together to get an harmonious overall effect is as important as finding the right outline for each one.

Remember that when doing the scheme of a drawing, the outline must always be progressive. There may be provisional lines that are the basis of complex forms and also give equilibrium to the whole drawing.

Once the drawing is finished these lines will be erased.

To understand this better, do a simple exercise based on creating a composition from three basic forms, a circle, a square and a triangle. Inside of each of them the definitive objects will be drawn. Draw the shapes with a rapid outline. They, in turn, must fit into a rectangle that represents the picture itself.

Starting from these basic shapes, it will be easy to complete the drawing. The objects have to be fitted into the forms. Afterwards the superfluous lines will be erased.

BREAKING DOWN THE FORMS

Elements or objects that are formed by especially complicated shapes can always fit into simpler schemes. Once the general form has been decided on, smaller outlines can be made inside it until you arrive at the definitive form. This means that just as you can combine different objects and their forms to create a balanced still life, in the same way a complex object can be broken up into simpler forms, all of them fitted into elemental geometric shapes.

Bear in mind that any object which can be used as a model, however complicated it may be, can always be divided into smaller geometric shapes.

An artist must learn to see any model as a unit, and, afterwards, as the sum of different shapes. First, the artist must identify the form in the space that surrounds it, then its internal dimensions, and, finally, the combination of both.

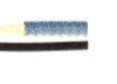

LEARNING HOW TO SCHEMATIZE

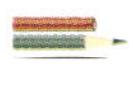

Learning how to schematize with geometric shapes makes drawing a lot easier, as does having a discerning eye for seeing the scheme of an object, a great help when you are faced with a blank piece of paper.

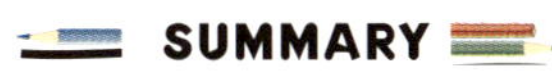

SUMMARY

THE OUTLINE

Simple shapes, which are easy to draw, help in the elaboration of more complex forms.

TRIANGLES AND RECTANGLES

A triangle is drawn by sliding the charcoal on one of its sides. Inside it, more complicated shapes can be fitted, like, for example, a bunch of flowers or a sailing boat.

A rectangle, too, is easy to draw. Inside it, forms, which in turn contain other shapes, can be fitted.

CIRCLES AND OVALS

Circular shapes, a possible base for more complicated outlines, are drawn freehand. This requires a steady hand and practice by the draftsman.

COMPLEX FORMS

Complex forms can be simplified by reducing them to groups of simple geometric shapes.

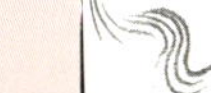

3 Exercices *Step by step*

THE OUTLINE. THE FIRST STEPS

The outline is nothing more than a guide which helps us to represent the forms of the objects. If you know how to draw a circle, a rectangle and a triangle, that is enough to get started on drawing more complex elements and forms.

The following exercise is about the outline. Starting out from a triangle, two rectangles and an oval we will draw a vase and a bunch of flowers. It is straightforward exercise, but special attention is required when elaborating the different geometric forms for they are the basis of all the drawing.

Bear in mind that the exercises put forward in each section assume that the learner has taken on board the concepts explained previously. In the following pages the learner is assumed to master flat strokes and charcoal point techniques.

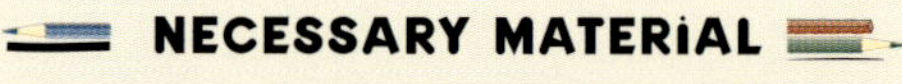

NECESSARY MATERIAL

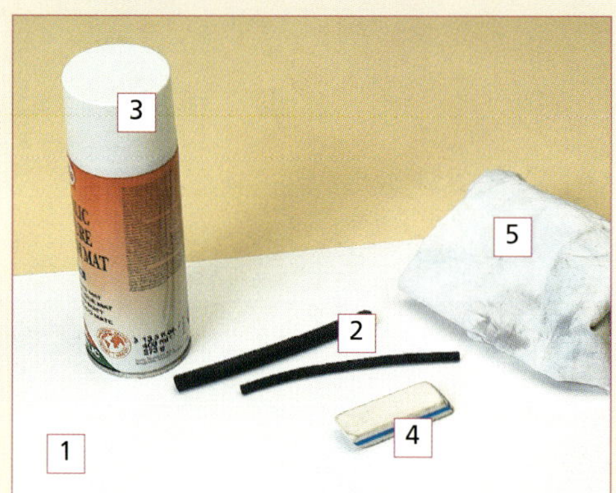

Drawing paper (1), charcoal (2), fixative (3), an eraser (4), and a cleaning cloth (5).

Always do the outline starting with the general shapes and then go on to more specific aspects. Every shape can have more complicated ones inside it.

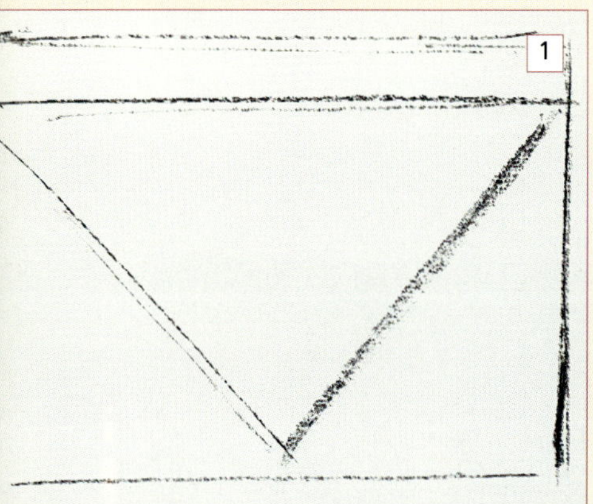

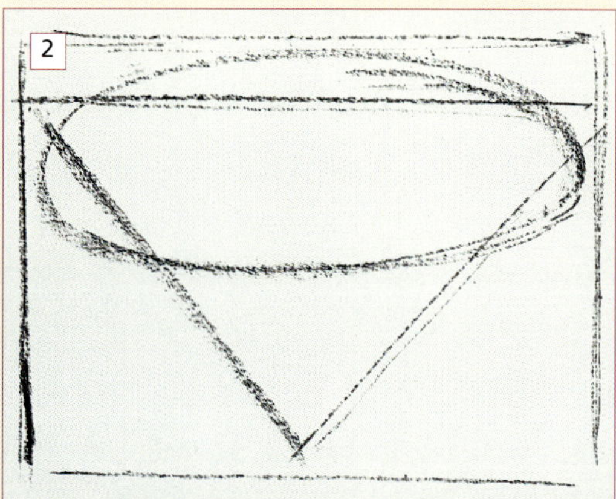

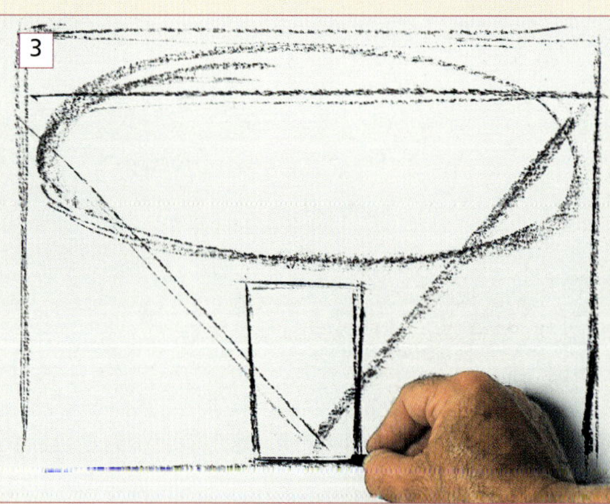

1· START THE DRAWING BY DOING THE OUTLINE. It is going to occupy all the space. Outline the four sides of a rectangle with the crayon flat, sliding the charcoal over the surface. Another alternative is to use the charcoal point.

HOLDING THE CHARCOAL FLAT, draw two diagonal lines from the top two corners down to the middle of the base to form a triangle within the rectangle.

AS YOU CAN SEE, general forms can have smaller forms inside them. The rectangle aids the drawing of the upside-down triangle, which in turn will be a reference for new shapes.

2· DO A FIRM, QUICK STROKE WITH THE CHARCOAL point to draw an oval shape in the upper part of the triangle; it actually goes beyond the triangle top and almost touches the upper limit of the rectangle. Do not worry if it is not perfect: it is an outline and not a technical drawing.

AS THE DRAWING IS QUITE BIG the curves should always be guided by the forearm and not the wrist.

3· THE NEXT STEP IS TO DRAW THE COMPLETELY rectangle and vertical outline of the flower vase.

THE REFERENCE POINTS FOR THIS NEW RECTANGLE must be the base line of the bigger triangle, the vertex of the triangle, and the bottom of the oval. It is easy to place a simple rectangle between these points.

4· THE OUTLINE OF THE VASE AND FLOWER forms is now completely constructed. So you can start to draw using the structure as a guide.

THE DRAWING ITSELF IS STARTED with some quite schematic flowers placed inside the oval and done with strokes with the point.

CONTINUE TO DRAW THE FLOWERS USING THE POINT. It is not necessary to draw precisely: what matters is the overall perception and not the details of the petals.

THE FLOWERS are schematized with curved, not too hard lines.

Outlining a flower vase based on simple formas

5· BY THIS STAGE we have now completed the objectives of this exercise in combining outlines. From now on you can continue to practice the drawing of the vase and the bunch of flowers.

6· USE THE ERASER TO ELIMINATE THE LINES that are no longer useful. If the eraser were dirty it could smudge the paper by getting into the pores.

HOLD THE CHARCOAL flat and start to darken the background, marking round the shape of the vase and flowers.

FINISH OFF THE DARKENING OF THE BACKGROUND but bear in mind that the rectangle frame-lines you did at the start allows the edges of the drawing to be seen.

7· PUT DOWN A FEW DARK TOUCHES on the vase and the bunch of flowers to give volume. Afterwards, spray the drawing with fixative so that the charcoal clings to the paper.

AS WE HAVE SEEN, it is not difficult to draw when the complex forms are fitted into simple geometric shapes.

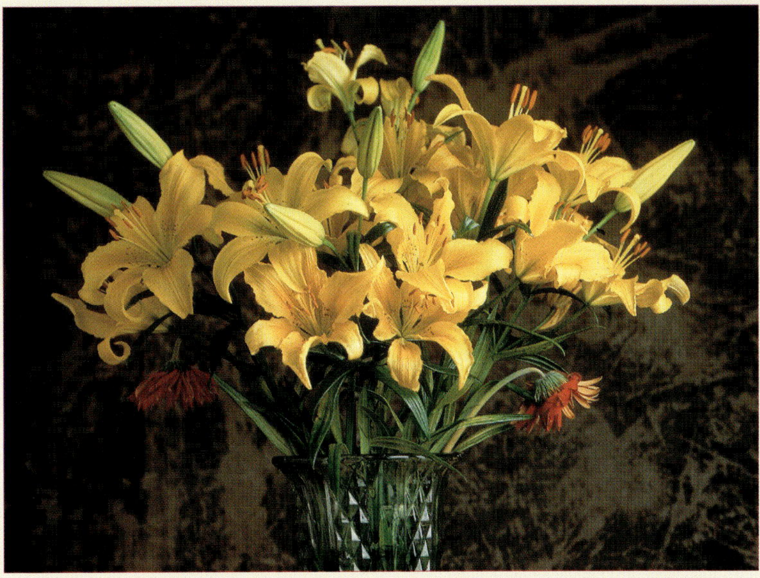

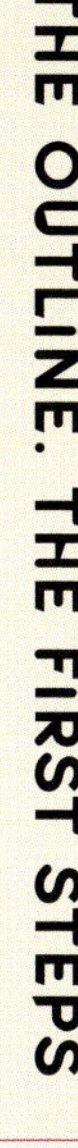

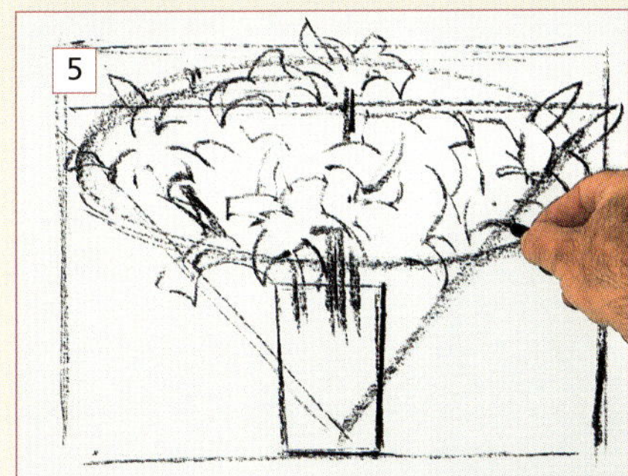

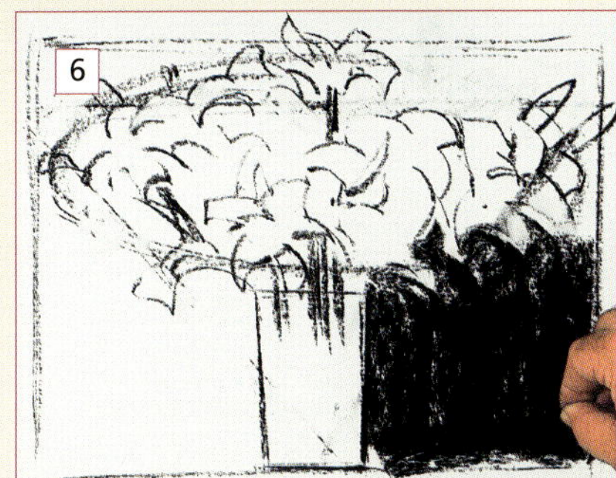

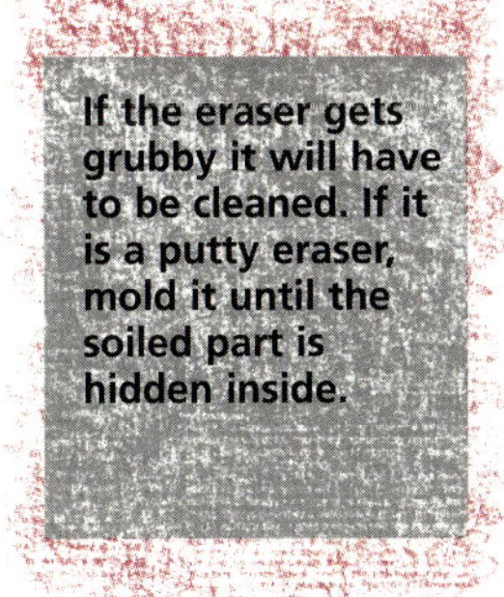

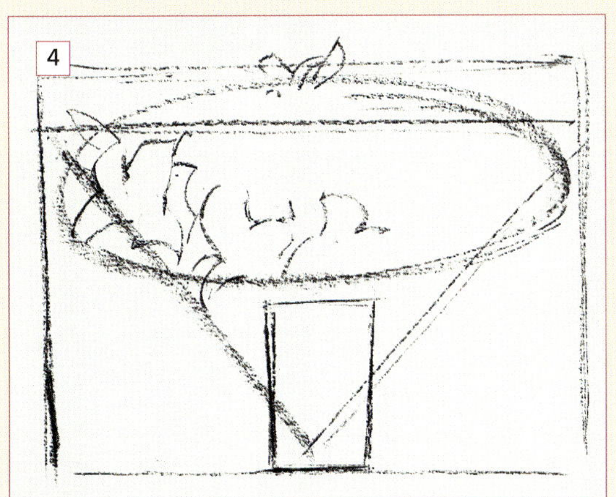

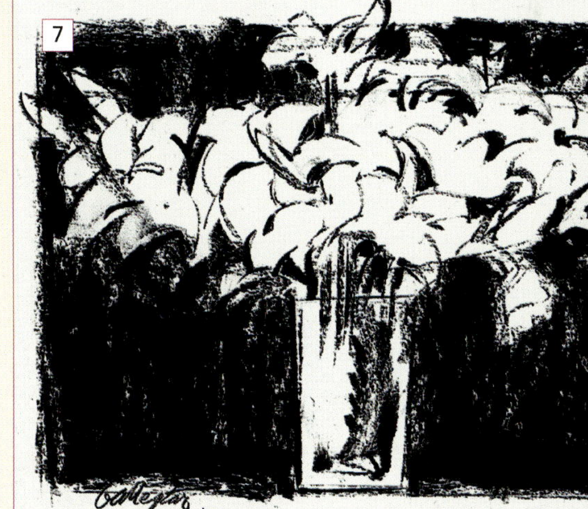

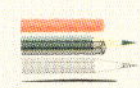

SUMMARY SCHEME

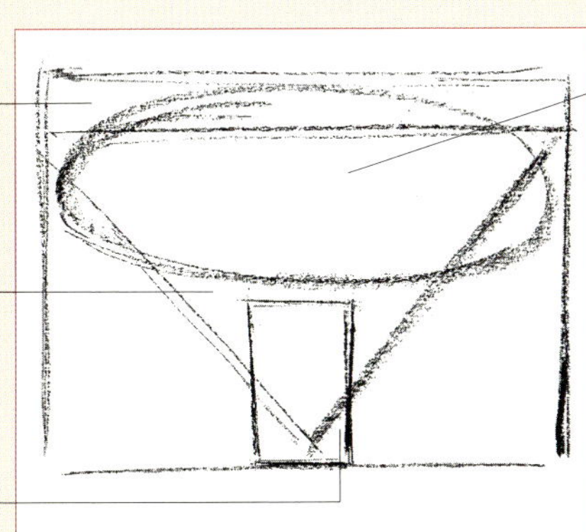

Do the general outline of the drawing.

e general form of the flowers triangular. The outline is done before drawing.

To separate the form of the bunch of flowers from the vase, outline the flowers inside this elliptic shape.

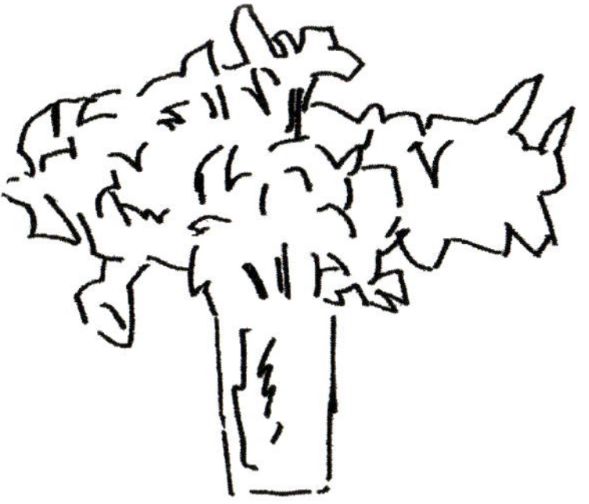

Once the scheme of the outline has been completed, you can start to draw the details.

FRAME-LINES, COMPOSITION AND OUTLINES

Before starting to draw on paper you must study where the different objects, both the main forms and the complements, are going to be placed. The first issue is to decide the frame-lines of the picture, meaning how to treat all the space that the drawing will occupy. Secondly, the outline has to be done. As we have studied, this implies drawing straightforward lines which mark off the model. Finally, the composition has to be decided on. This will depend on the artist"s viewpoint and how he or she lays the forms of the model out on the paper, always looking for maximum harmony with the space around them. However, before putting pencil to paper the artist should contemplate the model and try to structure the picture in the mind"s eye. Keen observation goes a long way to making a good drawing. Another point to bear in mind is that everything we learn related to frame-lines, composition and outline will be vital for later work, not only drawing but for any type of pictorial representation.

Before starting to draw, structure the forms and then mark on the paper the frame-lines, the composition and the outline.

THE FRAMING

When deciding the space that the picture is going to occupy -the space within the frame-lines- the artist must study the different possibilities so that the best is chosen. Although the paper may be rectangular this does not necessarily have to be the shape of the picture. Although frame-lines is part of all pictorial techniques, it actually belongs to drawing, which is the basis of all representations.

RECOURSES FOR DOING GOOD FRAME-LINES

To get the frame-lines right, as well as being a good observer of the model, the artist must also follow these guidelines:

Look for a point of interest in the model, for example a particular building or a highlight.

Avoid monotony shifting the point of interest away from the center.

As far as is possible avoid cluttering up any part of the space with too many elements.

Give space to the tone contrasts. For example, allow there to be light and shadow zones in a landscape.

When you believe it is necessary, modify the format of the picture to go with the frame-lines. You do not have to be limited to formats available in the shops. You can use long stretched formats, or even round ones.

FRAME-LINES WITH CARDBOARD

This tool is made at home by cutting out two black L-shapes. It is essential that the right angle is exact.

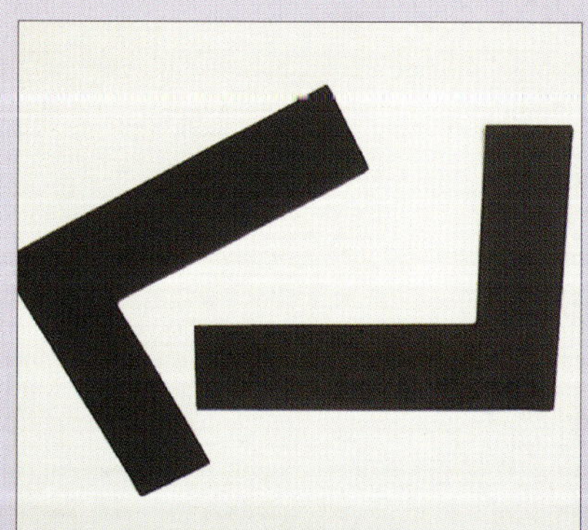

Afterwards, frame the object that is going to be drawn opening and narrowing the inner rectangle until you hit on the required frame-lines and the part of the model you are going to draw.

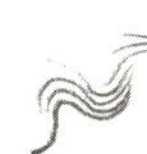

Now that we have studied the stroke and the outline we will see that new questions come into play when we do the drawing. We must learn how to layout the objects of the composition, which perspective to give them, and where to place the principal object.

4

COMPOSITION TYPES

In general a good composition has a basically simple geometric structure. This is demonstrated by the masterpieces of painting, and, in fact, a good method of practicing frame-lines and composition in drawing is to study how the classics were done. Place a sheet of tracing paper over the picture and use a ruler and a pencil and look for the basic composition by drawing lines that enclose the main forms. For example, in the oil painting **"Hippomenes and Atlanta" by Guido** Reni (1575-1642), now in the Prado Museum, you can observe a fine example of a trapezium composition. The oil painting **"Danae receiving the golden rain" by Tiziano,** also displayed in the Prado Museum, is an interesting example of a triangular composition. In the beginning it may be difficult to see simple forms in quite complex pieces, but with a little observation and practice you will discover that the most complicated shapes are based on simple elements.

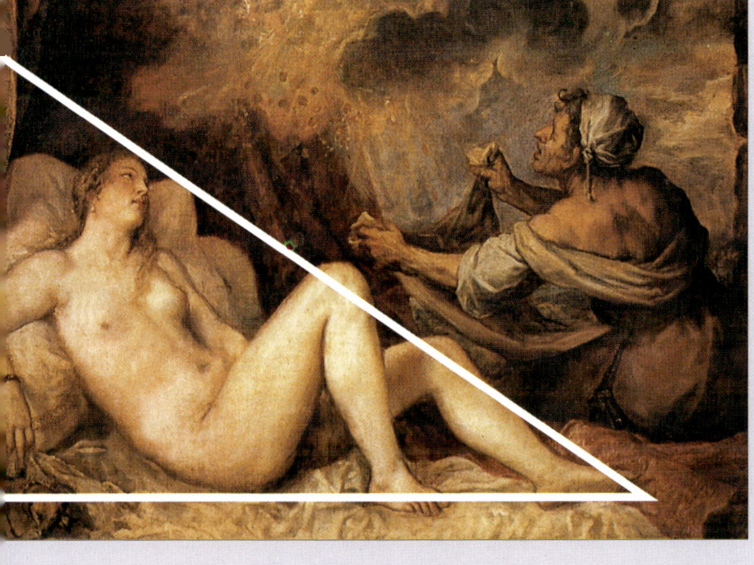

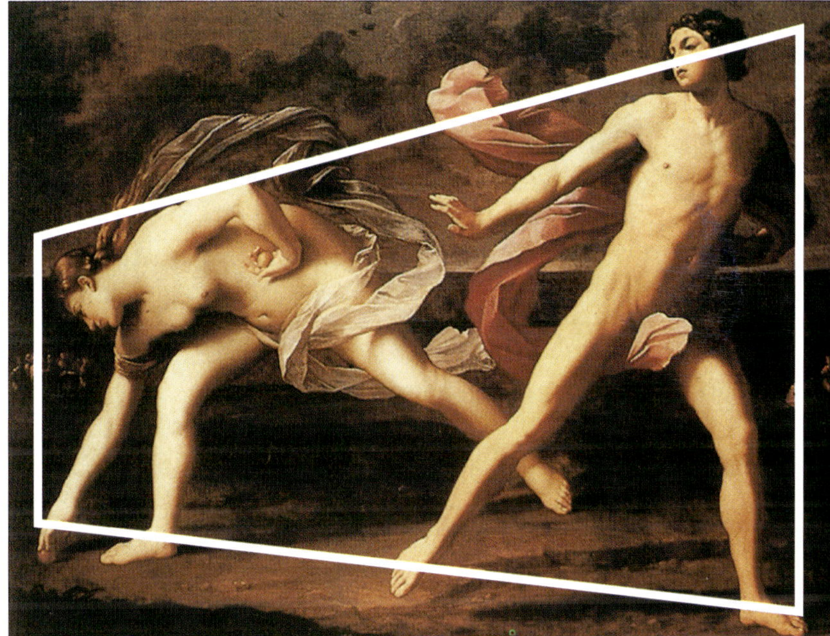

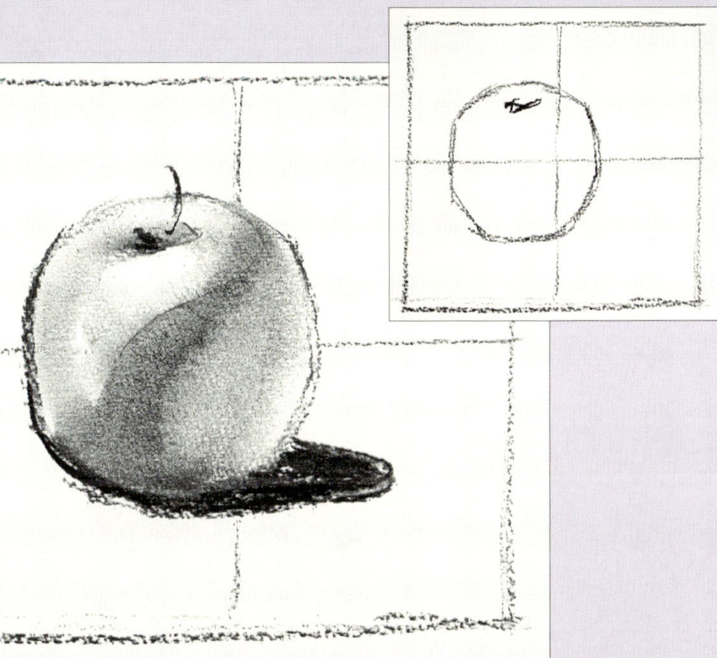

Firstly do the frame-lines of the drawing, and afterwards draw two axes to fix the center of the image. Outline the model form, here it is an apple, shifting it subtly away from the middle to get an interesting composition.

After outlining the form, start to draw the shadow of the apple. This new element will compensate the composition.

WORKING WITH LITTLE FRAMES

When you choose a model or an object to draw or paint, it is not always easy to decide on the best frame-lines. It can be a great aid to try all the possible framings by using two home-made L-shaped pieces of cardboard. This mobile, flexible frame will help you with your choice. When you are viewing the different framings, close one eye so that the frame works as a viewfinder. This same system can be used when working with photos as models, sliding the cardboard over the pictures.

OUTLINES AND FRAME-LINES

Once you have studied the frame-lines, it is necessary to draw the outlines: represent the forms with simple geometric shapes which mark off the object or model.

Having said this, it is worthwhile doing an exercise which ties both concepts together and puts them into practice in a drawing. To do this we are going to try square frame-lines for the drawing of an apple. Inside the square put in two axes that divide it horizontally and vertically. You can now locate the center of the drawing. Draw the apple slightly off center to make the framing more interesting.

Now that the fruit is outlined, proceed with the details: darken the right side with the charcoal and then gently pass your finger over.

Finally, paint the shadow of the apple with an intense charcoal stroke. The dark shadow is part of the drawing and gives equilibrium to the frame-lines.

THE COMPOSITION

The third factor, after the outline and frame-lines, which must be borne in mind when sketching is the composition, the aim of which is harmony between the shapes and the space they occupy. Although composition involves many subjective elements, there are basic rules that objectively contribute towards obtaining a sense of balance.

The elements of a drawing should be neither too centered, nor too cluttered, nor too far apart. Composition is a question of genuine equilibrium among the shapes.

GOOD OR UNSATISFACTORY FRAME-LINES

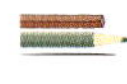

This landscape is going to be done with rectangular frame-lines and a horizontal line drawn across it as a reference point for the horizon. The curved composition of the river starts from this line and above it the rest of the elements have been drawn with direct, gestural strokes. In the first two pictures the frame-lines shift the river to the left, but in the third it has been centered, thus producing a certain sensation of disequilibrium.

The horizon line is placed slightly above the half way line. The curve to the right of the river starts in the lower left quarter and finishes almost in the middle of the picture.

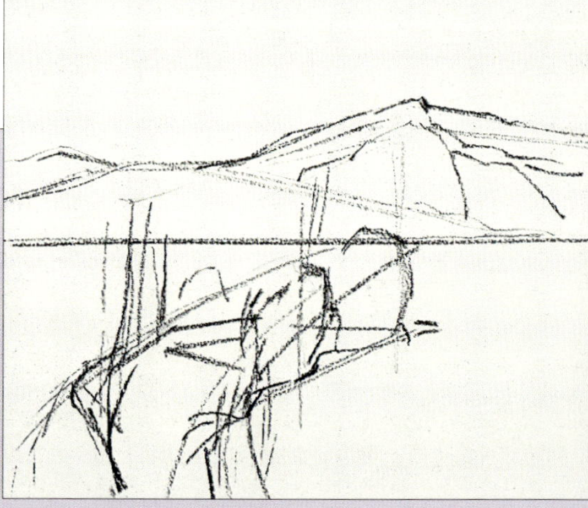

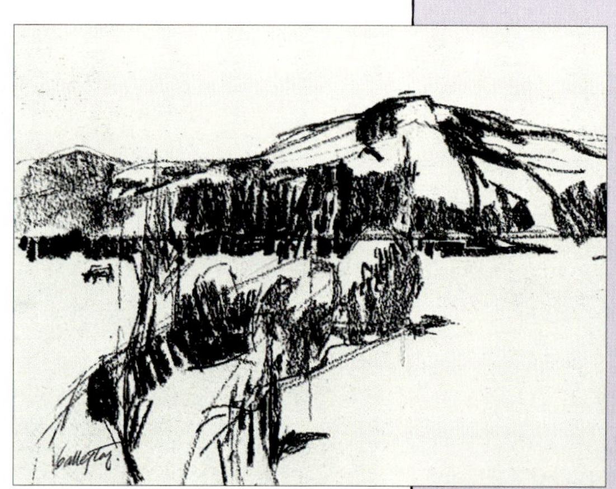

Compare the result of this image, realized with an inadequate composition, to the one on the left. The drawing is not bad but it has been spoiled by placing the river exactly in the middle.

The elements that complete the landscape can easily be added to the composition. Note that this composition pushes the river to the left within in the frame-lines.

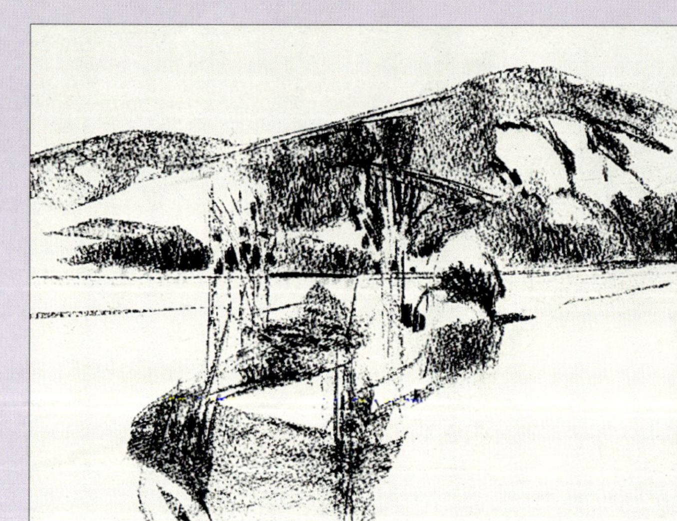

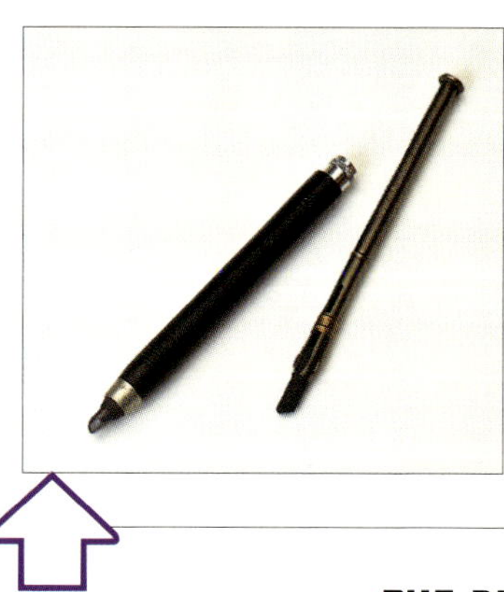

THE PROPELLING PENCIL

When drawing often the feel of the charcoal or sanguine becomes uncomfortable, especially when you are doing a fine stroke. If you place the crayon in a propelling pencil you will ensure a steady grip. This simple tool enables you to wield the charcoal with greater freedom, as if it were a pencil. Moreover, you can carry it around without fear of breaking the crayon. There are also holders available which allow you to get the most out of almost completely used up charcoal stubs.

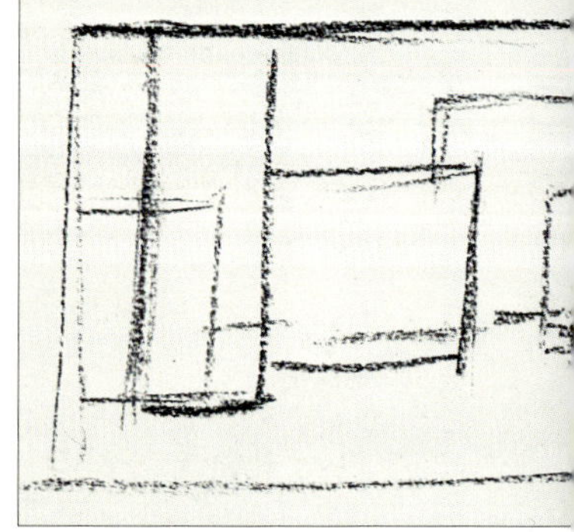

COMPOSITION AND FRAME-LINES

The frame-lines and the composition, important considerations in any picture or drawing, are closely linked. The more you paint or draw, the more fined tuned your sense for frame-lines becomes. Also you develop an instinct as to which models will make good images and how to arrange the composition.

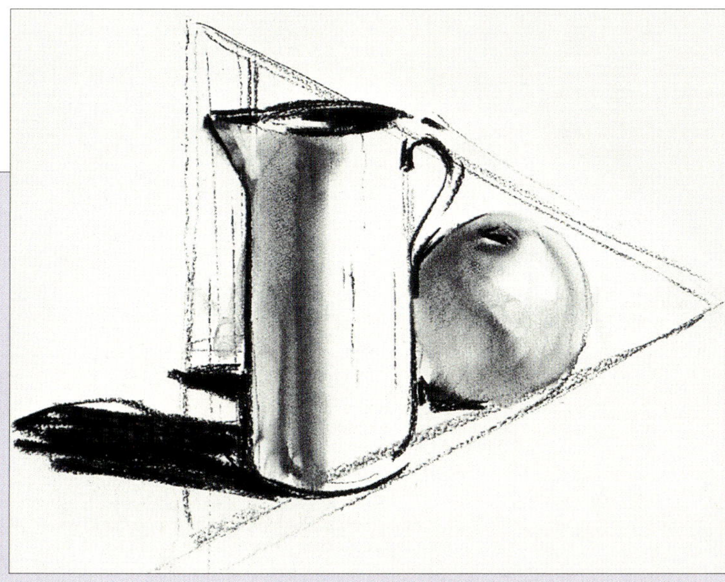

Once the frame-lines, the composition and the outlines have been done, continue to work on the figures and the shadows.

An exercise in composition. Draw a right facing triangle and inside it outline a jug and an apple. Logically, the jug is drawn in the wider part of the triangle while the apple is towards the vertex.

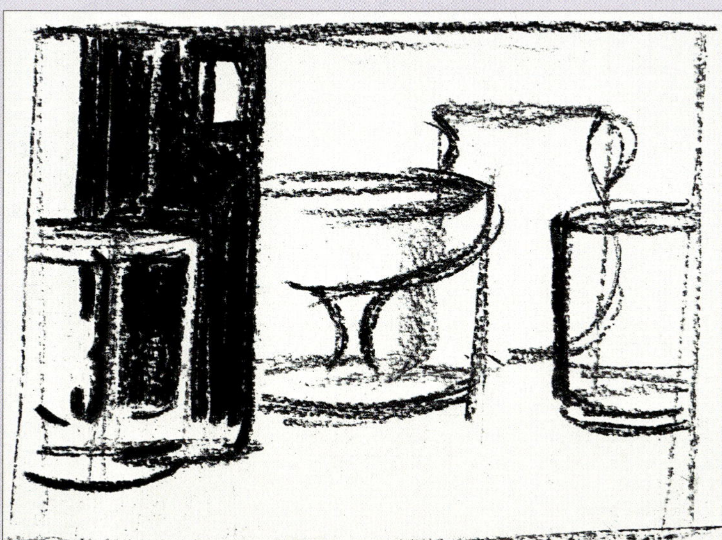

Getting the composition scheme and the outlines right means that you now have a solid base to go on to do an accomplished drawing.

Many types of composition are possible depending on the subject, the format, and even the artist"s intention and style. However, the rules of composition are equally applicable to any model, whether it be a figure composition, still life or landscape.

To a great extent the composition of a landscape depends on the frame-line it is given. Therefore, if a good landscape does not come off for some unknown reason, and its forms are balanced, special attention should be paid to the frame-line. Flawed frame-lines can spoil a good drawing.

COMPOSITION AND OUTLINE

In the same way that we learned how to outline a model with simple lines, so too must the composition be structured with basic guidelines. Inside this basic form we can fit in the shapes that make up the model. The idea is to use the outlines to layout the compositional elements of the picture.

However, never lose sight of the fact that outlines are to enable us to reduce complex shapes to simpler ones, something which has nothing to do with the general equilibrium or composition of the picture. All the same, the composition does build on the form outlines on the paper or canvas.

MEASUREMENTS AND THE COMPOSITION

To compose a drawing skillfully it is necessary to know how to do the outlines and to have a great capacity to see the model, two qualities which are learnt with practice. The fit of the composition must also be used to establish the proportions of the objects in the picture. Expressed in another way, this means that when a composition is done, for example inside a triangular scheme, the objects must be in proportion. The guidelines used to compose the picture are also valid for deciding the size of each object.

SUMMARY

THE FRAME-LINES

The frame-lines situates the model on the paper. The same model can have a great variety of frame-lines.

THE COMPOSITION

Composition means spreading out the elements of the model in a balanced way within the frame-lines. It is normally geometric.

MEASUREMENTS AND COMPOSITION

The composition scheme allows the proportions of the different objects to be established. The outlines are a great aid for the composition.

FRAME-LINES AND COMPOSITION IN LANDSCAPE

A landscape is subject to the same composition rules as any other model. However, in the case of landscapes, distributing the elements on the paper is closely related to moving the frame-lines.

4 Exercices *Step by step*

The fit is a guide which helps in the representation of the object forms. On the other had, the composition is aimed at achieving perfect harmony between these elements, which, of course, must always be correctly closed off with a frame-line, something which allows the composition of a model to be shifted.

In the next exercise we are going to do a straightforward composition consisting of a bottle and fruit still life. As can be seen, the frame-lines have already been decided on: the elements are slightly off-center in the picture.

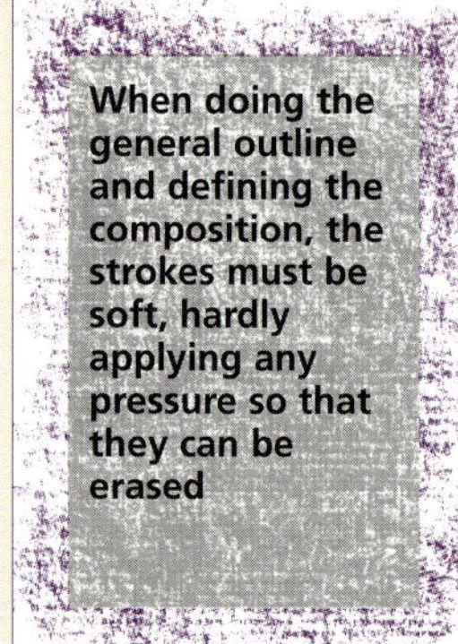

When doing the general outline and defining the composition, the strokes must be soft, hardly applying any pressure so that they can be erased

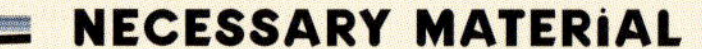

NECESSARY MATERiAL

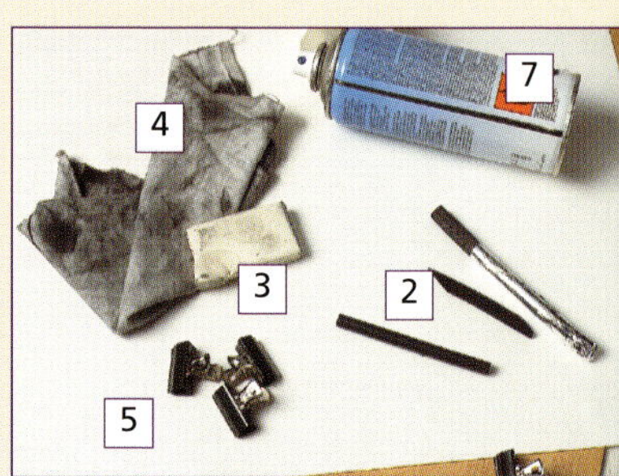

Drawing paper (1), charcoal (2), a putty eraser (3), a cloth (4), clips (5), a board (6), and spray fixative (7).

WHEN YOU LOOK AT THE MODEL you can see that there is a triangular-like composition in which the vertex coincide with the bottle lid and the side of the fruit. This composition is principally conditioned by the bottle, which is slightly to the left of the triangular form.

1· DRAW A VERTICAL LINE AS HIGH AS THE BOTTLE, and from the peak draw two sides to the triangle so that the fruit fits in.

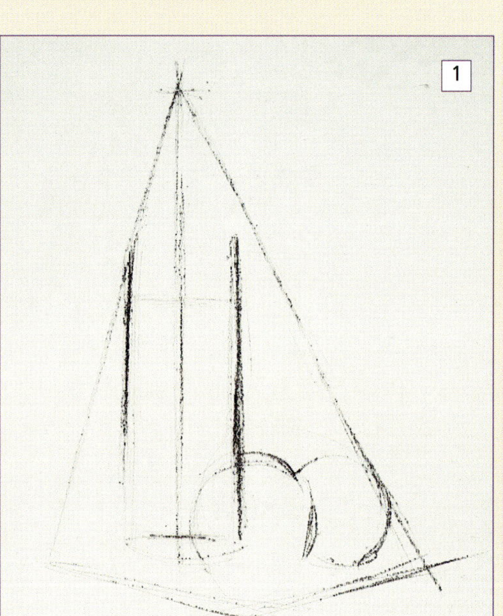

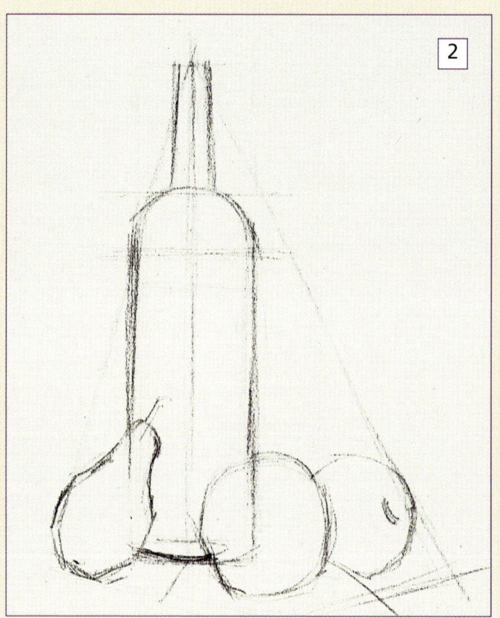

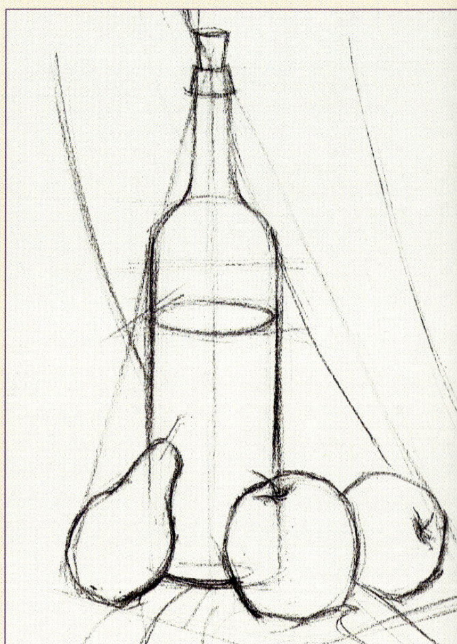

THE BASE OF THE BOTTLE IS ABOVE the line that marks the bottom of the fruit. This means that the triangle is somewhat deformed at the base. Mark the lower part of the bottle with a small vertical line to define the center. Now that the base of the bottle is established, draw the width of its body with two parallel lines.

TO THE RIGHT OF THE BOTTLE, start to do the fit of the apples with circles.

2· FIT THE PEAR IN TO THE LEFT OF THE BOTTLE. Be careful to make sure that its curve coincides with the side of the triangle.

MARK A NEW LINE where the left side of the bottle touches the triangle. This line is to initiate the curve of the bottle which will be done with a semi-circle.

AFTERWARDS, DRAW THE BOTTLE NECK with two not completely parallel lines.

HAVING DONE THESE LAST LINES, the outline of the composition is now completed. Now you have to soften the forms.

3· AS THE DRAWING IS DONE ON AN ALREADY STRUCTURED SCHEME, the new strokes, which must be precise, are guided by this base and can correctly define the forms.

DRAW THE OVAL THAT MARKS the wine level. Use free strokes to outline the folds in the cloth.

4· AS WE CAN SEE IN THIS STEP, NUMBER 4, the superfluous lines are rubbed out having served their purpose of constructing the fit. You can erase easily with a cloth or an eraser. Until the charcoal is fixed it does not stick to the paper.

A still life with a triangular composition

4

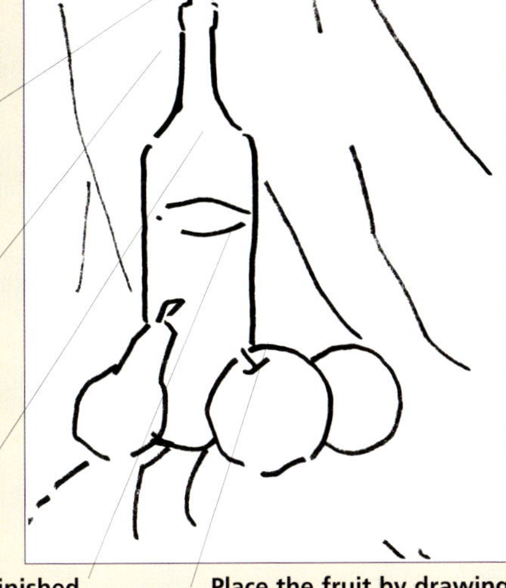

Define the triangular composition starting with the height of the bottle.

The curve of the bottle forms a semi-circle.

The wine level is represented by an oval.

Once the outline is finished, define the dark areas and finish the drawing in gray.

Place the fruit by drawing simple circles.

WHEN ALL THESE UNNECESSARY lines have been rubbed out, make the definition firmer by going over the lines with a new stroke.

5· NOW THAT THE DEFINITIVE FORMS OF THE FIT ARE MARKED, this still life composition exercise is finished. However, it is worthwhile continuing with the following steps to practice working with gray charcoal shades.

HOLD THE CHARCOAL FLAT, and without pressing too hard, color the dark zones of the still life and the dark areas in the background.

ON TOP OF THE GRAYS ALREADY DONE, emphasize the densest dark zones by pressing harder.

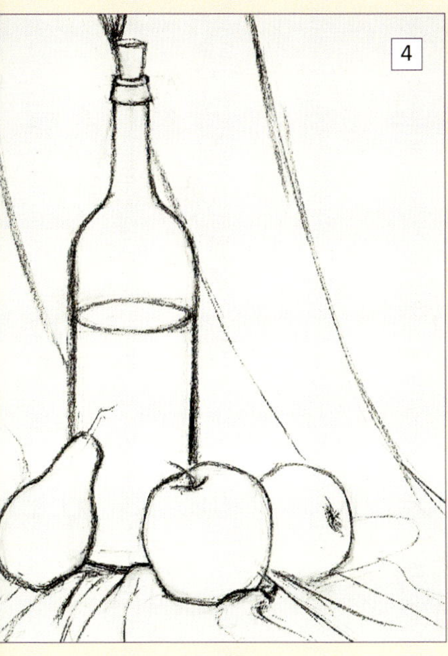

4

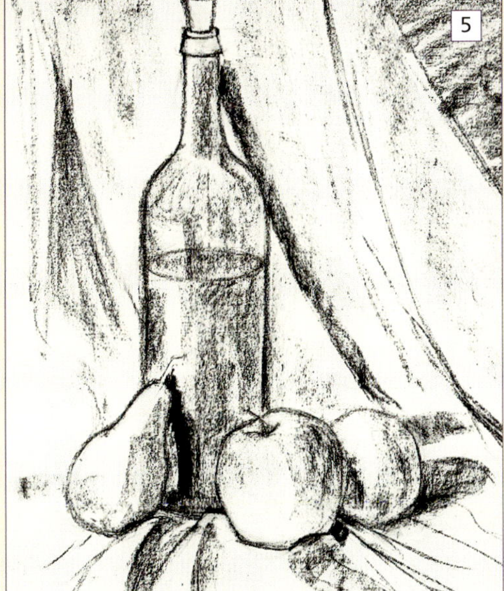

5

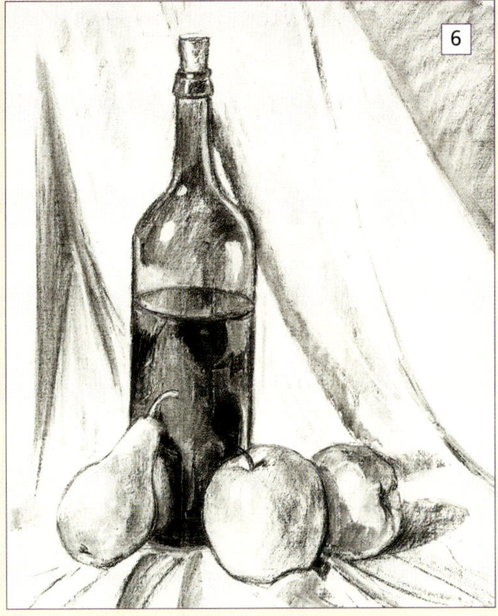

6

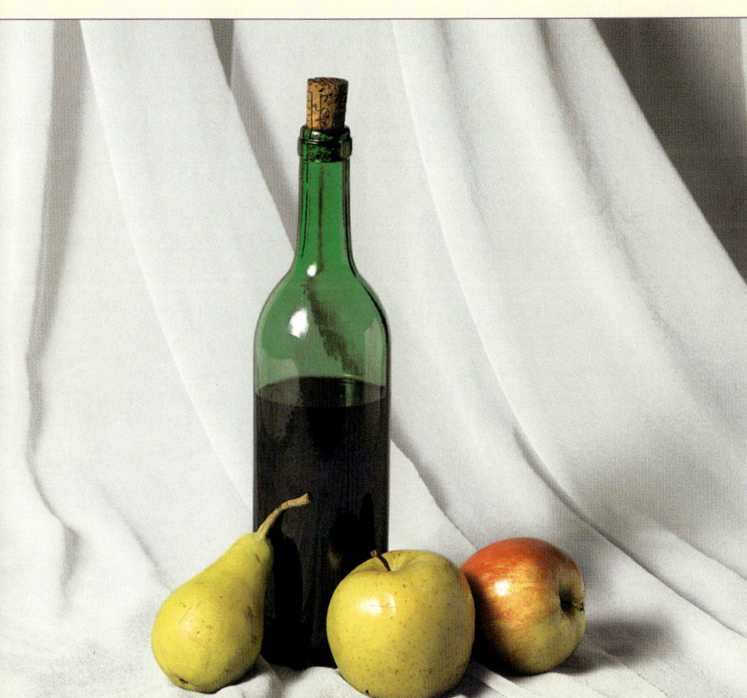

6· RUB AWAY PART OF THE DARK ZONES to get lighter grays. Observe how we have taken advantage of the rear apple shadow to adjust the form of the apple to the fore and to balance the composition with a new dark area.

USE THE FINGERS TO STUMP the most noticeable strokes in the background. Blend the strokes of the bottle and of the fruit.

PROBABLY STUMPING HAS LEFT THE PAPER GRUBBY so use the eraser to eliminate any smears. Open up a few highlights in the light zone of the fruit, on the bottle and in the background.

ALL THAT REMAINS TO BE DONE is to fix the drawing so that it is not spoilt by accidental contact. The charcoal is fixed with a spray held at about 30cm approximately.

COMBINING SANGUINE AND CHARCOAL

Working with charcoal is always an advantage because it is easy to correct and does not require many complementary materials. However, the range of grays possible can limit certain works. This is why it is worthwhile practicing combining charcoal with sanguine. Both use the same stroke technique and you will be able to add the range of red sanguine tones to the charcoal grays.

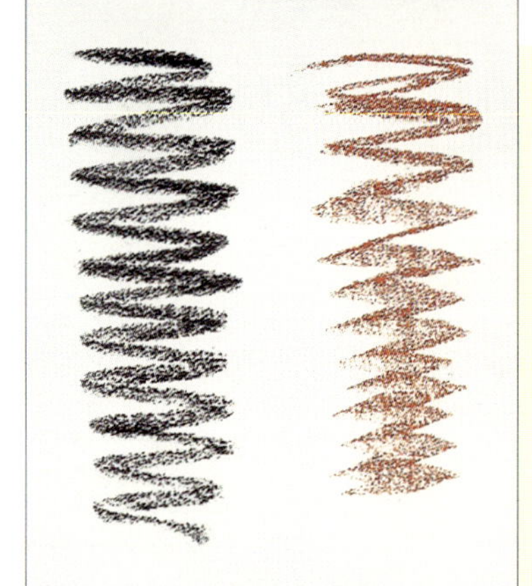

Before starting to do pieces in sanguine and charcoal, it is recommendable to try them out on paper. Sanguine is somewhat harder than charcoal.

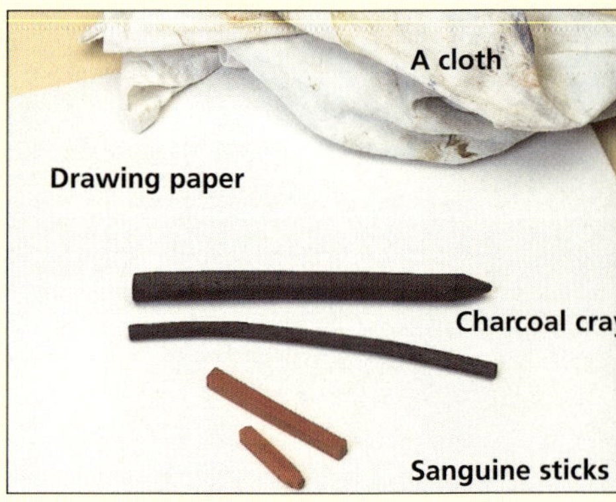

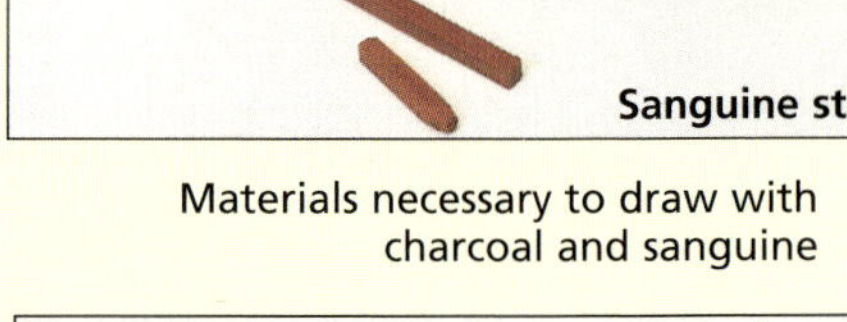

Materials necessary to draw with charcoal and sanguine

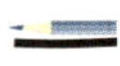

COMBINING TECHNIQUES

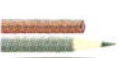

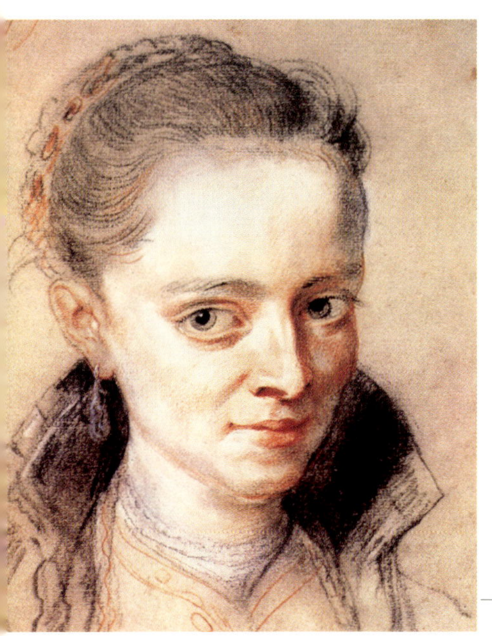

If there are many possibilities with charcoal alone, when another drawing medium is introduced, for example sanguine, then the results can be eye-opening, especially to those inclined to be colorists. They are both dry media which leave scuff marks on the paper, making them easier to blend. In this drawing by **Pedro Pablo Rubens (1577-1640)**, which successfully mixes both media, there are zones so delicately stumped that you cannot appreciate where the charcoal commences and the sanguine finishes. The gradations are perfect for giving volume to the face and achieving color differentiation between flesh tones and hair.

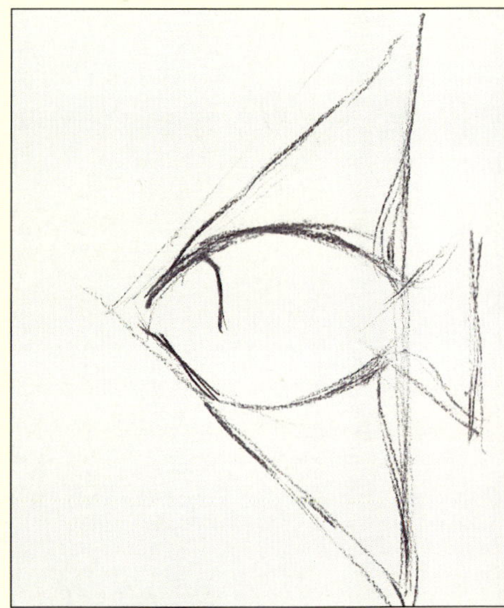

In any piece that combines charcoal and sanguine techniques it is better to do the fit in charcoal because when the drawing is finished it will be easier to erase.

THE MATERIALS

Charcoal is vegetable in its origin and produces black and gray strokes that come, as its name suggests, from the carbonization of wood.

Sanguine is a reddish mineral made of iron oxide, to which chalk and gum Arabic have been added. It is a medium somewhat harder than charcoal but it has no more adhesiveness.

To practice combining charcoal and sanguine the following material is necessary:

Sanguine sticks.
Charcoal crayons.
A cloth.
Drawing paper.

Combining charcoal and sanguine enables you to do drawings rich in tones.

Materials necessary to draw with charcoal and sanguine.
Drawing paper.
Charcoal crayons.
Sanguine stick.
A cloth.

As sanguine and charcoal are very delicate, touch-sensitive materials, many varied drawing exercises can be done with them working on the strokes and blending tones. Always start out from simple schemes and build up to the complicated forms.

COMPARING STROKES

When using any drawing medium, here sanguine and charcoal, it is worthwhile trying out a few strokes on paper beforehand to see how hard the crayon is, and how it responds. The softer it is, the denser the line will be.

When you do a stroke in sanguine you can maintain a fine line for longer than with charcoal due to the hardness of the former. This means that sanguine is more difficult to rub out than charcoal.

Bear in mind that in any charcoal and sanguine drawing, the white paper ground plays an important role. Not all the paper should be colored with marks, only the areas you have deliberately set aside. If you stump a zone, and the charcoal or sanguine spread too much, use a cloth or an eraser to eliminate the tone. The cloth will leave shadow-like, faint traces, but the eraser will restore the original white.

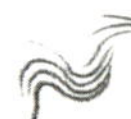

5

Charcoal is an ideal medium for going deeper into the technique of drawing for it permits all types of strokes and is easily corrected. Sanguine is the perfect complement because it is used in the same way and offers a wealth of tones and pictorial possibilities, suggestive forms and plastic values.

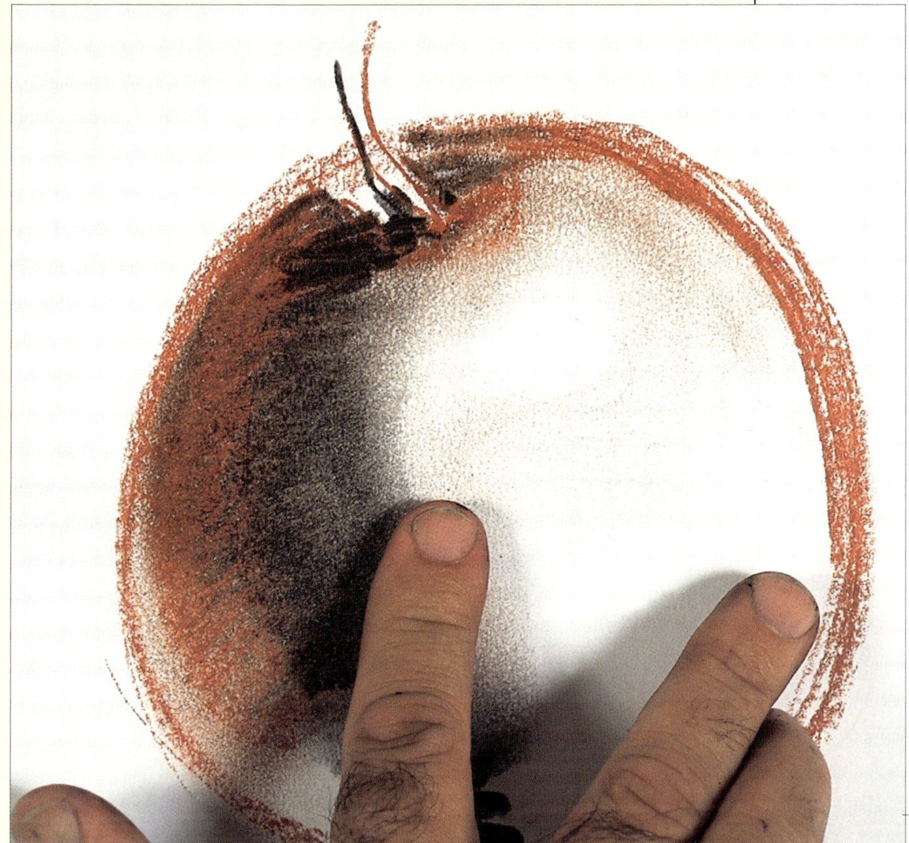

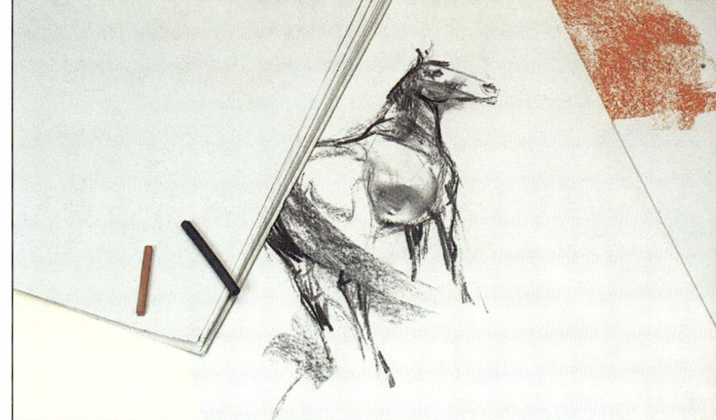

Gray papers or paper sold by weight are good options for doing tests and sketches.

PAPER FOR SKETCHES

When you are a dedicated draftsman it is recommendable to have a good supply of papers on which to do tests handy. Quality papers tend to be expensive and therefore are not suitable for testing. Use rough papers, or cheap ones that are sold by weight.

Combining charcoal and sanguine enables you to do drawings rich in tones.

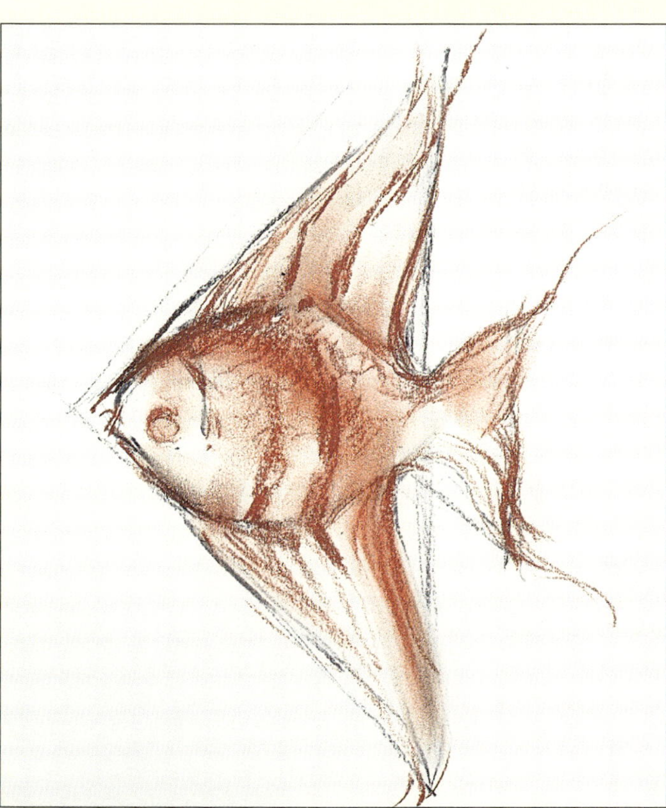

Once the charcoal fit has been done you can use sanguine to put down the strokes of the forms. Afterwards the fit lines are erased.

MAKING THE OUTLINE EASIER

When you have decided to work with charcoal and sanguine together, it is helpful to know which one you are going to start with and their different functions in the drawing.When deciding with which medium to use for the first strokes, compare the possibilities of rubbing them out. Charcoal comes off much more easily than sanguine. Bearing in mind that the fit is always temporary, when the lines of the are established it is erased, it is logical to use charcoal.

In contrast, when the drawing scheme is simple and quite definitive you can start drawing directly in sanguine. A sanguine stroke, even though it can be corrected like charcoal, always leaves a slight color mark on the white paper. This is not a problem if you plan to cover all the white spaces with the media.

COMBINING SANGUINE AND CHARCOAL.

BLENDING TOGETHER THE TWO MEDIA

Although sanguine is harder than charcoal this does not make it a more limited medium. In fact, both media have practically the same qualities for drawing. This can be proved by a simple exercise which consists of stumping two strokes, one of each. In previous chapters we saw how to stump charcoal. First a stroke is made and then a finger is passed over to spread it out. The same technique is used to stump sanguine.
When you do the exercise you will observe that the sanguine stumping is finer and more precise. However, both media blend together quite easily without having to press too hard when rubbing.

STUMPING WITH THE FINGERS

The best tools for working with dry media are, without doubt, the hands for they can give great subtlety to the piece and perform different types of stumping. There is a lot of freedom as to which finger to use, but, obviously, the thumb is most suitable for smudging large areas and the little finger for small details. The fingers must always be dry and grease free to enable you to stump comfortably.

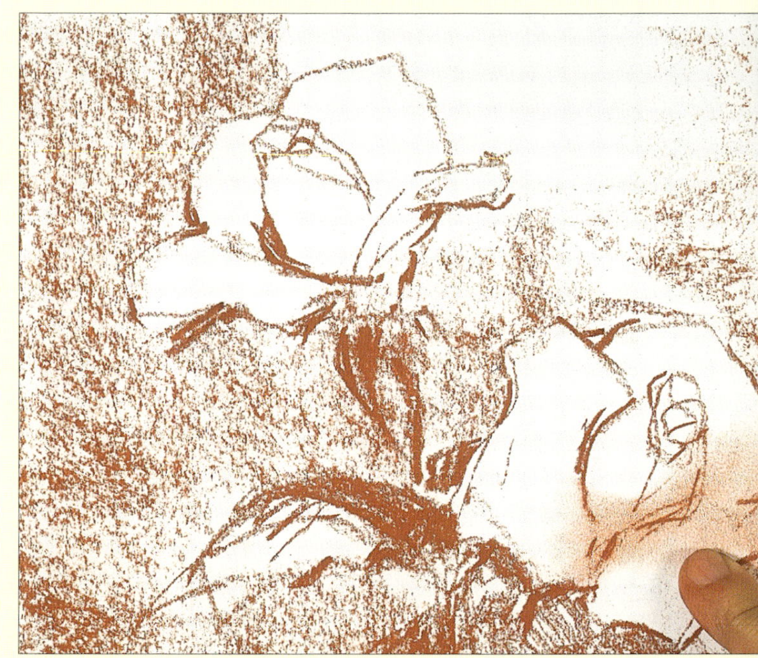

This drawing of a bunch of flowers was done in sanguine. The little finger gently stumps part of a flower.

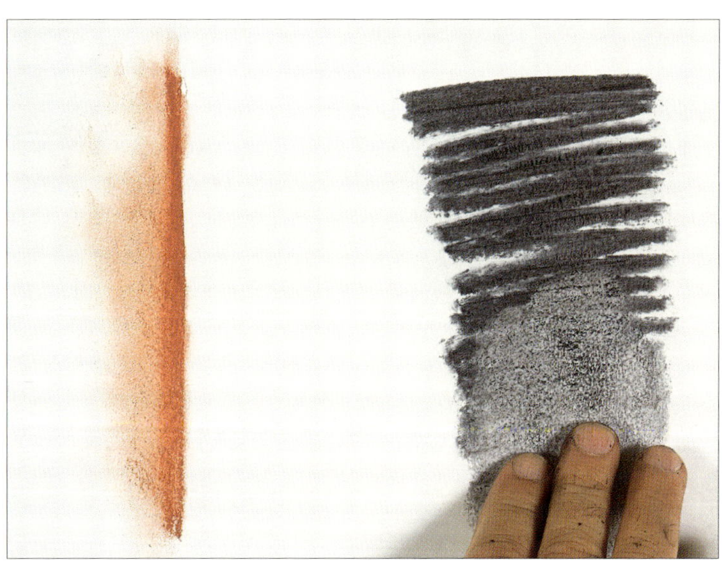

An example of a stumping with charcoal and sanguine. The strokes are different for the sanguine stumping is finer than the charcoal one.

A PAD OF DRAWING PAPER

One of the most vital materials for the artist is a pad of drawing paper. It must be good enough so that the strokes are clean and contrasted. There are many types and sizes and the final choice depends on the artist"s interests and preferences. To be of acceptable quality the paper must have the following characteristics.

- It must have good sizing.
- It must be thick and of the right weight.
- The grain must be suitable for the drawing technique.

CHARCOAL ON TOP OF SANGUINE

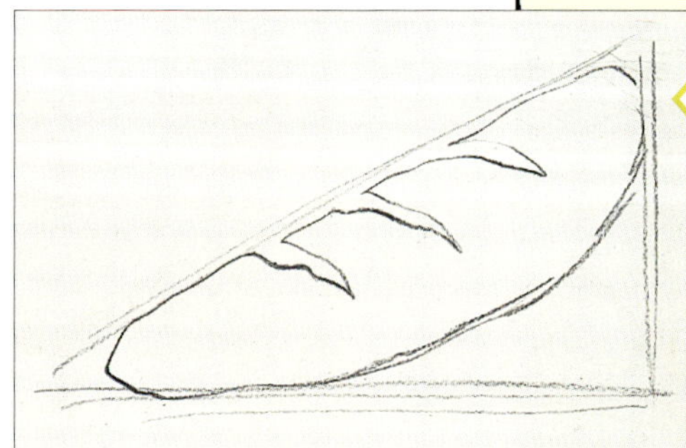

To get this drawing started firstly do a triangular fit. The form of the bread is done with soft strokes.

On top of the sanguine stumping draw with charcoal. Use the point so that the lines are finer. The areas that have not been stained will allow the white paper ground to be seen through the strokes.

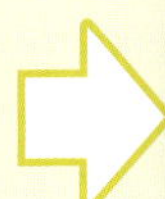

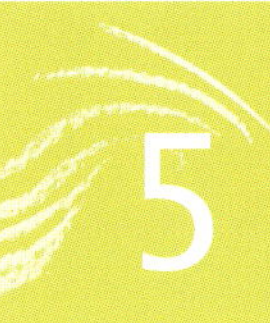

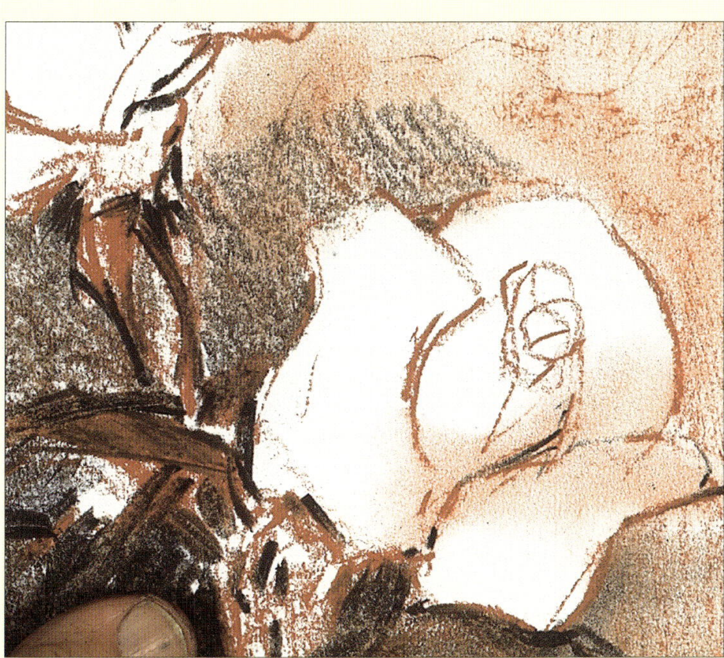

Afterwards draw in charcoal and darken zones as necessary. The wider areas are stumped with the thumb.

DRAWING WITH STROKES AND WITH STUMPINGS

When drawing the strokes can either remain clearly visible or they can be masked over with a stumping. Both possibilities can be combined in a drawing, always remembering that both charcoal and sanguine can be completely blended with the paper.
For example, on top of a stumped sanguine base you can draw charcoal strokes, either leaving them intact or blending them according to your intentions. If the charcoal stroke is blended over the sanguine, it will turn hazy and lose some of its definition, a possible preliminary step to a gradation that can go from black through to sanguine red. The dark color of the charcoal should always be set aside for the shadows. A gradated stroke can become a stumping but this has the disadvantage of losing some of the characteristics of the line. Combining strokes and stumped shadings in a drawing give it freshness and spontaneity.

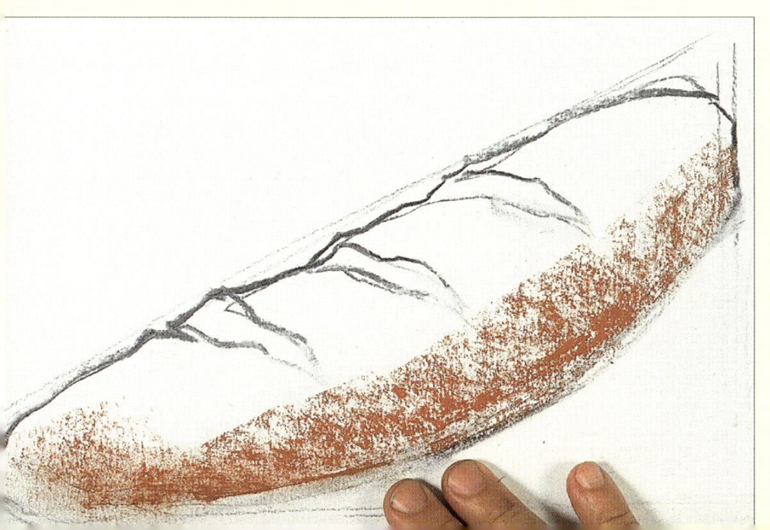

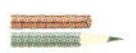

BEFORE DRAWING

Whenever sanguine and charcoal are combined, before drawing do the following:
- A simple outline.
- A firm approximation of the drawing lines to ensure they are correct.
- Make the strokes on the definitive lines firm.

Only when this has been done can the second medium be applied and any necessary stumpings be made.

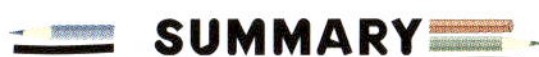

SUMMARY

COMBINING THE MEDIA.

A combination of charcoal and sanguine offers still richer coloristic possibilities the drawing possibilities. Sanguine offers the same recourses as charcoal but is harder and produces a stronger pictorial effect possible because of its chromatic value.

THE OUTLINE.

When the outlines are going to be totally erased it is better to use charcoal. Sanguine is only appropriate when the drawing is going to render the outline invisible, or when the scheme is straightforward and almost definitive.

STUMPING.

Stumping with sanguine is finer and more precise than with charcoal.

USING THE FINGERS.

The best way to stump the tones is with the fingers.

GRADATIONS.

When you draw in charcoal on top of a sanguine base and then stump it, a gradation is created that can go from black through to a reddish color.

When the strokes are firm you can start to shade holding the sanguine stick flat and painting broadwise. Do not press too hard so as not to close the pores. This shading can be stumped with the fingers.

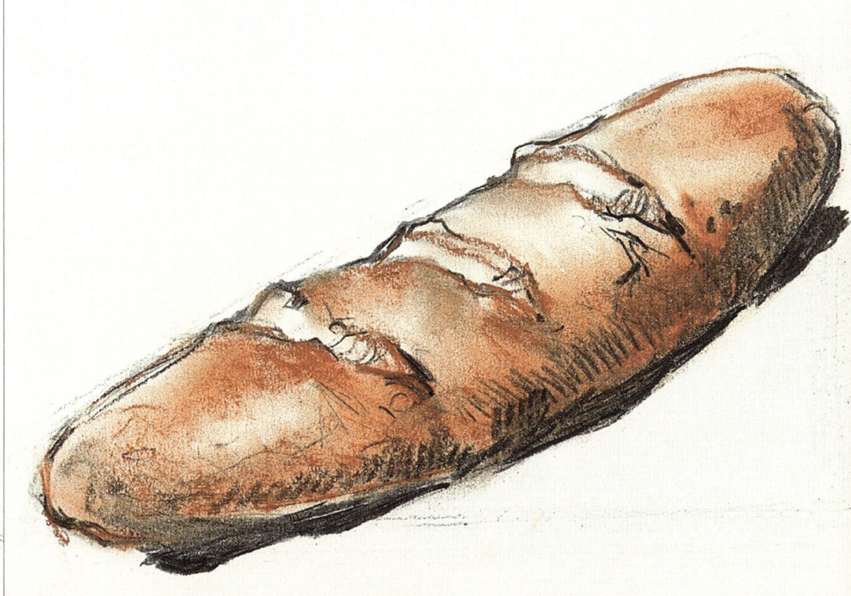

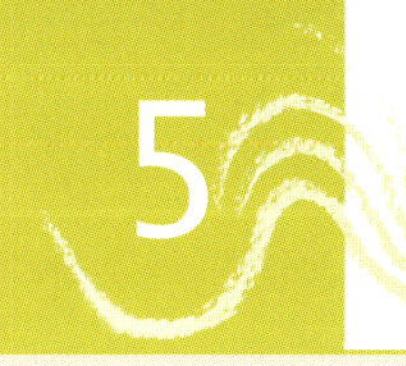

5 Exercices *Step by step*

A landscape is a perfect theme with which to practice strokes for it hardly requires a preliminary fit. Moreover its characteristics give you the opportunity to do different types of stumping, especially in the zones furthest away from the artist"s viewpoint.

NECESSARY MATERIAL

Charcoal crayons (1), sanguine (2), white chalk (3), and drawing paper (4).

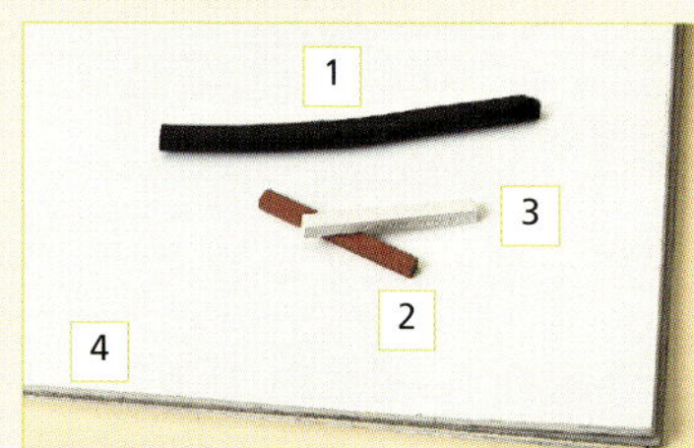

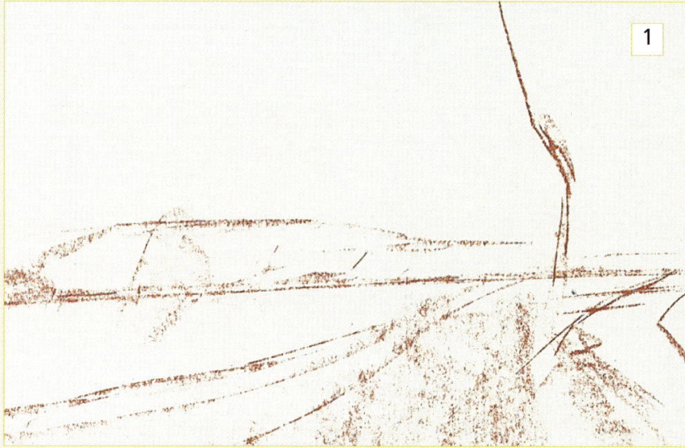

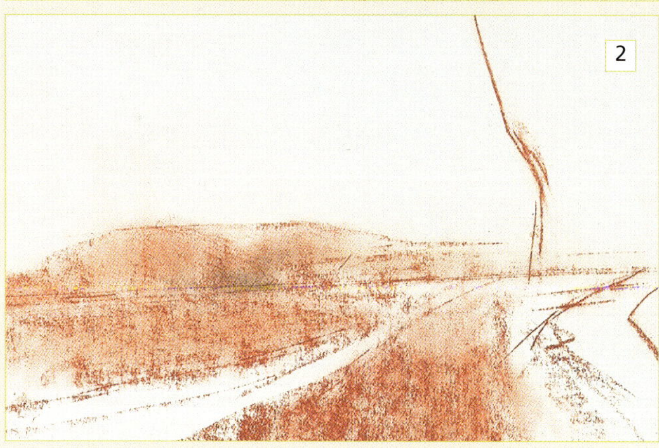

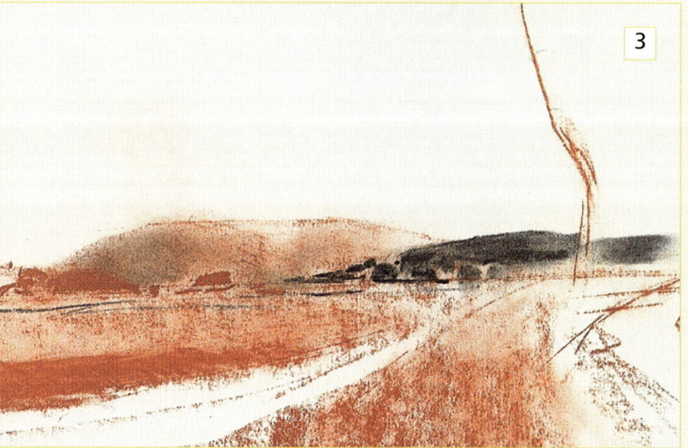

The objective of the next exercise is to practice combining sanguine and charcoal, with an increased emphasis on individual strokes, stumpings and gradations. Pay special attention to how hard you press with the sanguine in the first steps so that you can correct it if necessary.

1· START DRAWING directly in sanguine with hardly any preliminary outlines.

HOLD THE SANGUINE FLAT between the fingers to do the horizon line. This makes it easy to sketch the curve of the path and the stream.

START TO DRAW THE CENTRAL PART of the meadow moving the crayon flat across the paper. Do not press too hard so that you do not close the pores. Afterwards mark the outline of the tree trunk.

2· HOLD THE SANGUINE STICK FLAT and do sideways movements to color the earth area on both sides of the path. However, do not draw on the mountain in the background.

AFTERWARDS, AND PAYING SPECIAL ATTENTION TO THIS STEP, use the fingertips to softly blend part of the sanguine. Do not go into the path zone. Gently smudge the mountain in the background, it not being necessary to use the crayon directly. Once the blending is finished, clean the fingers with a cloth.

DRAW THE DARK ZONE next to the path and on the horizon using the point of the sanguine stick. This is the most intense tone obtainable with sanguine.

3· AFTERWARDS USE THE CHARCOAL to draw the smallest, darkest mountain.

SPREAD THE CHARCOAL WITH THE FINGERTIPS. Smudge the background mountain with the stained hand so that the sanguine and charcoal tones blend.

CONTINUE DRAWING THE EDGE of the stream in charcoal. Stump it with the tips of the index and ring fingers. Do not drag the fingers too hard for you could stain the paper.

4· ONCE AGAIN USE THE SANGUINE POINT to draw on top of the stumped zones as follows: on the horizon apply long strokes, and in the foreground, short, vertical strokes.

PUT DOWN A FEW SANGUINE STROKES ON THE PATH, zigzagged in the foreground, and then following the path as it goes into the distance.

5· USE CHARCOAL TO START THE SHADING of the grass in the foreground. This grass will be circular shadings with little unpainted spaces in the middle.

USE THE CHARCOAL POINT to darken the tree trunk and to start the drawing of the fence which runs beside the path. These lines come out of the dark sanguine zone and end almost on the horizon.

A landscape with charcoal and sanguine

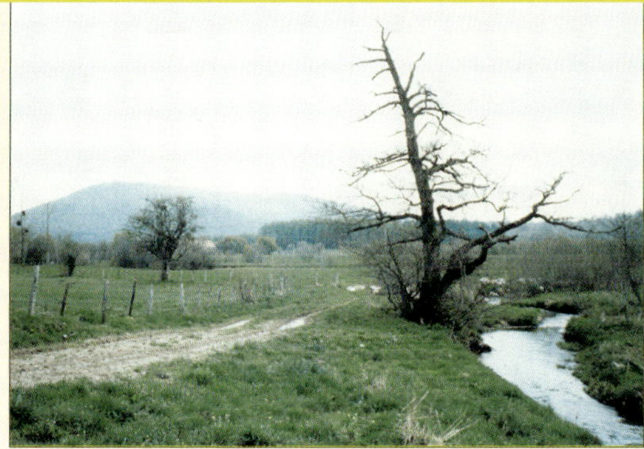

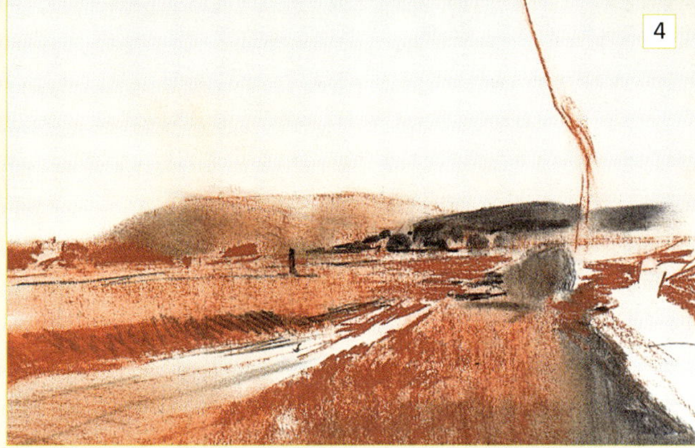

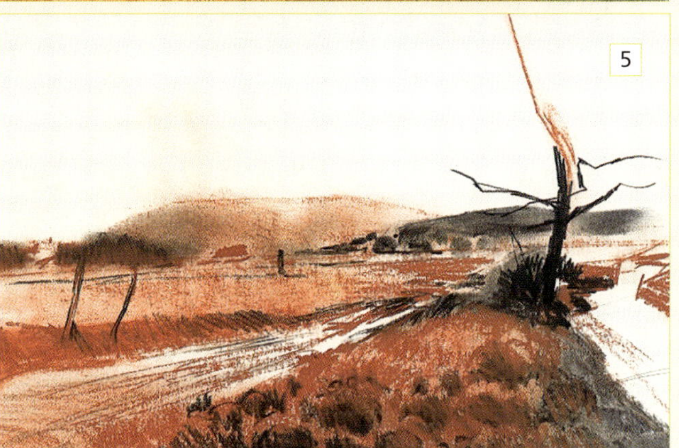

6· IN THIS CLOSE UP OF STEP 6 you can tell how the grass in the foreground has been drawn. It is only a few shadings on top of the background.

To erase a sanguine stroke, just flicking it with a cloth is sufficient. Do not press too hard with the hand for the skin oil will make the powder stick to the paper definitively.

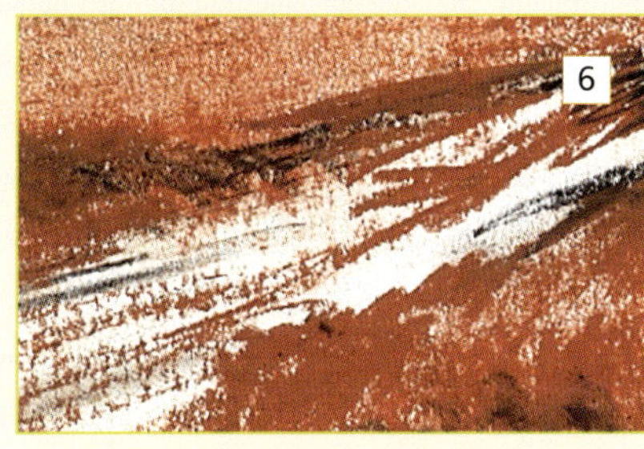

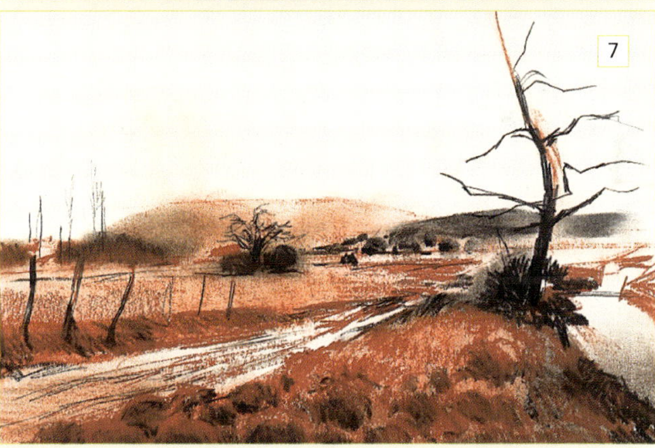

7· STEP SEVEN CONSISTS OF SMUDGING THE SHADINGS that make up the grass. Just rubbing the charcoal gently is enough to blend it with the sanguine.

DRAW THE TREES ON THE HORIZON and then make their form hazy by rubbing with the little finger.

FINISH THE FENCE BEING CAREFUL to make the posts smaller and finer as they go into the distance. Put branches on the tree that become thinner further away from the trunk. Intensify the dark zones on both sides of the stream and, once again, darken the grass in the foreground with charcoal.

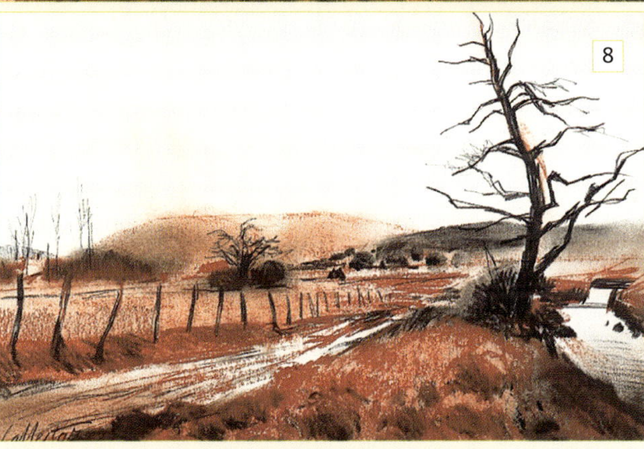

8· THESE LAST TOUCHES FINISH off this exercise realized in sanguine and charcoal. It is important to point out that the result does not have to be identical to the one shown here. What matters is to apply the techniques correctly, especially the stumping.

SUMMARY SCHEME

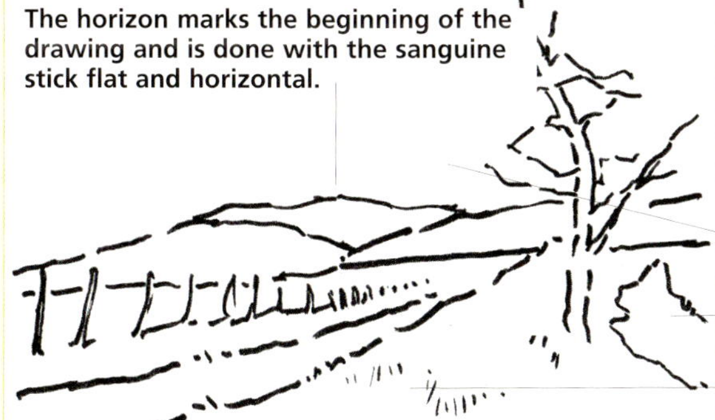

The horizon marks the beginning of the drawing and is done with the sanguine stick flat and horizontal.

The shadings in the background are done with the sanguine flat and vertical.

Along the edge of the stream, the charcoal is blended with the fingers as it merges into the sanguine zone.

The grass in the foreground is drawn with almost circular shadings.

6

FORM DEFINITION. THE SKETCH

Before approaching the strokes that will be definitive in a drawing, many factors have to be taken into consideration. In this chapter we will study how these early geometric forms become more defined as the sketch begins to resemble the model and the geometric character becomes less prominent. If all the following exercises are studied carefully, you will find it easier to understand the complex processes that appear later in the book.

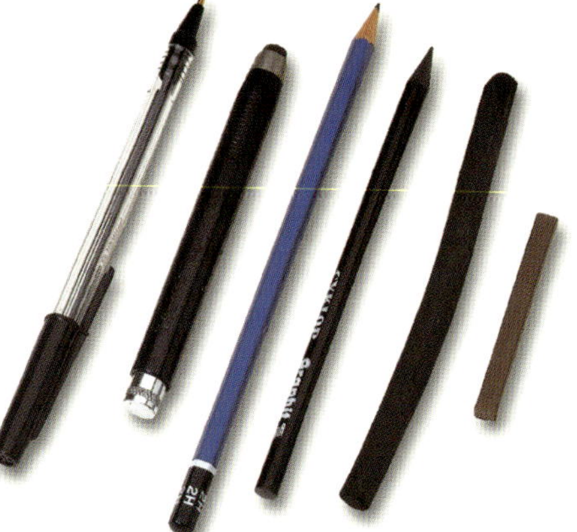

Any instrument that leaves a line can be used to draw, from classic drawing tools right through to the pencil and pen. All of these mediums produce different strokes.

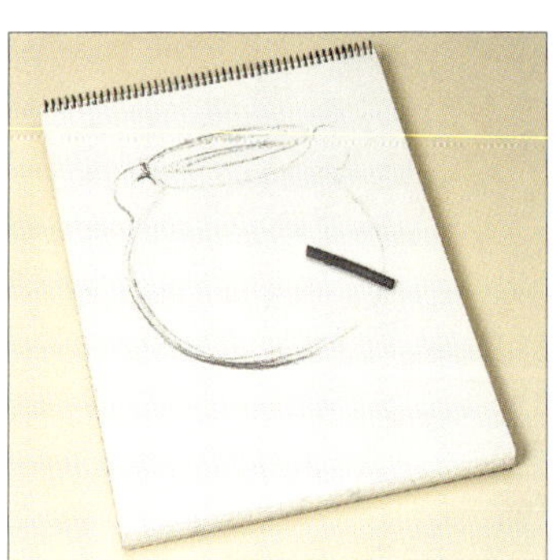

The sketch enables us to convert the initial lines into the definitive drawing. Set about it without reservations for the strokes can be corrected before the drawing is definitive.

FROM THE SKETCH TO DEFINITION

In reality a sketch consists of a few straightforward lines that help us to see how a drawing is going to turn out and help the artist to overcome any fear or uncertainty which may be provoked by the blank sheet. A sketch is never definitive: one way of expressing it is to call it the step between the geometric scheme and the final drawing.

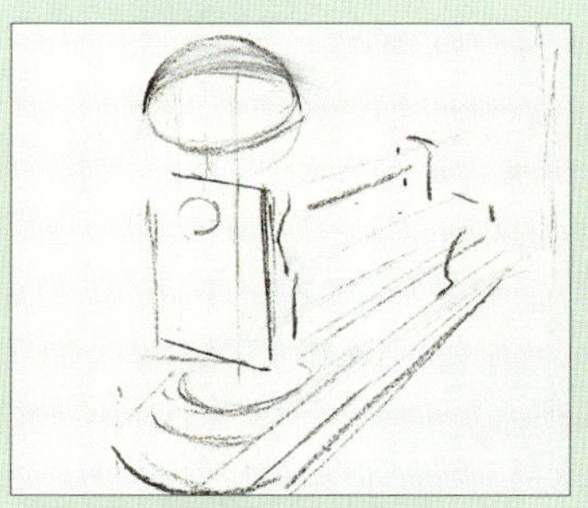

Draw the sides of the stapler with the charcoal flat and then do a preliminary scheme of the other initial lines.

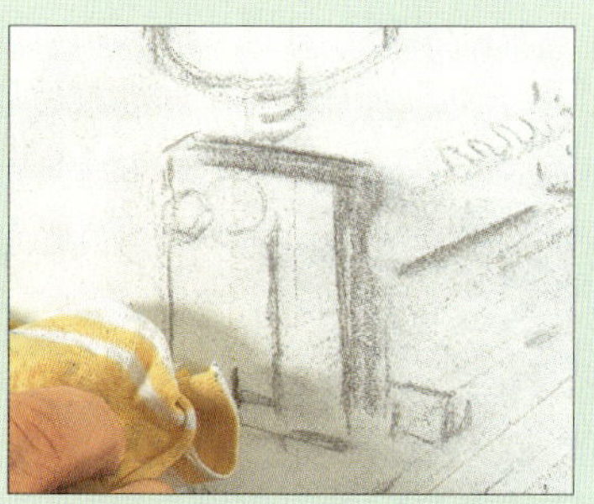

Use a cloth so that the strokes are hardly noticeable but will guide you later.

The first lines, which will be almost straight, will make a fit of the geometric scheme. They will be straightforward but well structured and on top of them we will do more definitive lines.

As you can see in the figure above on the left, first of all the side lines were drawn, then the height was sketched in, and, finally, the strokes that give a rough form to the object.

REDOING STROKES

Constant practice is necessary to learn how to draw. Drawing lines on paper is always good practice for the hand and will improve your coordination and sensitivity. To start drawing, take any object, for example something on the desk, and get working on it. Here, we have chosen a stapler. We are going to use charcoal for this drawing for the simple reason that it can be corrected by flicking it with a cloth or the hand. A pencil would require an eraser.

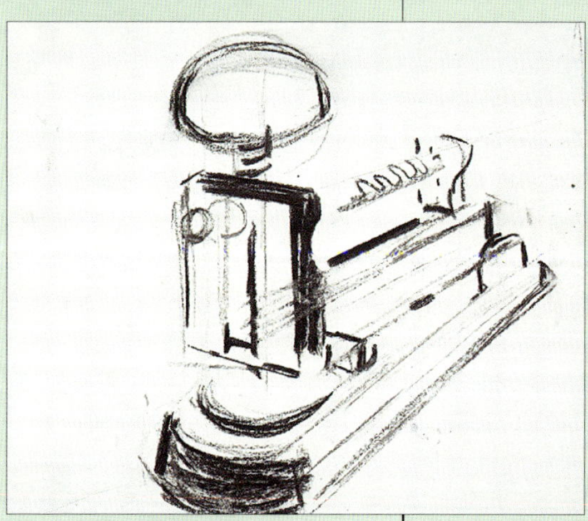

Once the first sketch is established, go on to mark the most prominent dark zones.

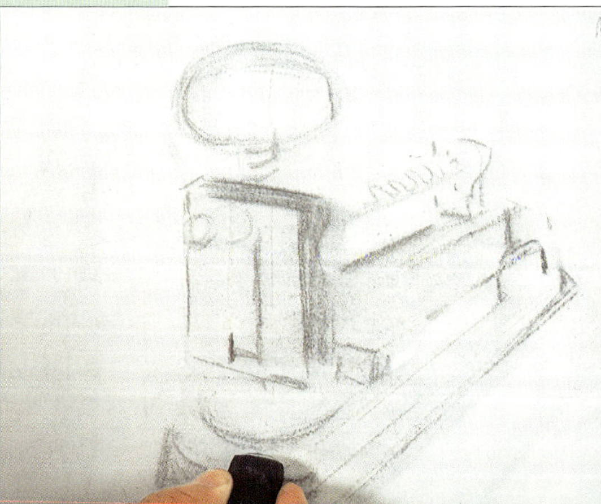

Clean up any areas that may have become grubby.

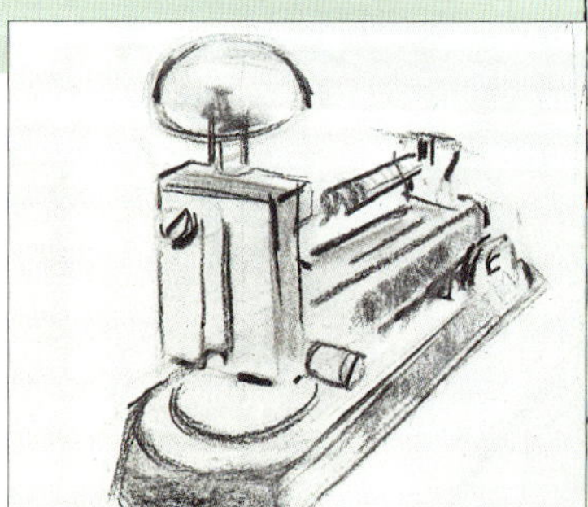

On top of the faint lined drawing, go over the strokes but this time definitively.

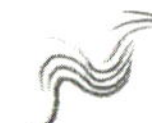

When a drawing is started the lines express a general scheme; the definitive forms do not appear until later. Gradually these geometric schemes become elements which are similar to the model until eventually the representation takes shape.

6

WORKING ON THE SKETCH

The contrasts generated enable us to see in the sketch a general idea of what the drawing is going to be like. This does not imply that it is the definitive drawing. On the paper, work on the contrasts, combining them with the initial lines that constructed the drawing. The definitive form is coming into shape, but what is most important at this stage is to get the dark contrasts in the right plane.

CORRECTING WITH THE CLOTH AND WITH AN ERASER

Once you have marked the first dark areas that insinuate volume, you must unify the different zones so that you can continue working on the sketching. This joining together is much simpler when using charcoal and sanguine than with a pencil, or graphite stick. Just flicking a cloth over is enough to remove any excesses, leaving a faint line that can be a guide later.

After having cleaned up the charcoal strokes it is possible that there are a few grimy areas. An eraser can restore the original color to the paper. Although it is not difficult, practice will help you to perfect your technique for cleaning up the lines.

A FIRM, CLEAR STROKE

Once the preliminary sketch has been cleaned you have a good guide for the drawing.

This work can be slow but it will ensure the definitive drawing is perfectly constructed. Once you have neatened the lines with the eraser and a cloth, go over the faint lines with charcoal to give a firmer and clearer stroke.

SKETCHING ON TOP OF THE OUTLINES

In the last section we studied how the preliminary sketch is used to do much firmer strokes. This approach is valid for all themes. Working on top of a faint, insinuated outline aids the evolution of the drawing, as if you had tracing paper. Working with a preliminary sketch that permits the strokes to be corrected makes for a more definitive structure.

We will continue to explore the possibilities of charcoal by doing an exercise which takes advantage of its malleability. This time the strokes will be freer than in the last exercise, but stick to the same principles: do a preliminary sketch, neaten up the lines and then do the definitive drawing.

The pencil lead shown above is poorly sharpened. The knife has cut into the wood too steeply.

As far as is possible, a pencil lead should be as shown below. The movement of the knife follows the line of the pencil to give a long tip.

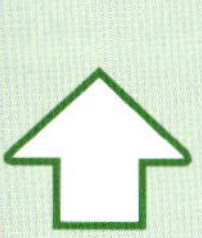

SHARPENING THE PENCILS

The charcoal point can always be kept sharp. As you can draw with all its surface, just turn it in your hand looking for the finest edge. In contrast, the pencil tip is constantly worn away, but it does have the advantage of permitting much finer and more delicate lines. A knife is the best sharpening tool. At first it will be difficult, but once you get the trick you will obtain a longer, sharper tip than with the traditional pencil-sharpener. The latter is not recommend for drawing techniques. When cutting with the knife, make a long, flowing movement to get a long tip. A short tip becomes blunt immediately and lacks the precision of a long one. However, when drawing with a long tip you can wear away the point to get a form that will help you with your drawing. If a stroke begins to wane, just turn the lead and use a still sharp edge.

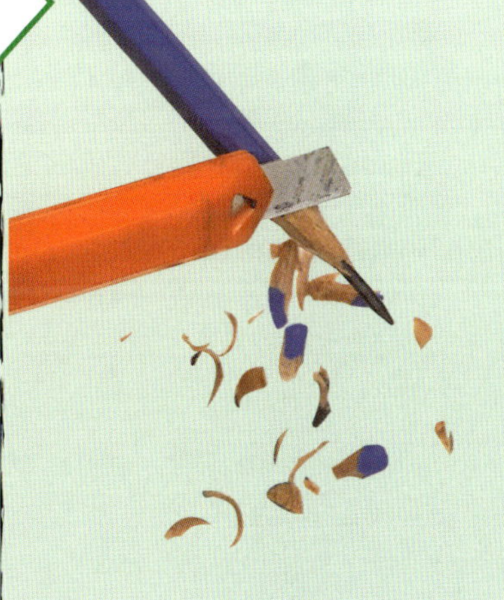

A knife gives a much better sharpened point than the pencil sharpener.

6 FORM DEFINITION. THE SKETCH

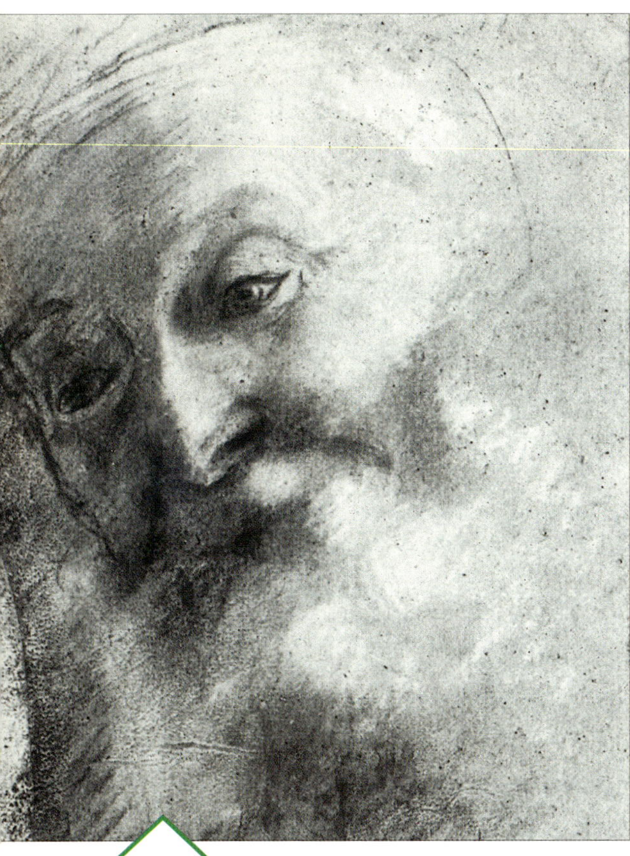

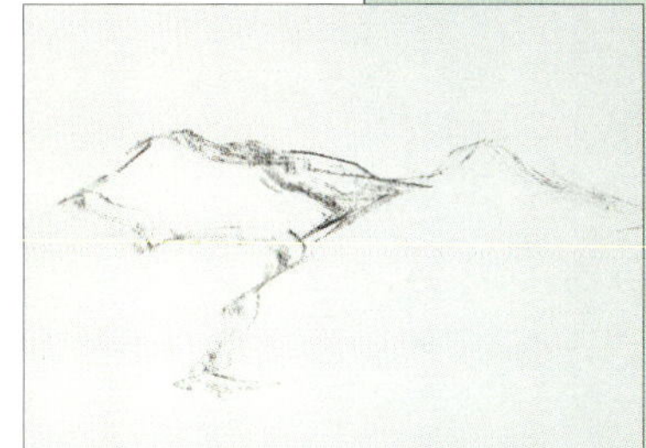

First of all draw the mountains in the background with soft lines, not pressing too hard.

Use the cloth to erase superfluous lines.

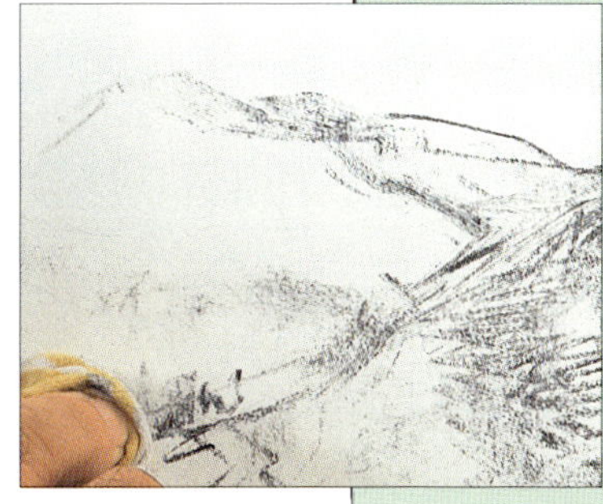

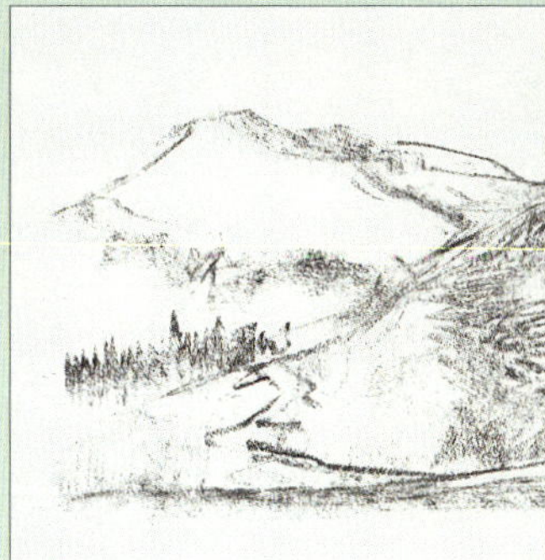

On top of the preliminary sketch it is much easier to construct the landscape using different stroke intensities.

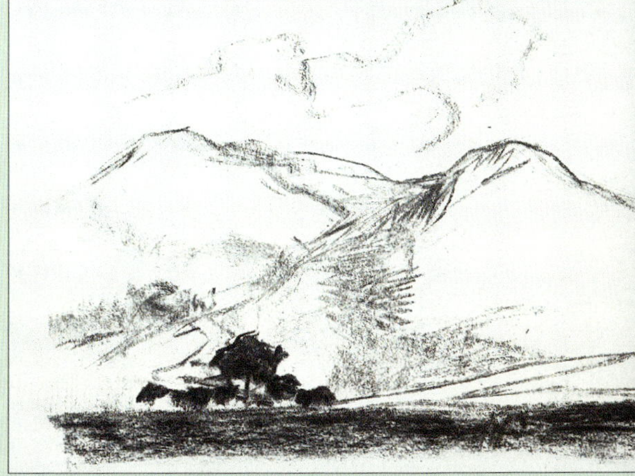

The strongest contrasts in the foreground stand out against the faint strokes in the background.

THE MASTER LINES OF THE DRAWING

When you look at a finished drawing it is unusual to be able to appreciate traces of the lines that helped to structure it. However, these invisible lines were crucial for the construction of the drawing. In his drawing **"The head of Zacharias"**, now kept in the Albertina Museum, Vienna, **Federico Barocci (1528-1612)** was very careful to eliminate all traces of the original sketch before continuing and finishing the work. This type of piece demands a thorough construction because the proportions and lighting can completely deform a drawing if they are not based on the initial scheme.

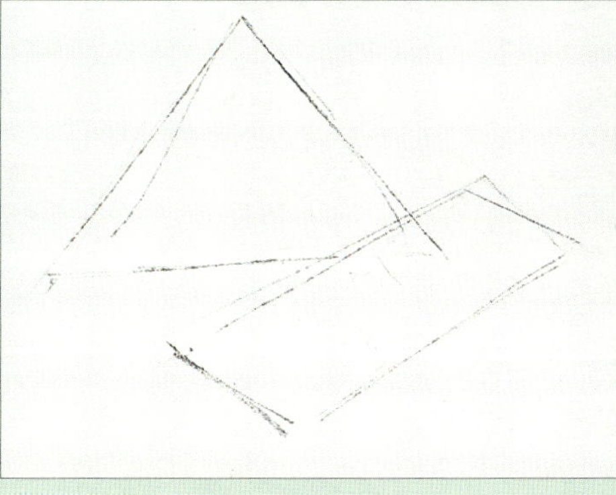

These simple forms give structure to the boats in the preliminary sketch.

THE PRESSURE OF THE STROKE

This exercise involves an undemanding landscape. Start by carefully combining horizontal and vertical strokes to sketch the mountains in the background.

The initial strokes can be done flat or lengthwise, a choice which will be noticeable in the final result. If the charcoal is flat you can do a stroke as wide as the crayon. If you do a lengthwise stroke, the line will be totally straight. Both strokes can be combined to get different effects with shades of gray and with the widths. In the early stages do not press too hard for although charcoal lacks adhesiveness you could close up the pores and prevent future corrections.

FINISHING THE PRELIMINARY SKETCH

Once the principle lines have been insinuated in charcoal, go on to do the fit of the essential lines of the drawing. Just as we did in the last example, before making the definitive lines firmer, tone down the strokes that will guide the drawing later on. Use a clean cloth, not rubbing too hard so that the initial sketch remains faintly. The aim is only to remove excess marks.

The drawing can be redeveloped with more definition on top of these insinuated lines. All this process is carried out in a short time period and soon, with practice, you will be able to do any theme regardless of its difficulty.

As you lay down new strokes you must increase the pressure, but not uniformly for a monotonous gray tone would make the drawing dull.

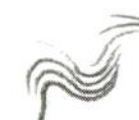

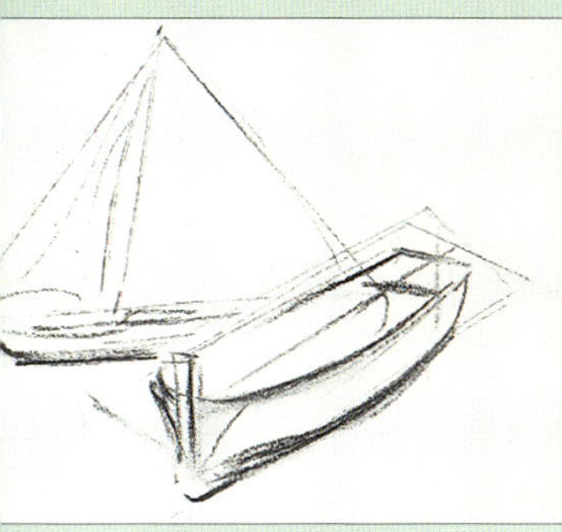

Working on top of the straightforward geometric figures it is easy to construct the form of the boats.

Working on the just finished faint charcoal lines you can draw the different planes exploiting distinct charcoal intensities. The background is left only sketched delicately to give the sensation of distance. It is in the foreground that you exploit the charcoal strokes to make the forms stand out. Firstly develop the ground and then use the charcoal point to draw the trees precisely.

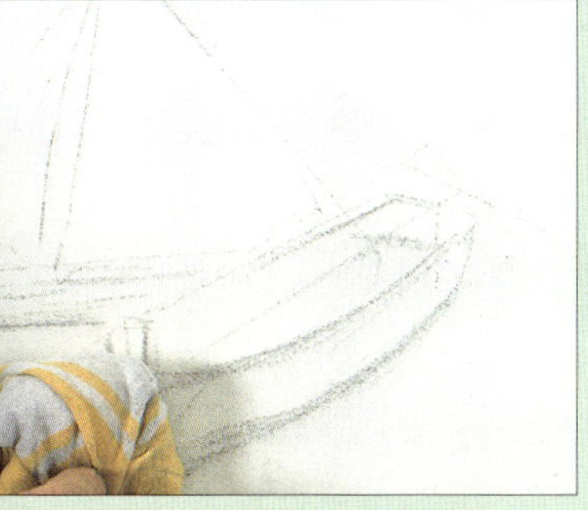

A cloth must remove the lines that have no purpose. Unfortunately some definitive lines will also be dragged away.

PROTECTING THE FIRST SKETCH

When doing the previous sketches you will have come across the problem of inadvertently rubbing away correct zones. A solution is to fix the preliminary sketch at an early stage so that however much you may erase and correct the lines the initial scheme remains.

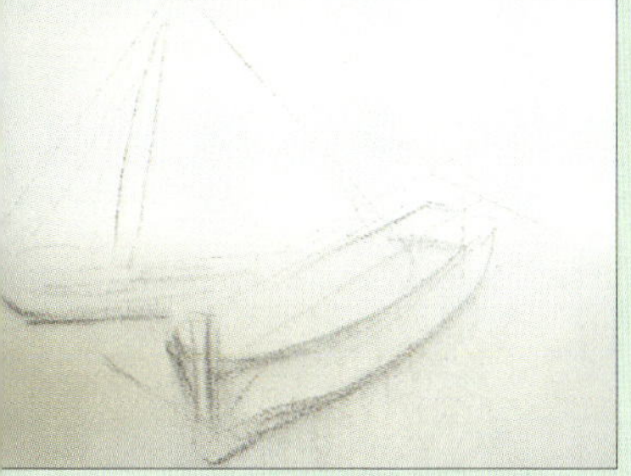

Hold the spray fixative can 30 cm away. A light layer is sufficient to stick it to the paper.

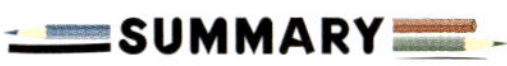

SUMMARY

THE PRELIMINARY SKETCH.

The first lines fit the form into a simple geometric scheme. The strokes must be neat and well structured.

CONTRASTS AND STROKES

The contrasts help to understand the first vision of the definitive drawing.

CLEANING UP

Use a cloth to make the stroke marks less noticeable. This will leave you with a high quality basic scheme.

STARTING FROM A GOOD SCHEME

Once you have neatened up the lines with an eraser and a cloth, the charcoal will enable you to develop firmer work.

ELEMENTAL FORMS

The basic form of any object, however complicated it may be, can be simplified into more straightforward and schematic elements. Although we dealt with this subject in other chapters, it is no less relevant now. Now we are going to draw some boats. In theory it does not seem an easy theme but notice how, thanks to the preliminary sketch it is possible to convert two geometric shapes into boats, which are rather more complicated objects.
These straightforward forms give rise to the structure of the boats.

CONSTRUCTING, ERASING AND FIXING

Once you have done a preliminary sketch of the basic elements, you can start to outline the internal forms, something which is not difficult. A simple structure helps more than would appear at first sight.
Just as we did in the previous exercises, once the fundamental lines have been sketched, make the strokes less noticeable with the aid of a cloth. Erase the structural lines, but in so doing it will be impossible not to rub away some of the lines that form the boats. The cloth is perhaps too clumsy to be controlled perfectly so some valid lines may be lost.
Before going on it is worth checking that the lines still on the paper are a good enough base for the drawing. The lines must be sufficient to construct the drawing, but superficial lines must not invade zones that should remain white. Any superfluous stroke must be erased away to obtain a drawing that looks like the one above. Now is the moment to fix it.

Once the fixative is dry, you can start to draw again, correcting and erasing without eliminating the fixed layer.

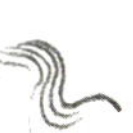

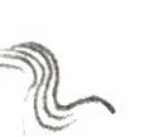

Exercices *Step by step*

The preliminary sketch, together with the outline, is the surest way of approaching the drawing. The first lines are gradually taken over by firmer, constantly elaborated and reworked strokes.

This exercise is not too demanding. However, there are a few complications that must be overcome before going on to more complicated exercises. Sketching the first outlines requires concentration, but if you follow the steps as shown the solution will be simpler than would appear at first.

NECESSARY MATERIAL

Charcoal (1), block of drawing paper (2), an eraser (3), a cloth (4), and spray fixative (5).

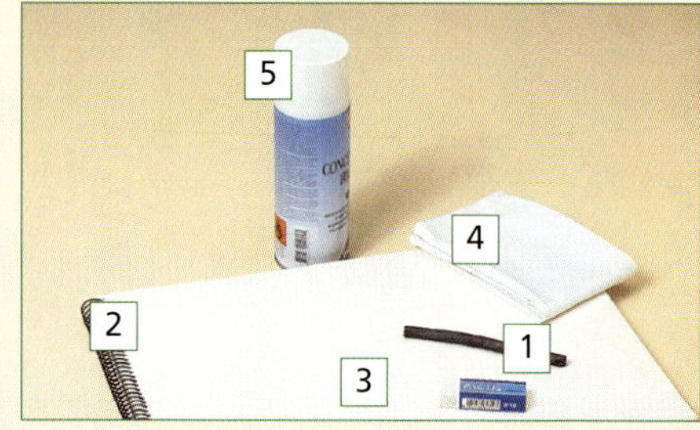

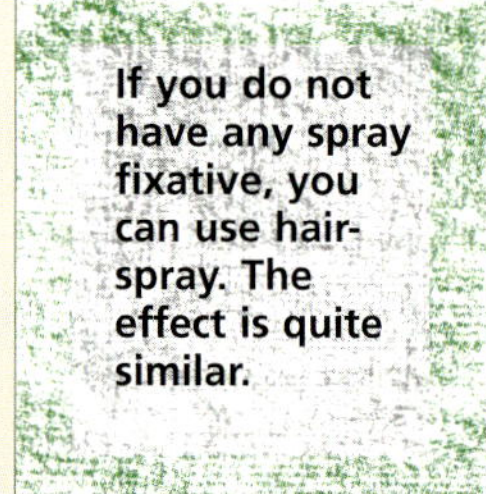

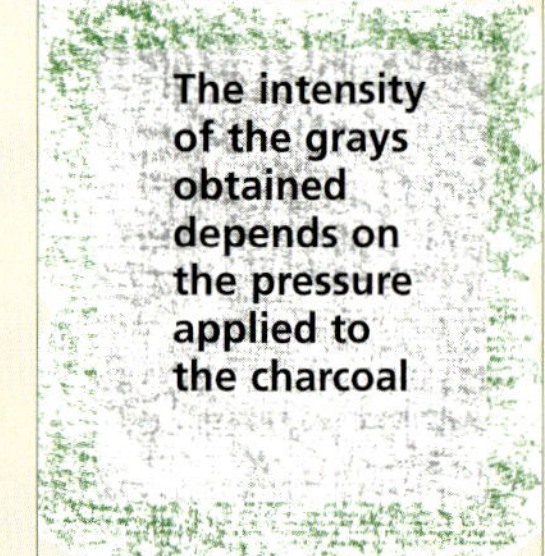

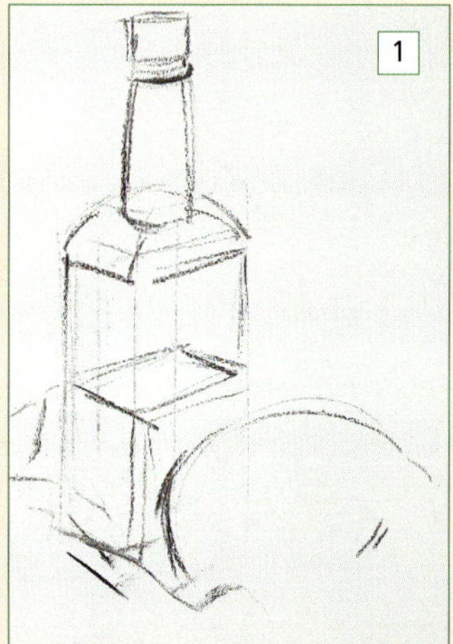

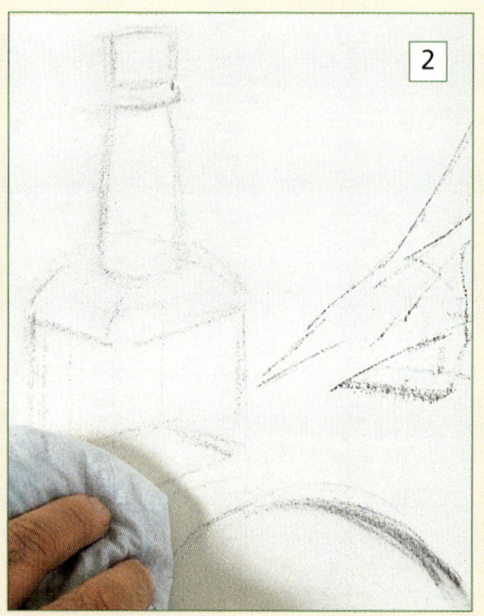

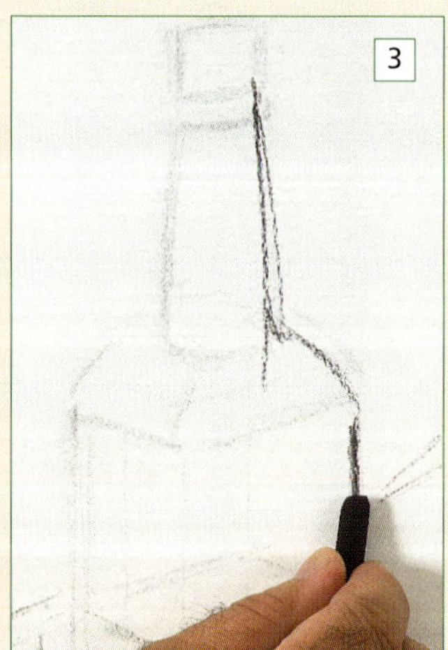

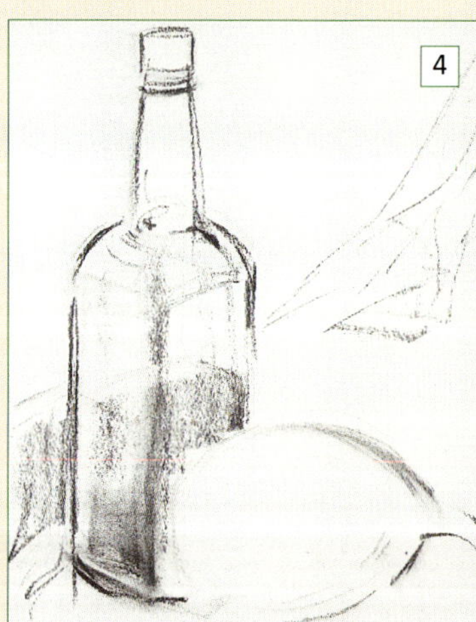

1· **START TO SKETCH THE OUTLINE** with the charcoal flat and in lengthwise strokes. In this way the strokes will be firmer and more definitive from the outset.

FIRST OF ALL DO AN OUTLINE of the bottle based on straight lines. Draw the bottle base and then four lines straight up which leading into the bottleneck. As the lines become more established you can increase the pressure of the strokes. Once you have done a scheme of the bottle in almost geometric forms, draw the pumpkin with one stroke.

2· **WHEN THE PRELIMINARY SKETCH OF THE TWO** elements has been finished, use the cloth to remove the majority of the lines. You must not rub too hard to avoid erasing all the sketch. The more definitive lines, as they have been drawn pressing harder, tend to remain even though the cloth takes away most of the rest.

USE THE ERASER TO CLEAN UP ANY GRUBBINESS. It is important to do this because after the next step the drawing will be fixed and any shading will thus become permanent. Reconstruct the drawing on top of the faintly insinuated sketch, this time with a more definitive stroke. The guidelines are almost transparent but remain visible.

3· **USE THE CHARCOAL** vertical to sketch the outline of the bottle and the bottle neck. For the time being only do the most important lines.

4· **INSIDE THE BOTTLE,** do horizontal strokes to produce a uniform gray.

A still life of a bottle and a pumpkin. 6

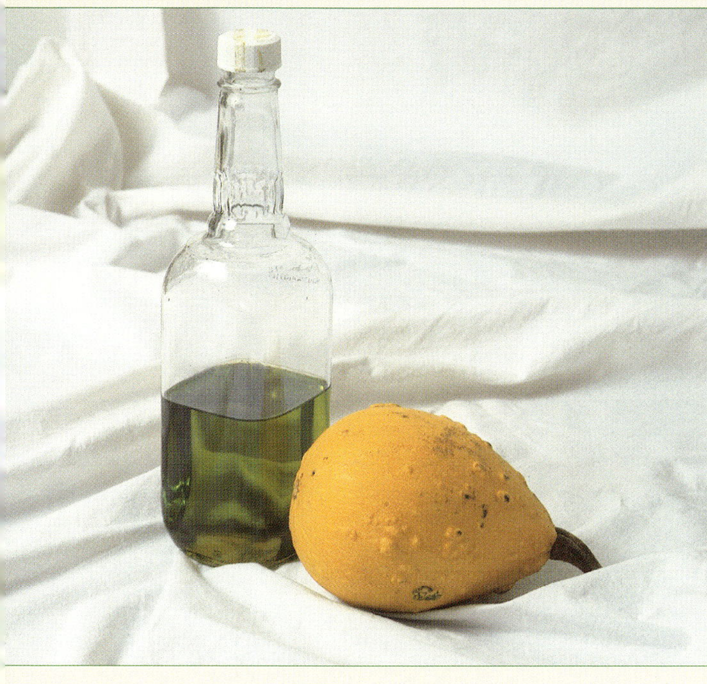

SUMMARY SCHEME

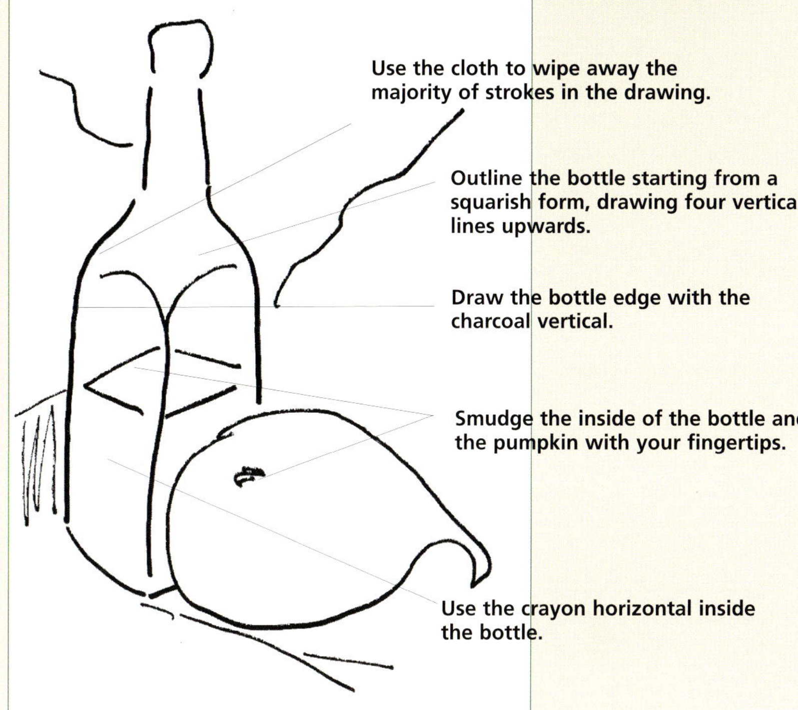

FORM DEFINITION. THE SKETCH

5· ONCE THIS STAGE IS FINISHED, clean up the zones that have become grubby and then fix the drawing with spray. Everything that is fixed now will remain intact although it is rubbed or smudged.

BY NOW THE PIECE IS QUITE ELABORATED. As it is an exercise in sketching we are not very concerned about developing it further.

6· WORK ON WHAT IS ALREADY DOWN ON THE PAPER. Use the fingertips to smudge the strokes inside the bottle. Afterwards softly tone down the stroke and use your dirty fingers to darken the most shady corner of the bottle.

7· WORKING OVER THE DEFINITIVE sketch lines you draw with greater liberty because any corrections will be made on a fixed base. Use the charcoal flat to do the gray of the pumpkin, pressing hard to do the dark part on the underside. The strokes to outline the folds in the tablecloth must be softer and subtle.

8· THIS LAST STEP CONSISTS OF INTENSIFYING the dark zones using the charcoal point, which allows you to get a much more precise stroke.

AS THE DRAWING WAS FIXED before a fine layer has been formed which makes the charcoal much denser and contrasted.

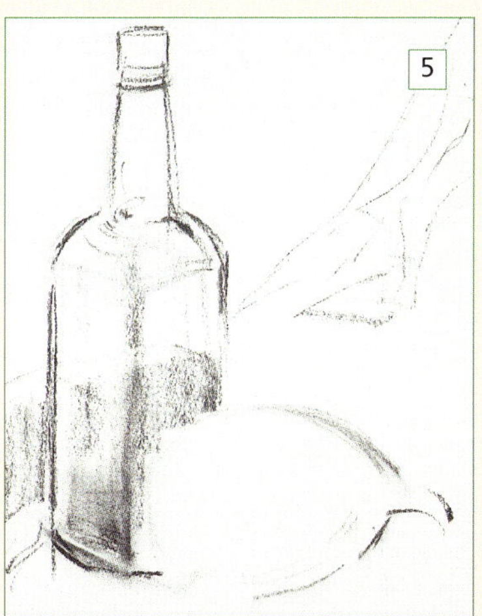
5

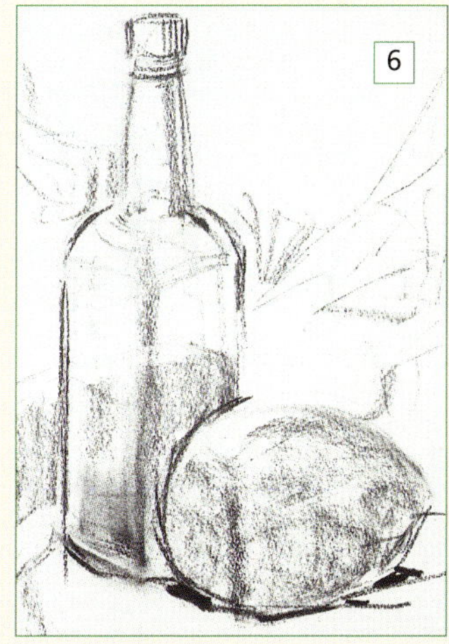
6

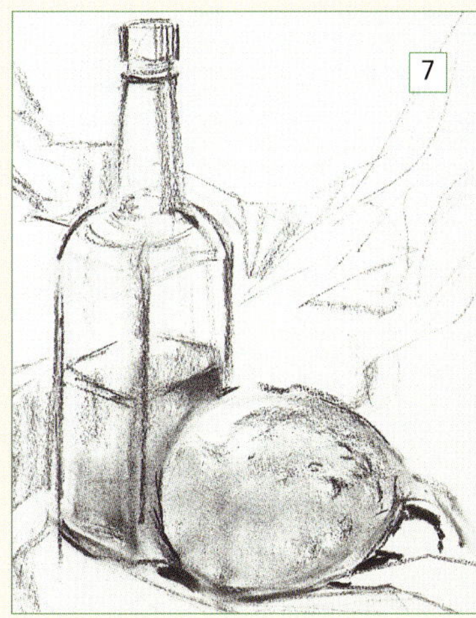
7

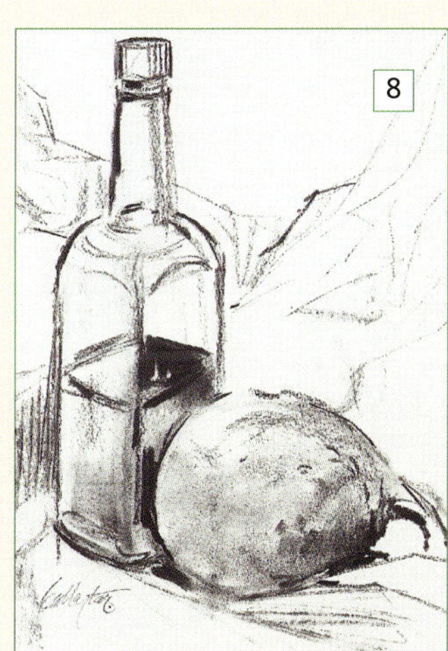
8

7 SHADOWS AND THE TONE SCALE

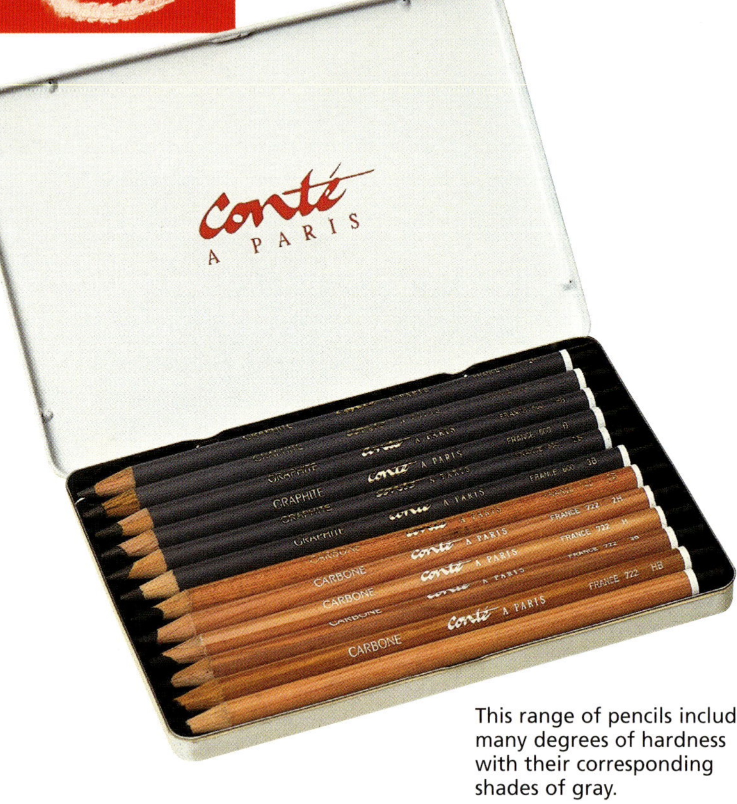

This range of pencils includes many degrees of hardness with their corresponding shades of gray.

The possibilities offered by drawing are not just limited to doing lines or strokes. In the other chapters we have seen how stumping and tone creation can be applied to other techniques. In fact, correctly exploiting grays is the way to represent shadows. In this chapter we are going to work on a series of theoretical ideas and exercises dealing with shadows in drawing. It is important to remember that drawing is the basis of all pictorial techniques and so knowing how to use grays is always vital to represent shadows. As you will see later, the shadows depend uniquely on the light that falls on an object, which is therefore depicted by the intensity of the grays correctly distributed on the different planes.

DEFINING THE SHADOWS

Each drawing medium behaves differently when stumped and this determines the shadows that can be created with it.

Right from the beginning we have examined how charcoal, sanguine, and pencil strokes can be smudged or stretched with the fingers, giving different shades of gray. Each drawing medium offers distinct gradations, which, in turn, means different shadows.

Shadows are produced by light falling on an object and not reaching other parts. However light does not fall uniformly, rather it comes across obstacles. The final effect is that there are luminous areas and dark, shady zones.

THE HARDNESS OF THE MEDIA

Each medium can be distinguished by its hardness, determined by the density of its structure. The softer a medium is, the wider the range of grays obtainable from it and its maximum gray will be more intense. In Fine Arts shops you will find ranges of products varying in hardness which enable you to take on works enriched by the subtlety of the grays.

APPROXIMATING THE TONE SCALE

Once you have found out about the different degrees of hardness of the drawing media it is worth practicing until you can get the most out of all the different grays produced by each one.

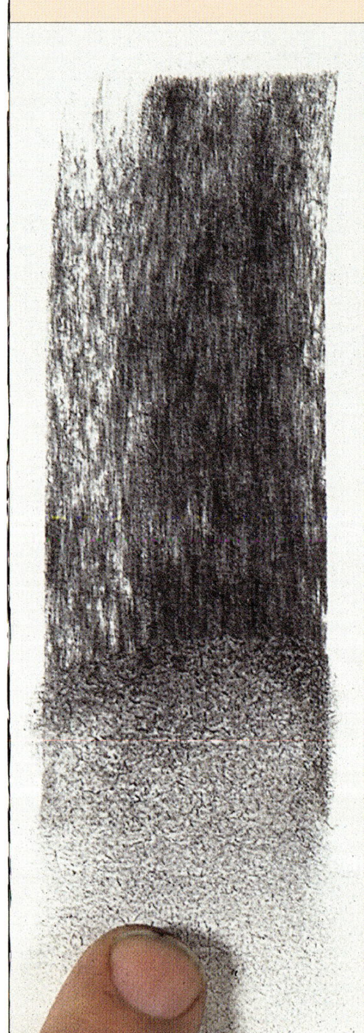

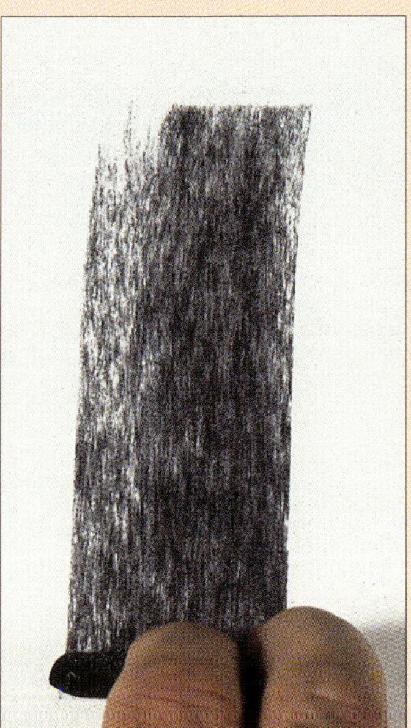

Stumping a charcoal stroke is as easy as drawing it. However, control the pressure when dragging your finger. The softer the gray you want, the less charcoal the finger must take with it.

CHARCOAL

Charcoal is the softest drawing medium. As it so precarious it offers a wide range of gradations. Just doing a charcoal stroke and then running your finger along it produces a rich sequence of tones.

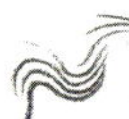

In drawing the reality of three dimensions is reduced to two which means that the shadows and depth of the objects is an illusion rendered plausible by the shades and nuances of gray in the picture.

7

PENCIL HARDNESS AND GRADATIONS

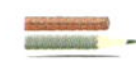

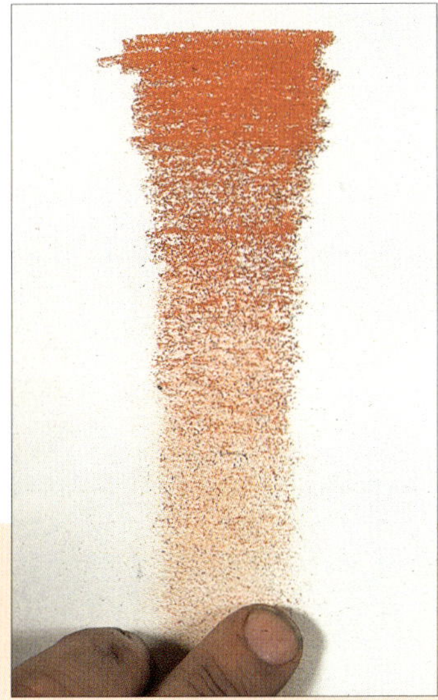

When working with charcoal the gray tones can be developed intuitively. Your choice is simplified because there is only one hardness. However, graphite pencils come in so many different degrees of hardness that each pencil offers its own range of grays: the harder the pencil, the more limited the range. In general, the pencils are classified with a number and a letter at the top which indicates the hardness. The softest pencils belong to the B range: an 8B is much softer than a 2B. The range of soft pencils is adequate for artistic drawing and are easier to erase than the hard ones. The latter are classified with the letter H.

Nevertheless, it is worth remembering that a sanguine stroke is harder than a charcoal one.

OILED CHARCOAL

Oiled charcoal is a soft and very compact medium. It has a pleasant feel as it leaves a soft mark on the paper. As you can see in the image above it gives a very dense black and intense tone gradations.

GRAPHITE PENCIL.

The variety of the plastic effects produced by a pencil depend on its hardness, ranging from blending by delicately rubbing a finger, through to pure graphism. Pencil gradations can be very rich in tone.

Although sanguine is harder than charcoal, there is no difference in the way of doing gradations and obtaining grays.

SANGUINE

Sanguine is another relatively soft drawing medium the feel of which is much rougher than charcoal"s. It produces a varied range of grays, and, in addition, its colors enhance the warmth of the drawing.

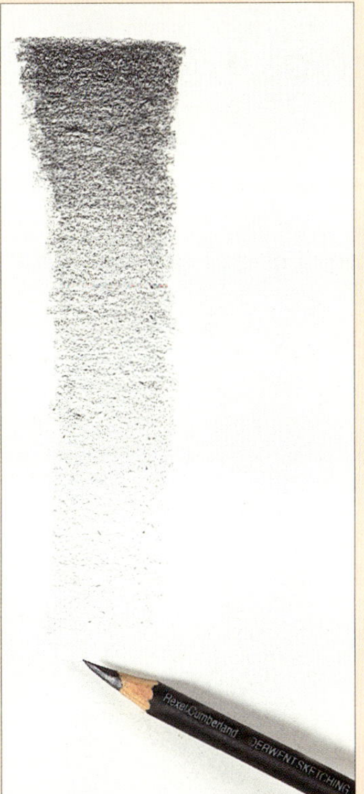

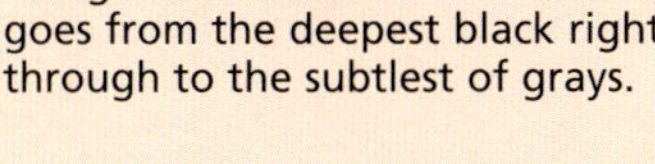

The gradation with oiled charcoal goes from the deepest black right through to the subtlest of grays.

A graphite pencil, depending on its hardness, can develop a rich and wide range of grays.

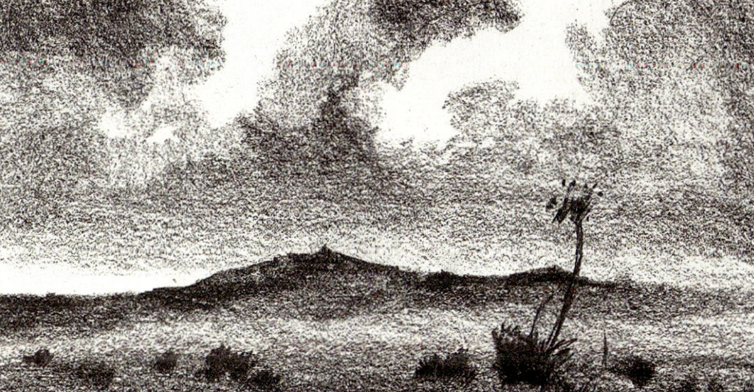

CONTROLLING THE GRAYS

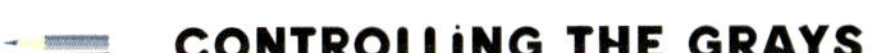

So many grays can be obtained by one unique drawing medium that often the artist only needs one pencil to do the drawing. This "Sketch of clouds" by Vicenç Ballestar (1929), now in a private collection, is a superb example of what can be achieved with one very soft graphite pencil, a 9B. He pressed hard in the upper part of the clouds, while the lighter parts were done gently caressing with the pencil. The whites of the clouds are where the paper was left untouched.

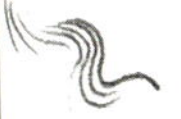

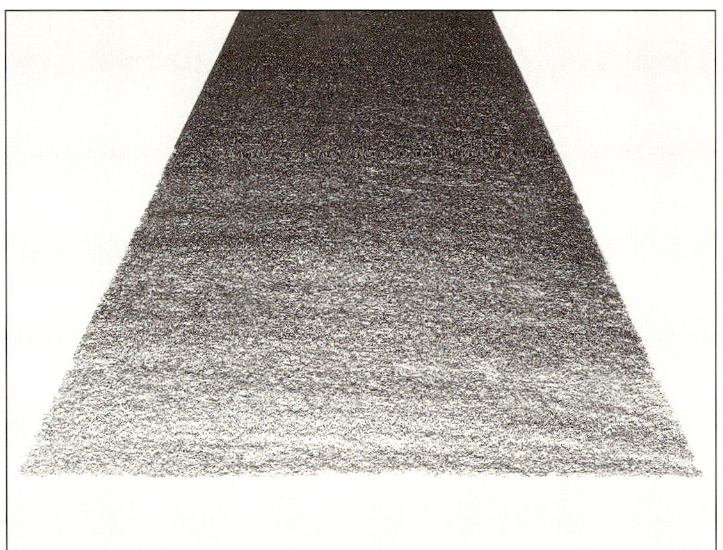

With this gradation we will practice elaborating planes in perspective.

A GRADATED RECTANGLE

Once we have seen how to do gradations with the different drawing media we can start to practice in drawings. In reality, the difference between practicing strokes and doing a complete drawing is that in the latter the gradations must be in a concrete zone.

The exercise we are going to do is apparently straightforward, but there is more to it than meets the eye. It is a rectangle in perspective, something which amplifies the sense of profundity. So that the lines finish exactly place a sheet of paper over the drawing paper. This will prevent the area outside the rectangle from being inadvertently stained when doing the rapid graphite strokes.

THE TONES OF A CUBE IN PERSPECTIVE

In the last section we saw how gradating on a rectangle in perspective produces the visual effect of depth. This same effect can be used to create shadows around simple geometric shapes, like, for example, a cube. In the next exercise we will do a cube in perspective, and on top of it we will apply sequences of gray and gradations to give shadow effects

THE DRAWING AND CONTRAST

Drawing any object in perspective is not a straightforward task, but practice will help you to advance. As you can see, all of the visible planes of this cube are drawn so that if the upper and lower lines were extended they would meet in the distance.

Color all the background with oiled charcoal, a drawing medium that allows intense blacks and soft, controlled gradations. This first addition of gray will create an impacting first contrast.

Blacken all the upper part, protecting the cube area with a sheet of paper, and then start to gradate with your fingers until the tone begins to blend with the white of the paper. Move the masking sheet of paper around until all the background is covered while the cube remains totally white.

GRADATING THE SHADOWS

All the background of the drawing has been completely darkened by the gradation in this plane. Now start to draw with pure graphite on the darkest side of the cube. In the image below you can see that the darkest graphite tone is lighter than the oiled charcoal black. The graphite only gives a dark, dense gray. Continue working on this side of the cube in the same way as you did the oiled charcoal gradation. The volume effect will be intensified by the contrasts between the planes. The same drawing medium does not have to be used for all the cube faces. To practice more gradations we are going to use the sanguine stick with its warm tones and therefore ideal for the half-shadows. Do the same with the sanguine as you did with the graphite: the strokes follow the upper line. The top face of the cube is left completely white. The contrasts produced by the gradations of the different media are evident. Although this has only been a practice exercise, the results can be applied to any object with straight edges.

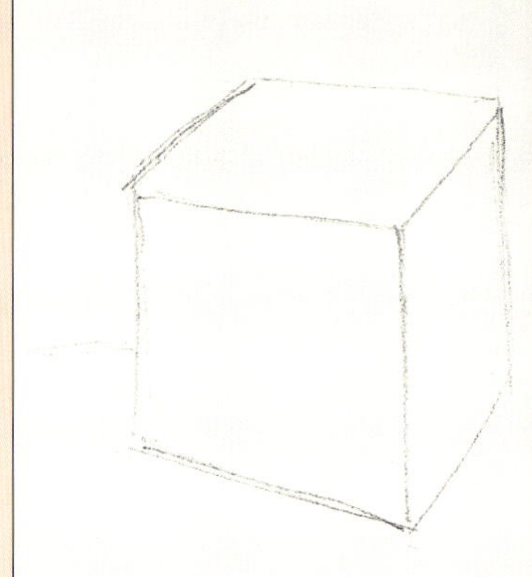

Before starting on the grays it is paramount that the cube forms are perfectly defined.

SKETCH GRADATIONS

In the previous chapters we studied how to resolve simple form sketches. Now it is time to learn how to resolve shadows using gradation grays. To practice we will do two spherical forms that eventually will be apples.

FORM APPROXIMATION

These forms are much easier to do than the cube in the last exercise. However, the gradations on the cube were not complicated because of the planes, whereas here they are more difficult. Drawing perfectly defined organic forms, not just doing the outline, is simpler than pure geometric objects.

This exercise will be done with a pure graphite stick. Firstly, softly outline the apple in the background with a circular stroke, and in front of it, outline the apple in the foreground. Erase away excess lines. The shapes are not completely round and, therefore, there is a certain margin of error.

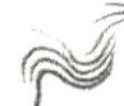

SHADOWS AND THE TONE SCALE 7

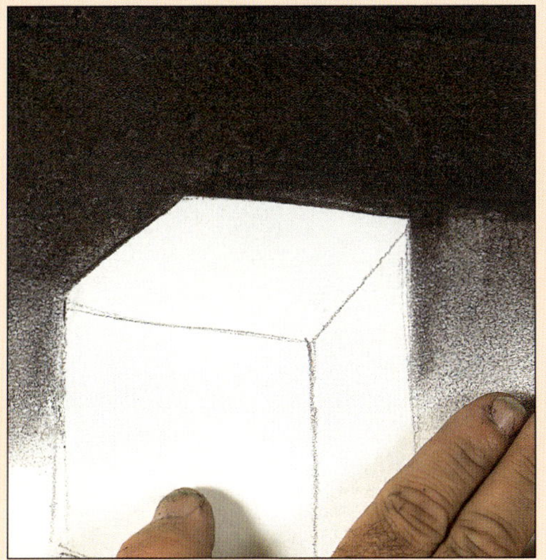

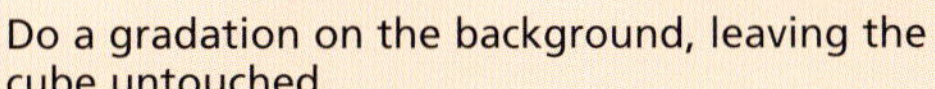

Do a gradation on the background, leaving the cube untouched.

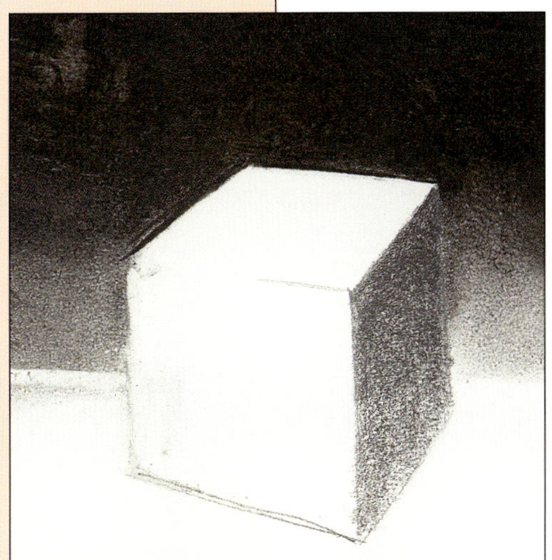

The darkest side of the cube is finished by doing a graphite gradation.

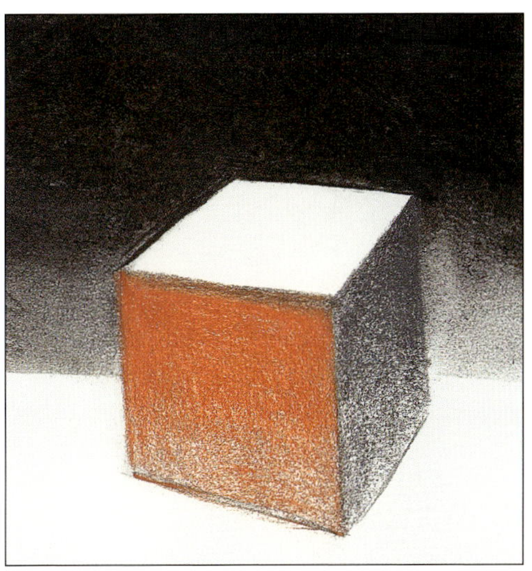

The front face is done with a sanguine gradation.

THE SHADOW IS THE GRADATION

If you go over the last exercise you can appreciate that the gradated tones are done starting from the upper line of each plane. In this new case, the planes are not straight, rather the surface is spherical. Gradating a spherical surface is very different to doing a flat one. On round forms the light zone is concentrated on one spot and the shadows gradually wrap around the object, their gradations surrounding the highlight.

GRADATIONS WITH STROKES

Up to now we have seen how grays can be resolved easily by softly rubbing the fingers until the tone is blended into the white of the paper. Graphite offers the chance to do a much more graphic gradation using strokes. The closer together the strokes are, the denser the dark area will be. Draw the lines of the shadows of the apples. Finally, rub a finger over the nearest apple to softly blend the strokes and make the zone more homogeneous.

SUMMARY

THE SHADOWS

The shadows are represented by the different intensities of gray given by each medium.

THE TONE SCALE

Each drawing medium varies in hardness and therefore offers its own particular tone range.

THE TONES IN PERSPECTIVE

The light falling on each object plane is different and, therefore, the tones applied in perspective are not done uniformly, but rather as a gradation.

GRADATIONS AND STROKES

The range of grays can also be obtained with varied strokes.

DOING SHADOWS STARTING FROM THE GRADATION

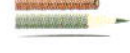

Do the outline quickly with straightforward, circular strokes.

The initial stroke, which surrounds the main highlight, is slanted. On the apple in the foreground, a new stroke crosses the old one near the highlight, superimposed on top of the gradation.

The strokes allow the shadows to be gradated. Finally, rub a finger over the foreground apple to blend the graphite strokes.

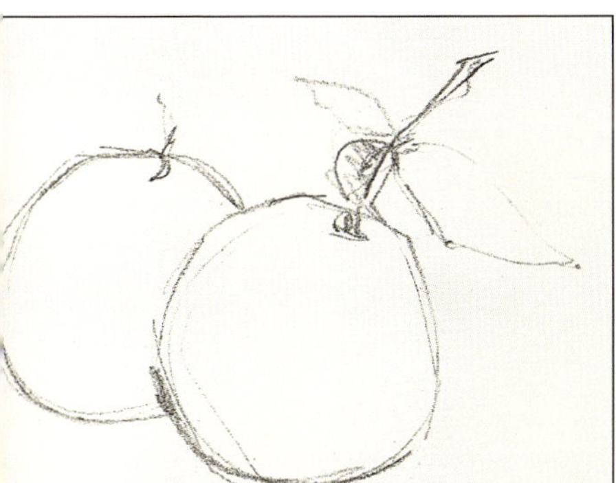

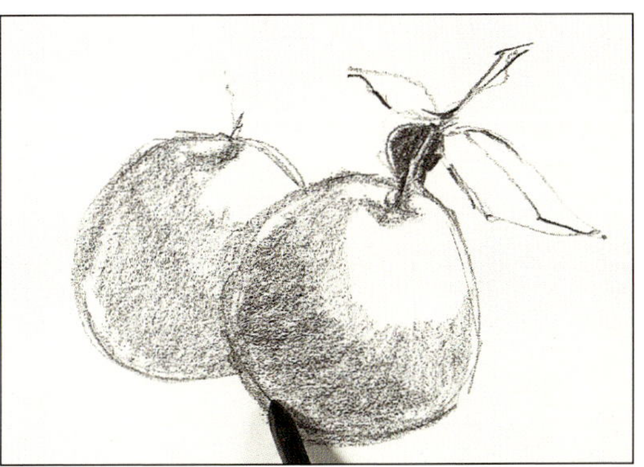

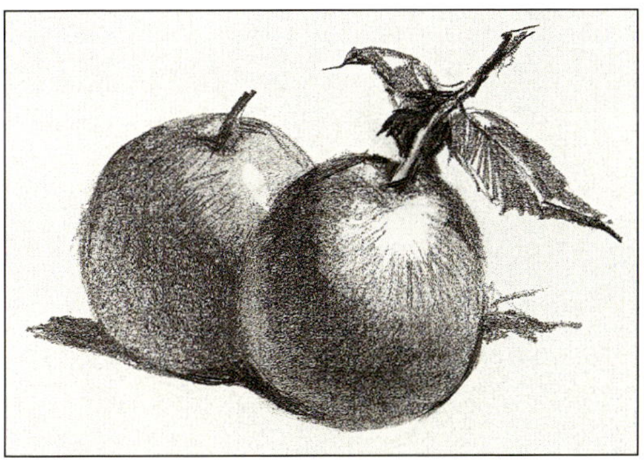

7 Exercices *Step by step*

In the following exercise we are going to develop what we have learnt in this chapter to do a somewhat more complex drawing. Although simple, this model was not chosen at random: the aim was pedagogic.

As you can see the forms are simple, but they both have different planes and, therefore, representing them with gray gradation demands special attention. Once the learner has finished the exercise, take similar objects and draw them following the guidelines given here.

NECESSARY MATERIAL

A graphite stick (1), drawing paper (2), and a cloth for the hands (3).

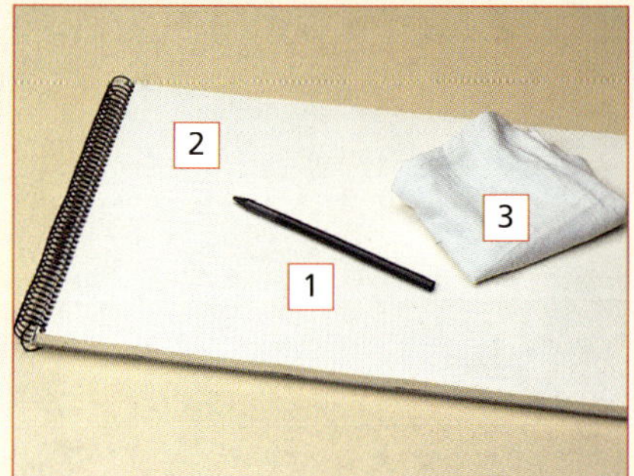

Do not leave the corrections to be done when the drawing is already in the advanced stages. The sketch must have the right forms and proportions.

1· THE OUTLINE IS VERY IMPORTANT BECAUSE the definitive form is based on these simple lines.

FIRST, DO A PRELIMINARY sketch and then gradually define the forms, increasing the firmness of the lines as you advance. Always respect the sense of proportion of the objects. It is crucial that any correction to the form, the perspective or the planes, be done at this stage.

IN THIS EXERCISE IT IS NOT NECESSARY to rub out any element. The corrections are superimposed on top of the lower strokes, becoming firmer and more definitive. The preliminary sketch will end up becoming a firm structure on top of which to continue the drawing.

2· ONCE THE FIRST STAGE IS COMPLETED, draw the different light and shadow planes of all the drawing, which is what really matters now. Firstly, do the background with a slanted stroke, cutting out the form of the objects. Afterwards do a new set of strokes that cross the previous ones.

THE DARKEST PLANE OF THE CUBIC tin is done firstly with vertical lines, and afterwards it is darkened with slanted strokes. The round container is done only with vertical strokes, leaving the highlights untouched.

3· NOW WE ARE GOING TO WORK ON THE DARK ZONES gradually, adding strokes that give shape to the shadow gradations, and, therefore, to the object planes.

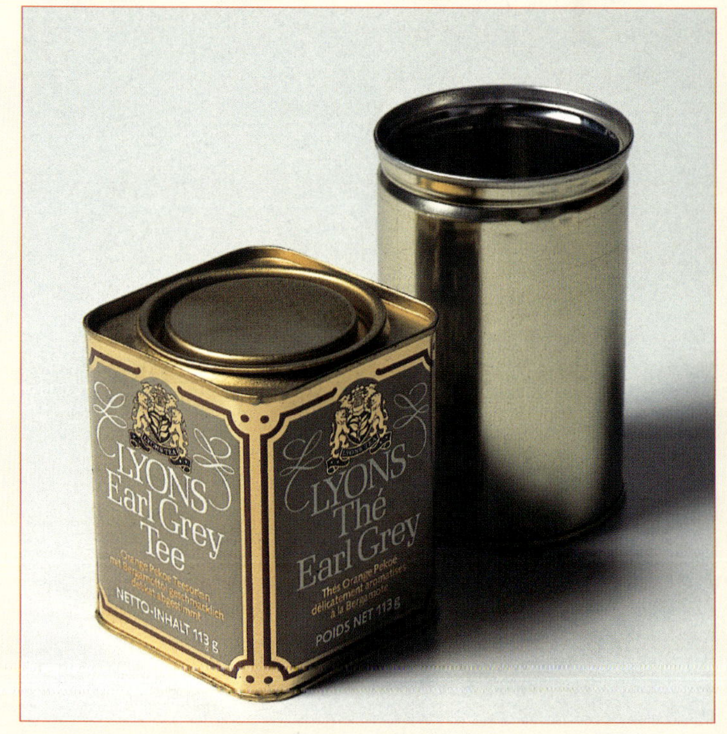

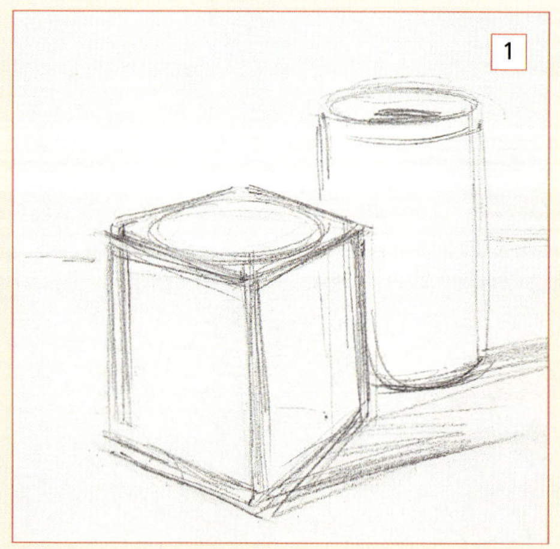

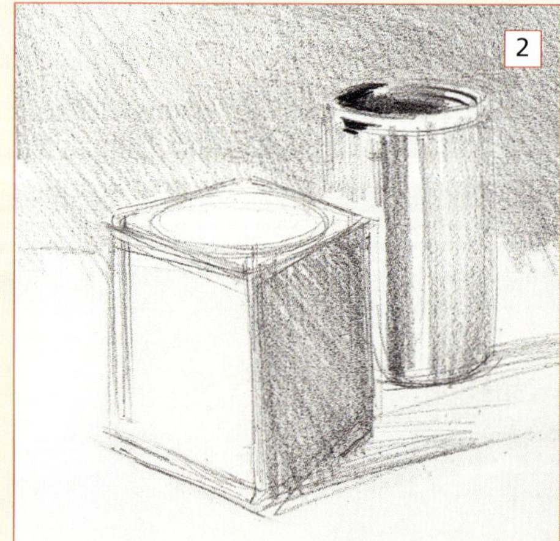

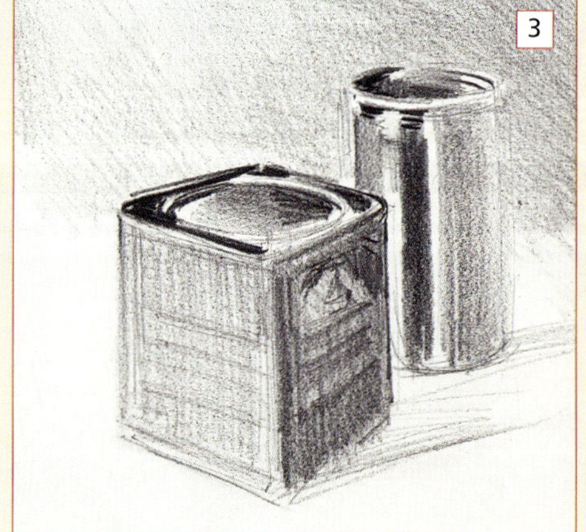

Geometric elements

7

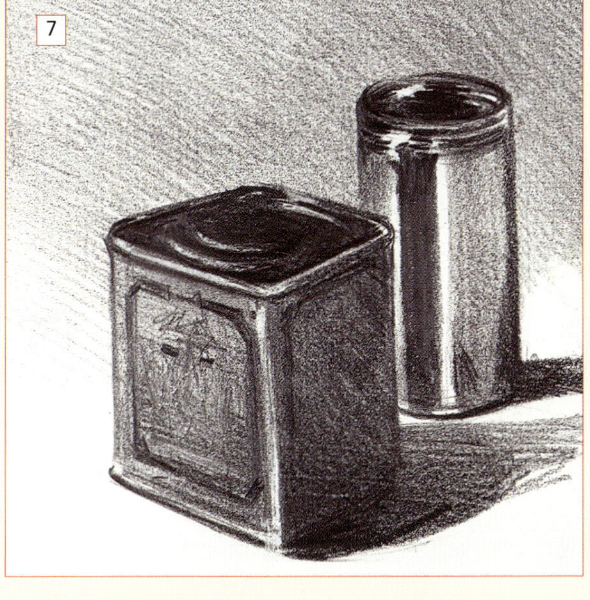

SUMMARY SCHEME

The outlines are done progressively, going over the forms as they are corrected.

The first gray is drawn in the background and marks out the forms of the still life.

The white reflection of the round container increases in luminosity when the dark area is more contrasted.

The dark face of the square container is contrasted by darkening the illuminated face.

4· THE MOST ILLUMINATED FACE of the cube is darkened by soft lines that follow, on one side, the plane direction, and on the other, the vertical line. Increase the strokes on the dark side, letting some of the gray done initially show through. On the round container increase the contrast of the reflection.

5· STRONGLY CONTRAST the upper part of both containers, leaving the highlights perfectly marked out.

CONTINUE WORKING ON THE PLANES OF EACH CONTAINER. On the square container, increase the contrast on the illuminated face with a straight stroke that goes in the direction of the upper line. This makes it necessary to increase the contrast in the darker zone. The contrast is also increased on the round container, so that the highlights appear much more luminous.

SO FAR THE DARK PARTS have been done almost entirely with the graphite point. To do soft gradations and to tone down the stroke effect, use the conic zone of the point. Pass it gently over the zone to be contrasted. When this is finished both containers will be adequately contrasted.

AS YOU CAN SEE, WHEN AN ILLUMINATED zone is darkened it is also necessary to increase the dark contrasts in the drawing at the same time, balancing the grays in each zone. Once again, use the point of the point to insinuate the contrasts of the decoration on the illuminated face of the square container.

BY NOW THE PIECE IS VERY ADVANCED. However, different modifications can be made which, while they will not change the overall effect radically, will give greater realism to the drawing.

6· ON THE DARKEST SIDE INCREASE the contrasts in the lower part in such a way that they almost match the shadow cast. Complete the definition of the decoration in this zone, avoiding a too blatant stroke effect.

DARKEN ALL THE DRAWING AGAIN to strengthen the contrast of the shadows. The highlights that are too visible are softly gone over with graphite, but do not completely cover them.

7· THIS WILL FINISH OFF THIS INTERESTING exercise related to the way grays can contribute to a drawing.

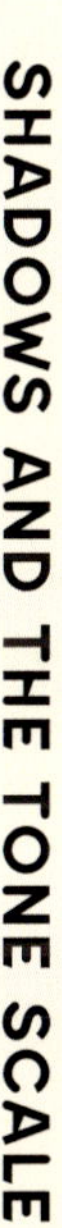

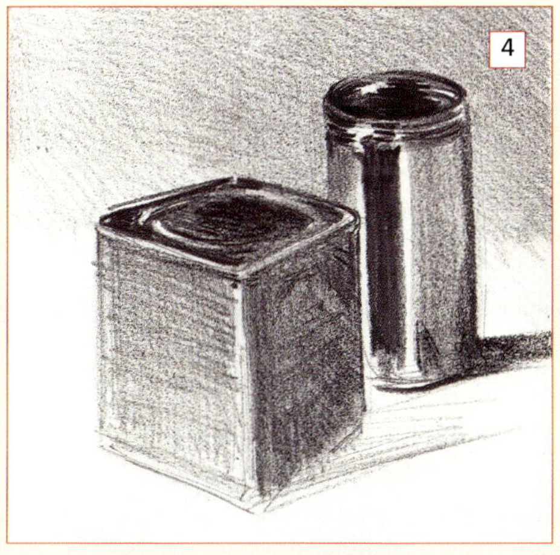

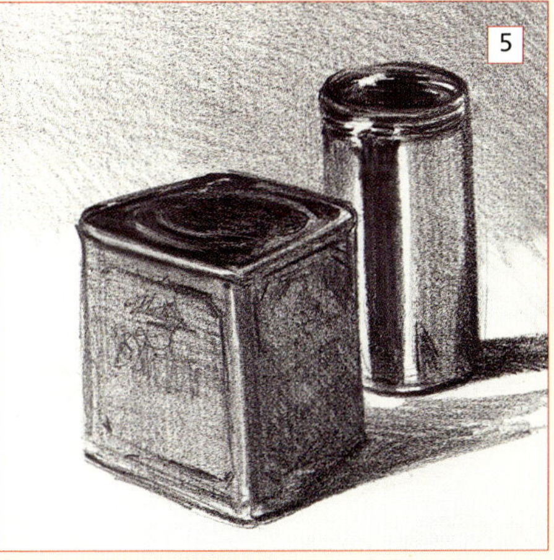

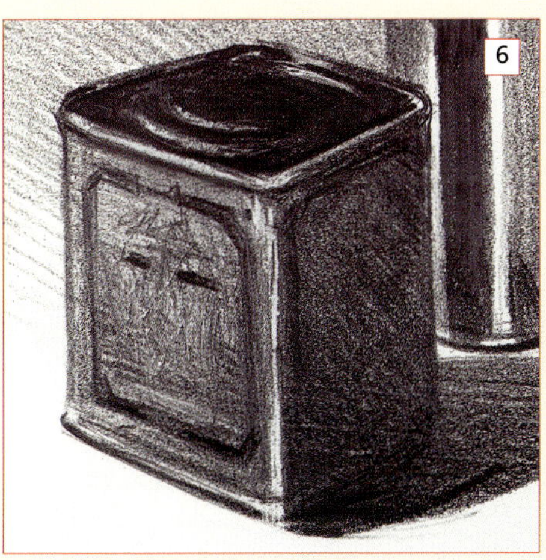

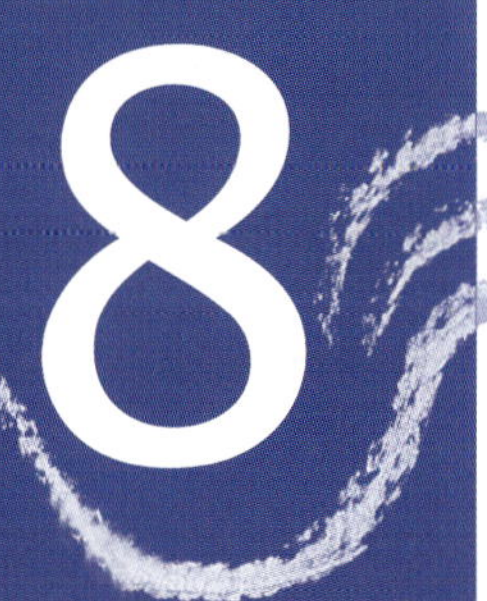

8 FIGURE COMPOSITIONS. THE FIRST OUTLINE AND PROPORTIONS

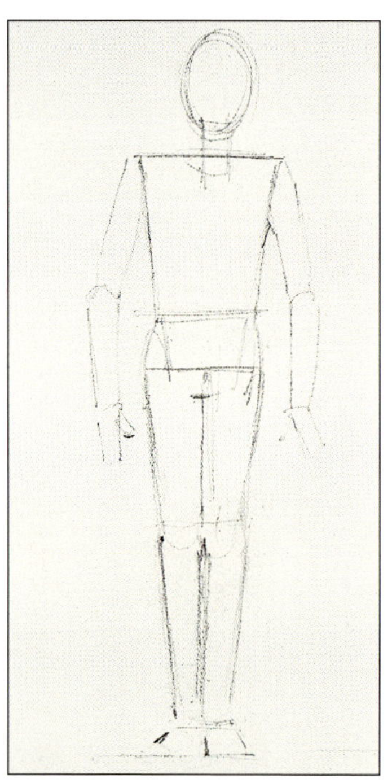

Synthetic forms can be used to represent the human body in simple geometric shapes. The man's chest is wider than the woman's, but his hip is thinner.

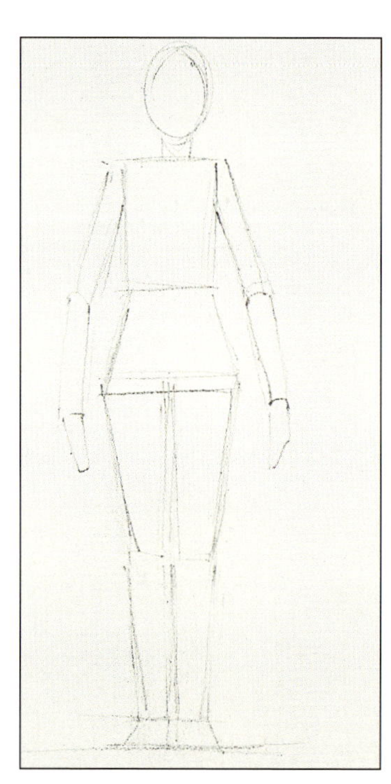

Compare the sketch of the woman with the man: although the forms are the same the proportions are different.

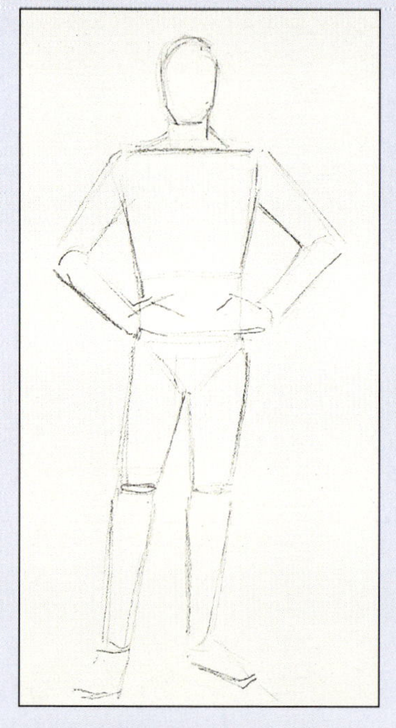

Starting from a basic scheme the figure can be represented in any position. Observe how this pose is softer and more fluid than the original one.

We must now set about learning how to master the techniques for drawing figure compositions. Landscapes and still lifes enable you to learn drawing and painting techniques which aim at getting a result that looks like the model. However, figure compositions require perfection in these techniques.

This chapter deals with figure composition and how to calculate the proportions, and one of the fundamental questions in this field: canons (these are standard measurements). Through the concepts explained you get a clear idea as to why the body must have a certain proportionality. As figure compositions are quite

THE CENTER OF GRAVITY

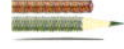

In pose studies, although there need not be symmetry between the right side and the left side, there is equilibrium, something which comes from establishing the center of gravity, or the vertical axis of the figure. The body weight must be in equilibrium on either side of this axis.

You can easily understand how the center of gravity concept works by practicing with your own body. If you stand upright with your legs together and your hands by your sides and then start to lean, you will eventually fall. However, if you raise a leg and lean in the other direction, you will stay on your feet longer. The raised leg is a counter weight which shifts your center of gravity. When doing any figure composition, always study this center of gravity effect so that the figures look stable on their feet.

Once the figure has been sketched you can perfect the forms, outlining each part of the body. Use the center of gravity to distribute the weight in a balanced pose.

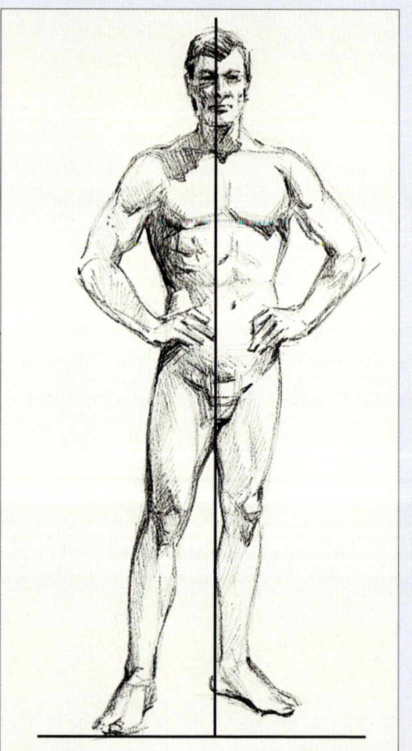

Only when you have done a preliminary sketch is it possible to do a figure like this, in which the effect of the center of gravity on the pose has been carefully studied.

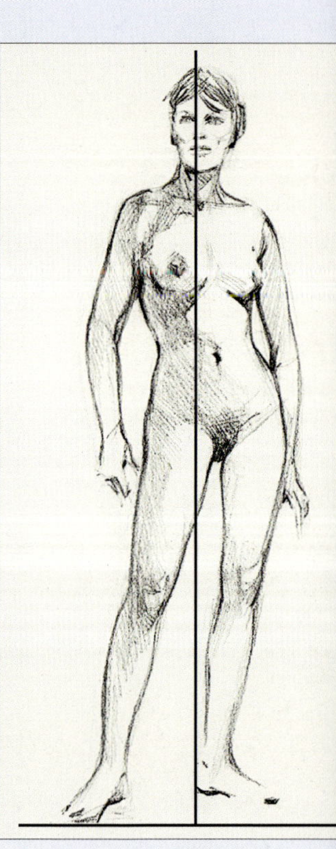

When elaborating a figure composition all the techniques you have learnt play a more important role than with landscapes or still lifes. An error in an apple or a tree may go unnoticed but errors always show up on a figure. The proportions and the outlines must be considered first.

8

complex, both this chapter and the next are dedicated to this subject. Progressing logically we will deal with outlines, proportions, anatomy and how to draw. The examples on the following pages need not be copied exactly. The aim is for the learner to become familiar with the proportions and to learn how to do schematic forms.

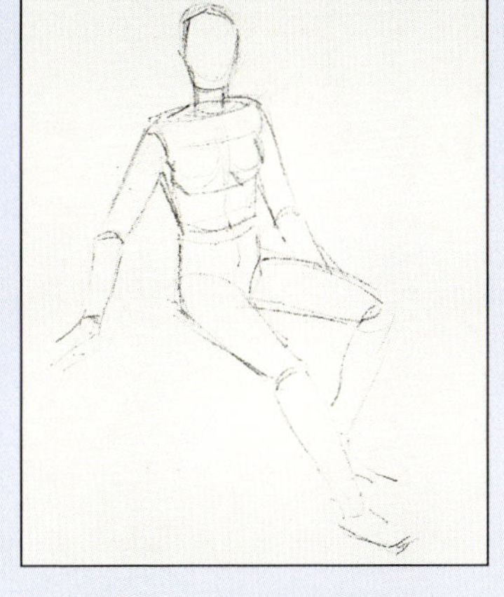

Drawing a schematic figure enables you to represent any pose however complex in may be. Sometimes body parts are partially hidden by others.

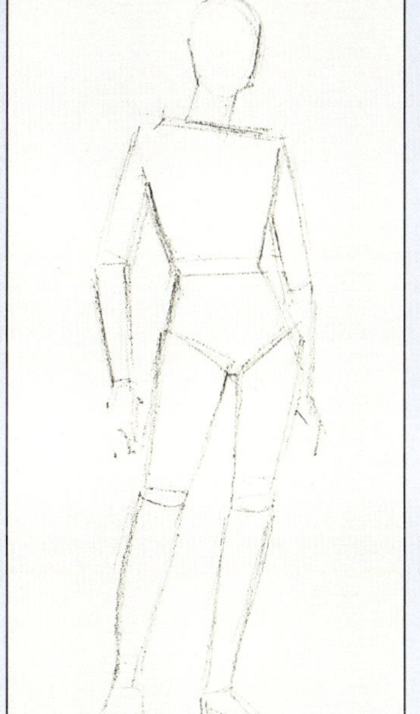

Natural poses are rarely static or symmetric. When part of the body is affected.

FROM STRAIGHT LINES TO FORMS.

If you have paid attention to the earlier chapters it will be easy to do the first outlines of a figure composition. Like any other element in nature, the human body has to be broken down into simple straight line forms and then constructed as if it were a dummy. This dummy can be used as the base for all types of poses and figures. Later we will learn more exact ways of doing outlines and proportions.

Outlining parts of the body.

Any figure can be outlined using simple shapes. Here we are going to outline a man and a woman which can later be used as a model for any figure in any pose from any viewpoint.

OUTLINING PARTS OF THE BODY

Any figure can be outlined using simple shapes. Here we are going to outline a man and a woman which can later be used as a model for any figure in any pose from any viewpoint.

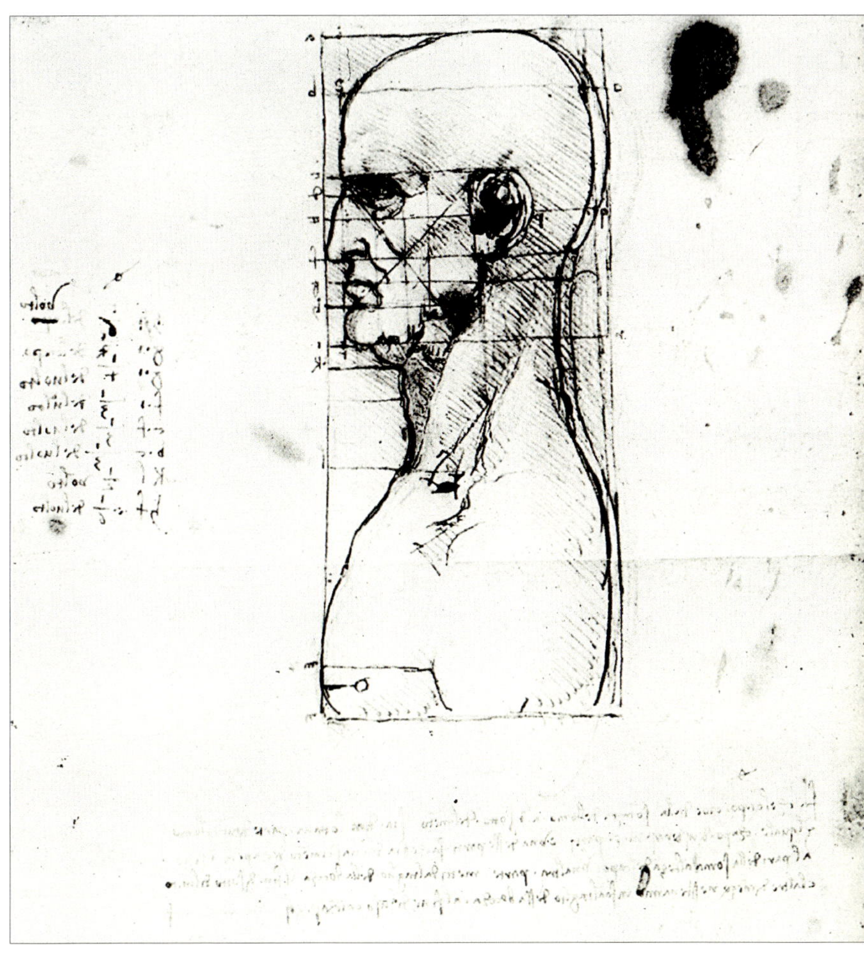

This study by Leonardo shows how one of the great masters worked on the anatomy starting from basic, linear schemes.

STUDYING THE BASIC FORMS

When the forms are complex, it is best to start the outline by doing a schematic study of each separate part of the body. Both the man's head and the woman's head are drawn with an ellipse shape.

The neck joins the head to the shoulders and is represented by a small cylinder. A man's chest is basically a trapezoid, much wider at the top than the woman's chest, a shape somewhere between a rectangle and a trapezoid. The waist line must be established and used as the base for the hips. These too, for both sexes, are a trapezium shape wider at the base. The male hip is lower than the female's and therefore the trapezium is smaller. The legs start from the hips and require approximately as much space as the trunk. Both arms and legs are tube-like, the elbows and knees being marked, of course.

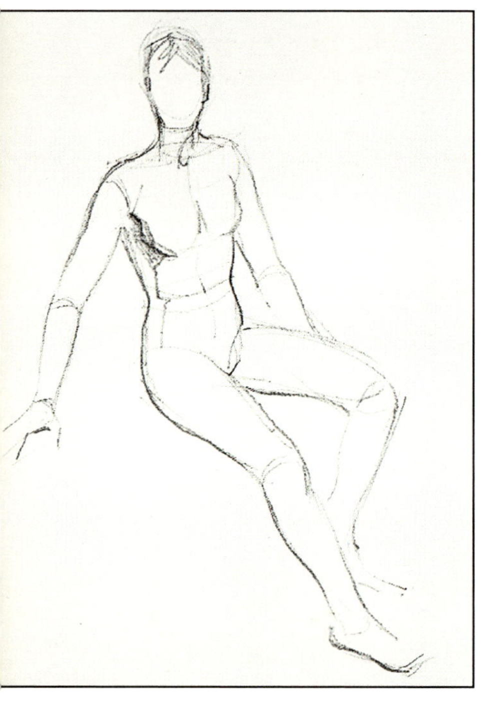

Starting from the preliminary sketch, join the forms and soften them. They then become more human in appearance.

THE SITTING DOWN FIGURE

A schematic figure can be used to do any pose provided that the parts of the body respect the center of gravity. The arms and legs are not only counterweights, they are also supports. Here we are going to do a sitting figure following the same guidelines as in the earlier exercises. As you can see, the dummy scheme has been reproduced sitting down.

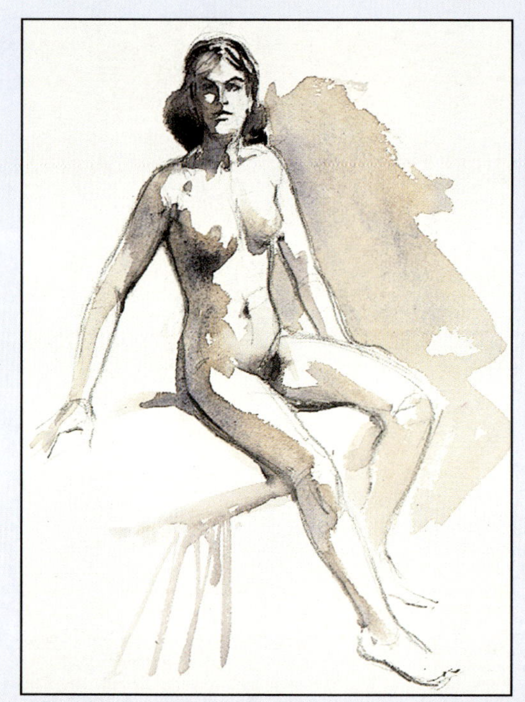

Once the superfluous lines have been erased, darks and lights finish off the figure composition. Here the work was done with a wash.

SCHEMES AND SHADING THE FORMS

The essential forms done with geometric shapes are the basis on which the figure is constructed precisely. On these pages some schemes are shown as a guide for doing more complicated poses. Simple shapes can be used to build up any pose, though natural, and therefore unsymmetrical, ones are better . Even when resting, the human body is rarely so still and balanced that it is perfectly symmetrical. It is much easier to fill out the forms starting from the preliminary sketch.

The study of the pose -the preliminary sketch- is the first thing that has to be done.

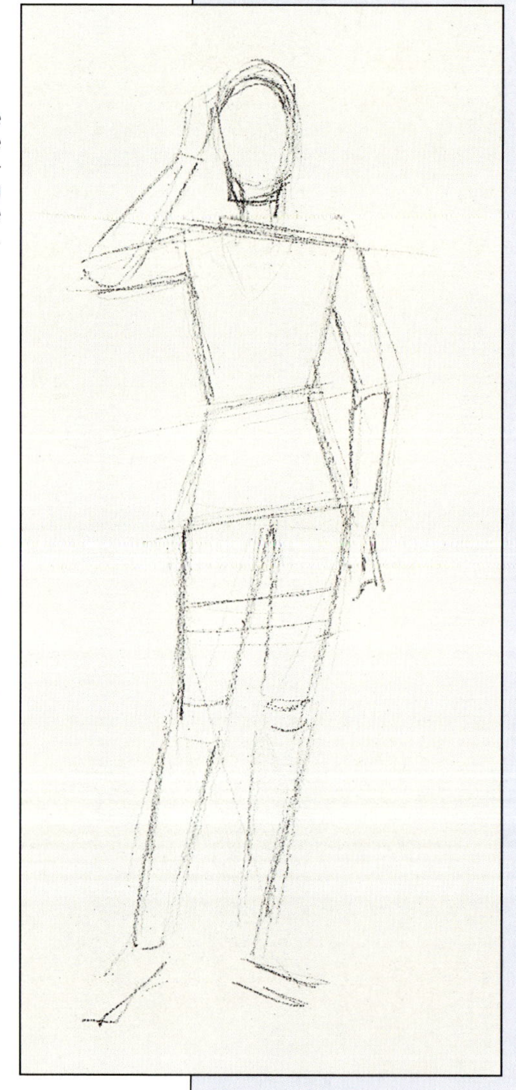

Although this figure is going to be dressed, it is fundamental that its internal structure is sketched as if it were naked.

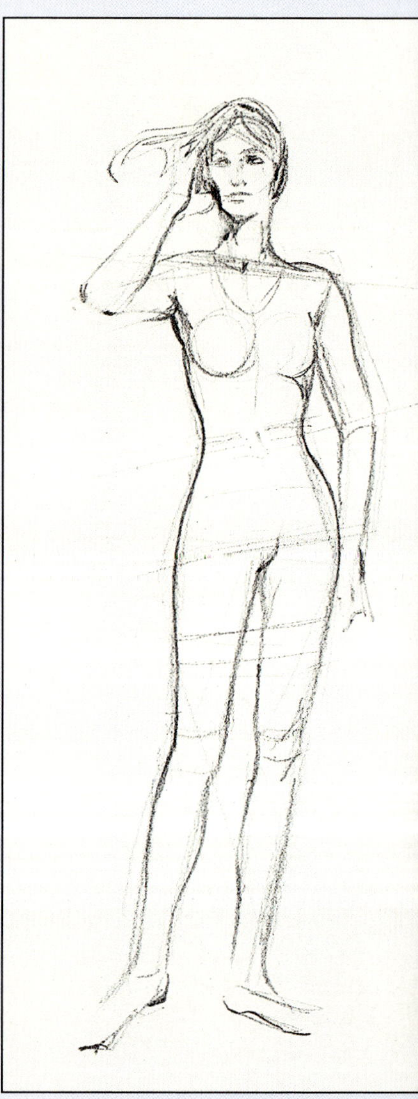

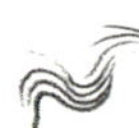

FIGURE COMPOSITIONS: THE FIRST OUTLINE AND PROPORTIONS 8

JOINING THE FORMS

Building on the preliminary sketch the forms of the balanced figure can be turned into a much realer anatomy. This drawing procedure is enriched by the different stroke possibilities. Soft, fleshy curves can be put in and the line loses its straightness. Once the lines that support the figure are in place, the accessory ones can be rubbed out. Though necessary in the first steps, they are not needed now.

Joining the different forms gives unity to the outlines. As you can see, drawing in this way means that the piece evolves more solidly.

Everytime unnecessary lines are removed the figure becomes more realistic as the preliminary sketch fades away. Then the figure composition can be completed with any of the mediums. This example has been finished with watercolor wash.

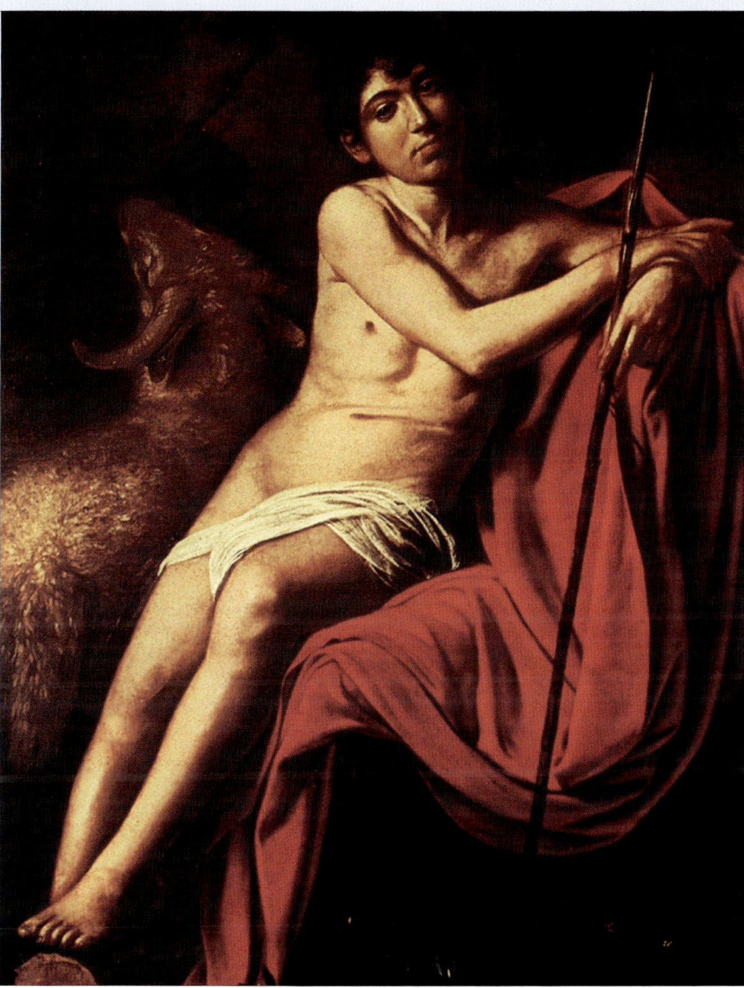

STUDYING THE POSE

However complicated a figure composition may appear, behind it there is always an original structure based on simple forms. This enables the artist to start the work free from the pressure of doing an intricate study. Nevertheless, this does not mean that the drawings of the great masters had preliminary sketches as elemental as those shown in this chapter, but they did do various studies before deciding on the definitive pose. This would have been the case of the Italian artist known as Caravaggio (1573-1610) before painting 'John the Baptist', which is now kept in the Borghese Gallery in Rome. Obviously, the more figure drawing is mastered, the less reliance there is on the preliminary sketch: the outlines become more fluid as the artist becomes more skilled.

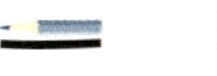

STUDYING THE CLOTHES

Studying the folds made by the clothes is a good exercise. It is not necessary to draw the entire figure, just do a rough preliminary sketch of the body part the clothes will cover and then work on the creases. Leonardo da Vinci's study of the clothes of a kneeling figure is complex, but the other two examples are not. Ask someone to pose for this exercise. A flexed arm or leg will show you that drawing woolen clothes is different to drawing cotton.

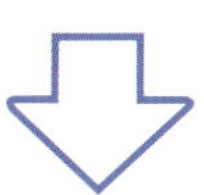

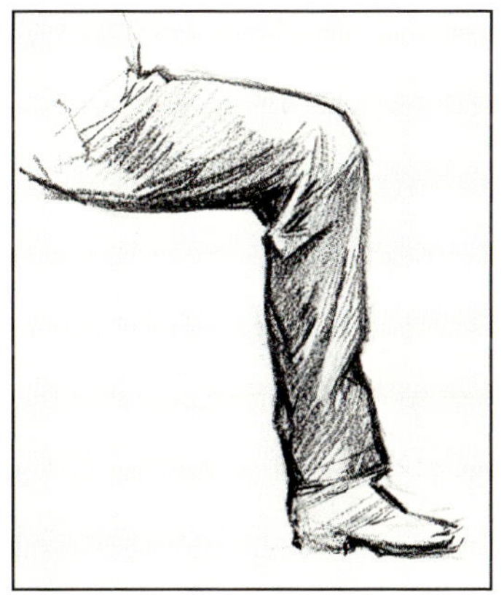

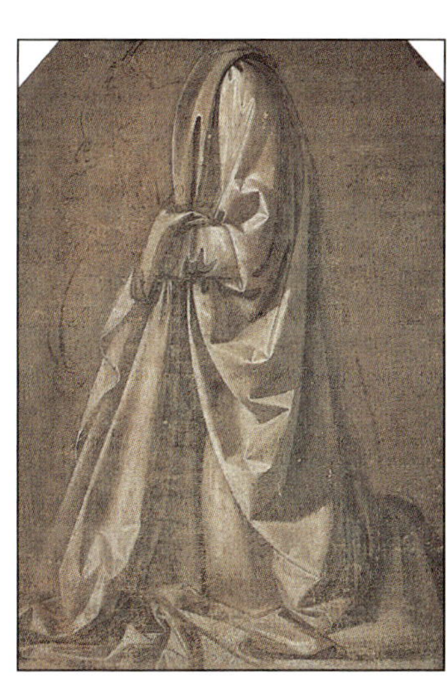

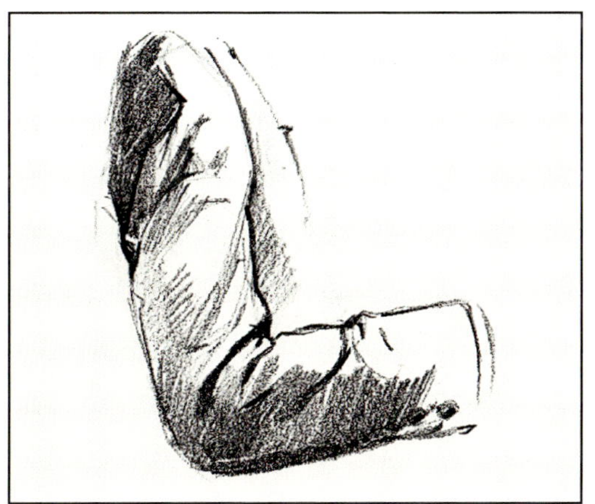

8 FIGURE COMPOSITIONS: THE FIRST OUTLINE AND PROPORTIONS

THE DRESSED FIGURE

All the examples done on these pages are aimed at showing that starting from a dummy, all imaginable poses can be developed. Try doing as many different poses as possible. Later on we will work on figure compositions using proportions and getting by without the drawing of the dummy. However, at the moment it is a good recourse for schematizing the figure's forms.

In this exercise we will do a figure that will be dressed later. The purpose is to show that even clothed figures need a perfect internal structure.

STUDYING THE POSE AND THE ESSENTIAL LINES

The first lines of the figure come from the preliminary sketch of the pose. It is in this first step that the parts of the body are decided on and their interrelationship. As can be seen in the drawing below, the different parts of the body can be arranged so that the figure adopts a natural pose, but always having a vertical axis. With these first sketch lines, any pose can be adopted by shifting the arms and legs.

A handy trick. To draw a pose study without having to do the scheme every time, cut out a cardboard outline of a dummy. This simple recourse will allow you to study any movement or pose naturally, and also to see which parts are hidden from the viewer.

THE FIGURE NUDE BEFORE DRESSING IT

Clothes cover real volumes, not a scheme of lines.

The scheme must be as like a well defined body as possible, otherwise any intervention you do on top will be lacking in realism. However, if the figure drawing has been correctly done, it is straightforward to complete it before putting on the clothes.

When the body of the figure is defined no essential part must be hidden, and, therefore, the construction lines have to be clear and free of any traces that could mislead the artist in later work.

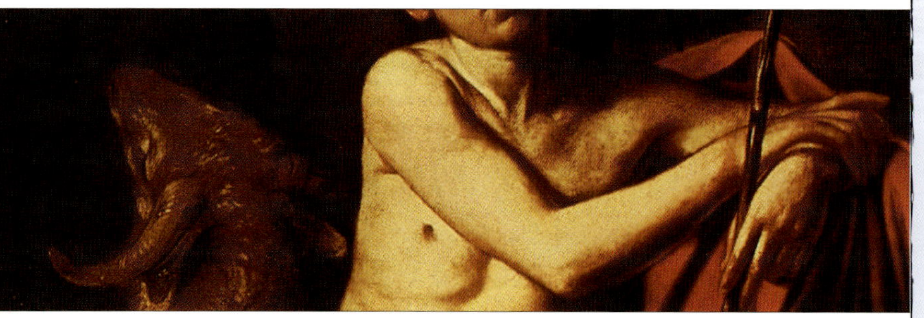

Before dressing the figure, always ensure that the preliminary sketch is perfectly structured.

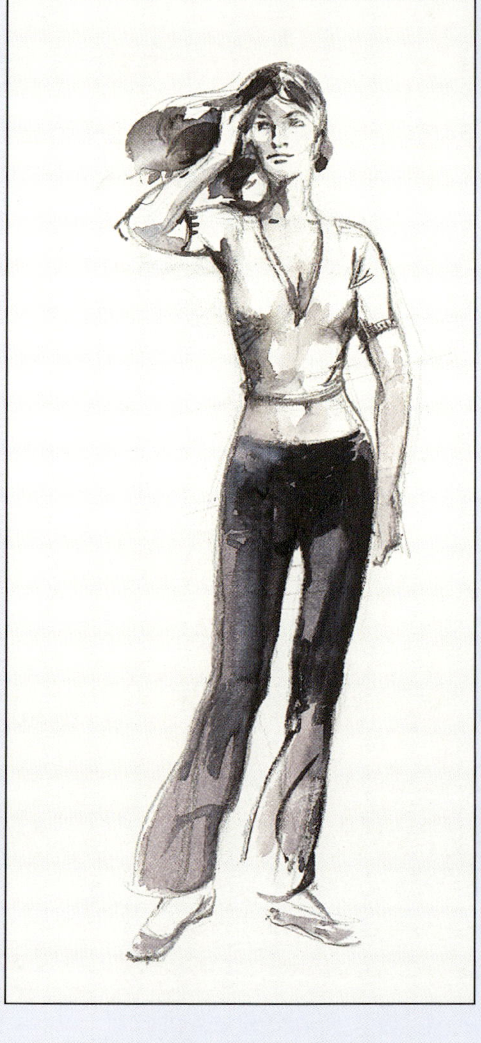

ADAPTING THE CLOTHES TO THE BODY

When the figure scheme is well structured, the geometric construction lines erased, and the body parts joined by the outlines, you can start to tackle the clothing.

It makes no difference if the clothes are loose fitting or tight, what matters is that the figure is perfectly defined so that the clothes can be correctly drawn.

SUMMARY

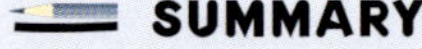

PRELIMINARY SKETCH

The preliminary sketch, or scheme, is based on pure shapes.

FINISHING THE FIGURE

Working on the preliminary sketch, do a study of the body form. Fix the principal lines and eliminate the others.

THE POSE AND THE PRELIMINARY SKETCH

Being familiar with the elemental figure forms will allow you to do any pose however complicated it may appear.

THE DRESSED FIGURE

Before dressing the figure it must be well structured.

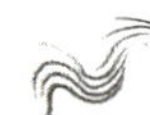

A figure study

8

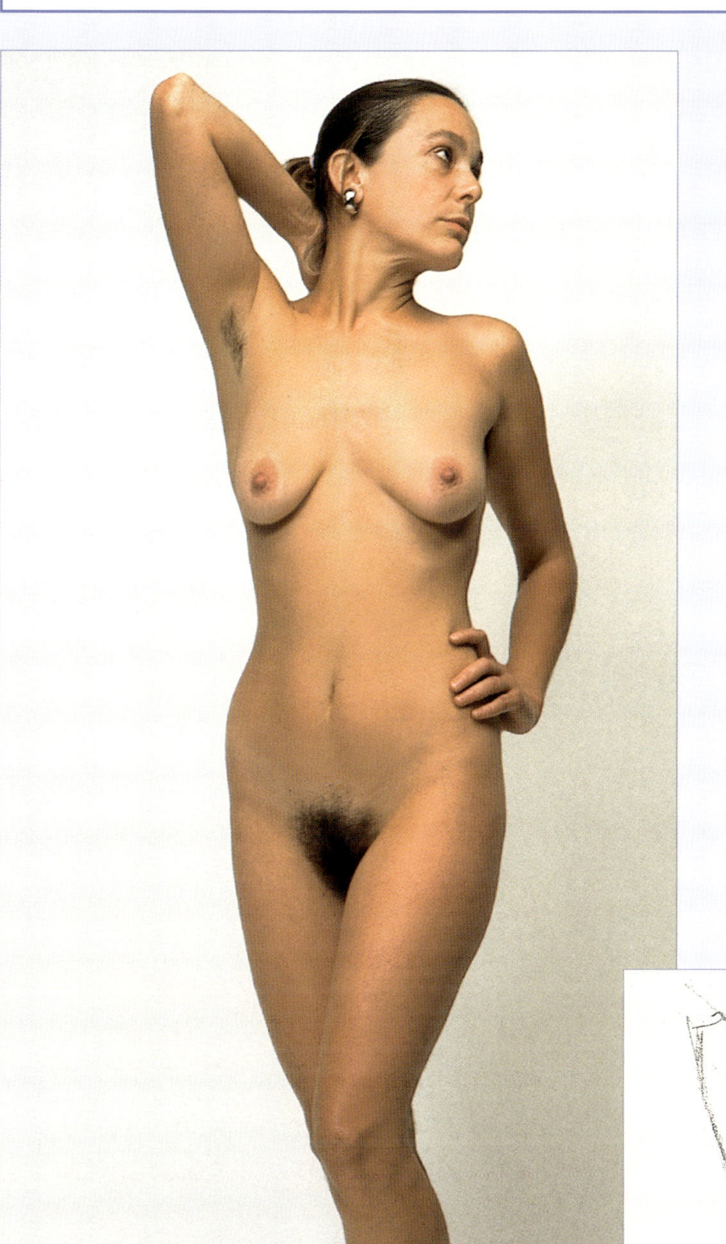

In this chapter we have studied how the a figure can be schematized with simple shapes and an outline done as if it were a dummy. This next exercise is no more complicated than any exercise done up until now, but it requires a great deal of attention from the learner because the arms and legs, as you can see, are not symmetrical. If you follow the steps and study the drawing's evolution, many of your initial doubts will become clear.

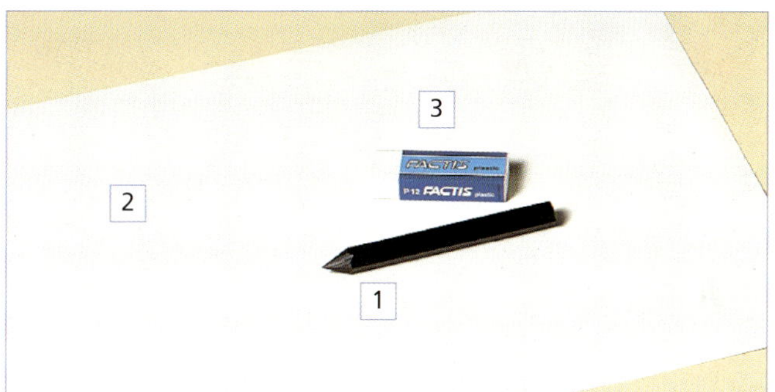

(1) graphite crayon, (2) paper, and an eraser (3).

WHEN STARTING THE DRAWING take into consideration the measurements of the body parts and how they can affect the initial scheme. The outline based on simple shapes always helps to do the figure, above all when the pose is complicated. Here you can see how one leg is in front of the other and how the arms produce different planes. The arm tucked into the hip appears shorter because of the depth effect.

Exercices *Step by step*

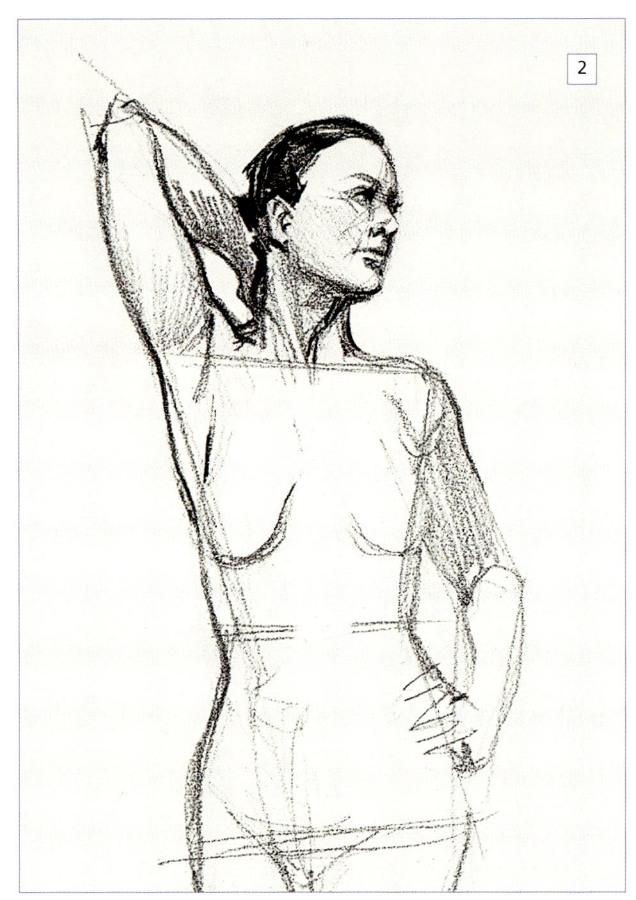

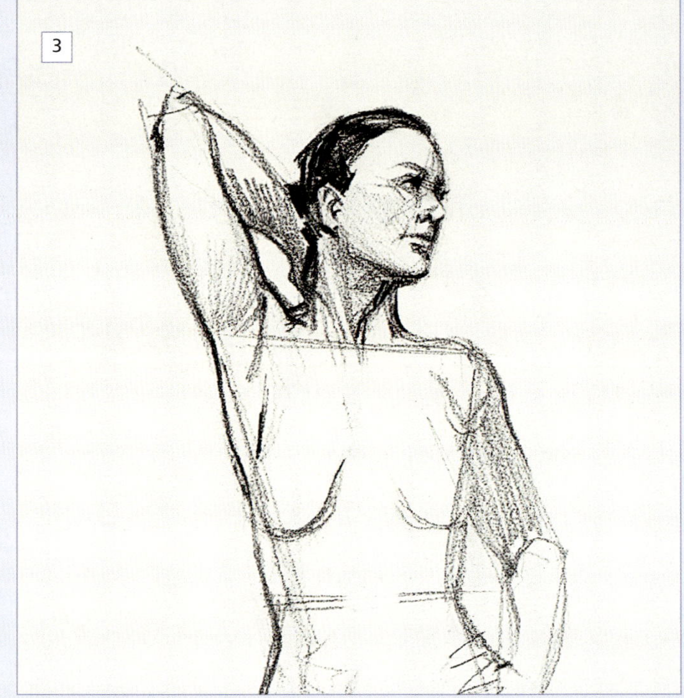

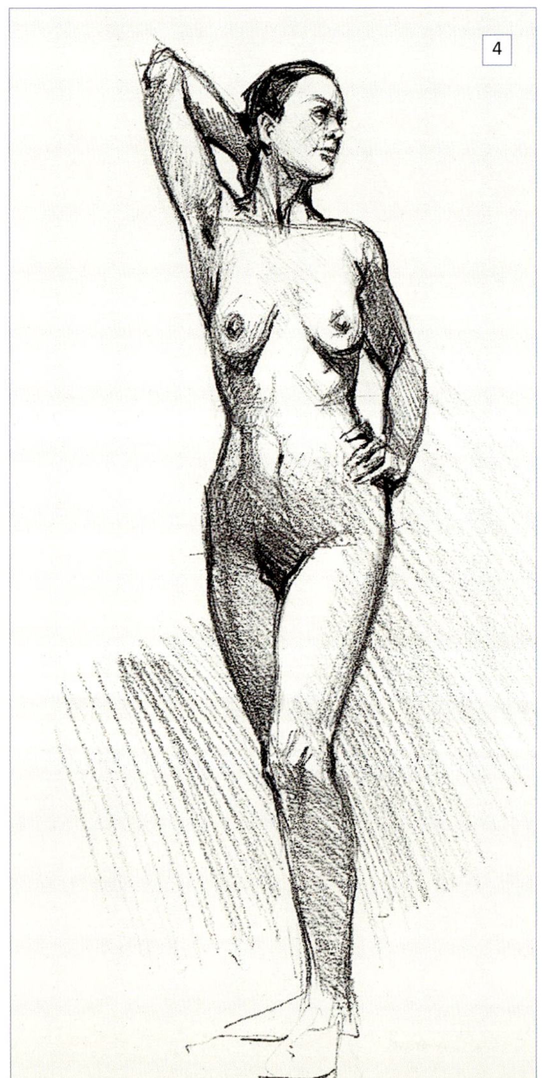

AS YOU CAN SEE, the torso and the hip are represented by trapezoids.

2· IN STEP TWO, once the initial scheme is completely developed and the spatial planes resolved, you can start on the forms of the drawing with a much more definitive stroke.

NOW IT IS NECESSARY THAT ALL the parts be understood not only individually but also as part of the whole.

3· IN THIS CLOSE UP, you can see how the different parts of the body are joined together. The hidden lines are now unimportant for it is the outlines that bestow cohesion on the drawing.

IF YOU COMPARE THIS FRAGMENT with the first 'step by step' picture you will see the importance of the stroke when giving form to the parts of the figure.

4· ONCE THE PRINCIPLE LINES ARE FIRM, the preliminary sketch is no longer necessary and can be eliminated carefully with the eraser.

EVEN THOUGH IN SO DOING YOU MAY RUB OUT a few definitive lines, do not worry because a small trace always remains as a guide. Start to shade the first darks to give form to the figure.

LONG STROKES ALLOW THE BACKGROUND behind the figure to be darkened, outlining the human form with the contrast.

A figure study

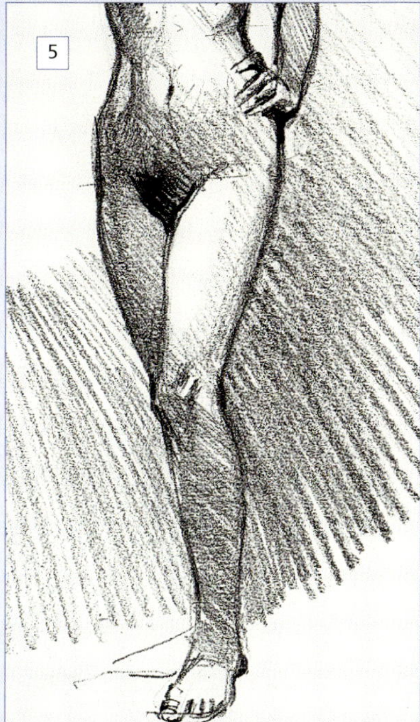

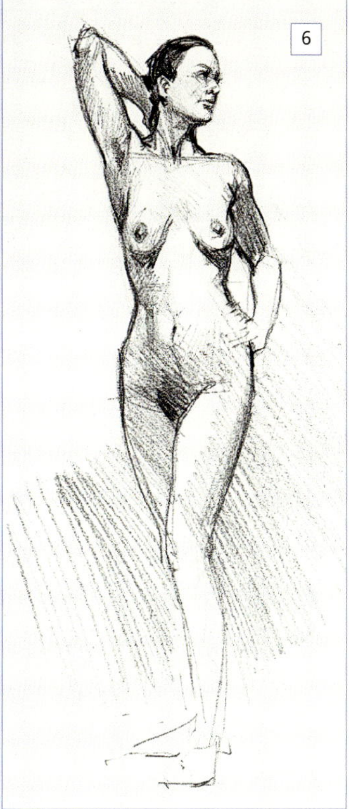

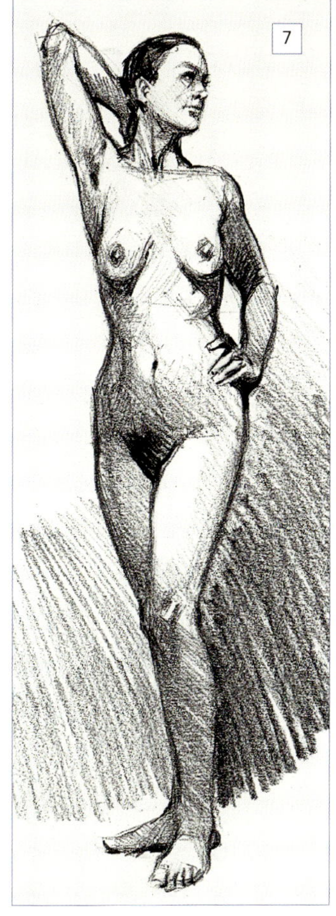

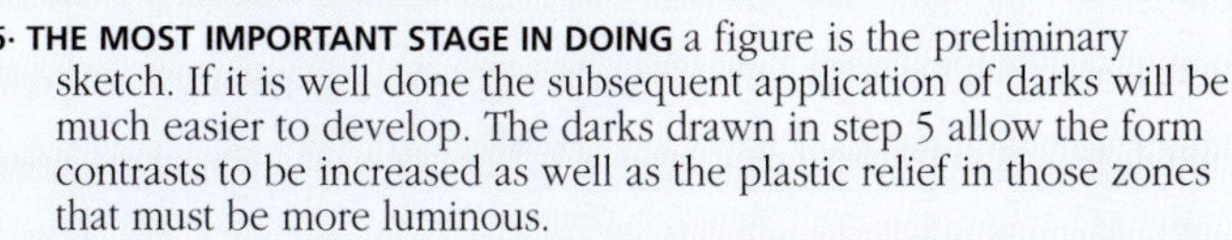

5· THE MOST IMPORTANT STAGE IN DOING a figure is the preliminary sketch. If it is well done the subsequent application of darks will be much easier to develop. The darks drawn in step 5 allow the form contrasts to be increased as well as the plastic relief in those zones that must be more luminous.

OBSERVE THE RIGHT SIDE OF THE FIGURE: compared to the last step there has been a notable darkening of the shadows while the luminous zones appear brighter due to the contrast.

AS THE DARKS ARE INTENSIFIED, the figure contours take shape, as you can see in the lower part of the legs.

6· THIS CLOSE UP FROM STEP 6 requires special attention. A foot could be quite complicated to do, especially if there is no scheme. However, if the initial structure is schematized in simple shapes, it will be much easier: look at the model and try to do the principle darks synthetically, ignoring superfluous elements.

7· ALL THAT REMAINS TO BE DONE IS TO INCREASE the contrast of the main background darks.

USE THE ERASER TO CLEAN the zones that have become smeared in the drawing process.

NOW YOU HAVE finished this figure study.

The preliminary sketch is constructed with simple geometric shapes, as if it were a dummy.

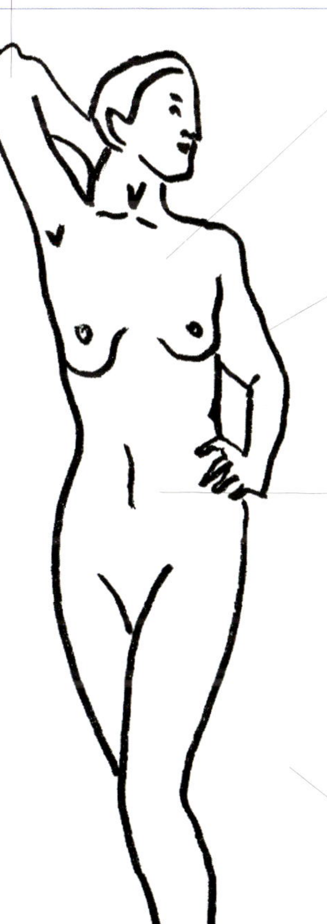

Inside the figure get rid of lines as they become unnecessary.

The darks help to explain the way the light falls on the body. The arm supported on the hip is darkened as the drawing progresses.

Draw the form outlines by superimposing a line over the straight line sketch.

Darkening the background helps to contrast the figure.

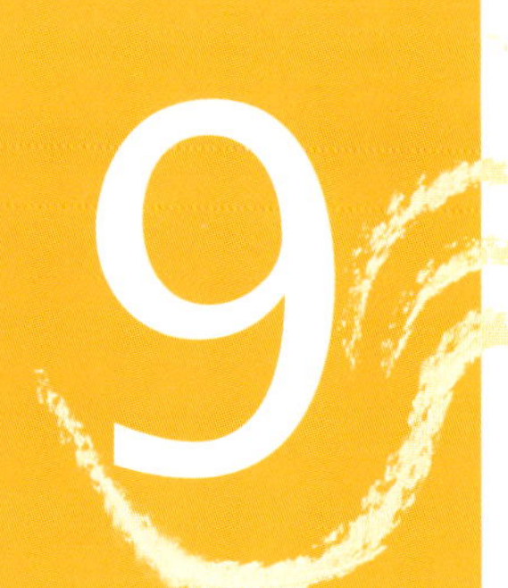

STARTiNG THE MODELiNG

In this chapter we will deal with one of the principle questions in technical academic drawing: modeling through tone values. This subject will also come up in progressively more complicated forms in later chapters.

GRADATIONS AND TONES

Modeling, as its name suggests, aims at representing the forms of the object by studying how the light falls. When you observe any object you can see that the shadows are different tones of the same color; the less light that falls, the darker they are. Just one drawing medium can produce gray tone scales. If these tones are stumped the result is the modeling of the shadows and the lights.

All the dry drawing mediums allow different tones to be established by varying the pressure on the paper. As you press harder you will near the maximum tone obtainable with the medium. If you vary the pressure exercised in a series of strokes, you can obtain a gradation from the darkest tone through to the gray closest to the paper color. Gradations give tone scales which permit the modeling of objects and make the tone value process easier.

Simple gradations like this allow modeling and tone value effects.

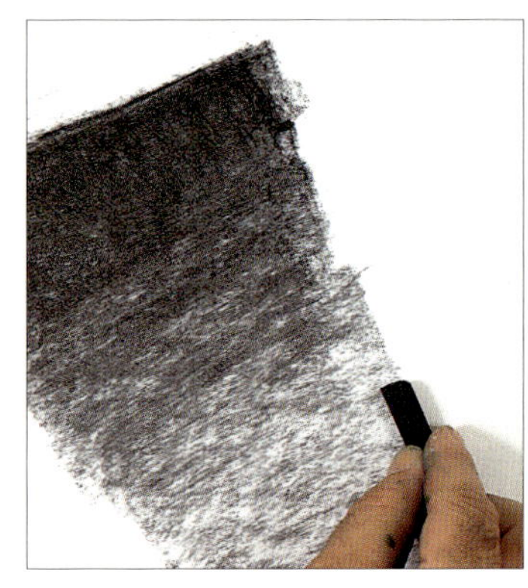

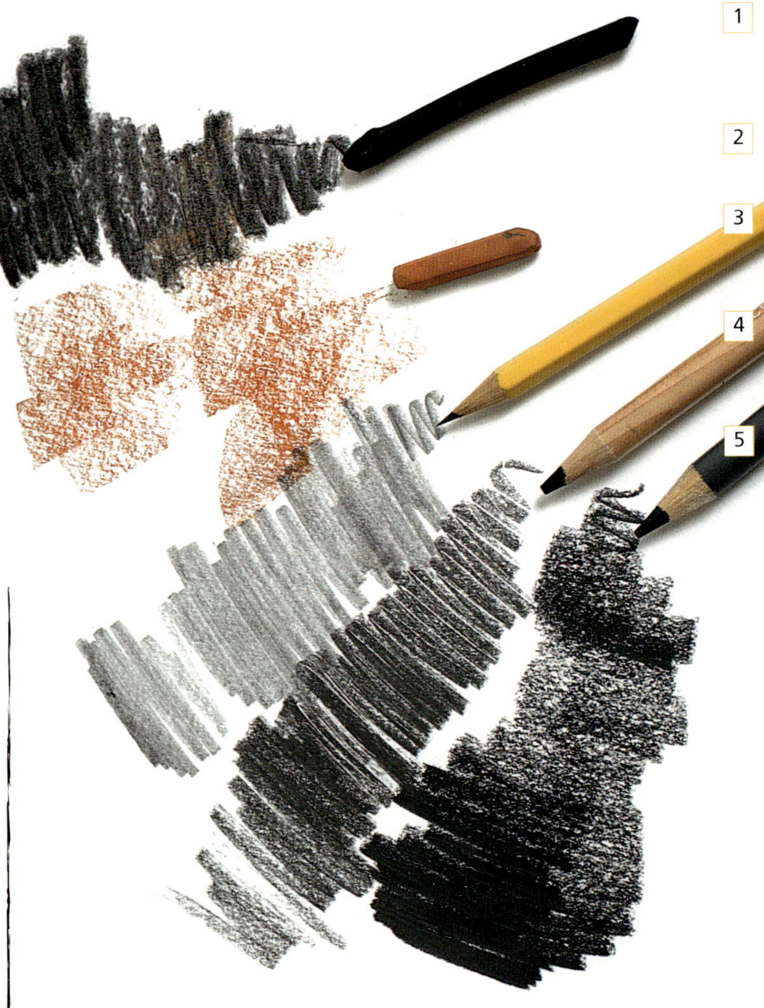

All of these dry mediums offer different gray intensities: charcoal (1), sanguine (2), 2B pencil (3), and conté pencils (4 and 5).

TONE VALUES

Valuation is the process of establishing different tones of gray for the shadow and light zones on the model. The darkest parts can be the starting point: less pressure on the paper will give lighter tones to reflect the intensity of the light. Tone values, in fact, mean establishing the degree of lightness or darkness on the paper.

We can do a simple exercise, the medium is not important, to understand the effect of tone values on a drawing. Firstly draw the circle of an apple. Hold the chunk flat between the fingers and press as hard as you can. The difference between the white and the black is the first valuation.

The stump can be used to precisely spread any shading done with a dry medium.

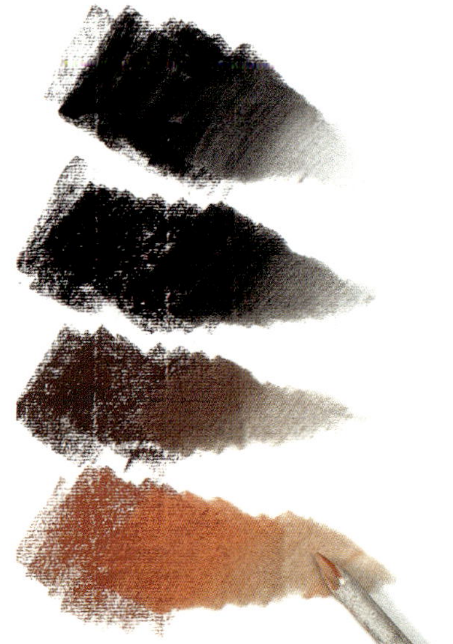

THE STUMP

When you have to spread the mark of the medium over the paper, a stump is used. It is a simple tool that allows the stroke to be dispersed. However, as you have seen before, it is the best tool for working on the tones, although sometimes it can be too imprecise for fine lines.

A stump is a piece of paper rolled up with a point sufficiently stiff that it can exercise pressure and not crumple.

Try the following practice exercise. On the paper do various strokes in

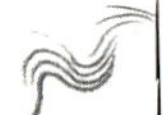

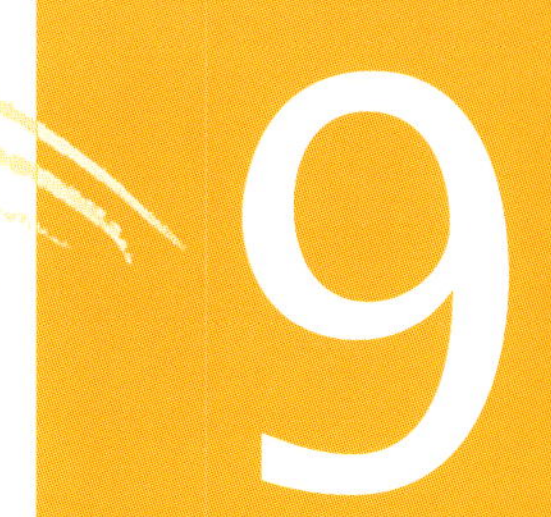

In all dry mediums the tone is controlled by varying the pressure on the paper, a characteristic which differentiates them from the fluid mediums and is especially useful when modeling.

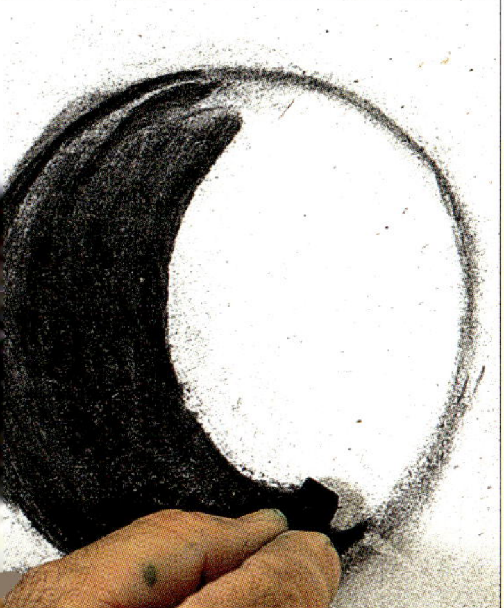

The process of valuation is started by establishing the principle dark and light tones on the paper.

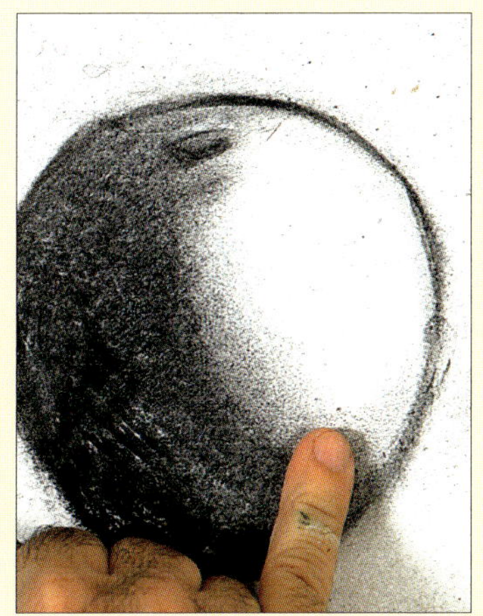

Rub a finger softly over the shading that differentiates the two tones of light.

charcoal, chalks and sanguine, holding the crayons flat and aiming at the maximum darkness that the mediums can produce. Use the stump to rub the end of the strokes as you spread the tone and impregnate it into the paper. The shading becomes gradated. The stump pressure, just like the charcoal and sanguine crayon pressure, can be controlled to decide the tone.
Once the stump point is stained you can draw with it just like other drawing mediums.

MODELING

Modeling the grays on the paper is based on the tone values. Dry drawing mediums can easily be spread by gently rubbing the stroke and thus they are gently blended into the ground. Working on the tone values, the modeling is realized by this merging with the paper ground. To model the grays, follow the form of the drawing plane. Going on with the apple tone values example, use your fingers to soften the hardness of the dark tone contours against the paper. Soft rubbing will produce plastic, volume effects on the object and will give form to the shadows as the charcoal is dragged.

COMPENSATING THE CONTRAST AND THE GROUND

One of the principle problems when doing tone modeling is finding the equilibrium between the brightest and the darkest tones. A tone has to be intensified or lightened so that it produces the desired effect alongside the surrounding tones. If it were excessively darkened it would make nearby light tones too luminous. If a medium gray is applied to the ground, the tones are compensated and an equilibrium between the light and shadow zones obtained. When graying the background, bear in mind the simultaneous contrasts of the two zones: a dark next to a light zone provokes a simultaneous contrast.
Lay down more strokes next to the luminous zone to darken the background. The light zones will thus become more luminous.

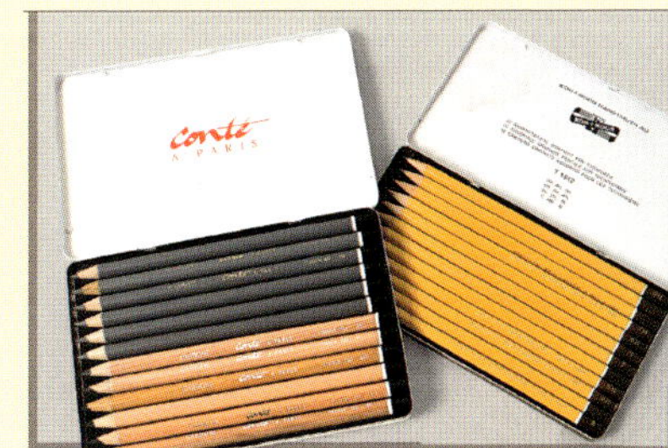

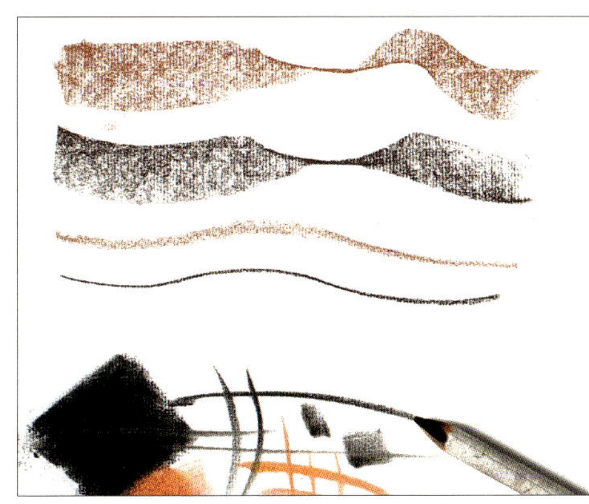

Once the stump is stained, you can use it as a drawing tool. Do strokes while the stump is still impregnated.

GRADATiONS AND MODELiNG

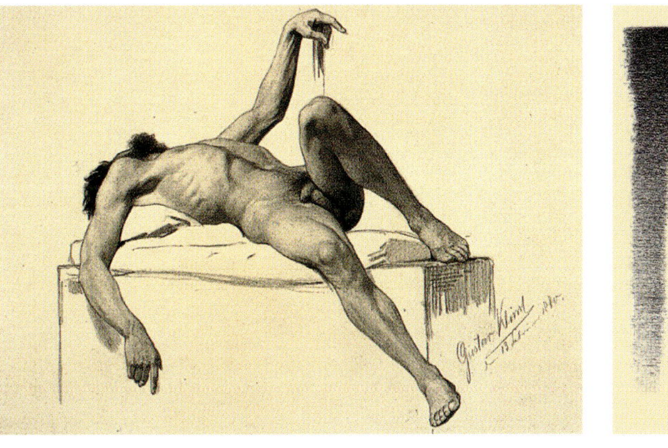

'Nude male lying face upwards' by the Austrian painter **Gustav Klimt (1862-1918)** is a masterly example of anatomy work. In addition to the perfect anatomy, it is surprising the way he uses tone contrasts to get almost photographic realism in the volume effect. As can be seen, the darkest tones softly gradate into the most luminous. Even the most illuminated zone has a dark tone modeled by the shadow. To master the technique to such an extent many modeling exercises must be done until you perfectly control tone scales.

TONE RANGES

Each different drawing medium has characteristics which distinguish it from the others. Some of them give a dense stroke with an intense tone. Others cannot go beyond a soft gray. When working with tone values and modeling, bear in mind the maximum tone of the medium. Fine Arts shops have pencils with different degrees of hardness so that a variety of tones can be obtained.

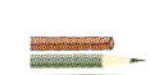

9 STARTING THE MODELING

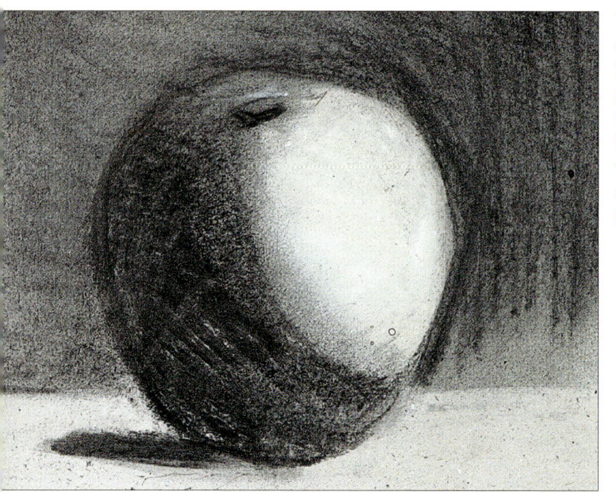

To compensate the strong contrast, the background is shaded with a medium gray. Along the edge of the illuminated part, increase the contrast of the darks by compensating the simultaneous contrast.

Working with white chalk allows the brightness to be increased, but working with it means that the paper must not be completely white.

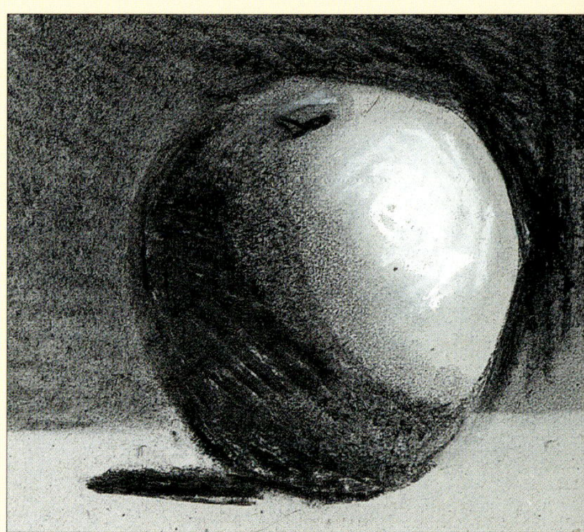

A COMPLETE CRAYON CASE

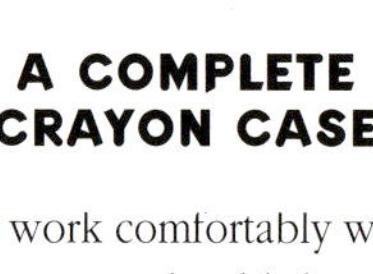

If you want to work comfortably with tone value and modeling, you should buy a case that includes all the necessary mediums for the different methods. The white chalk, sepia, sanguine, pure graphite, oiled charcoal and ordinary charcoal crayons will vary in hardness so you will have available a complete range of grays and earth colored chalks. One of the advantages of this type of case is that every drawing medium has its own compartment for when not being used.

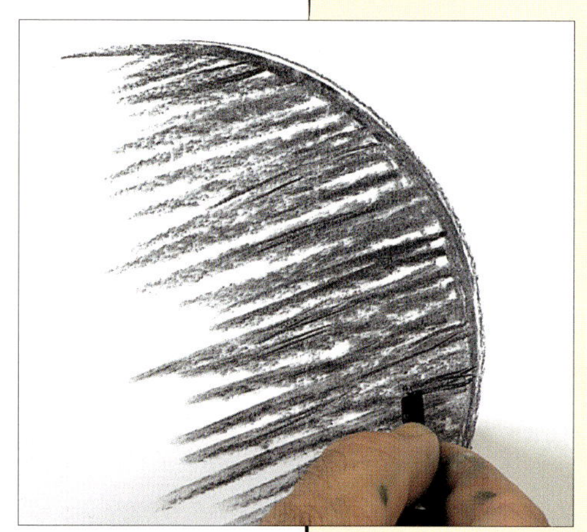

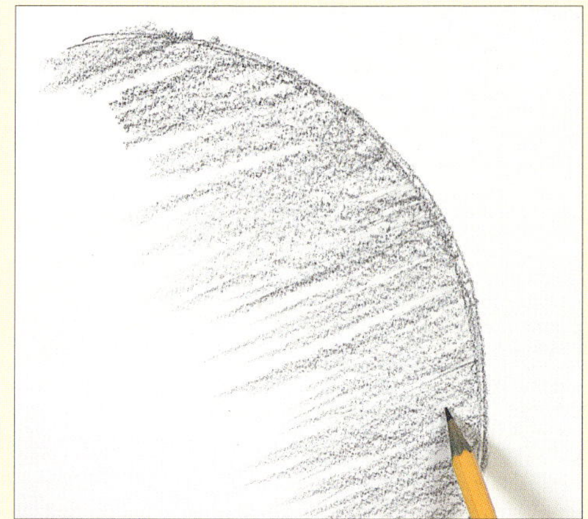

Dark, superimposed pencil strokes are made to darken the fruit.

Straight charcoal strokes will also darken the fruit.

INCREASING THE BRIGHTNESS

In all tone value and modeling work different mediums are used to increase the brightness of the most illuminated zone. This must be done after the modeling work and to make the marks more luminous than the paper itself, white chalk will have to be used. However small the contrast offered by the background may be, this dry medium will stand out. If the paper is only slightly darker than white, white chalk can be used to gain brightness. The darker the paper is, the more intense the contrast with the white chalk will be.

DARK STROKES WITH DIFFERENT MEDIUMS

Each drawing medium has a different feel on the paper. Charcoal yields very easily just by dragging its tip, and its softness is reflected in a dense, black stroke lacking in adhesiveness. At the other end of the scale, a graphite pencil can come in varying degrees of hardness. All drawing mediums are suitable for tone value work, all that changes is the shading process on the paper.
Tone value work with a pencil is quite different compared to charcoal although essentially the result is the same. The latter allows a rapid, easy stumping process, while the stumping obtained from a graphite pencil is much less obvious.

RECOURSES FOR MODELING

The lights can be modeled by working with parallel strokes, but you will always have to use soft pencils from the B range. After shading the darkest zones, increase the shadows by doing more intense strokes. You need not start pressing hard. It is always better to begin the shading with soft lines and then to superimpose darkness on top. This will produce tone value effects similar to those you get with charcoal. Perfect plastic modeling on top of the pencil work can be done by softly rubbing the graphite powder with the fingers.
Graphite pencils offer many possibilities and a wide range of dense grays. Later on we will study this technique.

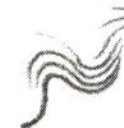

DRAWING IN SANGUINE AND CHARCOAL

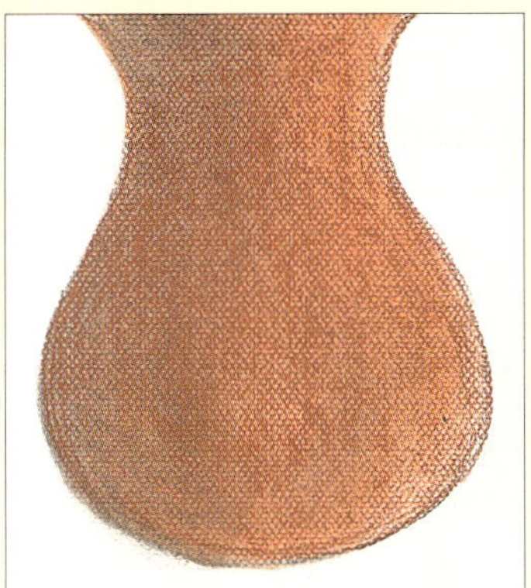

Blend both tones with your fingers.

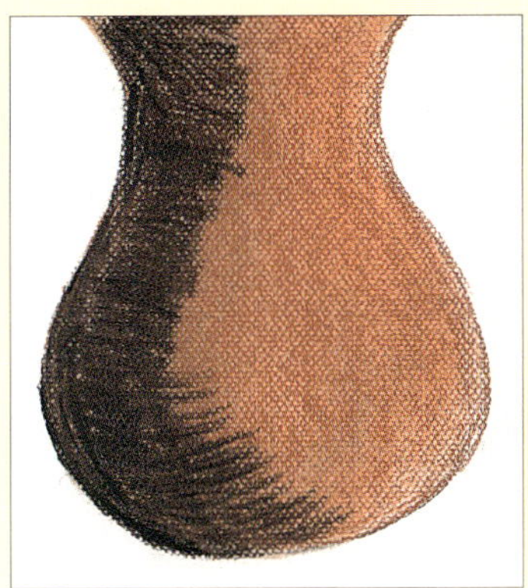

Do charcoal strokes in the shadow zone.

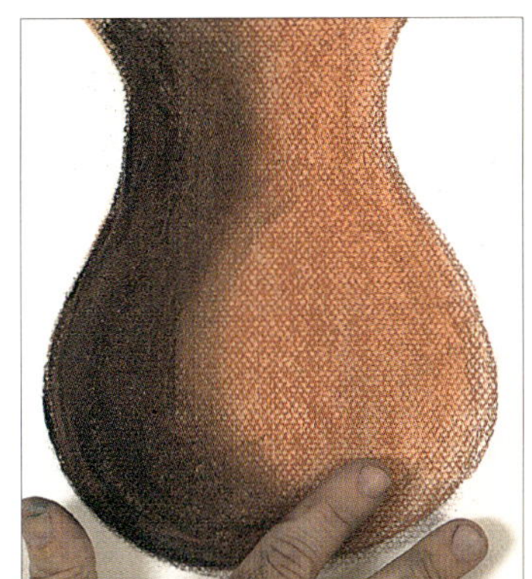

Draw and shade a form in sanguine.

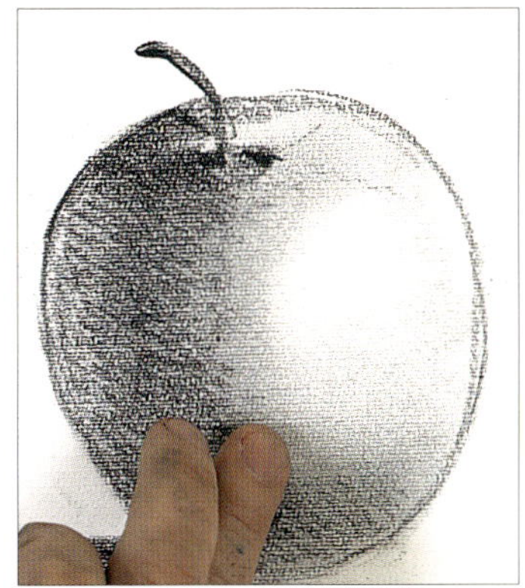

Model the tones with your fingers, softly superimposing strokes.

MODELING WITH SHADING AND STROKES

As time goes by you must learn how to control the density of the different mediums to get the desired result. As they practice, each artist acquires their own resources which will help to obtain gradations. For example, if you want to exploit charcoal, you can play with its blending and stumping possibilities. A tone value gradation is nothing more than a correctly applied scale of grays. The first shadow, the densest, can be started with a strong stroke and the secondary tones with a series of lines, a process which only serves to place the right quantity of charcoal in each zone. Afterwards, tone blending will give the plastic modeling effects.

All that remains to be done is to unify the zone by blending the strokes. Finger action will give perfect modeling.

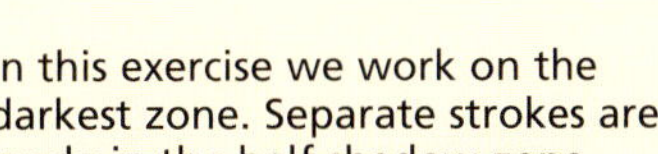

In this exercise we work on the darkest zone. Separate strokes are made in the half shadow zone.

PAPER, SANGUINE AND WHITE CHALK

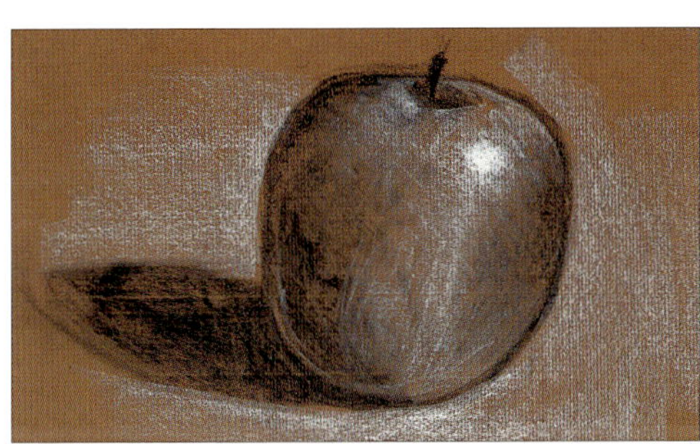

We studied the effect produced by using white chalk to give a bright area on non-white paper. If, instead of an off-white paper, tinted paper is used, the white chalk stands out much more strongly due to the contrast. Similarly, drawing in sanguine on tinted paper gives tones which are not possible on white paper. The drawing mediums can be blended, superimposed or mixed to obtain tones and light effects.

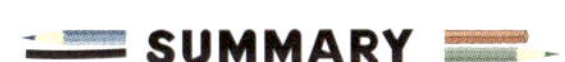

SUMMARY

TONE VALUES

Each zone has its own gray tone and intensity.

MODELING

Blend and model the different tone values of the zones.

INCREASING THE BRIGHTNESS

White chalk allows the brightness to be increased on non-white papers.

SHADING AND STROKES FOR MODELING

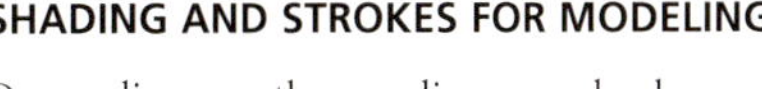

Depending on the medium used, charcoal shading or superimposed pencil strokes can be applied

SANGUINE AND CHARCOAL

Sanguine and charcoal are perfect complements to establish different tones in the valuation process.

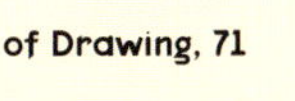

9 Exercices *Step by step*

STARTING THE MODELING

By blending dry mediums the gradation of any tone can be perfectly controlled. However, tone values can also be done by direct strokes, increasing the intensity in the darkest zones and letting the white show through in the lightest zones.

As we saw, blending, superimposition and mixing the different mediums produce different tones and light effects.

This exercise involves two different pieces of fruit. Firstly we will do a nectarine with charcoal and sanguine. Afterwards, we will do an apple working with charcoal and white chalk. Both processes are elemental, not difficult to get right if you pay attention to each step.

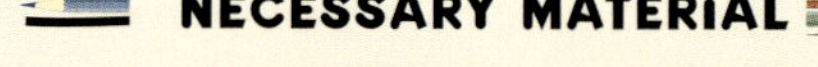

NECESSARY MATERIAL

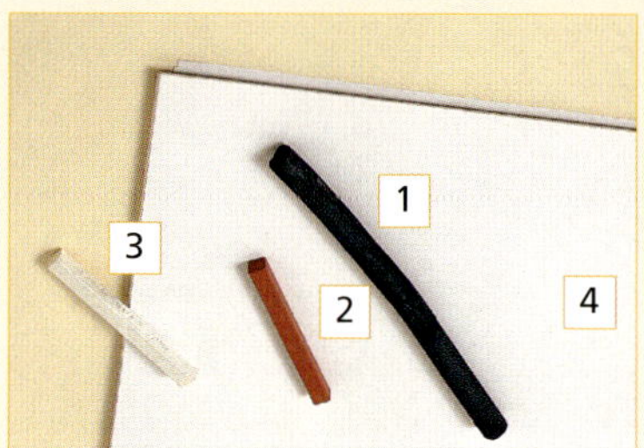

Charcoal (1), sanguine (2), white chalk (3), and drawing paper (4).

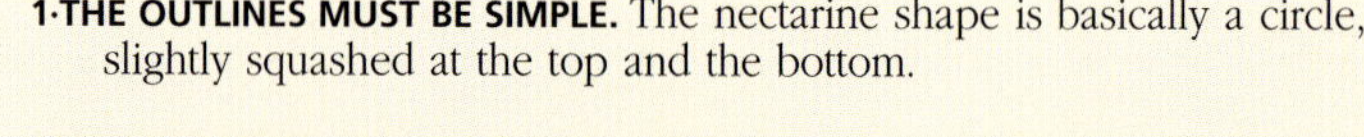

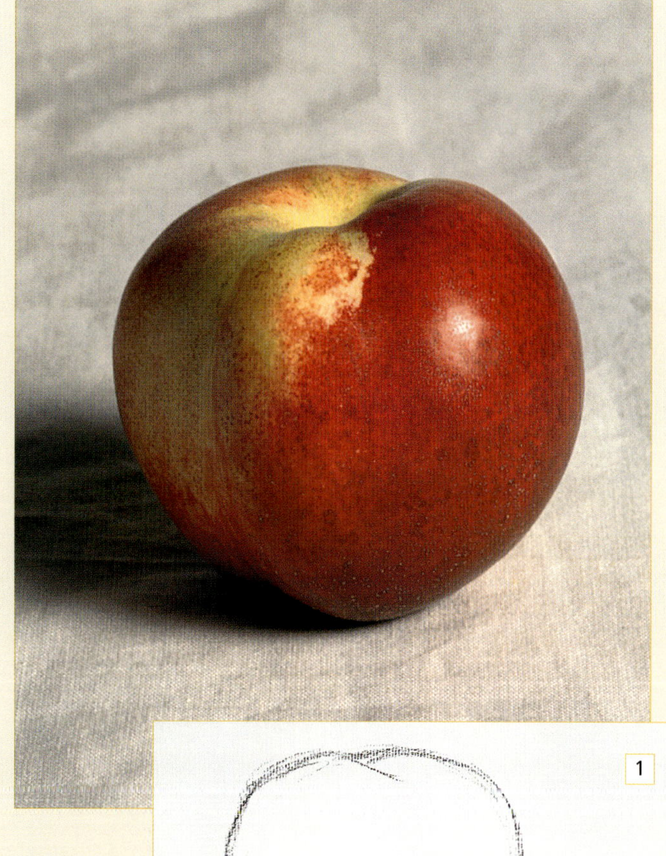

1·THE OUTLINES MUST BE SIMPLE. The nectarine shape is basically a circle, slightly squashed at the top and the bottom.

WHEN YOU START THE DEFINITIVE LINE, draw the small mark at the top with a delicate but firm hand. This tiny detail is important to give the fruit volume.

2· IN THE LEFT ZONE, RUB THE CHARCOAL only gently without working on the first tone. On the right, however, the pressure is much greater.

DRAW THE SHADOW, pressing hard with the charcoal.

3· SOFTLY FLICK OFF CHARCOAL in the zones where there is too much contrast.

USE YOUR FINGERTIPS TO GENTLY STUMP the darkest shadow. Afterwards, increase the form definition with the sanguine crayon, reserving in white the zone for the highlights.

4· FINALLY, IN THIS FOURTH STEP, do soft sanguine strokes, but insist in the zones that must be darker.

THIS WILL FINISH off this simple but interesting tone value exercise.

ON TOP OF THE COMPLETED OUTLINE, shade the dark parts of the nectarine with the sanguine stick flat between the fingers.

NOW WE WILL START ON MODELING THE SECOND FRUIT. The elaboration process is basically identical to the last one, the only change being that it is on tinted paper, and that, instead of sanguine we will use white chalk to increase the highlights.

1

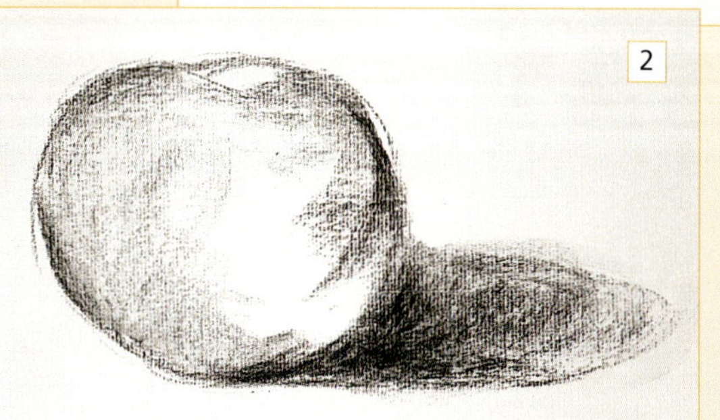

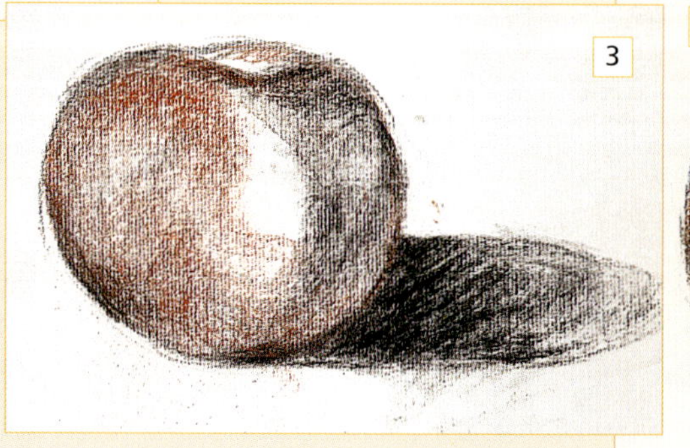

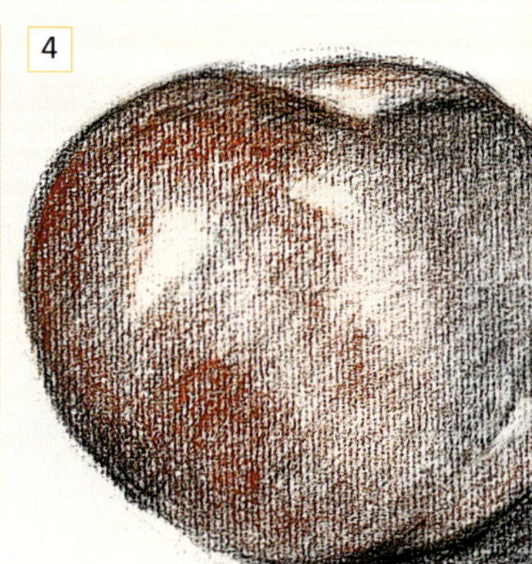

A nectarine and an apple

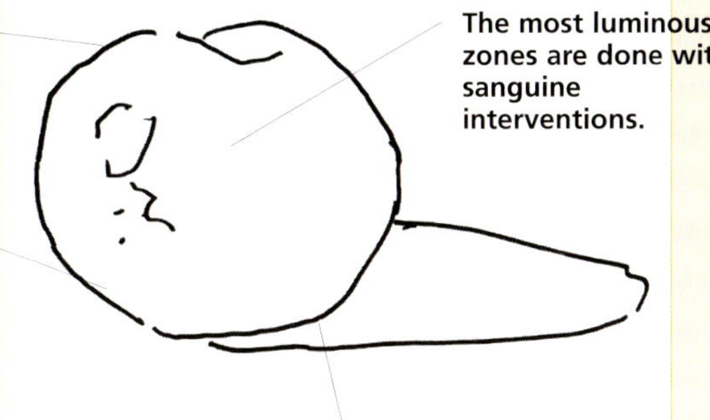

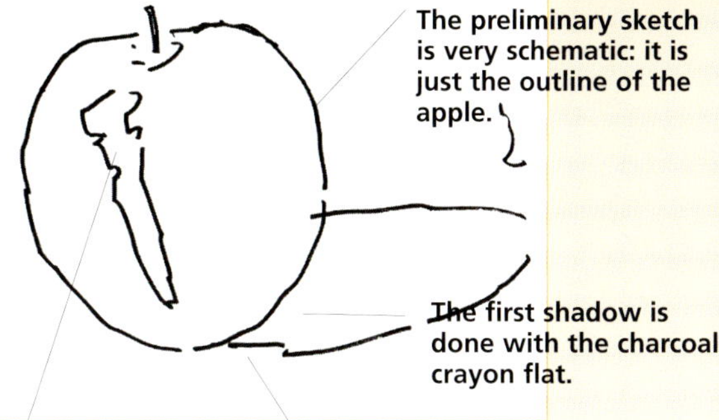

1· **OUTLINING THE FORM IS ALWAYS** fundamental in a drawing. Generally, it is a process so simple that little attention is paid to it by many learners and as a result the quality of the final drawing. Without a good outline it is not possible to do a satisfactory drawing.

DRAW THE FORM OF THE APPLE as cleanly as possible, without shadows, just the principle lines.

2· **ON TOP OF THE PERFECTLY STRUCTURED OUTLINE,** do about 3 cm long charcoal strokes to mark the main shadow zones. Hold the charcoal flat between the fingers.

THE MOST LUMINOUS part is left reserved, untouched.

ALSO DRAW THE SHADOW THE APPLE CASTS. This gray is much darker than the strokes inside the apple. Use your fingertips to stump the charcoal inside the apple. You must obtain a darker contrast in the lower right part.

3· **USE WHITE CHALK TO SHADE ALL AROUND THE FRUIT,** which will now stand out more against the paper. The color of the tinted paper is integrated as if it were just another color.

INSIDE THE APPLE, paint strongly with the white chalk in the most luminous parts. On the intermediate highlights, the pressure of the white chalk is minimum.

FINALLY, do some dark shadows with the charcoal.

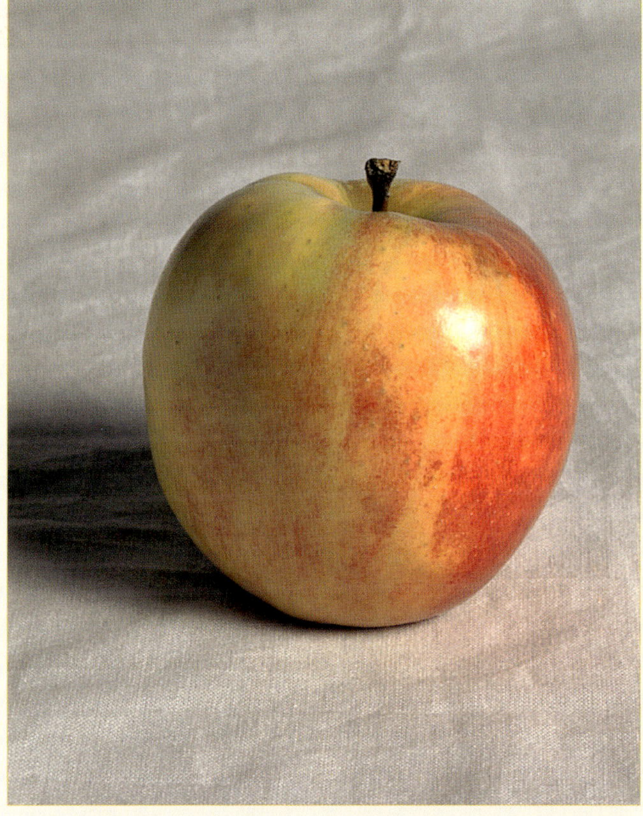

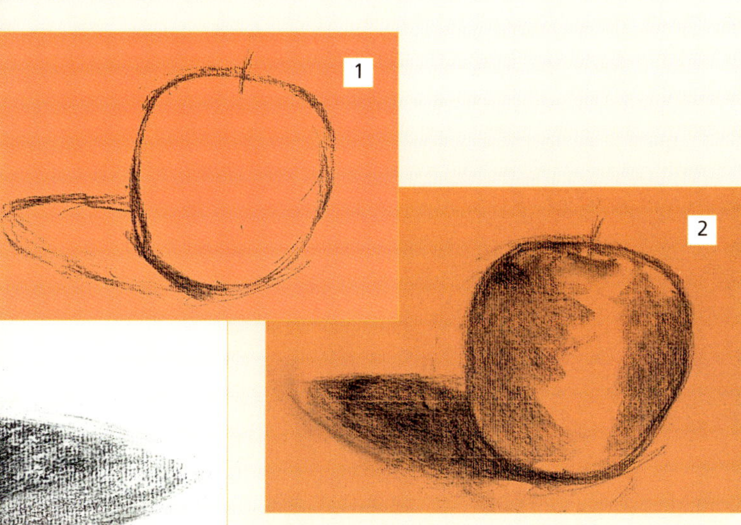

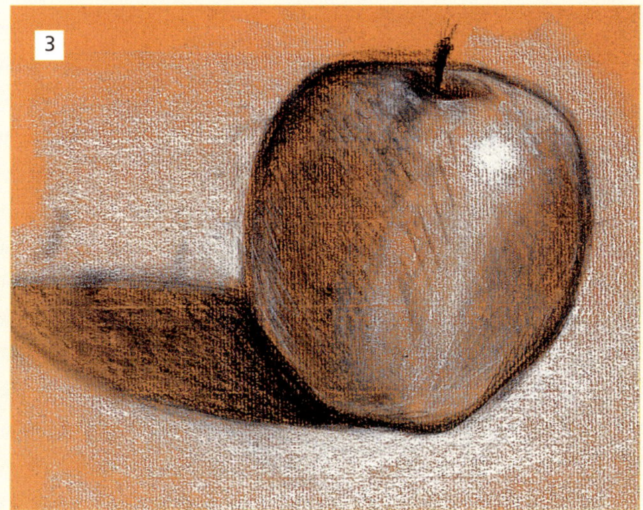

10 OPENING UP WHITE SPACES

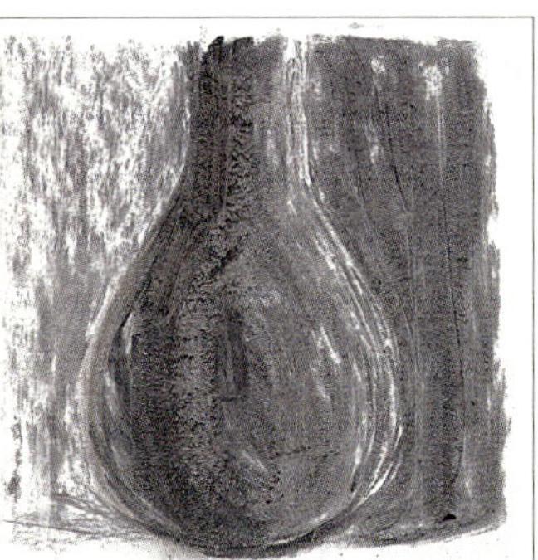
Strokes with different grays will aid in the process of placing the white spaces.

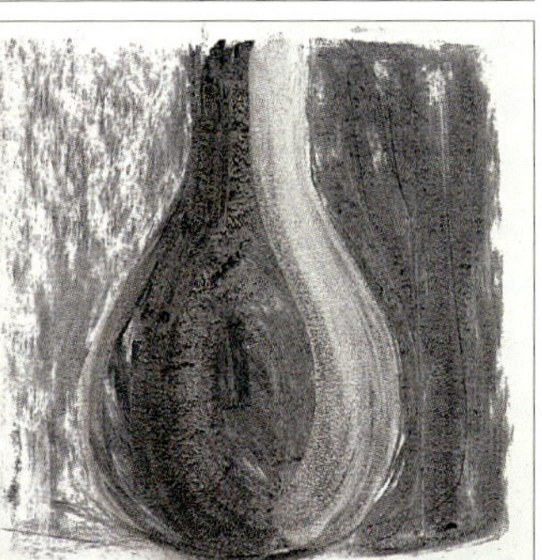
Use the tip of your thumb to open up a white space along the illuminated edge.

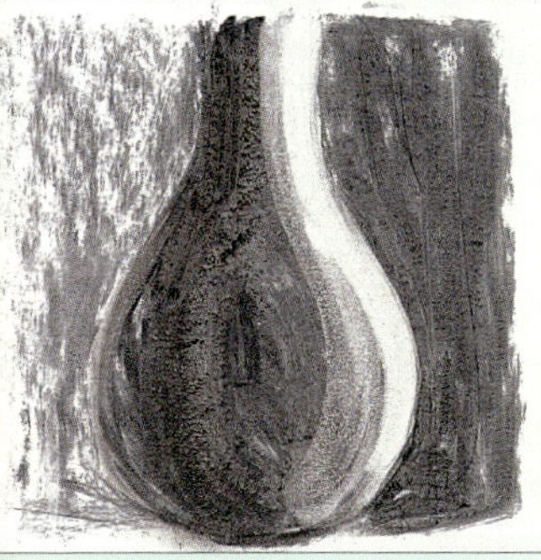
On top of the white just done, superimpose another much more luminous. Use the eraser.

Draw the horizon line and shade all the sky background in charcoal.

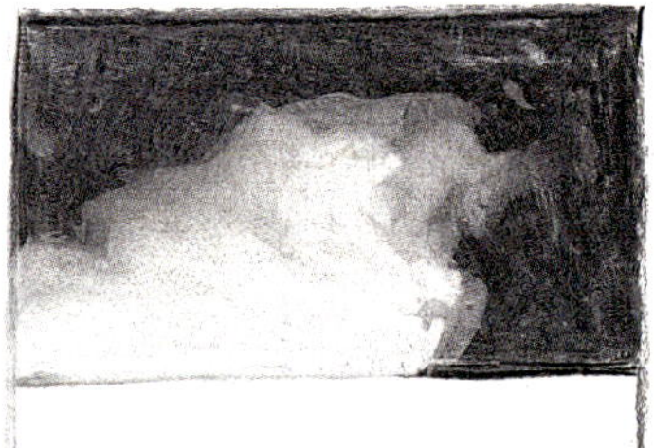
Open up the cloud shape with your fingers. Afterwards, use the rubber to open up a new more luminous white space.

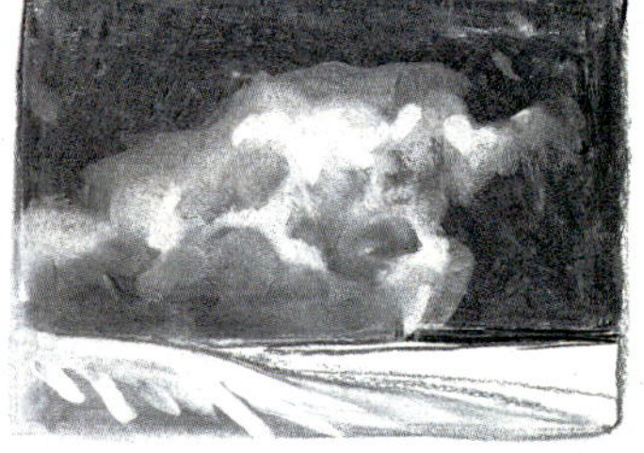
On top of the white of the clouds, smudge the charcoal once again.

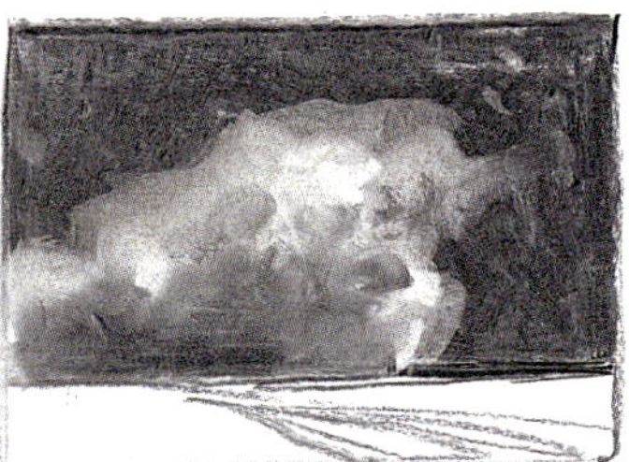
The eraser allows you to do strokes as if it were another drawing medium.

Often the artist's intention when using modeling is frustrated by the dark tones that clutter up the picture. They must then open up white spaces, something which can be done by different procedures, all of which have different degrees of whiteness: your hand, a cloth or the stump.

In previous chapters we presented different tools, among which the eraser stands out especially. In this chapter we are going to deal with this subject in greater depth.

DIFFERENT PROCEDURES AND DEGREES OF WHITENESS

We do not always want to obtain maximum whiteness on the paper. Sometimes we are after a smudged gray and not a radiant white and, therefore, different methods are employed, each one suitable for a special type of opening.

HALF WHITES WITH THE HAND

The principle drawing tool is neither charcoal, nor a pencil, nor an eraser. Although hard to believe it is the hand. A stained hand can draw. In fact, all the other implements are just to make the stroke easier and more practical. The hand can be used not only for smudging and doing strokes but also for correcting and opening up white spaces.

To learn fully about how to open up white spaces, it is recommendable to practice exercises like the following.

DIFFERENT PROCEDURES TO VARY THE WHITENESS

Draw a circle and shade it in charcoal. Try not to scratch the surface.

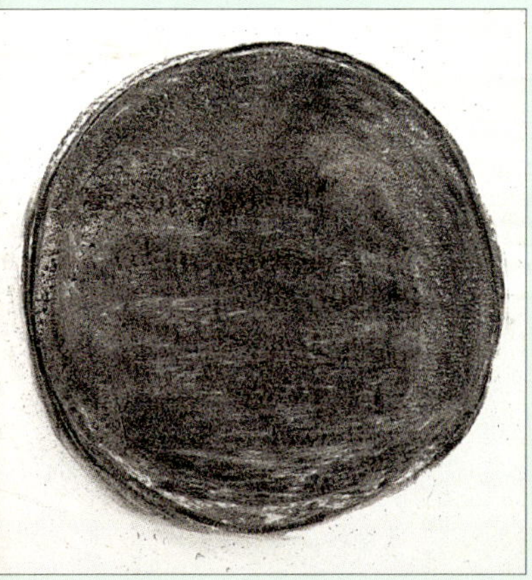

The edge of your hand allows you to open up wide white spaces in the shaded area.

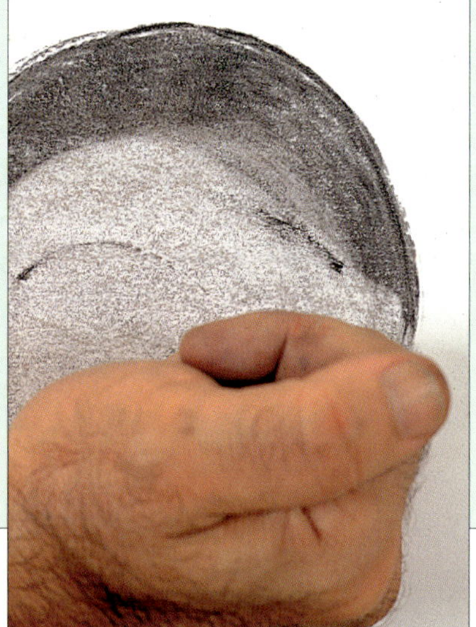

The biggest white space is perfected with the fingers.

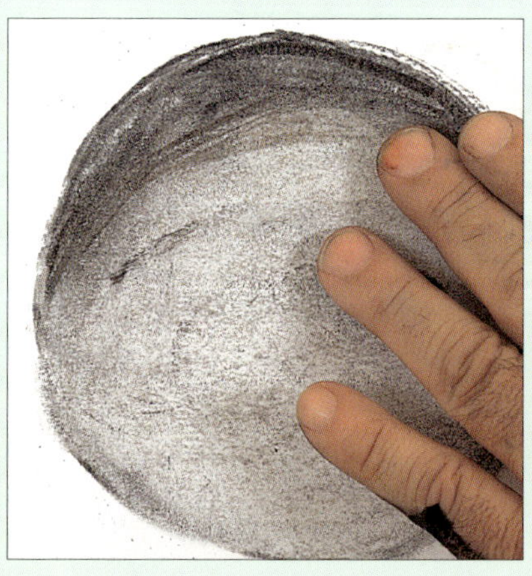

The background has been shaded with charcoal to increase the contrast. Use the little finger to open up more precise white spaces.

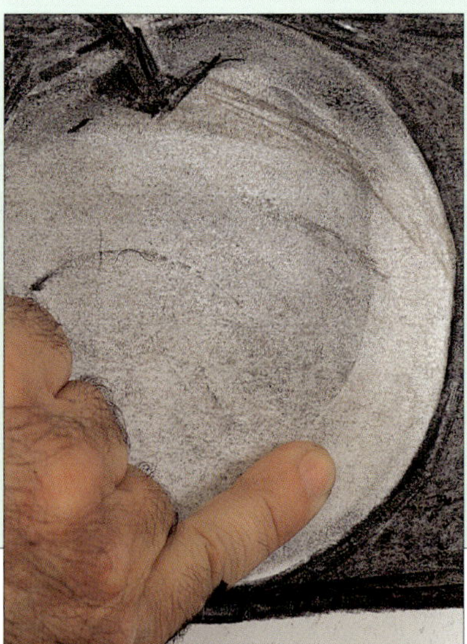

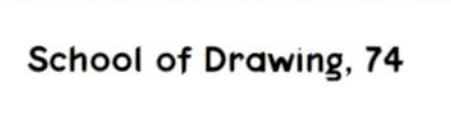

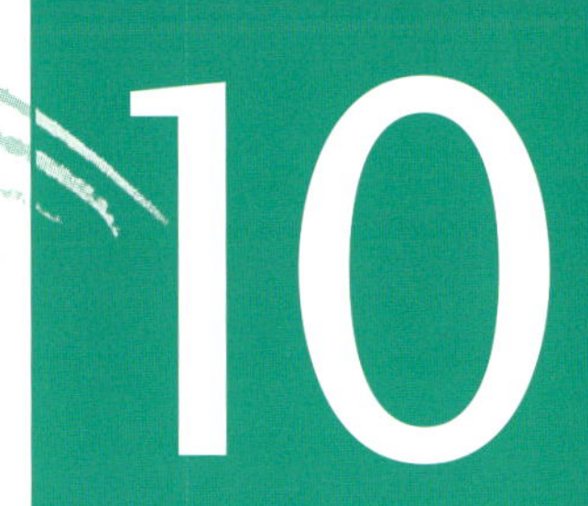

Drawing allows a tonal interpretation of the different colors of the model. However, usually the paper is accidentally stained by gray shading and smears. Fortunately the most common drawing mediums can all be rubbed out.

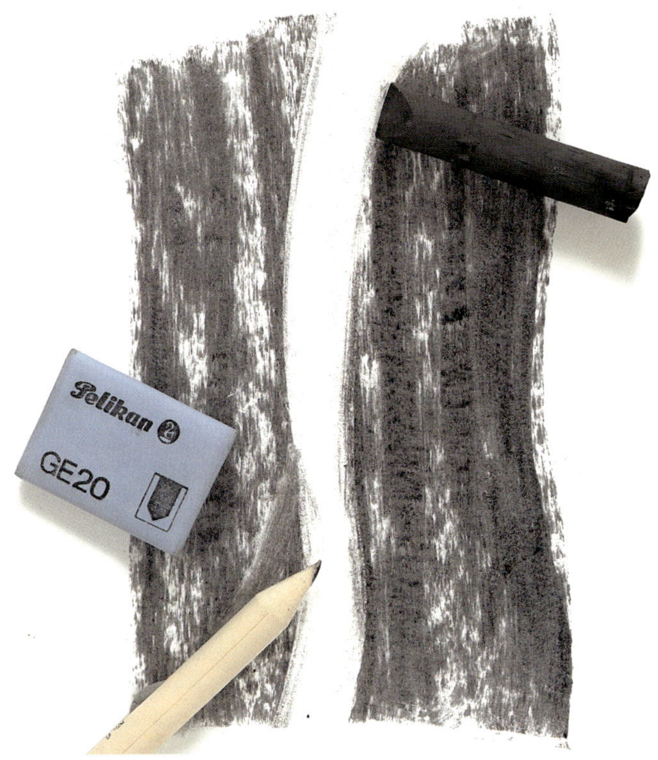

A stump and a putty eraser, two tools closely linked to drawing which as well as adding charcoal tone can also take it away.

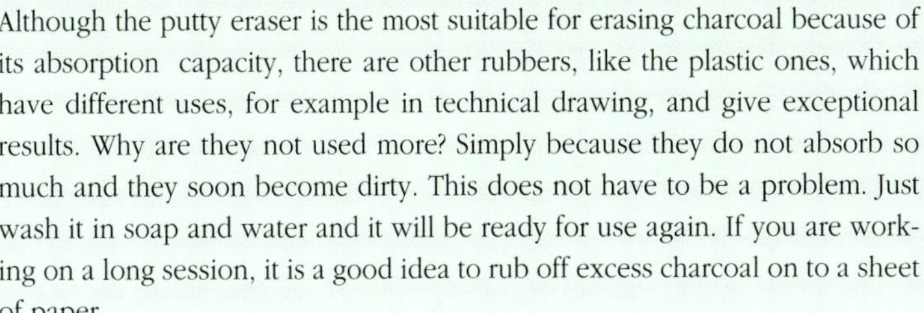

THE CLEANLINESS OF THE PLASTIC ERASER

Although the putty eraser is the most suitable for erasing charcoal because of its absorption capacity, there are other rubbers, like the plastic ones, which have different uses, for example in technical drawing, and give exceptional results. Why are they not used more? Simply because they do not absorb so much and they soon become dirty. This does not have to be a problem. Just wash it in soap and water and it will be ready for use again. If you are working on a long session, it is a good idea to rub off excess charcoal on to a sheet of paper.

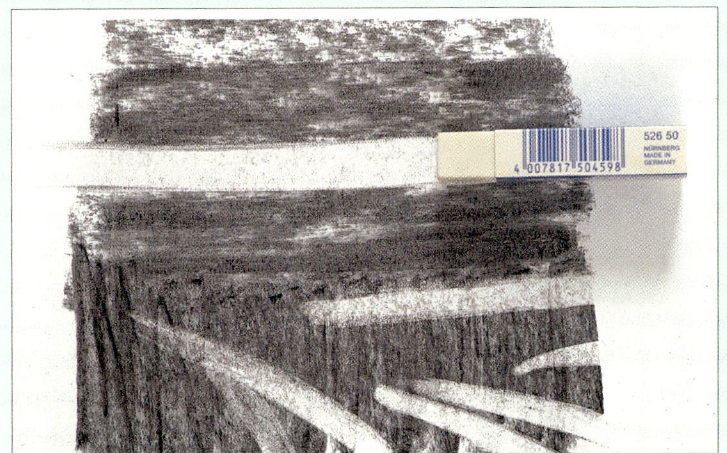

A plastic eraser gives perfect whites, but it has to be kept clean.

In the earlier chapters about drawing we have opened up some white spaces. This is a very common practice as just wiping the hand over the paper is enough to take off the charcoal. However, obviously it is not possible to restore complete whiteness.

In this example we are going to start with a sphere drawn completely in charcoal, as you can see in the first image at the bottom. The density of the stroke is not important because provided it does not scratch the paper, the charcoal can always be removed.

OPENINGS WITH THE HAND AND WITH THE FINGERS

The edge of your hand can open up wide white spaces in the charcoal. Do not press too hard so that you do not block up the pores. The central part of the edge gives you good control of the opening, but you will have to use your fingers for the exact edges of the white space.

All of the hand does not offer the same degree of control in taking off the charcoal. Different parts of the hand are good for different purposes. The little finger is perfect for fine lines and small white dashes in the middle of already established openings.

COMBINING OPENINGS

Opening up white spaces with the hand gives rise to medium grays but it does not restore the original whiteness to the paper. However, the white created still remains valid. In fact, broken whites and half tones can be very interesting, especially when combined with very luminous white spaces done with the eraser.

THE CHARCOAL INTENSITY

As we saw in previous chapters, the pressure applied determines the intensity of the gray. Bear this in mind before starting to open up whites because it will help you to integrate the white forms with the grays.

FINGERS AND THE ERASER

On the surface marked by charcoal, open up a white space with your thumb tip, as we saw before. Even though the opening goes all along

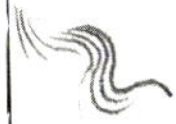

10 OPENING UP WHITE SPACES

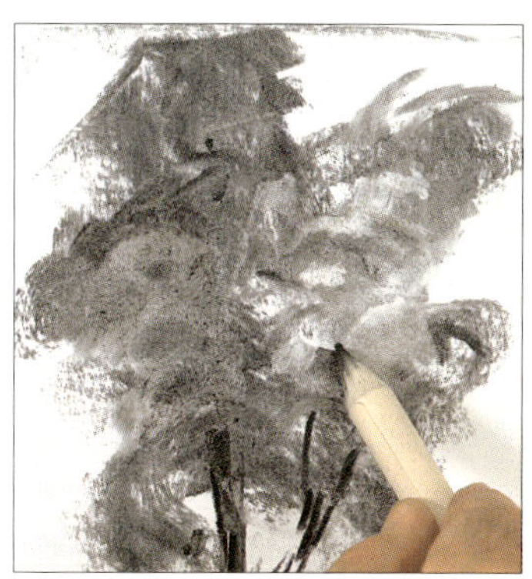
Use the stump very softly on the charcoal strokes.

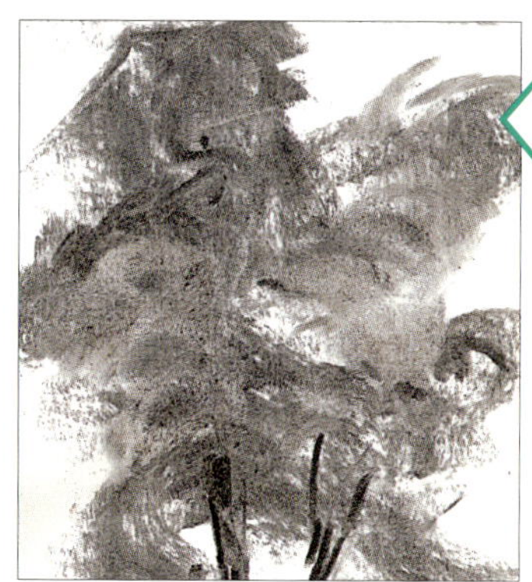
This is the maximum white obtainable with the stump. The action is always soft and discrete.

OPENING WHITES WITH THE STUMP

Some implements are very useful for opening defined whites or smudging a particular area. A stump is a pointed piece of rolled up paper. It can be used both for stumping and for eliminating excess charcoal. They come in different sizes but all of them are pointed. They work on charcoal and on sanguine but are never able to create perfect whites. A stump is not an eraser but it can still create useful medium tones. To practice working with a stump, we are going to do a picture based on flat, circular movements with the charcoal to draw something that could easily be the top of a tree. On top of the charcoal shading, use the stump to open up some light spaces. As you can see, pressing harder does not give a cleaner white. The white spaces from a stump are always soft and discrete, ideal for all types of interventions.

the illuminated edge, the white space is not perfect, so you will have to resort to the eraser to get a more luminous white. When using a putty eraser, mold the cleaning edge before rubbing. If you opt for a plastic eraser, get rid of any charcoal which has stuck to it to make sure you get a perfectly clean effect.

WHITE SPACES WITH THE ERASER

The characteristics of the eraser stroke can be very varied. In the last example we studied how to combine openings with the fingers and with the eraser. In this quick exercise, similar in technique to the last one, we are going to study how to use the eraser to open up white spaces and then intervene later with charcoal.

SHADINGS AND OPENINGS

As we have seen in earlier chapters, charcoal has great covering capacity. It crumbles on the surface of the paper and can fill the pore. However, unless you use spray fixative it will not stick to the paper and your hand could dislodge it.

We are going to draw a little landscape. Draw a straight line for the horizon and shade the sky completely with charcoal until the white of the paper disappears.

Form a cloud by flicking the charcoal away from one zone to eliminate it gradually, increasing the finger work as you progress until the ground is whiter. In the middle of the gray cloud, use the eraser to open up a white space. In this way, as we saw in the last example, the two openings complement each other.

THE IMPORTANCE OF WHITE IN THE DRAWING

White is not only the color of the paper ground. In drawing it means a lot more: it is the most intense light obtainable without using white chalk. This can be perfectly seen in this work by Gustav Klimt (1862-1918), a male nude on a pedestal. The highlights opened in the background make it almost photographically realistic. Any zone that appears completely white in a drawing is because it has been cleaned. If you look at the whites in this drawing, you will see the perfect way they have been opened up among the grays.

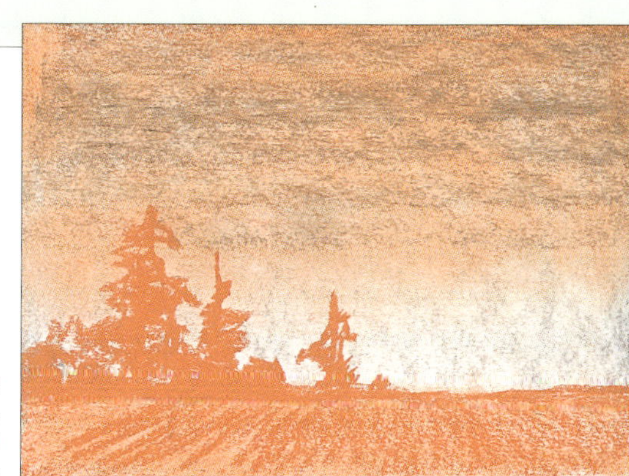
On top of the sanguine drawing, shade the sky in charcoal.

A NEW SUPERIMPOSITION

A white space can be smudged or colored again and then reworked. White space can be opened up on gray areas and vice versa: new grays can be formed on white zones.

Going on with the sky picture: stain the lower part of the white clouds with charcoal and then spread it upwards with the finger. The white just done with eraser, which finishes the cloud forms, must not be

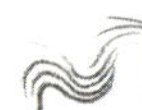

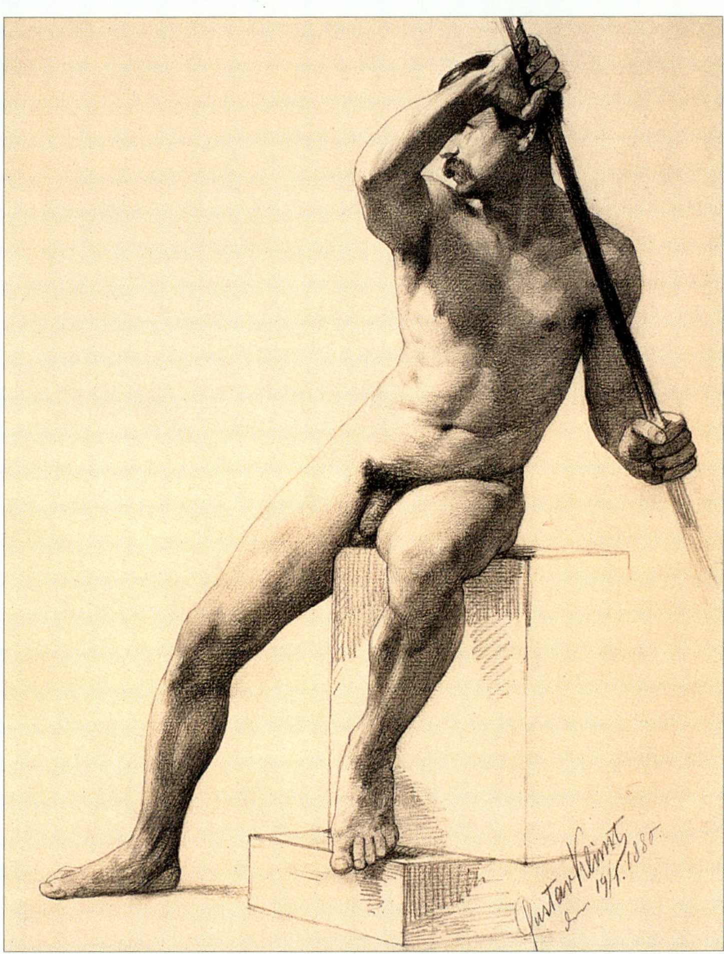

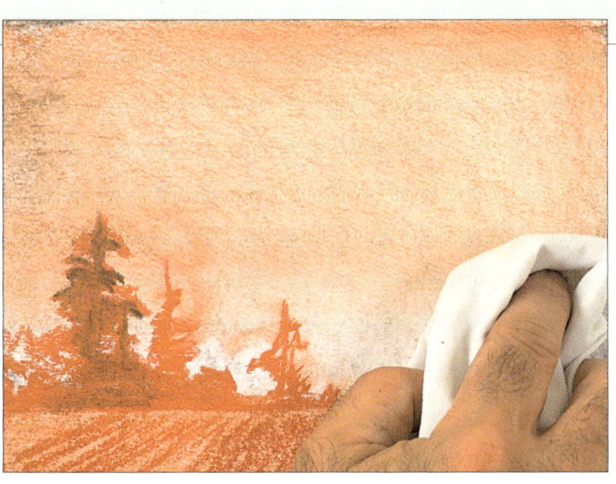

Use a cloth to blend the charcoal with the sanguine.

completely covered. Now in the earth zone, blend the gray, and then immediately go over it several times with the eraser.

CHARCOAL, SANGUINE AND WHITES

Sanguine is much more adhesive than charcoal but this does not mean that clean openings cannot be made. This characteristic permits charcoal to be used on top of sanguine like a fixed ground. Later, white spaces can be opened with the eraser.

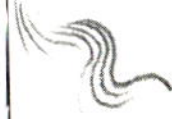

SUMMARY

OPENINGS WITH THE HAND

Different parts of the hand can be used to obtain distinct whites. However, the complete whiteness of the paper can never be recovered.

COMBINING OPENINGS

Working on top of an off-white opening, the eraser can be used to get total whiteness.

GRAYS ON WHITES

New blendings can be done on top of whites just opened up.

SANGUINE, CHARCOAL AND THE ERASER

This is one of the best combinations for drawing. Sanguine is more adhesiveness than charcoal. This characteristic means that you can get a lot of play from sanguine and the eraser.

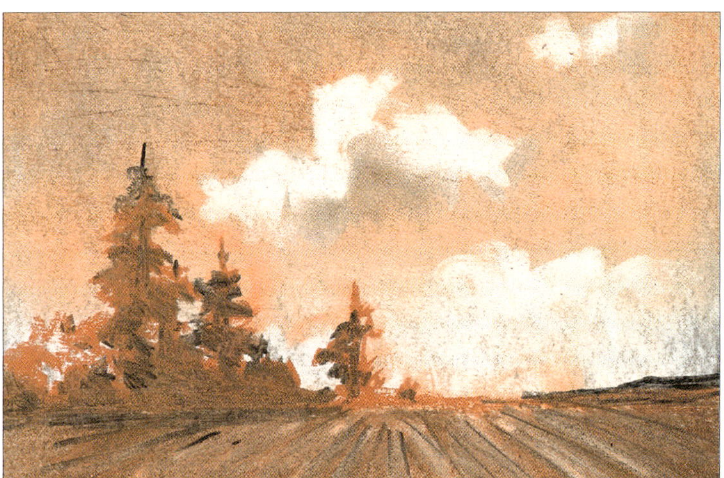

Once the landscape has been contrasted in charcoal, open up clouds in the sky with the eraser.

CHARCOAL ON SANGUINE

A straightforward practice exercise is the best way of explaining how to open up white spaces in charcoal and sanguine. We will do a simple landscape in sanguine.

Firstly, draw the horizon line. Then, in the sky zone, do a soft gradation. Immediately afterwards, in the lower part, draw some trees with a very schematic stroke using the sanguine point. Do not press too hard so that you do not close the pores of the paper. Draw the lines on the earth.

In the sky, use the charcoal flat to softly darken this area. Blend the charcoal over the sanguine with a cloth. As you can see, the background has hardly been altered.

DARKENING AND OPENING WHITES

Some very attractive contrasts can be obtained by repeated interventions with the charcoal. They will give form to the landscape.

Finally, use the eraser to open up very luminous white highlights in the sky in the shape of a cloud.

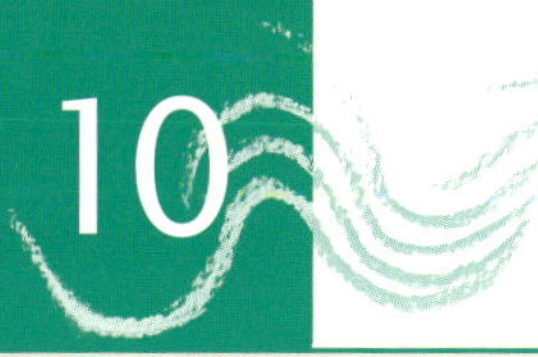

10 Exercices *Step by step*

As the drawing mediums are easy to correct, the eraser is a useful tool. You can draw in negative with it. In this landscape we are going to practice opening up white spaces with the eraser.

The process is quite natural and logic. When drawn on, the paper will get dirty and the eraser will restore its cleanliness, making possible the opening up of light areas, clouds and highlights.

NECESSARY MATERIAL

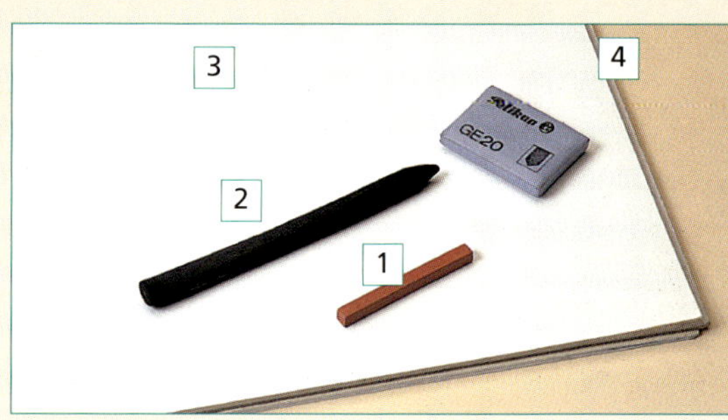

Sanguine (1),
charcoal (2),
paper (3),
and an eraser (4).

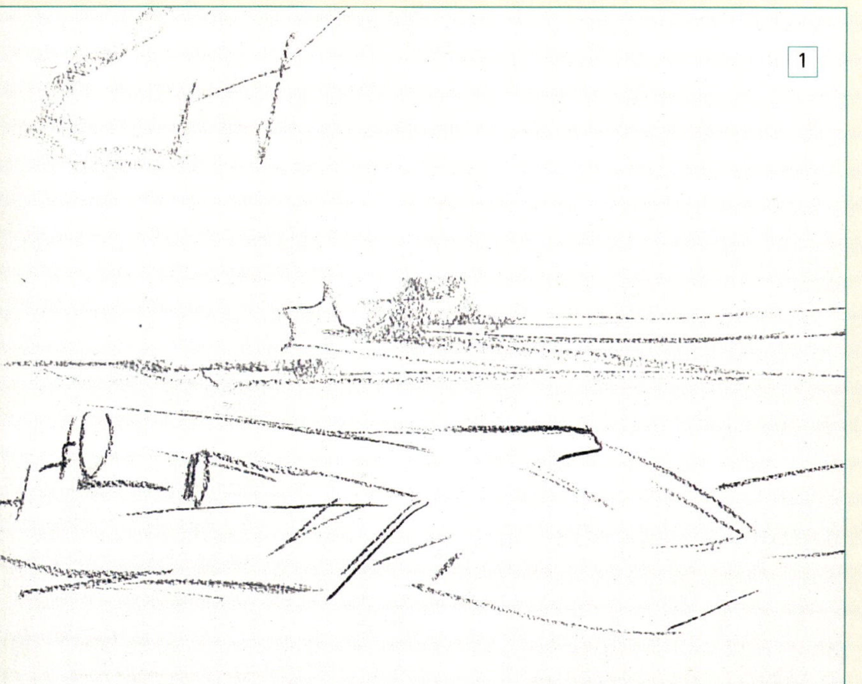

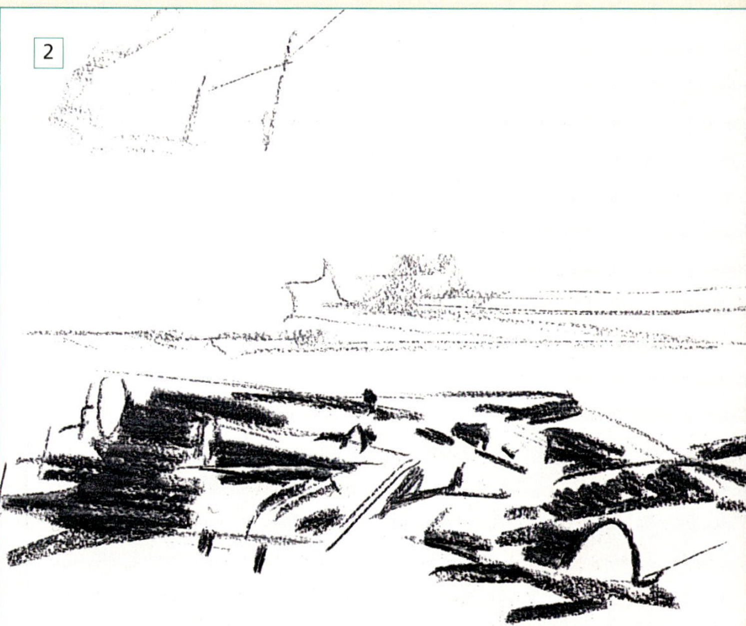

1· START THE DRAWING WITH SIMPLE CHARCOAL STROKES. In all drawings or pictures the principle elements must be correctly located from the outset, before starting to draw the details or specifics.

THE FIRST STROKES ARE DONE ABOVE THE HORIZON line to separate the sky from the land. They are drawn with the charcoal flat and broadwise. The pile of trunks is schematized with a few strokes.

The charcoal tone is very easy to blend on top of the sanguine.

On top of the charcoal, you can draw directly in sanguine as it is a dense, opaque medium.

2· TO DO A MODEL WHICH CONTAINS MULTIPLE FORMS, the best approach is to start with the dark masses that define the principle shadows. At the same time as you draw the dark parts of the shadows with dense black shading, mark off the most luminous parts of the trunks.

Landscape with openings

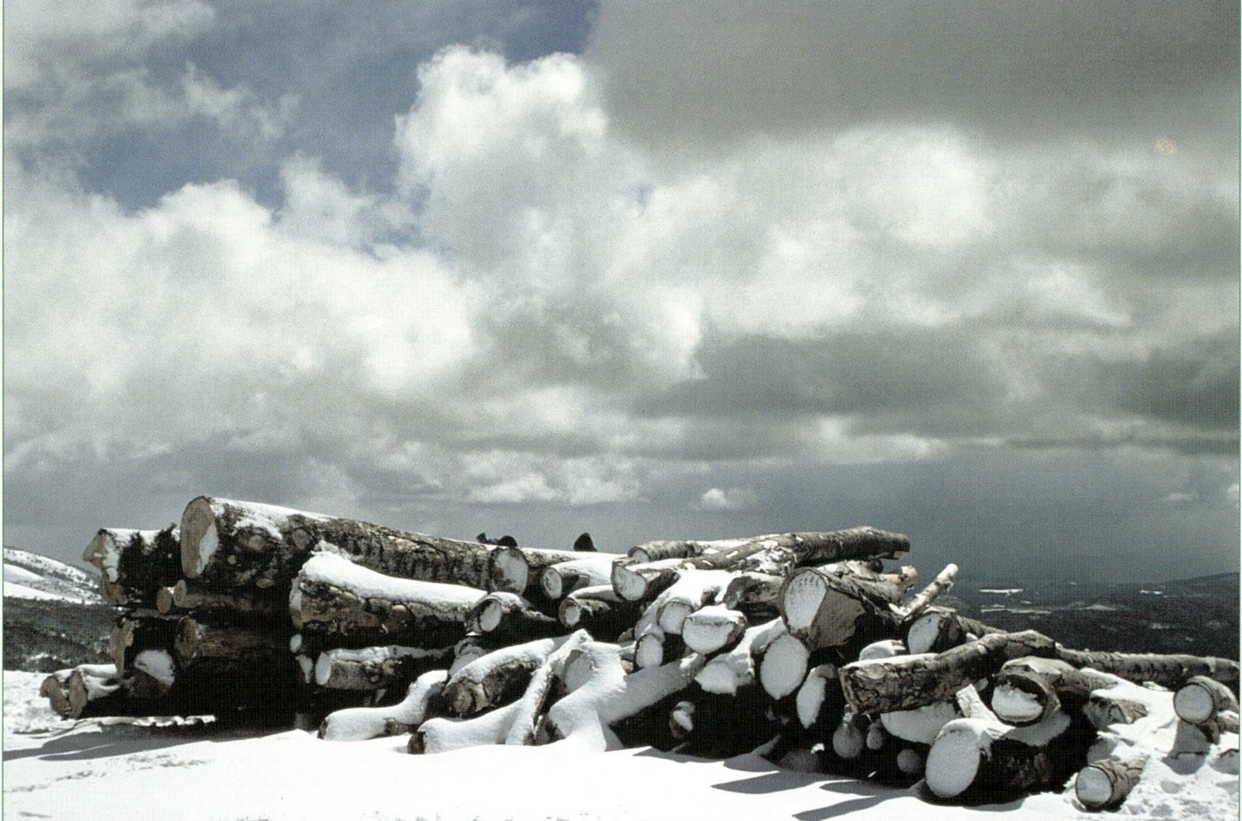

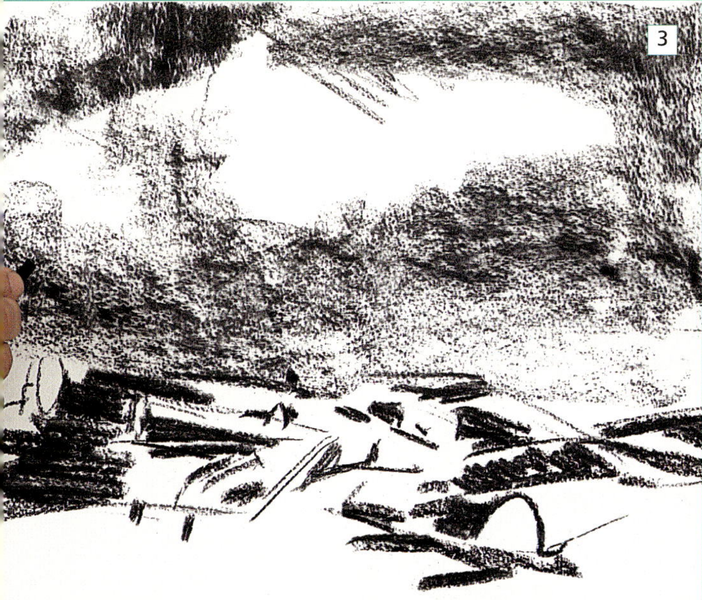

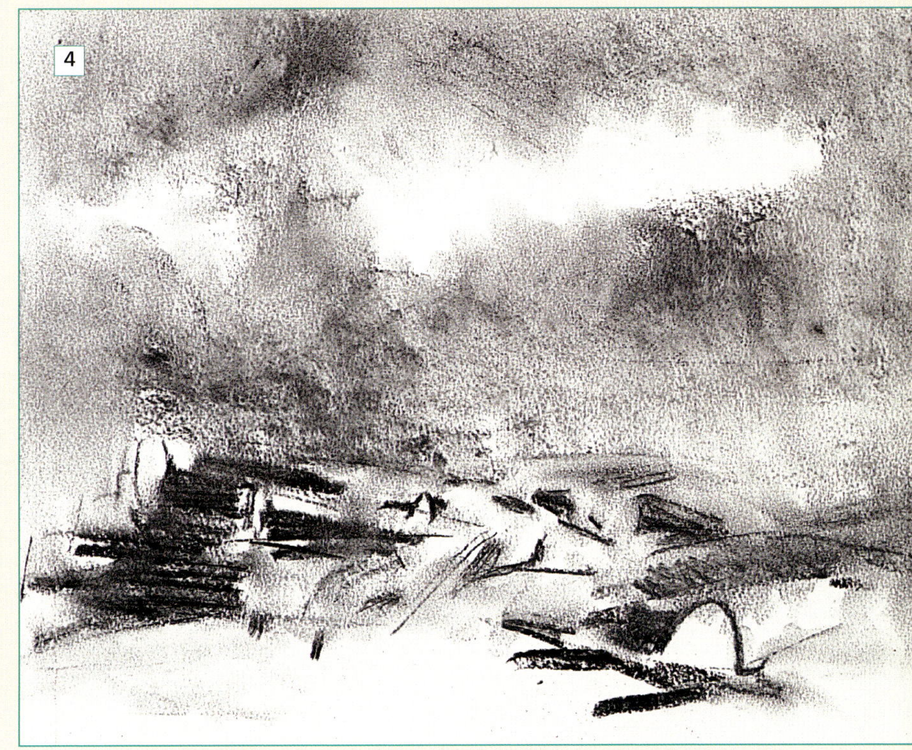

3· **USE THE CHARCOAL FLAT BETWEEN YOUR FINGERS** to shade all the sky background. With the charcoal flat, the pressure gives a uniform medium gray. The central cloud mass is left unpainted.

4· **OUTLINE THE FORM OF THE CLOUDS** with a charcoal gray tone. As you can see, the line that used to mark the horizon is absorbed by the charcoal stroke.

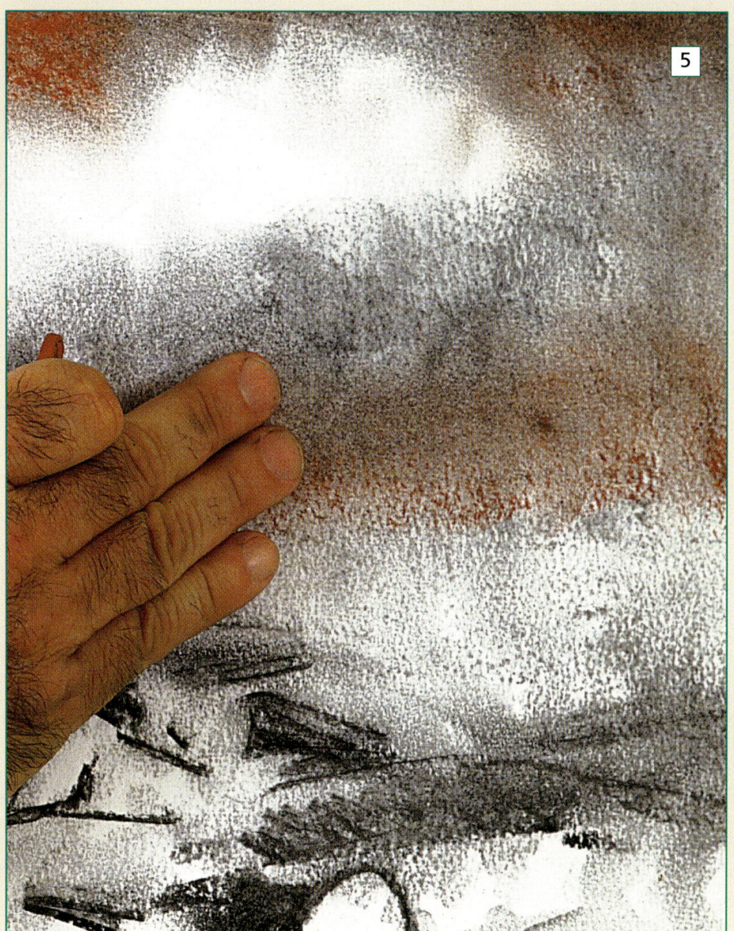

OBSERVE THE UPPER ZONE and you will notice that the sanguine pressure has been quite substantial. When you blended the tones, the sanguine strokes revealed that they were more adhesive than charcoal.

THE ERASER IS ONE OF THE MOST USEFUL drawing tools, especially for drawing in negative and for opening whites.

AS WE SAW IN THE FIRST PART OF THE CHAPTER, the eraser is suitable for tasks other than correcting errors or cleaning dirty zones. In this example, the eraser's principle function is to open up white spaces, a process which starts when the drawing is well advanced, as is the case here.

6· IN STEP 6, FIRSTLY, finish the form of the clouds giving them volume. The whites that are opened with the eraser contrast against the grays creating highly luminous zones. After drawing the cloud forms with the eraser, clean some parts of the pile of trunks on the snow.

5· USE YOUR FINGERTIPS TO BLEND all the background that has just been shaded. In some zones, the gray tone is completely stumped. In other zones, in contrast, the charcoal shading is preserved fresh and reveals the paper grain texture.

JUST PASSING YOUR HAND OVER THE ZONES that must be faded is enough to blend the stroke. Use your fingers stained in charcoal to smudge some white spaces on the paper.

SANGUINE IS MUCH MORE ADHESIVE and opaque than charcoal and therefore can paint on any surface however dark it may be.

USE THE SANGUINE FLAT to shade the upper part. Apply little pressure to shade the lower zone of the sky. Then rub gently to blend the tones of charcoal and sanguine.

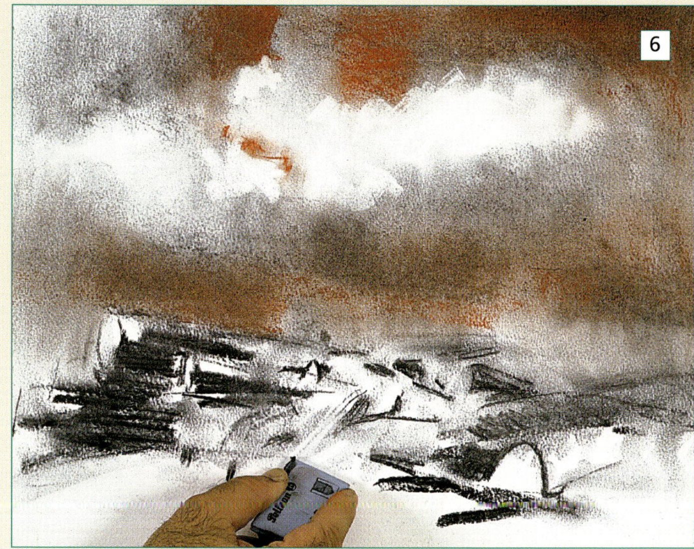

7· IN STEP 7, start to draw in sanguine in the definitive white spaces, the background on the right and the trunk shadows.

THE CUT TRUNKS ARE DIVIDED into two zones. A dark zone in which the white spaces are outlined, and a lighter zone in which the flow of the lines plays an important role. Use the eraser to finish cleaning the

Landscape with openings

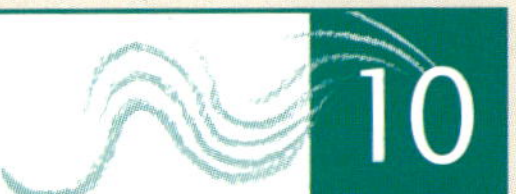

10

SUMMARY SCHEME

Graying and smudging the sky.

Whites opened up in the clouds with the putty eraser.

Sanguine is much denser and compact than charcoal. It is more difficult to rub out with the hand so you have to use the eraser.

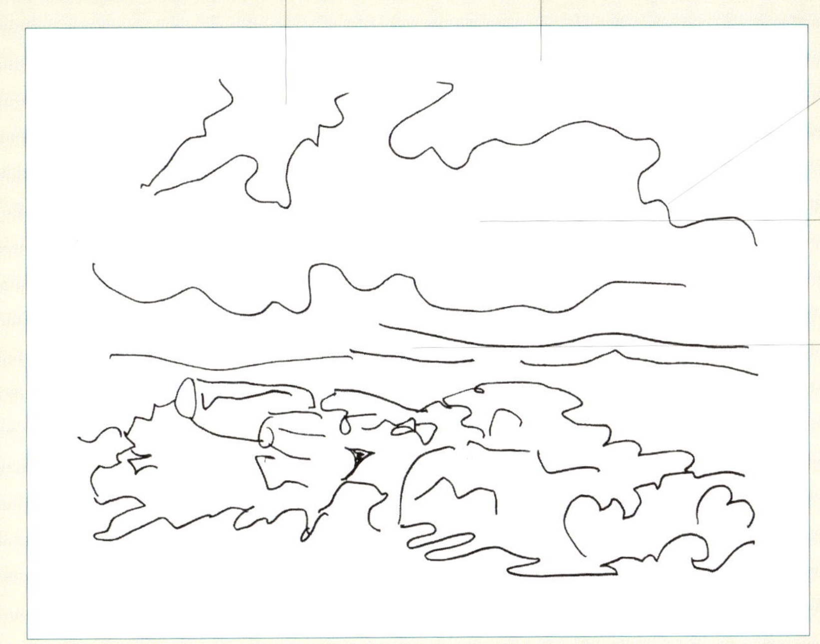

Sanguine superimposition over the charcoal background.

Mix of sanguine and charcoal.

Opening of white spaces in the pile of trunks.

FINISH THE DEFINITION OF THE DARKS on the cut trunks with charcoal. The most luminous zones are left undrawn. If, by accident any white area is dirtied, restore it with the eraser. As any shape can be given to the putty rubber, it can open up both fine lines or wide spaces.

TO FINISH THIS LANDSCAPE WITH WHITE SPACES, clean up any zones that may have been accidentally stained by charcoal or sanguine.

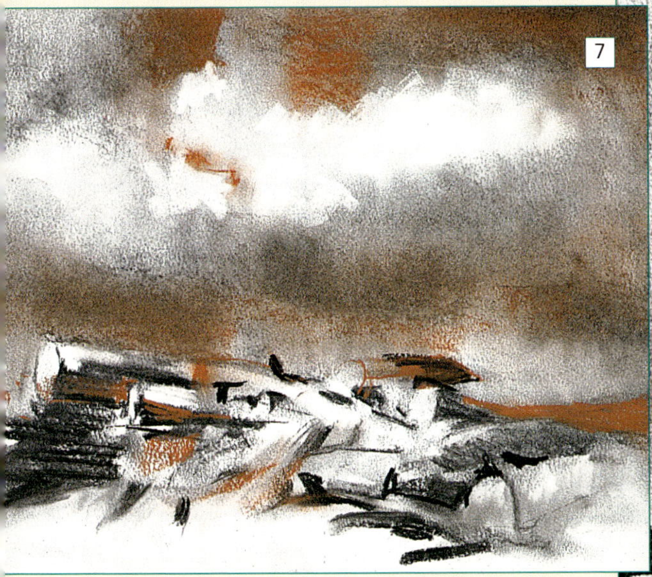

7

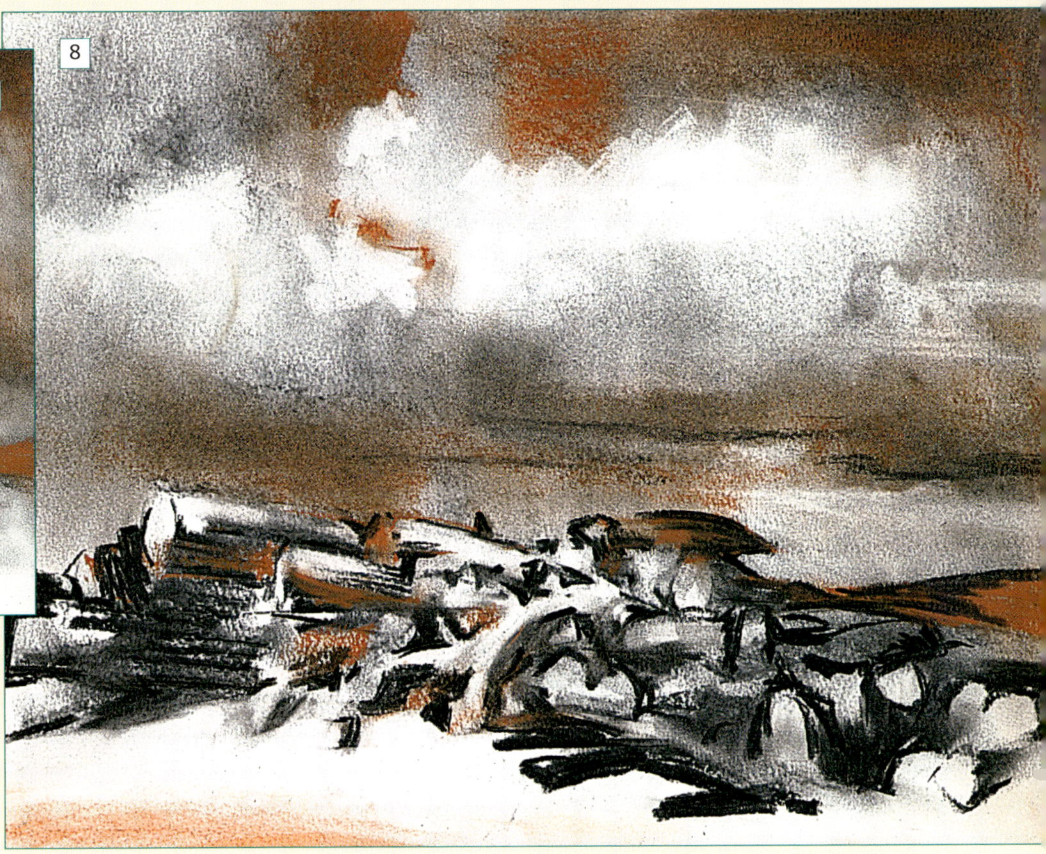

8

DRAWING WITH THE ERASER

In this chapter we are going to work drawing with the eraser on an area previously shaded in charcoal. The exercises are simple and do not differ from the normal drawing procedure. Moreover, if you make a mistake with the rubber, just spread a little charcoal already on the paper to cover up. Using this method the enthusiast can learn a series of interesting concepts about drawing in negative (with the eraser) and in positive (with a medium).

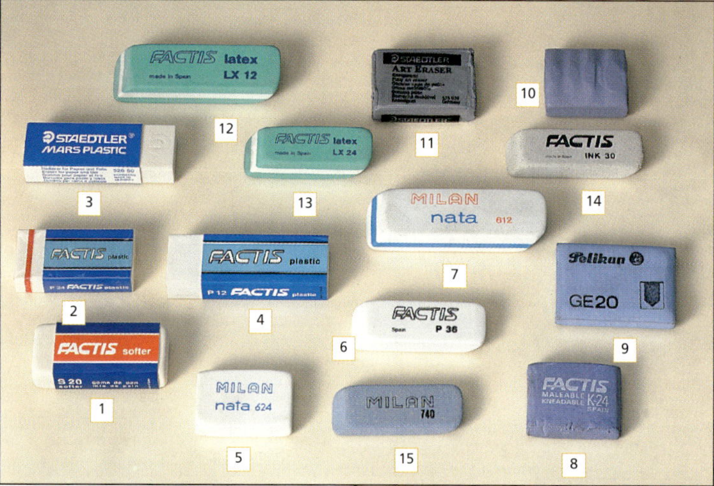

NECESSARY MATERIAL

Here is a wide range of erasers, each one especially suitable for a particular drawing medium. Plastic erasers (1 to 4); latex erasers (5 to 7); putty erasers, specially for charcoal and sanguine (8 to 11); soft kneaded erasers (12 to 14), and a hard eraser for ink (15).

Cover all the paper in charcoal and blend it.

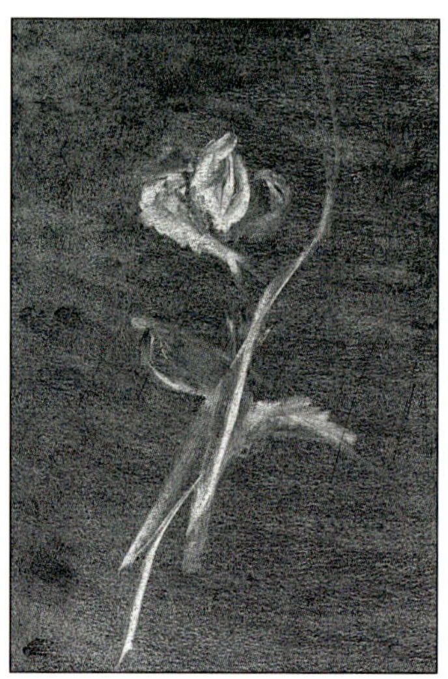

The first strokes place the principle elements. It is only an outline.

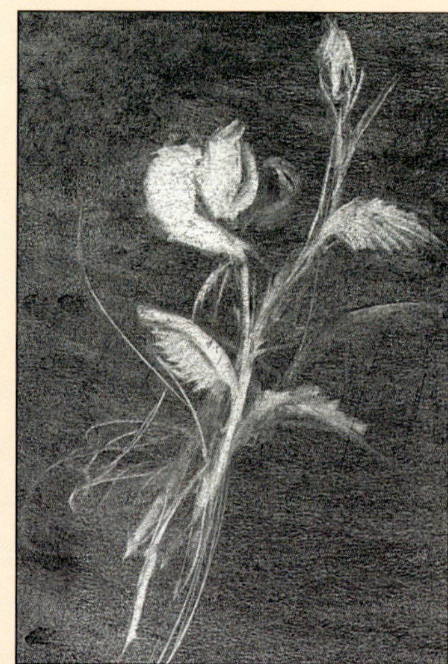

When the background is cleaned the forms become more outlined and luminous.

CLEANING THE ERASER

As the eraser eliminates charcoal it becomes increasingly grubby until, finally, it is black and unable to open up new white spaces. If it is a putty eraser, the grime can be pushed inwards. Kneaded and plastic erasers can be washed in soap and water, but leave them to dry before reusing them. All this can be awkward in the middle of a drawing session, so have handy some sandpaper and give your eraser a quick clean. Little rubber is wasted. Alternatively, use a spare, clean, eraser during the session.

DRAWING IN NEGATIVE

Drawing is normally passing a dark or toned medium over paper to leave a contrasting mark. The eraser has exactly the opposite function: it must take the medium off the paper, restoring its original whiteness or something similar.

The capacity of the eraser to open up white spaces is greater than what we have studied up to now. This converts it into an ideal, if somewhat different and surprising, implement for drawing.

FORM SKETCHES

To start drawing directly with the eraser, all the paper has to be previously shaded with the right drawing medium. Any medium may be used provided that it can be erased. Remember that the less adhesive it is, the easier the work will be. If you use an oily medium, like graphite, the eraser will quickly become clogged.

All the exercises in this section can be done in charcoal on white paper. The first step is to shade all the surface with the stick flat. To quicken the work process, use a thick, straight piece of charcoal about 7 cm long. Do a zigzag stroke, filling horizontal stretches until all the sur-

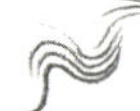

11

Charcoal is the less adhesive of all the drawing mediums. Any mark made on the shaded surface can be eliminated by passing your hand over. The effect is much stronger if the eraser is used.

face is shaded. Then blend the strokes with your fingers, be careful not to leave any evident marks so watch the rubbing pressure.
As we saw in the last chapter, just passing the eraser over the paper is enough to open up white spaces. This will be put to good use to get interesting effects. Once you have started to draw with the eraser, do not stain the paper with the grease on your fingers because you then would not be able to rub out. Also, you could remove charcoal in the wrong place. However, if you make a mistake with the eraser, you can correct it by doing a subtle stumping.
Here we are going to do a flower. First, draw the petals. The zones that are going to be dark must not be rubbed out. Only the illuminated parts are opened up. After doing the white spaces, work on the stem and the leaves. This part of the drawing is done with quick, firm strokes.

CLEANING THE BACKGROUND AND OUTLINING THE FORM

When the eraser has outlined the drawing, you can start to work on the most important shapes like the upper part of the flower and the leaves. To give definition to these forms the paper background must be literally cleaned so that the whites are more luminous and the drawing is precise. The spotless background will also outline better the forms. For example, look at the flower petals. When you have cleaned inside them with the eraser, their form is much more precise. The same applies to the recently drawn leaves.

The darkest details are drawn with the charcoal tip once all the tones have been opened up.

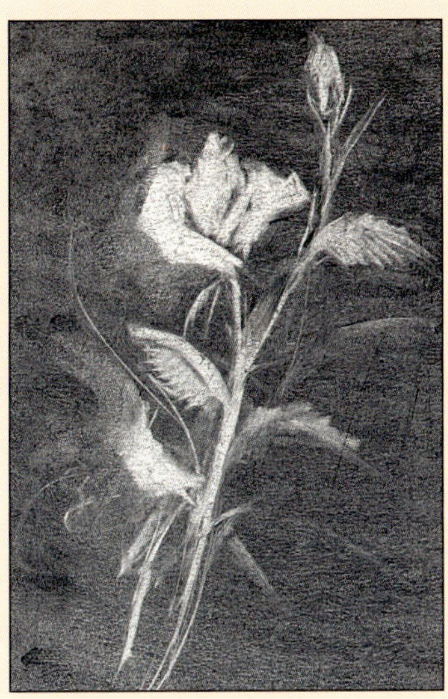

The leaves on the right are done by erasing hard to create different tones of white in the drawing.

INTENSIFYING THE DETAILS

Erasing with the rubber can be a highly perfected skill. We are only at the beginning of all the possibilities offered and which can be applied to any drawing theme.
Once the preliminary sketch has been done, precise and luminous details can be realized. We will have to practice the different tones obtainable as we enrich the drawing with luminous whites and a scale of grays between charcoal and the color of the paper.

When a background tone next to the flower is intensified, the contrast also increases as the whites appear more luminous.

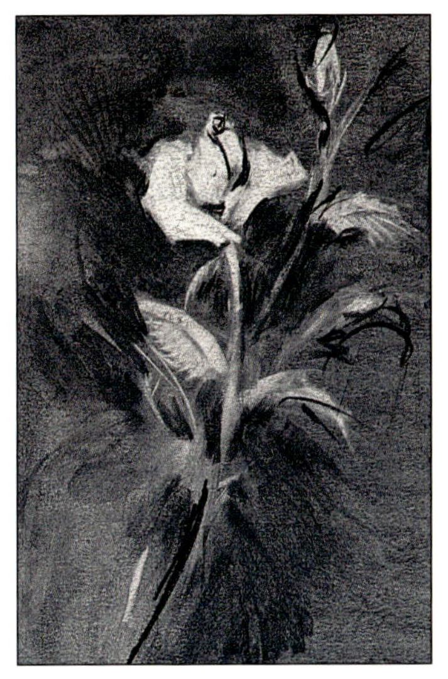

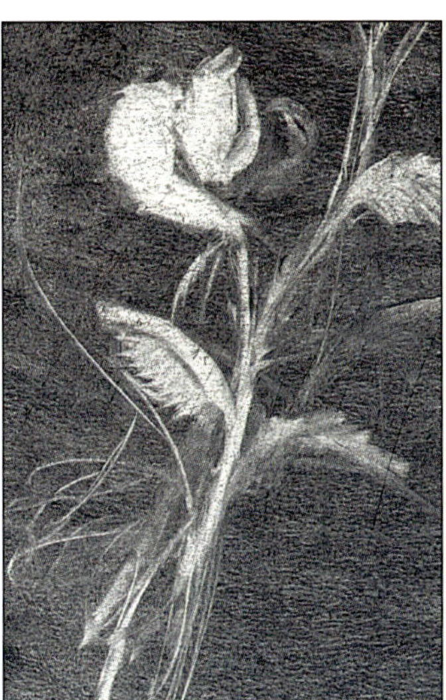

DARK CONTRASTS

An eraser can open up white spaces but it cannot give darks. Charcoal, or oiled charcoal for dense blacks, must be used again to obtain them. Any maximum contrasts obtained from charcoal must be drawn at the end of the process, when all the tones have been opened up. These darks can increase the depth sensation in the background, which was shaded gray before.
Charcoal is also used to redo the small details of the flower shapes and the background. On top of any new intervention, you can do blendings that mix with the background. Whenever you draw with sanguine or charcoal, fix the drawing so that your work is not lost.

CARDBOARD PROTECTION

Many methods are possible when using an eraser. In the last section we studied how to draw in negative. Now we are going to do an entertaining piece using a cardboard shape to protect the shading.
The eraser will not touch the drawing protected, or reserved, underneath the cardboard.

The rest of the composition elements will be drawn after doing the light parts of the landscape with the eraser.
When you have cut out the card-

11 DRAWING WITH THE ERASER

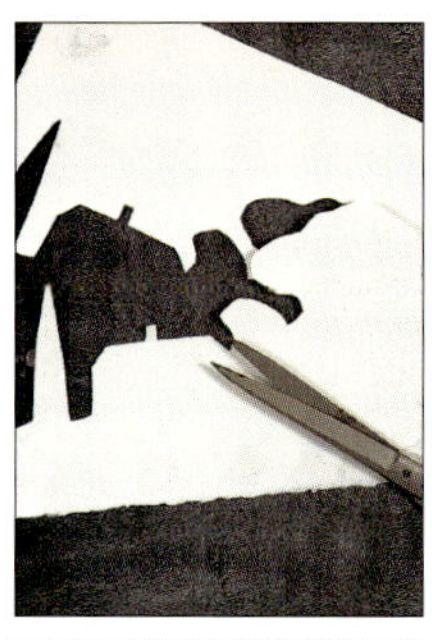

Firstly, cut out the cardboard protector -or 'frame'- in the shape of the reserve. In this exercise we are going to do a simple landscape with a house and some trees.

Once the cardboard frame is ready, place it on the paper without touching the charcoal with your fingers. Then start to rub out inside the shape to form the tree top.

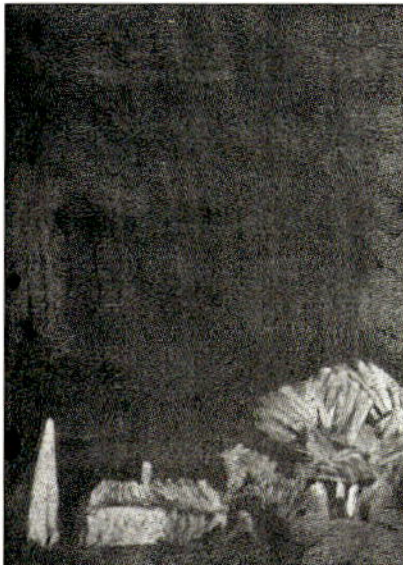

Once the frame has been removed, carry on working on the landscape forms. Firstly, work on the light parts which were inside the frame.

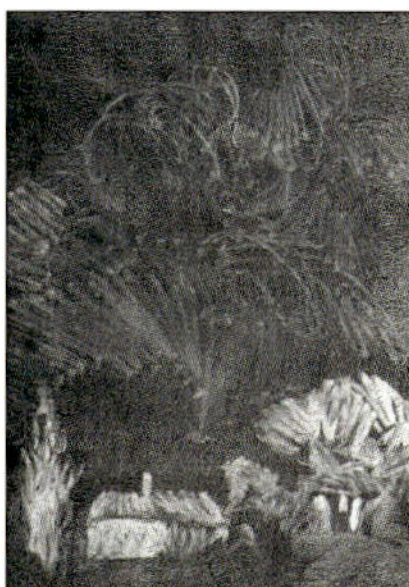

Use the somewhat dirtied eraser to insinuate the shape of the clouds with quick strokes. After cleaning the eraser, open up new, more pristine, white spaces in the cypress tree on the left.

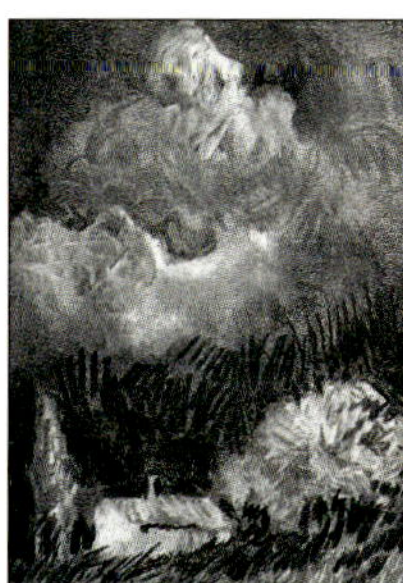

When you have medium grays and new light spaces, start to do the darkest contrasts. These contrasts will make the grays and whites more luminous.

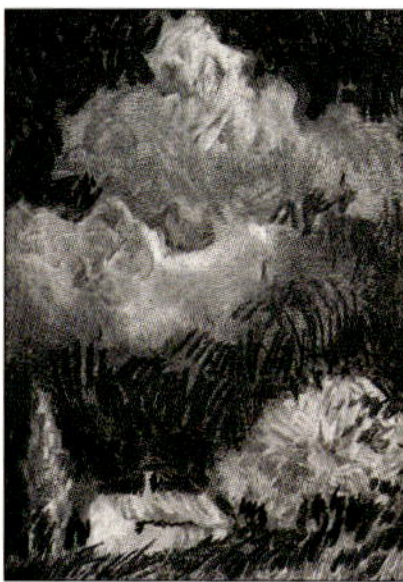

The simultaneous contrast effect is always present in drawing techniques and depends heavily on the white of the paper.

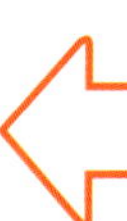

THE CARDBOARD TECHNIQUE

board shape, you will have to decide on the composition. When trying out different possibilities with the cardboard be careful not to smudge the charcoal, nor touch it with your fingers -do not forget that human skin is oily. You could leave stains or marks. Use the eraser to start opening up the main elements of the landscape. Of course, the cardboard recourse is not limited to landscapes: it is also valid for other themes like still lifes or even figure compositions. It has two advantages: it guides you and prevents shading in the wrong zones.

REDOING THE FORM

Just as you worked on the tree inside the cardboard frame, carry on with the other elements. The movement of the eraser must not be uncontrolled: you have to follow the plane of the elements you are working on, like, for example, the house roof and the cypress tree on the right. Once the outline of the frame is on the paper, you can remove it and polish the forms. You need not rub out all the shading inside the frame. The aim is to exploit the difference between the charcoal and the whiteness of the paper restored by the eraser.

NEW WHITE SPACES

The frame has now served its purpose and you must work with the eraser to do the light elements of the landscape. Before cleaning the eraser, form some graphic clouds with quick strokes. Little pressure and the dirtiness of the eraser combine to give a soft stroke that does not completely cover the white of the paper. Clean the eraser by rubbing it on fresh paper or on sandpaper. Now it will give very clean whites, which are very good for around the cypress tree.

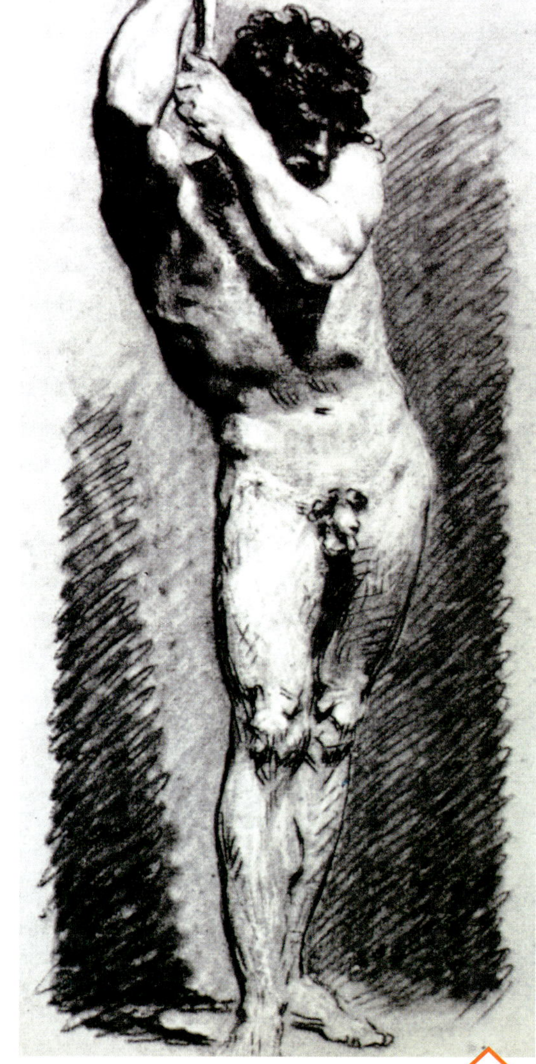

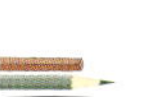

CORRECTING SHADING

The French painter **Pierre-Paul Prud'hon (1758-1823)** did the masterly **'Nude study'**, kept in the Bonat Museum in Bayonne, in the south of France. Correcting the shading was an important recourse for the artist to achieve the luminosity of the muscles. He started with gray tones and then worked on them, rubbing out and adding contrasts with plastic modeling and white chalk.

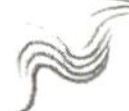

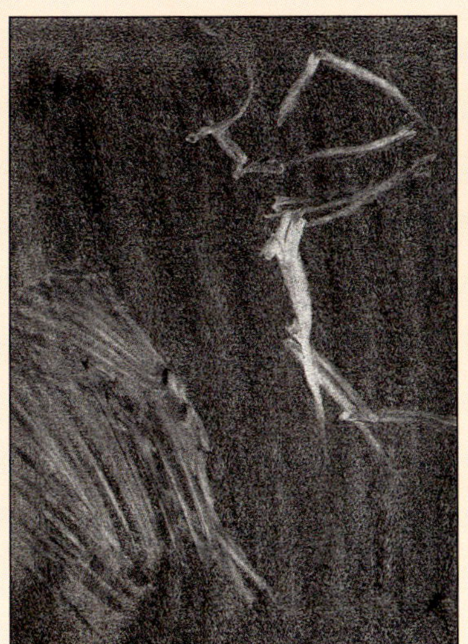

The outline of this model seen from behind is insinuated It starts from the luminous part on the right.

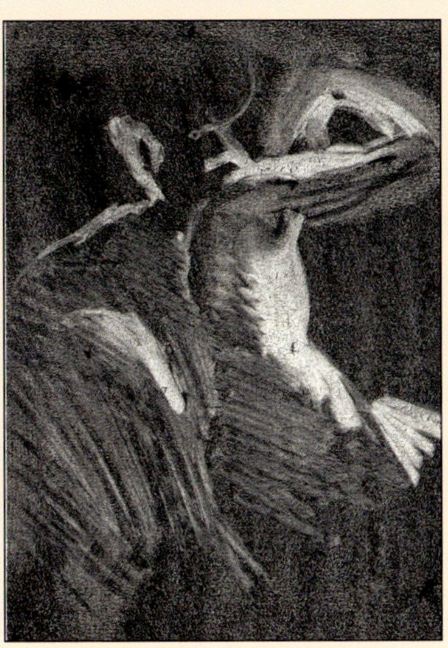

Once the necessary corrections have been done, new white spaces can be opened up and the pre-existent ones intensified.

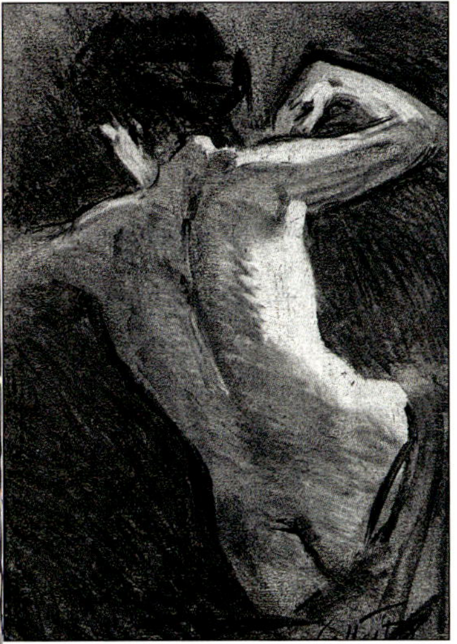

Use the charcoal point to darken the contours of the figure. Afterwards, correct the form of the left side.

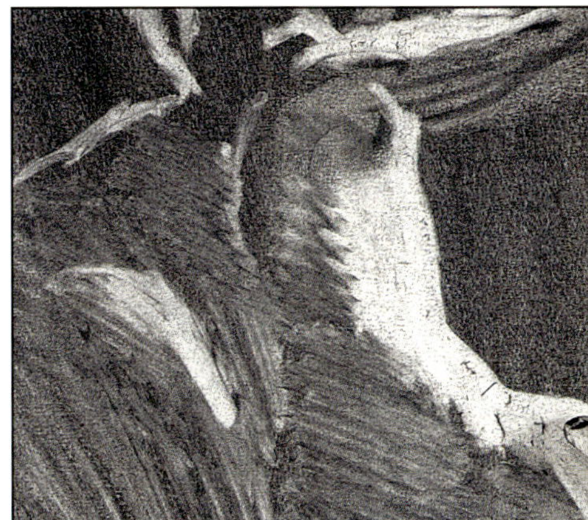

The very luminous whites, as seen in this close up, are the fruit of repeatedly passing the eraser over.

GRADATIONS AND GRAYS

Use the same stroke as before to insinuate the volume of the clouds. Open up some very luminous whites in this zone. On top, smudge with your fingers to blend some new grays and to form a good base for the definitive highlights of the clouds.

Draw new contrasts in oiled charcoal around the main forms. This will enable you to separate the planes and to obtain a texture that would have been impossible with the eraser. When you draw the new darks, you will be able to observe the simultaneous contrast effect: the grays and the whites become more luminous, a recurrent theme in drawing.

WHITE DASHES

In previous chapters we have seen the effect of whites opened up on a smudged charcoal shaded area and the importance of simultaneous contrasts. Now we are going to do a figure seen from behind. The corrections will be easy to do. The highlights opened up with the eraser will need contrasts beside them to give more luminosity.

THE OUTLINE

Any line unnecessary for the development of the drawing can softly be reintegrated into the gray. The hand can wipe out any stroke made by the eraser. This is how you start to draw in negative on the smudged surface. Before starting to draw, go over all the exercise so that you have a good idea about the forms that appear and the most illuminated zone -the right side, which is the center of attention in the drawing.

CORRECTING THE FIRST LINES

When you look at the outline, it can be seen that the highlights on the left make the back seem too narrow. This is very easy to correct in this type of work. You can draw with free strokes because the dark tone of the paper can quickly be restored by smudging with your fingers. If the white space opened up is too wide and has to be corrected, darken it again with charcoal and then blend the new tone in until it is homogeneous. Once the original tone has been restored, open up new white spaces with the eraser.

CONTRASTS AND WHITES

The principle contrasts do not only come from opening up whites. In a complex drawing the highlights can occupy a wide area, as in this example, and will therefore need something to compensate the tones established. The darkest contrasts help to make the light areas more luminous. Draw around the figure with the charcoal point, turning the background gray into an intermediate tone. The white on the side now stands out more.

SUMMARY

FIRST RUBBINGS OUT
As in all drawing processes, the first lines have to insinuate the fundamental scheme of the model. These lines do not have to be pure white.

RANGE OF WHITES
The luminosity of the white paper will depend on the pressure exercised and how much you insist.

A FRAME
A simple frame can be used to erase only in the right places and to define undrawn forms.

COMPENSATING CONTRASTS
Charcoal can intensify the contrasts and establish great differences between the tones.

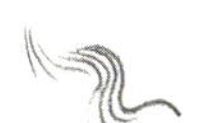

11 Exercices *Step by step*

DRAWING WITH THE ERASER

As we have studied in this chapter, the eraser is one of the most useful tools for opening up whites. It can produce highlights, create textures on the charcoal shaded surface and make strokes and marks similar to those of any drawing medium. However, all of this is in negative. It the opposite to what white chalk does on tinted paper.

In the next exercise we are going to do a beautiful landscape, getting the most out of the eraser recourses. It is not a complicated exercise but, as with any drawing, requires attention as you progress.

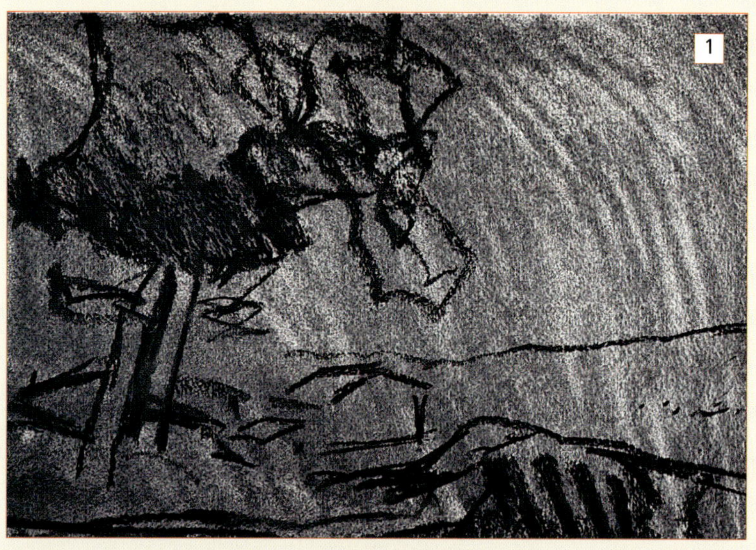

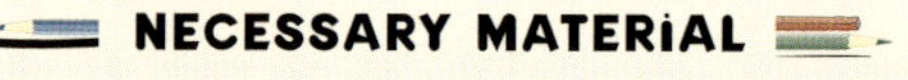

NECESSARY MATERIAL

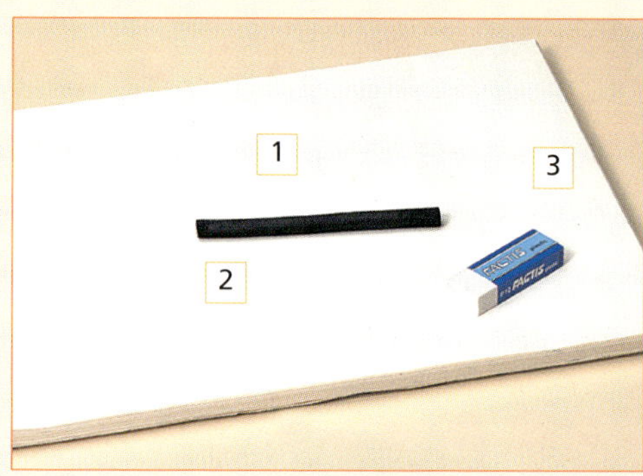

Charcoal (1), drawing paper (2) and an eraser (3).

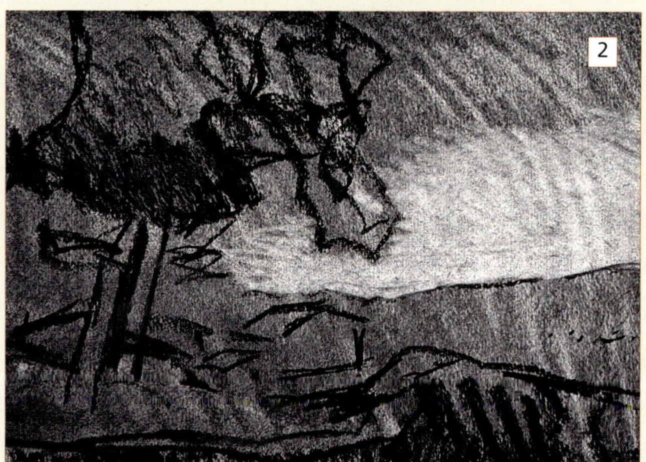

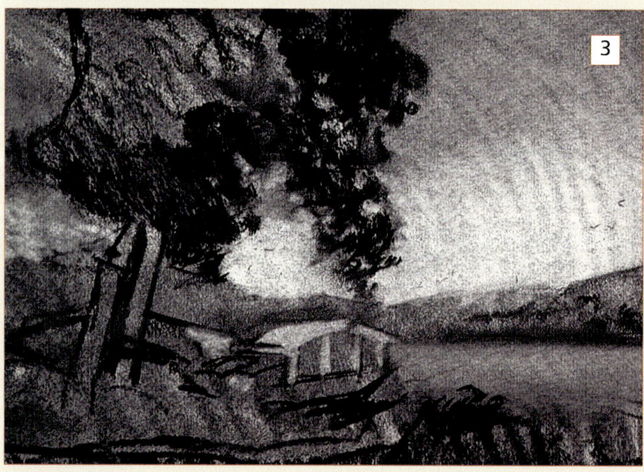

1· FIRSTLY, SMUDGE ALL THE BACKGROUND of the paper without the stroke standing out too much. Use the charcoal broadwise at half pressure. Cover all the paper completely so that you have a gray surface on which to draw in negative.

ONCE ALL THE BACKGROUND IS SHADED, soften the stroke with your fingertips until the shading is homogeneous. The white paper, now gray, is a perfect drawing base for the charcoal point. Do a scheme of the landscape.

IN THIS PRELIMINARY SKETCH it is important to mark out the principle masses.

2· USE THE TIP OF THE ERASER TO START TO DO strokes in the background, in the lower part of the sky.

WHEN THE ERASER IS DIRTY, it is very important to clean it thoroughly so that the charcoal does not clog up the paper pores. Just as charcoal can mark with all its faces, the eraser too can draw with all sides. To open up these white spaces, use an edge.

USE A SLOPED STROKE TO RUB OUT THE SKY. On top, blend the charcoal from the upper zone. It is not a good idea to dirty the just cleaned zone too much. If this did happen you would have to re-erase and reblend the charcoal over the white zone.

3· OPEN UP A NEW, not excessively luminous, white space, above the haystack by rubbing softly. The details can be left until later.

IN THIS CLOSE UP, you can observe how new white spaces have been opened up in the foreground with the eraser. These openings are not regular. Instead they are like the teeth of a saw. Opening up whites with an eraser has as many creative stroke effects as other mediums, although, as we are observing in the practices, the light areas tend to join together.

THE WORK NOW FOCUSES on the great tree which dominates the scene. Firstly, do the light areas on the trunk, making it stand out against the background. Afterwards, clean some parts of the tree top. Here the white spaces are realized with precise marks with the eraser point.

Landscape with the eraser as a recourse

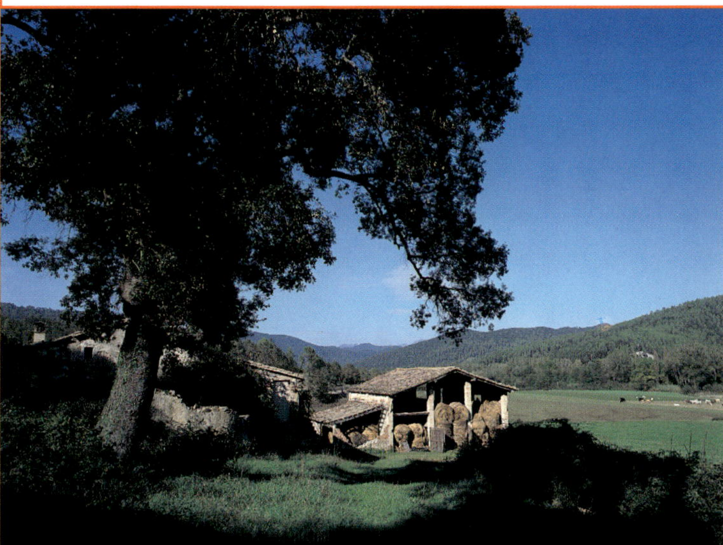

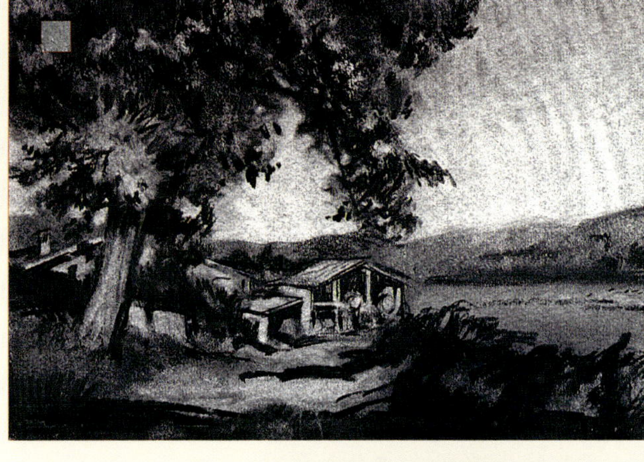

The putty eraser is very simple to use but the plastic and kneaded erasers are more practical because they aid the stroke

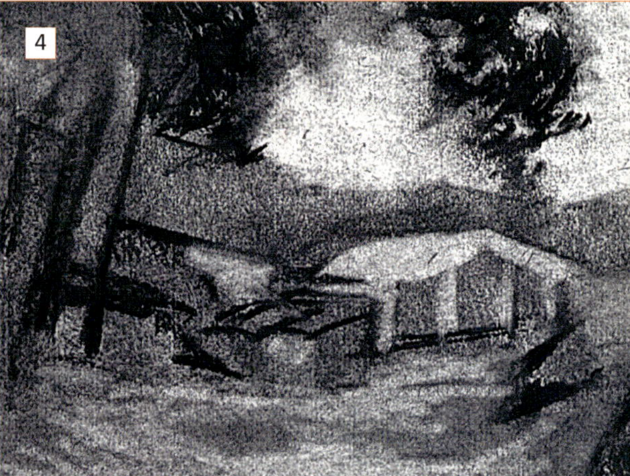

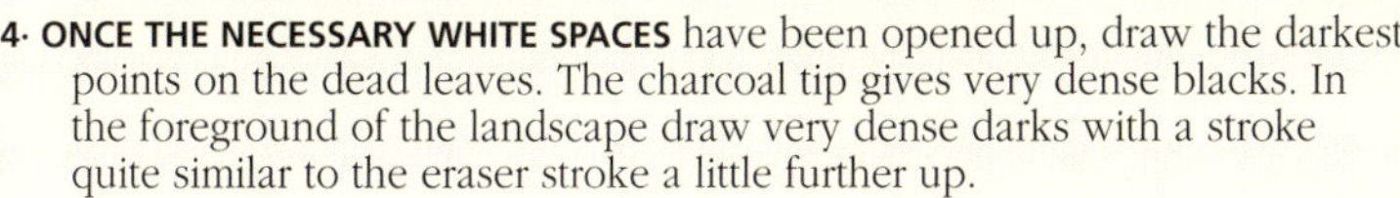

4· **ONCE THE NECESSARY WHITE SPACES** have been opened up, draw the darkest points on the dead leaves. The charcoal tip gives very dense blacks. In the foreground of the landscape draw very dense darks with a stroke quite similar to the eraser stroke a little further up.

USE THE CHARCOAL POINT TO FINISH the dark part in the lower zone. Establish a spatial plane between the foreground and the midground.

5· **INTENSIFY THE DARKS ON BOTH** sides of the tree trunk. This will make it appear much more luminous and shiny because of the contrast effect.

IN CHARCOAL, GO OVER THE TRUNK and use the eraser to open up whites again to give it texture. All that remains to be done are some small details on the haystack and the tree branches.

6· **OBSERVE THE DRAWING** when it is finished. As you can see, the plastic effects achieved are very different from those when drawing in positive. The character of the drawing comes from the work done on the whites and in some ways it resembles an engraving.

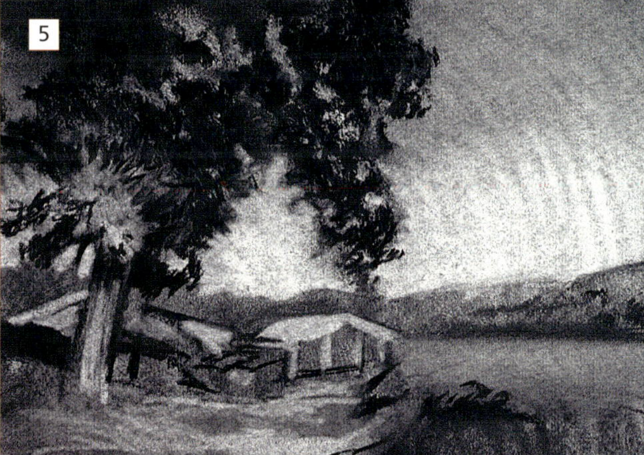

SUMMARY

Smudge all the background so that you have a gray charcoal base on which to work with the eraser.

The first whites are realized in the lower part of the sky in slanted strokes that are later blended with the darks.

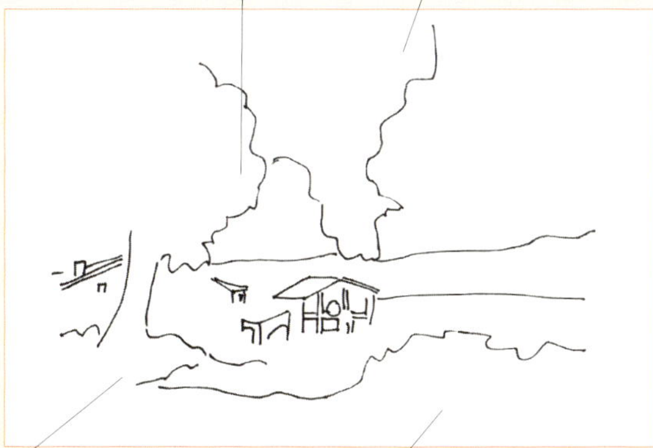

The tree trunk and the haystack are done by rubbing out at the beginning and drawing the details at the end.

In the foreground, rub out with saw-like strokes. In the lower part, place an intense dark.

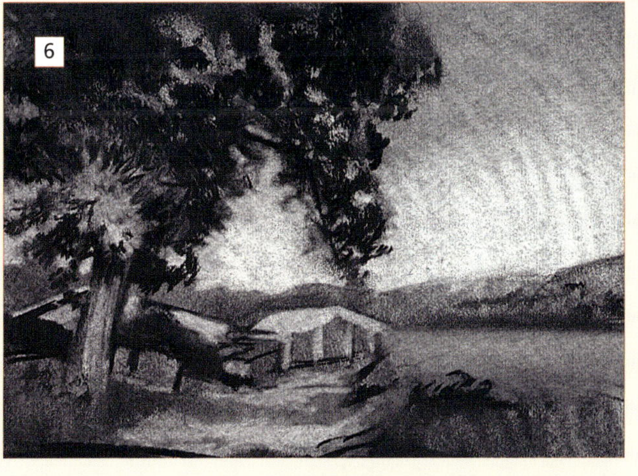

12 MODELING

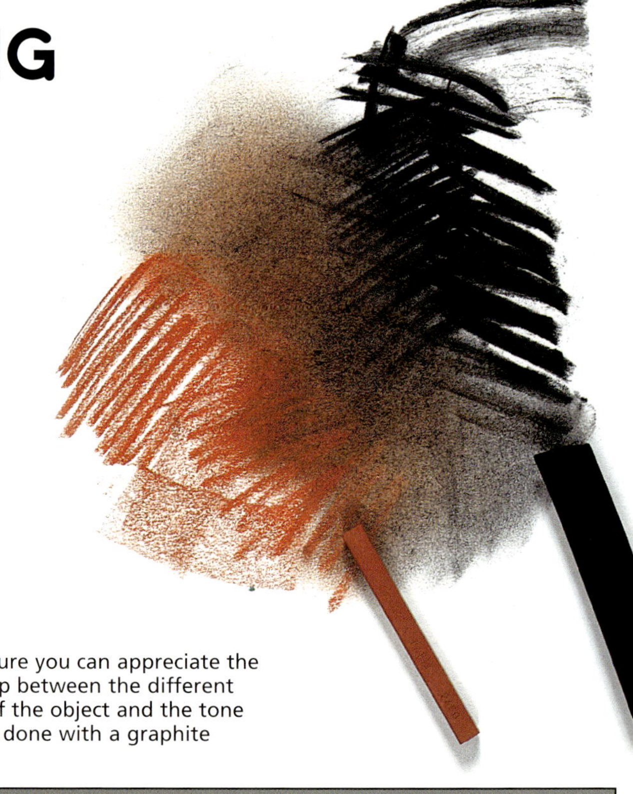

Sanguine and charcoal combined can produce tones that go from the darkest black to soft half tones.

In drawing there are many techniques which permit a model to be represented with its forms realistically interpreted. The most classic, and the one which also allows the best study of the model, is modeling, the starting point of which are tone values. When learning to draw, modeling must always contribute to the creative process. It is not sufficient if it comes up once in a while: it is a process that must be continuously developed. In the different chapters on drawing, modeling will be applied to distinct themes -fruit, objects, figure compositions- and we will progressively deepen our understanding of it.

THE TONE ON THE OBJECT

The shape of an object means that light does not fall on it uniformly. Some zones are fully illuminated, others are in soft or very hard shadows.

The different shadows do not start suddenly, but rather there is a soft gradation between the two tones, except when there is a radical change between two planes of the object. The shadows vary considerably in each of the illuminated zones and they are joined by half shadows.

STUDYING THE SHADOWS ON A PLASTER MODEL

To study the shadows of an object a useful comparison can be made between the tonal gradation done in any drawing medium and a plaster model, obtainable from any Fine Arts shop. There are a great variety of models, from simple geometric ones through to complex reproductions of classic sculptures. They are, logically, white, which makes easier a thorough study of the exact tones of each shadow. Doing this exercise will help you to understand the different shadows and the transition between the tones.

SANGUINE OR CHARCOAL

Sanguine and charcoal offer tones from intense black to soft half tones. Before starting to draw you have to decide which medium you are going to use first and thus the consequent complexity of the drawing. If the drawing involves complicated techniques, it is better to do the outline in charcoal because any corrections are easier and quicker.

In this picture you can appreciate the relationship between the different shadows of the object and the tone gradation, done with a graphite pencil.

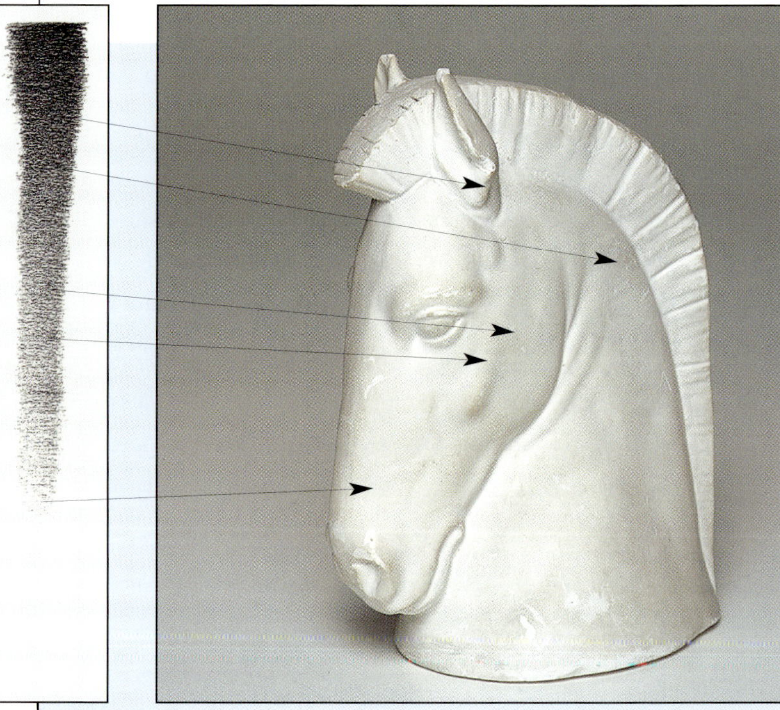

INTENSIFYING THE TONE VALUES

When working with tone values in charcoal and sanguine, the former can be used to intensify the sanguine contrast without radically changing its original tonality.

The drawing is normally started in sanguine: the highlights are opened up in the right places and then the shadows are drawn in charcoal. Blend them in with the tone underneath. Finally, all that remains to be done is to open up white spaces where appropriate.

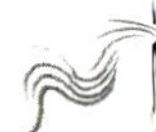

Different drawing mediums can produce a series of gray scales known as valuations. These scales are blended and give rise to the modeling in which each shadow tone has its own gray tone.

12

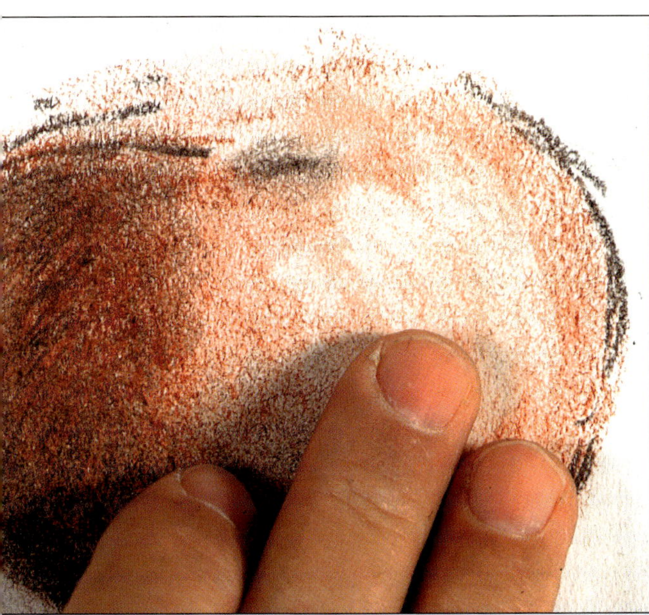

Blend the charcoal over the sanguine drawing and model the form with your fingers.

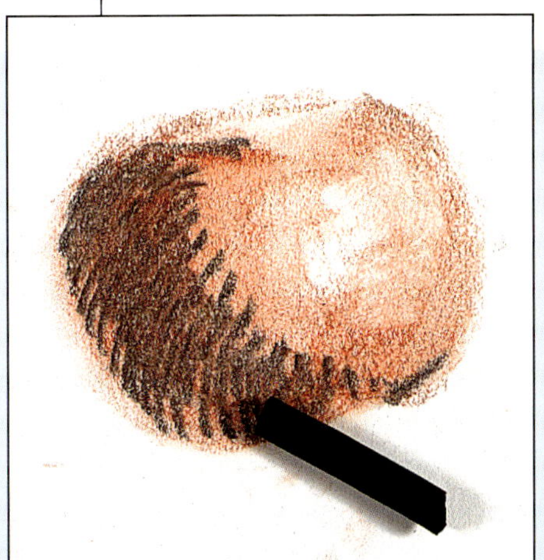

On top of the sanguine drawing, do charcoal lines.

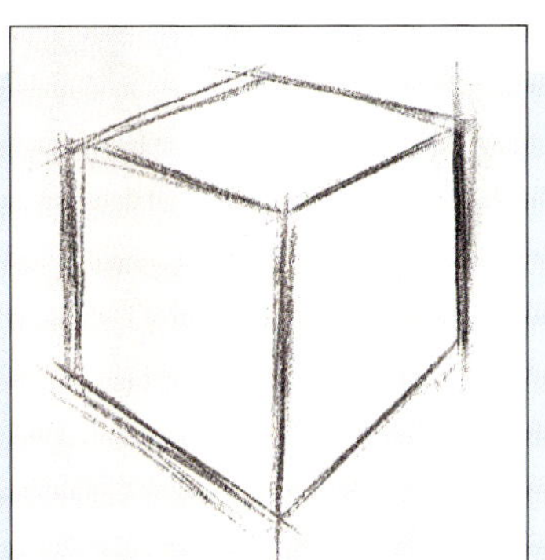

Only the essential lines of the cube scheme are done. Work on the basis that observed from this point of view, the cube is seen as a rhombus, as are the two visible sides.

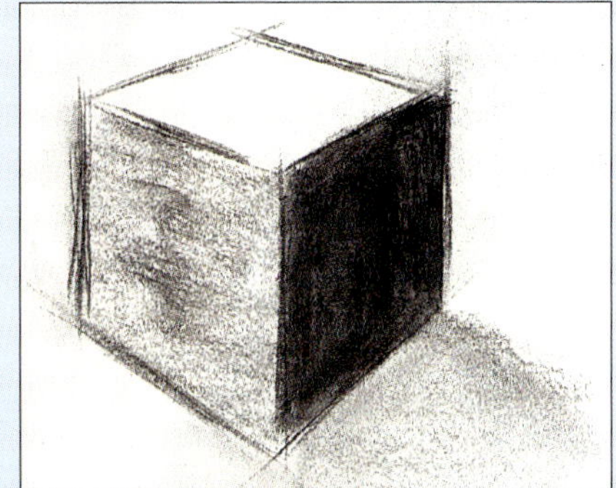

The darkest side is drawn with the charcoal flat and pressing hard. The half tone face is shaded in a medium gray and the most illuminated one is left white.

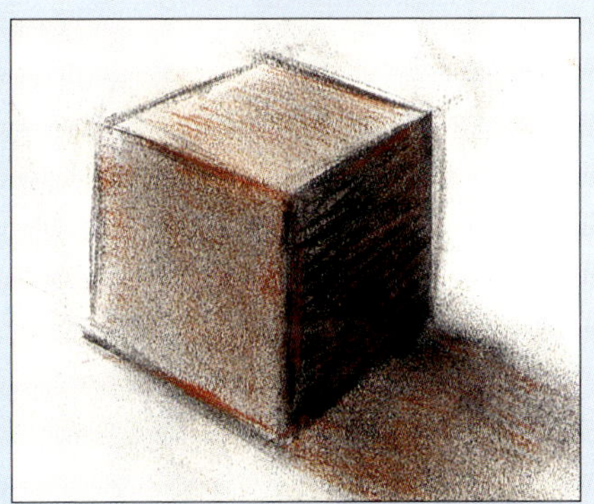

Use the sanguine to intensify the densest tones. The new tones will give the drawing a warmer look.

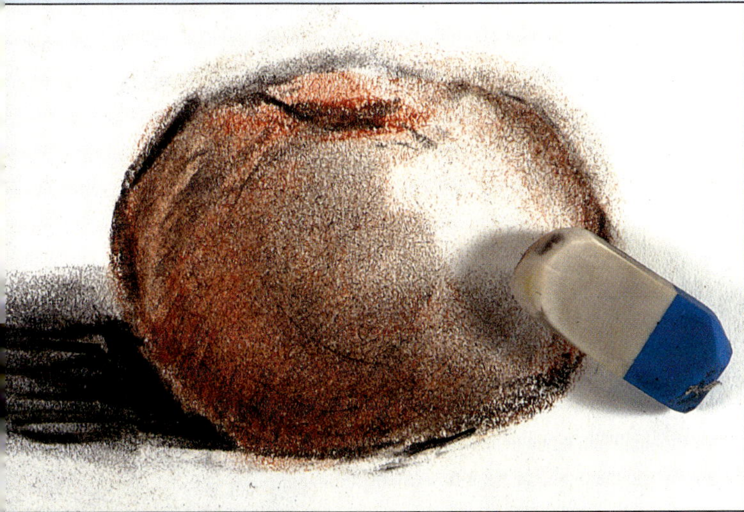

Afterwards, open up the highlights with the eraser.

MODELING GEOMETRIC FORMS

We started by studying how to model spherical forms. They are accessible and allow you to work on one plane. Many forms can basically be a sphere but many other relevant ones are geometric. They must not be left aside in the learning process. Now we are going to model two geometric objects with different planes and faces: a cube and a cylinder.

THE CUBE

The cube is a complex form, especially because of the way the light must be treated on the different faces. The scheme must always be based on a square. The base, in fact, will not seem to be square when looked at from above. It will appear as a rhombus.

Later on we will deal in depth with drawing in perspective, but for now we are only concerned about modeling geometric volumes.

Representing this cube starts with a scheme initiated at the base. Draw upwards the sides and then close off the cube with the 'lid' face.

On any object, one face receives more light than the others, and, conversely, there is a dark side. The maximum highlight in the modeling of the cube is uniform on one entire face.

Continue to draw the cube in charcoal, remembering to apply the right tone and intensity on each face. The determinant factor for the result is the

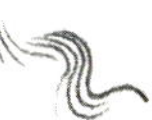

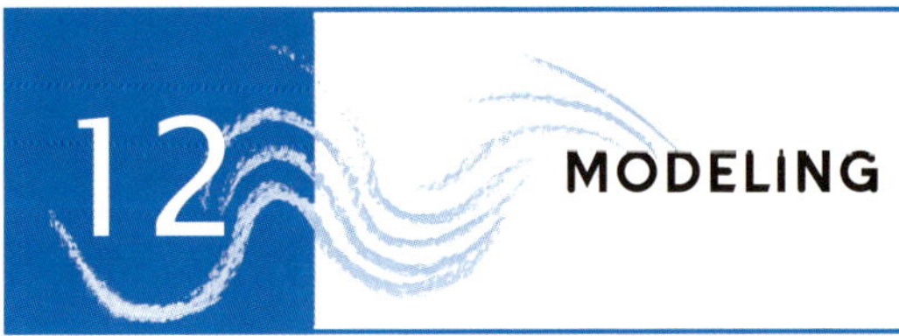

12 MODELING

JOINING THE FORMS

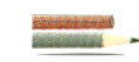

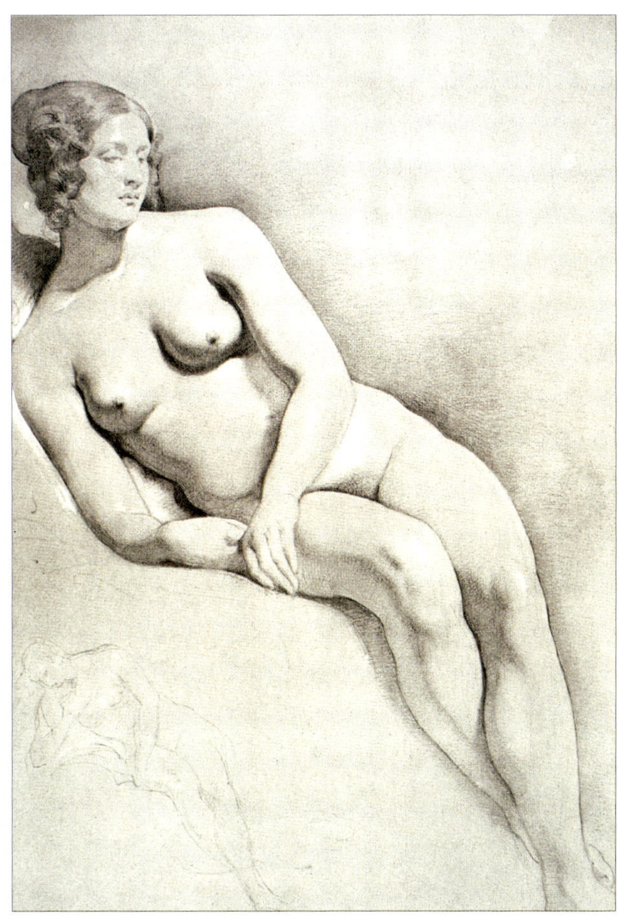

When modeling complex elements, like the human figure, the forms must form a coherent body, but they must also be comprehensible individually. This **'Leaning nude'** by **'William Frost' (1810-1877)** is a masterly example of modeling. If you look at all the feminine forms separately you can make out simple elements like spheres (breasts, buttocks and knees) and cylinders (arms).

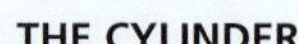

pressure.
Now we will use sanguine. When you have placed the main tones in charcoal and have blended them adequately, you can start working in sanguine. The light can be treated more softly as the strokes are less noticeable after the blending.
Once the charcoal has been blended, you can go over the strokes to stress the contrasts.
Finally, use sanguine to intensify the tones and to give warmth to the drawing..

THE CYLINDER

A cylinder consists of only three planes: a curve and two circular planes. It is much easier to construct than a cube, being based on a circular base and the vertical side as wide as the diameter. Although the cylinder is easy to draw, its modeling is not so evident as the cube's.
Once the cylinder has been constructed, a not too complicated task, the work becomes more demanding

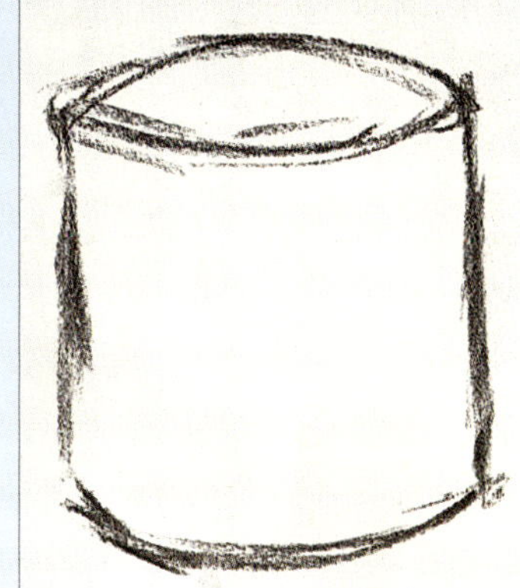

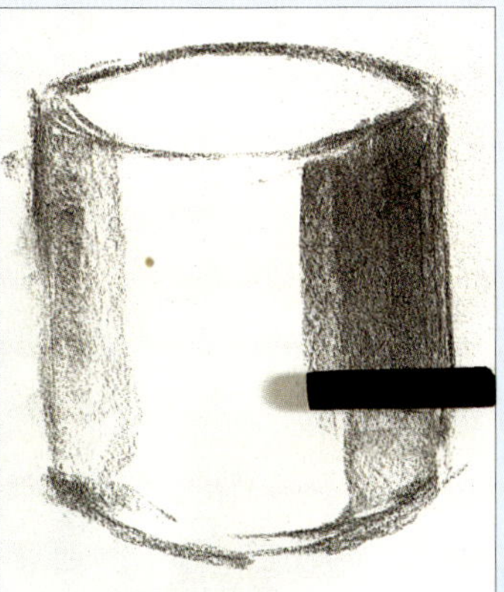

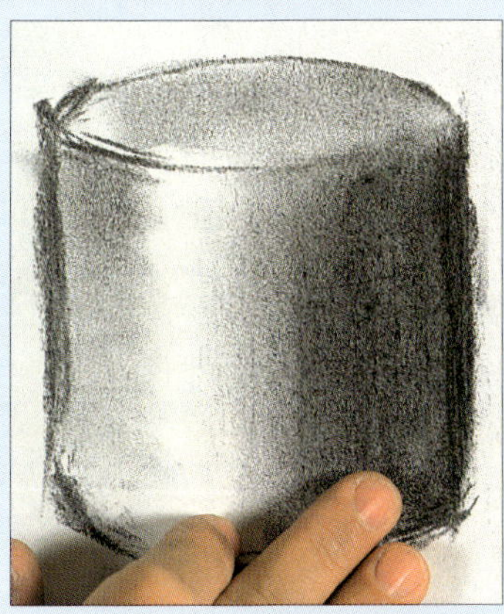

FROM LIGHT TO SHADOW

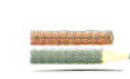

The transition between tones is done by gradations and finger blending. One shading can give rise to many tones if it is correctly stumped. In principal, shadows are realized by starting with a tone and then gradating it to lighter shadows, eventually arriving at the most luminous zones. In this exercise we will practice modeling on a spherical object. Firstly, draw the curve of the plane with the sanguine flat between the fingers. This will be the main shadow. Use your fingers to blend the stroke until the texture is unified. Following the plane of the object, stump the stroke until it is blended with the light zone. Once the principle shadow has been drawn, work on new tone values in charcoal, just as you did with sanguine. Charcoal will enable you to obtain more contrasts and to make the highlights stand out more.

The shadow zone is done with the sanguine flat between the fingers.

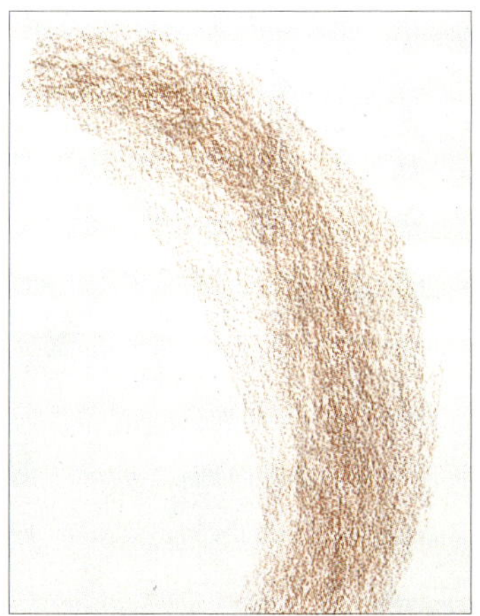

Once the darks have been drawn in sanguine, add new tone values in charcoal and stump them.

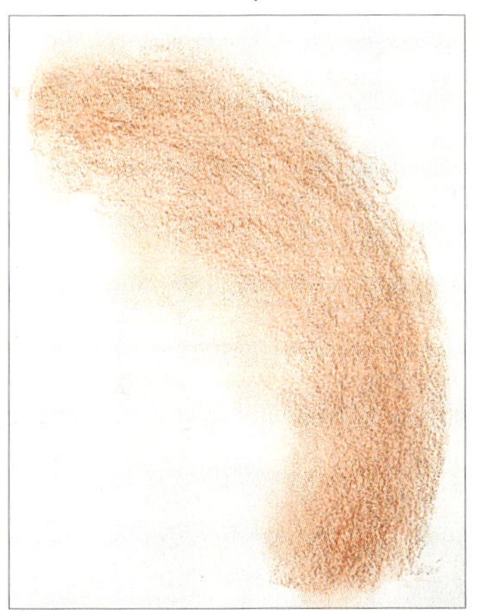

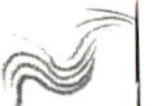

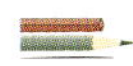

as you set about the shadows. Charcoal allows dense, continuous shadows, suitable for all the shadow on the side. If necessary, go over the paper twice to ensure that the pores are closed. On the other side, the shadow is fainter so press more softly.

The shadow highlight. Gradate the darks by stumping and they will become blended tones. Note where the light zones are so that you leave them almost untouched. In theory, the blending has to be done following the plane of the cylinder and leaving the maximum highlight unspoiled. On the cylinder, both the shadows and the highlights are vertical. Once the shadow forms have been outlined, you can start to work on modeling the gray in the plane direction.

When modeling a cylinder shaped element it is important to remember that the curved surface gives rise to a varied shadow. Pay attention to the zone in which it is lighter and where the contrasts are formed. This lightening can be done with the eraser or a finger.

COMPLEX GEOMETRIC FORMS

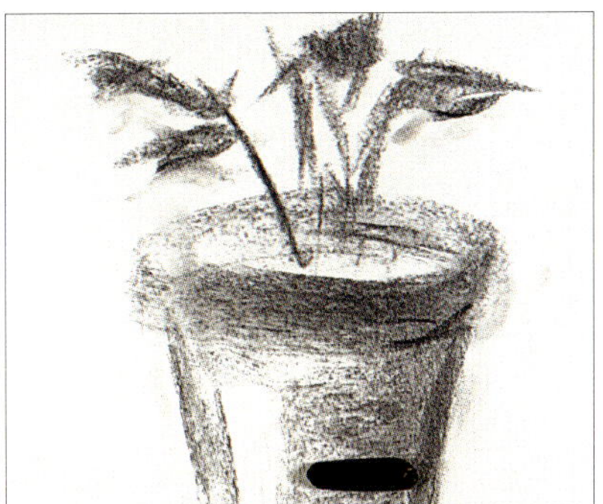

Complex forms, like a flower pot, are outlined in the same way as the cylinder, but narrower at the bottom.

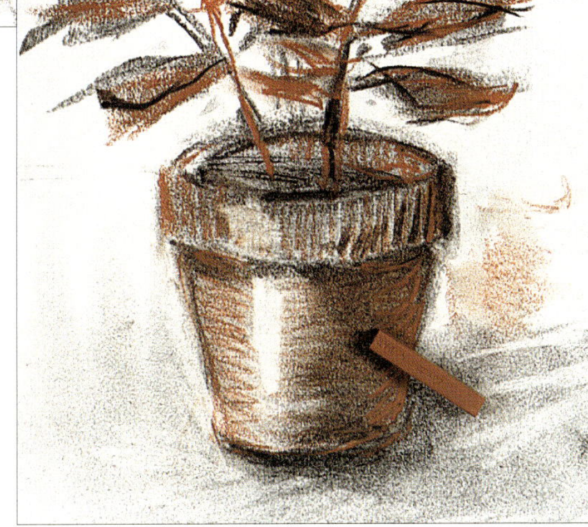

Once the charcoal tone values have been done, use sanguine to distribute the principle tones. The strokes follow the form of the main plane.

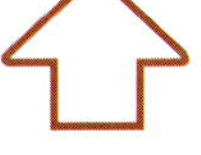

The sphere, seen from this angle, looks like an ellipse. The cylinder is constructed by an ellipse and the vertical plane.

Use the charcoal flat to do the main shadow zones. They are dense and continuous.

Once the shadows have been drawn, blend them so as to soften the contrast with the main highlight.

When the shadow tone values have been realized, open up a highlight on the side plane of the cylinder.

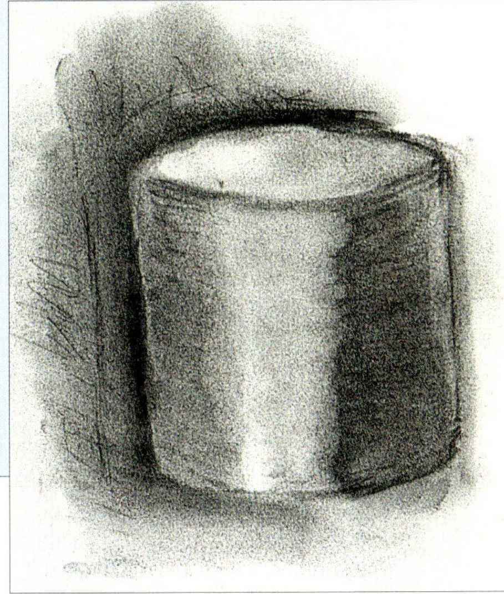

Stump the stroke with your fingers until it is unified with the light zone.

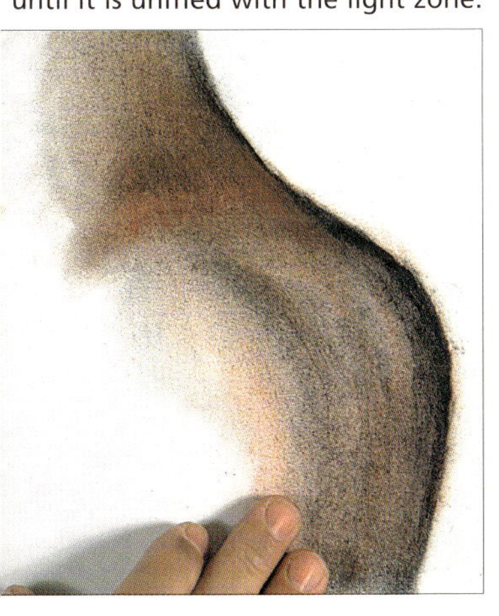

Often various elements have to be combined to model complex forms. In fact, it is not correct to say that one form is more complex than another. They just have to be developed in the right way. For example, to draw a flower pot, you can start from the modeling of a cylinder, adapting the shadows to the new form. A flower pot is only a truncated cone, or a tapered cylinder. The highlights and the shadows are applied as on the cylinder.

Tones are added placing darks around the shadow highlights. After stumping the charcoal tones, use the sanguine to do plastic modeling with the half tones. The sanguine stroke must follow the object plane that has just been worked on.

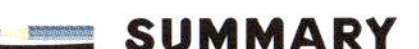

SUMMARY

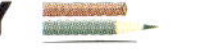

STUDY THE SHADOWS OF THE PLASTER MODEL
The plaster model allows a thorough study of the modeling.

SANGUINE AND CHARCOAL
Sanguine and charcoal complement each other and create new tones.

MODELING GEOMETRIC FORMS
The cube and the cylinder are two forms that require the planes to be studied.

THE SHADOW HIGHLIGHT
The shadow on the cylinder has an intense highlight due to its curve.

COMPLEX GEOMETRIC FORMS
Complex geometric forms are based on simpler shapes.

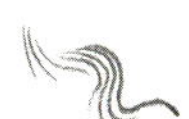

12 # Exercices *Step by step*

MODELING

Modeling is the drawing technique which gives form to the objects by using light and dark tones. The light is studied so that the model is realistically represented.

For this exercise, a female seen from behind has been chosen. The body forms are very suitable for this type of work. You do not need to know how to draw anatomy to practice modeling. This is why a very specific fragment has been chosen.

NECESSARY MATERIAL

Charcoal (1), sanguine (2), paper (3), a stump (4) and an eraser (5).

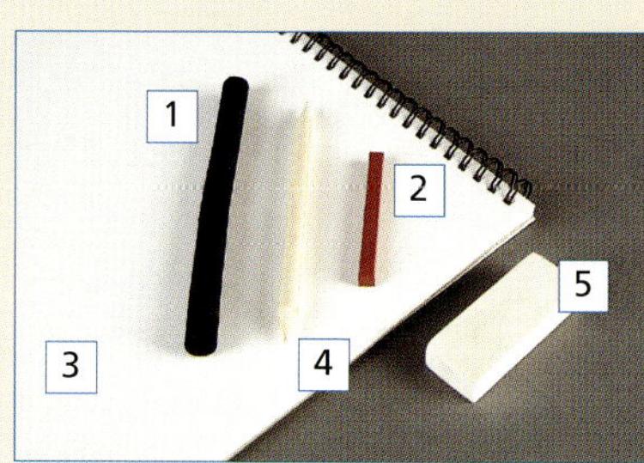

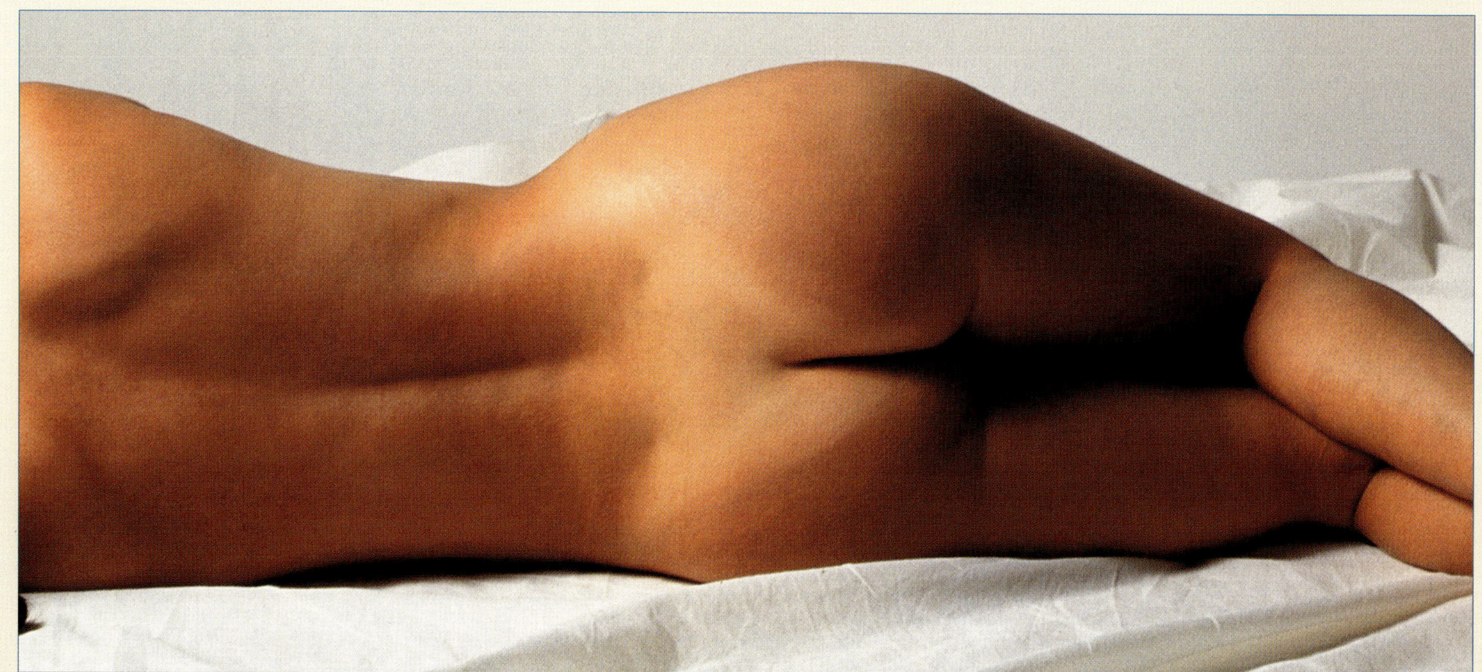

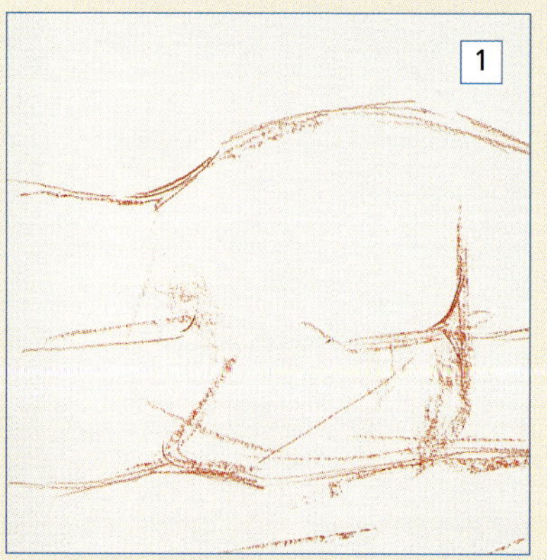

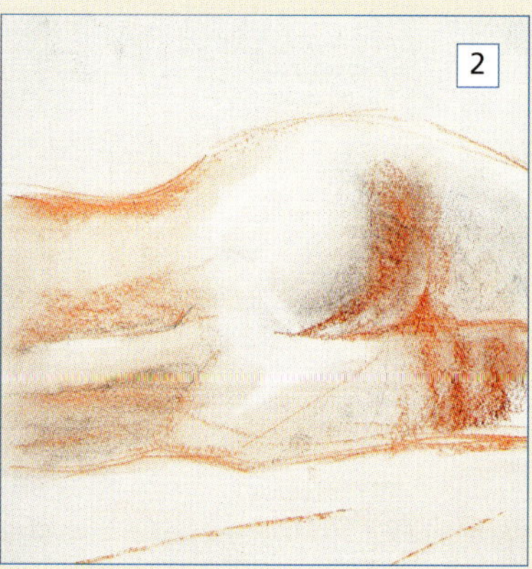

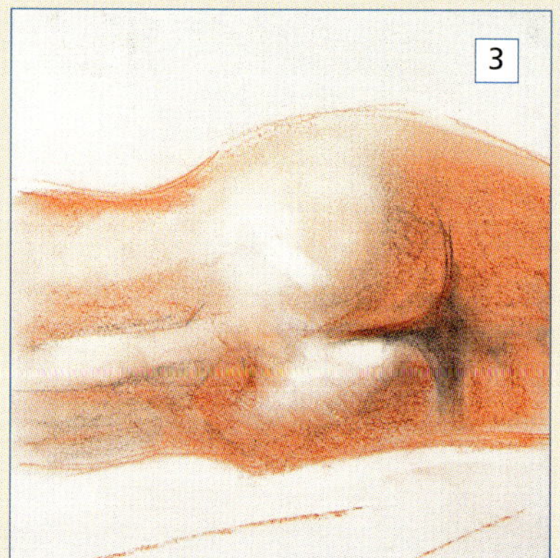

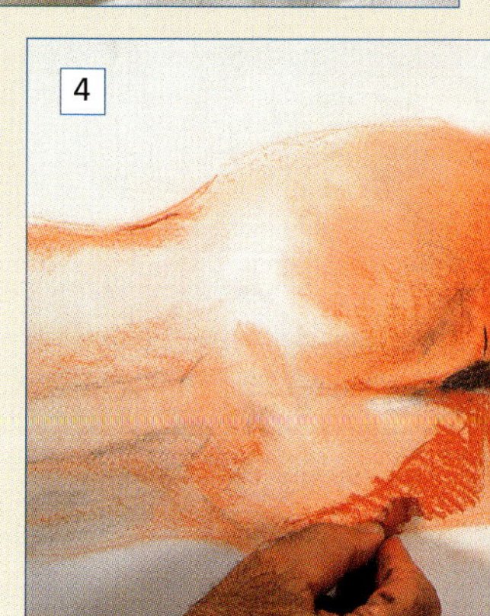

1· THE INITIAL OUTLINE IS DONE ONLY IN SANGUINE, a medium much more definitive than charcoal so do not press too hard on the paper. Any correction would have to be done with the eraser and not the hand or cloth.

THE FORMS CONSTRUCTED ARE STRAIGHTFORWARD but pay special attention to the separation between the lines and the proportions.

2· DO THE FIRST SHADOWS, on the upper side, on the spinal column, under the right buttock and on the left leg, working from the outline.

THE WIDEST SHADOWS ARE DRAWN with the sanguine flat between the fingers. Smudge the paper with your fingers.

3· OPEN UP THE MOST LUMINOUS white spaces with the eraser. The modeling has been started, firstly with shadow tone values and, now, with the highlights.

A female back in sanguine and charcoal

SUMMARY SCHEME

The highlights establish the principle tone values.

The outline is started in sanguine.

The first shadows on the buttocks are done with the sanguine flat.

The first charcoal intervention establishes the hardest contrasts.

The charcoal is applied in curved strokes.

The highlights soften the modeling.

The highlight is constantly redone with the eraser.

USE THE SANGUINE FLAT BETWEEN THE FINGERS to draw the main shadows, not pressing too heavily so that the pore is not closed. Draw with charcoal in the darkest zones.

GENTLY RUB AGAIN WITH YOUR FINGERTIPS each of the zones until the different gray values blend together. On top of this background, do fresh sanguine strokes, especially where the model is leaning.

USE THE ERASER TO OPEN UP a white space on the right buttock and another on the illuminated part of the left buttock.

4· IN STEP 4, the tones are added together, stumped and contrasted continuously. In this close up, you can see how a new dark is done with the sanguine point.

AT THE MOMENT, THE CHARCOAL is reserved for the darkest zones.

5· IN STEP 5, softly blend with your fingers the strokes done in the last step. Apply contrasts on both sides and in the shadow zones on the legs.

ON TOP OF THE PERFECT SANGUINE TONE VALUES, start to draw in charcoal. On the right hip, do a continuous, soft, long stroke. On the darkest leg, do curvy strokes.

ONCE THE CHARCOAL tone values have been done, use the eraser to open up the highlights on the hips again.

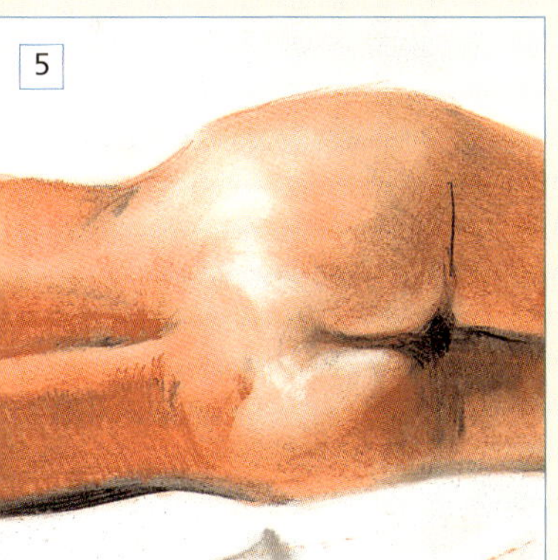

6· IN STEP 6, the forms are modeled with your fingers. In the general zones, softly rub with your index, ring, and middle fingers. The parts that require a more precise shadowing are blended with the thumb. Soften the highlight zone so that the white of the paper is integrated into the gradation.

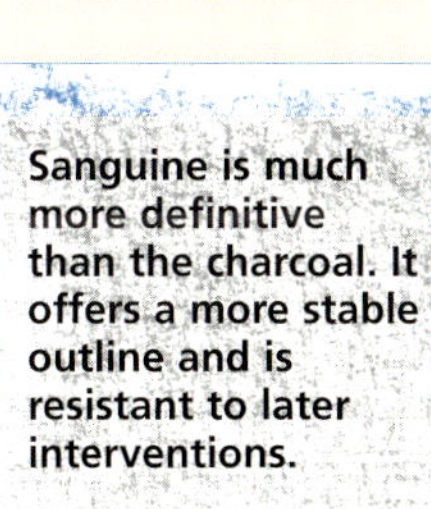

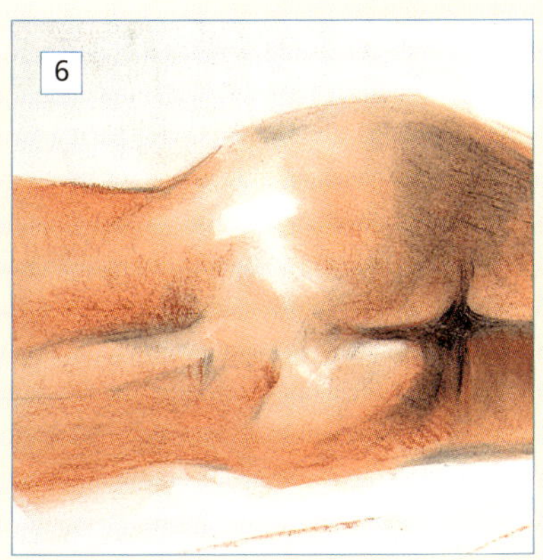

ON THE BACK, DRAW SANGUINE strokes much darker than before.

ON THE DARK PART OF THE BUTTOCK, do a new sanguine intervention and then, immediately, stump the tones below.

7· FINISH THE MODELING by blending the last tones put down on the feminine forms.

FINALLY, DRAW ONCE MORE IN CHARCOAL where the forms overlap. A soft stumping will integrate these dark lines into the work.

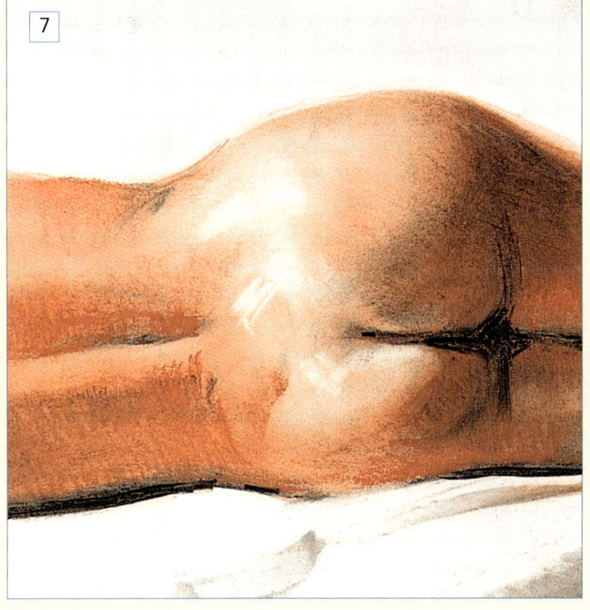

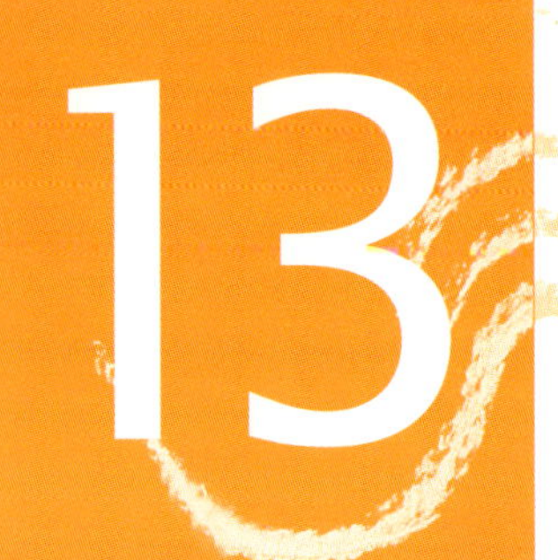

DRAWiNG: VALUE AND PLASTiC RELiEF

In earlier chapters we studied concepts related to shadows, opening up white spaces, highlights and contrasts so it should not be to difficult to deal with valuation and modeling. This chapter is fundamentally about the principle differences between the ways of representing shadows in drawing. As you can see, the objects used for the first practices are simple elements and you will not have to worry about proportions or complicated figures. We will do still lifes to learn about the basic principles of value and modeling.

TWO DIFFERENT CONCEPTS

Value and modeling are mentioned repeatedly in drawing exercises. In fact, the names themselves are sufficiently descriptive, although both can be studied separately.

As an introduction, we will say that valuation consists of establishing on the paper different intensities of gray to represent the light and shadow tones. Modeling is the blending of these tone values. Valuation does not necessarily imply a modeling process. However, modeling does imply valuation. These differences can be seen in the following exercises.

VALUATION IN THE DIFFERENT HIGHLIGHTS

Valuation is nothing more than an ordered tone gradation. To progress with this subject, we will do an exercise to study the different highlights on a simple object. Any drawing must be sufficiently defined so that the distinct tones can be developed on the relevant planes. This teapot is based on a very elemental scheme: an almost spherical base is sufficient to define it neatly. As you can see, in the initial drawing the shadows are not included. Two lines are enough to describe the spherical plane of the object and to indicate the form of the valuation in the drawing.

Once the preliminary sketch has been done, you can work on the first shadows, as shown in the second picture on the last page. In fact, these shadows only show a valuation process just beginning and take in the situation of the principle highlights. In this step, do a stroke on the side of the shadow and insinuate the object form, a process very useful for rapidly visualizing the plane form, in this case almost spherical.

SIMULTANEOUS CONTRASTS WITH ONE TONE

Simultaneous contrasts enable you to establish tone values between a dark tone and a light one. If you now draw a darker strip on the shadow side, a new gray tone value will be established. However, at the same time, the tone value of the white paper will be changed. Observe in the first picture above these lines the tones of the paper on both sides of the darks. On the left, the widest side, the white does not seem so luminous as on the right. However, the whites on both sides of the valuation still have not been touched. This optical effect is due to the simultaneous contrasts. The dark tones make light ones seem brighter.

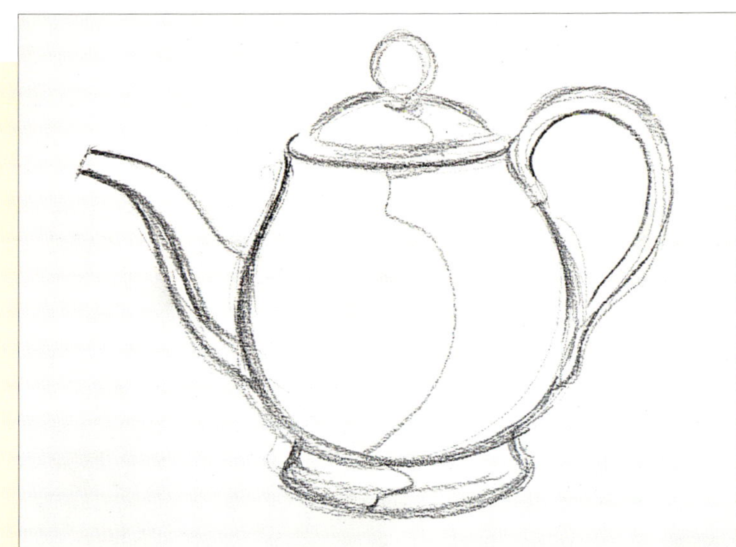

The preliminary sketch must be very simple. It must indicate the form that the tone value process will follow.

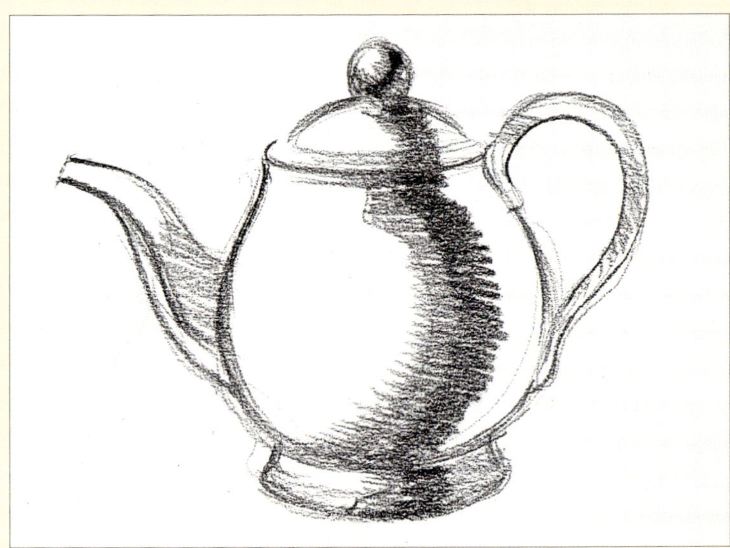

The first tone allows the lighter tones to be established for they can be compared to the tone of the paper.

VOLUME AND HALF TONES

On the darkest side of the shadow, draw in a very dark black tone. Its intensity depends on how the other tones have been drawn. If they are not very differentthe densest shadows will have to be compensated.

Tone values must always be added gradually so that the volumes can be

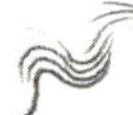

Some of the most important parts of a drawing are the shadows. Two fundamental processes come into play to obtain them: valuation and modeling. Valuation does not necessarily imply modeling. However, modeling does require tone values.

13

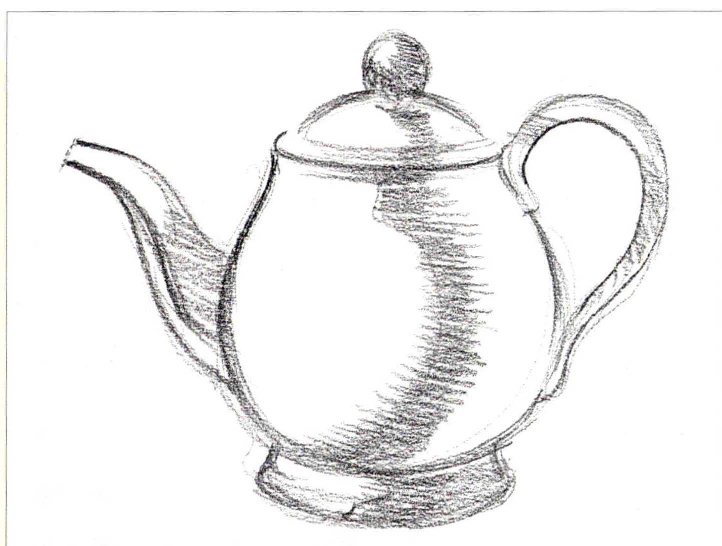

The valuation strokes must follow the plane of the object perfectly. Here the shadings follow the form of the teapot.

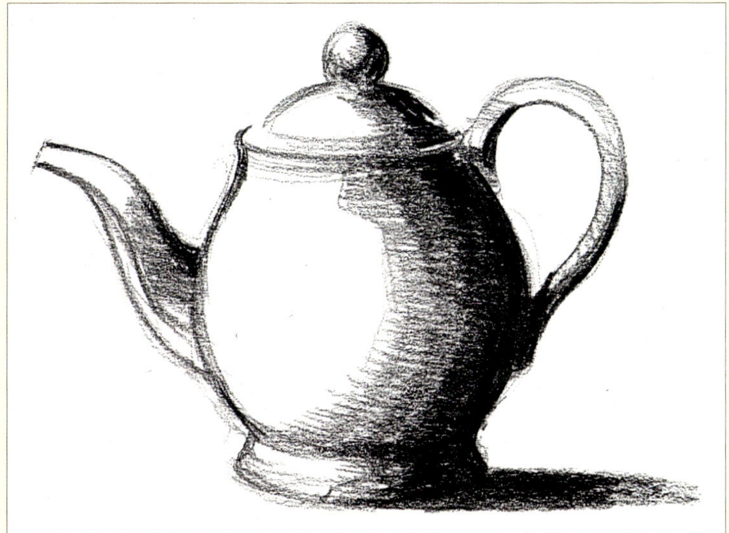

In this tone value work, the limits of each part of the shadow are clearly defined.

insinuated. That is the way shadows are in reality, too. As you can see in this example, the volume effect has been achieved starting from the medium tone in the center. This is the equilibrium point between the lightest and the darkest tone.

TONE VALUES AND MODELING

The valuation carried out in the last exercise did not involve modeling. It only consisted of obtaining a gradually superimposed tone scale, but not blending. When we speak about modeling we are referring to the way of getting volume effects using tone values. Indeed, it is possible to go even further and to eliminate the visual distinction between tone scales. There are several methods of doing a soft gradation between tones, the first of which is blending.

BLENDINGS

To do a tone blending it is not necessary to establish a tone scale as in the last exercise. The gradation can be done using the drawing mediums on the paper. What is necessary is that the material be soft enough to be manipulated by your fingers. The objects which will be drawn have spherical forms and therefore offer all the possibilities of modeling and tone valuation.

First of all, do a good outline of the figure to which the tone values and modeling will be applied. This preliminary sketch has to be simple, without sharp divisions inside.

Here the first step in the valuation process is quite different from the last example. There is no defined dividing line between light and shadow, although both are perfectly located. The blending between the two tones is produced in the modeling. The illuminated zone has sufficient charcoal for it to be spread with the fingers and to give form to the object by stumping. Rub the charcoal towards the white part of the paper. The dark tone will be stumped and will become a more luminous tone. This simple process establishes tone values through modeling.

We now have a good base on which to do any alteration to the gray gradation texture. We can use an eras-

A MODELING MASTERPIECE

Federico Barocci (1528-1612) did this study **'Moses and the Serpent'**, which is kept in the Louvre Museum, Paris. He used the majority of modeling processes normally practiced in drawing. Firstly, you can admire the tone gradation which gives a great volume effect. The dark tones blended into the paper make the light zones stand out more. Besides taking advantage of the light color of the paper, the modeling has been stressed by using white chalk for plastic relief. Take a look at the simultaneous contrasts. The highlights are intensified when surrounded by dense darks.

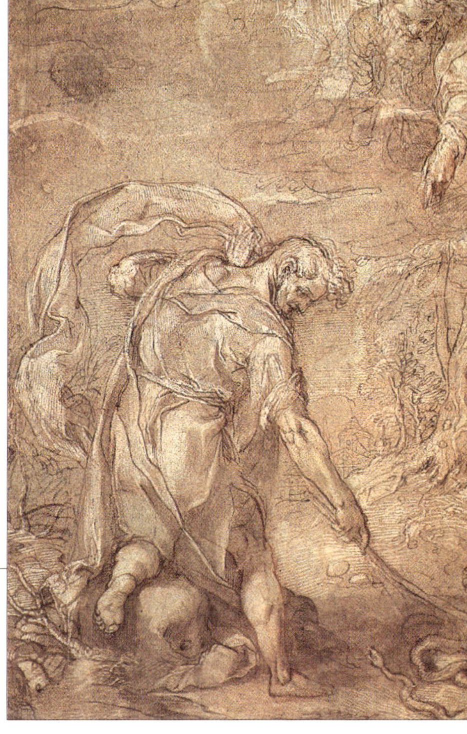

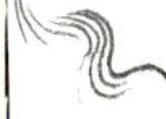

13 DRAWING: VALUE AND PLASTIC RELIEF

er to open up little white spaces and give texture to the form. As we saw in the last chapter, the eraser is a vital tool for doing all types of corrections on the shaded paper. In this process the eraser must be very clean so that it does not stain the paper by dragging charcoal.

The shadow edge. The shadow in modeling does not have a defined limit: it extends softly over the object, blending into the white of the paper. This does not mean that the shadow area has to be very wide. Even a narrow strip can be blended into a wide illuminated zone.

The darks must be worked on gradually in the modeling process, just like when you blend them over the light tones. The contrasts are increased progressively and are blended into the background, which is already quite dark. Soften the gradation in the illuminated zone with your fingers. On the newly darkened area, contrast fresh tones even though the texture of the object is based on direct strokes.

VALUATION AND MODELING IN SERIES OF LINES

Up until now we have studied modeling by blending the dark tones with the fingers. It is a possibility that requires not very adhesive mediums, like charcoal and sanguine.

Another option is to model the object by using hatching or cross-strokes and can be practiced with all the mediums, regardless of their hardness or softness. It even works with inks. Hatching is a series of lines very close together in part of a drawing. The closer together they are, the darker the gray will be as less white comes through.

FROM THE DRAWING TO VOLUME

A plain drawing line has no volume. However, it is vital for the subsequent modeling. Time dedicated to outlining and schematizing the model will help you at a later stage. It is not wasted time.

In the first step of valuation of the object, it is important that the shadow lines define the form. For example, in the bottle on the right, the main shadow is developed with lines not drawn randomly. The curved bottom of the bottle is a good start for doing the shadow. To do this shadow zone, do two series of lines, one downwards and the other slightly upwards. At the bottleneck, the shading becomes slightly tighter: the line is shorter but its form is similar.

CONTRASTS AND VOLUME

With the hatching process it is not difficult to do a tone gradation. Take the bottle background as a reference and start to do strong, tight, dark hatching in the zone to be gradated, as can be seen in the first picture on the next page. The tone reduction process could have been started before but we preferred to cover all this zone to establish a strong contrast with respect to the principle element in the composition.

Use the same recourse on the bottle to do the round part of the neck, although here the tone is much more luminous than in the background and so the pressure must be less and the lines softer.

THE FORM OUTLINE IN MODELING

The modeling process starts from valuation carried out principally with the fingers. Although they are ideal tools, the fingers do not have the same precision as the tips of the drawing mediums. Do not worry if you smudge finished zones. This is part of drawing. As the contrasts are increased and they are blended over the background, the details done in earlier steps tend to blend and disappear. They can be recovered with new strokes, or, in the case of the highlights, with the eraser.

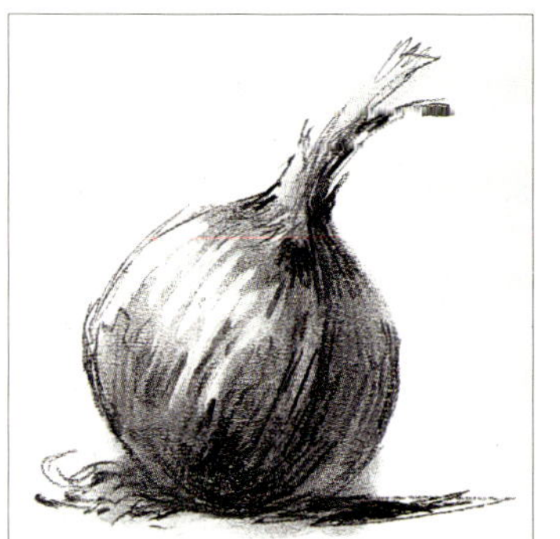

When modeling, the original highlights may be lost but they can be restored by reopening them with the eraser.

The lines follow the object plane. As they cross over, darks and lights can be obtained. The darkest tones are obtained by highly intense criss-crossing.

MODELING

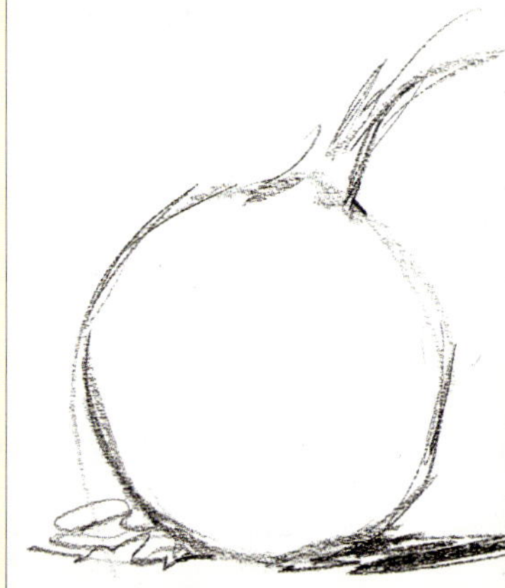

Once again, just like in the tone value exercise, it is important to do a good outline. Here it is the figure which is going to receive tone values and modeling.

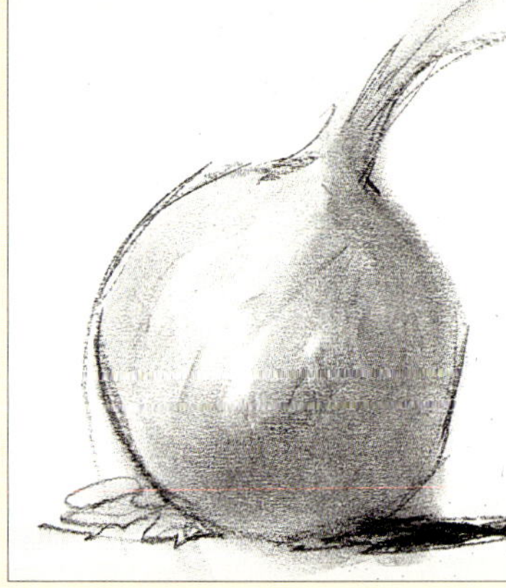

Use your finger to rub the zone shaded in charcoal towards the white of the paper. The dark tone is stumped and becomes much more luminous.

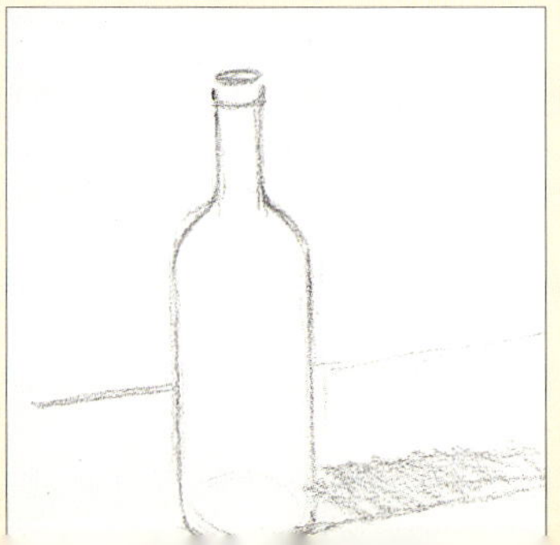

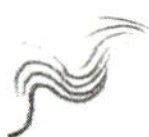

The clarity of the bottle is made to stand out by the lines behind it. Afterwards, we can return our attention to the background. As the work progresses, the strokes become less intense, an effect that is visible in the second picture and appears like a tone gradation. If the reduced pressure is accompanied by the lines being further apart, the tone gradation is more stressed.

BY BLENDING

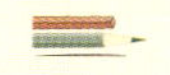

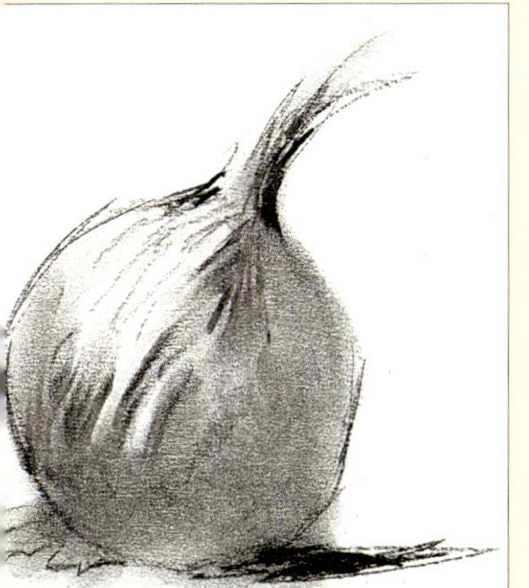

When modeling, white spaces can be opened up which, due to their great luminosity, contrast with the other tones.

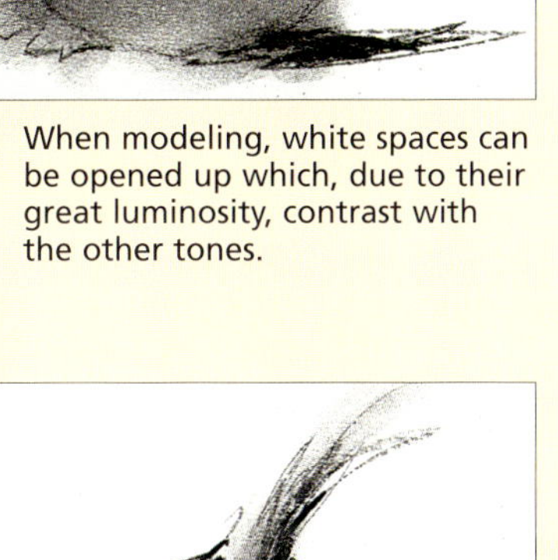

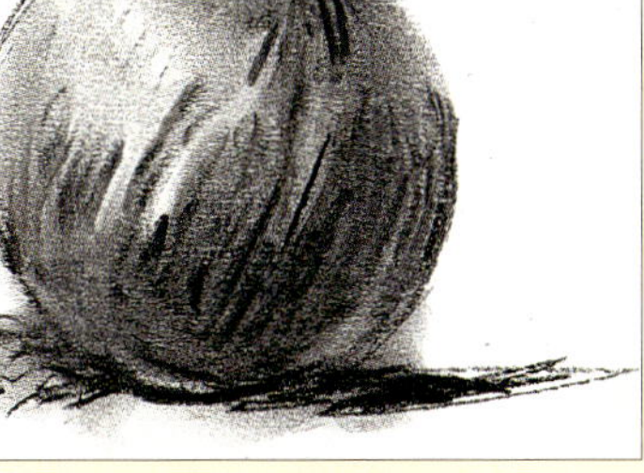

Intensify the contrasts but continue to blend them with the lower tones. New, direct interventions make the modeling more realistic.

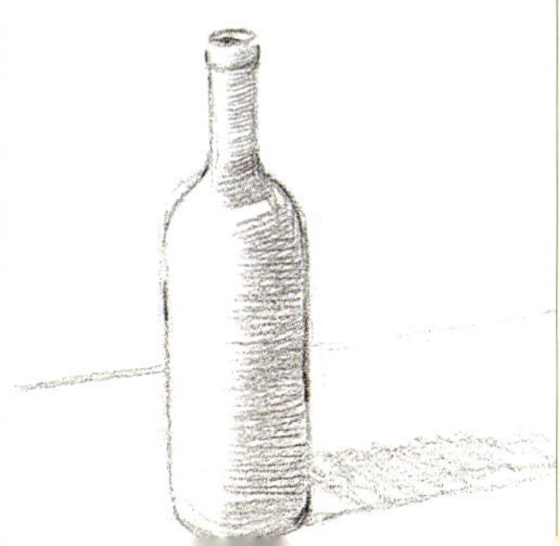

THE FINAL CONTRASTS

What really give volume to the objects are the contrasts, without which the drawing would appear flat and unrealistic.

Once the principle contrasts have been drawn, do crossed strokes to intensify their tone. On top of this, do new darks, by drawing dense lines, which are similar to the first shadows. This process is carried out both on the bottle and in the background, as you can see in the third picture on this page. In this last step it is very important that the darks are in the right place in the composition and that the highlights are correctly reserved.

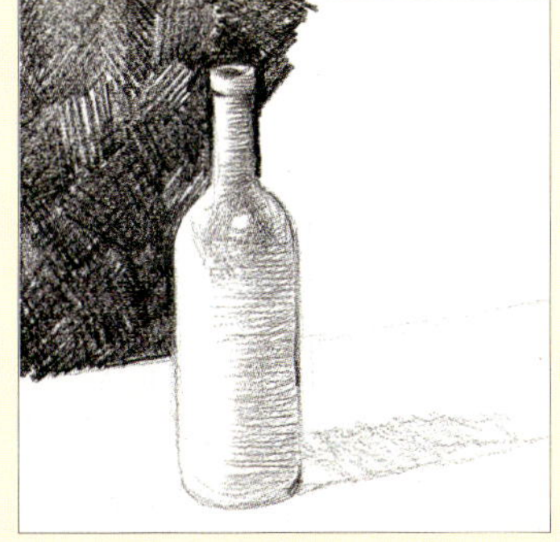

This modeling procedure is based on tone values and hatching. To start it is essential that the drawing indicates the form.

The maximum contrasts help to establish the medium tones and the brightest whites. On the bottle, the hatching outlines the highlight.

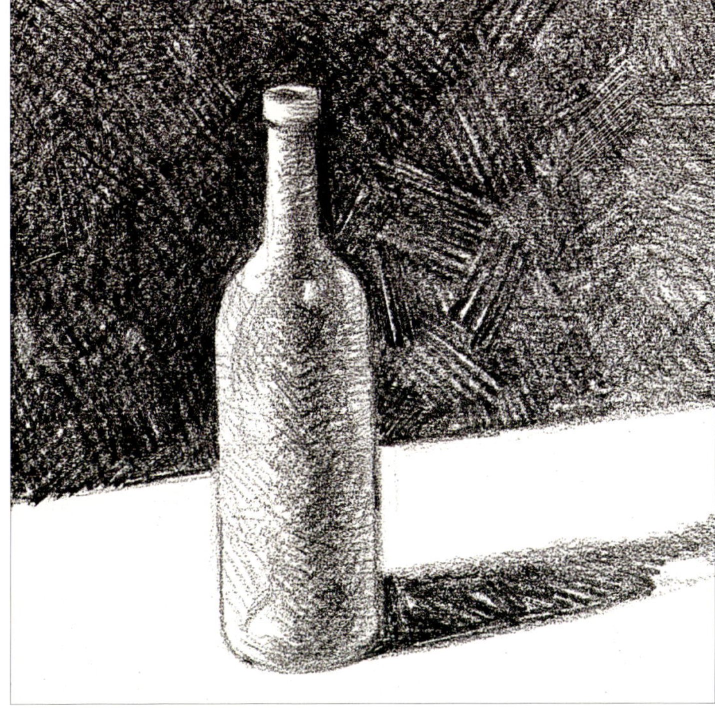

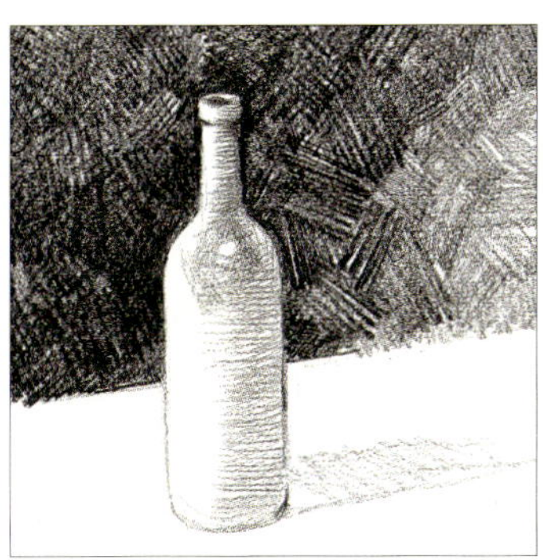

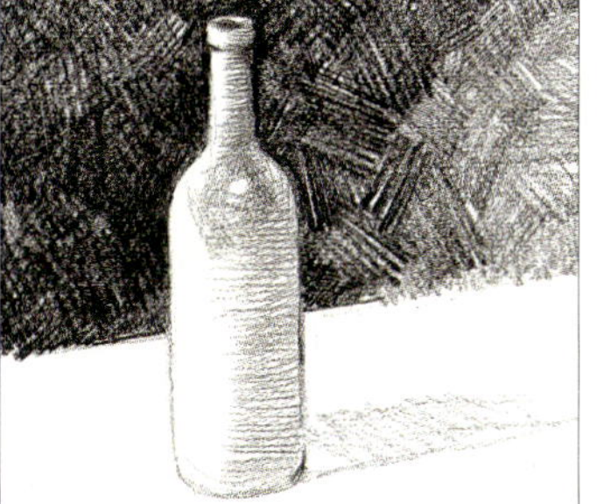

The gray gradation is produced by a modeling effect without tone blending. The gradation is based on the density of the lines.

In the background the grays are modeled according to the number of lines. On the bottle the modeling depends on how close together the lines are.

SUMMARY

VALUATION
Valuation is the tone progression depending on the light that falls on the model. With valuation the tones are established in a gradated order but they do not have to blend.

MODELING
Modeling is part of valuation. Although there is no evident difference between one tone and another, they blend together through different drawing processes.

CONTRAST IN MODELING
The contrasts must be applied progressively to balance the grays. Bear in mind the role and impact of the simultaneous contrasts.

BLENDING
Blending is one of the methods to obtain a soft gradation between tones.

THE FORM AND MODELING
Depending on whether the modeling is done with the fingers or with the lines, the character of the form will vary.

13 Exercices *Step by step*

The best theme for practicing modeling and valuation is a still life because the artist will not be conditioned by the rigidity and complexity of other models. However, this composition is a little more complicated than ones done up until now.

In this example we will be able to study how the elements interact through the contrasts in the light planes and shadow planes. The exercise will be done through modeling with lines, and not by blending tones. Blending will be insinuated by gradually reducing the number of lines, going from the shadows to the light zone.

Before starting to work on the different light and shadow zones, it is vital to do a good outline and to compose the still life with simple lines. Do not press too hard so that you can draw over them to get the definitive form. The outline is straightforward, even for the beginner, because the fruit and the eggplants have elemental forms.

NECESSARY MATERIAL

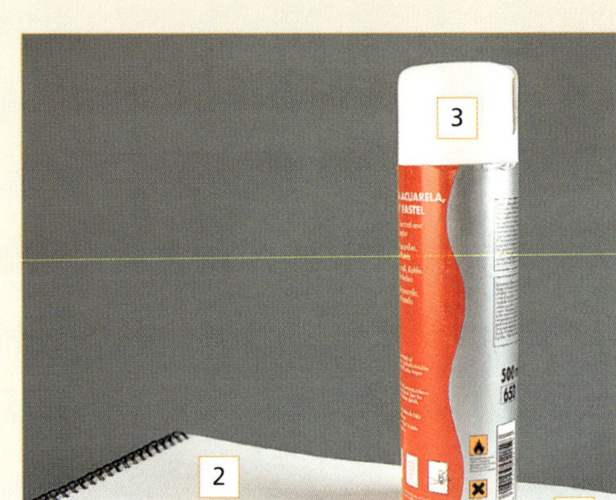

Drawing paper (1), sanguine (2), and spray fixative (3).

1· **BEFORE STARTING TO WORK** on the different light and shadow zones, it is vital to do a good outline and to compose the still life with simple lines. Do not press too hard so that you can draw over them to get the definitive form. The outline is straightforward, even for the beginner, because the fruit and the eggplants have elemental forms.

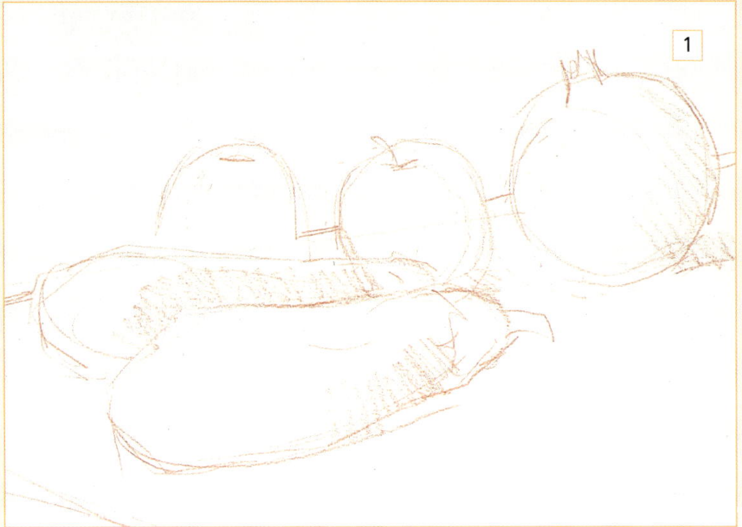

ONCE THE OUTLINES have been correctly placed, start to work on the first shadow zones. The first tone is soft. Just do a few strokes that timidly mark the principle light zones.

ONCE THE OUTLINE IS COMPLETE, you can start to work further on the shadow zone. Here the strokes are more intense than before, but do not press too hard or cross lines yet. The function of these strokes is to perfectly separate the light planes from the shadow planes.

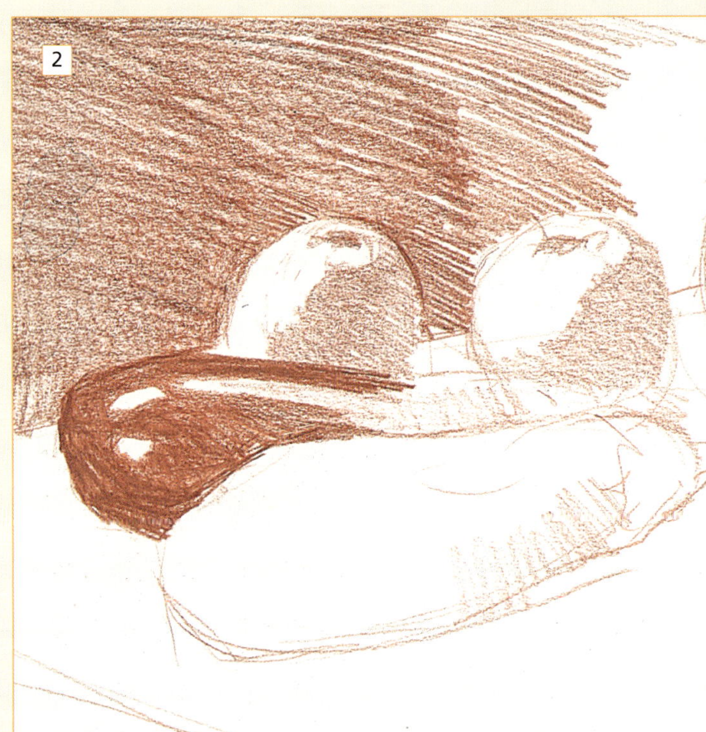

2· **TO DO THE FIRST GRAY TONE VALUES,** do a denser and darker gray in the background. The highlights of the fruits are clearly outlined and defined.

The highlights of a still life

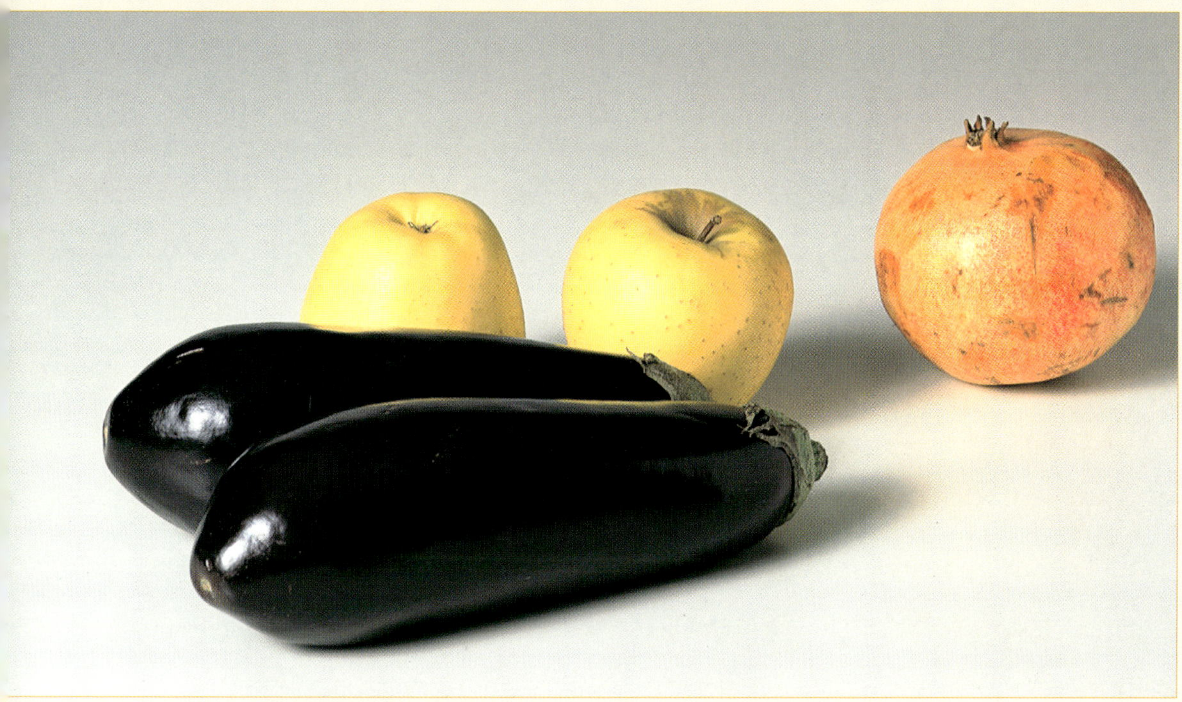

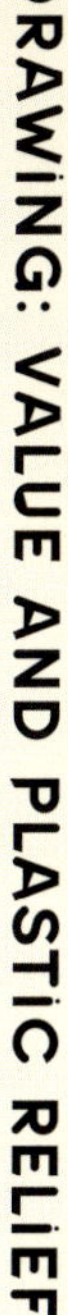

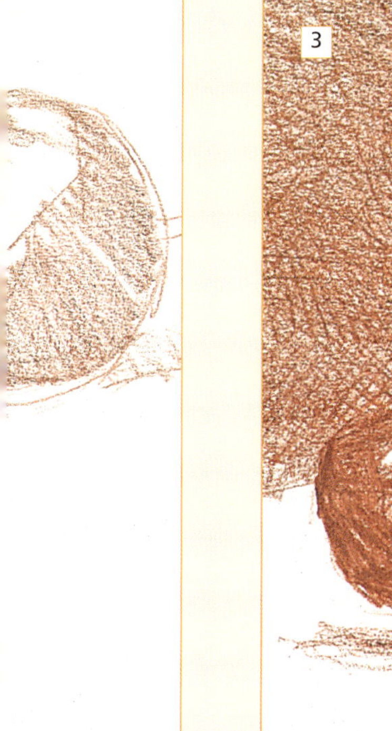

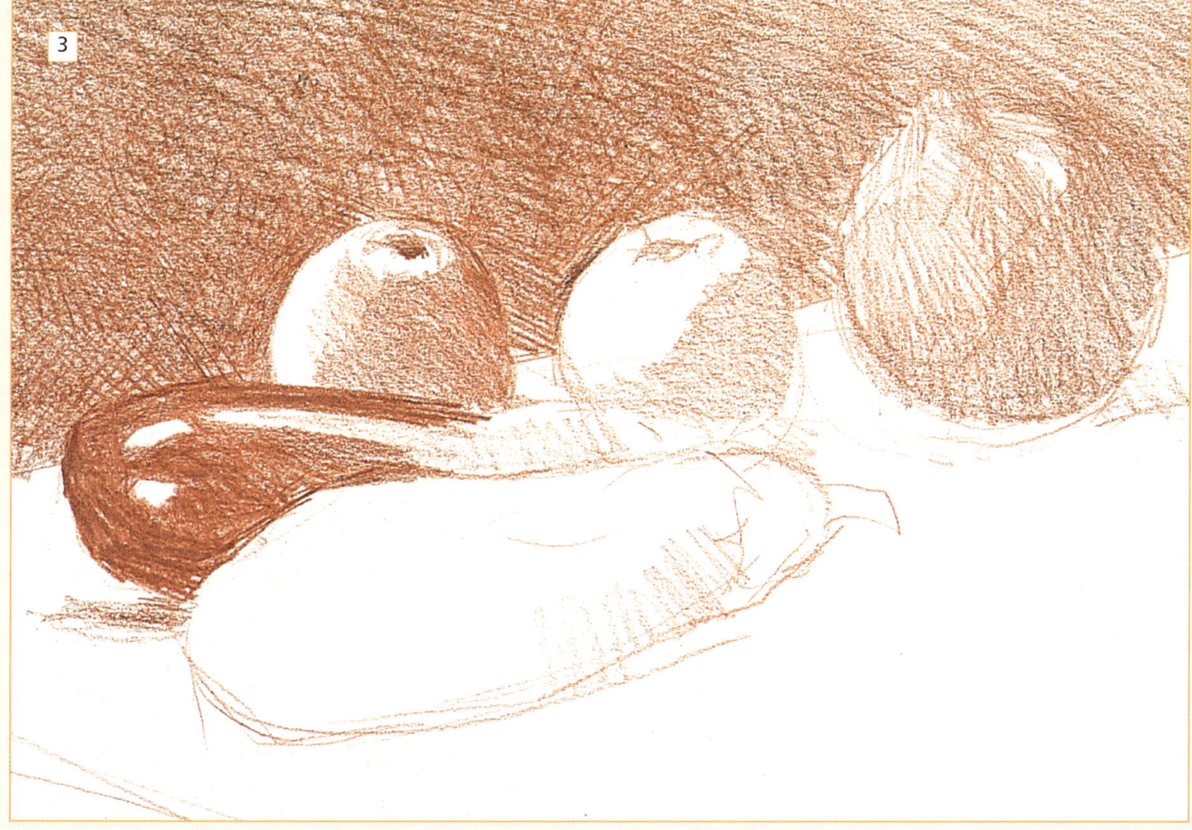

3· ESTABLISH THE DIFFERENT TONE VALUES of the still life. The maximum darks will be on the eggplants. Start drawing on the eggplant in the midground. The highlights on the eggplant are outlined by the darks.

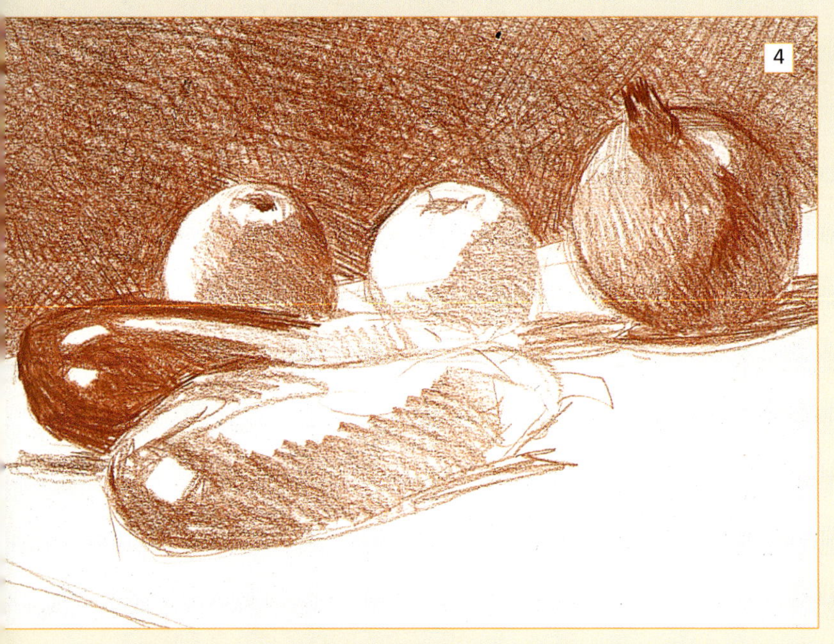

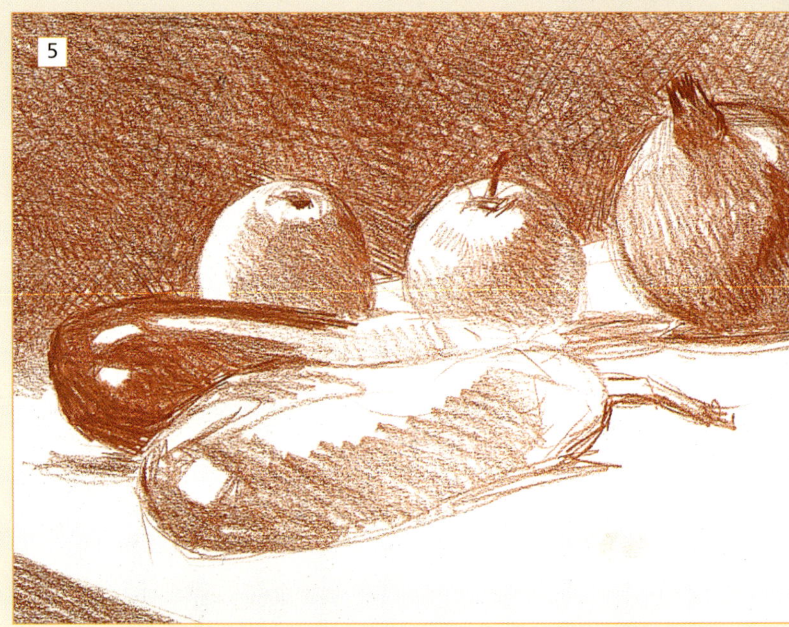

4· IN THIS DRAWING WE ARE NOT GOING TO USE STUMPING. All the grays and darks will be done with hatching in sanguine.

USE THE POINT OF THE SANGUINE crayon to darken the background. The process is straightforward: criss-cross the lines. The more lines there are, and the closer together they are, the darker the grays will be.

TRY TO GET THE SAME effect on the fruits, although less intense.

5· IN THIS STEP, CONTINUE WITH THE DARKENING of the background. It need not be a complex task. Just control the number of lines and reduce the intensity to model the grays.

ON THE POMEGRANATE ON THE RIGHT, try to model the shadow by developing the point of maximum darkness. This stroke, firm and dark, turns into shading which fades away in the illuminated zones.

ON THE EGGPLANT IN THE FOREGROUND, outline the shadows in the same way as you did on the other one.

INTENSIFY THE SANGUINE on the shadow side of the apple in the center of the composition. The stroke is toned down until it is completely integrated into the light zone.

6· THE LARGE WHITE SPACE OF THE TABLECLOTH is cut in the bottom right corner by the dark which indicates the table edge and the change of plane. This detail is highly important to balance the grays in all the drawing.

JUST AS AT THE BEGINNING OF THE VALUATION process the first eggplant was darkened, now do the same with the second one.

IT IS VERY IMPORTANT TO OUTLINE the highlights in the exact point on all the elements in the still life. This will ensure that the light focus and quality will be perfectly defined.

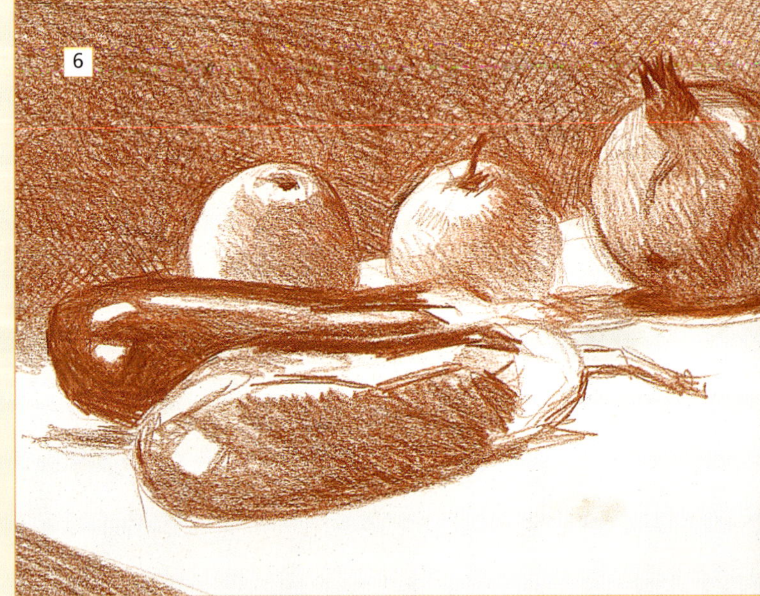

You must always bear in mind the nearness of the tones and how they contrast with each other.

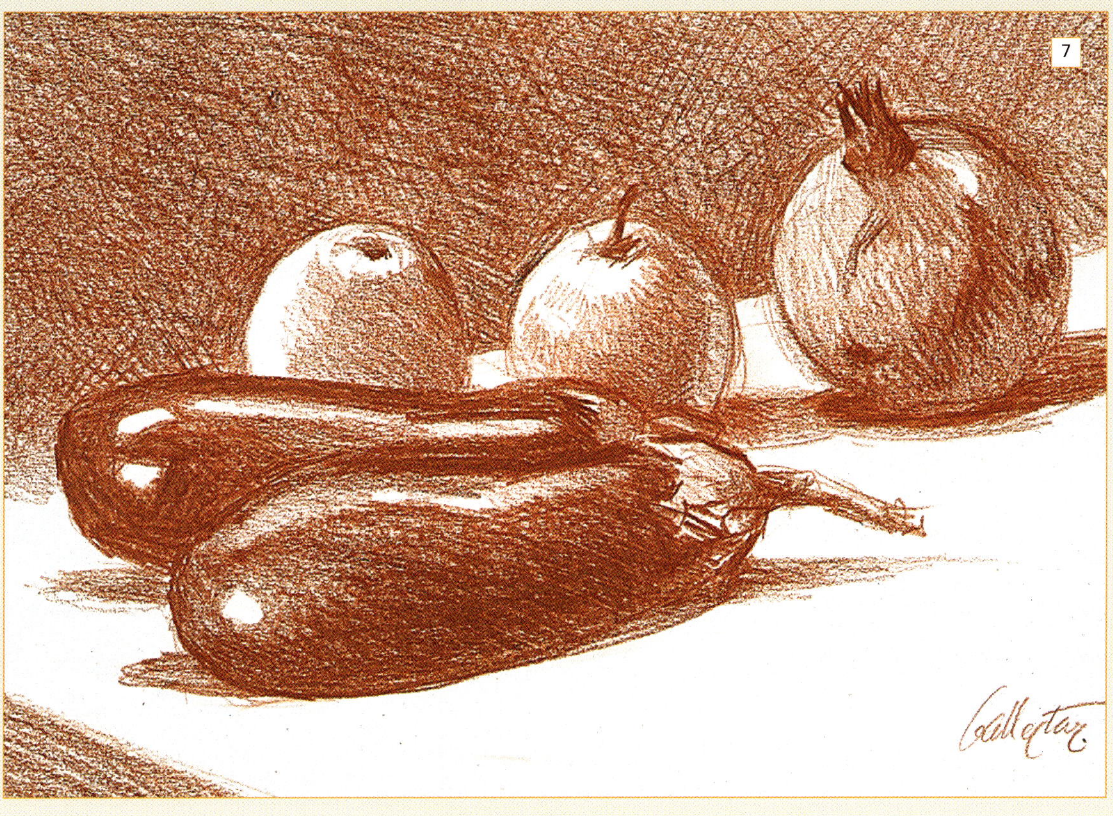

7. THE GENERAL INCREASE in the contrasts is achieved by doing more intense lines. However, you must not lose sight of the effect produced in the different planes by the type of hatching used. For example, if you look at the apple in the middle, you can see how the lines follow its spherical form.

THIS WILL FINISH THE EXERCISE. The main part of the work has been the tone valuation and the modeling of each of the light and shadow zones.

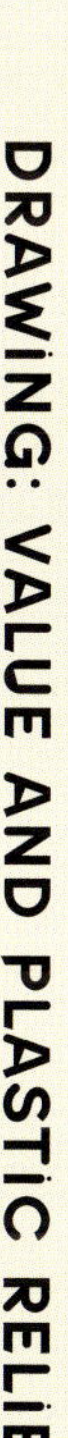

SUMMARY SCHEME

The drawing outline allows you to mark the first difference between the light zone and the shadow zone.

The background is darkened by hatching that becomes less intense and so produces a gradation.

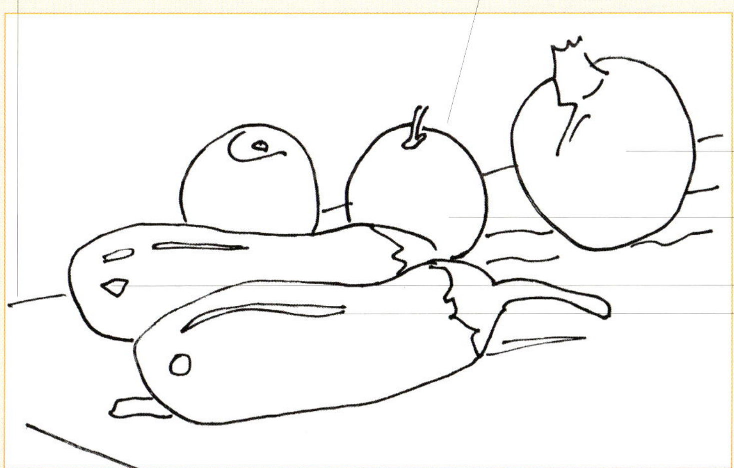

The strokes on the apple and on the pomegranate are done by following their planes.

Do the densest darks on the eggplants, leaving the most luminous tones outlined.

DRAWING IN COLORED CHALKS

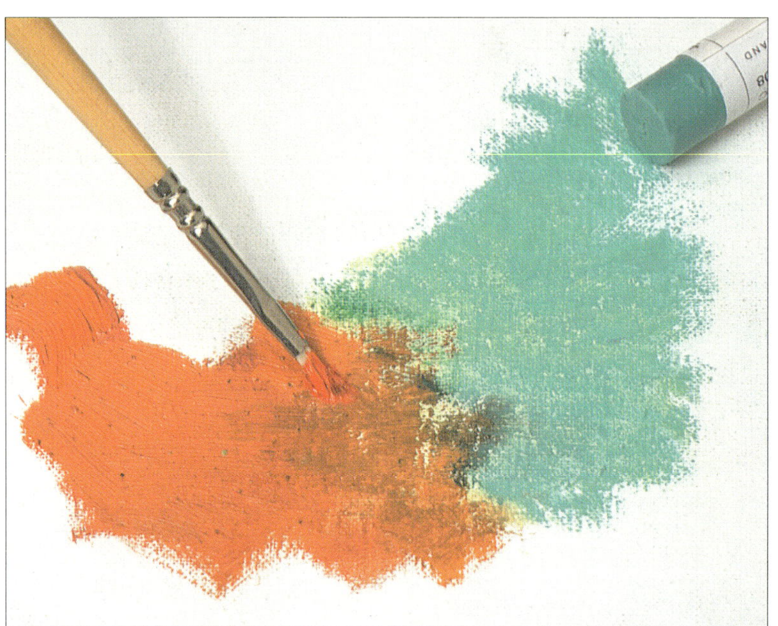

Colored chalks are a drawing medium manufactured from synthetic calcium carbonate mixed with sizing and pigments. They are sold in stick form and can produce a variety of strokes and a wide range of possibilities. Their appearance is similar to pastel, although they are harder. In this chapter we are going to study drawing with colored chalks and some of the many possibilities offered by this medium. If the artist is familiar with charcoal, sanguine or oiled charcoal, chalks will not be too difficult to get used to. The chalks make a unique contribution to the drawing. Not only the tones obtained from each stick must be considered, but also the contrasts established between the colors, and, of course, the possibility to take advantage of the paper color.

CHALK CRAYONS

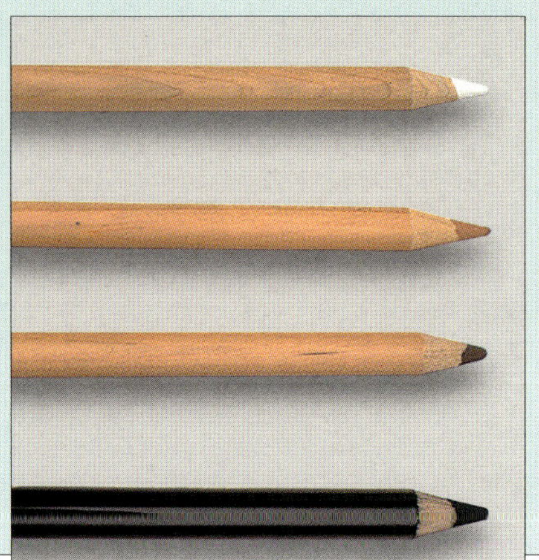

Chalks can be bought in crayon form as well as in sticks. Chalk crayons, like charcoal crayons allow a much more linear and defined work than the sticks. They are fragile and should not be sharpened with a pencil sharpener because the tip breaks easily. A knife gives better results.

CHALK STROKES

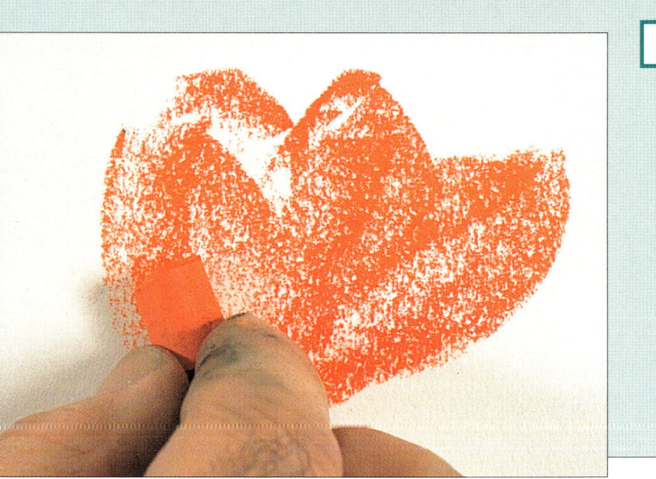

The feel of the chalk strokes on the paper is quite similar to charcoal or sanguine, although it is somewhat harder.

TONES AND CONTRASTS

Chalks produce very varied color ranges. However, in drawing the classic range are the earth tones. Nowadays an extensive chromatic range is manufactured, but in Ancient times basically only white chalk and a few earth colors, like sepia or sanguine, were available. Any color chosen will enable you to draw. In fact, it is quite common for an artist to use colored chalks to prepare a painting.

THREE EARTH TONES

Although the artist can work with any of the chalk colors available in Fine Arts shops, the basic and most widely used ones are three earth tones. They offer extensive ranges and when applied to white paper give one of the most interesting effects in drawing: plastic modeling phenomena in white chalk.

CHALK COLOR RANGES

We have just seen the most common chalk presentations, but now we are going to focus our attention on how to get the most out of the chromatic ranges.These very complete ranges enable the artist to incorporate rich

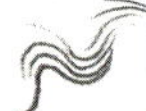

Drawing should not be limited to the gray and black tones possible with the normal mediums like charcoal and graphite. Beside these, another medium which can link drawing to painting must be considered: colored chalks.

14

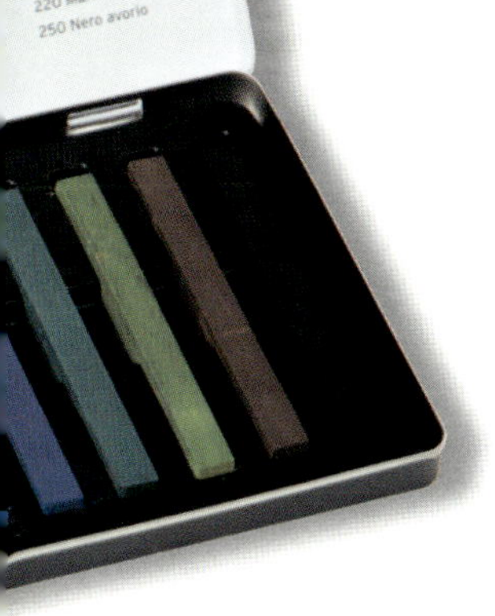

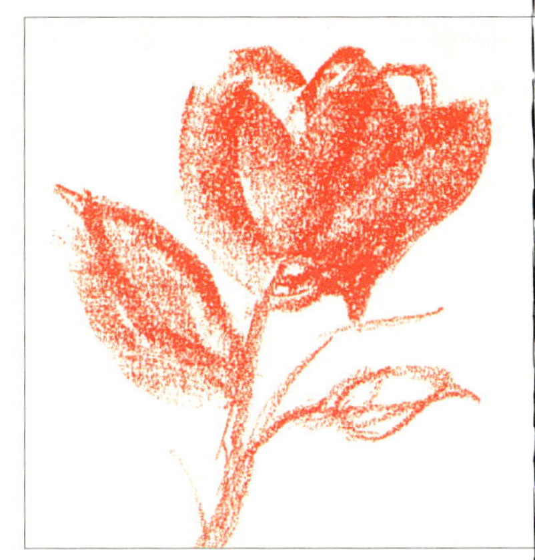

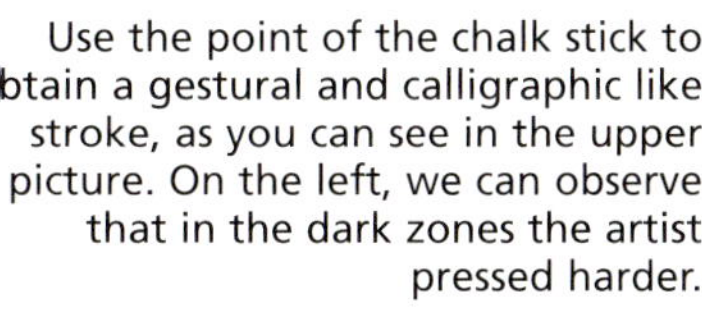

Use the point of the chalk stick to obtain a gestural and calligraphic like stroke, as you can see in the upper picture. On the left, we can observe that in the dark zones the artist pressed harder.

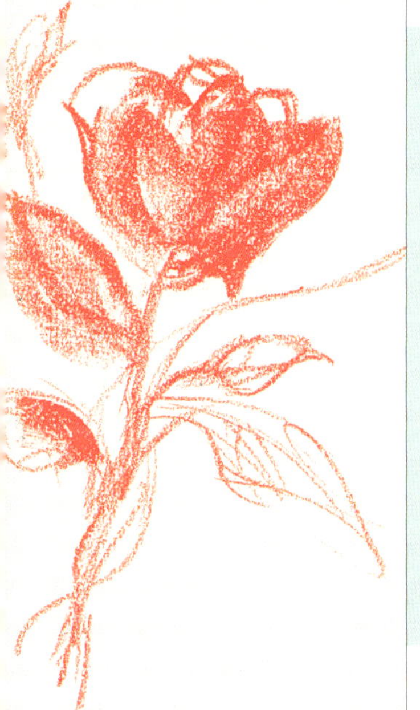

CONTRASTS POSSIBLE WITH CHALKS

While normally the common drawing mediums are worked on white paper, color chalks can draw on varied tinted papers, just like pastels. The most intense contrasts come from luminous colors on dark papers.

contrasts into their work. However, do not forget that we are working with a drawing procedure and that the stumping possibilities of chalk are less than those of soft pastels.

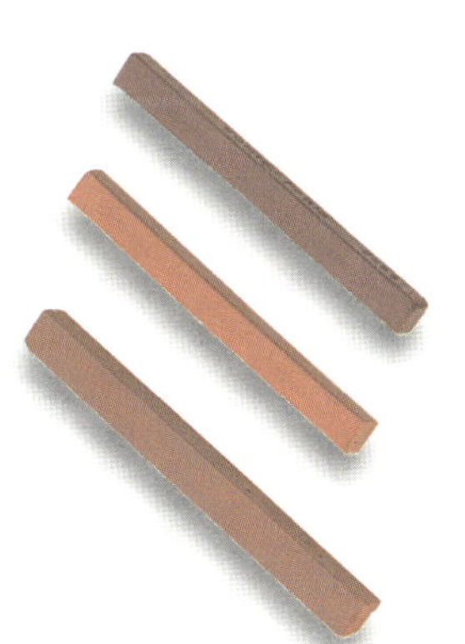

STARTING WITH ONE COLOR

To start practicing with chalks it is best to do one-color exercises, or at the most start with a limited range. This will enable the learner to see how this procedure compares to others, such as charcoal and sanguine. Drawing with just one chalk color gives results similar to those obtained with charcoal, oiled charcoal or pencil. All types of tone values and modelings are possible, using both shading and lines. If you pay attention it will not be difficult to follow these exercises.

PRACTICING THE STROKE

The strokes done in chalk, as with the other drawing mediums, are richly expressive and offer many possibilities. In the following exercise you will observe that the strokes can often be simple lines or shadings that are suddenly cut or interrupted by turning the wrist. In this exercise we are going to paint a flower. Pay attention to the strokes in each of the zones. The images illustrate the process.
The chalk stick held flat is useful for doing these first strokes, both curved and straight, and you can quickly cover each of the flower's petals. You can softly turn the stick and use it to paint lengthwise.
The stroke obtained depends on the position of the stick. Broadwise rubbing allows you to quickly cover wide areas, and using its point gives highly exact and defined lines. Drawing with the point reflects the gestures of the wrist and fingers. In this example, the stem and the leaf on the right have been drawn in this way.
Using the tip of the stick means that the stroke is controlled by the fingers. In contrast, the stroke of the flat stick offers different tone intensities depending on how you draw and the paper grain.

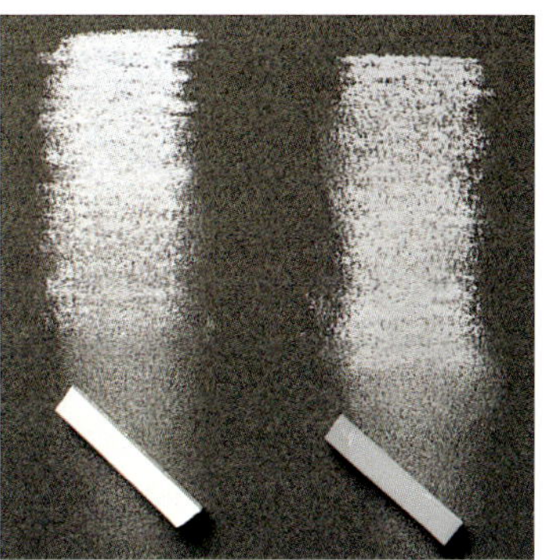

In this picture the results of white chalk on tinted paper are shown.

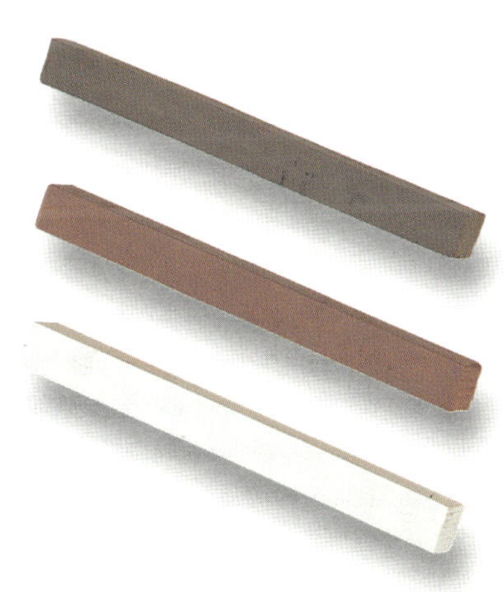

14 DRAWING IN COLORED CHALKS

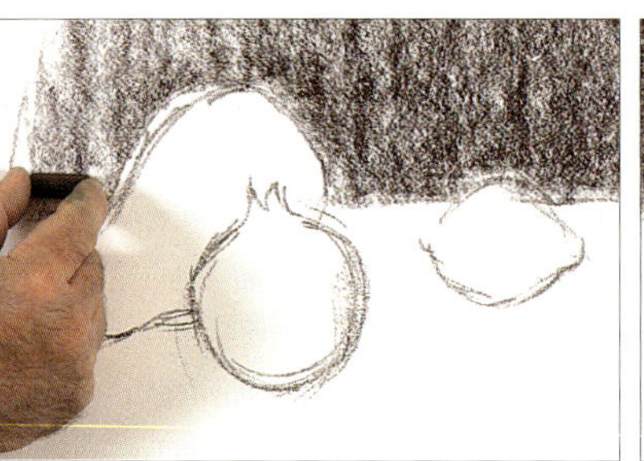

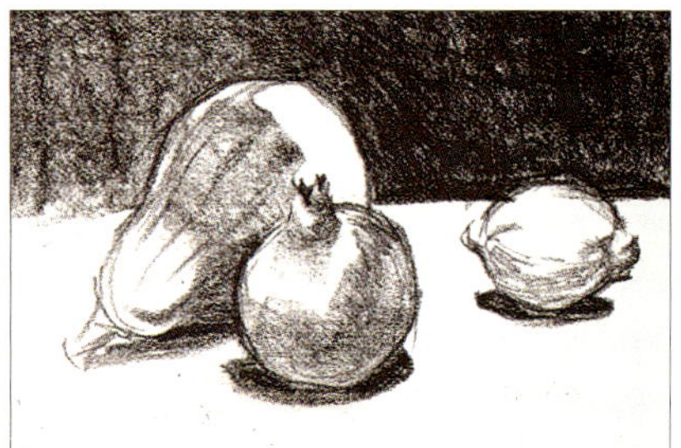

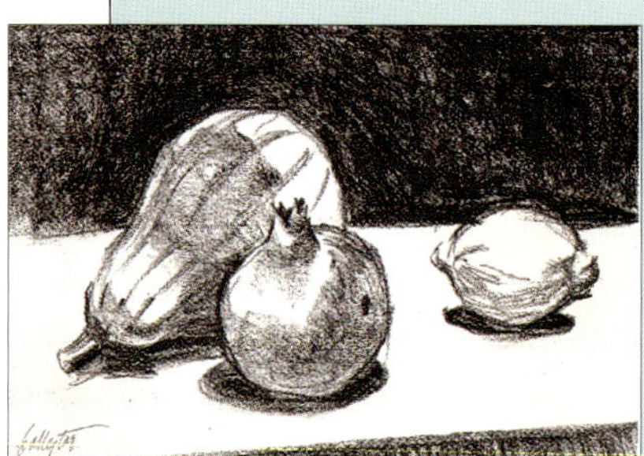

The background is painted holding the stick flat. Increase the intensity where you want more tone contrast.

To do the pumpkin texture you must combine flat strokes with point strokes, playing with the pressure on the stick.

The drawing is finished by doing interventions with the point of the stick to obtain exact outlines and contrasts.

THE IMPORTANCE OF TONE WITH CHALKS

The last exercise was very simple. Now we propose something more complicated, but we continue working in monochrome. Although the drawing mediums can be similar, each procedure has a different feel on the paper and, therefore, it is important that the learner becomes familiar with all of them and is aware of the technical possibilities. In this still life exercise, we are going to deepen our knowledge about the possibilities of just one chalk color. Pay special attention to the way the simple forms help to understand the more complicated ones. As we have already seen in practice, any face of the chalk can be used to paint. Paint the background with vertical movements, holding the stick flat. If you do not press too hard, the pore will not be totally covered. In contrast, high pressure will give intense darks. Do this to obtain the darks on the right.

ONE COLOR SHADINGS AND INTERESTING EFFECTS

Many different effects can be obtained from the same stroke. In this part of the exercise we will also use the stick flat but the application will be different to the background. In the second picture, you can see how the stroke is slightly curved, outlining the form of the drawing. In some parts of the drawing the grain continues to show; in other parts it does not. Use a flat stroke to draw the inside of the pumpkin. Here the pressure is minimal so that the pore remains open. On top of this stroke, use the point to draw the furrows.
To darken a zone that has already been shaded, you will have to insist with the chalk. The darkness is limited by the intensity of the color being used. In the background, redraw the outlines of the still life forms, increasing the contrast especially on the left, where the tones were faint. To finish this exercise, use the point of the stick to do some shading in the lower part of the composition.

MORE COLORFUL

One of the differences between drawing with chalks and other drawing procedures is that the former is much more colorful.

WORKING WITH COLORED CHALKS

We are going to do some flowers with a complete range of colors. The basic lines of the structure are always the first to be drawn. Simply and synthetically, they form the outline, which will later aid the elaboration. In chalk work, these lines are not definitive. The work is done step by step, securing each phase of the drawing. Within the preliminary sketch, fit in the flower forms.

The first colors. Once the drawing structure is on the paper, you can work on much more precise forms and then eliminate the construction lines. Depending on the way the drawing progresses, they can either be rubbed out or covered by new colors for chalks are opaque. Once this is finished, it will be beneficial to fix the drawing so that it does not get dirtied by the hand or the wrong chalk color.
On top of the definitive scheme, draw the first colors. It does not matter if they are dark or light because due to their opacity chalks permit a degree of superimposition. It is fundamental to take into consideration the color of the paper and the possible tone reserves. In this example, the first colors are put down with the stick flat between the fingers. The background color is integrated as if it were just another color.

Handling the stroke. The chalks can be blended together or applied with different drawing styles. Both recourses must be well controlled from the beginning of the shading process. The blended zones can have new strokes laid over them.

Black can be used to develop an extensive tone range, although when it is blended with other colors the stroke presence is lost.

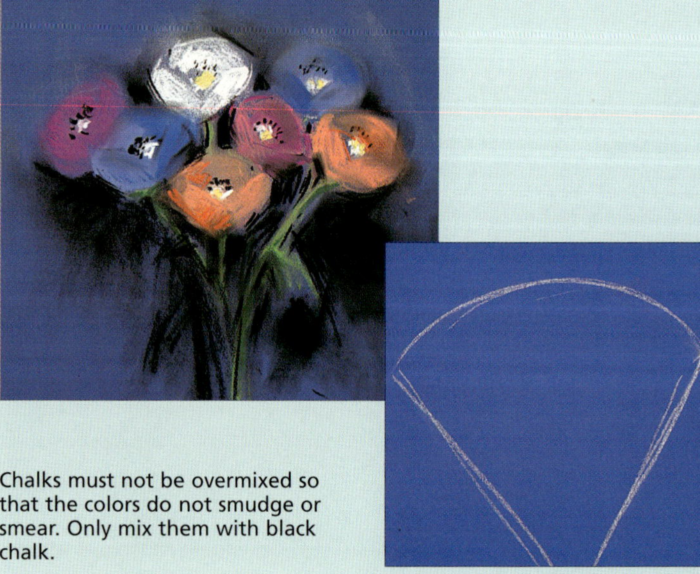

Chalks must not be overmixed so that the colors do not smudge or smear. Only mix them with black chalk.

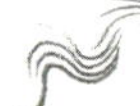

Hold the stick flat between the fingers to paint around the clouds without shading them. The lower part is done schematically.

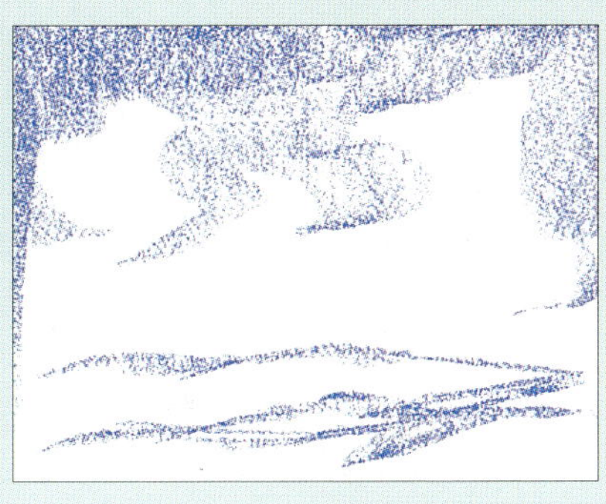

Where you must do a uniform tone, draw with a flat stroke, hardly pressing on the paper.

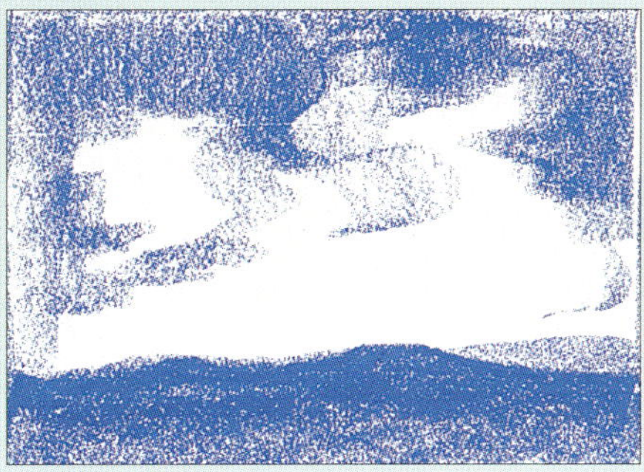

The strokes for the final details are very meticulous. This is necessary when doing the mountain and tree outlines in the foreground.

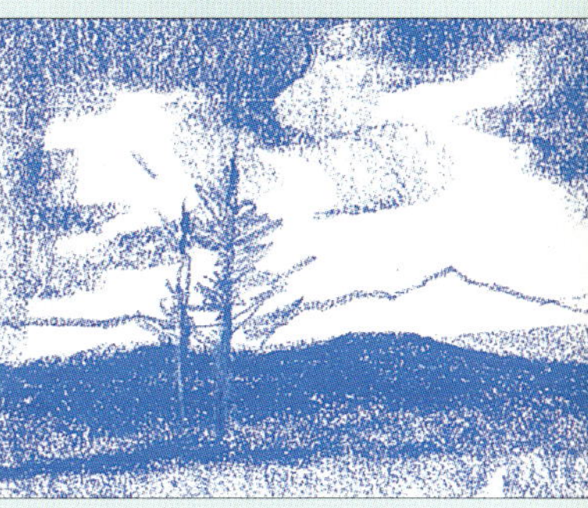

COLORED STROKES

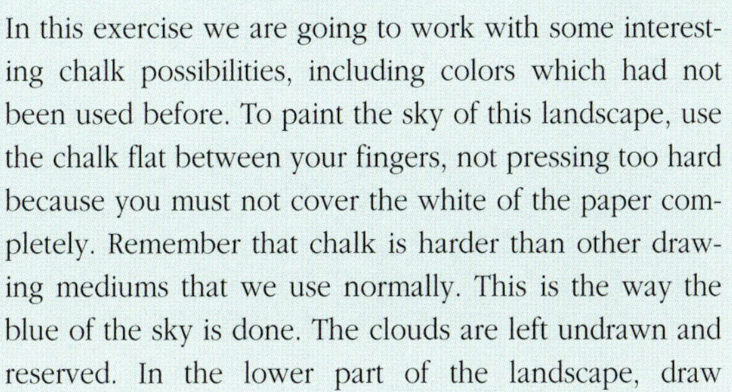

In this exercise we are going to work with some interesting chalk possibilities, including colors which had not been used before. To paint the sky of this landscape, use the chalk flat between your fingers, not pressing too hard because you must not cover the white of the paper completely. Remember that chalk is harder than other drawing mediums that we use normally. This is the way the blue of the sky is done. The clouds are left undrawn and reserved. In the lower part of the landscape, draw lengthwise with the stick flat between the fingers to do a rapid but firm preliminary sketch.

Once this sketch is done, you can go on to do firmer lines. The chalk outline is distinct to the charcoal one in that colors, too, can come into play at this early stage, and not with just tonal differences. This phase is done with the stick flat, painting broadwise. As you have already done the landscape scheme, you can now work on the contrasts.

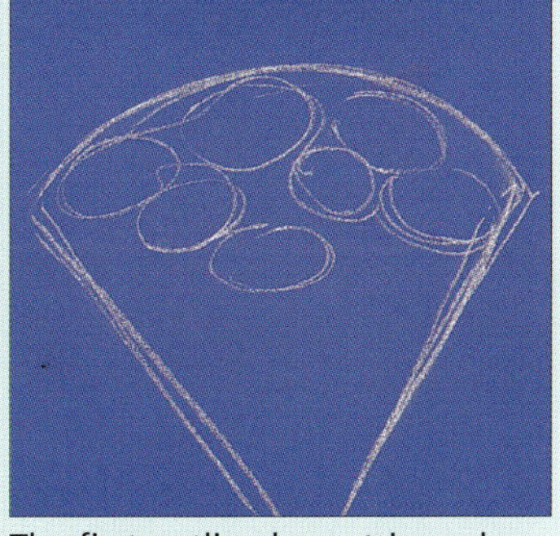

The first outline has a triangular form. It will later contain more complex elements.

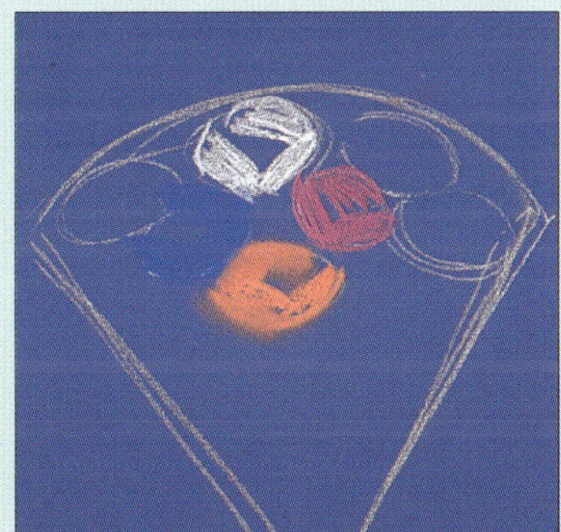

After doing the preliminary outline, complete the forms that must be included inside.

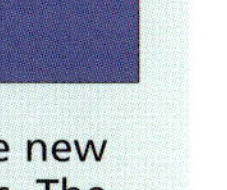

On top of this, superimpose new lines to define the contrasts. The color of the paper must be considered as just another color.

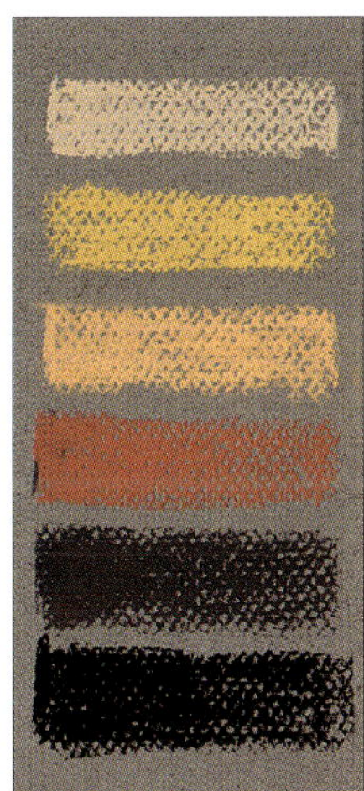

Besides the earth tone range, other colors can be used in chalks, for example, harmonious cold colors (blues, greens, greeny yellows and violets).

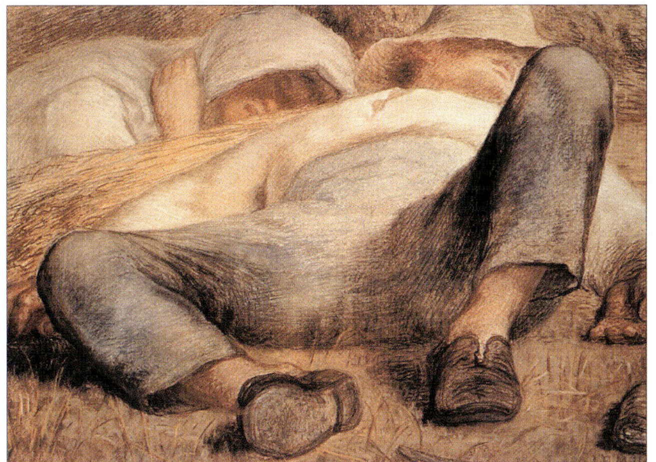

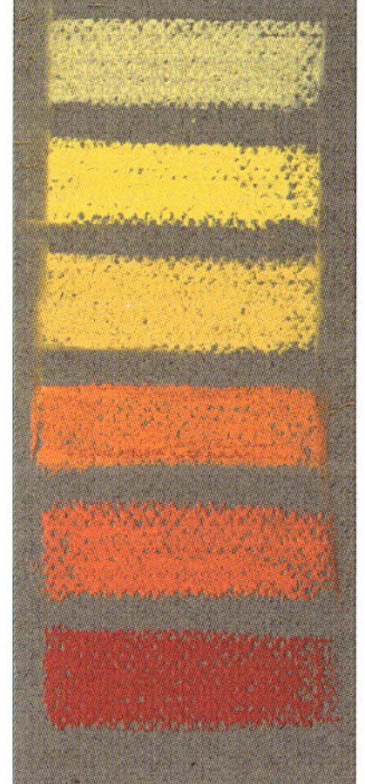

Additionally, as in any pictorial medium, warm color ranges can also be used (reds, yellows and oranges).

MASTERLY USE OF CHALKS

The world of the countryside and the humble folk who live there was a favorite theme of **Jean-François Millet (1814-1875)**. One illustration of his skill is the piece **'The Siesta'**, kept in the Philadelphia Museum of Art, Pennsylvania, USA. To do this drawing, colored chalks have been used masterfully. The artist did not play with color superimposition, rather he did the opposite. He seems to have aimed at isolating some white zones of the paper with dark tones, without ever covering the pore of the paper.

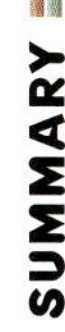

SUMMARY

CHALKS AS A DRAWING MEDIUM
Chalks allow all sorts of strokes to be developed, just like charcoal and the other dry mediums.

DIFFERENCES WITH OTHER MEDIUMS
Chalks offer wide color ranges and can be painted on tinted papers.

THE COLOR PROCESS
Drawing with chalks is somewhat similar to painting in pastel, although it is less expressive pictorially.

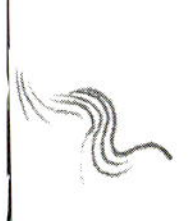

14 Exercices *Step by step*

When draw with colored chalks the color of the paper acts as just another color, becoming integrated into the range. The following exercise is a landscape done with two very different but complementary colors.

The exercise will be done on cardboard, a texture very different to paper. The color of the support will form part of the tone range of the drawing.

NECESSARY MATERIALS

Two chalk colors (1), gray cardboard (2) and a cloth (3).

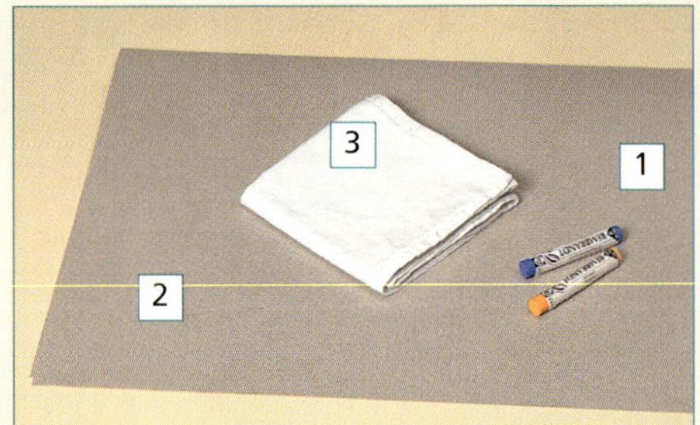

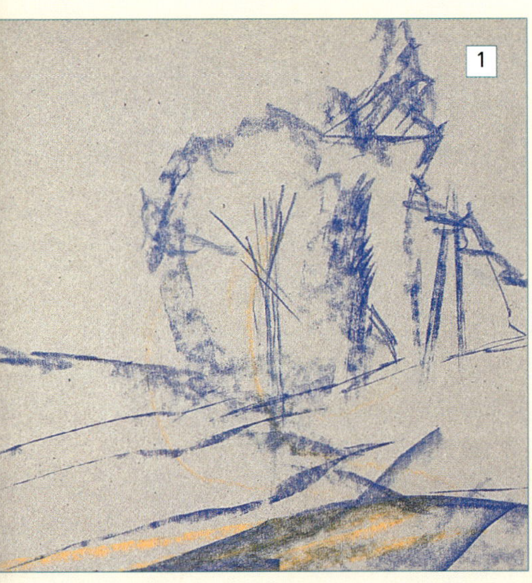

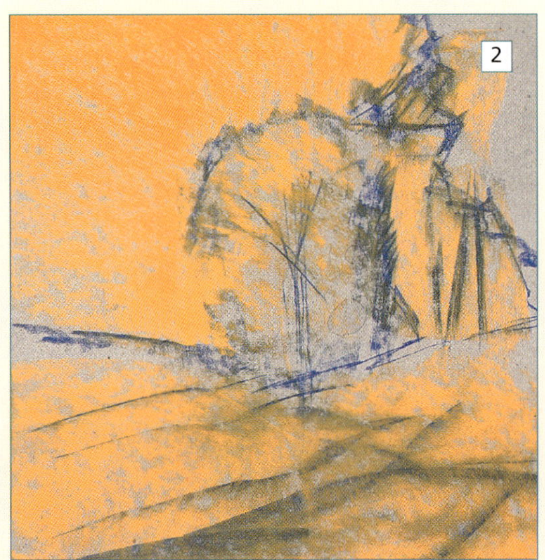

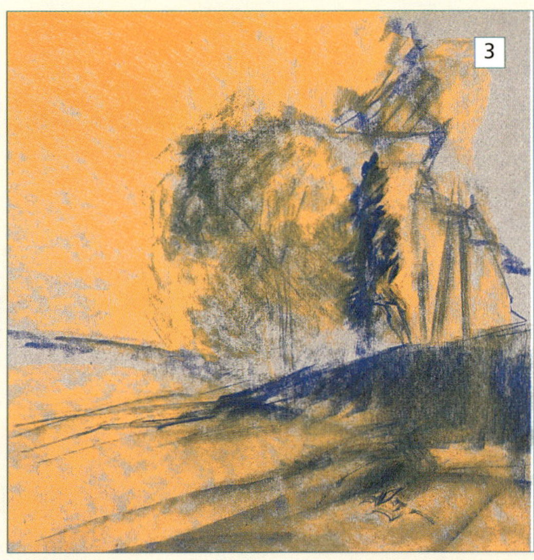

DRAWING IN COLORED CHALKS

1· THE PRELIMINARY SKETCH OF THE LANDSCAPE are the first lines and they will situate the different masses of the model on the cardboard. Just as we did at the beginning of this chapter, draw using the different possibilities that the stick offers flat between the fingers: broadwise and lengthwise.

THE UPPER PART OF THE TREES IS DRAWN gently passing the stick over in a broadwise direction. However, the stroke is lengthwise in the lower part, and very dense. The chalk tends to slip over the glossy surface of the cardboard.

THE CHALK APPLIED TO THE CARDBOARD is much more adhesive than on the paper. This color layer can close the pore.

2· ON TOP OF THE PERFECTLY DEFINED DRAWING, start to paint in orange chalk, holding the stick flat between the fingers without covering the cardboard surface completely. The color stands out against the stroke texture.

WHEN YOU PAINT IN ORANGE ON TOP OF THE BLUE, drag the first color to obtain a slightly green blending. The blue chalk will permit contrasts that define the shadows and the most important outlines of the drawing, while the orange chalk will provide the necessary luminosity.

3· GO BACK TO DRAWING in blue and start to do the fundamental contrasts.

AS YOU CAN SEE, it is important to maintain the tone presence of the support despite the different color applications. The dark contrasts, drawn in blue chalk, make the small dips, in which the cardboard color can be observed, stand out.

4· ON THE RIGHT OF THE PICTURE, paint with the necessary pressure so that the blue is dense and opaque.

THE TREE IN THE MIDDLE OF THE LANDSCAPE is drawn alternating the two colors. Immediately, they are softly blended with the fingers but not completely removing the stroke presence.

DRAW MIXING AND BLENDING the colors in the bushes in the background. The trunks are drawn against the light. When these darks are laid down, both the color of the cardboard and the orange in the sky stand out more because of the complementary contrasts. The tones blend and are superimposed, giving rise to different intensity mixes.

USE THE BLUE STICK TO INTENSIFY the contrasts in some zones. This is not done equally in all the picture. In some parts, the orange of the background continues to come through.

5· NOW THE WORK IS CONCENTRATED on the foreground. Firstly, draw the contrasts of the land. Afterwards, on top of the darks and the already blended zones, do a series of direct interventions in orange.

A landscape with colored chalks

14

It is important to get as much as possible out of direct interventions with the chalk.

Drawing with the stick flat between the fingers helps to give a good, firm and synthetic scheme.

ON THE RIGHT, draw softly in orange.

6· BLEND THE EARTH TONES SOFTLY and then superimpose some very direct orange interventions.

7· FINALLY, PAINT THE MASS OF VEGETATION on the right, increasing its size considerably. The background color comes through the lines and the shading. We have now finished this landscape full of contrasts.

SUMMARY SCHEME

The cardboard is painted orange. The stick flat between the fingers allows an open stroke through which the background color can be seen.

The preliminary sketch is realized with the stick flat between the fingers. It will tend to slip because the support has a very closed pore.

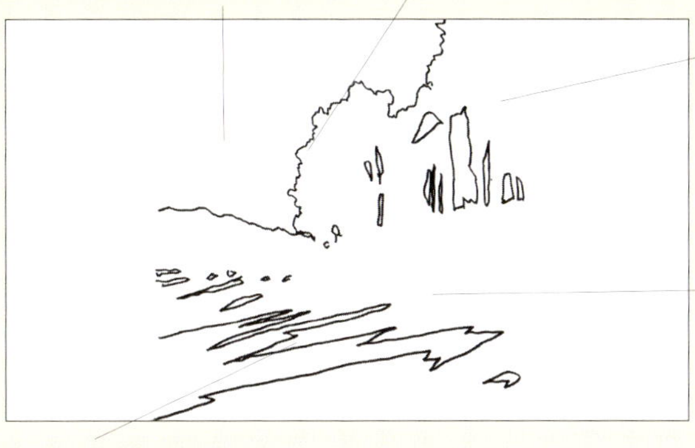

The contrasts are painted in blue, a color which allows backlight effects to be represented.

When painting in orange on blue, drag part of the lower color.

The direct orange interventions give luminosity to the land and strengthen the complementary contrasts.

DRAWING IN COLORED CHALKS

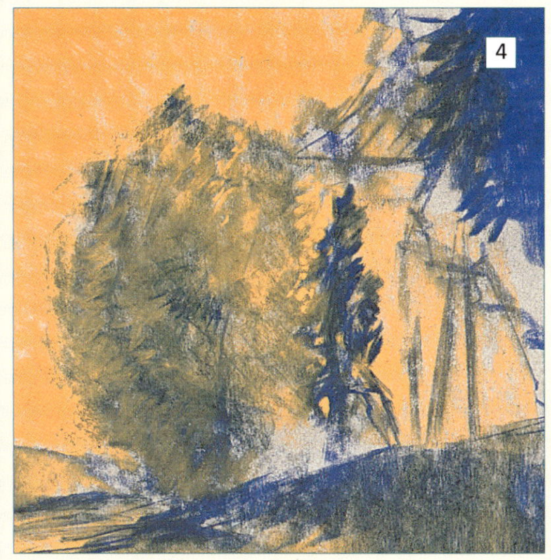

4

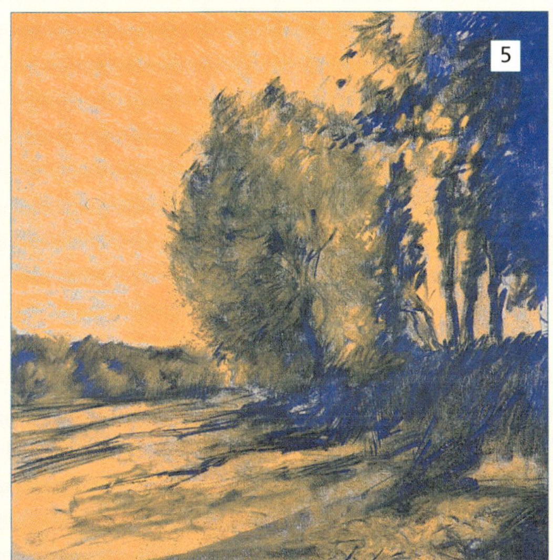

5

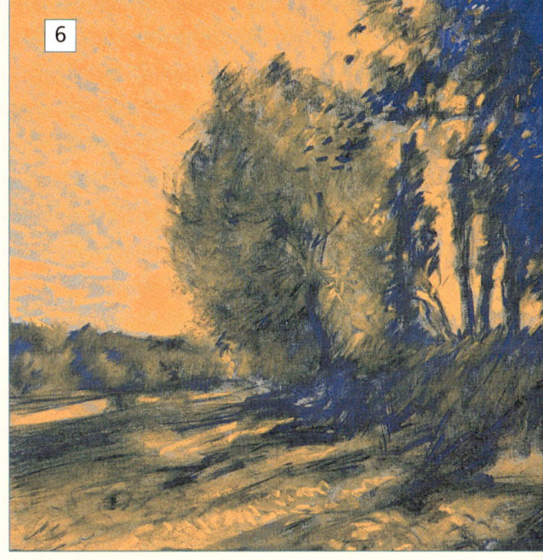

6

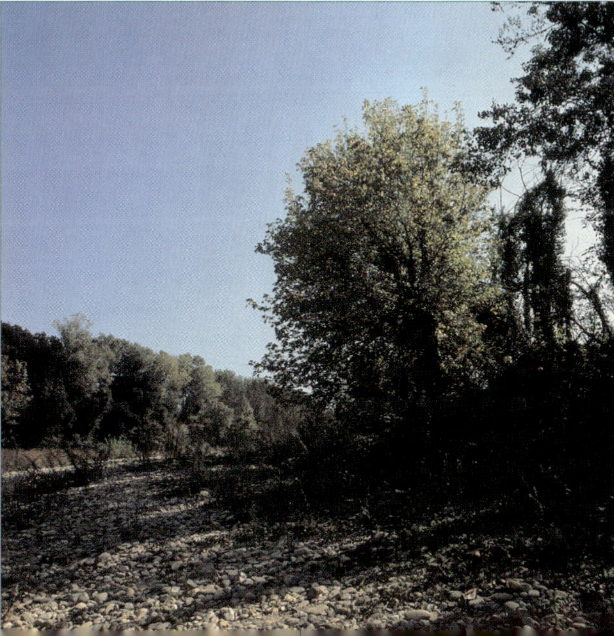

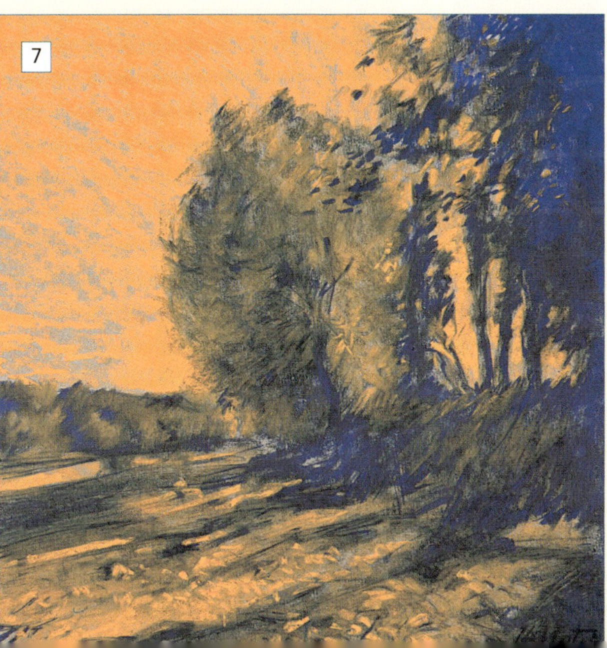

7

15 INK AND PEN

Pens are traditional drawing tools which give satisfactory results as they can produce a whole range of drawing effects such as grays, blended lines and even stumpings.
In this chapter we are going to study a classic drawing procedure, although it is not as common as the dry mediums. Using a pen and a brush produces rich stroke effects. Although the pen stroke is clearly related to the quill, it is more similar to the grays obtained from the dry mediums. When drawing with a pen, the most important aspect is to control the amount of ink on the nib that forms the stroke, all types of which can be produced in different intensities of gray.

Depending on the pressure and the amount of ink on the pen all types of strokes can be done, even in gray.

STROKES AND SHADING

To start drawing with the reed pen we are going to do a landscape that offers the possibility of trying out different strokes with the nib. Before starting to draw, remember that the nib leaves a gray mark even when the ink load has run out. A waxing and waning stroke is gray and loses intensity as the ink in the pen diminishes. Shading is done with a continuous stroke, either straight lines or hatching to obtain different shades of gray. Have an identical piece of paper at hand so that you can try out the tones before drawing.

STROKE PRACTICE

Try not to waste the ink: make the marks in the right places. Dip the pen in ink and you will be able to start with black strokes for clearly defined zones, like the horizon. Before redipping the pen, when it is beginning to run out of ink, you can do some gray zones. When even the gray is beginning to wax and wane, redip the pen.

WANING STROKES

The principal quality of the reed pen is that it offers a waning stroke similar to the grays of other dry mediums. Fountain pens cannot produce this stroke because they are not porous enough. When the stroke wanes you can draw grays that vary in intensity depending on the ink remaining in the pen and the pressure applied. Returning to the drawing exercise, outline the clouds against the sky. As you can see, these grays are rendered lighter by the contrast of the fading ink. Once the gray is completely run out, new grays cannot be drawn. Reload the pen to draw the darks on the horizon. In the background, combine different shadings, varying the grays according to the amount of ink left on the nib.
The nearer to running out completely the pen is, the softer the grays are.

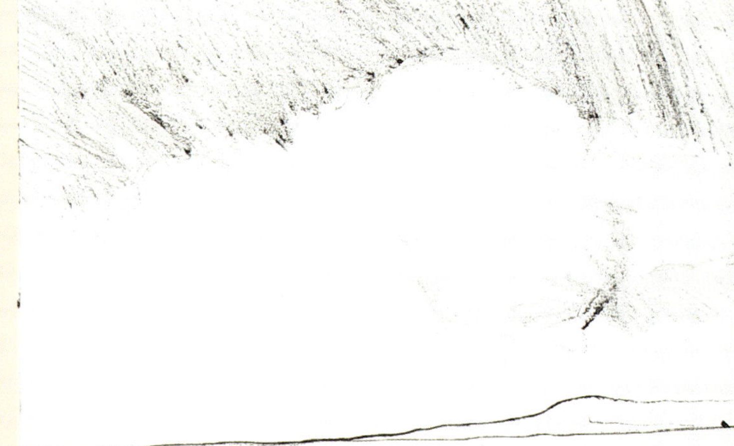

Once the ink used for the horizon is running out, draw the sky with the faded stroke.

THE MARK OF THE PEN

The reed pen can make a rich variety of strokes. Although it may seem a rigid tool, it is highly flexible, offering thick or fine strokes depending on the pressure and the ink load. When you have put down a loaded stroke (for example, the trees along the path), you can do finer strokes simply by dragging the wet ink with the nib. This is how you do the tree branches and the grass in the foreground without having to redip the pen in the pot. First do a few strokes heavily loaded with ink to contrast with the grass. Afterwards draw the rest rubbing the still fresh ink.

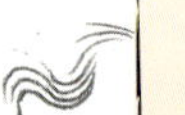

A drawing can be done in many ways and with any medium that leaves a mark on the paper. Generally, dry mediums, like graphite, charcoal and sanguine are used. However, it is also possible to draw with ink and any tool sharp enough to give a fine line.

15

NECESSARI MATERIALS

To draw in ink not many materials are necessary to give amazing results. The principal drawing tool for this technique is the reed pen with a sharp nib. The reed pen is very hard and therefore allows you to draw continuously without wearing out its point. It is sold in Fine Arts shops or in shops for artisans. There is nothing mysterious about its elaboration: it is only a shortened and sharpened piece of cane.

Ink is another indispensable material for drawing with a pen. You could draw with watercolors or even with anilines (a black dye) but the blackness of Chinese ink gives tone intensities that other medium cannot match.

Paper is the third indispensable material. As the reed pen is hard and coarse it can draw on any paper but it is recommendable to use special paper for ink which has the right degree of absorption. Stucco paper is especially suitable for drawing with Chinese ink. One of its advantages is that it allows very precise corrections with the aid of a razor blade.

Optional materials include kitchen roll or blotting paper, which soak up excess ink from the drawing paper.

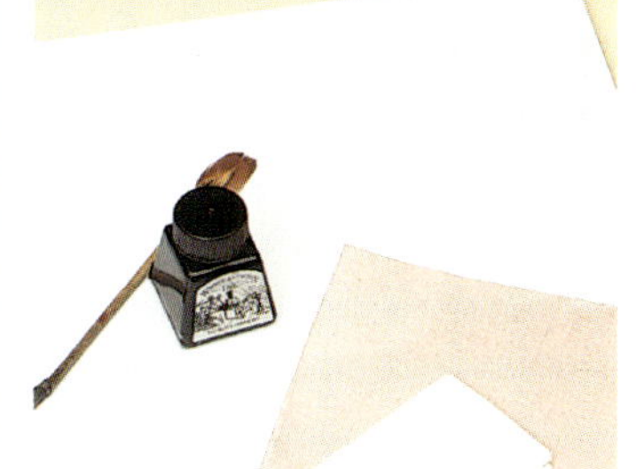

Chinese ink, stucco drawing paper and a reed pen are necessary to get going with this technique. Blotting paper is optional for cleaning.

The less ink there is, the softer the grays are.

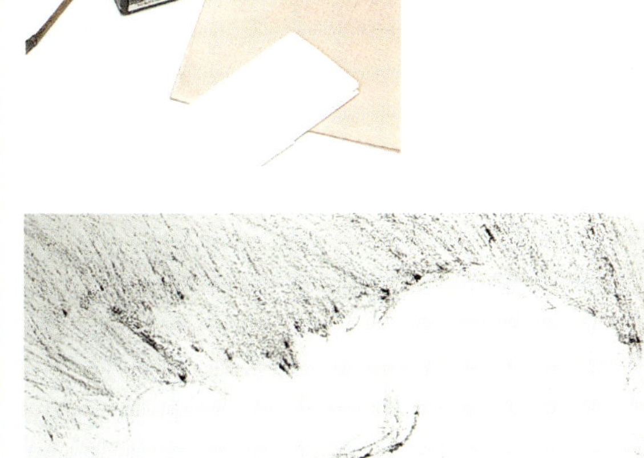

The darkest strokes are done at the end, complementing the contrasts that balance the whites.

FROM LIGHT TO THE DENSEST DARK

As would logically be guessed, the ink tone changes progressively. Contrasts are painted on light tones and on whites so that the different tones are always added progressively, starting from the clear grays. On top, do denser strokes. Finally, you can contrast the darkest shades of the drawing.

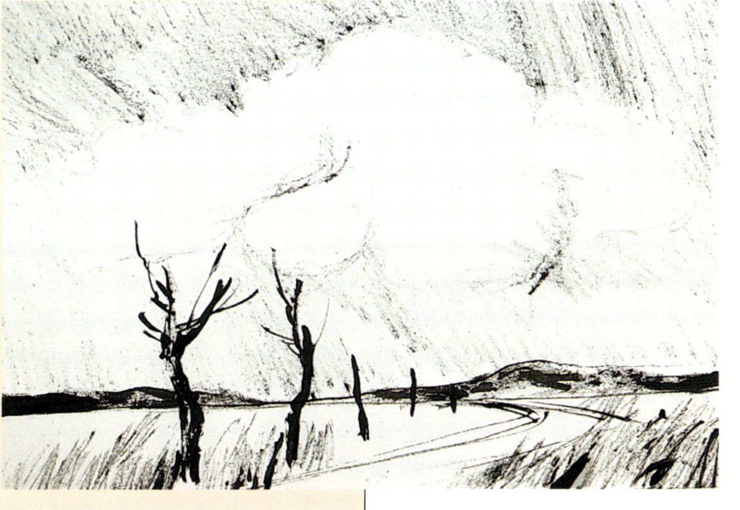

The mark of the pen depends on the ink on the paper.

15 INK AND PEN

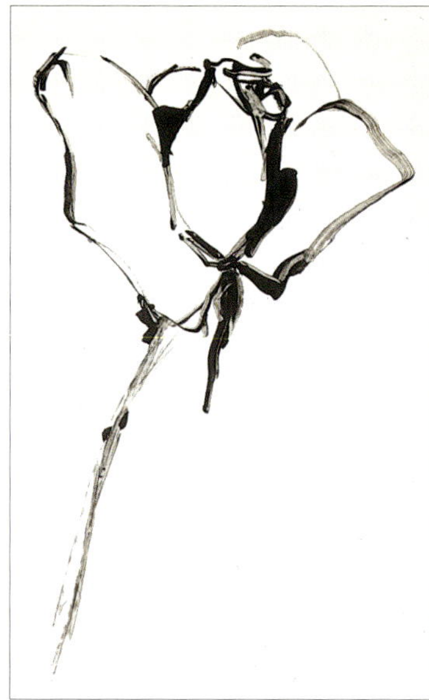

The flower is drawn in one go, starting with the petals and finishing with the stem.

SHADING, STROKES AND CORRECTING

Chinese ink is more famous for shading than any other painting medium. It is not uncommon for the learner to stain their clothes, and nothing seems able to clean it off. On the paper the dry ink produces the same effect, although it can be corrected.

Correcting the ink depends on the quality of the paper. At the beginning we said you could draw on any paper, although the most suitable was stucco. On normal paper the ink penetrates right through to the fiber and makes it impossible to erase. However, with stucco paper the ink does not penetrate, instead it stays on the surface and therefore can be scraped off with a razor blade. Stucco paper has enough body to resist the attack of the razor, but be careful not to cut or tear it.

We are now going to do a simple exercise to practice the reed pen stroke again, but this time we will do an important correction in the dry zone.

Do not cut your fingers with the razor blade.

COMBINING PEN AND BRUSH

So far we have seen some of the qualities of using a pen. It can work together with a brush, which makes it much easier to cover wide areas. We are going to do a landscape using alternatively the pen and the brush. Always be on the lookout for ways of getting more out of the pen when using it in tandem it with the brush.

FINE LINES TO CONSOLIDATE THE DRAWING

To start, outline the drawing by doing a preliminary sketch of the principal lines with the pen. Rapidly and agilely draw the lines of the landscape and the shadows in such a way that the forms and planes are comprehensible. Each of the planes is resolved with the most suitable type of stroke: curved and horizontal strokes for the land and long, slanting strokes for the mountains. Varying the stroke enables different textures to be insinuated.

DRAWiNG AND CORRECTiNG

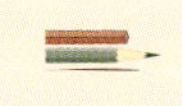

Good drawings in Chinese ink need not be 'lost' for good if you make a mistake. You can retrieve them with a razor blade. We are going to draw a rose. Do the first strokes, starting individually with the petals, directly without a preliminary sketch. Finally, draw the stem. The darkest contrasts of the flower are drawn with completely black shadings on both sides of the petals.

Once the principal form has been done, draw the darks that surround the rose with rapid strokes in the same direction as the flower. The closer together the strokes are, the darker the background will be.

Open up whites by scratching with the blade.

When the leaves have been drawn in negative, draw on the details and intensely contrast the background.

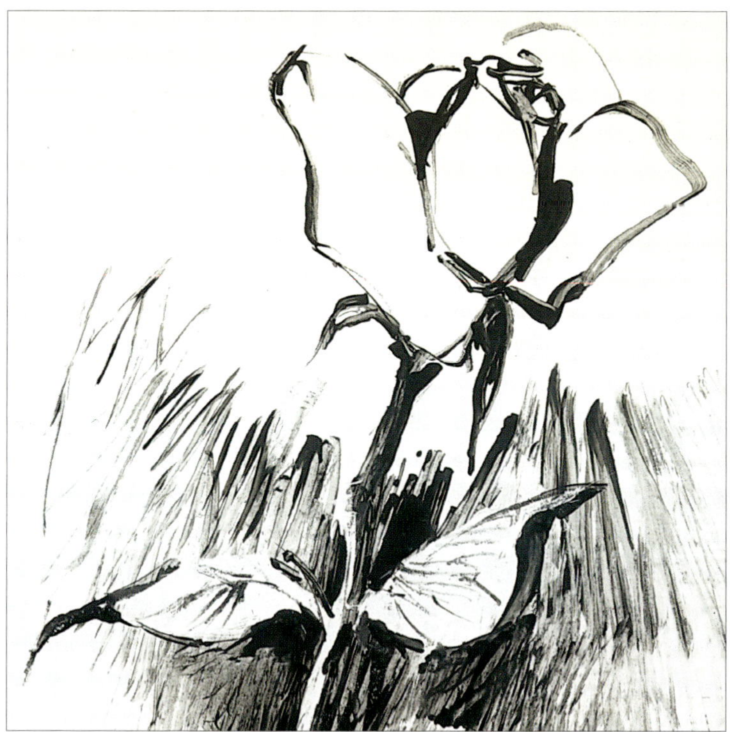

Pay attention to this step: we are going to work on the flower leaves with the razor blade, but only when the ink has completely dried, either naturally in the air or by using blotting paper. Do not rub the ink, only press down on the wet zones.
Once the ink is dry, start to scratch delicately, dragging the blade broadwise. You will see that the paper stands up well to tone scraping.
Once the necessary whites have been opened up, you can finish the drawing of the leaves. The strokes for the leaf veins blend in with the rest of the picture. Draw contrasting, intense blacks around the fresh whites.

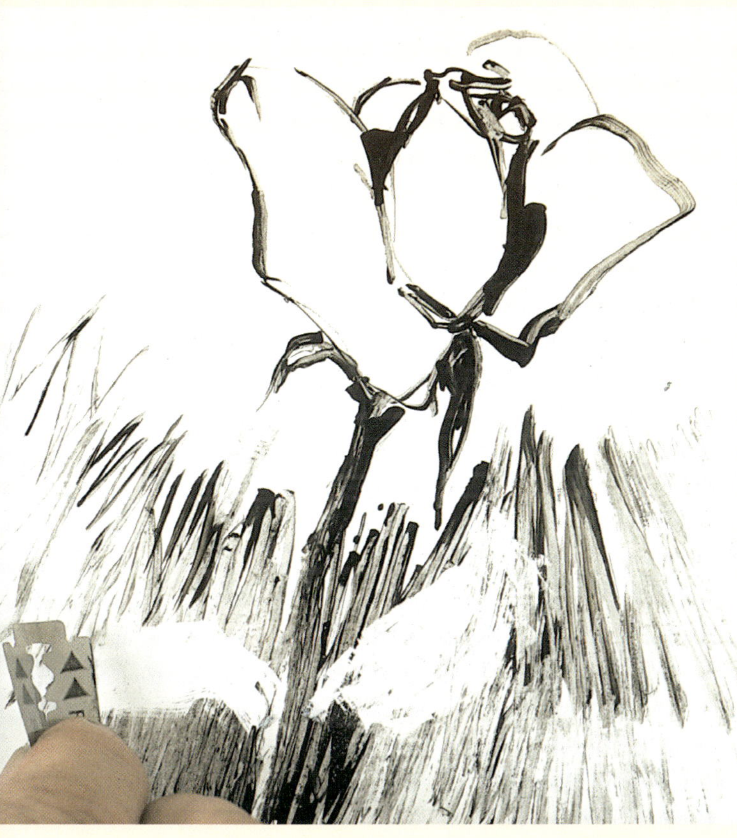

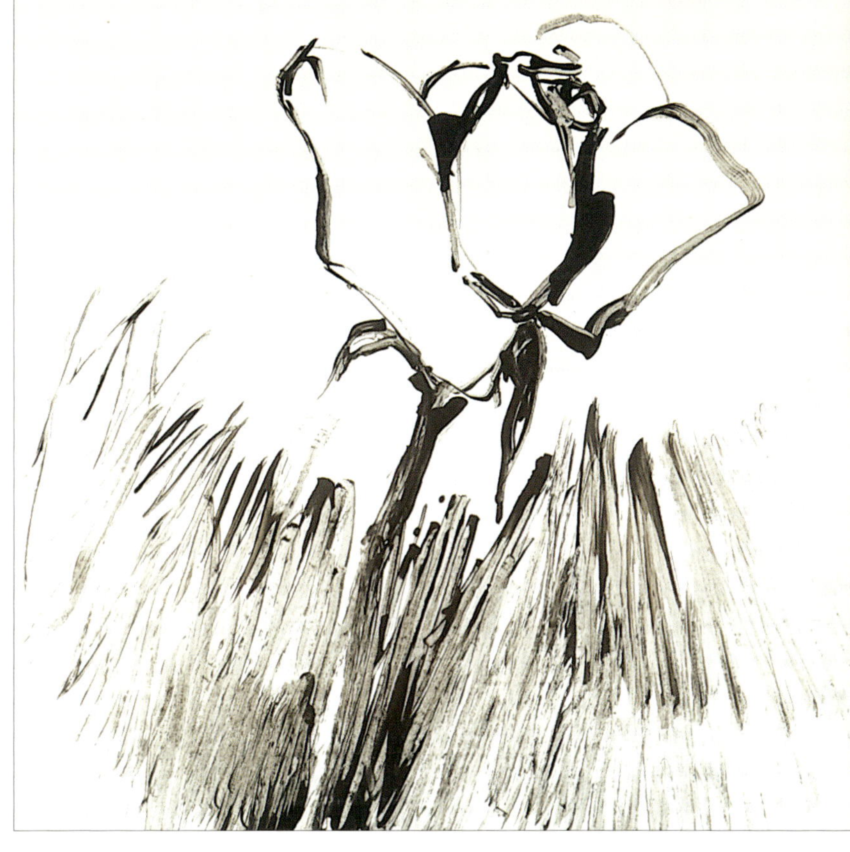

Draw the darks on the flower with quick, continuous strokes.

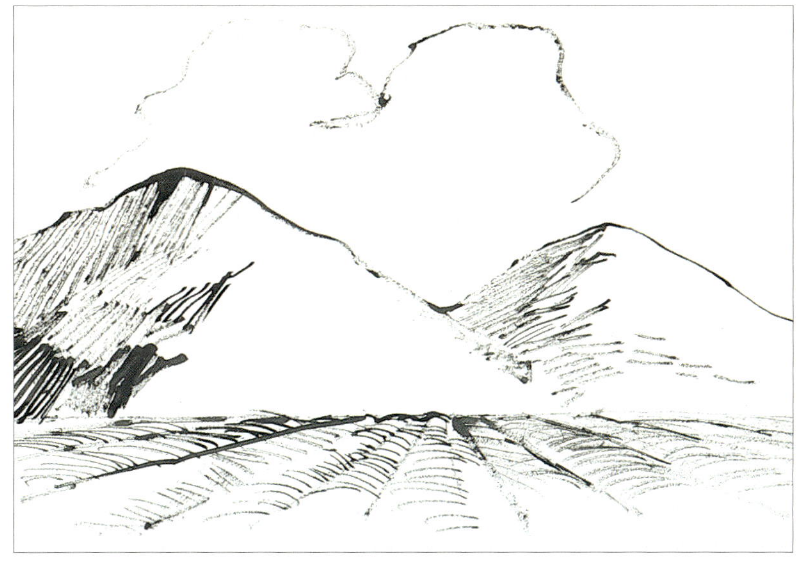

The lines on the ground are horizontal and curved. The mountains are done with long, slanting strokes.

BRUSH WORK ON DARK AREAS

Once the principal zones of the landscape have been drawn, and the details that identify each plane, you can use the brush to do the darkest shadows. The name 'block style' is given to the method of drawing shadows as pure blacks. The darks appear as compact blocks of ink and thereby facilitate the creation of intense simultaneous contrasts between the lights and the darks.
Dip the brush in ink to do the dark parts of the landscape. Do not soak it too much because ink spreads a long way, and, anyway, it is only to be used in concrete zones.

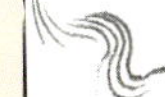

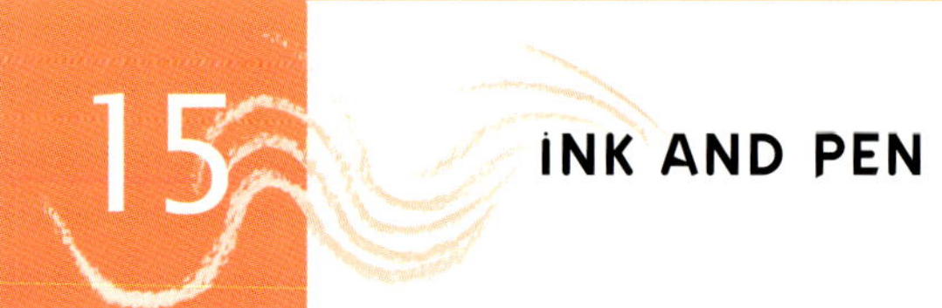

Use the brush dipped in ink to draw the darkest parts of the landscape in compact black blocks.

The drawing is finished alternating the two drawing mediums. The brush is for the black, compact zones. The pen is for the flowing lines that require more of a drawing technique.

COMBINING DARKS AND LINES

Working with ink, and especially using a pen, enables a very elaborated style of drawing. One recourse that is widely seen in imaginative artwork is the combination of perfectly defined zones with others hardly insinuated. The result is a fresh, gestural and energetic finish.

FROM THE PRELIMINARY SKETCH TO THE FIRST DARKS

As we have already seen, you can start working directly in ink. You do not need to do a first outline in pencil, although it is an option to be considered.

We are going to do a pine tree. Do the preliminary sketch with a very faded stroke; only the outline of the top and the trunk matter. Once the tree is outlined, rewet the pen and do a firm, bold stroke on the right side of the trunk until the ink begins to run out. Take advantage of the gray to do the pine needles texture.

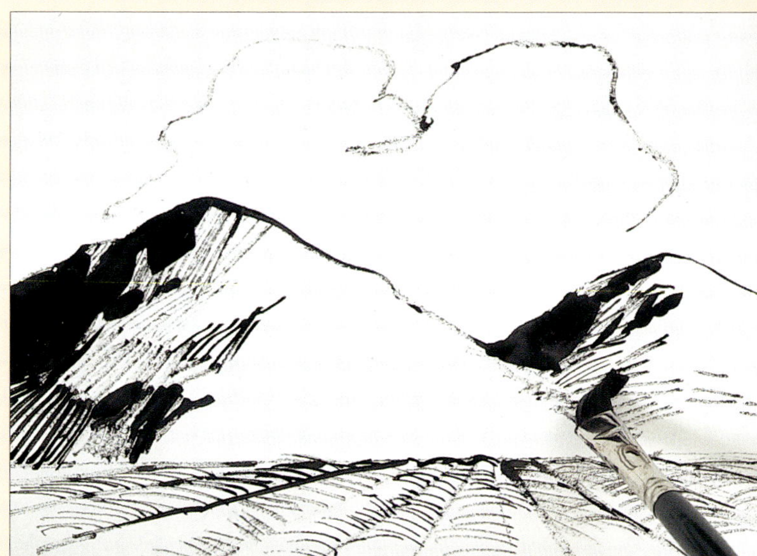

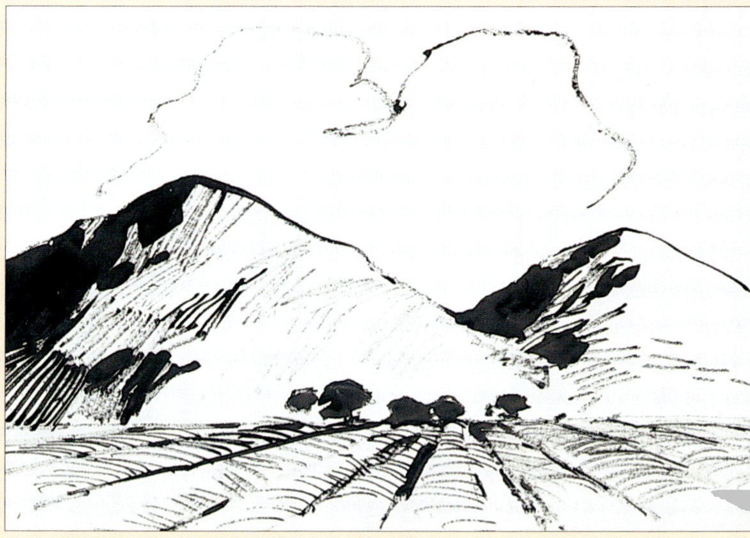

After drawing the side of the tree trunk, outline the dark zone to the left of the tree top.

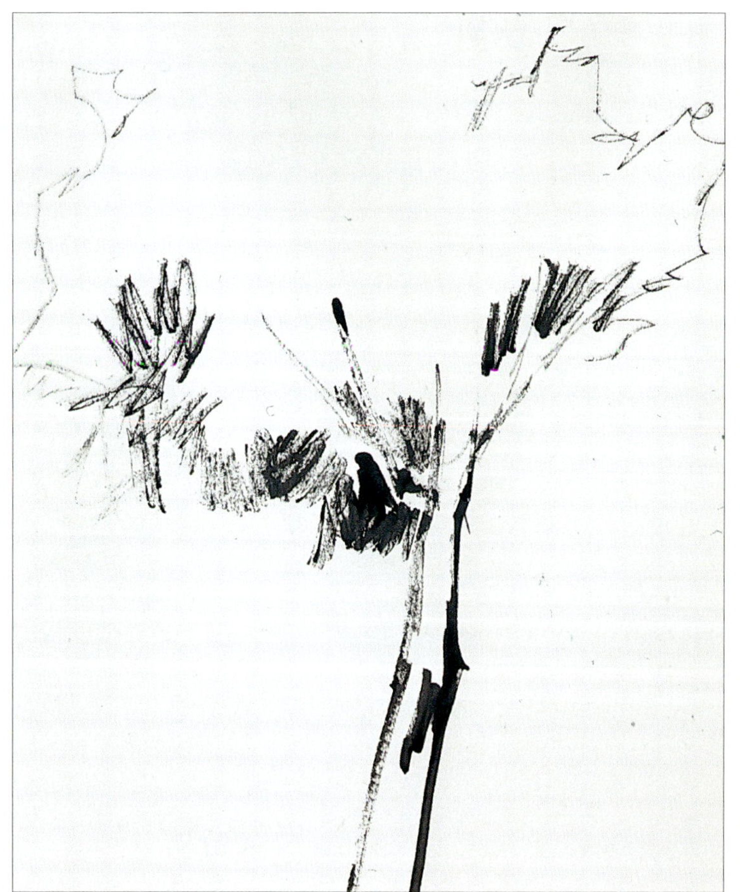

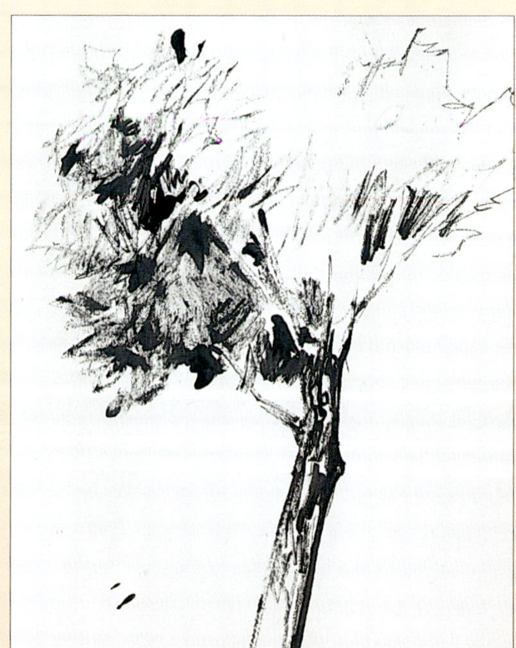

The final contrasts are drawn with dense, very direct darks, markedly graphic in their style. This introduces different languages into the drawing.

The contrast work is centered on one side of the tree; the other side is barely insinuated.

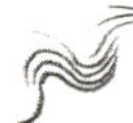

Use the brush dipped in ink to do the darkest zones of the landscape in black blocks.

INTENSIFY THE CONTRAST

The maximum contrast is only on one side of the tree, although there is to be no clear division between the two halves. As you can see, different strokes are combined for distinct effects: faded strokes for the gray trunk, clean strokes for the densest darks, and stainings for the intensely black shadow zones.

This is how the finished landscape looks. Strokes, fine lines and shading have all come into play.

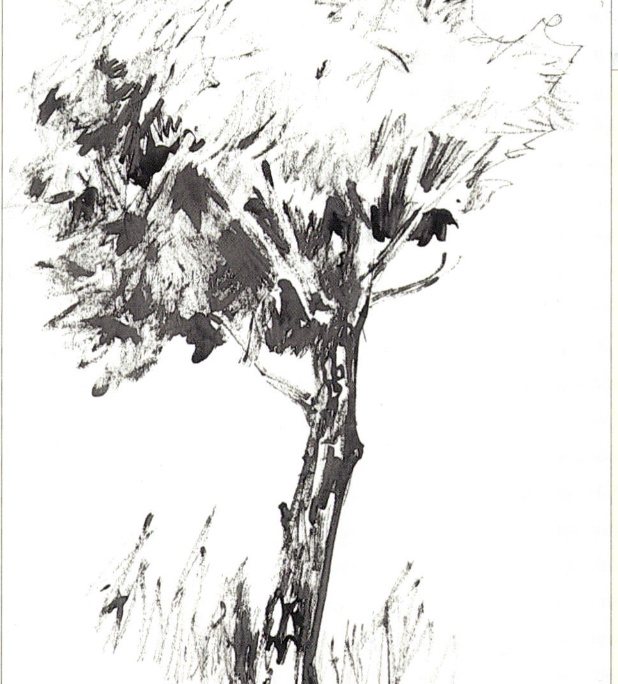

BLOCK STYLE

Drawing with a reed pen or cane has been a tradition throughout the history of art. In Daumier's work you cannot help admiring the spontaneity of his gestural strokes and the intelligent use of blocks for the shadows to create a chiaroscuro.

Honoré Daumier (1808-1879). Two men seen from the waist up and with their heads bowed. Pen and Chinese ink on paper. The Louvre Museum, the drawing room.

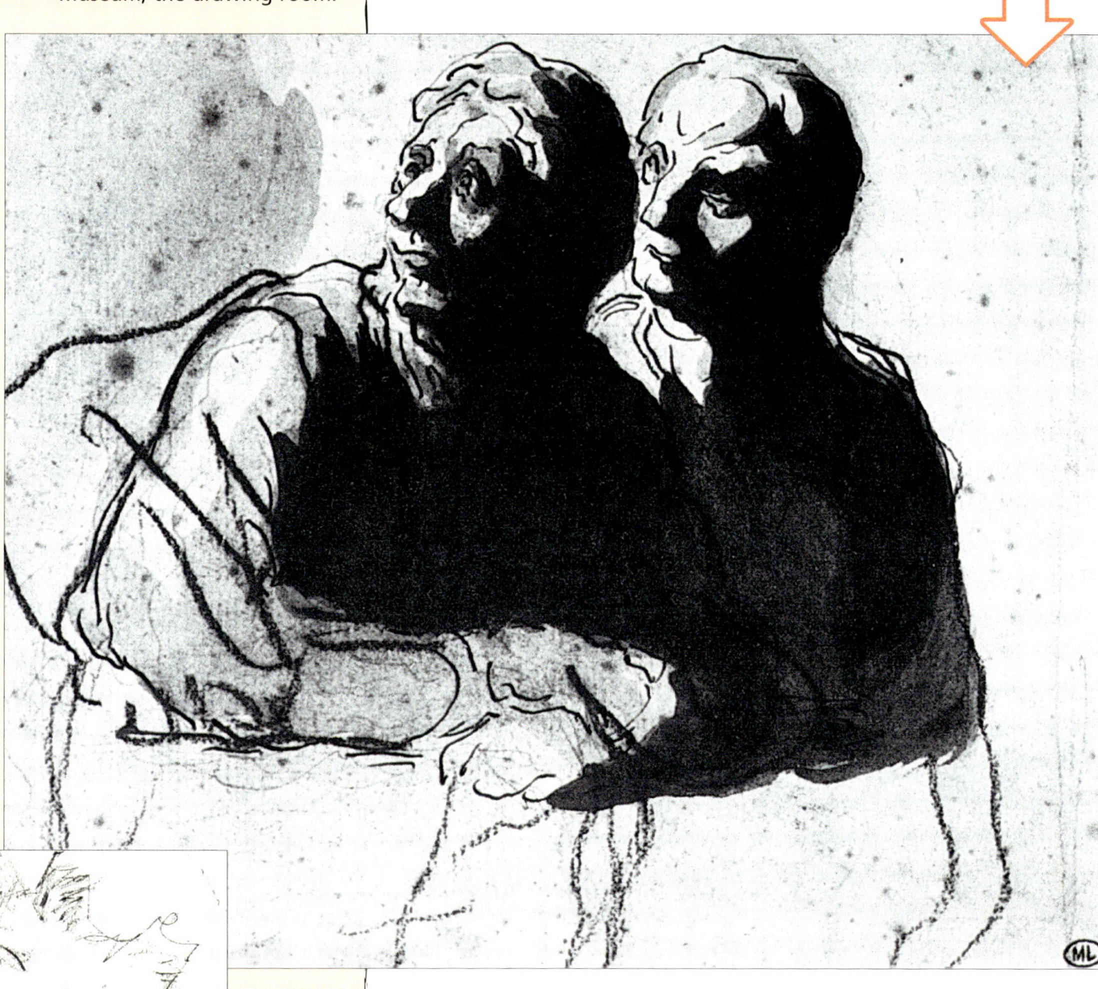

SUMMARY

THE PEN STROKE
A pen permits firm, individual strokes. However, when the ink is running out medium grays can be obtained.

THE INK
As far as is possible try not to take more ink from the pot until it is completely exhausted.

CORRECTIONS
Ink drawings can be corrected with a razor blade provided that stucco paper is used.

COMBINING TECHNIQUES
Brush and pen complement each other to intensify the strokes for the darks.

15 Exercices *Step by step*

Representing a landscape is always pleasant and rewarding. The elements can be so varied that a permissivity in the form interpretation is allowed that is not possible with figure or still life themes. So we have chosen a mountain landscape to practice with the reed pen. The pen stroke, depending on the ink-load, can go from a strong deep-black accents through to gray tones. As you can see, we have chosen a forest overflowing with little details. Right from the beginning, take care to respect the white reserves.

NECESSARY MATERIAL

You can draw not only with a sharpened bamboo cane: a wooden stick or an ostrich feather can also be used. The results and stroke quality will vary.

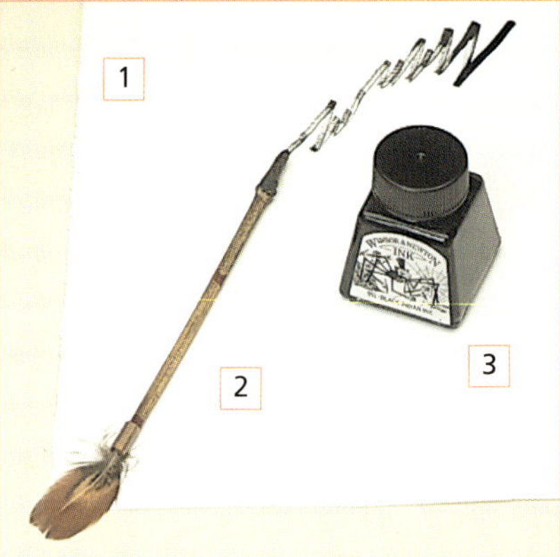

Paper for ink (1),.
The reed pen for drawing (2),.
Chinese ink (3).

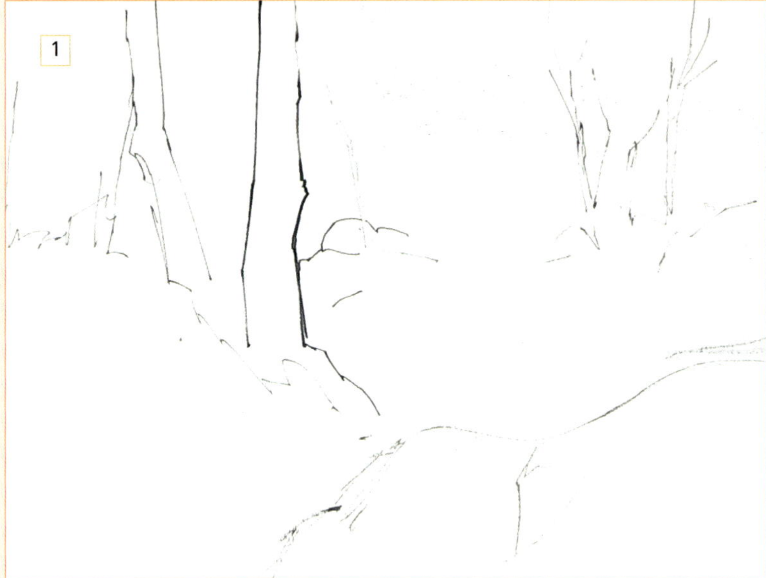

1· DO THE PRELIMINARY SKETCH IN INK. It is not a problem if later you have to do corrections because working on the blacks will retrieve any errors. Start work on the outlines of the two masses in the foreground, the trees in the midground and the rocky background. In the preliminary sketch the line must not be too bold so do not overload the pen. Test the pen on spare paper beforehand.

START TO DRAW THE LEFT-HAND side of the rock torrent. Long, slanting parallel strokes will help you to get the gesture right. Just above do a dark shading during which the ink should run out. Do not reload the pen, instead start rubbing part of the black until the first grays are formed. The blades of grass under the trees on the left are drawn with the pen out of ink but the nib still moist. The light parts of the trunks are left reserved. Observe how we are following the rule of doing the medium grays when the ink is fading.

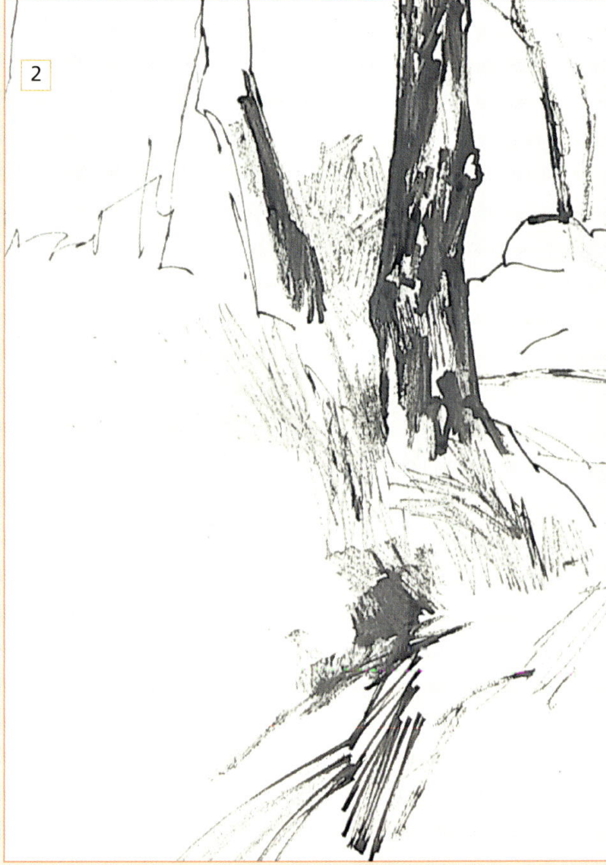

2· CONTINUE WORKING ON THE TREES ON THE LEFT, always leaving the most luminous zones reserved. In this exercise the model does not show these zones, so exactly how you do them is up to you. However, inside them you must use the fading stroke to do medium grays. Every time you are nearly out of ink, before refilling, try to do a light gray zone, like the upper left part of the trees.

A landscape

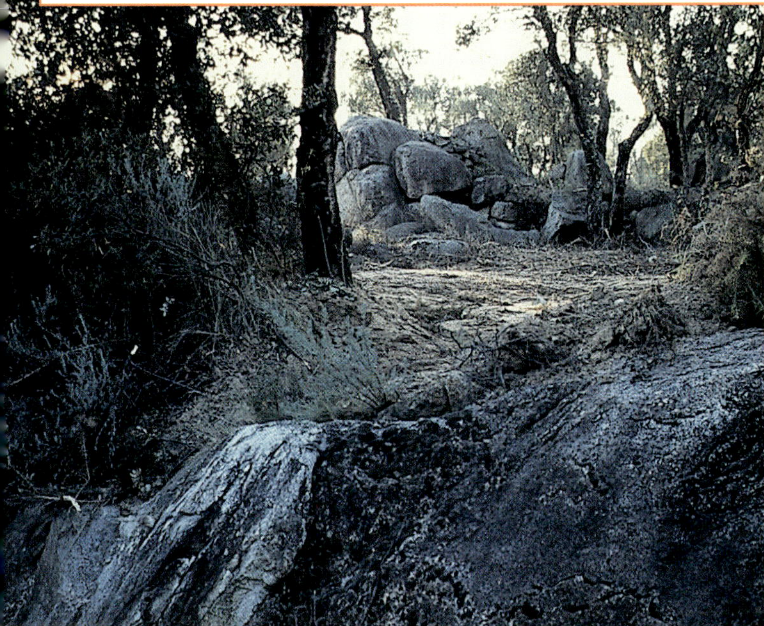

To get a gray stroke there must hardly be any ink in the pen. Rub it purposefully over the zone which is going to be gray. The resulting stroke is similar to some dry mediums.

3. **THE TREES IN THE BACKGROUND** on the left are much more contrasted than those in the foreground. Their completely black trunks establish a clear spatial plane between the grounds of the landscape. Before the ink runs out completely, draw the grass in the background with a clean stroke, not pressing too hard. Go over the rocks in the background and put in a few soft contrast details. Now that the ink mark is almost faded, draw the vegetation on the right.

3

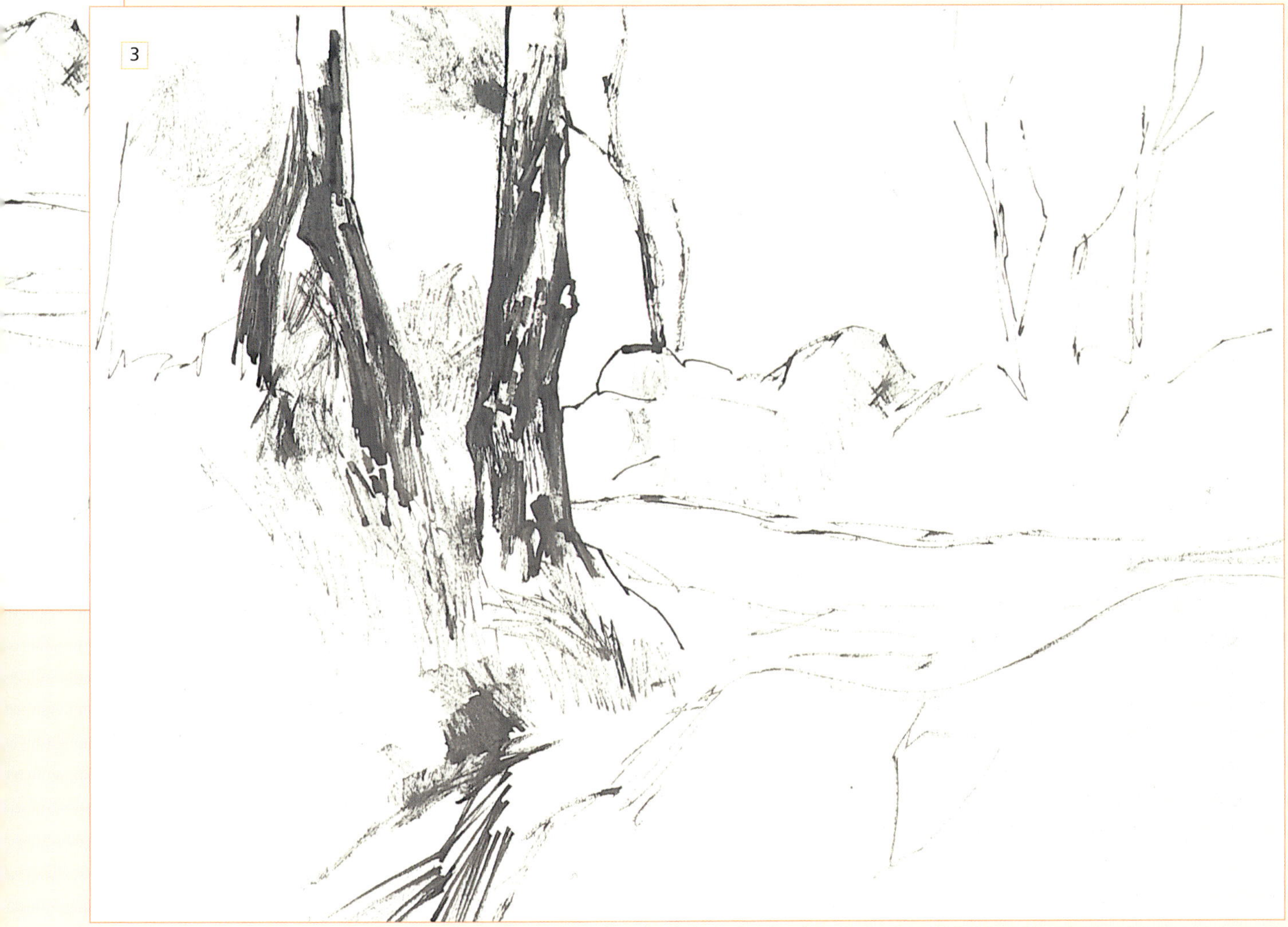

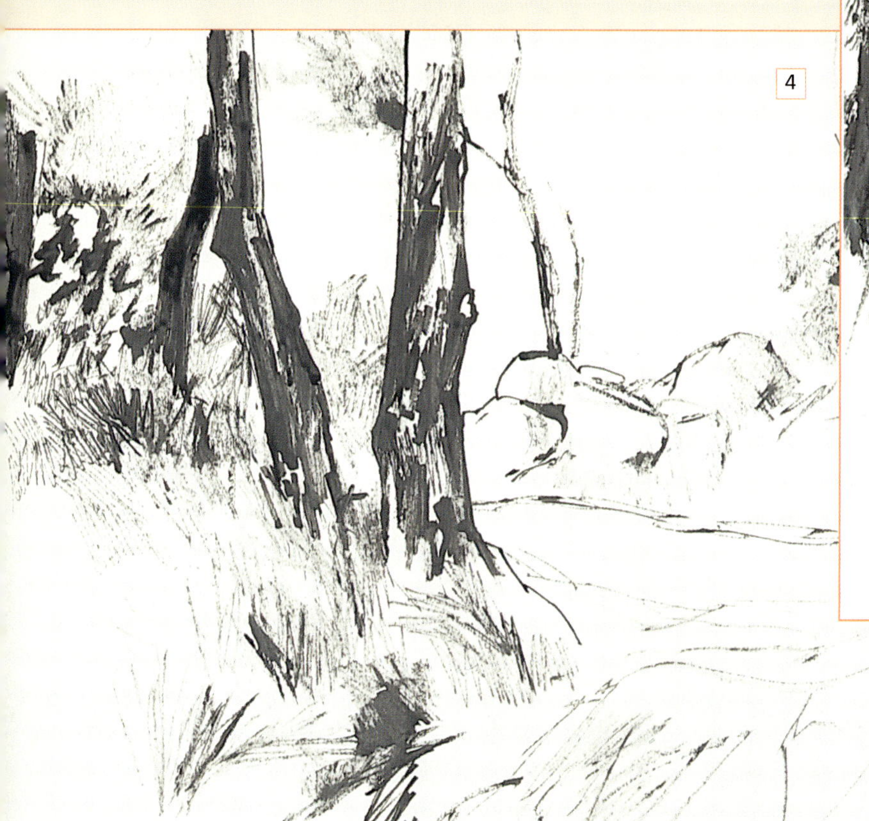

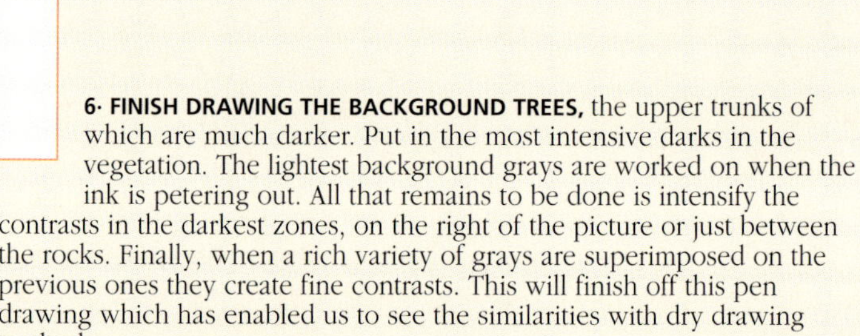

6· FINISH DRAWING THE BACKGROUND TREES, the upper trunks of which are much darker. Put in the most intensive darks in the vegetation. The lightest background grays are worked on when the ink is petering out. All that remains to be done is intensify the contrasts in the darkest zones, on the right of the picture or just between the rocks. Finally, when a rich variety of grays are superimposed on the previous ones they create fine contrasts. This will finish off this pen drawing which has enabled us to see the similarities with dry drawing methods.

4· THE WORK ON THE BACKGROUND GRAYS is done with the pen almost out of ink, rubbing persistently all the areas to be grayed. Every refill is an opportunity to work on the stronger contrasts in the background, like the bush on the right, above the rocks. Do the dark stainings but always be watching for when the ink starts to fade so that you can continue working on the grays. Draw the rocks in the foreground with long strokes at the end of which you leave a little blot of damps ink to be stretched later.

5· NOW FOCUS ON THE FOREGROUND. Do hatching, criss-crossed not excessively contrasted lines, sufficiently dense to give a realistic grass texture. This ground will be quite a contrast to the midground, in which there are numerous whites.

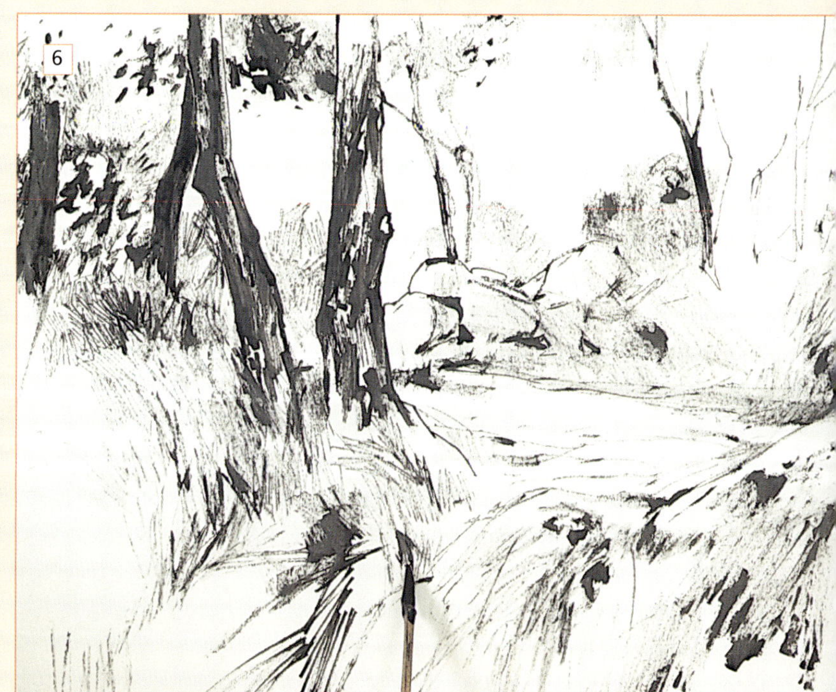

A landscape

15

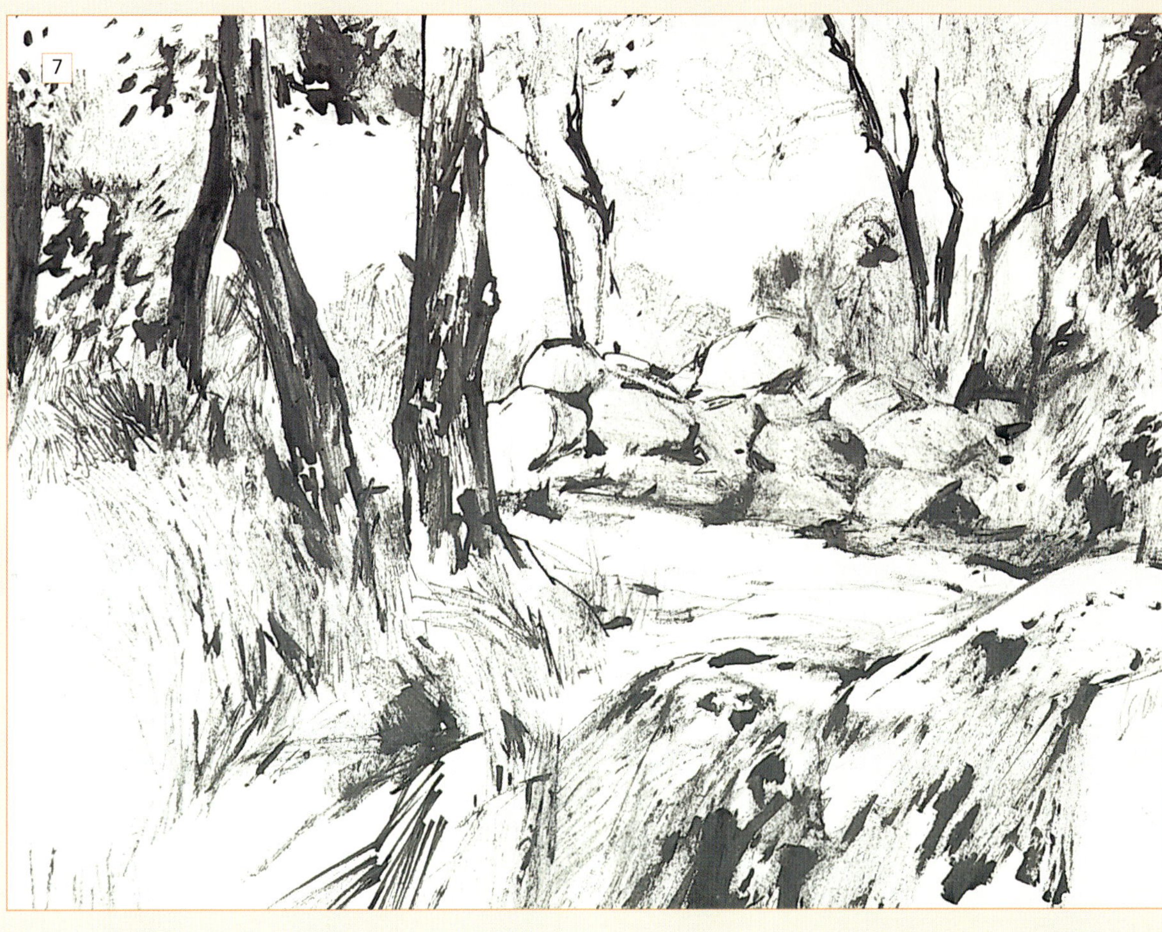

INK AND PEN

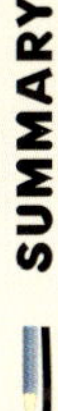

SUMMARY SCHEME

1.The preliminary sketch is done linearly. Only the tree outlines and the spatial planes are drawn.

4·In the background the softest grays are done pressing lightly with the nib almost out of ink.

2· Paint the first contrasts ower the trees on th left.

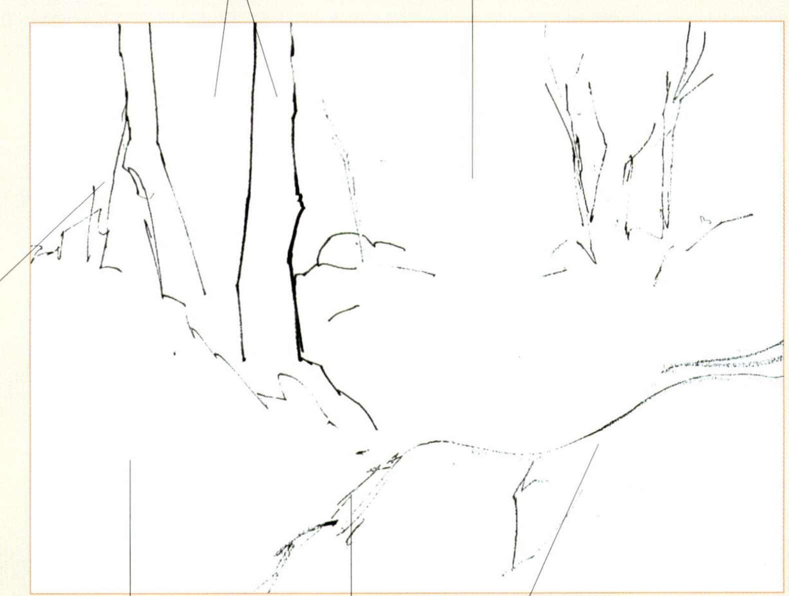

5·The foreground vegetation is drawn half out of ink. Attempt to get the texture right.

3·The grays in the foreground are produced by the fading strokes.

6·The strokes for the rocks on the right are contrasted. Little ink droplets are left at the end and spread out later.

16 TONE VALUES AND THE STUMP

The stump is a tool eminently suited to drawing. It is different to the other drawing mediums because it has no stroke or shading of its own. So what is its function alongside the other drawing tools? Although a stump cannot shade on its own, this does not rule it out of the shading process. Its role is to redistribute on the support what other tools put down. Like a propelling pencil, it does not draw on its own, but must be loaded with charcoal or graphite to be able to draw, or there must be a stroke on the paper to be smudged.

In this chapter we are going to do a series of exercises that reveal the most important possibilities with this work tool. While getting familiar with the strokes obtainable with the stump it will not be difficult to equal the results shown on these pages.

CHARCOAL AND GRAPHITE POWDER

When working with a stump, a piece of absorbent paper rolled up into a point, remember that you need a material that can be smudged. There are two ways of working with a stump. The first is more intuitive and has already been seen: directly smudge a charcoal, sanguine, graphite, or any other dry medium stroke. The second way is what we are going to practice now. Scratch or grate the charcoal or graphite with a razor blade and collect the powder on a piece of paper and then impregnate it into the stump.

Graphite powder, stumps and paper.

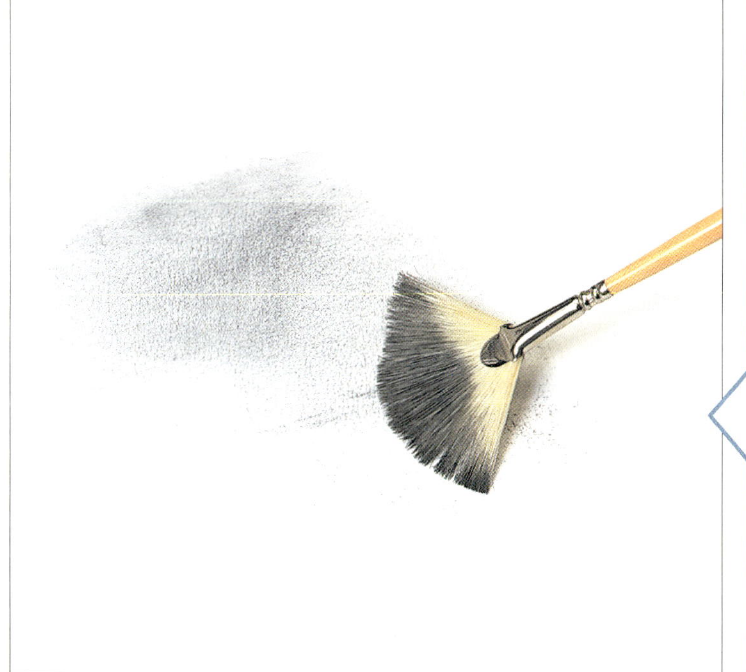

USING THE STUMP

In the majority of exercises in this chapter we are going to use the stump not only as a means for spreading the tone on the paper, but also as the main drawing tool, actually transporting it to the paper. Therefore, we must learn to use the stump reloading it when it runs out. When the stump is out of charcoal powder, it can be used to blend the zones that are already drawn.

To get things moving we shall do a pear. Fruit is always easier to represent than pure geometric shapes. Impregnate the stump with graphite. Use the conical side of the tip as if it were a pencil to outline the pear. Smudge the background. The pressure of the stump varies as the point becomes gradually unloaded. Once all the background is gray, establish the medium pear tones without reloading. Persevere with the tone

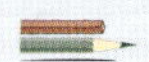

TRYING OTHER MEDIUMS

A stump can smudge graphite powder without any problems, but it would be a pity to limit yourself to this procedure for other methods give diverse tone possibilities on the paper. For example, you can use a brush impregnated with charcoal or graphite to draw.

A stump is a perfect tool for drawing. Unlike ofher drawing mediums on its own it has no stroke or shading capacity. So wath is its role among the other drawing tools?

16

in the middle of the shadow.
This work is done directly with the stump, without using the graphite crayon. The first tones have to be soft to start off the tone value work.

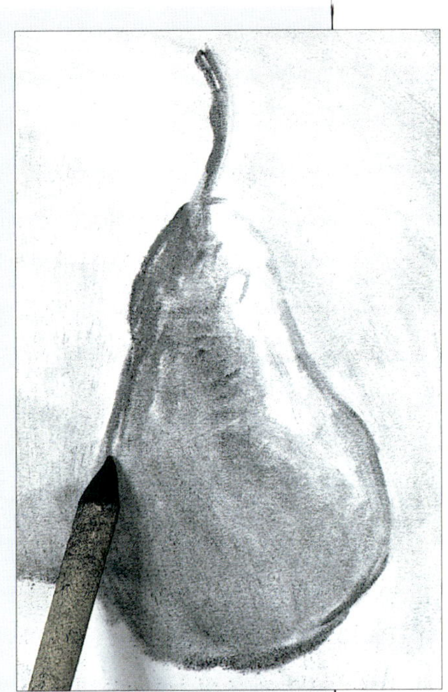

CONTRAST BETWEEN LINES AND STUMPINGS

Once the medium tones have been done, you must start to adjust the contrasts to get the right tone values. In the last step the drawing line had priority over the tone values. Now you have to intensify the tones of the darks until they absorb the tonality of the line. Impregnate the stump again, with a dense load, and start to darken the densest shadow parts. Softly blend the dark zone in with the light parts, trying to leave reserved the completely blank parts so that they are not stained by graphite. If necessary, any highlight can be cleaned with the eraser.

This work is done directly with the stump. Graphite plays no role. The first tones must be soft as you start work on the tone values.

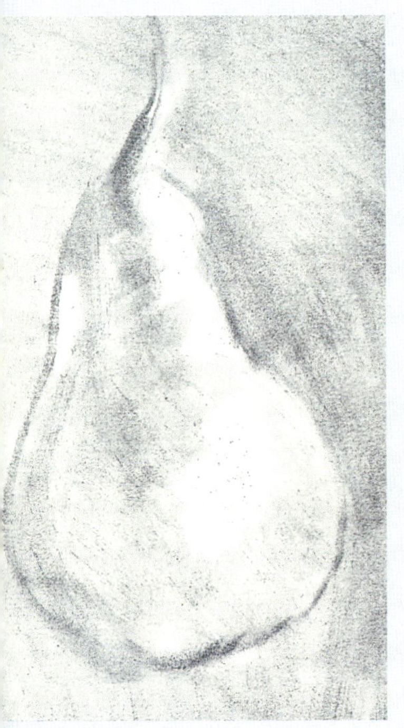

STUMP PRESSURE

The stump can continue to draw dark strokes on a stumped surface. When the point passes over the graphite, the tone becomes more concentrated. Use the point to shade the shadow parts. These strokes will stand out as quite pure lines that contrast even more with the dark gray tone.

Darken the shadow zones using a new graphite load. The tones have to be softened to integrate them with the light zone.

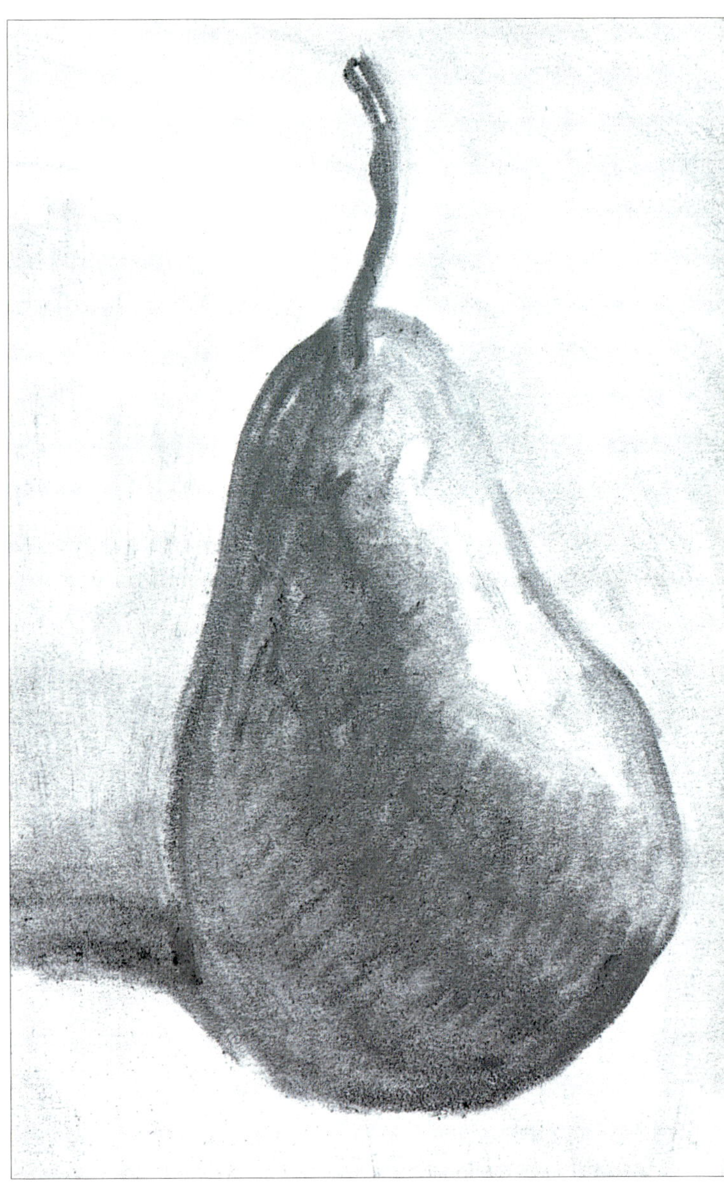

Use the stump point to do these strokes over the shadow zone.

TONE CHANGES

In the last exercise we saw how the stump was used on the paper, and these techniques will remain valid for the following ones, too. However, with any method it is wise to perfect the style and rule out bad habits, something which could occur with tone changes. Whenever working directly with a stump, remember that the tones are intensified progressively so the first applications must be soft. The shading, too, is gradual.

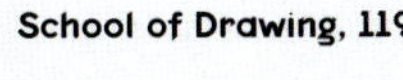

16 TONE VALUES AND THE STUMP

SHADING WITH THE STUMP

The stump basically creates shadings which can be lengthened into strokes or turned into grays in particular zones. This exercise provides the opportunity to practice both possibilities. Draw the circular form that will be the apple with the point. Put in the highlight, marking the shadow limit. It is now that you start work on the first shadings that alter the tone values of the apple shadow. Darken the edge of the shadow of the apple. This contrast will help the spherical effect and the illumination of the apple to be appreciated.

BALANCING TONES WITH DARKS

Once the first tones have been done, start to work on compensating the darks, for it is the dark tones which, in the final analysis, outline and define the highlights. Do strokes with the stump in the same direction as the apple plane.

The darks are intensified avoiding invading the medium tones of the highlights, the luminosity of which will increase with the contrast. In this final step, darken the most intense shadow. As you can see, the right part of the shadow becomes a luminous dark tone.

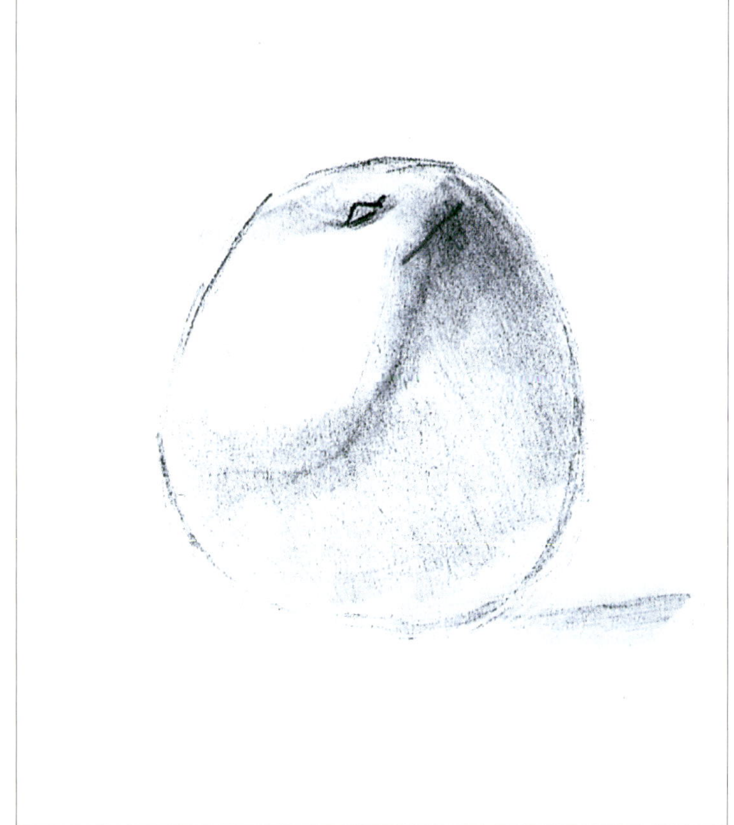

The most luminous zones on the shadow on the right are left reserved.

The shadow tone is done a little darker to intensify the modeling of the form.

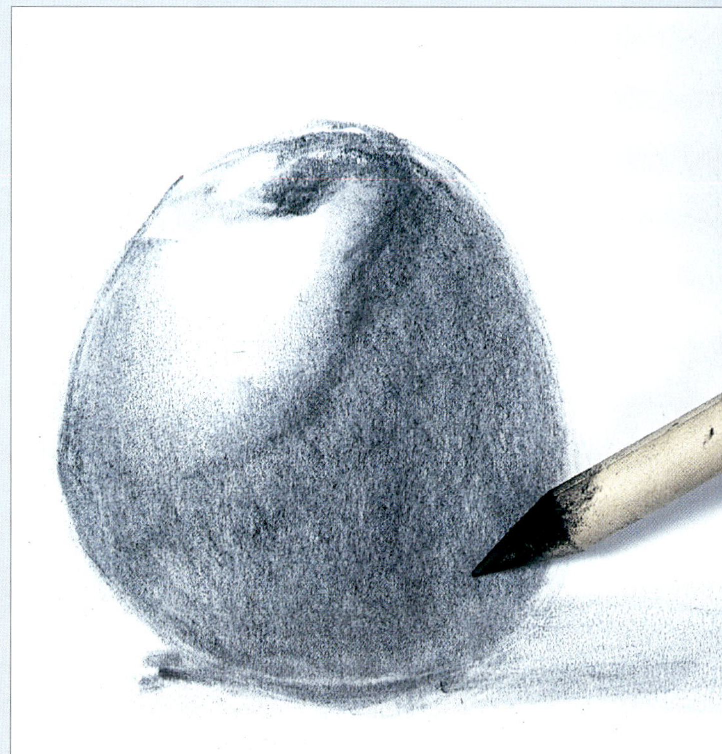

When the shadow is darkened, the side becomes more luminous.

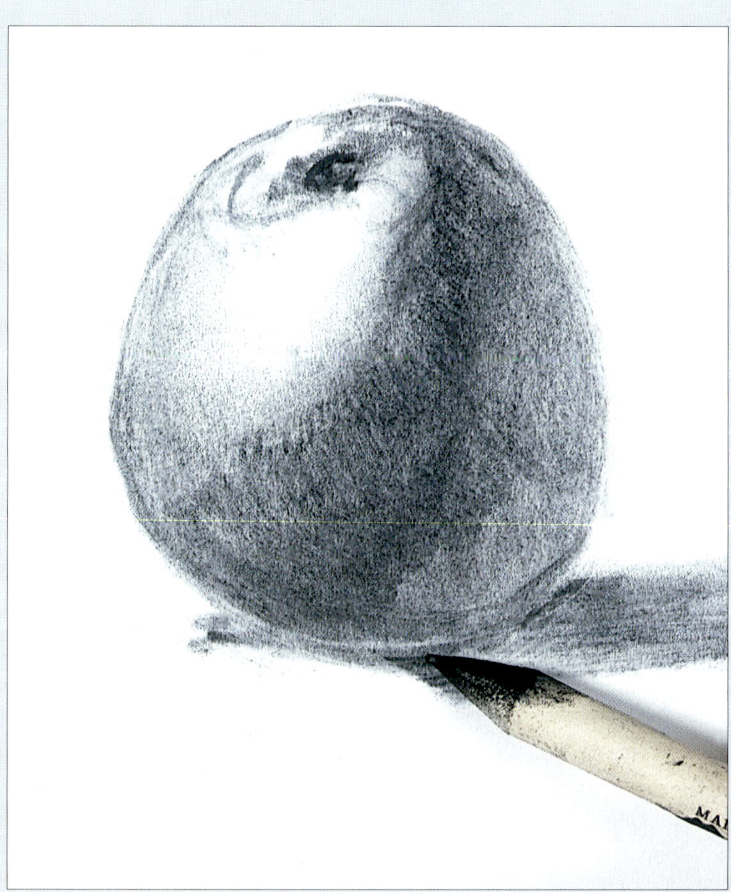

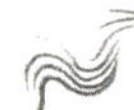

MASTERING THE TONES

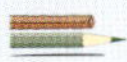

Gustav Klimt, Portrait of a youth, drawing on paper.
Getting the tones right allows perfect modeling of the forms and interesting texture effects. The softest tones come from gently applying the stump, almost imperceptibly, to do the transition between the grays.

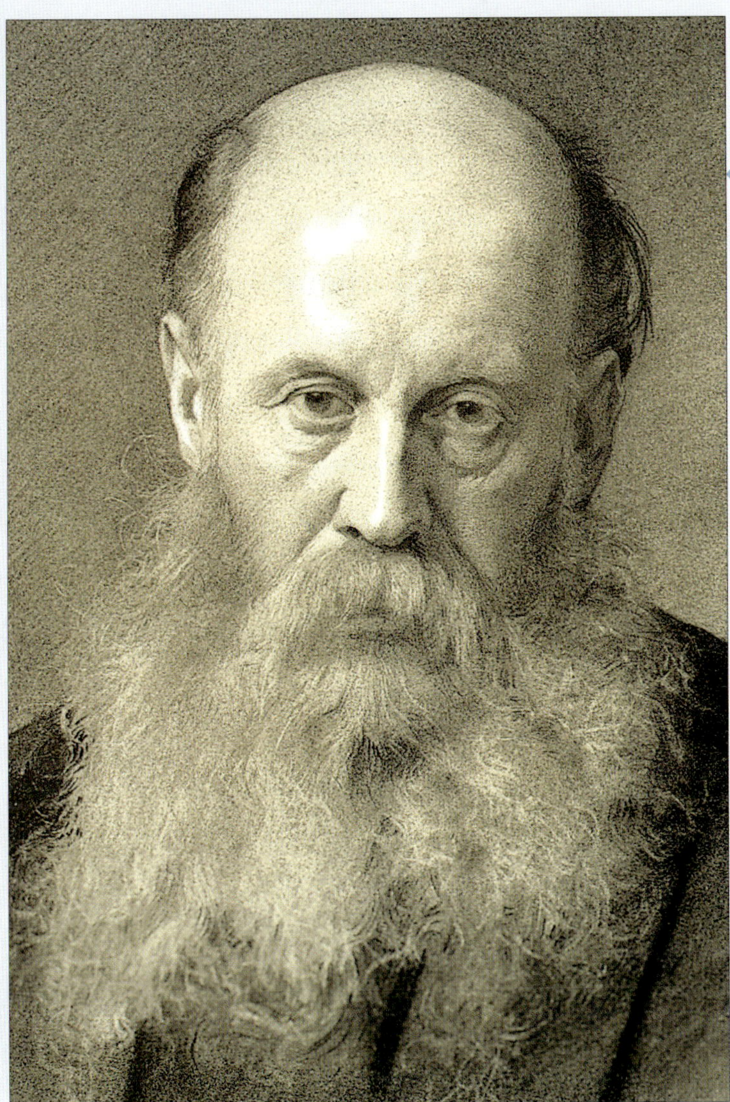

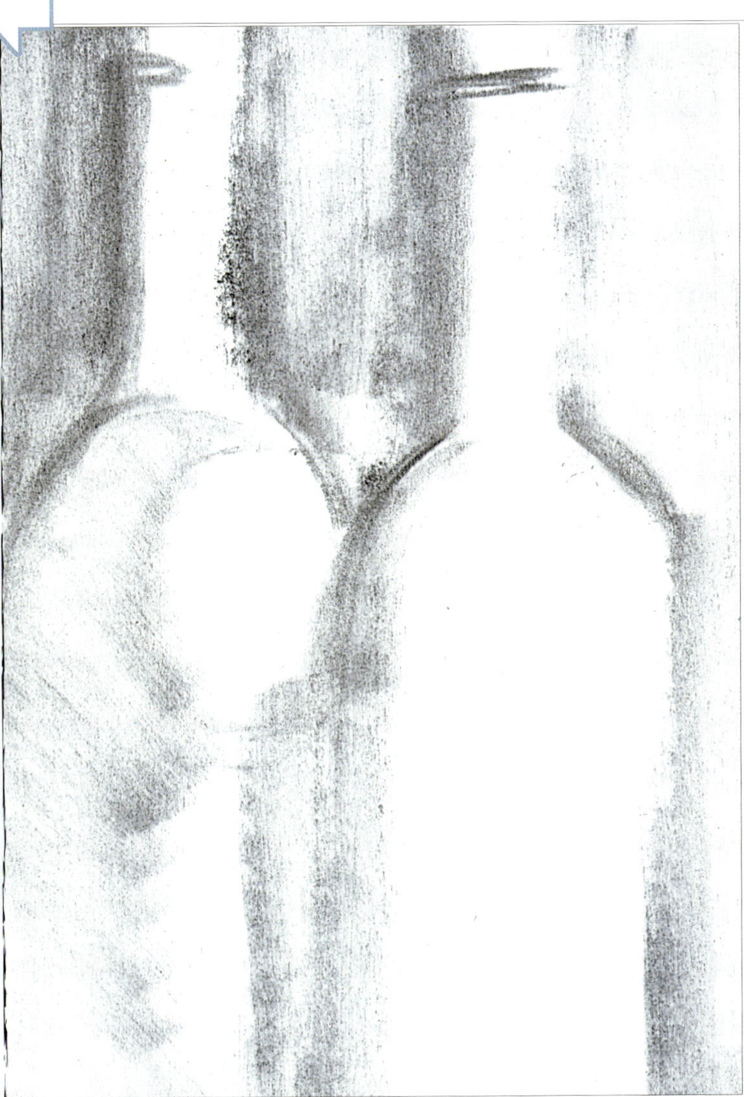

The first zone to be darkened are the bottle shadows, while the highlights are left reserved.

INTEGRATING STUMPINGS WITH CHARCOAL CONTRASTS

Until now we have used the stump alone to get grays. Even the darkest contrasts have been elaborated superimposing tones with the stump. The stump can be used as the drawing base, on top of which you can construct the most intense darks in charcoal. We will work on this in the next exercise, a still life with two bottles.

DEFINING FORMS WITH DARKS

Load the stump to do a scheme of the darks on the bottles. First, outline the forms, then the main shadows, and, finally, the dark background. The stump stroke enables you to do an approximate modeling of the forms and to outline the most luminous part of the still life. The darks will define the principal parts of the bottles. If necessary, reload the stump to do new dark zones.

INTENSIFYING THE DARKS

Impregnate the stump again with charcoal and start to darken the most contrasted zones of the still life. The first tones drawn on the background are now integrated with the less contrasted medium tones. Start to draw the densest darks on the right of the bottle with the stump well-loaded. Observe the strong contrast established between the different tones.

When all the modeling has been done with the stump, you can start work on intensifying the tone contrasts directly with charcoal on the drawing. The blacks in the background must also be intensified. Finally, go over with the stump, softening any forms that may be too dark.

APPLYING THE PRINCIPAL STUMPING TECHNIQUES

Throughout the exercises we have been able to study the stumping techniques, drawing, outlining, blending and smudging. In this final exercise we are going to do a female figure from behind, taking the opportunity to practice all the techniques used up to now. Moreover, we are going to incorporate brush stumping to get soft grays and a more delicate tone distribution than is possible with the stump.

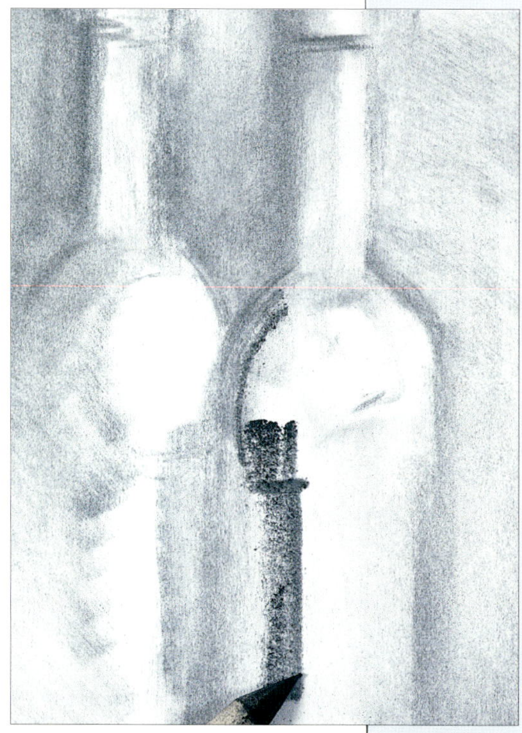

Intensify the darks progressively. The strongest contrasts are applied with the stump heavily loaded.

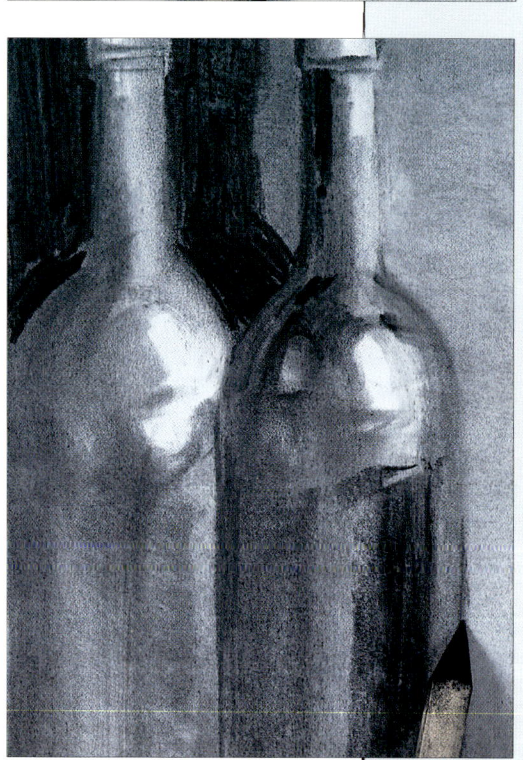

Draw the darkest zones directly and use the stump to soften the excessive contrasts.

OUTLINING THE FORM

Lay out the principal forms of the model with the stump lightly loaded. Be careful with this step because all the later work depends on it. If errors are made, they will have to be corrected with the eraser. Although the figure construction is started with the head, the proportions of the spinal column and the hip structures are important.

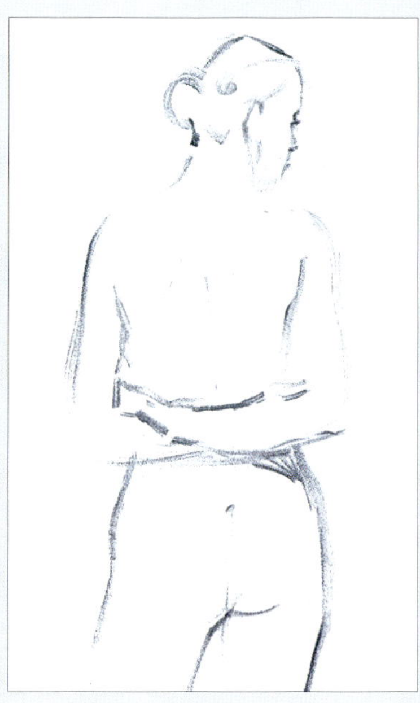

The preliminary sketch must be done carefully, getting the forms right before going on to work on the darks.

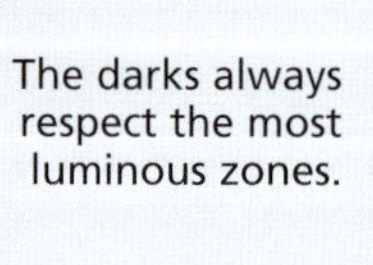

The darks always respect the most luminous zones.

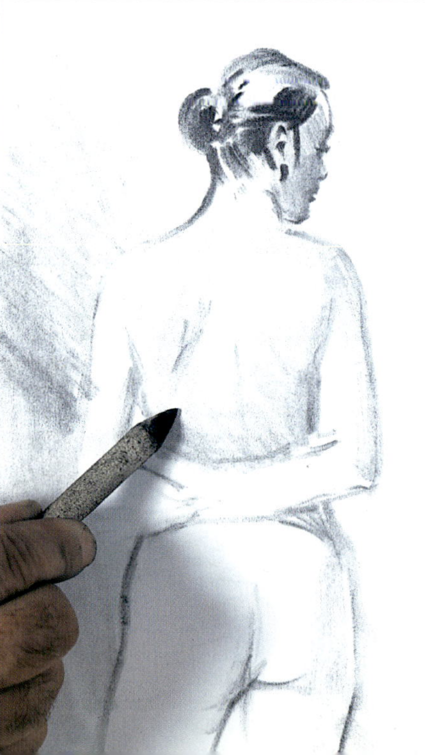

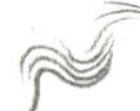

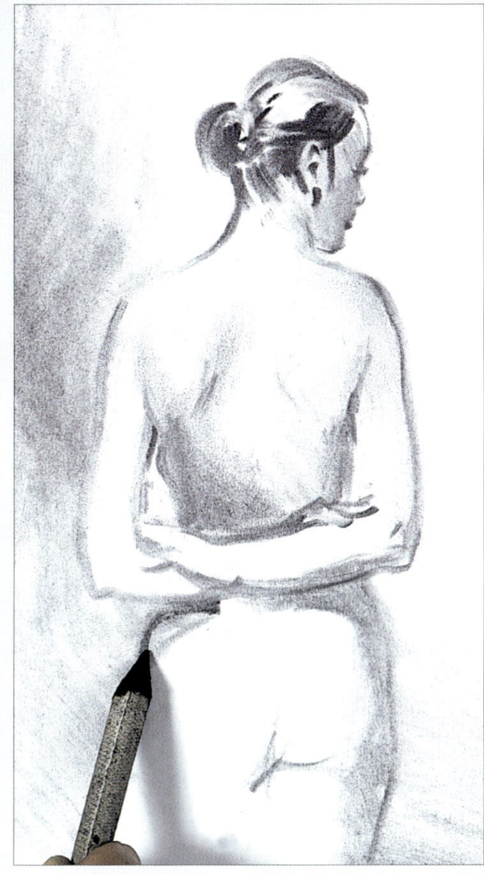

The softening of the forms is done gradually, applying the contrasts at the same time.

Finish the blending of the tones by going over them with the brush one more time.

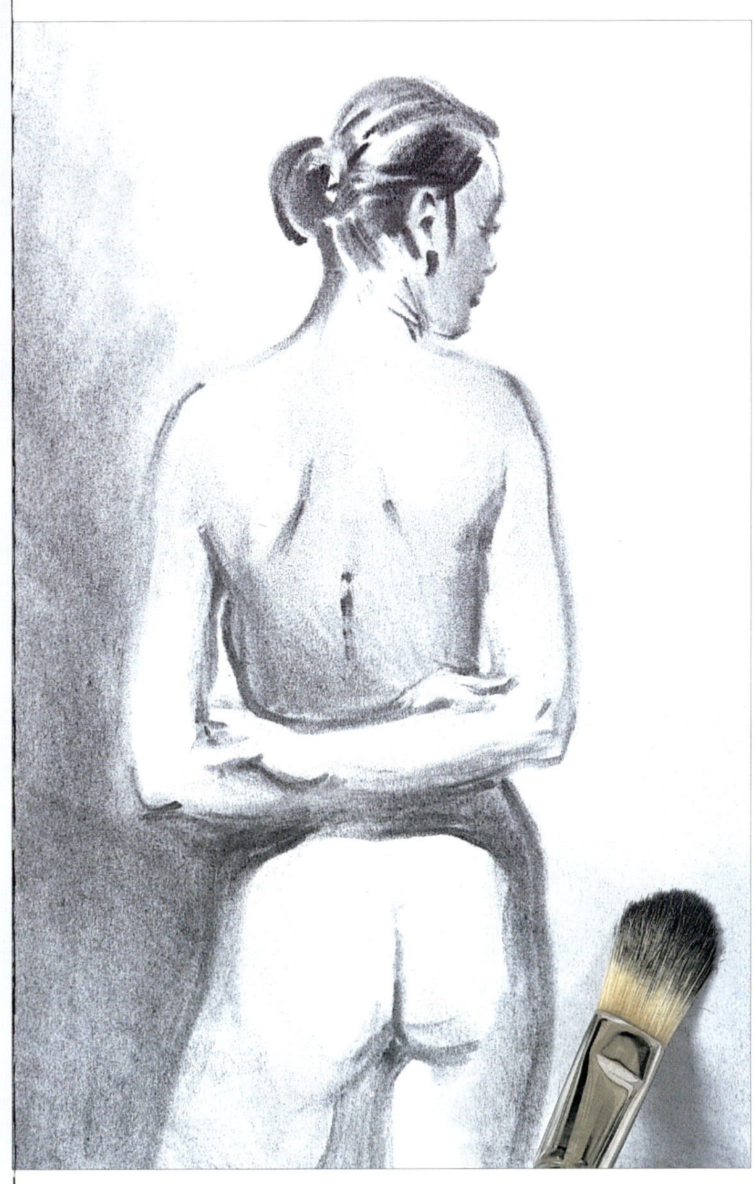

THE FIRST DARKS

Approach the first darks on the figure as you did in the earlier exercises. Once the background is darkened, use the stump loaded with graphite to start the modeling. Be softly insistent when doing the darks between the arms, never pressing too hard so that the transition is subtle. The highlights and the most luminous skin zones must be reserved, unsmudged, from the outset.

SOFTENING THE FORMS

Start to intensify the darks by adding tone, softly passing the stump over. The stump is constantly reloaded so as to increase the contrast. When a tone on the paper turns out to be too dark, spread it until the stroke brings the contrast into proportion.

BRUSH FINISHES

To finish this tone blending exercise we are going to use the brush. The principal darks are realized softly, trying to model the forms and balancing the darks by increasing the shadows on the rounded parts. Finally, all that remains to be done is to soften the grays using the brush. If the latter is impregnated with powder it will darken the tone, like the stump. It can also blend or stump. Here it is used to tone down the strokes in the background.

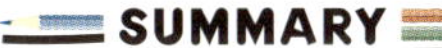

SUMMARY

THE ROLE OF THE STUMP
The stump can be used as a tool to spread the stroke or as a tone applier.

STUMPING AND THE STROKE
The stump helps to do gradations and to draw lines.

THE STUMPING PROCESS
Stumping must be progressive; first the medium tones, then the darker ones and, finally, the tone blending.

INTEGRATING WITH OTHER MEDIUMS
Drawing directly with the stump allows other mediums, charcoal or graphite, to be applied to intensify the contrasts or to blend the tones with a brush.

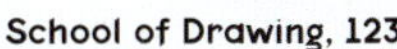

16 Exercices *Step by step*

Working with a stump allows the forms and tone values to be done in great detail. A still life is an excellent theme with which to practice what we have learnt in this chapter. So varied are the tone value and recourse possibilities offered that you can even get by without using graphite or charcoal crayons. If you use earlier exercises as references it will not be too difficult to get a good result in this one.

NECESSARY MATERIAL

Drawing paper. (1),
Graphite powder. (2),
Stumps. (3),
A paint brush. (4),
An eraser. (5),

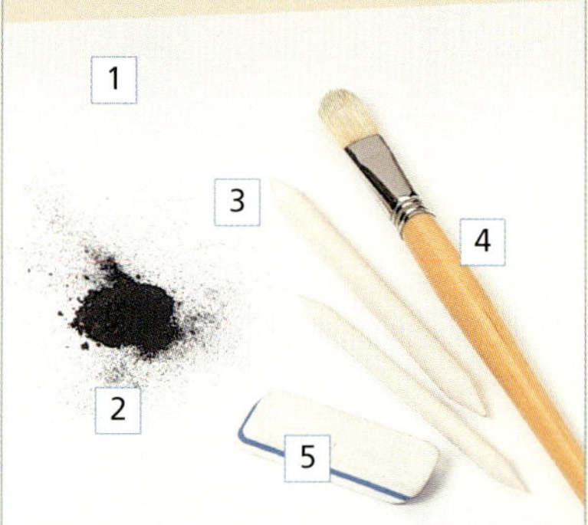

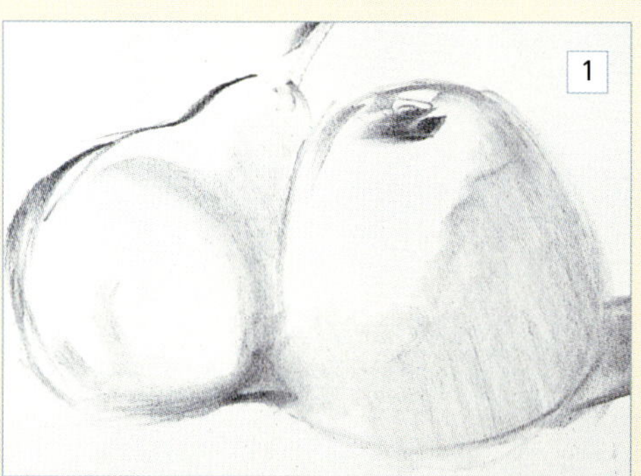

Using the brush gives great effects and allows very special strokes when applied loaded with graphite. However so much use will leave the bristles completely clogged up. Wash it in soap and water and leave it to dry.

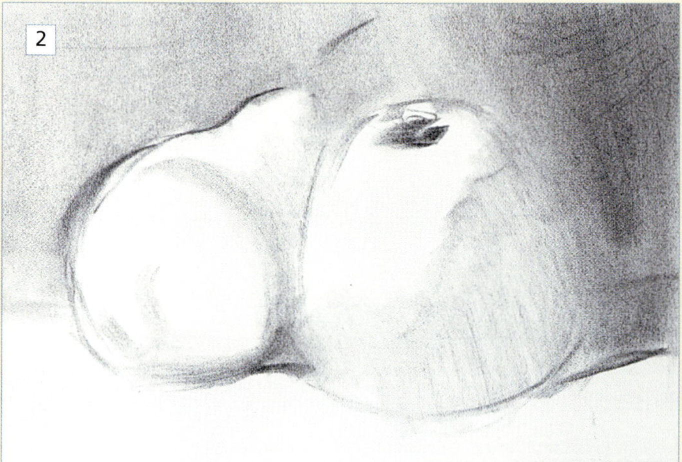

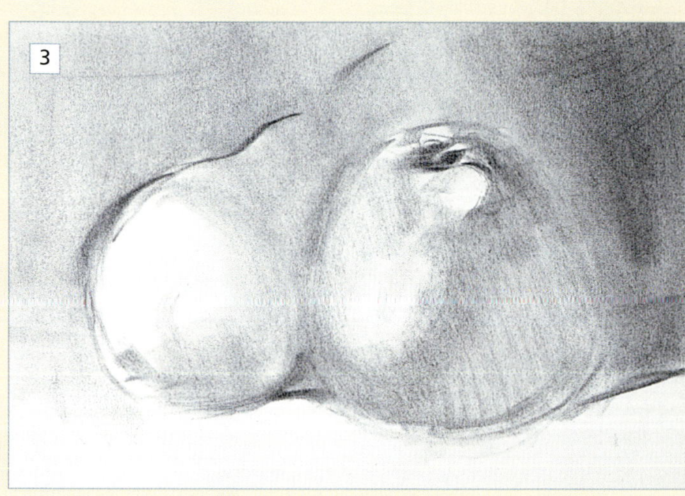

TONE VALUES AND THE STUMP

1· **FIRSTLY, IMPREGNATE THE STUMP** with graphite and outline the fruit, defining them and then doing the first shadows using the stump laterally. The conic side of the point, a precise tool, is softly dragged until the principal shadows are marked and well-defined.

2· **RELOAD WITH GRAPHITE AND MAKE** the background much darker than the shadows of the fruits, which now come across as duller than before. Insist with the stump on the right until this side is much darker. When you compare this step with the last one, you will see that before the apple shadows were soft yet well-defined. Adding darks has dimmed the tones of the apples considerably.

3· **ADDING GRAYS TO THE BACKGROUND** decreased the shadow contrast of the fruit. Now you have to compensate the grays and redarken the shadows. Impregnate the stump with graphite again and darken the shadow that runs diagonally across an apple. Blend this tone with the previous one, going over it lightly. Outline the pear and intensify the dark tone. The whites are now surrounded by shadows. Their definition can always be increased with the eraser.

4· **DARKEN THE SHADOW OF THE PEAR,** making the highlights brighter and more contrasted. To draw the dark zone that separates the pear from the apple, softly apply the stump each time the zone is darkened. Model the apple with a new graphite load, going around the highlights without shading them.

5· **IN THIS STEP INTENSIFY THE DARKEST** contrasts on the fruit until the tone intensity of the background is matched. This is the most important part of the modeling process because it will give the necessary

A still life with fruits

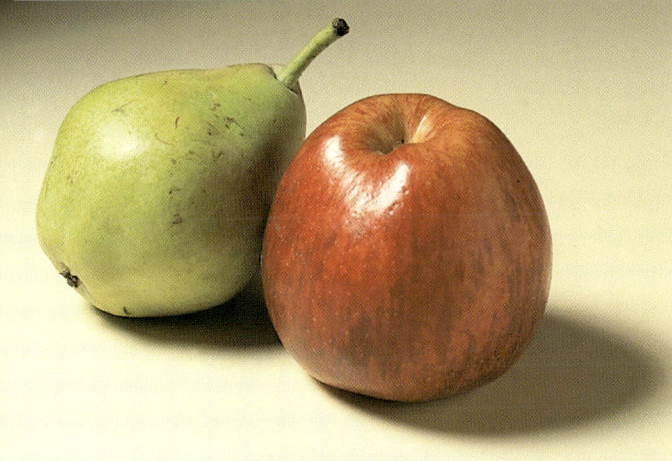

SUMMARY SCHEME

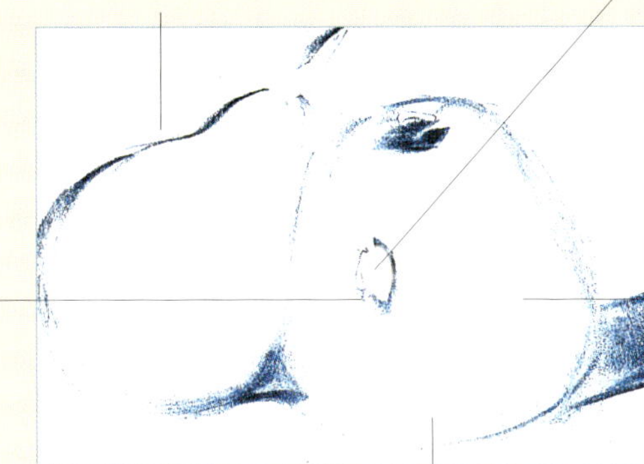

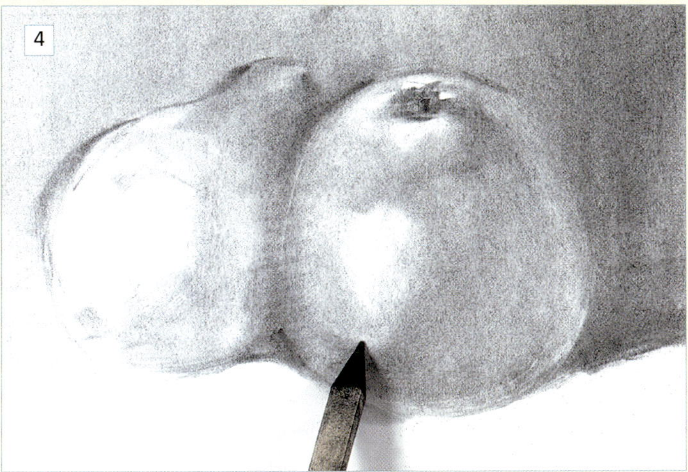

4

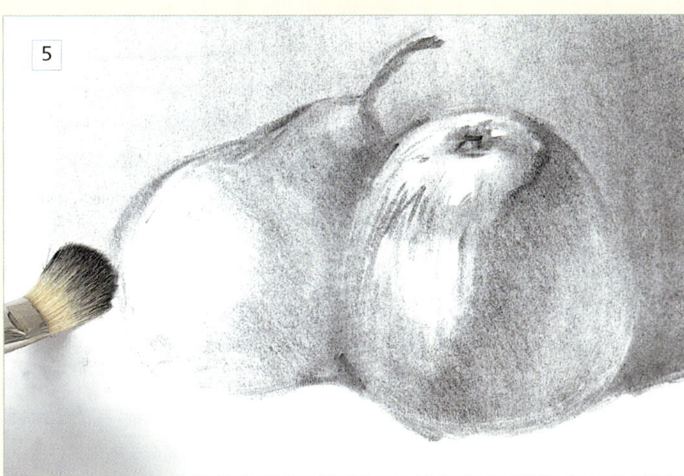

5

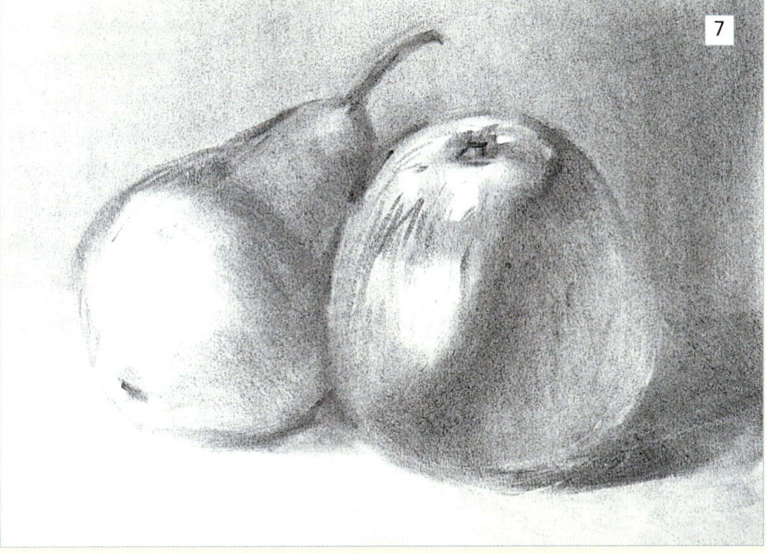

7

7· CLEAN THE LIMIT BETWEEN THE HORIZONTAL white and the background with the eraser, making an imperfect, straightish line. Use the impregnated stump to softly go over the fruit outlines, but only in the darkest parts. Finally, gently darken the table foreground with the brush.

volume effect. Work as you did when doing the middle part of the apple, but here the tones are much darker. Use the edge of the eraser to open up linear highlights on the apple and to outline those on the pear. Use the brush to start softening the grays.

6· IN THIS CLOSE UP YOU CAN SEE how the darkest zone of the apple has been intensified. Soften the shadow against the background so that the tone transition is subtle.

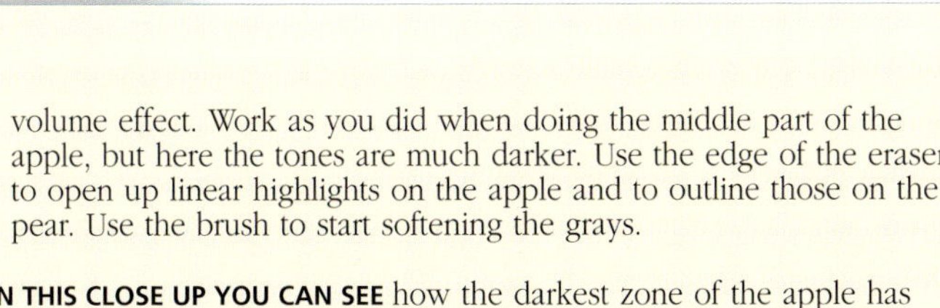

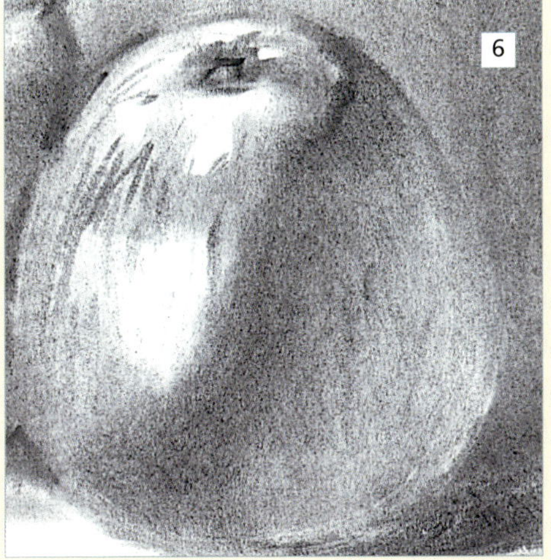

6

17 HOW TO SKETCH THE MODEL

A sketch is defined as a rough drawing done in the minimum possible time. As one does more and more, one's hand will become steadier. Moreover, one can learn tricks which will enable you to achieve all sorts of effects and overcome problems. In this chapter we are going to do a fair number of sketches. We have left out the intermediate steps so that more figure poses can be shown. Try to copy them and understand how they have been done. It is a good idea to repeat the sketches so that you get the feel of the strokes, the forms and the proportions.

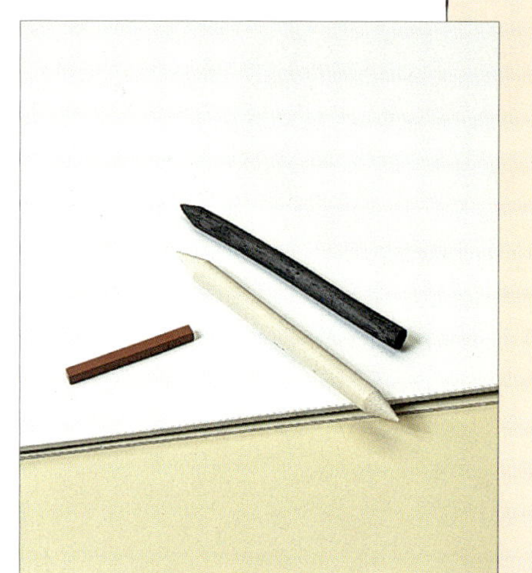

This material is ideal for doing sketches.

A WORK SESSION.

Sketch work doing a series of studies is called a session. The work is continuous and the aim is quick sketches without going into details but rather concentrating on certain aspects of the figure. In some sketches you will be going for just the line, in others expressing the poses through shadows, and in others movement with a few schematic lines. In all of the different exercises we do it is important to be concise with the details. By working on your sketching skills you will master drawing forms and pick up recourses which will help you to do all types of pictures later.

SKETCH ANYWHERE AND ANYTIME.

A sketch is a discrete exercise that can be done anywhere. All your need is a small piece of paper to do this rewarding exercise. In a café, in a bus or a public park, any place where there are people offers you opportunity to do some sketches.

FIRST OUTLINES

Start the session by doing synthetic and gestural strokes to warm up. At the moment you are only trying to capture the main lines with just a few strokes, even though the final result may end up not looking very complete.

The purpose of a sketch is not to have a finished look: many parts of the body do not even need to be outlined. In general, a sketch is about the principal forms which make the pose recognizable.

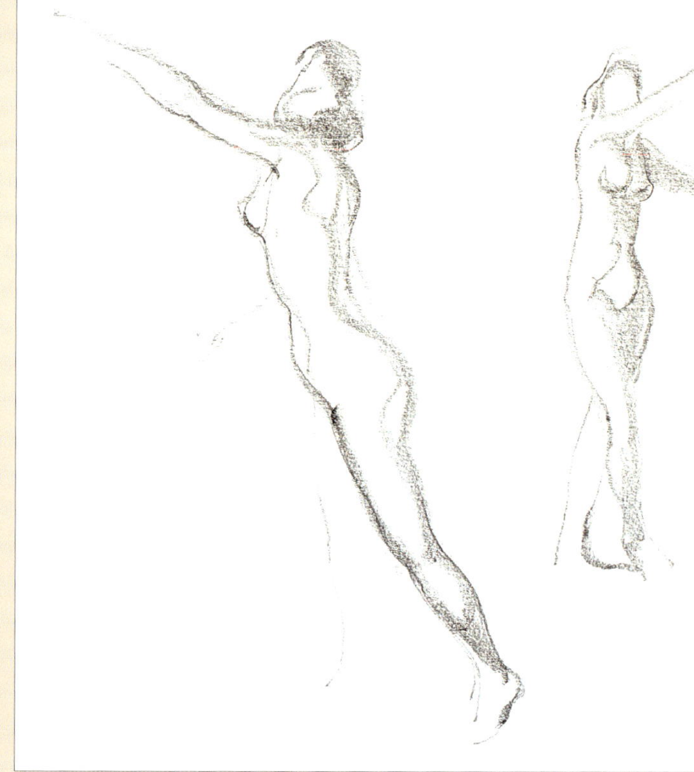

This sketch was done in less than thirty seconds in a public place. This type of work can turn waiting at, for example, the hairdressers' into an interesting 'session'.

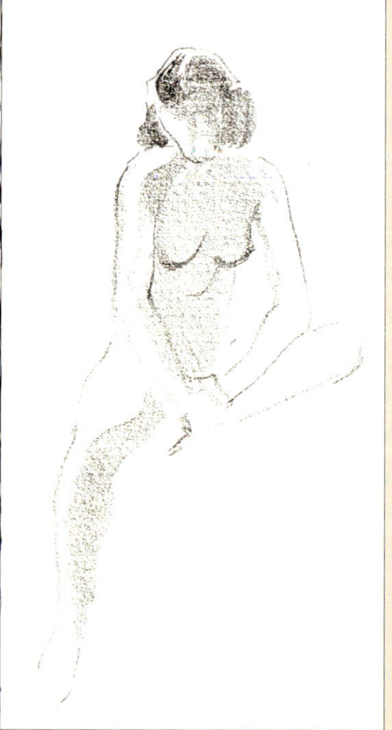

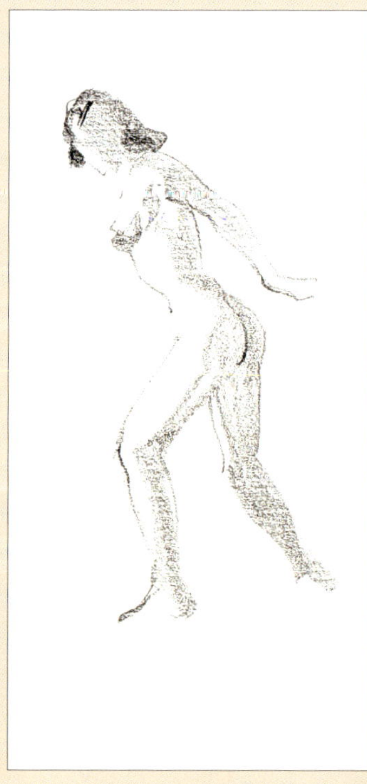

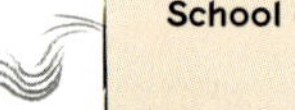

17

In drawing a learning process that is complex and requires patience and dedication is that of sketching the model. A learner, or anyone who aims at perfecting their ability, is constantly having to fall back on sketches

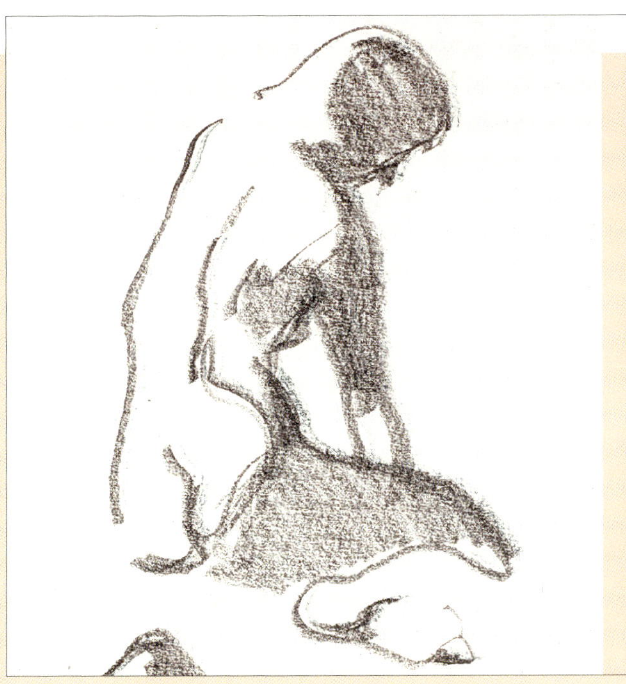

Observe the simplicity and speed with which the light and shadow zones are separated.

LINE AND STROKE RECOURSES

Model sketches must be realized in such a way that they do not slow down the work rhythm. Therefore you must leave aside tone values or the modeling of grays. One of the best ways of setting about a sketch is by doing a fine, clean stroke to define the figure's illuminated form, and a single thick graphite or charcoal stroke for the form of the shadow.

These sketches are done at the beginning of the session to express the form. Each drawing should only take a few seconds.

WHERE TO DO SKETCHES

Although it is fine to work from photos, there is nothing like a real model. This should not be a problem for the majority of learners because in many towns there is an art school where one can freely go to sketch a model. In some cities there are artists' associations which have a weekly session with a model. Another possibility is to hire a model: they are usually paid by the hour, and if several learners club together a couple of hours are not too expensive and give enough time to do a reasonable drawing. However, if it is impossible to draw a natural model, you can always fall back on photos, but remember it is not the best option.

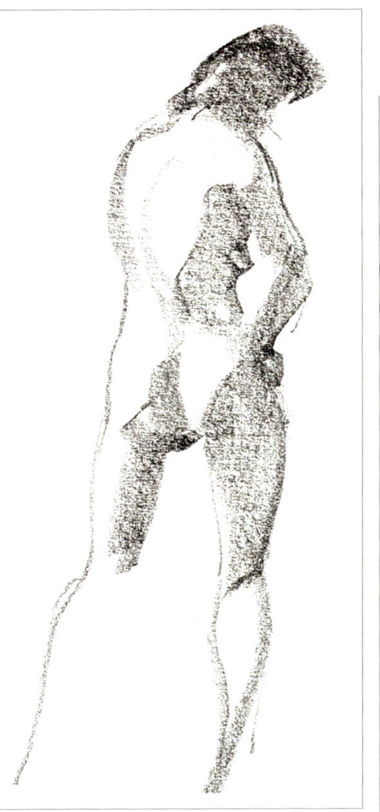

The proportions are much more evident on a standing up figure.

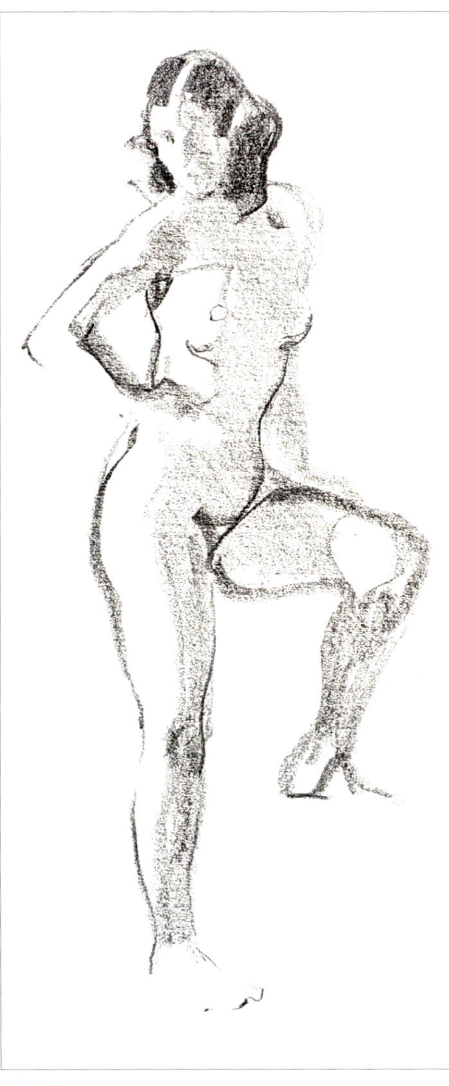

The figure must be constructed paying attention to the shoulder position with respect to the hip line.

UPRIGHT FIGURE SKETCHES

Once you have done a few rapid, gestural strokes, you can start on upright poses. It is necessary to do it in this order because, as you can appreciate, some poses are more complex than others. It is easier to perceive a figure standing up and to sketch it than one reclined or in perspective.

STATIONARY SKETCHES

The easiest sketches to do are those without time limits as it is possible to correct any errors. However, do not use an eraser. Instead correct on top of the false line so that you can use it as a reference of what to avoid. Moreover, the eraser means you waste valuable time. When doing sketches of standing up figures, bear in mind the following points: the proportion between the head and the body, the form of the spinal column, the inclination of the shoulders with respect to the hip, and the leg position and the way they are supported on the floor.

MORE THAN ONE VIEWPOINT

Whether doing stationary sketches or people moving, it is interesting to try it from several viewpoints walking round the figure. The same pose can appear completely different when viewed from a different angle. Moreover, constantly changing the work angle means that the draftsman does not become 'lazy' and too familiar with working with fixed references.

SITTING FIGURE SKETCHES

Sketching a sitting figure involves different complications to a standing one. The joints and limbs are not the mere continuation of the body: they are on different planes which have to be worked in with the strokes and shadows. Here a few sitting sketch figures are put forward, a little more complicated than the previous ones.

Pay attention to the form of the joints and remember that some parts may be hidden but they still play a role as reference points.

Try to do these drawings rapidly. Both sketches are of the same pose but from different perspectives.

THE THICKNESS OF THE SKETCH STROKES

The stroke must not have the same intensity in all the drawing. In some zones the stroke will be pressed down hard on the paper as it marks out a principal line. On other occasions it can be so fine that it almost disappears. These are some of the most rewarding recourses of a good draftsman: a zone that requires a lot of dedication is left undrawn but perfectly insinuated by the hard, firm strokes around it.

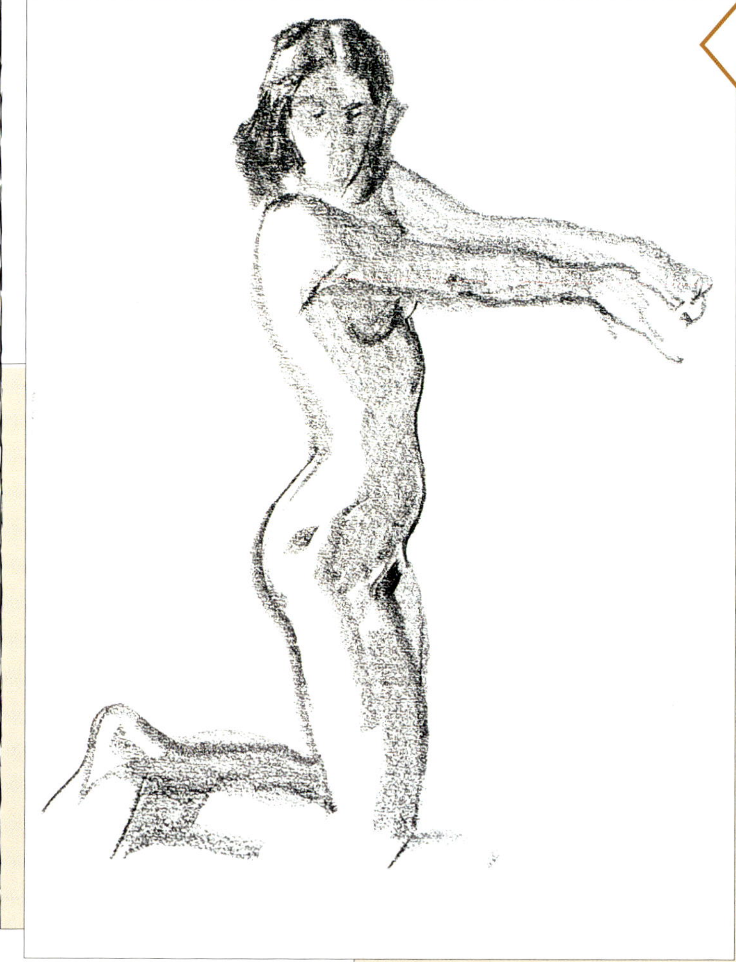

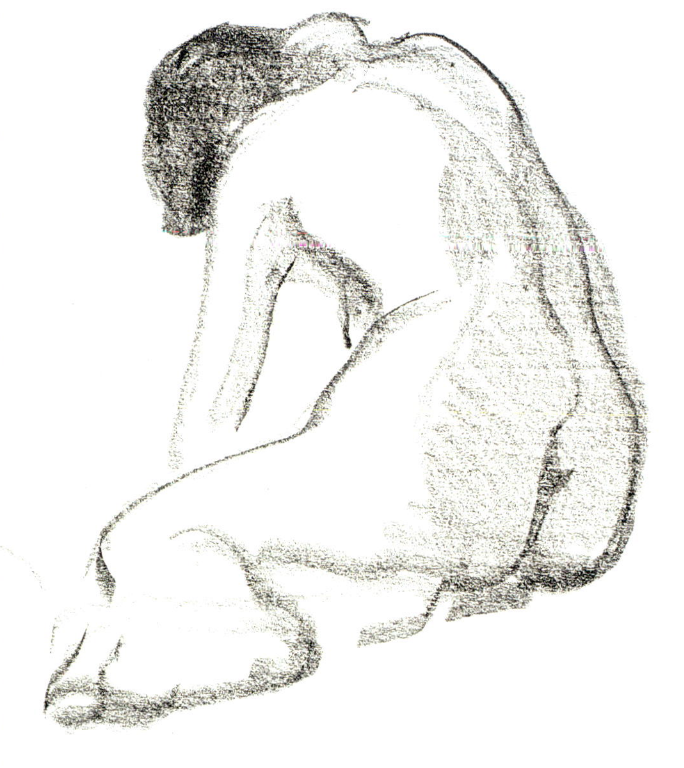

The body parts extended forwards start from the torso.

RECLINED FIGURE SKETCHES

A reclined figure requires an additional dimension compared to standing or sitting. It is one of the most complex forms to draw because it alters the sensation of space.

KEEP THE PROPORTIONS

If you have practiced the standing up figure sufficiently you will start with an advantage when it comes to the reclined figure. The proportions

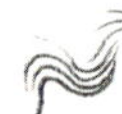

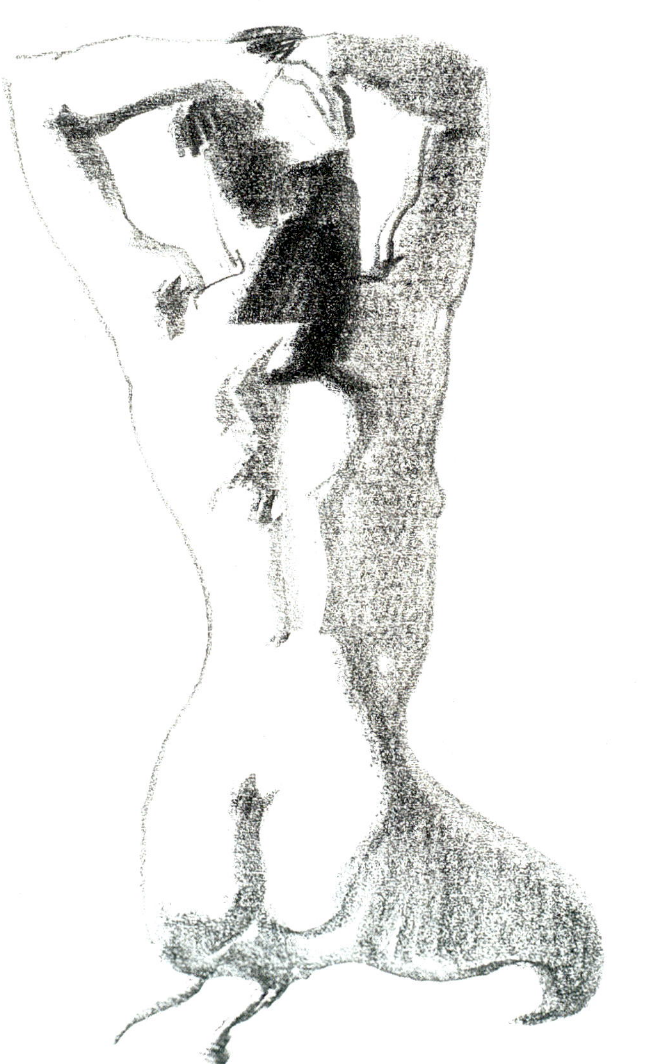

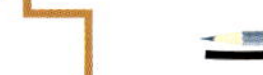 **OBSERVE BEFORE DRAWING** 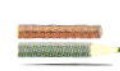

This must be one of the artist's habits before even approaching the first line. A figure that is not standing presents a series of complexities, especially the foremost leg and hidden body parts. You have to observe where all the lines start, where the joints are and how they are supported by the body.

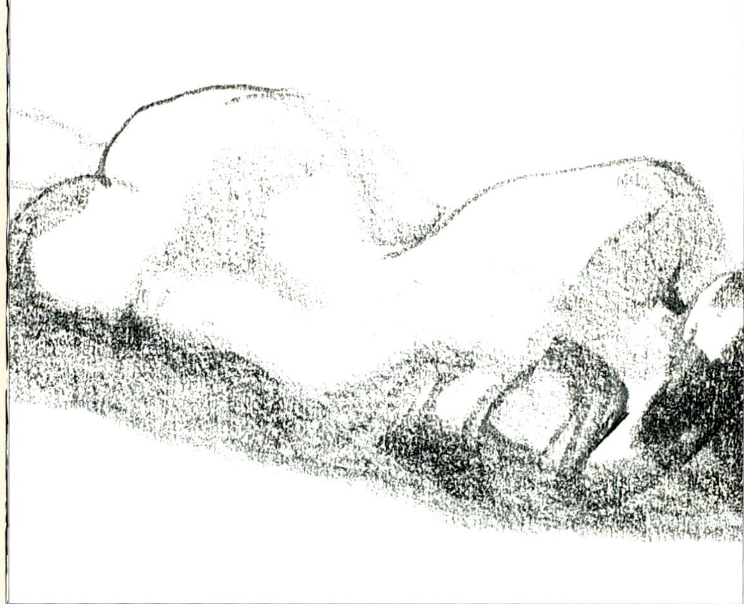

In this close up you can observe one of the most frequently used recourses for resolving the form.

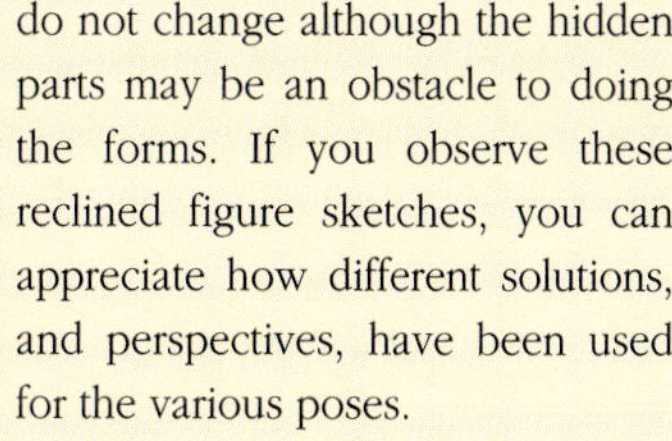

do not change although the hidden parts may be an obstacle to doing the forms. If you observe these reclined figure sketches, you can appreciate how different solutions, and perspectives, have been used for the various poses.

Observe how in this sketch the areas requiring most attention have been insinuated by perfectly defined, straightforward lines.

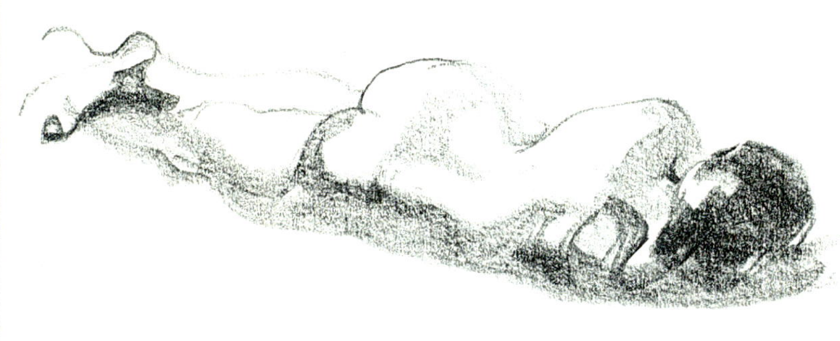

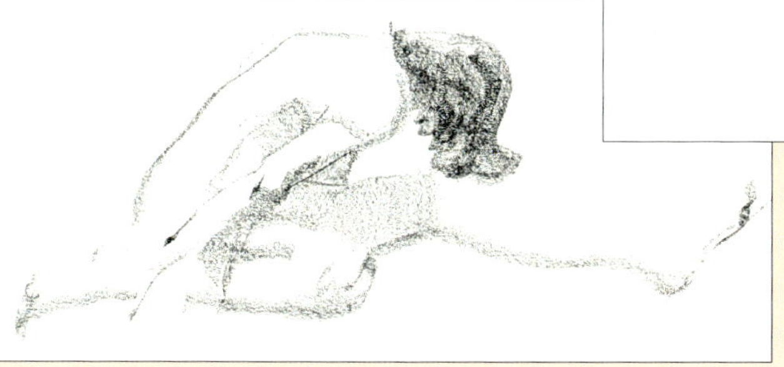

Pay attention to the bending of the joints.

COMPLEX RECLINED POSES

Drawing the figure foreshortened is the most complicated approach. It is recommendable to outline it again, at least mentally, as if it were a simple geometric shape composition. This will enable you to make the foregrounds appear logical in the eyes of the viewer, something quite tricky because the daring viewpoint means it is difficult to make credible. The most demanding poses are those in which part of the body is hidden by the head. In this case the torso is in a posterior plane and is also foreshortened.

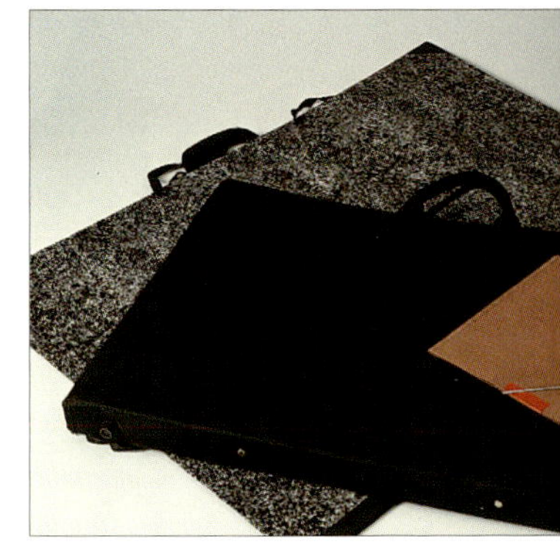

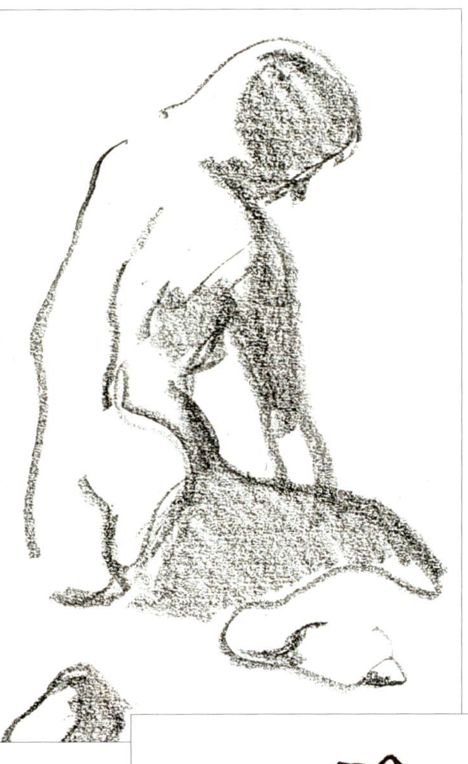

Pay attention to the proportions and how the limbs of the reclined body are situated.

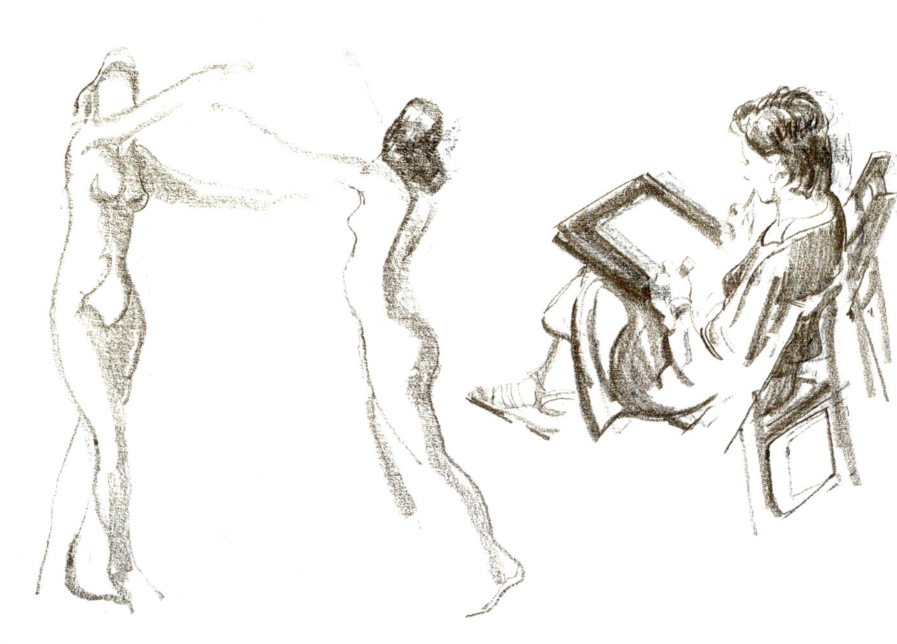

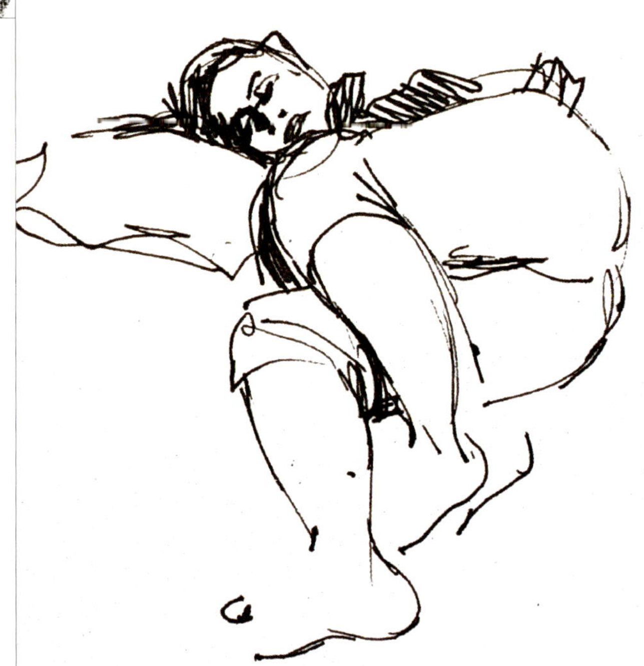

Use these sketches as references. As you can see, the body parts being out of proportion is due to the foreshortening.

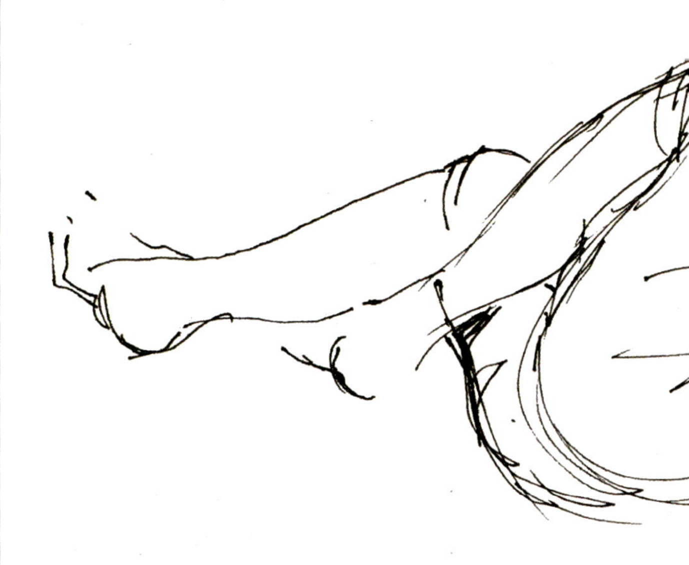

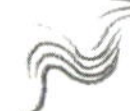

HOW TO STORE THE SKETCHES

When an artist is constantly doing sketches, they will soon build up quite a number in a short period of time. In one session twelve sketches can easily be done and could be a good inspiration source for later works, learning both from the good points and the things that did not come off. Sketches are important so store them safely in files, sorted according to the date and the size. Then they will always be ready to be revised, quickly and comfortably.

Take these sketches as a reference and try to do them as quickly as possible.

MOVING SKETCHES

To finish off the session of figure sketches, we can do a few of people in movement, which means they are especially difficult. Calculating proportions or neatly constructing the dg1 does not work here. What you must do is draw the principal lines in a few strokes, leaving out any element that could slow down the process or agility.

AN EXERCISE IN VISUAL MEMORY

This next exercise can also be taken as a game by the learner. As it is impossible to show a figure moving on these pages, we propose the following: observe the sketch for a second and then try to do it as quickly as possible without looking at the book again. At first it is likely that the results will not be perfect, but practice will make your hand steadier, improve your visual memory and knowledge of the human body.

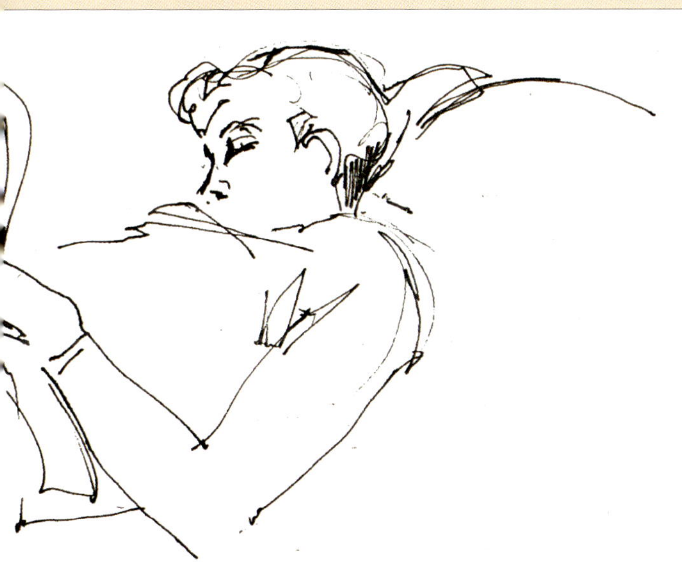

QUiCK SKETCHES

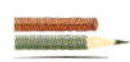

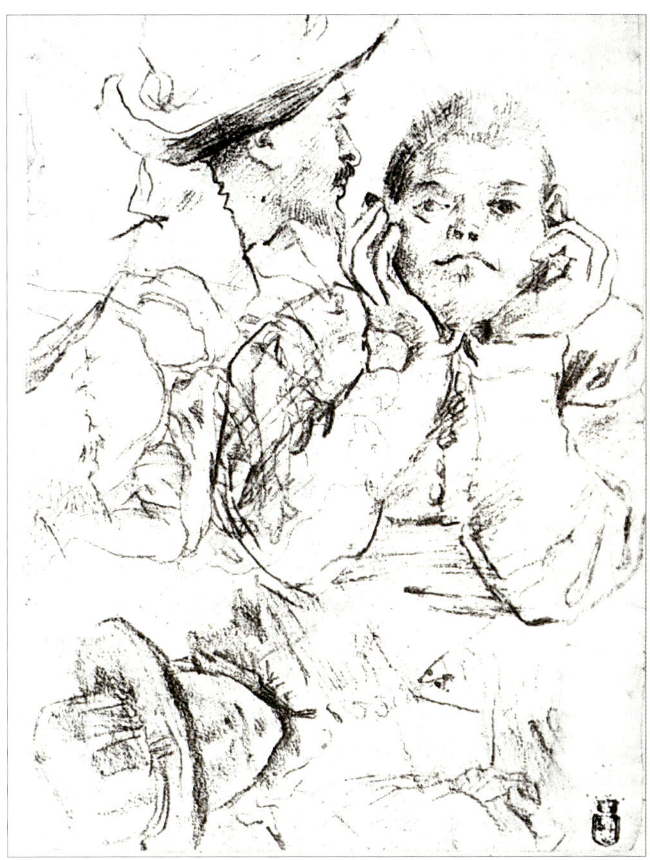

Annibale Caracci (1560-1609). Three studies of men, black stone. Private collection. Natural sketches teach you how to treat the forms spontaneously and to resolve the drawing. Here is a good example. Caracci's sketches are fresh, relaxed and full of spontaneous, free expression. The artist was not worried about getting a perfect finish, and therefore did the corrections directly over the drawing.

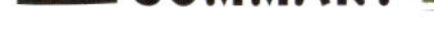

SUMMARY

STROKES AND SHADING
When sketching models use a rapid and firm stroke. The dark zones are done in one stroke.

STANDING FIGURE
Bear in mind the proportions between the parts of the body and the relationship of the shoulders and hips.

GOING AROUND THE FIGURE
The same pose can be done from different viewpoints.

COMPLEX FIGURES
Foreshortened figures are complicated so break the preliminary sketch down into simple shapes which help to make the structure clear.

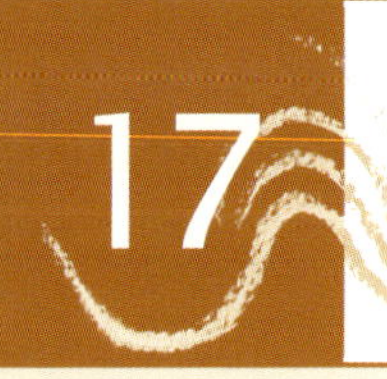

17 Exercices *Step by step*

Here we can do two pose exercises fairly quickly, working from photos which means that the results will be quite similar to a brief session of stationary figures. We are going to use these two poses: one standing and the other lying on the floor. Before starting to draw, observe how the weight is distributed, the shoulder line, the hip and the proportions between the limbs. Copy the steps that are shown, and once you have finished the work, do new sketches which will surely turn out better. Although in the first part of this chapter you were advised not to use an eraser, this is not an unbreakable rule. It is included among the material, so use your judgment.

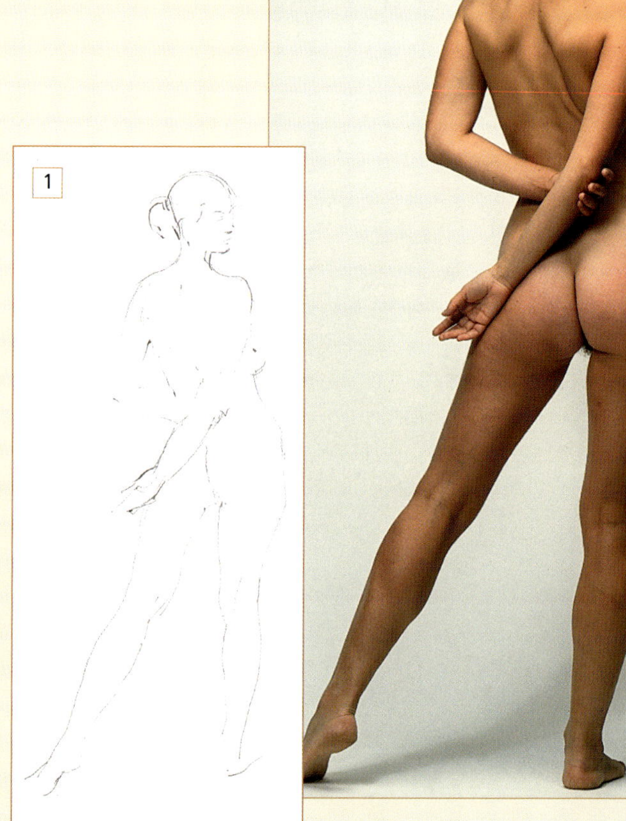

NECESSARY MATERIAL

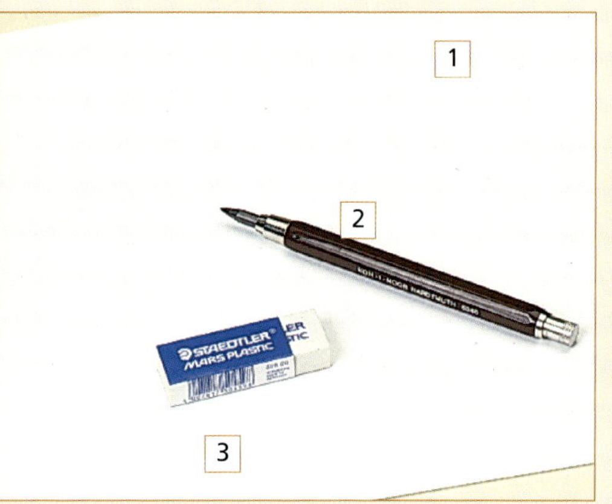

Drawing paper (1), Push button pencil with a graphite lead (2), Eraser (3),

1· **DO THE PRELIMINARY SKETCH QUICKLY,** starting with the head and the line of the back. The shadows are slightly twisted and this influences the complete pose: the right shadow is more curved than the left one. As you can see, the right hip is somewhat higher than the left one, stretching the leg and placing all the body weight on the opposite side. Observe how the elbows have been done, hardly drawn, just insinuated by the forearm and the arm.

2· **ONCE THE PRELIMINARY SKETCH** has been done, you can start on the shadow zones. As we saw in the first part of the chapter, shadows in quick sketches do not have tone values and, therefore, the anatomy has to be described with planes of light and shadow. Draw the darkest parts of the figure and you will notice how the most luminous parts stand out more. This work is done rapidly, paying attention to the model's light zones. The graying of the forms can be done with the side of the graphite crayon, or by taking a piece of lead out of the holder and drawing with all its surface.

3· **DRAW THE DARK PART OF THE LEGS** in the same way that you did the upper part of the trunk. The highlights on the right calf and on the buttocks are left blank. Finally, go over the main lines of the figure without doing excessive details on the finest parts, like the fingers.

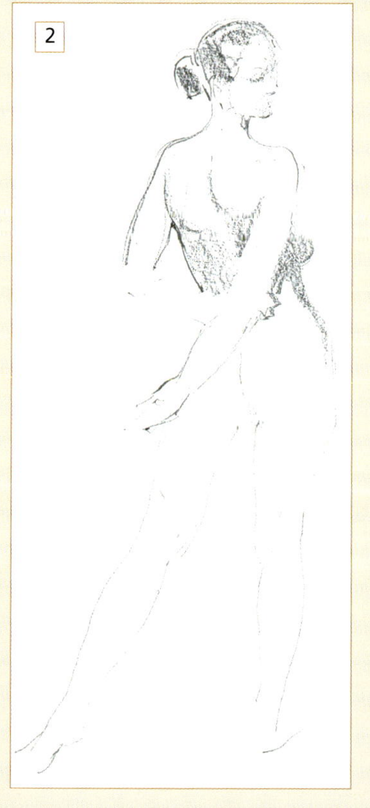

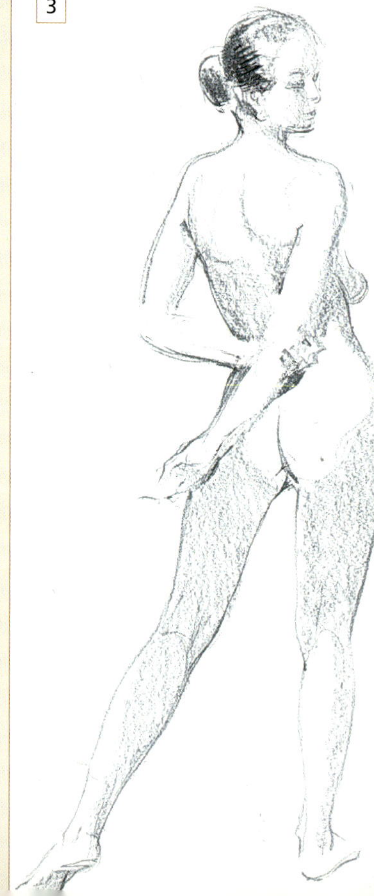

Two model sketches

17

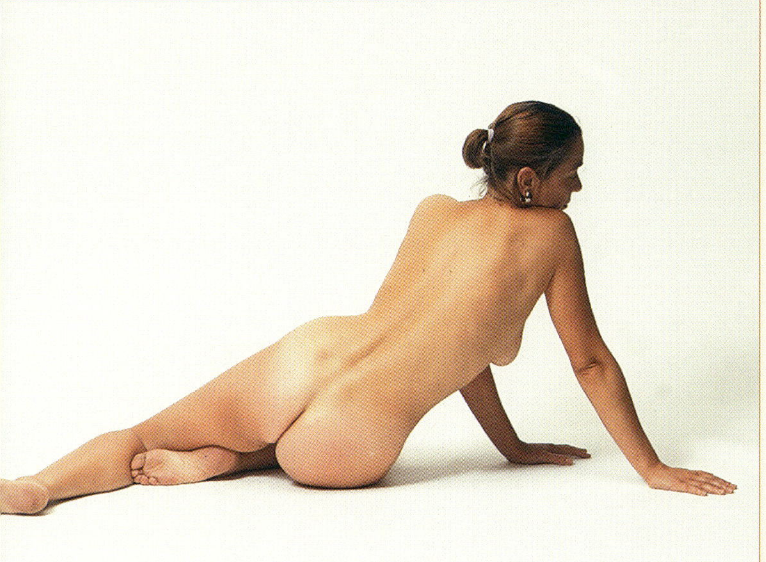

SUMMARY SCHEME

1. Start working neatly, studying the position of the shadows and of the spinal column.

3. The most luminous tones are outlined by darker tones.

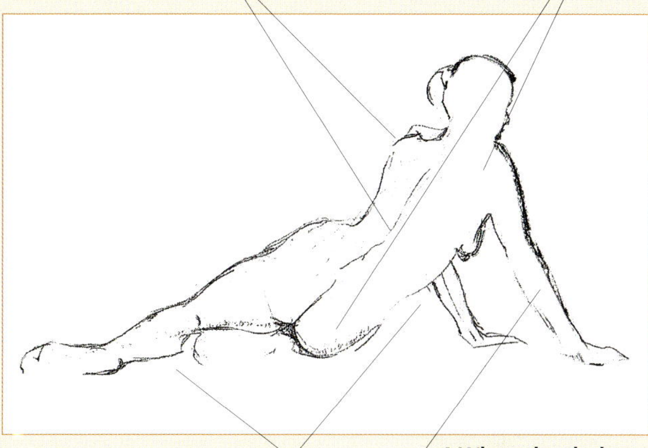

2. The darks are done with a thick, steady stroke, without adding tone values.

4 When the darks are finished, go over the drawing lines.

4

5

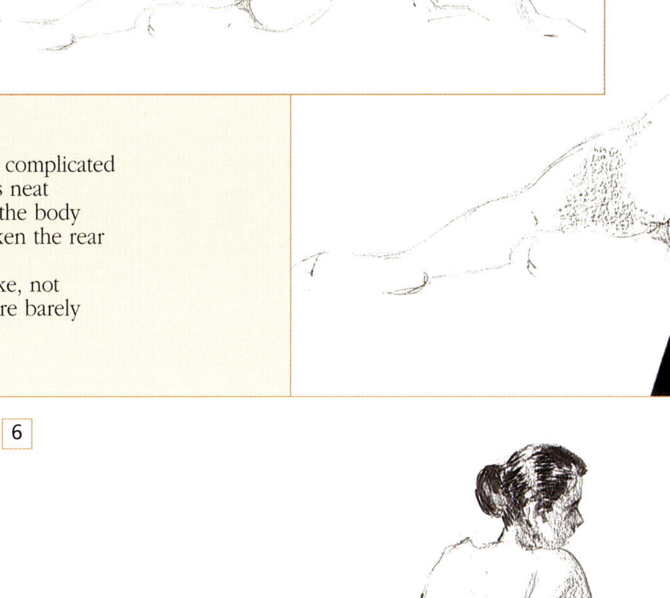

6

4· THE DRAWING STARTS WITH THE HEAD. Draw the shadow line so that both shadows are almost at the same height. The deltoid muscle covers part of the chin. As the pose clearly indicates the leaning of the spinal column, the drawing is made easier. In this drawing the back is easier to draw than in the last exercise because the arms do not get in the way and the spinal column is immediately visible. The hip line is sharply sloped to the right so the right buttock is supported on the floor. Pay attention to the way the lower left leg is slightly foreshortened as it is slightly to the rear.

5· ONCE THE SCHEME OF THE POSE IS FINISHED, the most complicated anatomical features are behind you. On top of this neat drawing you can start to draw the darks that give the body form. To foreshorten the leg, it is sufficient to darken the rear part of the left thigh.
Darken all the figure's right side with a quick stroke, not adding any tone value. The most luminous parts are barely insinuated.

6· TO FINISH OFF THE FORESHORTENING OF THE LEGS, do a strong dark between the right buttock and the foot. This gives an effective sense of spatial depth. To balance this very dense dark, do the same on the left arm, leaving the wrist and the hand scarcely insinuated by the light.

18 CROSSED STROKES AND HATCHiNG

Shaded zones can be crossed or parallel, and the resulting grays offer all types of drawing possibilities.
In this chapter we are going to study different ways of drawing based on hatching and shading. Stumping will not come into play but this does not mean that there will not be tone values.

A wide range of grays can be derived from shading. In the following pages we will study a variety of examples working with these ingredients.

LINES, SEPARATE AND SIDE BY SIDE

Strokes add up to form shading and the consequent gradations. As with the other drawing techniques, the way the shadows are constructed has to go hand in hand with the formal construction of the drawing, the tone values and the light lines. Shadows are an accessory which help to structure the drawing and must be used as tools or recourse.

SHADOWS FROM STROKES

Shadows can be created without there being any tone blending. This work must be intuitive, taking advantage of your knowledge of obtaining tone values from stumping. Darker shadows are obtained by pressing strokes hard together. The type of shadow developed will depend on the relationship between the plane in question, the different light zones and the breaks between the illuminated parts and the penumbra.

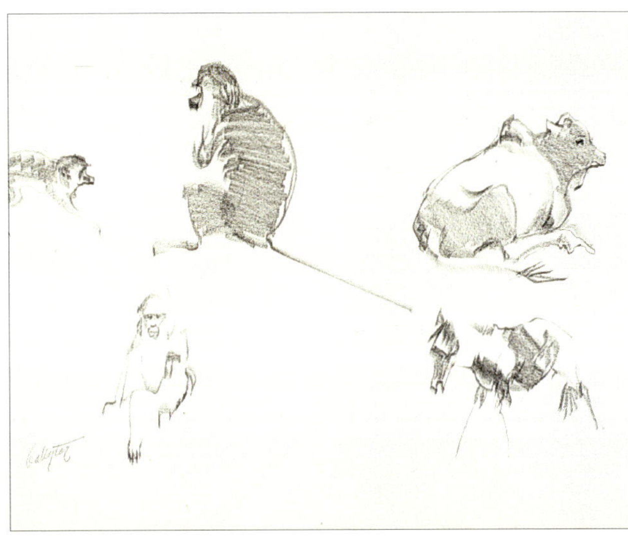

The light zone of these sketches is outlined by the shadows, created uniquely by rapid strokes. There is no stumping..

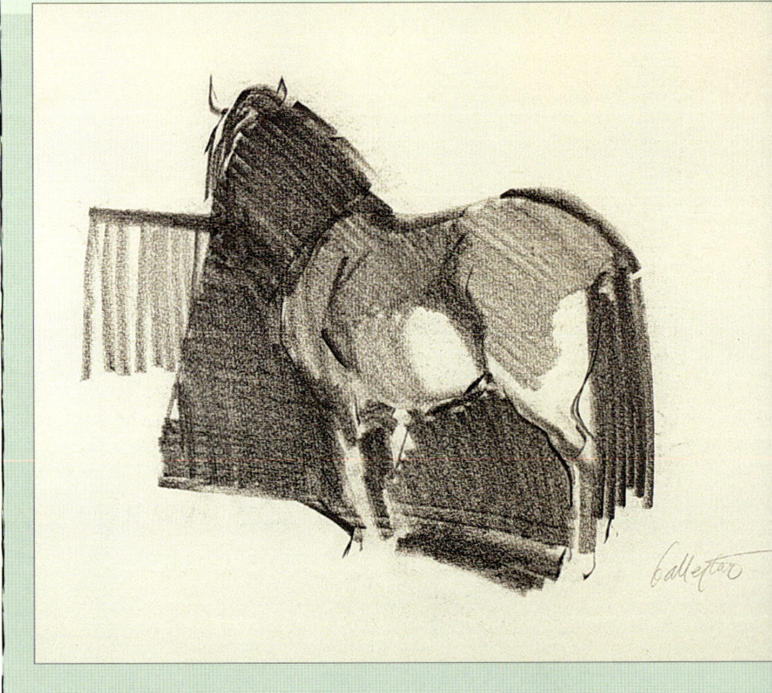

NO STUMPiNG iS USED

Strokes together, separate or crossed give an optical effect of shadows. The closer together they are, the grayer they appear. The white paper ground can be seen through the grays, but, of course, intense strokes blot it out giving a denser dark.

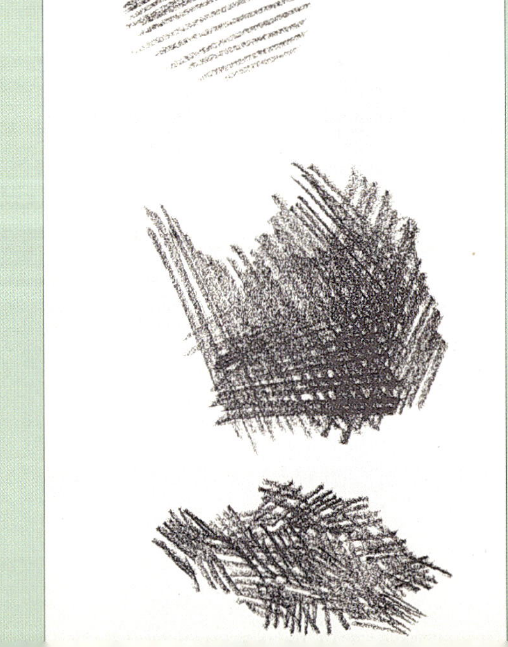

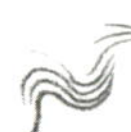

18

The most conventional drawing mediums offer endless possibilities that sometimes remain unnoticed because of the simplicity of the work tools. As you begin to understand drawing more profoundly, you will appreciate what the lines can contribute, compared with other processes like tone value. Lines can play off against each other or work together.

Observe the way this drawing is constructed. As you can see, the darks have been done with long lines close together. The medium grays have been realized with less pressure. This technique for doing the shadows, building them up with strokes, requires a perfectly constructed preliminary sketch.

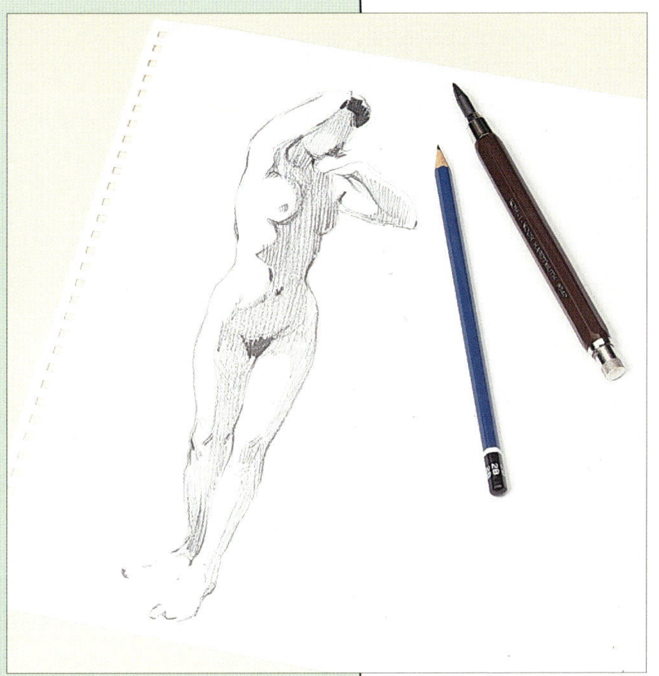

SHADOW AND VOLUME.

We are now going to practice developing different light and shadow zones. Above all remember that the first strokes must be softer as they prepare the zone where you will work on the shadows. You must make provision for the strokes that you will do later. All these sketches can be done in any normal drawing medium: charcoal, pencil, sanguine or pure graphite.

iDEAL FOR PENCiL

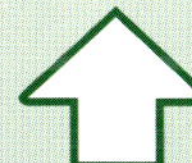

Pieces based on shading and lines can be done with any of the normal drawing mediums. This exercise will be done in pure graphite and pencil.

Shadows created by strokes can rapidly cover a large area. Often you need not completely cover the zone to be darkened, a quick shading will suffice, a technique ideally suited to the fine lead of a pencil: it can only cope with quick shadings, anything else takes too long. In this procedure the gray need be neither dense nor "closed".

After drawing the brick in perspective, each plane is done with a different stroke.

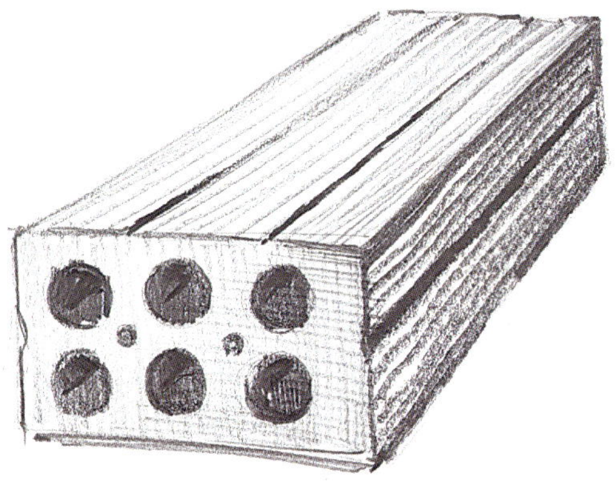

Darker zones are drawn with greater stroke pressure.

PAY ATTENTION TO THE STROKE DIRECTION

SWe are going to do a straightforward exercise to practice the strokes in different planes. A brick is a suitable object because it is straightforward to draw in perspective, the front face enabling the lines of the upper plane and of the visible side to be established. The strokes that define each of the planes must bear in mind the following rules:

The lines that define the sides are a guide for drawing the insides. Observe if the plane perspective means that the lines must be closer together or further apart.

Pay attention to the lighting of the objects. Not everything is illuminated in the same way.

There are always degrees of darkness and light..

A zone can be darkened with broadwise strokes. However, they must always go in the plane direction.

CROSSED STROKES AND HATCHING

The form must always be completely defined before starting the shadow, whatever technique is used.

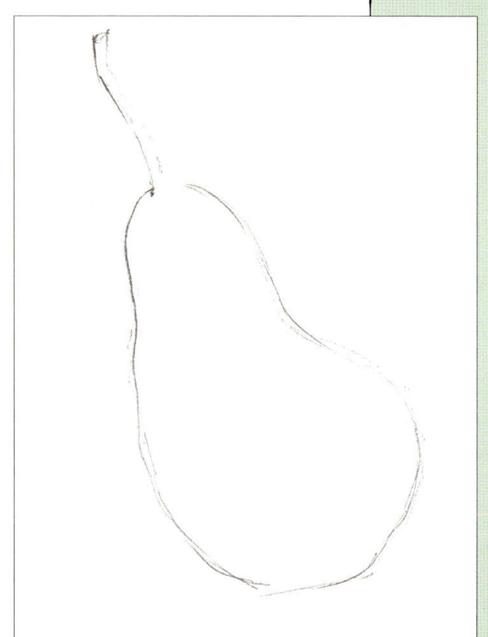

When deciding the stroke direction you must take into consideration the lighting of the plane. Darker zones are drawn with more pressure than lighter zones. Observe how the strokes have been employed on the different brick sides.

CURVED AND FLAT SURFACES

Not all the surfaces are drawn with the same type of stroke. The plane decides the stroke direction and how it joins up with the most illuminated zones of the object.
Curved forms are treated differently to straight planes for the shadows and values work in such a way that the darkening is progressive. Flat planes normally receive a uniform quantity of light on their entire surface, unless there is a uneven texture, something which may be brought out with a different stroke and light reflection.

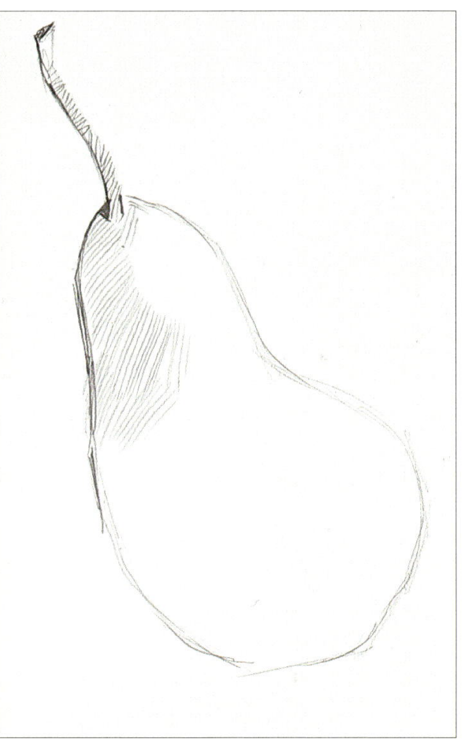

Start the strokes with a circular movement around the highlights..

SPHERICAL SURFACES

Working on a perfectly defined preliminary sketch, the spherical surfaces are resolved using the light that falls on them and the shadows cast on the rest of the object. As we said at the beginning of this chapter, doing shadows with lines is a recourse comparable with modeling by stumping. It is necessary to pay attention to the light and shadow effects before starting to model the form with grays.

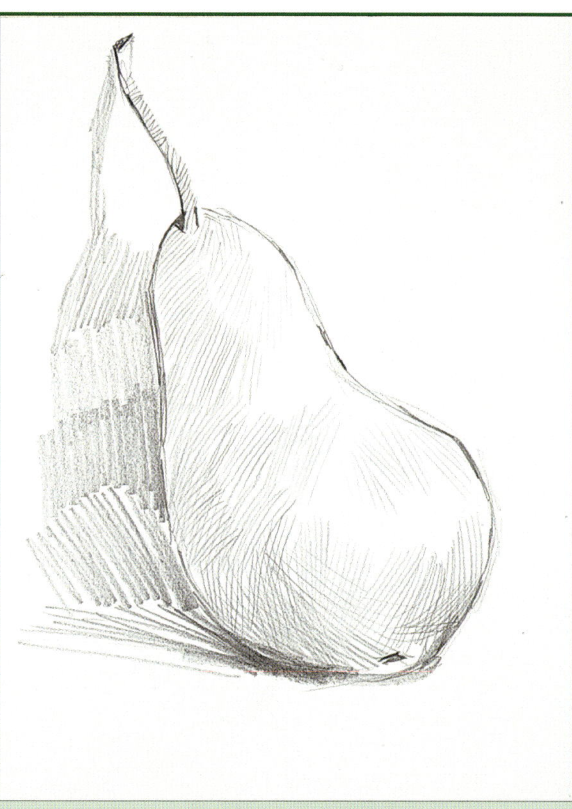

Do hatching around the two highlights of the fruit. The criss-cro direction and intensity depend on the form of the plane and th darkness of the shadow.

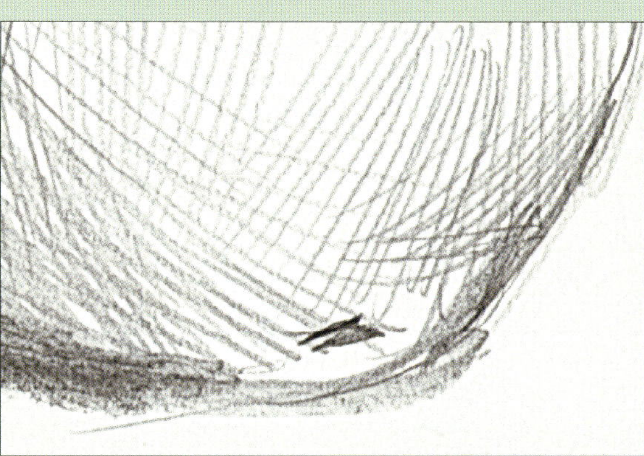

In these close ups you can appreciate how the crossed strokes in the different zones of the pear have been done.

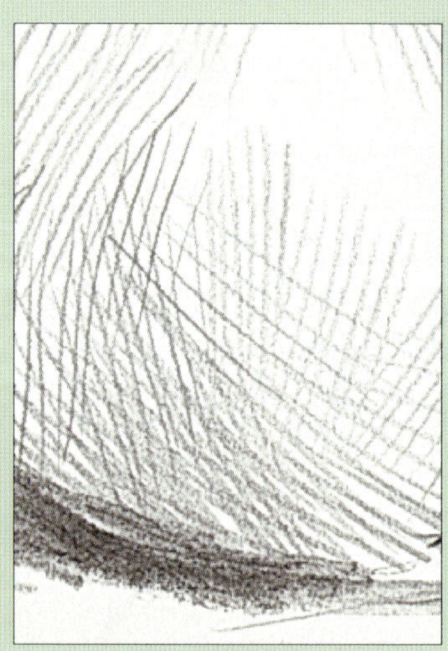

Start to do the lines around the light zone. Try not to cross over into this zone. Define the adjacent zones at the same time. If necessary, use the eraser to outline the highlight more exactly. Do radial strokes in the shadow zone, in the same direction as the spherical plane.

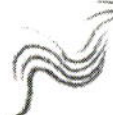

The shadow does not fall uniformly across the surface. The different forms create highlights with shadows around them. In this example, the pear consists of two spherical shapes, a small oval one on top, and below it a much bigger one. In the form at the bottom, the strokes are more crossed and the radial hatching starts from the highlight.

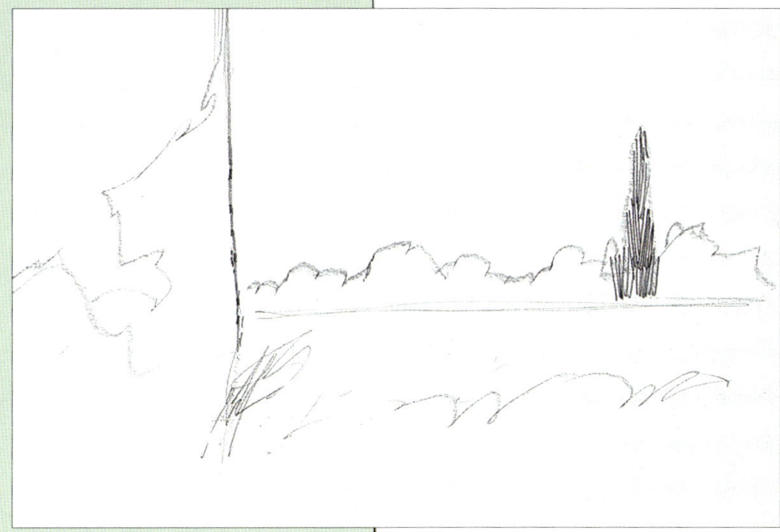

The preliminary sketch sets out the principal planes of the landscape, one of which is the house wall.

FLAT SURFACES

Flat surfaces could seem to be easier to draw than spherical or curved ones. However, bear in mind that these surfaces can be drawn in perspective and with uniform lighting. Rarely are different surfaces perfect or smooth and textures produce varied effects under the light. We are going to do a simple landscape example in which the wall of a country house offers an interesting texture.

The drawing must be schematic but straightforward, making the necessary separations so that the shadows can be formed by strokes and lines. Use completely vertical strokes to start the shadows of the wall. Where the wall changes texture the lines are darker and closer together. If you compare this plane with the rest of the drawing, you will see that there are many stroke changes in the other parts. On the wall there are only changes in intensity. Observe how the trees in the background are dealt with. The strokes are short, dense and crossed, but never superimposed.

Short crossed lines, superimposed on the vertical strokes, give texture to the wall surface. In some zones, draw long slanting strokes that crossover the initial strokes. Do the darkest parts using short, crossed lines to give the wall texture.

The flat wall plane is done with long, straight strokes. Only the intensity varies.

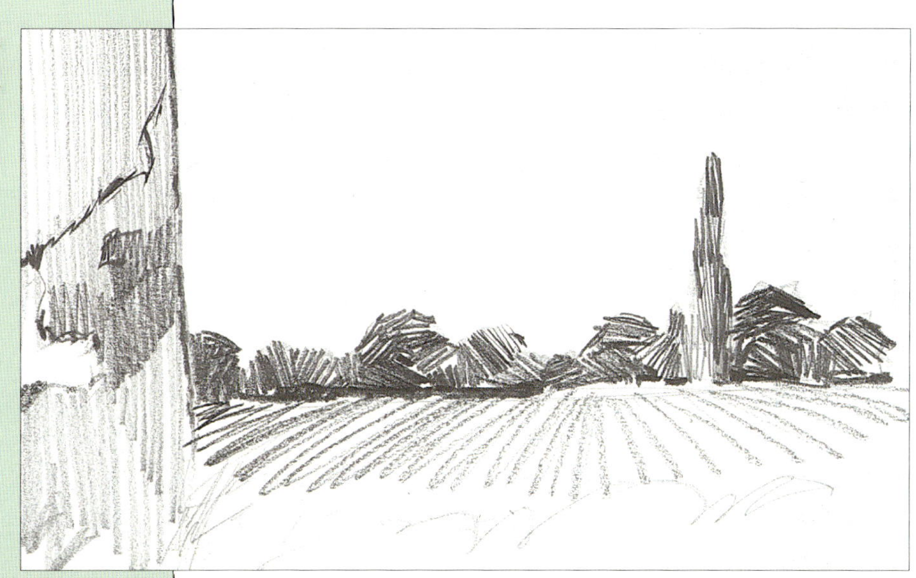

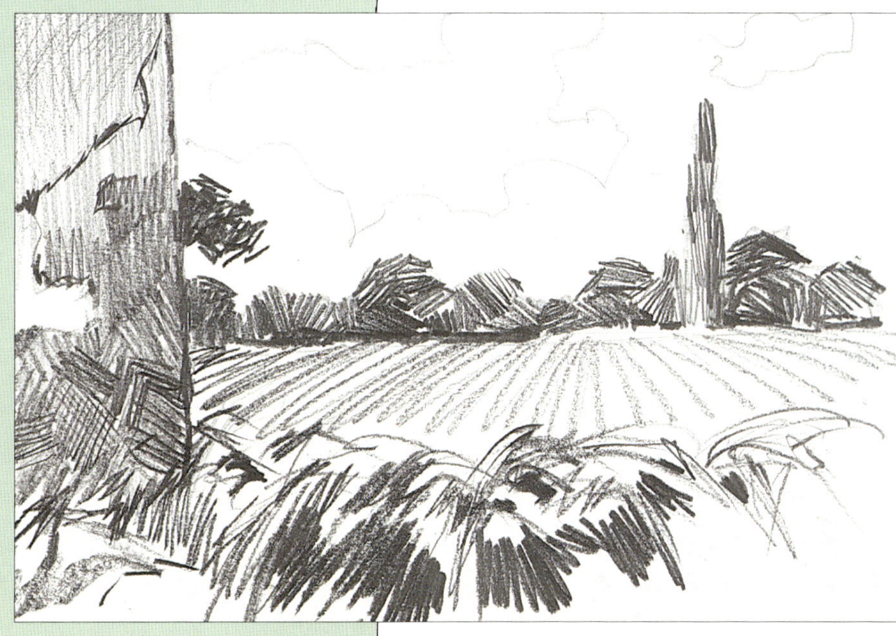

The lines that represent the wall texture are superimposed on the vertical strokes.

18 CROSSED STROKES AND HATCHING

THE IMPORTANCE OF PERSPECTIVE IN THE STROKE

As you have been able to appreciate in earlier examples, the stroke indicates the different planes of the object. Good perspective work can be done just by insinuating the plane direction with a few strokes that merge in one zone of the drawing.

We are going to do an example in which it is important to increase the sensation of perspective. The drawing revolves around the line that separates the sky and the land: the lower it is, the less ground there will be. Draw the curved path. Perspective means that two parallel lines tend to converge in the distance. Draw lines that mark the inside of the path. Trees are drawn on both sides of the path, getting smaller as they go into the distance.

First place the horizon and the lines of the path.

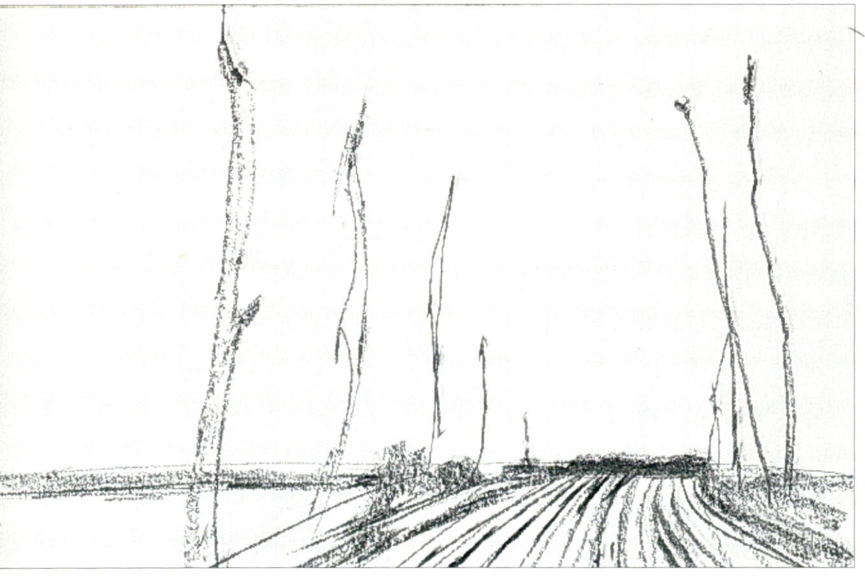

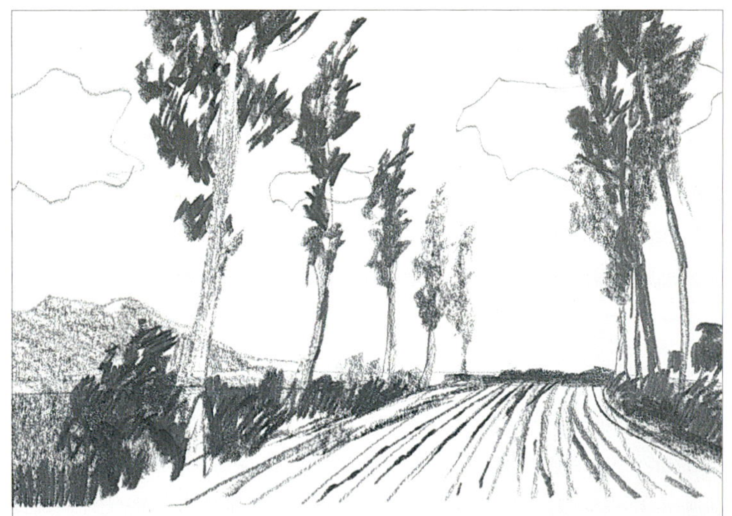

COMBINING STROKES

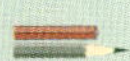

The varied ways of doing strokes mean that all the planes of nature drawings, and all those necessary for other drawings, can be represented. Try to do this straightforward example, observing how different types of strokes are applied.

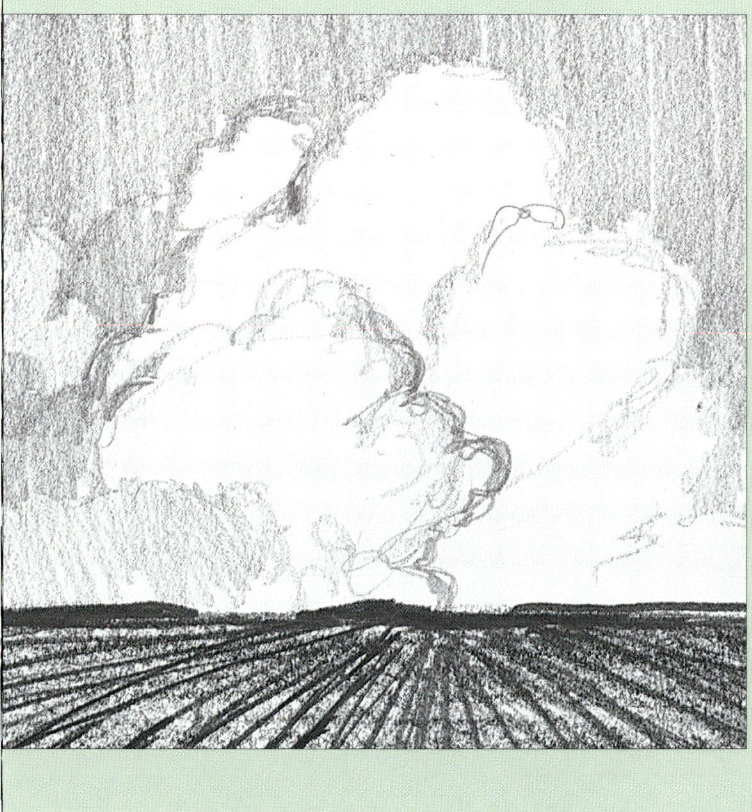

Finally, do the strokes that define the different zones of the landscape.

OPTICAL EFFECTS

Strokes together or separated provoke the optical effects of light intensities and shadows in the drawing. Planes can be separated by different highlights. In the same motif a single type of stroke can dominate, being cut in the light zone to create a volume effect. This case was already seen in this chapter with the pear. However, in the same vein, we are going to do a more complex exercise, a female nude. Pay attention to the form of the shadows. They are realized almost completely in vertical lines, while the lights that give shape to the plane are perfectly defined.

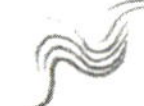

CROSSED STROKES AND HATCHING 18

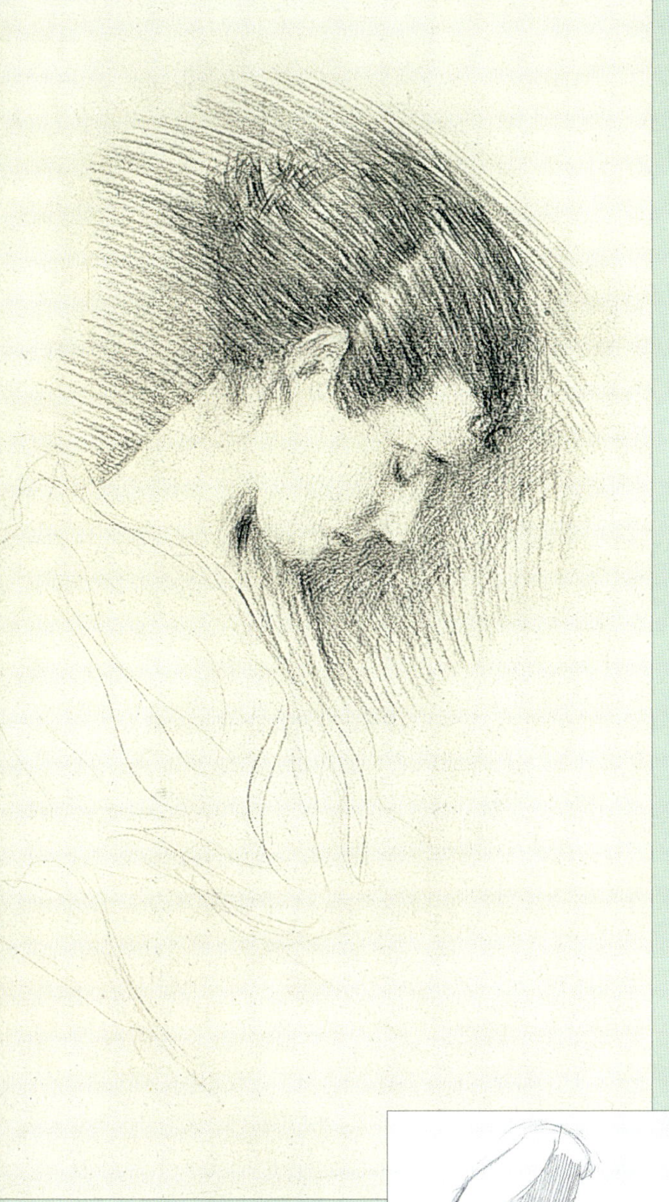

KNOW HOW TO USE THE RECOURSES

Gustav Klint, a portrait, drawing on paper.
It is not sufficient just to know the technique, you must know how to apply it to get good results. Klint was more than just a virtuoso in color and in drawing: his works are full of technical recourses that appear simple but are applied with great mastery and sensitivity. Observe how in this portrait he used the stroke to darken the contour of the face, which gives off luminosity. The crossed stroke on the right in the background intensifies this zone and bestows a greater plastic relief effect, although there are hardly interior details. Another area worthy of note is the hair where intense sloping strokes have been made.

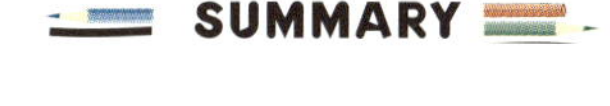

SUMMARY

LIGHT AND DARK STROKES
You can do different gray gradations depending on the direction and quantity of the strokes drawn in a determined zone.

DIFFERENT SURFACES, DIFFERENT STROKES.
Every surface requires a different type of stroke. Never forget the shininess of each zone.

STROKE AND DEPTH.
Planes in perspective can be constructed taking advantage of the distance and angle.

THE OPTICAL EFFECT.
Darks can be realized with strokes in one direction provided that the light zones are perfectly defined.

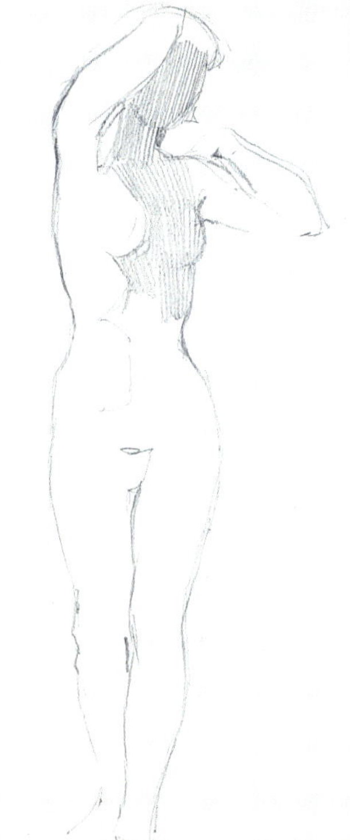

After drawing the figure, do the first shadows which perfectly outline the light planes in almost vertical strokes.

Once all the shadows have been placed, do small tone differences with dense, dark lines. The light zones are perfectly outlined and defined by the shadows and the optical effect gives a sensation of volume exploiting the dark contrasts and the pure whites.

The final strokes allow the light zones to be isolated, creating an optical volume effect.

19 VALUES AND PLASTIC RELIEF WITH WHITE

Adding white chalk to do plastic relief further enriches the effect. In this chapter we are going to study thoroughly how to do plastic relief on tinted paper, a not to complicated subject if the fundamental concepts of value and modeling are understood.

TONE AND THE COLOR OF THE PAPER

Drawing techniques always involve the same concepts: lines, shading and stumping. They seem to be simple questions and are, in fact, the tools with which the artist represents any object. They are sufficient to do the most complicated drawings, even risky foreshortened poses.

Although certain basic concepts were presented in earlier chapters, it is fundamental to bear them in mind when studying tones on tinted paper, before adding the white relief that will finish off the gradation process.

MODELING ELEMENTAL FORMS

When using modeling in a drawing the light zones are left very clear. Around these light parts grays are colored in which will convert the darkest tones into shadows. The model without shadows will appear flat, lacking in volume, while when well contrasted it will have lights and shades.

Draw a circle, just a line on the paper. Two values can be established, light and shade.

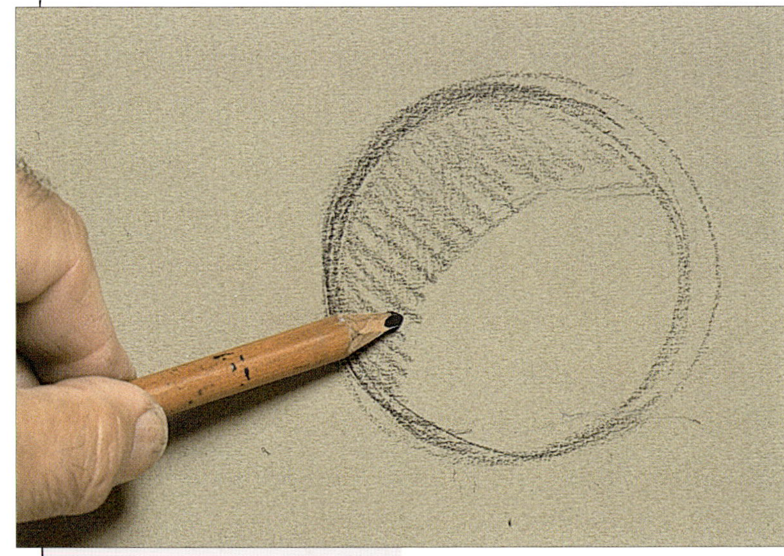

Use the finger to stump the line until it is blended with the highlight.

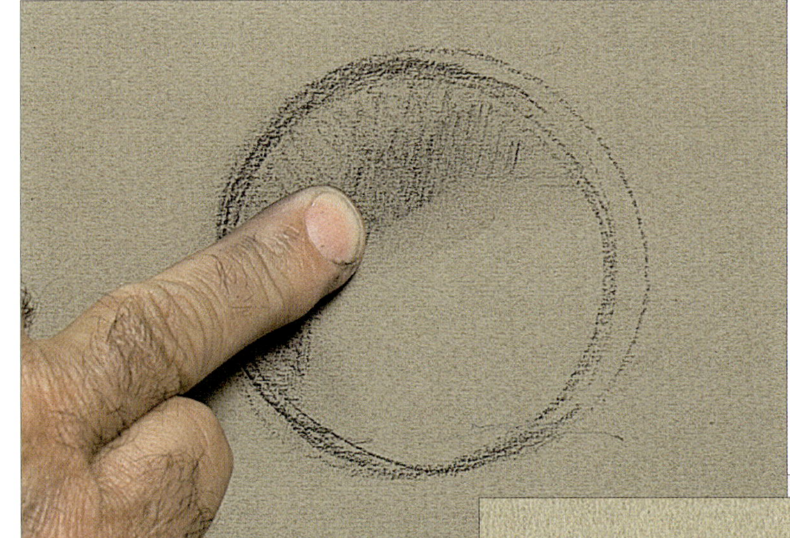

This badly drawn piece of fruit has hardly any volume due to the lack of contrast on the surface.

On top of this stump you can do a sanguine line. If you stump again you will create a new tone as the simple form becomes a perfectly modeled chest.

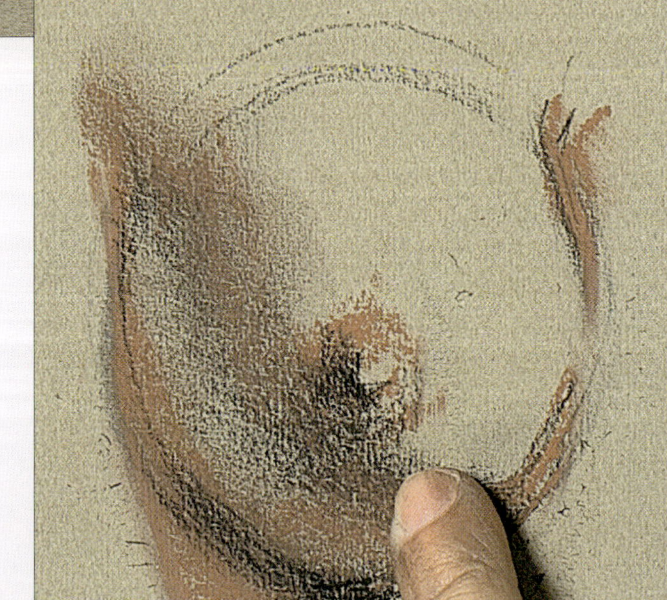

The shadows are created out of the modeling, by the valued contrast between the gray and the paper color. In this case the transition from the dark tone to the background color is done by stumping. The more subtle this transition is, the softer the light that falls on the model will be.

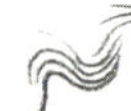

To give an adequate sense of volume to any object it is necessary to color some zones darker than others. As we have studied in previous chapters, tone values enable volume to be represented by different gray tones. However, it is possible to get more interesting effects if charcoal and sanguine are combined on tinted paper.

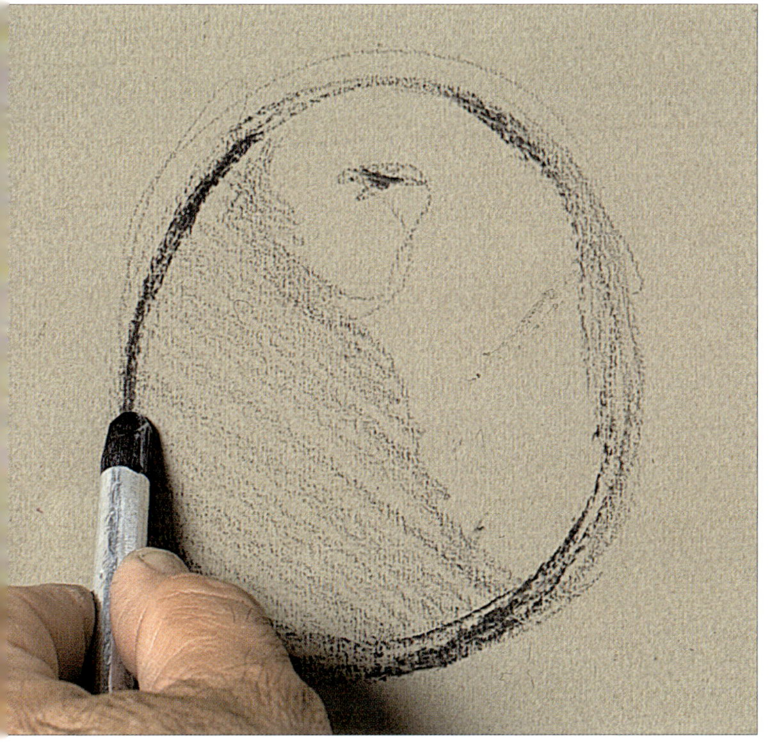

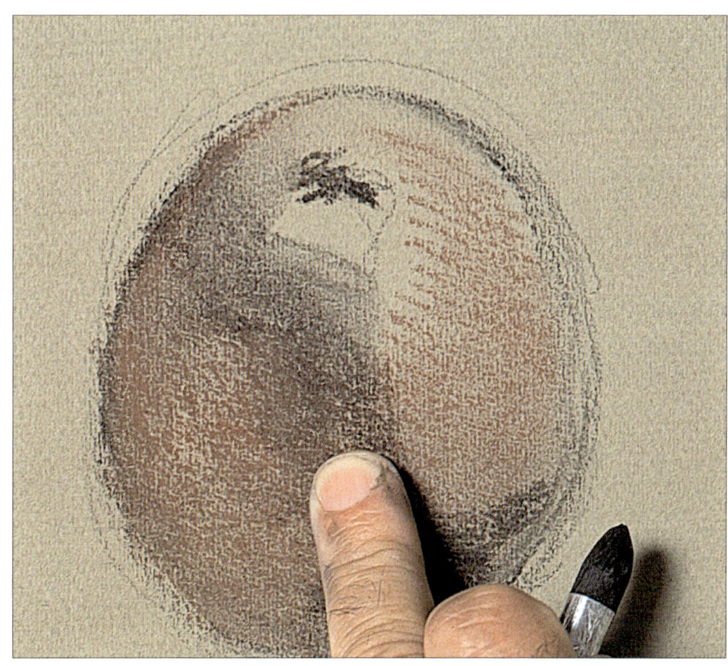

Use the sanguine to develop the light zone and the charcoal to shade the shadow. The result is more realistic. Mix the two tones with a finger around the highlight.

ADDING TONES TOGETHER

Charcoal and sanguine together give grays that can become different tones through stumping. When two mediums are used, like charcoal and sanguine, the first one does the tones of the light while the second allows you to do the well contrasted shadows.

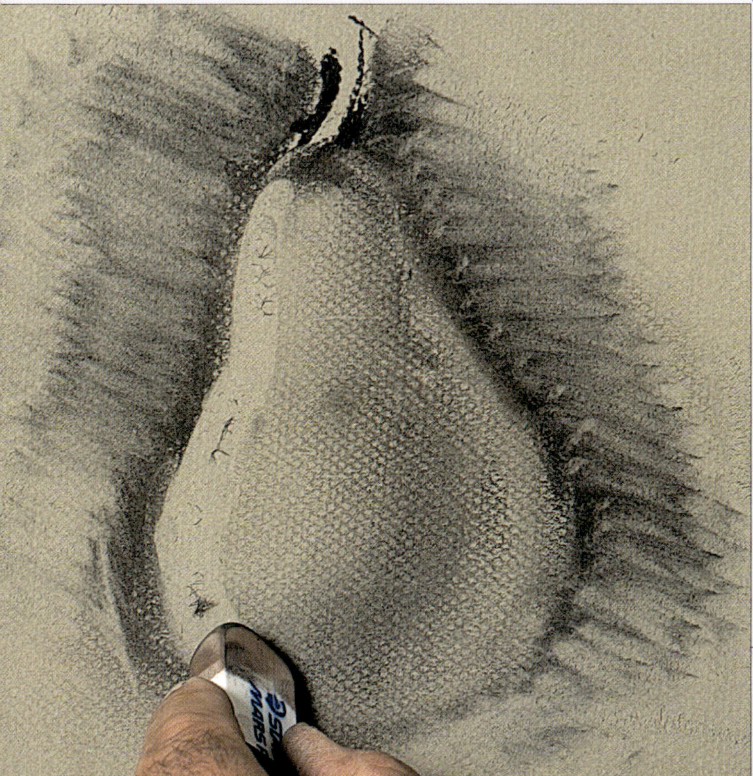

THE ERASER WHEN MODELING

When you are drawing an object with volume, whether it be a still life or a figure, the form and the shadows are influenced by the background color. The gradation may produce a slightly strange plastic effect. If so, you can use the eraser to open up highlights and to reoutline the form.

In this example the form is drawn with the volume producing gradations. The darkest grays outline the lightest tones, however, the highlight has not been adequately defined. Here the rubber comes into play, opening up different shades of gray. The background has been almost totally cleaned allowing the form to be reoutlined. The highlight has been opened up precisely and the volume effect is perfectly achieved.

The highlight opened up with the eraser allows the volume to be defined perfectly.

VALUES AND PLASTIC RELIEF WITH WHITE

THE ERASER AND TINTED PAPER

The eraser, a tool as useful as charcoal or sanguine, allows you to open up whites and to restore zones that have been overstumped. In previous chapters we looked at the function of opening up light spaces, but here we will go further and examine how light and shadow effects and plastic forms can be obtained from different shade intensities, using the eraser. This is why the eraser is basic when drawing on tinted paper.

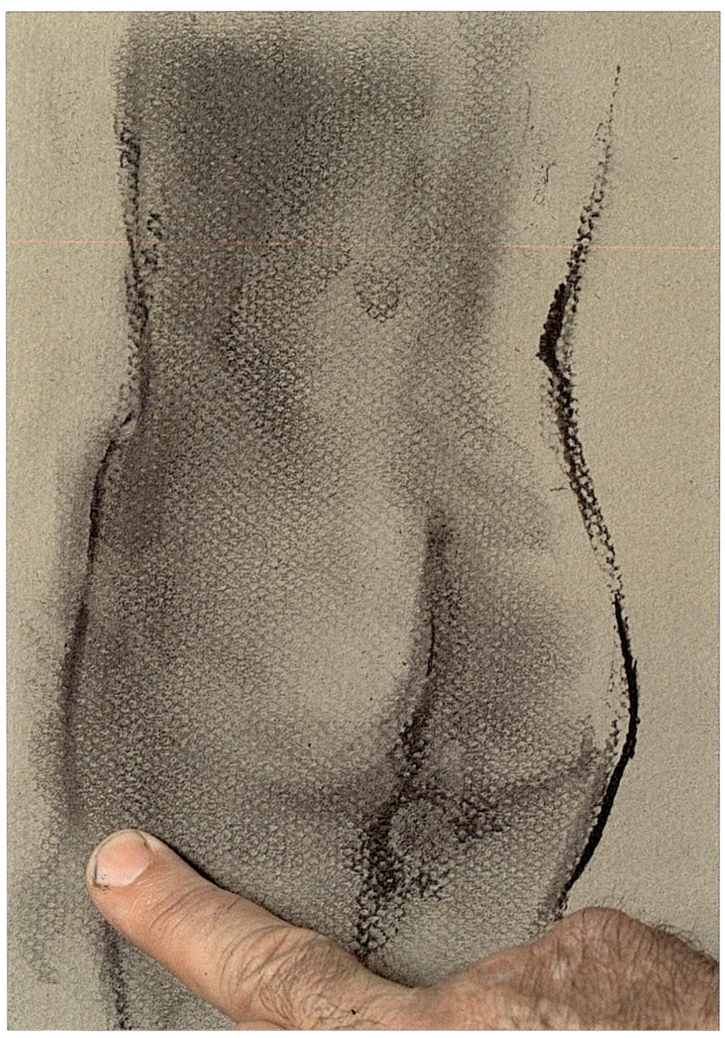

This drawing has been correctly stumped but the tone has been dragged where it should not have been.

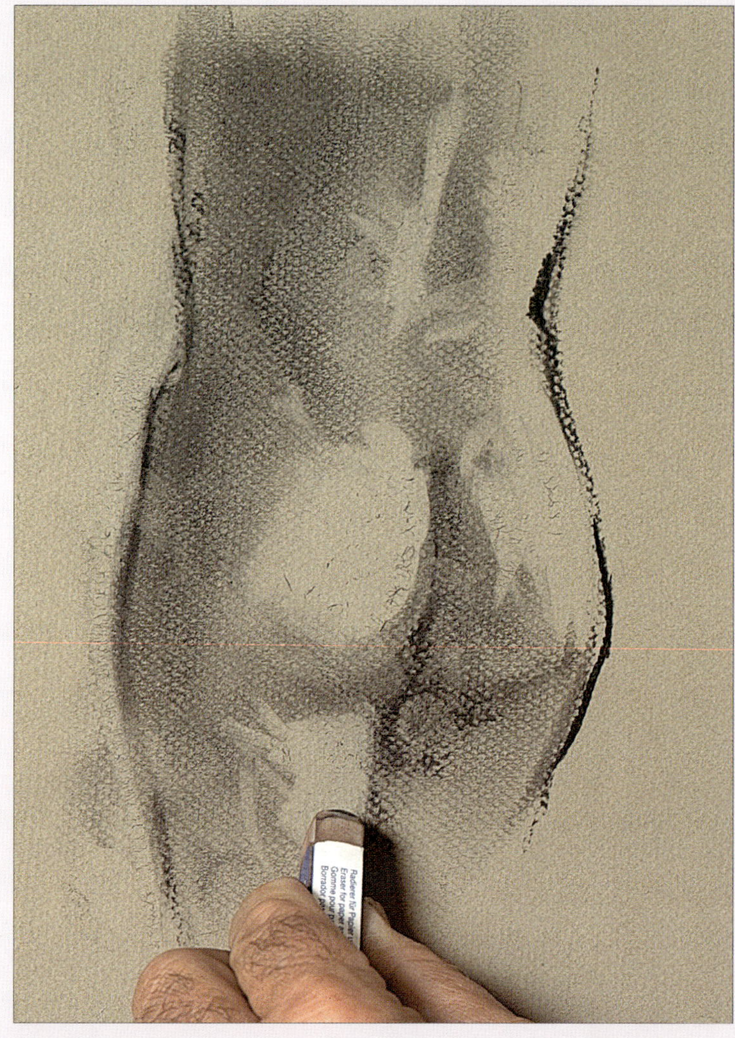

Use the eraser to open up the highlight in the right place. Do not press too hard so as not to spoil the paper. The shadow indicates how the light falls and allows the tone of the paper to be perfectly integrated into the flesh color.

THE EFFECT OF ADDING WHITE

On tinted paper you do not have to limit yourself to drawing with dark mediums. White chalk can be used to complement the gray tones and to give light and shadow effects with plastic form. The work gives vitality and contrast with the pencil color and the other mediums used. The white contrast increases the intensity of the volume effect.

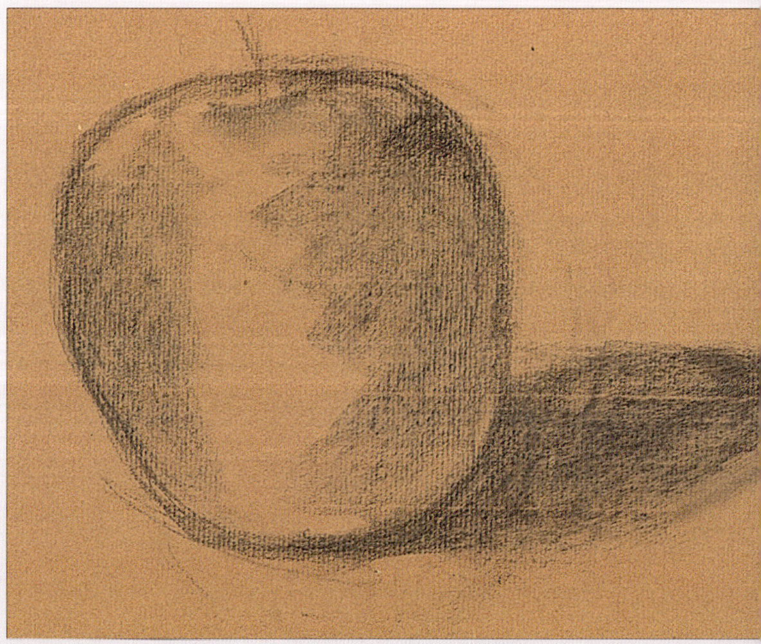

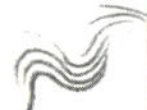

VALUES AND PLASTIC RELIEF WITH WHITE

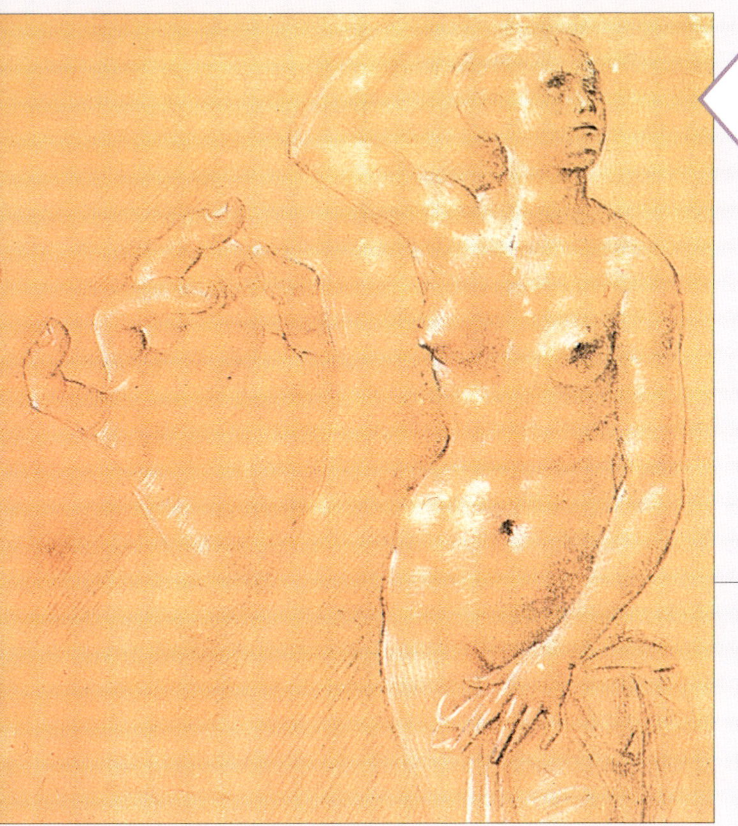

WHITE PLASTIC RELIEF AND VOLUME

The Florence workshop, fifteenth century. A study of Venus. Drawing with white chalk relief on tinted paper. Uffizi Gallery, Florence.

As you can see, this drawing was done on white paper. The lines are very clear and the volume effect was obtained with small white shadings to depict the flesh. Just a few white touches in the light zones were sufficient to give an almost sculpture like volume effect. If you observe the drawing carefully, you will see that all the parts of the figure have been depicted as if they were circles or spherical shapes. The chest is similar to an apple and the rounded stomach is given volume by adding a few white dashes in the illuminated part, as if it were a sphere. The white chalk produces very realistic forms. The color of the paper helped to create a contrast with the white.

HIGHLIGHTS AND VOLUME

We are now going to do a simple exercise in modeling, tone values and plastic relief in white chalk. As you can see, the reflections of light integrate the color of the paper as if it were just another color.

The white chalk must be applied progressively, softly at first, studying the form of the object you are depicting. Once you have given tonal value to the white to make it stand out against the gray background, you can increase its intensity.

When the principal white zones have been established, the contrasts have to be balanced with a dark medium, here charcoal. As you increase the tone the whites down on the paper appear much more luminous because of the effect of the simultaneous contrasts.

Draw dark tones in charcoal and do white strokes in the most luminous zones.

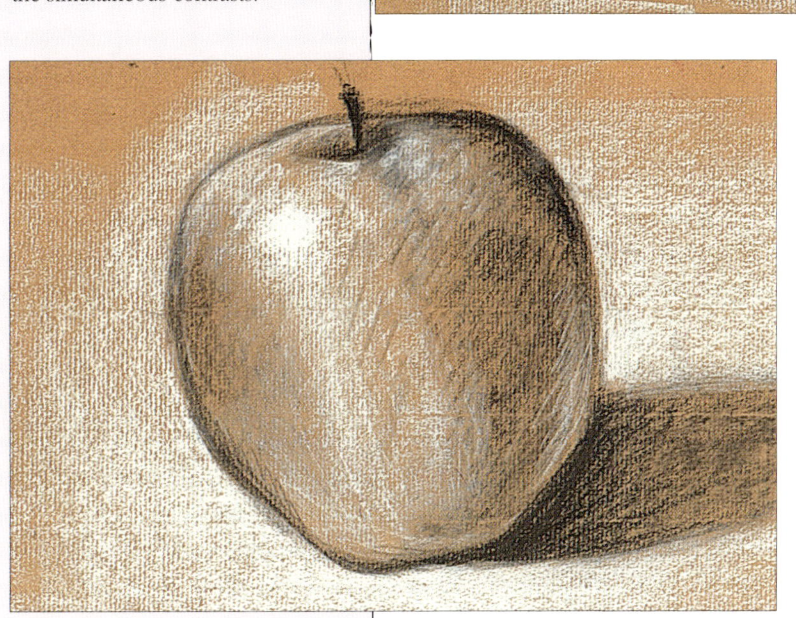

Draw the form in charcoal. Leave the highlight zone untouched.

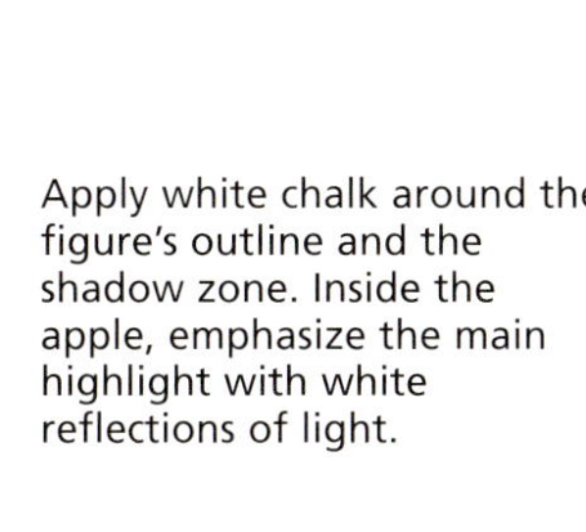

Apply white chalk around the figure's outline and the shadow zone. Inside the apple, emphasize the main highlight with white reflections of light.

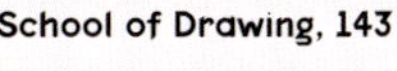

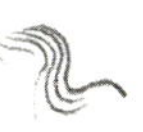

19 VALUES AND PLASTIC RELIEF WITH WHITE

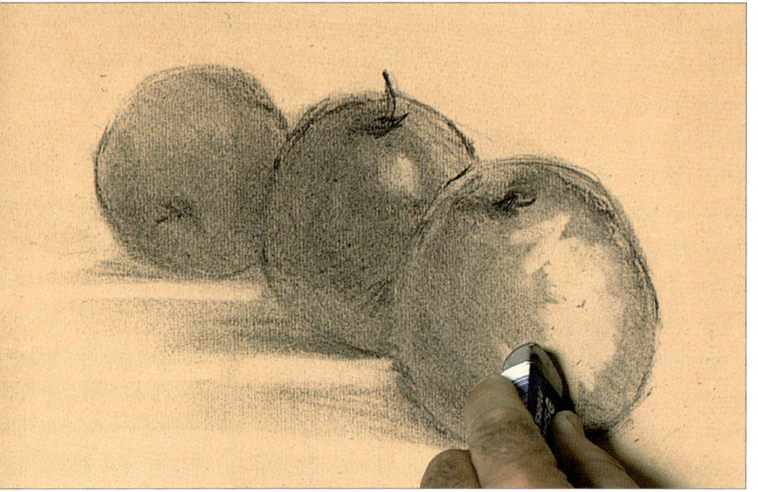

The whites opened up are progressive and decrease with the distance.

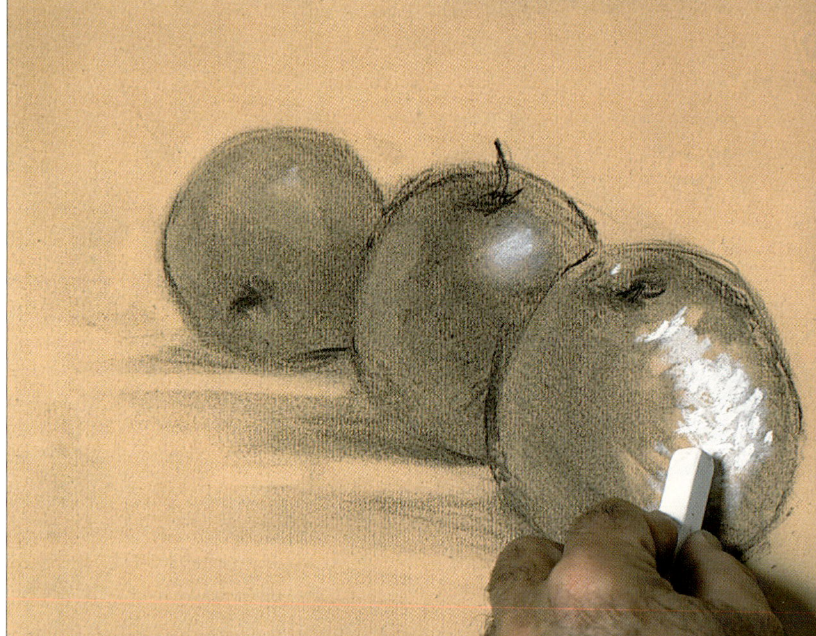

The white chalk allows the background to be integrated into the drawing as a medium tone.

GRADATIONS AND ILLUMINATION

It is the drawing of shadows with lines and shading that gives volume to the objects represented. Gray can be gradated by rubbing a dry finger along the stroke. The light zones must be situated around the brightest highlights. The smaller the white zone is, the darker the object will appear, and you can always use the eraser to distribute the grays. We are now going to do different gradations: in theory the tones of the fruits are similar but they will vary according to the nearness of the objects. Open up a large white on the first shape with the eraser. On the second shape, do another opening but smaller than the first. On the third shape the opening is minimal and has been stumped and gradated.

To get a striking light effect, apply white chalk accents in different intensities to get plastic relief, standing out more on the first shape and softly stumped on the second. On the third shape, white is only insinuated and there is no plastic relief.

THE HIGHLIGHTS

The light effect is enriched considerably when color paper is used. The most intense highlights are done with white chalk. There must be few of them and well placed as too much white would destroy the volume effect. A highlight done with a soft white chalk stumping is not the same as one which impacts strongly on the paper.

CONTRAST AND VOLUME

In this chapter we have studied how highlights and reflections of light giving surprising modeling effects and a highly realistic sensation of plastic relief on tinted paper. This next exercise offers the opportunity to join together all the concepts explained.

Draw very simple sanguine lines to outline the general form of this model, the back of a woman.

Use a simple stroke to shade the dark areas, thus defining the light and shadow zones. The body is perfectly outlined by the darkness and the background paper is integrated with the other colors.

Outline the form. The volume is insinuated with simple lines.

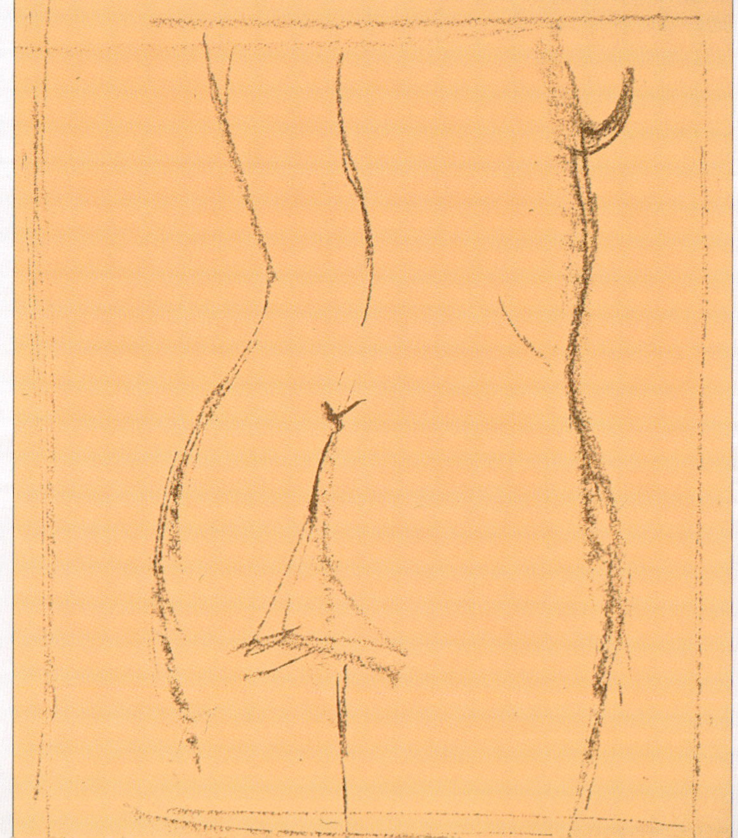

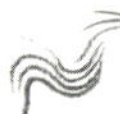

VALUES AND PLASTIC RELIEF WITH WHITE

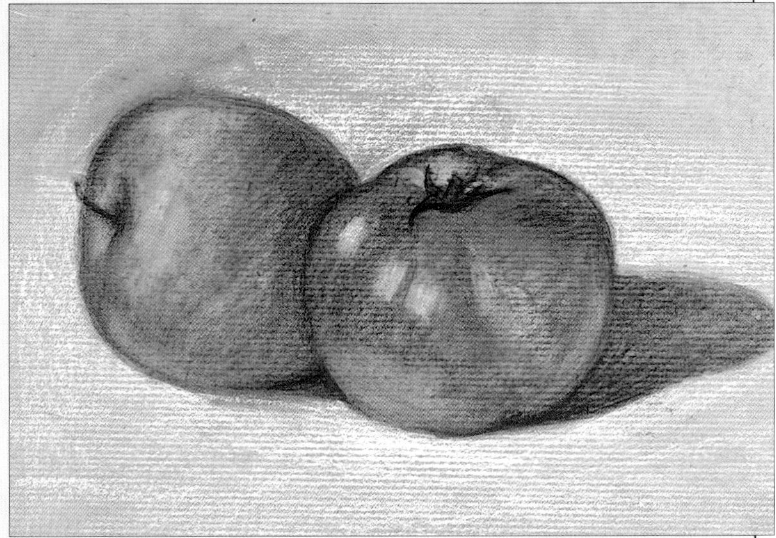

The combined effect of the contrasts means that the background paper is integrated into the composition. The highlights must be precisely placed so that they increase the contrast in the volume represented.

After doing the contrasts, clean the light zones with an eraser and apply the white chalk plastic relief.

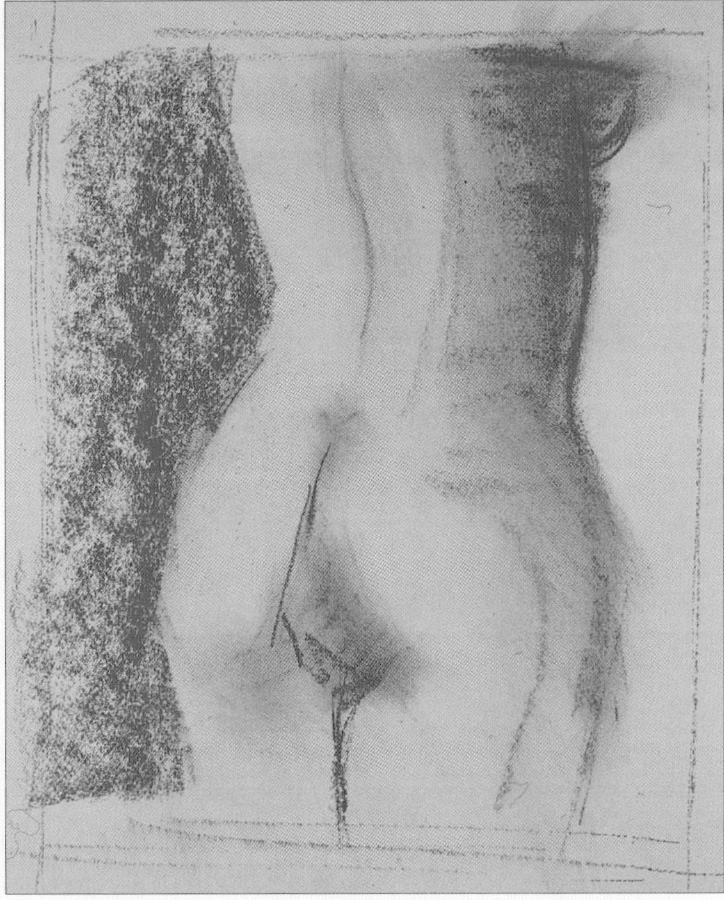

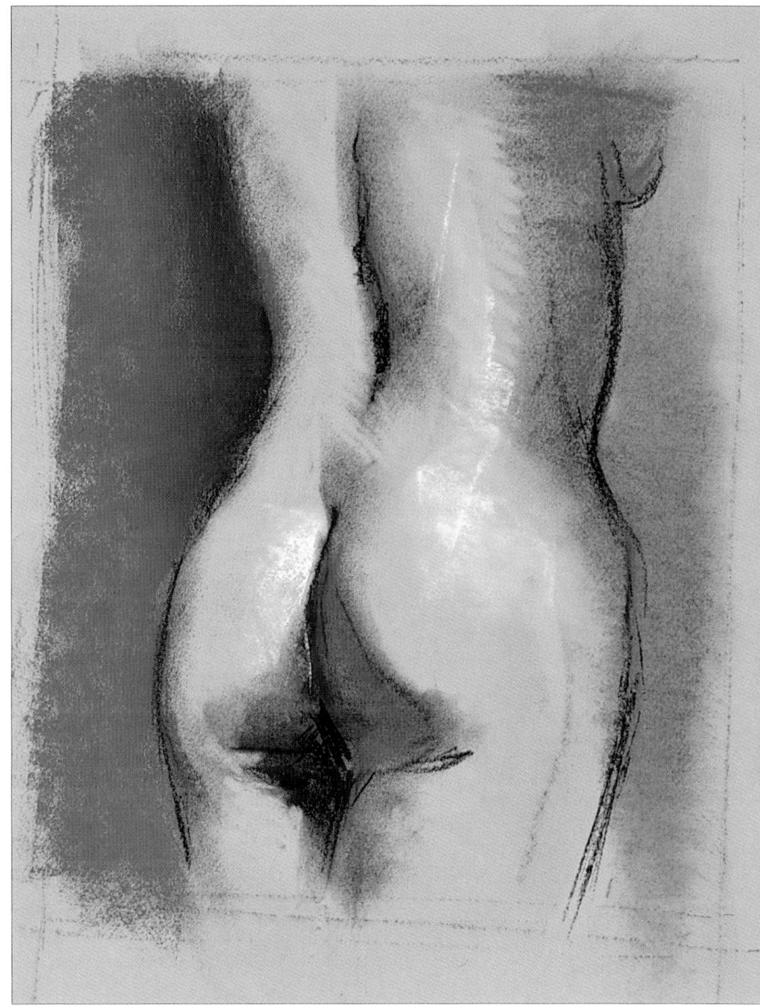

Increase the contrasts using charcoal and after the stumping open up whites with the eraser. White dashes of chalk provide direct light impacts. Do not press too hard with the eraser. Clean it regularly on a fresh sheet of paper.

Use a simple stroke to mark the difference between light and shadow zones. The background paper is integrated into the composition.

SUMMARY

DIFFERENT TONES AND VOLUME
When modeling objects different tones can be used to emphasize the volume. The color of the paper is one more tone that can be integrated into the form modeling.

THE ADVANTAGES OF WHITE
White chalk makes it easier to do plastic relief in the modeling on the tinted paper.

THE ERASER
The eraser aids in the opening up of light spaces that can be used for highlights.

REFLECTIONS OF LIGHT IN WHITE CHALK
Think out carefully where to apply the white chalk highlights. Its better to be sparing than to overuse it.

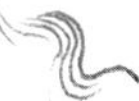

19 Exercices *Step by step*

The plastic phenomena in a drawing can be obtained in many ways, one of them is by modeling grays and using white chalk plastic relief. As we have seen before, gray shading in the shadows and white for the light zones give volume to the objects. Here we are going to use a female model to try out volume effects with white chalk plastic relief. A monochrome drawing with dashes of white produces an interesting result on its own. If we are drawing on tinted paper and use a second tone, impressively realistic volume can be obtained.

NECESSARY MATERIAL

Charcoal crayon (1), Sanguine crayon (2), Eraser (3), White chalk (4), sanguine (5), Charcoal (6), Canson Miteintes Havanna tinted paper (7).

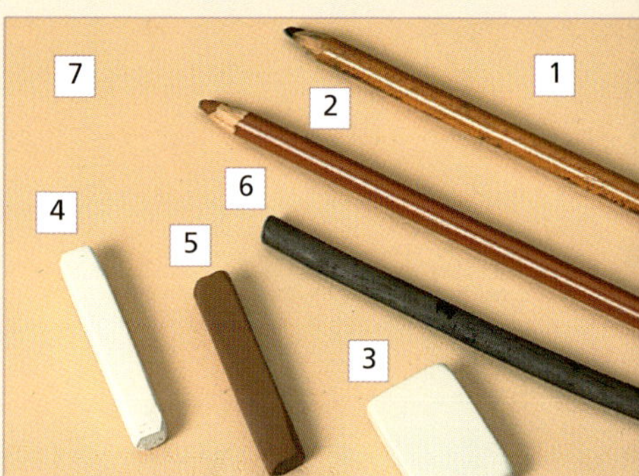

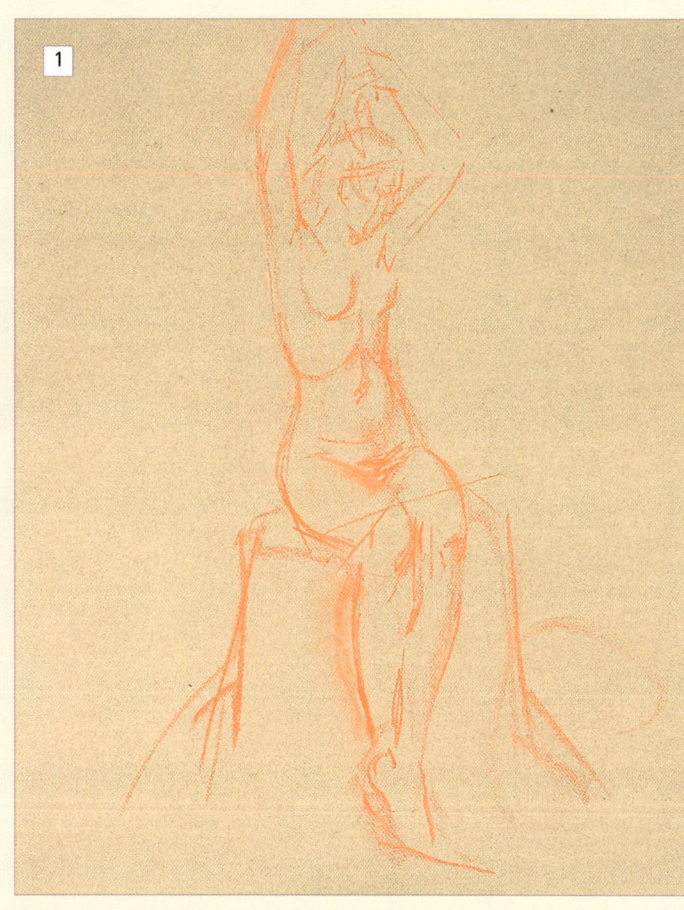

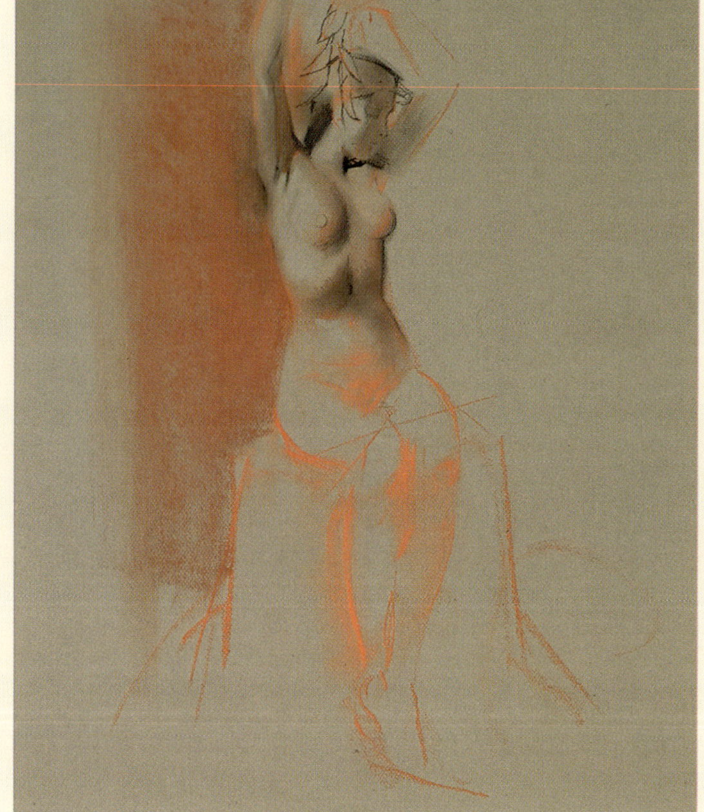

1· START TO DRAW THE FIGURE IN SANGUINE, starting with the lines that define the features of the face, the hairline, the shape of the nose and the mouth. In this zone use the point of the sanguine crayon because it enables you to draw much more precisely, as if it were a pencil. Fine lines define the thighs and the form of the calves.

2· WITHOUT RUBBING TOO HARD, use the fingertips to fade away the most evident strokes, insinuating the volumes through shadings which let you see the paper clearly. This will outline the principal lights. Use the eraser to bring out the highlights. The eraser edge can precisely marks off the stumped areas. Use the charcoal crayon to shade the gray areas on the chest, on the rear of the head and on the raised arm. Outline the figure with a very wide stumping in the background. Below the chin, draw in a very dense black, giving shape to the face in this zone.

A female nude

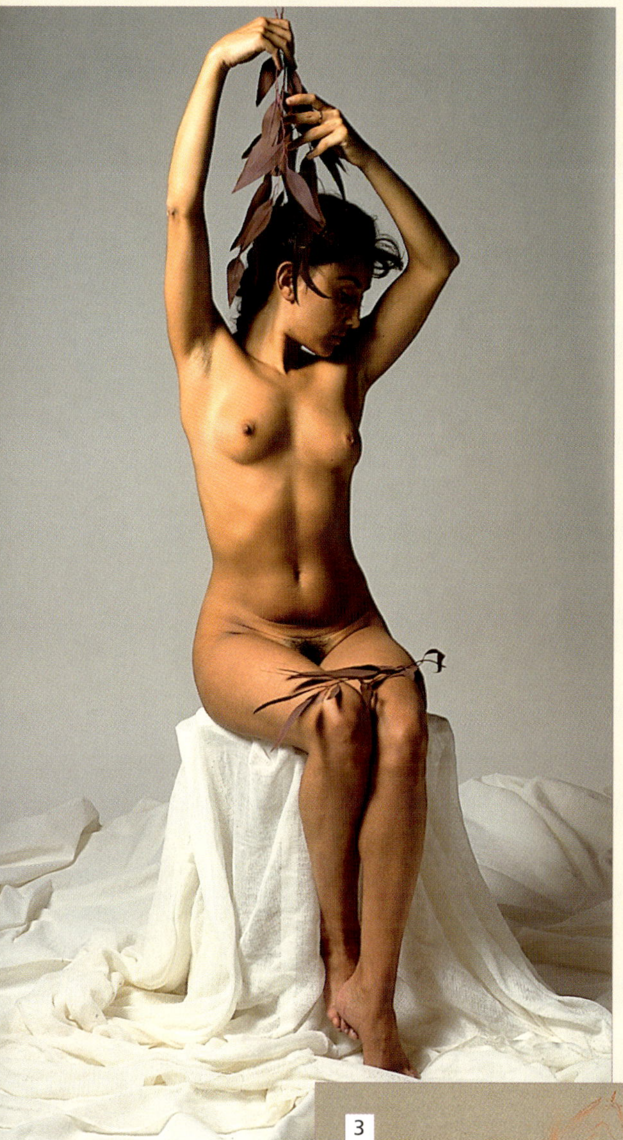

3· **IN THE STUMPED BACKGROUND INCREASE THE CONTRAST** with soft charcoal strokes, and then, once again restump the mix with the fingers. Continue with the charcoal crayon to darken the shadows on the chest. Touch up the charcoal contrast with the fingers and blend it into the sanguine color. The charcoal on the abdomen is softly stumped. Use the sanguine flat to restain the background and then stump it. Use sanguine to shade the zone on the right with a new tone. Use white to do the first highlights on the chest and on the side. Increase the contrast on the abdomen and stump with the fingers. The volume will be perfectly defined.

4· **USE THE CHARCOAL CRAYON** to increase the contrast of the darkest shadows. The highlights will now seem much brighter. Every time you apply charcoal, freshly stump with the fingers to blend the tone with the background and to model the form of the figure. Use the eraser to open up new highlights, making light strokes on the side and in the pelvic region. White intensifies the main highlights in the illuminated zone.

3

The furthermost back planes of the modeling can be blended into the background. The nearest parts are drawn with unstumped strokes.

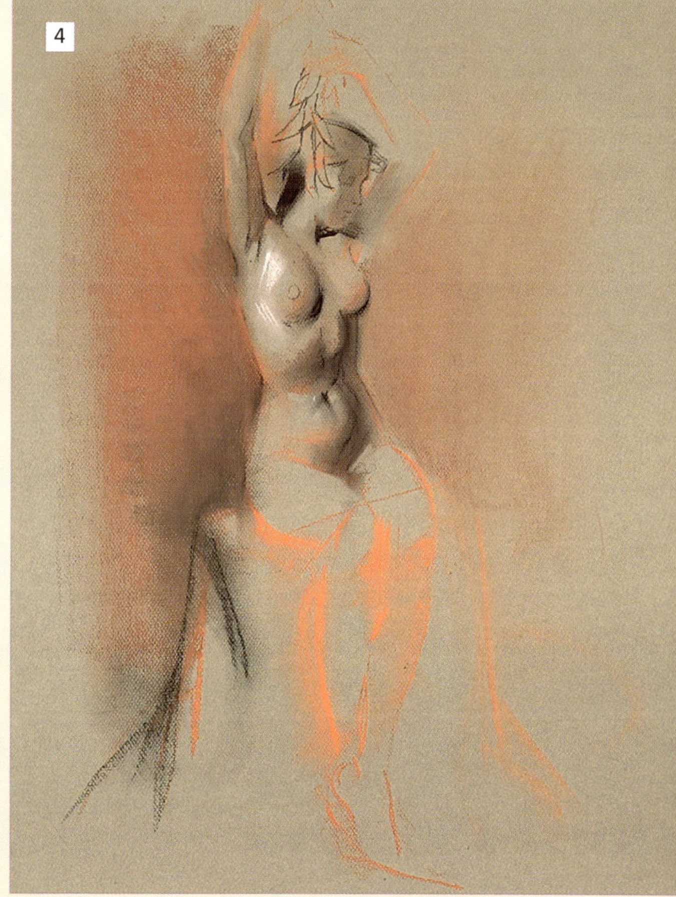

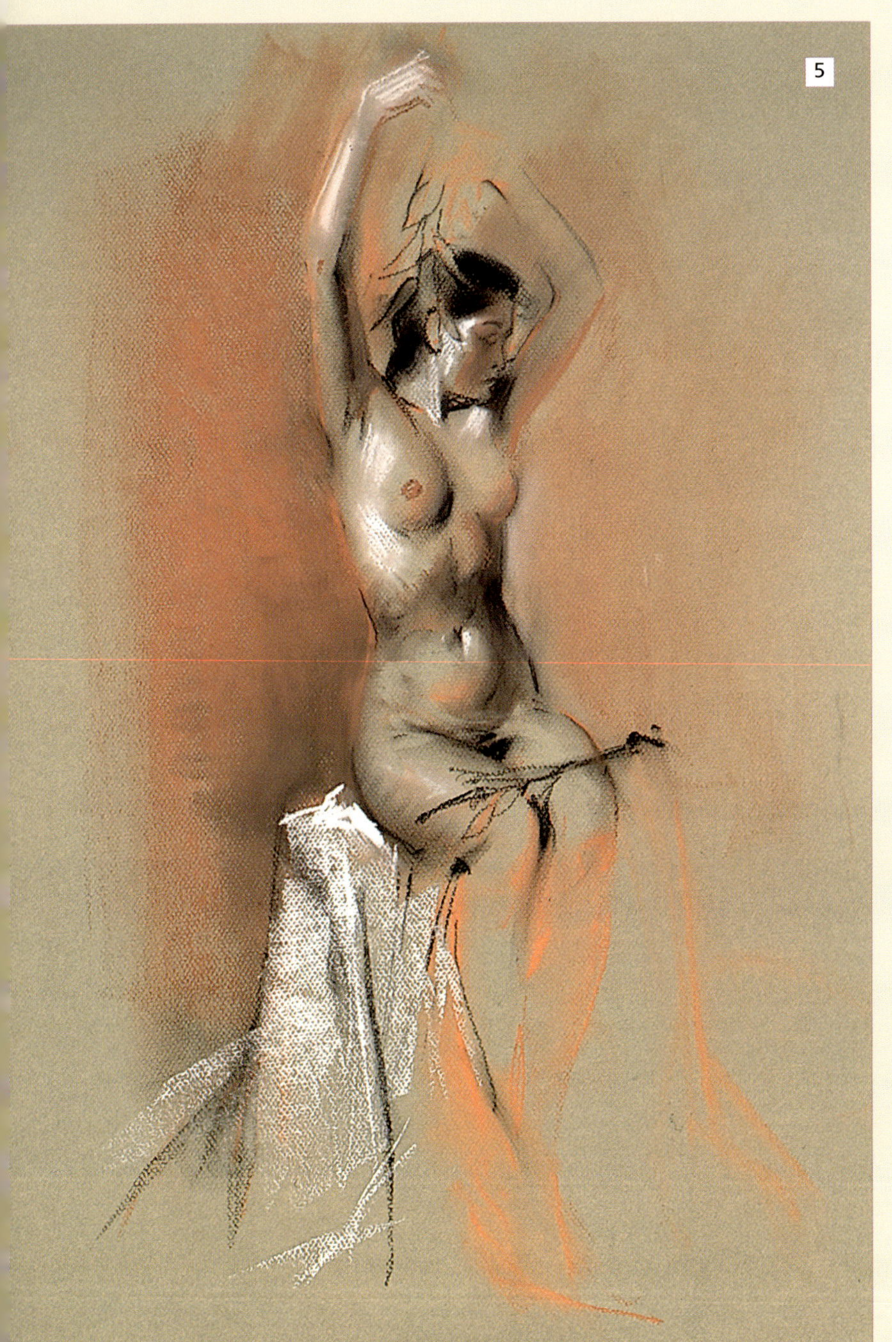

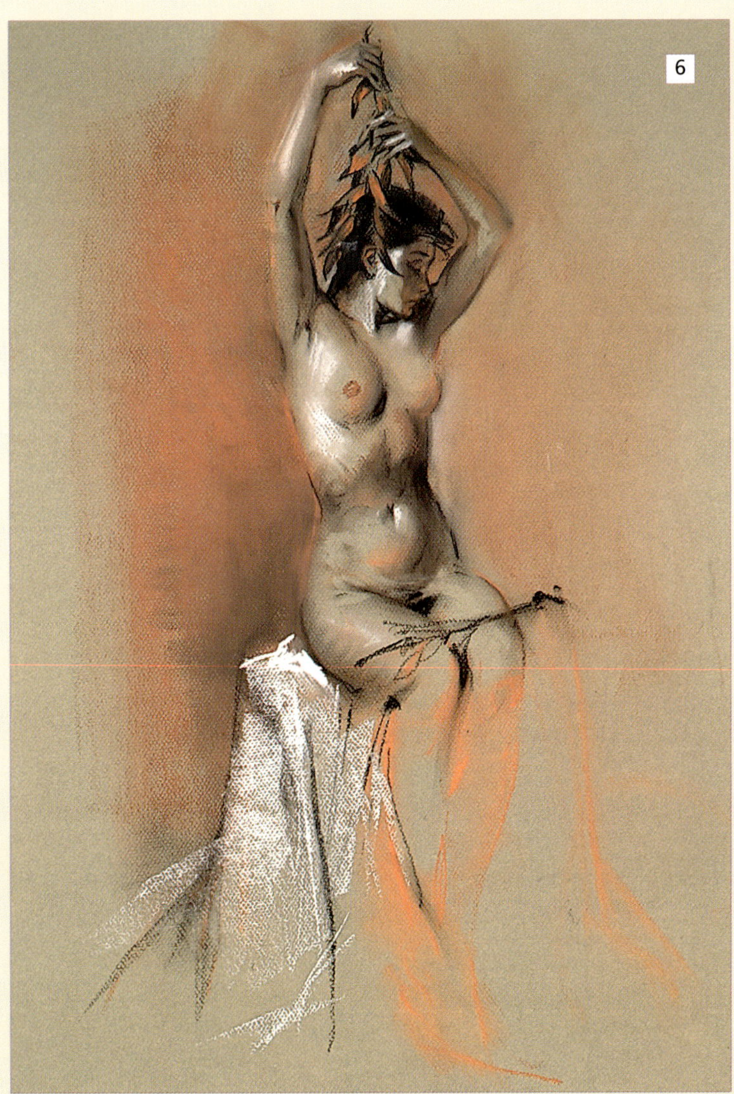

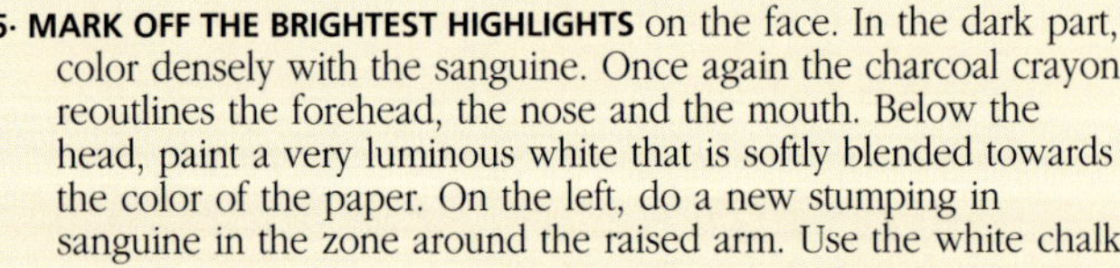

5· MARK OFF THE BRIGHTEST HIGHLIGHTS on the face. In the dark part, color densely with the sanguine. Once again the charcoal crayon reoutlines the forehead, the nose and the mouth. Below the head, paint a very luminous white that is softly blended towards the color of the paper. On the left, do a new stumping in sanguine in the zone around the raised arm. Use the white chalk flat to shade all the area around the seat and increase the contrasts on the arm and the navel. Use your finger to model the thigh, rubbing part of the charcoal away from the line. Open up a new white with the eraser, increasing the highlights with white chalk. Go over the right hip with black charcoal.

6· START TO DRAW THE HAND and the fingers with the charcoal crayon. Make sure that the dark lines only define the shadow zones for the light areas are left reserved. Outline the forms of the body, and the ear, in charcoal, insinuating the flesh color with sanguine.

7· THE FACE IS FINISHED OFF WITH MORE HIGHLIGHTS and by intensifying the dark tones. The highlights on the left hand are resolved with direct applications of white chalk. Define the fingers. Use the sanguine pencil to increase the definition of the face features. If you look closely, you can see that there is a small error of proportion in the length of the legs. This is no problem with dry mediums because they can be redone at any time. Use the sanguine crayon to reform the legs and to darken the background, emphasizing the figure and the volume.

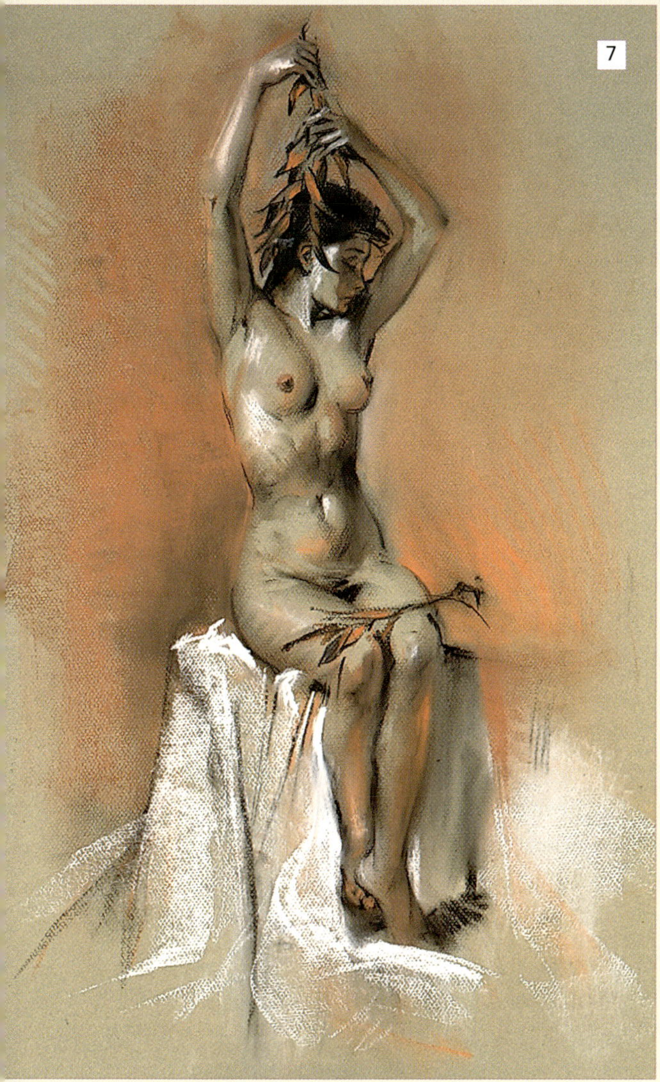

SUMMARY SCHEME

3. Contrast the background. The color of the paper is integrated into the piece.

1. Do a specific highlight around the stomach.

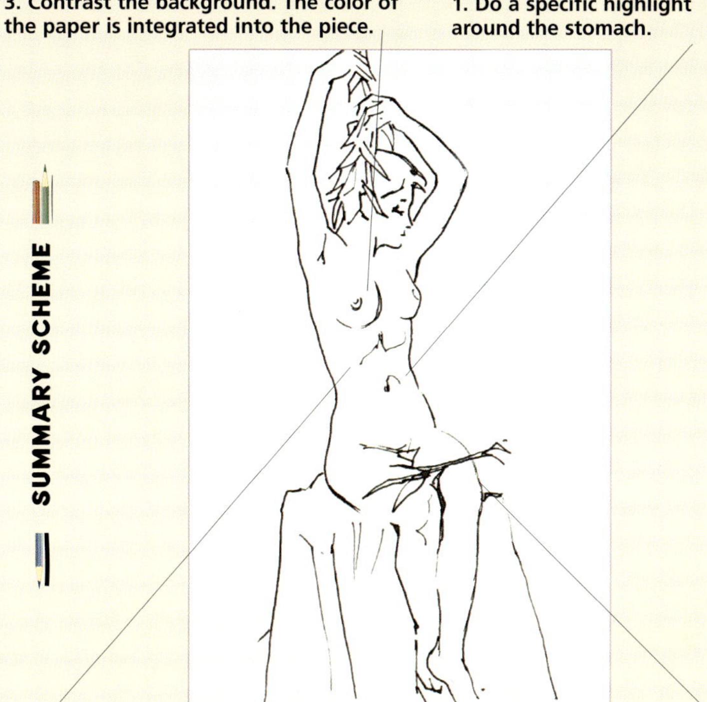

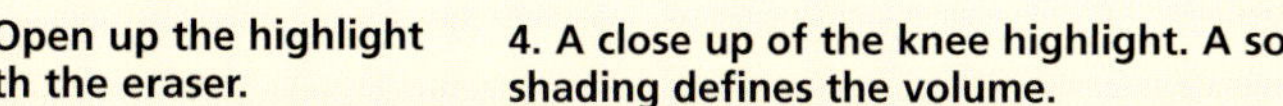

2. Open up the highlight with the eraser.

4. A close up of the knee highlight. A sole shading defines the volume.

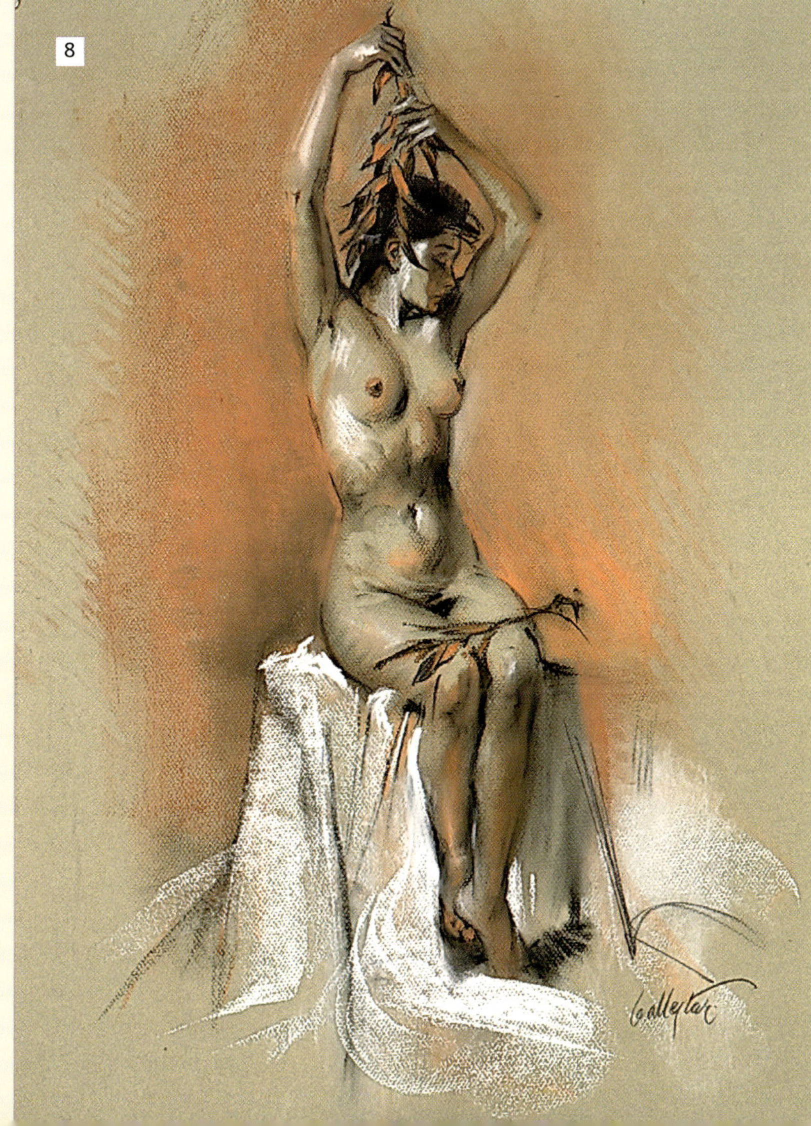

8· THE LEGS ARE DEFINED BY THE WHITES around them. Do the details on the figure adding small charcoal and sanguine accents, stumping them softly into the background with the fingertips. Add sanguine directly to the medium tone luminous zones on the legs. The contrasts will be achieved with charcoal, modeling the shadow zones by blending them with the background. Put in a few direct touches of white chalk on the knees and heel. Finally, finish off the outlining of the hands using sanguine. Just as the theoretical part taught us, the volume effects have been achieved by contrasting the lights with the aid of the white chalk plastic relief.

20 DRAWING TEXTURES

We have dealt with textures in previous chapters: smooth surfaces, shiny ones, water, etc. In this chapter we are going to go into the subject more deeply and we will study rough surfaces done with chiaroscuro, the reflections of light and contrasts that are created when working with tinted paper. It is strongly recommended to follow the cases explained on these pages and to repeat the processes, looking for new applications for the techniques.

COMPLEX TEXTURES

Subjects and themes are only difficult to represent if they cannot be understood. The most complex textures are usually made up of small, easy to comprehend zones which, however, add up to saturate the eye making the whole picture difficult to organize into planes. In the following pages we are going to do some examples of texture which require complicated techniques. Tinted paper will be used so that the white chalk plastic relief work is easier.

THE MATERIAL

It is important to have available different paper colors. Changing colors will help you to develop your creativity and to achieve different effects as the paper becomes totally integrated with the tones employed.

THE ROUGHNESS

Roughness can be represented by studying the light planes and the shadows on the model. However, as always, before starting to draw on the paper carefully study the object you are going to draw. Textures can be the repetition of light and shadow zones. If you understand and clearly perceive the model, representing it will be straightforward. The first exercise we are going to do is a crumpled piece of paper. Just screw it up in your hand and you have the model.

FROM THE PRELIMINARY SKETCH TO THE STUDY OF LIGHTS

As in all drawing processes the preliminary sketch is fundamental before going on to the next steps. Moreover, any texture representation can only be understood if it is

The preliminary sketch must be definitive before going on to the texture. As you can see, this drawing is not dificult.

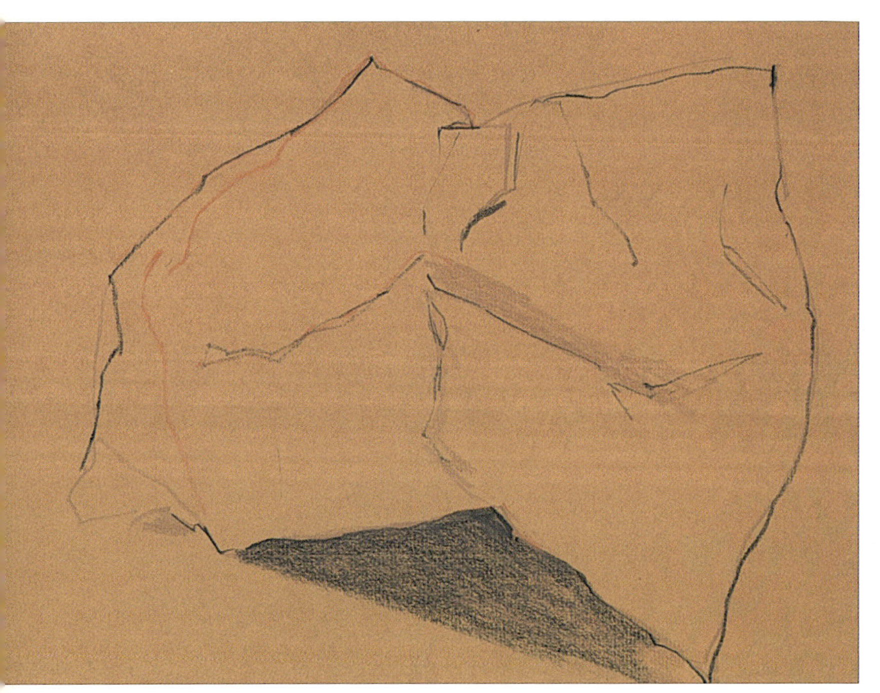

Use white chalk to do the principal highlights. These are forms along the most prominent folds. Some darks will be next to them, giving rise to interesting contrasts.

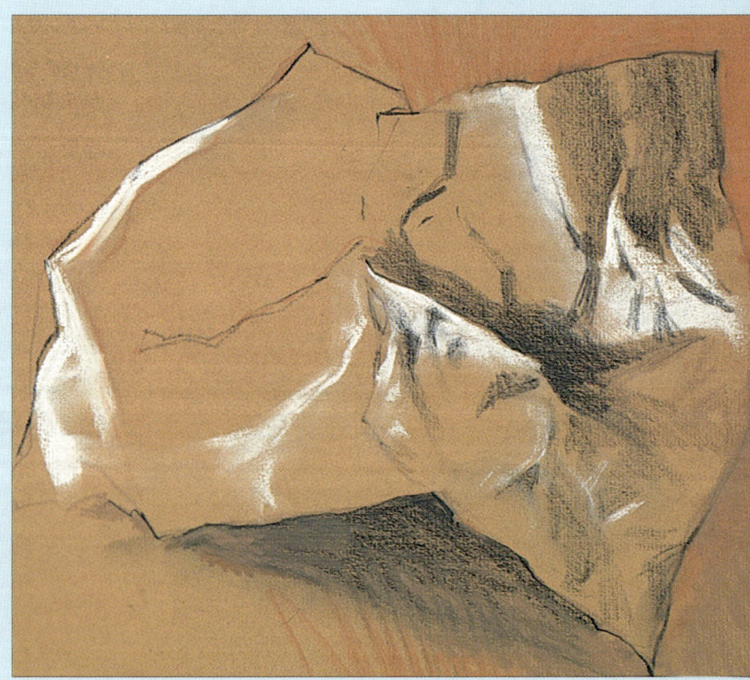

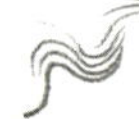

One can set about drawing textures with many different aims: going for the maximum realism using chiaroscuro or simplifying the form so as to study the surface of the object. However, whatever the case, drawing is a long way behind painting in this aspect for the latter can use a multitude of effects to represent the texture of the object. In contrast, with drawing the textures are always represented by visual effects and synthesis.

20

placed on a correctly drawn scaffolding. A fragment of texture blown up and out of context loses its meaning: the references and other forms around aid in creating the effect.

Once the drawing and shadows are complete, you have to study the light zones, something to be done with the aid of white chalk. White stands out strongly on any tinted paper enabling you to get the most out of the highlights. Only mark the most luminous zones. This will break up the internal zones of the figure using light as the criteria distinguishing between them. The texture work in this example can be applied in other drawings, all that changes is the stroke form. Study the folds and the forms created where the paper planes intersect. The folds of a crumpled piece of paper are straight and sometimes form triangular planes.

Do white lines softer than before to suggest less pronounced folds on the paper. Next to these lines, start to develop medium tones, on one side sanguine, on the other charcoal. These tones will give the sensation of depth to the folds in the paper.

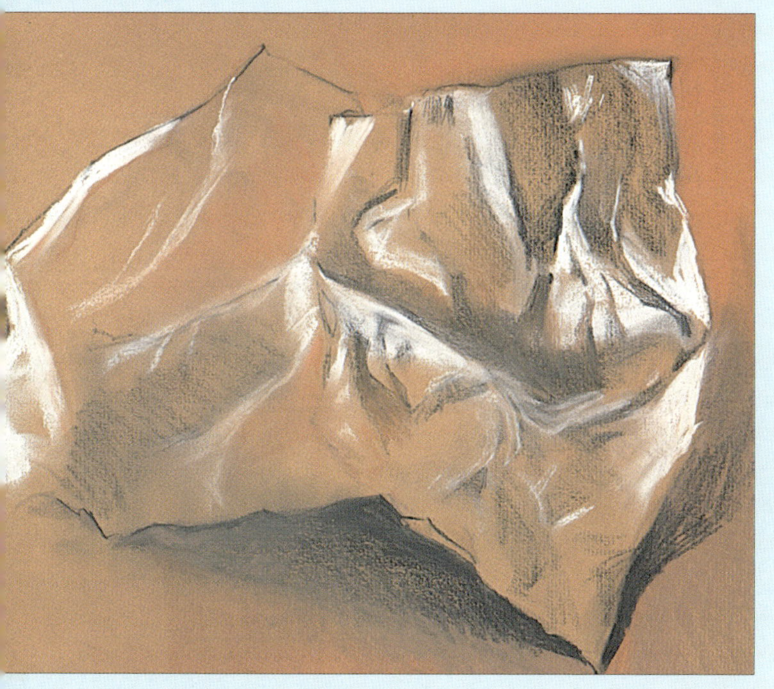

MEDIUM GRAYS AND OTHER TONES

Once the principal light zones have been put in, as they contrast strongly with the paper ground you can start work on form contrasts based on different medium tones. Here it is important to blend in the color of the paper so that it is just one more tone in the picture. In this example, brown sienna has been chosen, not a sanguine tone, and therefore the latter can be the union with the other tones in the drawing.

SMALL PLANES CUT THE LIGHT

We are now going to work on tone values and compensating different gray tones, but gradually without greatly affecting the contrasts or excessively increasing the tones. In this step it is important to study each of the planes that make up the forms. Each small zone of paper is defined according to the direction of the plane. Do rapid strokes and pay attention to the texture. Later, in the next exercise, you will be able to compare it. Each plane is done individually depending on its texture, but always with soft strokes to blend in the tinted paper ground.

Each plane of crumpled paper is depicted with a stroke that indicates the dividing line. White chalk, charcoal and sanguine are used depending on the amount of light.

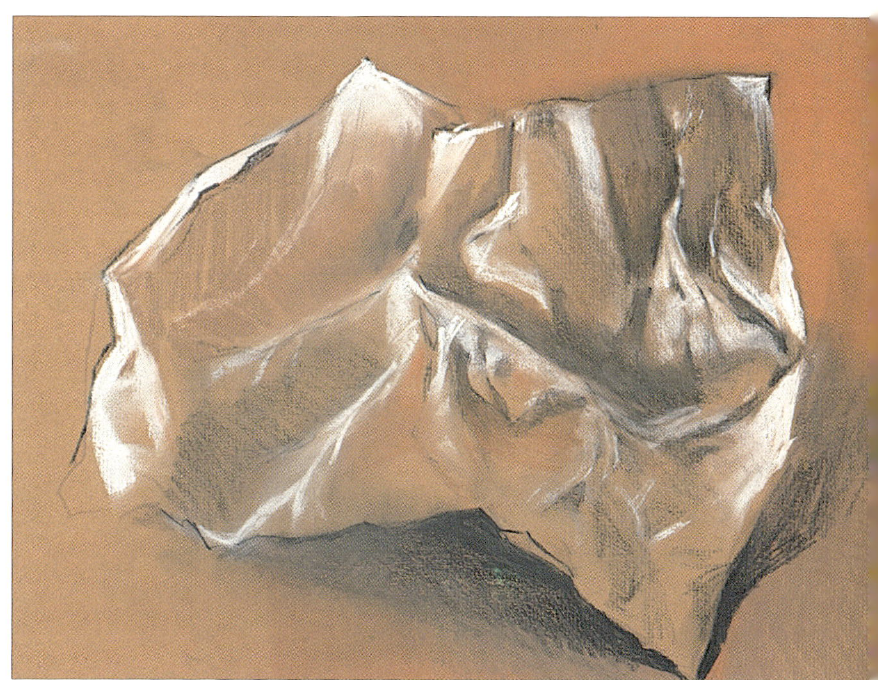

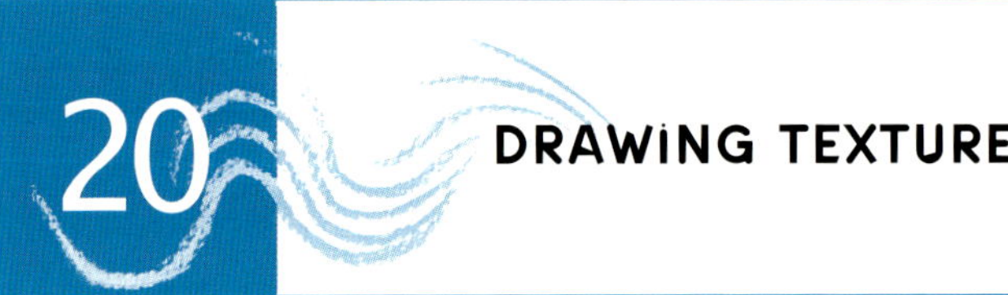

INCREASING THE CONTRAST

The contrasts must only be increased when the different texture zones are sufficiently depicted. Also, bear in mind that all the contrast work must be done in one go to get the values right and to compensate the grays. As we have seen in earlier chapters, simultaneous contrasts allow an increase in tone intensity. This means that if a strong charcoal contrast is placed next to one of the principal highlights, the light zone increases considerably in luminosity and the shadow, next to a pure white, appears much darker.

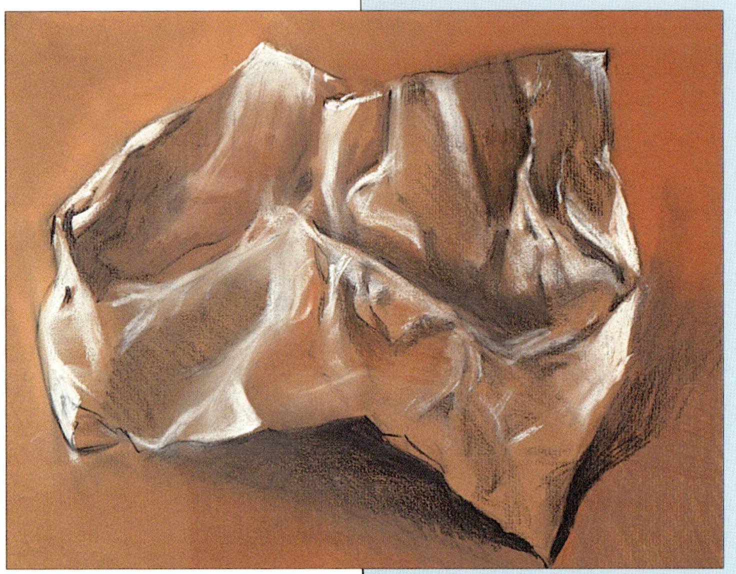

Darken the shadows in the center of the paper. This will make the highlights on the folds appear much more luminous and gives a greater sensation of volume.

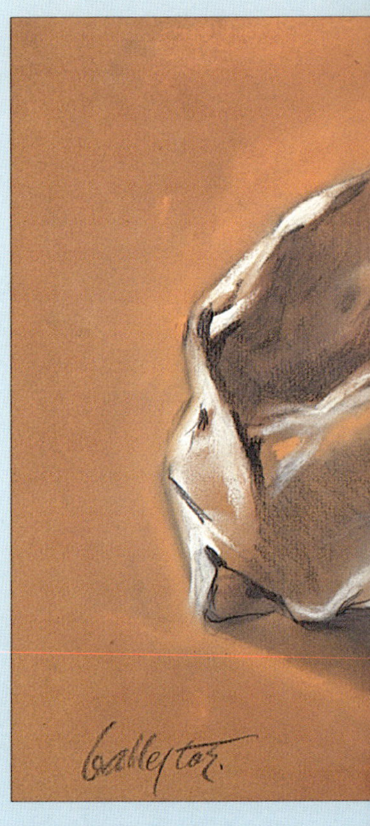

Finally, very small very defined contrasts, both dark and white, finish off the paper texture.

The texture must always culminate the most precise highlights, those based on final contrasts and values worked on the paper. Here do some blendings with your fingertips, but without breaking completely the hardness of the folds. Sanguine permits the complete integration of the tinted paper ground into the drawing as just another tone. In some zones this color must show through, while in others, for example on the right, it is covered by the sanguine in the shadow.

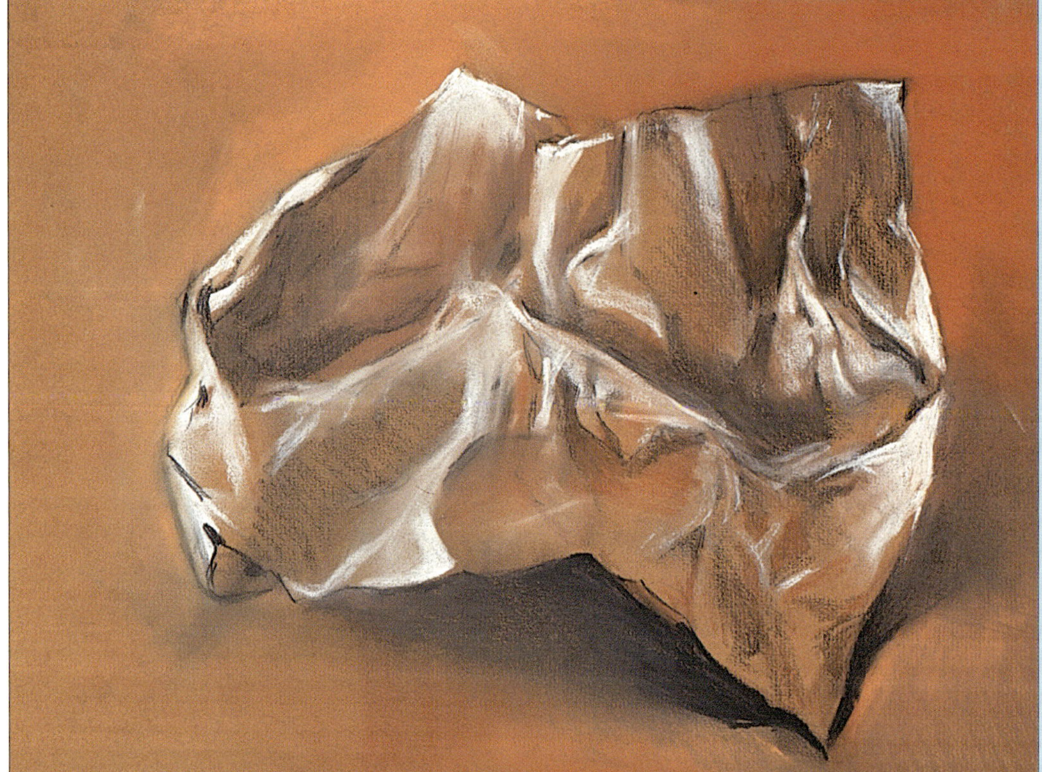

In this image you can appreciate how the shadow of the paper on the table has been intensified and how shadows have been added to the darks in the lower corner.

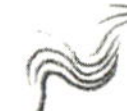

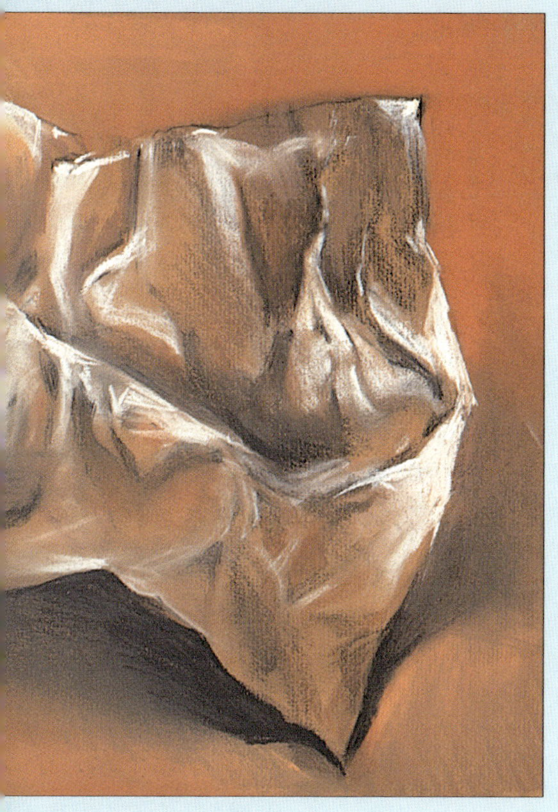

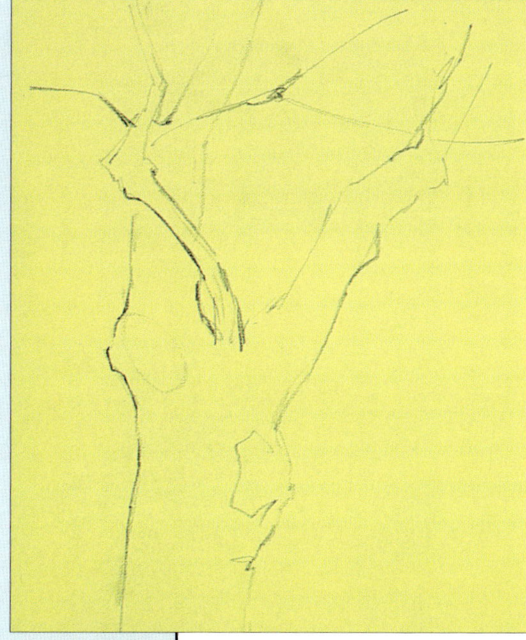

Do the preliminary sketch in graphite on green tinted paper. This will help you with the tree texture.

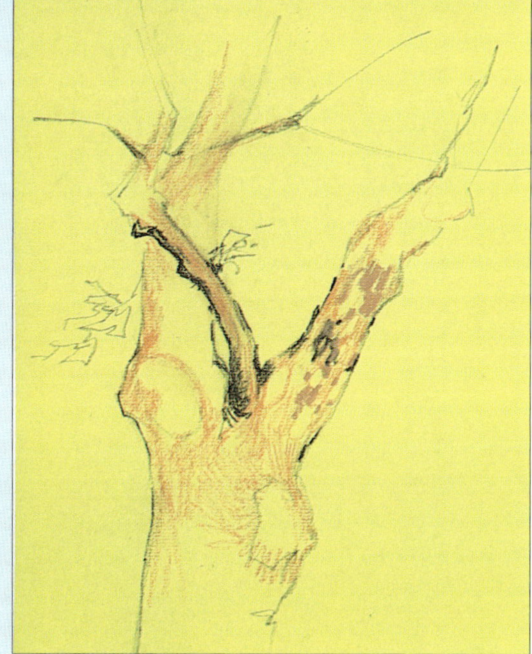

Use rapid strokes to schematize the volume of the tree, marking out the knots. On the bark of one of the main branches do small dashes with the sanguine crayon.

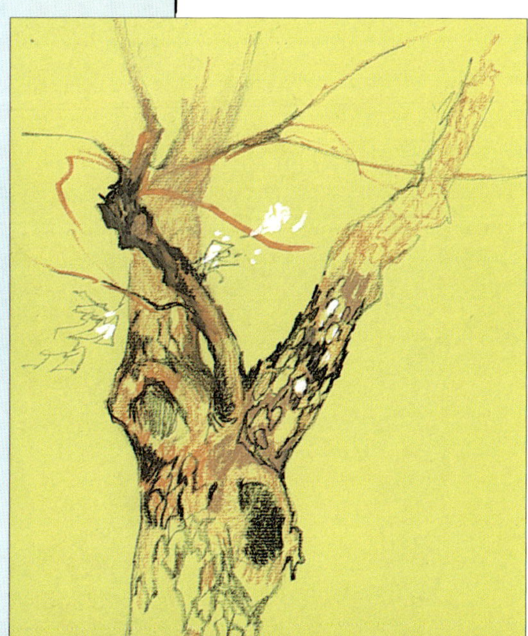

Combine shading with line effects to get this texture. The foregraund is more defined than the branch behind.

BARK TEXTURE

In the last example we studied how to depict a stiff, crumpled texture, something very different to a cloth as we saw earlier. Texture study gives form to the object being depicted. In the last example the paper was composed of multiple planes running into each other. However, textures are not always based on short planes. An object can have a rough, continuous covering wrapped around it. This is the case with the bark of a tree.

THE STROKE FORMS THE PLANE

The preliminary sketch and the drawing need not include the texture. A completely linear drawing can be done without any texture work. The latter is another recourse which must always enhance and support the forms done in the original drawing. In the next exercise we are going to develop the texture of the bark of a tree. The preliminary sketch must be as exact as possible and any corrections must be done before going on to the next stage.

The next step is to give form and volume to the tree. We still have not started work on the texture because, so far, the only concern is to show the volume. Use a sanguine crayon to outline the principal highlights. These strokes must faithfully follow the cylindrical shape of the fragment being drawn. On the trunk, the principal knot is surrounded by circular strokes. A little further up, many short lines enclose small elliptic shapes and here you will start the bark texture adding tiny, precise dashes of sanguine.

A CLOSE UP IN THE FOREGROUND

In the foreground the texture must be more obvious than further back. Never forget this when you are doing complex textures. The thinnest branch of the three is in front of the thick one. To do this drawing avoiding confusion due to the richness of the textures, give priority to the foreground texture work, in this case the thin branch. The branch behind will be done more superficially and less contrasted.

The trunk texture work is identical to what you did at the beginning, short, intense sanguine strokes

superimposed as if they were scales. On top outline the bark with an oiled charcoal contrast. These darks are drawn both as shadings and as contours around the edges of the pieces of bark. White chalk is used for the reflections of light on the most illuminated bark.
To get this texture effect it is necessary to work with shadings and lines. The foreground is more defined than the branch at the back.

DEPICTING LIGHT ON TEXTURES

It is the small contrasts on the trunk texture which will give the realistic effect that we are after. Some zones must be intensified, like the thin branch, by increasing the darkness. This produces a greater separation from the plane behind. Enrich the texture by increasing the contrasts, both light and dark, following the line that defines every chunk of bark.

DEFINING THE TEXTURE WITH DRAWING WORK

The definitive texture of some materials is not fully depicted, as is the case with bark, until the darks complete the form outline. When drawing the chunks of bark, take into consideration the light direction. Only do strokes in the dark part of each fragment. The realism of the texture to a great extent depends on the way the light is handled.

The branch to the fore is more intensely contrasted so that it is separated from the one behind. The tiny highlights and contrasts make the texture more realistic.

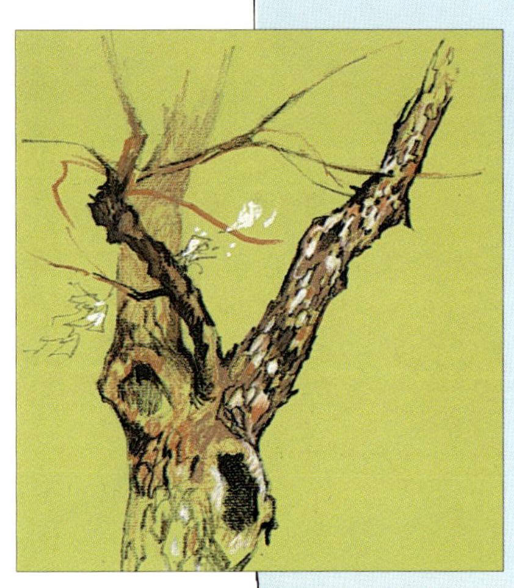

Complement the small shadings and increased contrasts by drawing in the darkest parts on the bark.

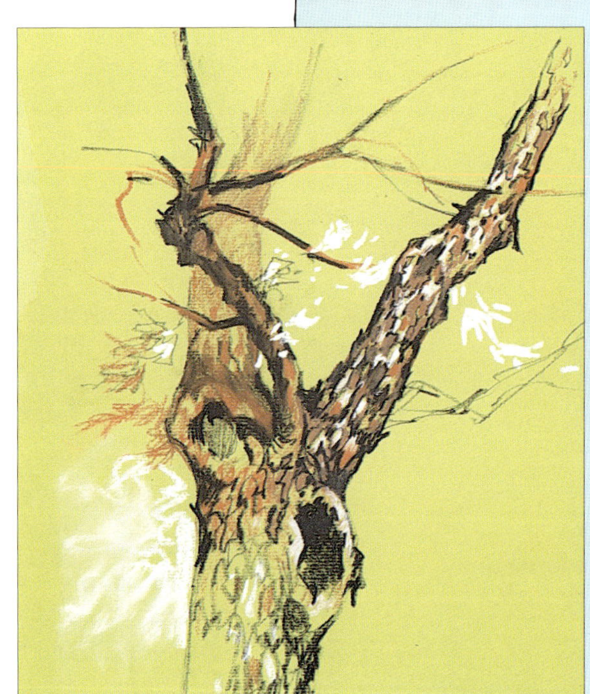

In this amplified close up of the last image you can see how the chunks of bark were done.

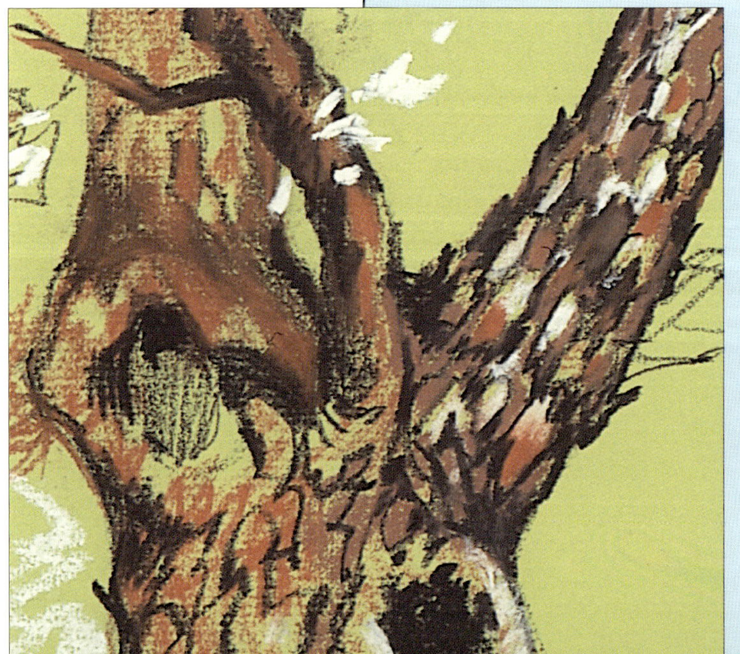

ORGANIC TEXTURE

One of the most complex textures to represent is wrinkled skin or peel. This is because the skin clings to the object. The peel of a stale fruit is a good example with which to practice. As in all the examples in this chapter the color of the paper plays a fundamental role as it is going to be blended in as if it were another tone.

TEXTURE AND TONE VALUES

Start the drawing with a simple scheme, as you have done so many times with fruit, because it enables us to understand modeling and tone values on basic shapes. Once the apple has been schematized, start work on the light and shadow values using a very soft stroke. The modeling of the fruit is based on a gradated shadow that divides the fruit in two and is slightly more contrasted nearer to the viewer. Gradate the faint shadow at the back. When starting on the shadow tone values it is also important to approach the peel texture. Sketch the texture with soft lines covering all the zone where the contrast is most intense.

PERFECTION COMES FROM SYNTHESIS

Texture work mixes complexity with simplicity. Every now and then we come across masterpiece examples, like this work by Casas. Observe closely how he did the dress texture. Such was his ability that a few black strokes stumped on a black background give a highly realistic effect. To avoid cluttering he left the cloth unfinished in the lower part.

Ramón Casas (1866-1932). The muse of Montmartre. Charcoal on paper.

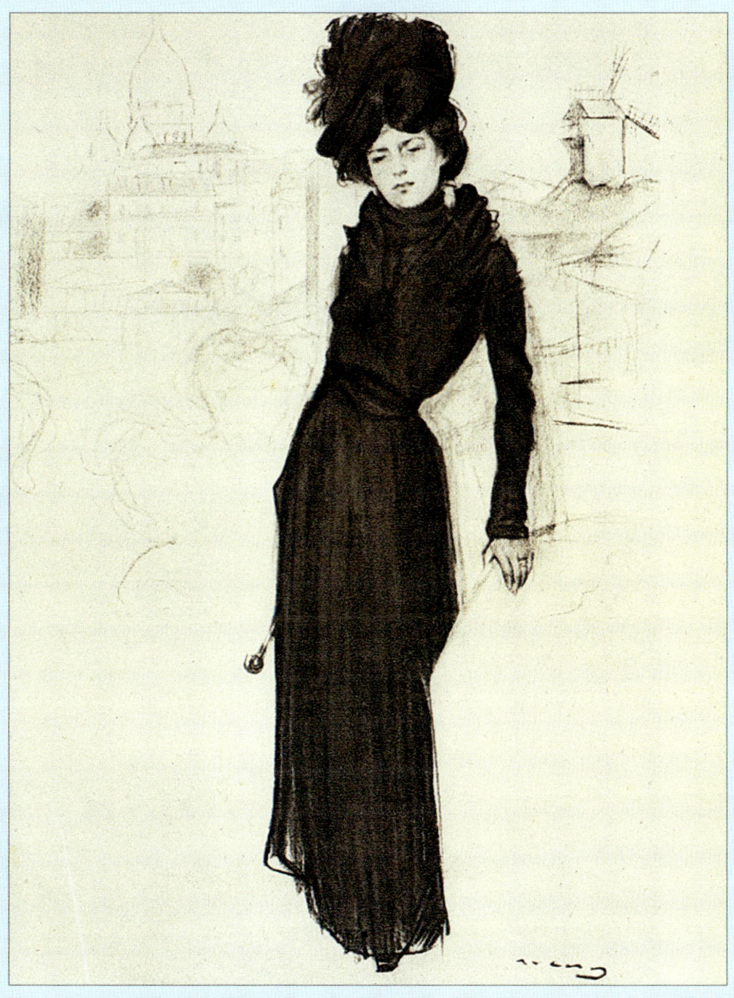

CONTRASTS IN DIFFERENT ZONES

When the tone values are well contrasted, increase the depth of the wrinkles in the peel. This is done by combining graphite and sanguine, always going in the same direction as the plane of the fruit. The darks of the texture are drawn in zones, always leaving a small gap between the darks.

Once the wrinkles in the peel have been worked on, you can continue with the tone values. Darken the shadows but be careful not to completely close up the paper pore. Use white to do the texture of the most illuminated zone: the broken stroke indicates the roughness here. To finish the texture effect, and therefore the exercise, increase the light and dark contrasts.

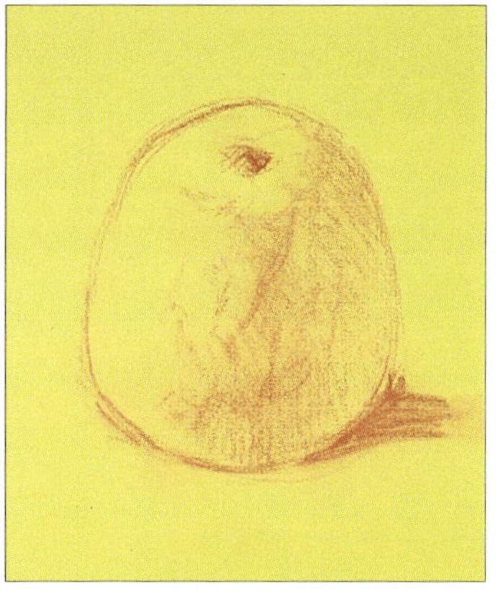

The texture work must always go hand in hand with the tone values.

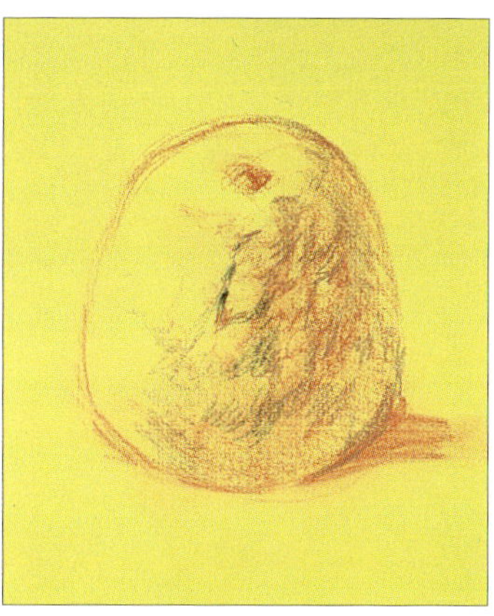

The process of contrasting means exploiting the shadowing, especially in the wrinkles on the peel.

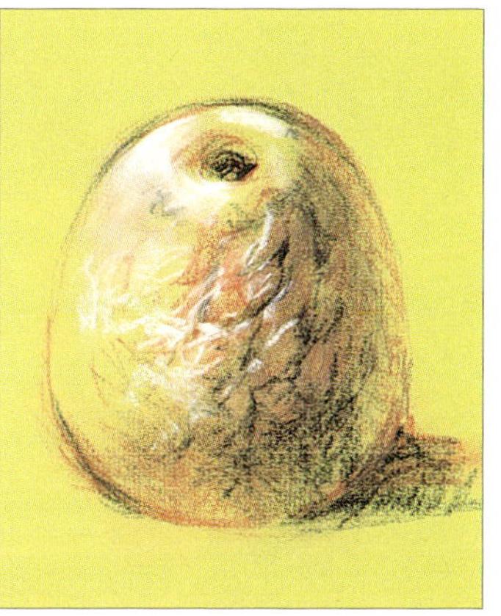

The dark tones are done zone by zone. They give shape to the original texture.

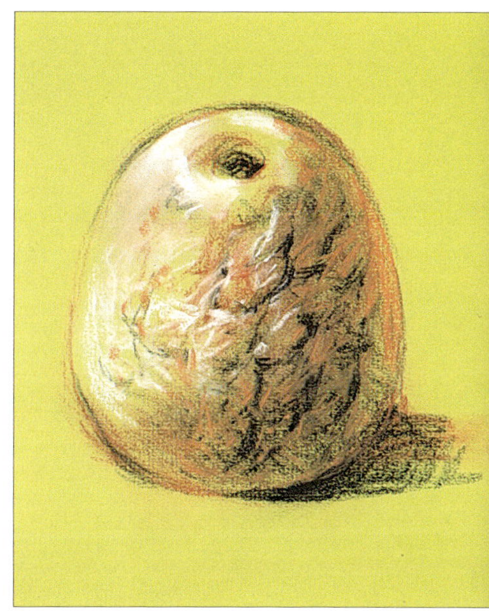

SUMMARY

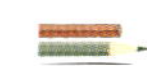

GRADUAL ELABORATION
The textures must be elaborated gradually together with the rest of the drawing.

ROUGH TEXTURES
The light and shadow planes cut into each other. The corners are intense highlights.

FOREGROUND PLANES
When different planes are superimposed, the foreground must be more defined so that the separation is clear.

MODELING AND TEXTURE
When the modeling involves complex textures, work simultaneously on texture and tone values.

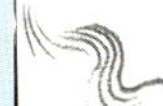

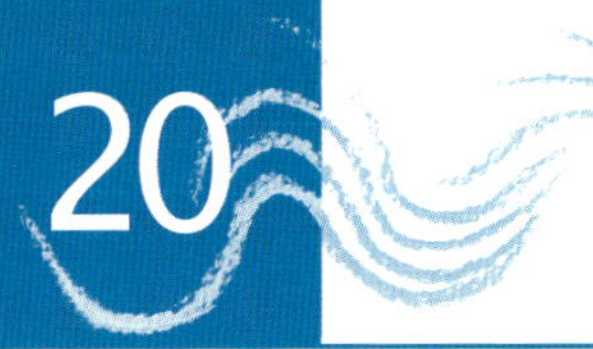

Exercices *Step by step*

DRAWING TEXTURES

Drawing textures can be a stimulating challenge for figurative painters. Effects which imitate reality can often be striking and surprising, above all when applied in the right measure. To put into practice some of the concepts studied in this chapter we are going to draw a curious still life.

It is important that the artist learns to improvise models. Sometimes the most straightforward one can also be the ideal one. Now and then simplicity prevents the learner from seeing the drawing opportunity before him or her. Some leaves and a thread compose this still life in which we will work on wood and leaf textures.

NECESSARY MATERIAL

Tinted paper, **(1)**
Sanguine crayon, (2)
Sepia crayon, (3)
Charcoal crayon, (4)
White chalk, (5)

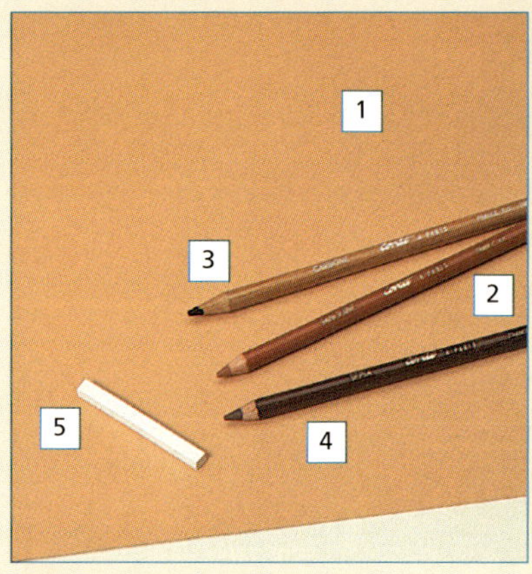

The textures must be done progressively, starting with the lighter tones and increasing the contrast as the drawing becomes firmer.

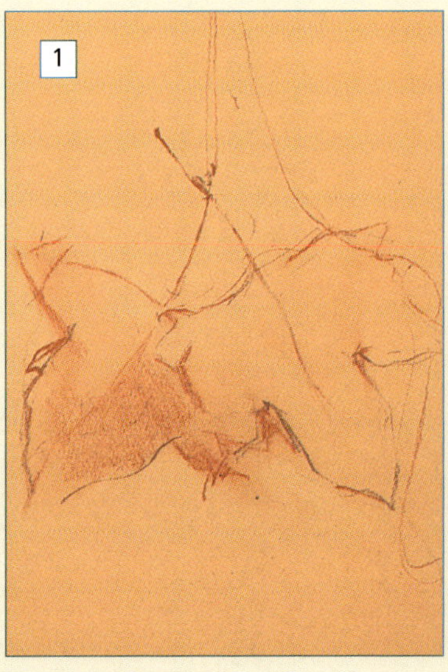

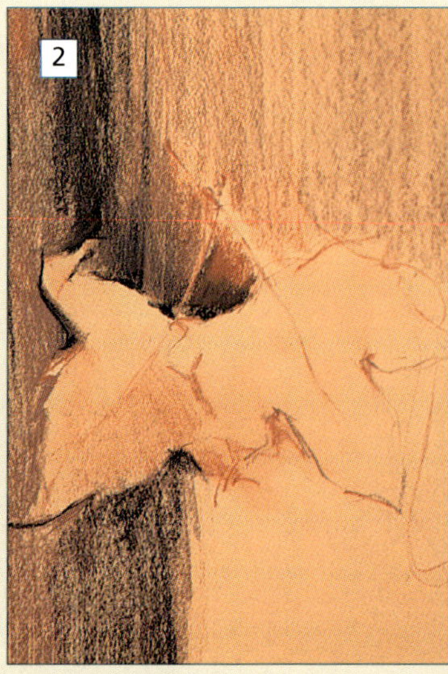

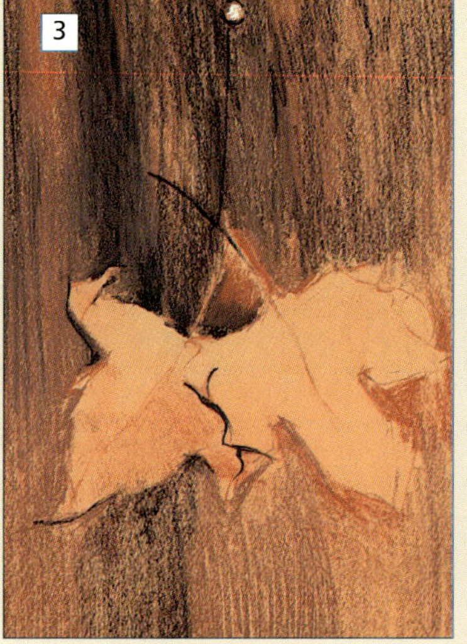

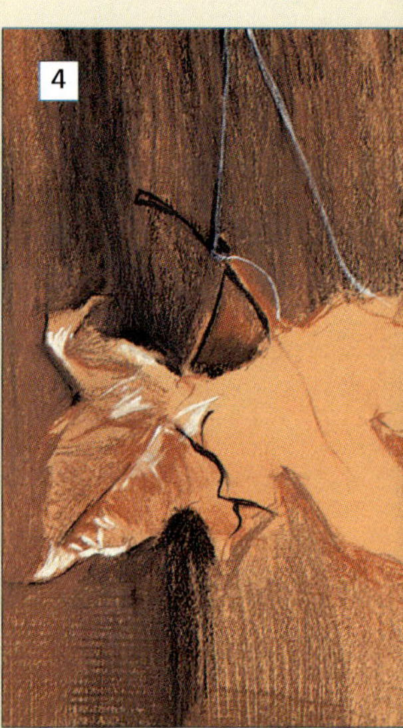

1· **THE PRELIMINARY SKETCH IS DONE** as in the earlier examples. Here the composition must be painstakingly constructed because the model is completely centralized so it is important to break the symmetry by pushing the leaves to one side and counterbalancing with the thread across the board.

ONCE THE LEAF FORMS HAVE BEEN done you can separate the planes by stumping and darkening the rear leaf.

2· **START TO WORK ON THE CONTRAST** of the board which holds the leaves. A very dark, uniform vertical stroke insinuates the wood texture without going into details. The darkening of the background means that the color of the paper is blended with the leaves.

NOT ALL OF THE BACKGROUND is shaded in the same intensity. Charcoal is used to increase the dark strokes in the background.

THE TEXTURES MUST BE WORKED on progressively, starting with the light tones and increasing the contrasts as the drawing becomes more definitive.

3· **COMPLETE THE BACKGROUND BY DOING** wide sepia and charcoal strokes. Now the leaves are perfectly marked out by the background.

GO OVER THE DRAWING IN SANGUINE in the lower part of the leaves. As we have studied throughout this chapter, dark next to light gives rise to simultaneous contrasts that make the tones more intense.

COMPARE THIS STAGE OF THE DRAWING with the last one. The leaves have become more luminous due to the darkening of the background.

4· **START TO WORK ON THE TEXTURE** of the leaf on the left using sepia and sanguine on both sides of the central vein. White chalk intensifies the most luminous parts of the texture. A rough, silvery aspect can be created by a few dashes of white chalk. Draw the thread that supports the leaves in white, too. The contrast with the background is strong.

IN THE LOWER LEFT PART, DO HATCHING IN SEPIA. These horizontal lines will later be stumped with the fingertips.

A drawing of leaves

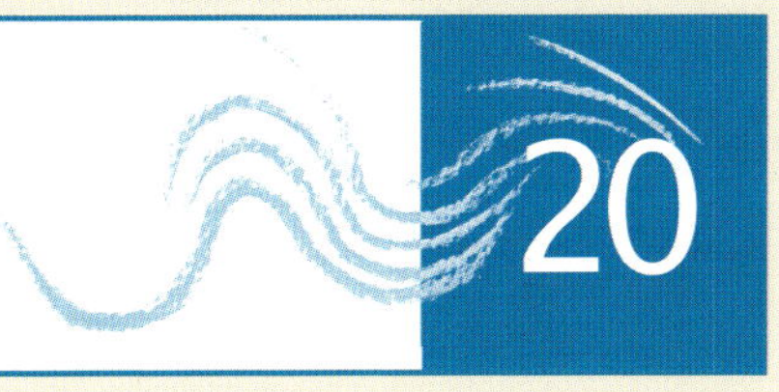

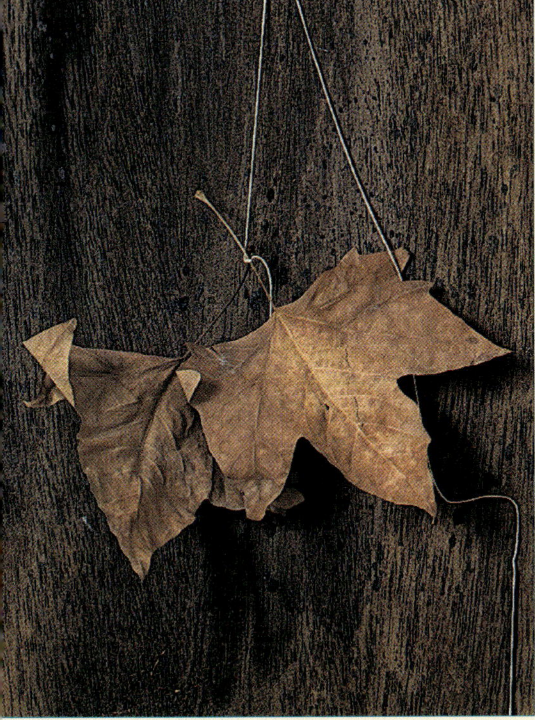

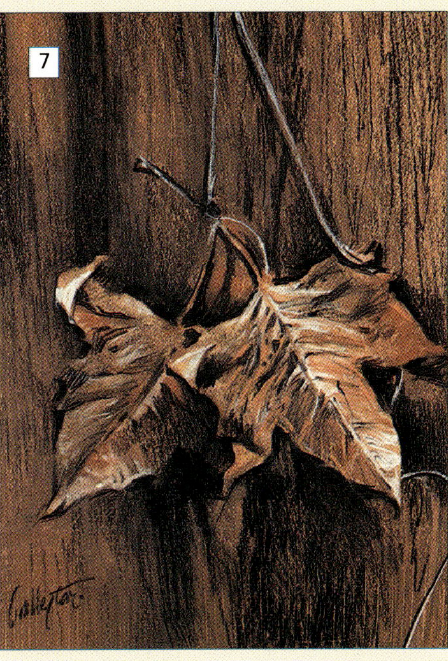

SUMMARY SCHEME

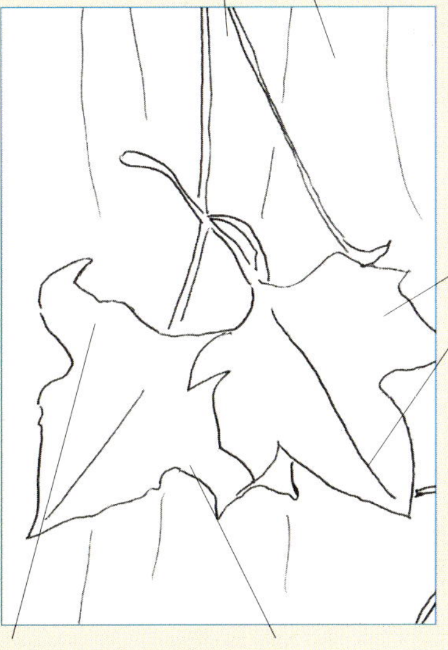

5· SHADE IN SANGUINE ON THE RIGHT in the background and then immediately smudge it with the hand, making vertical stumping strokes but do not completely smear away the sepia drawn at the beginning.

WHILE THE HAND IS STILL covered in sanguine powder, smudge the sepia zone on the background. Intensify the darks on the leaf on the left using the charcoal crayon. Observe how the leaf texture is made. The lines drawn before now show through these shadows laid on top.

6· START WORK ON THE TEXTURE of the leaf on the right. First use a slanted sepia stroke on the texture. After intensify the shadows that outline the lower part of the leaf. Finally, intensify the contrast of the leaf on the left.

USE SIENNA TO DRAW SOME DARKS on the leaf on the right. These darks take on the form of the veins on this side of the leaf, making the tones much lighter. Now the principal light zones on this leaf are defined. Draw the brightest parts in white chalk.

7· USE A STRONG, VERTICAL charcoal stroke to intensify the contrast of the background.

IN THIS FINAL STEP WE ARE AIMING at contrasting all the textures. start in the background, taking special care with the wood streaks. Use charcoal and sepia to do long strokes that contrast with some background zones.

LIKEWISE, INTENSIFY THE TEXTURE contrast on the leaves going over the white lines. Intensify the darks.

FINALLY, ALL THAT REMAINS TO BE DONE is to finish the leaf shadows on the wood.

Do not fix the drawing yet. The complexity means that perhaps some zones will have to be corrected later.

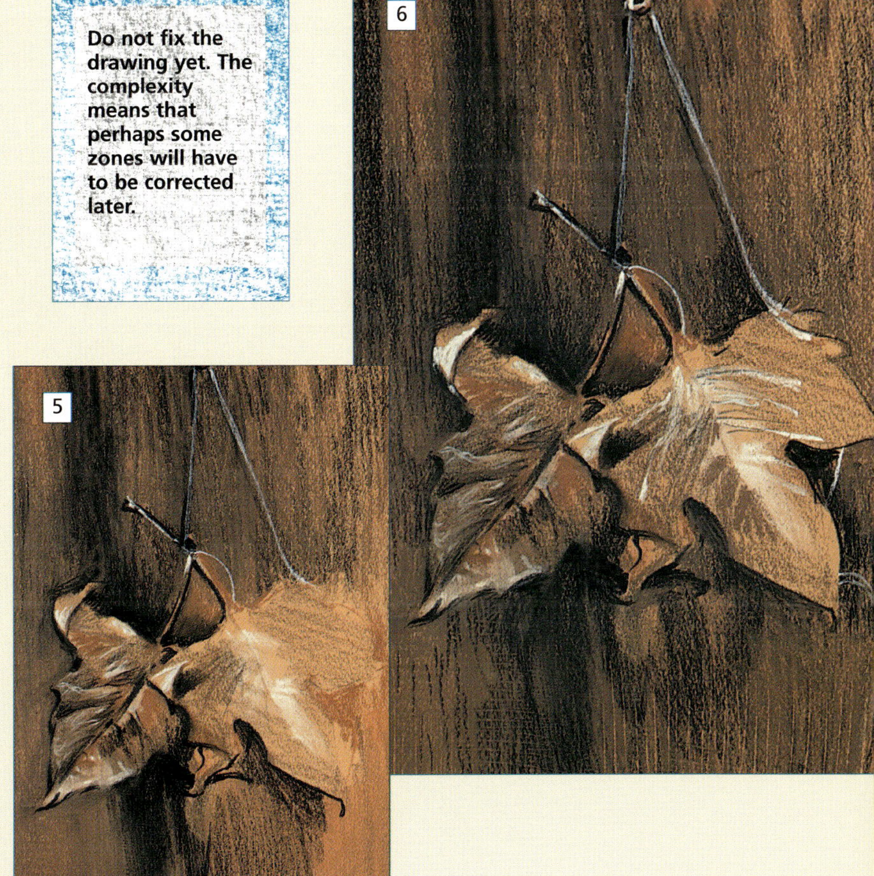

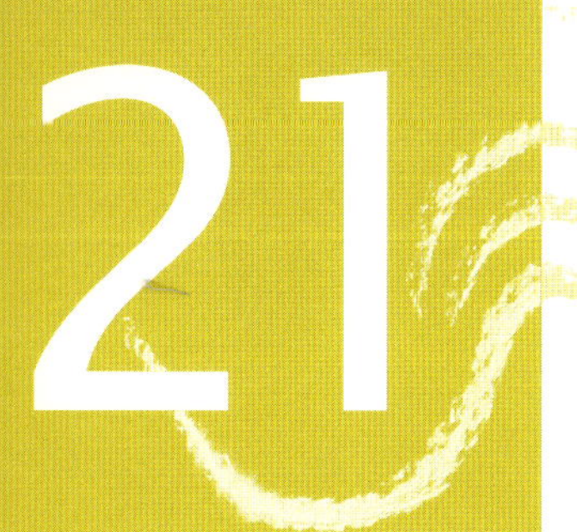

21 DRAWING WITH AN REED PEN

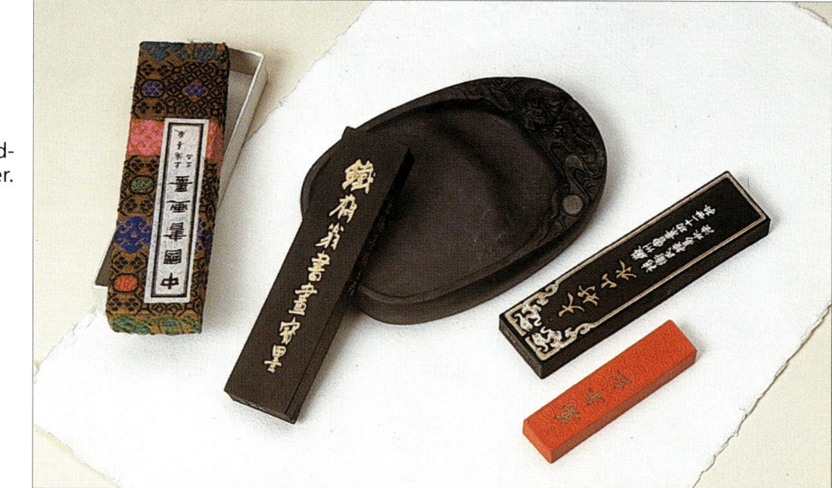

Ink sticks, a stone and hand-made paper.

In this chapter we are going to study a rather unconventional application of the reed pen. Its normal use requires patiently dissolving the ink in water and using the traditional wash technique. In the following pages this work is going to be simplified considerably: the brush will be a complement and we will draw directly with the wet stick.

THE REED PEN

Chinese ink, or India ink, is the name given to black drawing inks derived from the soot of exceptionally hard woods, such as olive or grape vines, or from the fatty lampblack of the oil flame. Gum-arabic is mixed in as the binder. Various other ingredients are frequently added to improve its performance. However, this limited description fails to do justice to this carefully elaborated drawing medium.

The ink is made over a small stone recipient, into which a little bit of water is added, just enough to be able to rub the wet stick. The latter crumbles to form the classic black color. So subtle is the preparation process that the way the ink is rubbed against the stone determines the characteristics of the black.

Chinese ink in sticks still has to be imported from the Orient, the principal exporters being China and Japan. During centuries it was the drawing method used by the majority of artists but gradually it was pushed aside by the more practical liquid Chinese ink. Recently it has enjoyed a resurgence.

THE REED PEN STROKE

When the reed pen is fresh it must be wetted and dragged across the wet stone to get an intense enough black. If you paint with a continuous, black line, the stick must be wetted, softened, and well rubbed. Otherwise, if the stick is not very wet, the stroke can be broken, almost charcoal like. Just because the reed pen is thick does not mean the strokes have to be thick for you can use any of the sides or edges. A thick stick can do fine, precise strokes to make drawings as direct and as defined as those of any other drawing medium. These lines can be enriched by the shades of gray

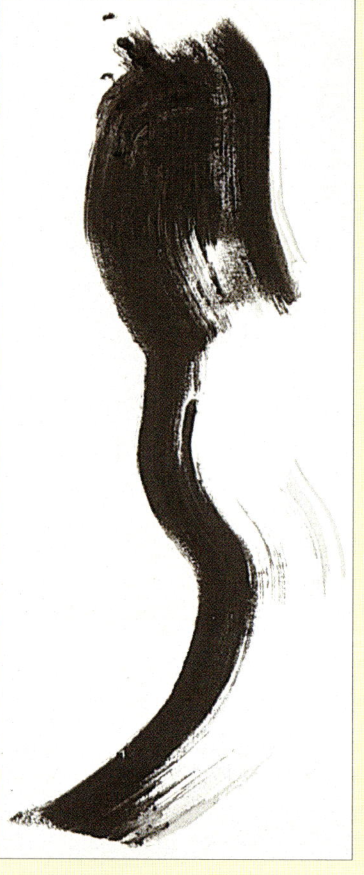

A stroke done with the stick wet but not very rubbed.

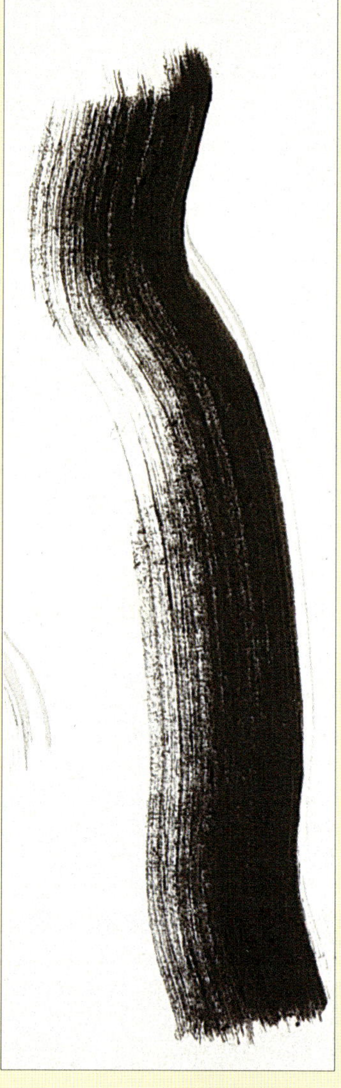

In this stroke the stick is soft enough so that the line is not broken.

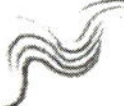

The reed pen, comes from China and has been used in the Orient for thousands of years. Today the majority of plastic painting and drawing mediums are perfectly integrated into western art. Indeed, you will see how the medium has advanced with new applications to what was previously intended to be a brush method.

21

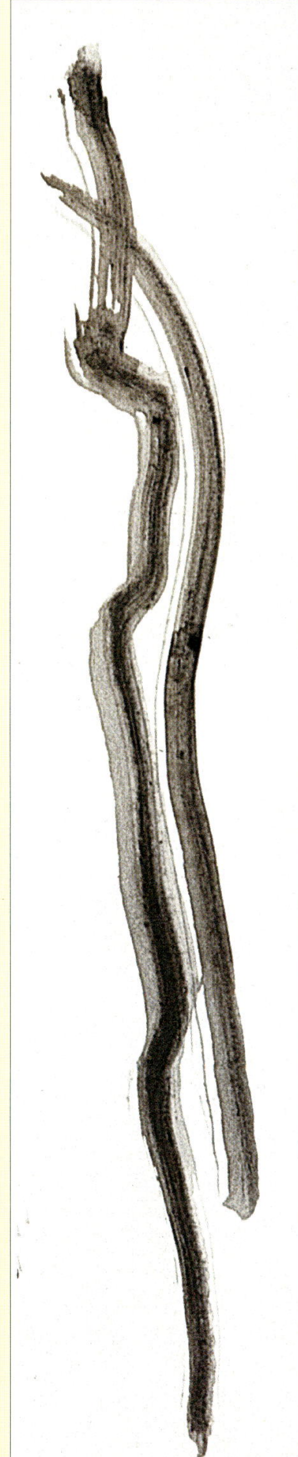

obtainable from the washes. Before starting to draw, although the learner may already master other drawing processes, it would not go amiss to do a few tests on paper to become familiar with the medium. Do not put too much water in the stone recipient, just enough to fill the deepest part of the bored through stone. Treat this stick as if it were a pencil, wetting it as you drag the dissolved ink towards the water. When the stick starts to slide over the stone you know that the ink has already been formed and it is the moment to start to draw. As you can see, when the stick is soft and wet, it gives a continuous stroke. When almost dry, the stroke is more faded and broken.

A constant stroke made with the wetted edge of the stick. Do not move the stick too rapidly.

Strokes made with the corners of the stick.

A series of strokes with the edge of the stick.

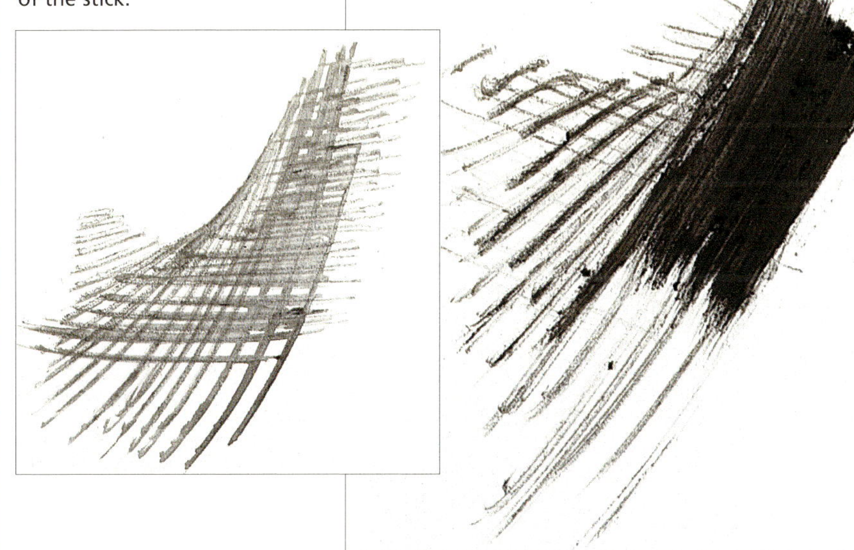

Firstly, the thick stroke was done with all the width of the stick. The hatching was done rapidly with the edge of the stick.

PRACTICING DRAWING WITH THE REED PEN

We have just studied some of the strokes possible with an reed pen. Before going on it is necessary to point out something which although obvious could be overlooked by a new-convert to working with ink. Despite having the appearance of a

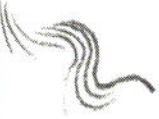

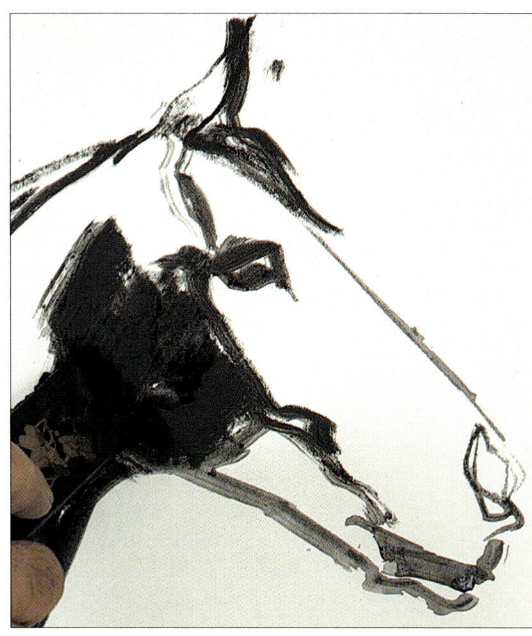

dry medium, the ink stroke, once down, is irremovable so apply it carefully but being bold enough to get the most out of it. Always start the work with the essential lines and once they are firm you can put down wider, more direct strokes and shading. If the learner is intimidated by starting on a blank piece of paper, the preliminary sketch can be done with a pencil.

THE FIRST STROKES

We are going to draw a horse's head, which should be easy if you follow the steps laid out. Firstly, wet the stick and rub it against the stone. You are not after a very black stroke so when the ink starts to flow, dip the stick in water to loosen any excess color. The first lines are fine: outline the head, starting with the forehead and going down to the snout. Use the narrow part of the stick to draw the line of the mouth and the rear of the neck. Now, with the preliminary sketch complete, drag and soften the ink in the stone deposit before working on the darks of the face.

Once the main lines have been placed, add in greater contrast using the wet, well softened stick. To enable you to draw with intense blacks, the reed pen must be rubbed hard against the sloping side of the stone recipient, dragging the exact measure of water so that the stone abrades the reed pen. Apply the medium grays to the horse's face using the reed pen almost dry. The line produced is similar to other dry drawing mediums.

You can build on the lines put down before.

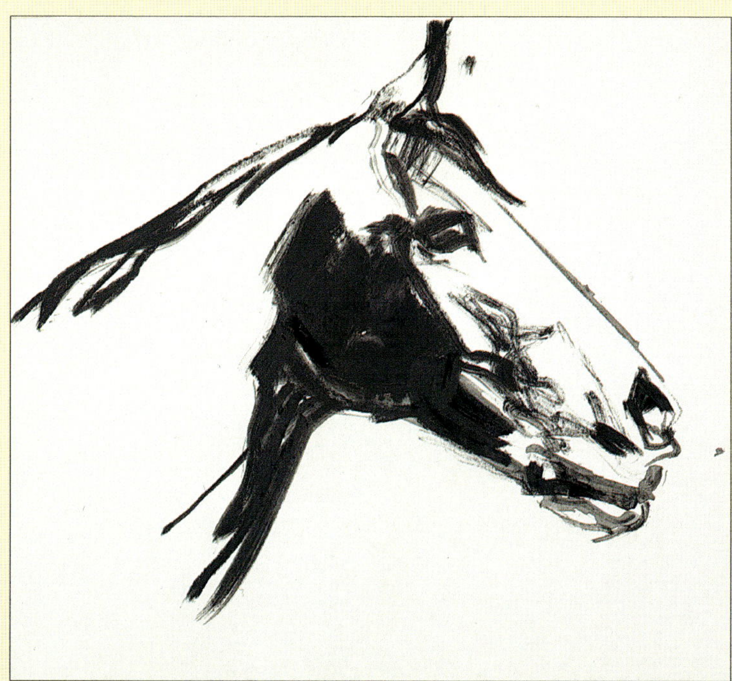

Once the principal lines have been done you can go over them with thicker strokes and start to look for effects with the worn away stick (just a little moistness).

The lines of the neck are made with a rapid stroke, started and finished without rewetting the stick.

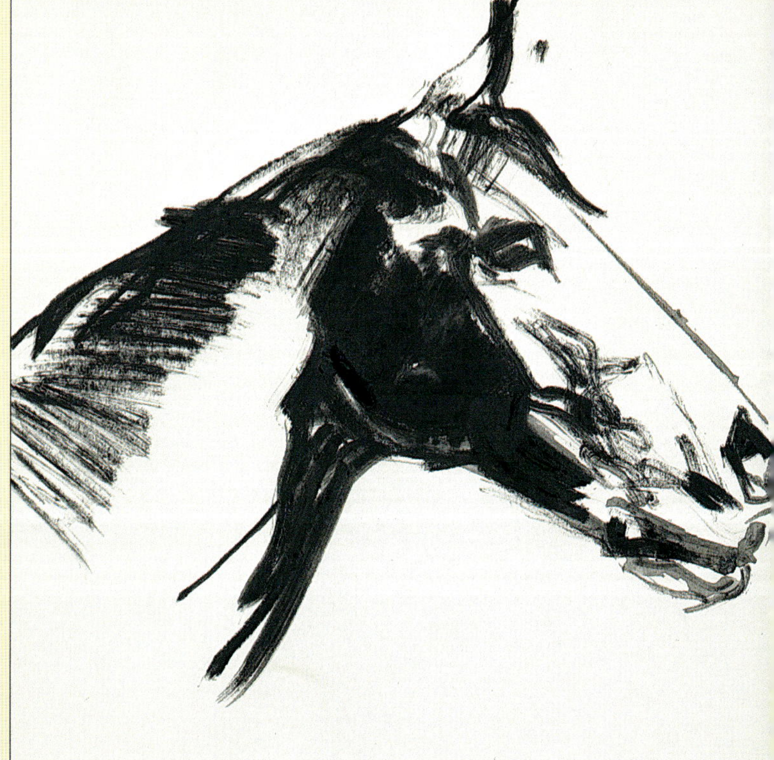

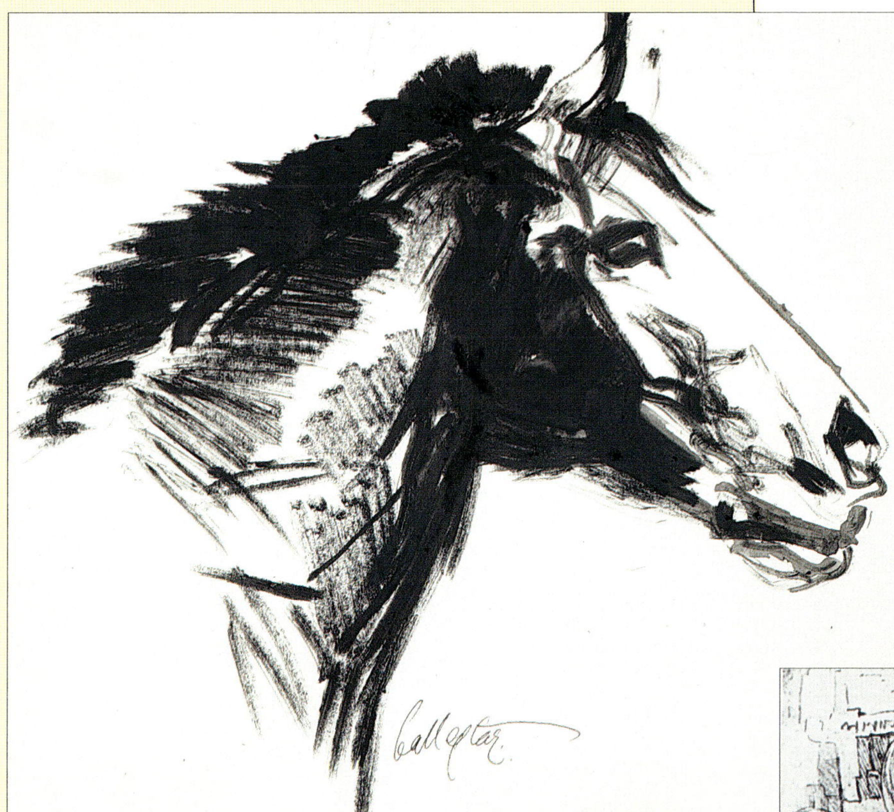

After drawing the lines that structure the head, complete the dark zones of the animal. When the stroke begins to run out of ink, before redipping the stick, do some medium tones on the neck.

THE DENSITY OF BLACK

When you are trying to get blacks in a dry medium it is necessary to do a great variety of strokes close together. The strokes are different if you want gray. For this work we are not using a dry medium, but a fluid one even though the stroke appearance indicates the opposite. However, the ink is applied in a way very similar to other dry mediums. Do rapid strokes to darken the rear of the neck and to emphasize the illuminated zone. Wet the ink and rub it until it flows freely over the stone and then start to draw the neck with rapid strokes. At first the lines will be black but if you do not wet the stick again they will turn gray and progressively clearer.

DARK CONTRASTS

As you can see in this exercise, the hair is elaborated gradually. Add darks once the light zones have been sufficiently defined by the supporting lines. The initial lines enabled the darks of the shadows to be placed, but always being careful not to shade areas that have to be reserved. Soften the reed pen and darken the horse's mane and the lower part of the neck. Every time part of the stick is worn away, take advantage of the texture to apply medium grays where necessary, for example on the neck.

A STROKE EXERCiSE

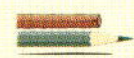

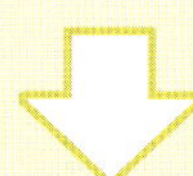

Leonardo. A study of a great explosion.

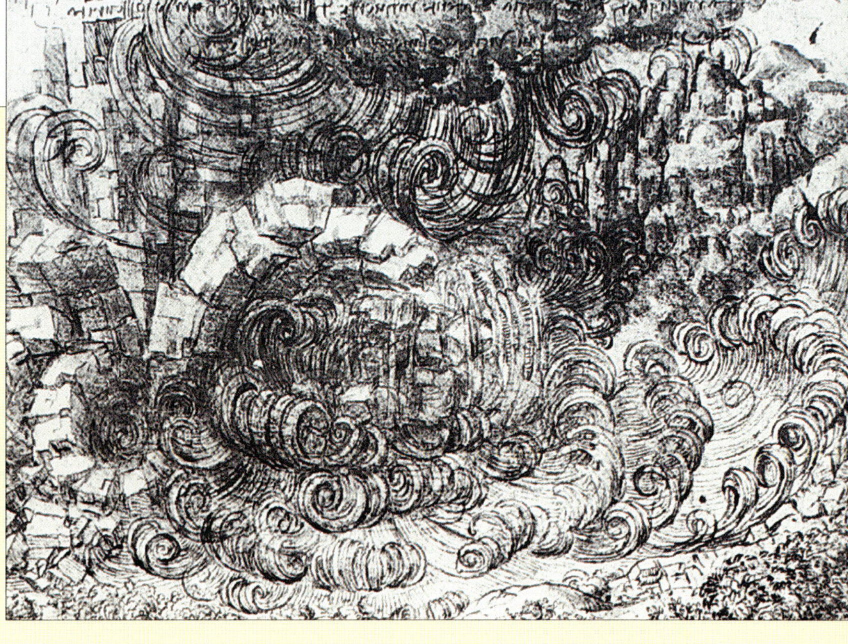

The best way of learning is practicing. A stroke is the result of hand gestures and therefore the great masters were constantly exercising and trying to develop in all their works. By continuously practicing strokes you will learn to express what you have in mind. Do not limit yourself to doing what you already know how to do. This was the approach that Leonardo took as he tried to depict his thoughts, even those beyond reason. Anxious to portray reality the great master did this study of the dynamic of an explosion. Observe the lines of all the forms: there are no signs of tiredness or carelessness. Every line is drawn precisely and the effects perfectly studied beforehand.

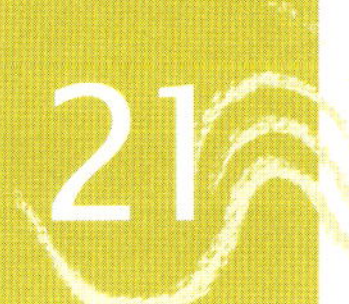

21 DRAWING WITH AN REED PEN

THE BRUSH AND THE REED PEN

In the last example we studied the principal applications of the reed pen when it is applied directly on to the paper. As you saw, ink is soluble when wetted in water and it can therefore be turned back to liquid if it is wetted by the brush when on the paper. In this exercise we are going to study how to use the stick and the brush together: a technique half-way between pure drawing and the wash.

DEFINITIVE LINES

It is worth doing this exercise after doing the previous one, without letting too much time go by so that you can compare the fundamentals of drawing in comparison with the new possibilities. Another reason is to take advantage of the ink that is dissolving in the water. The ink is not densely black because the aim is not to do an ink wash but rather to paint directly with the stick on the paper. Use dissolved ink from the stone to do the definitive lines and the shadings that blot the clouds in the sky. Construct the form of the path and the mountain line. In the stone, prepare a denser gray with the reed pen and use it to darken the initial strokes.

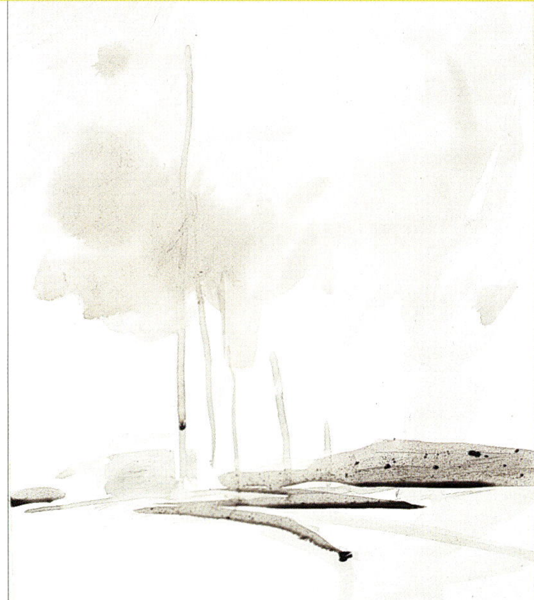

Wet the brush in the inky water to shade the principal lines and landscape forms.

RUBBING ON THE PAPER OR ON THE STONE

In the last exercise we studied how the ink can be wetted, rubbed, dissolved and softened on the stone. If the paper is moist and the stick sufficiently soft after use, you can draw directly with the stick on the moist zones of the paper. The paper texture abrades the ink to give a dense and black stroke.

Put this effect to good use by doing the principal darks of the landscape, horizontal strokes on the right and small vertical strokes on the left. On the house walls do both types of stroke using the width of the stick.

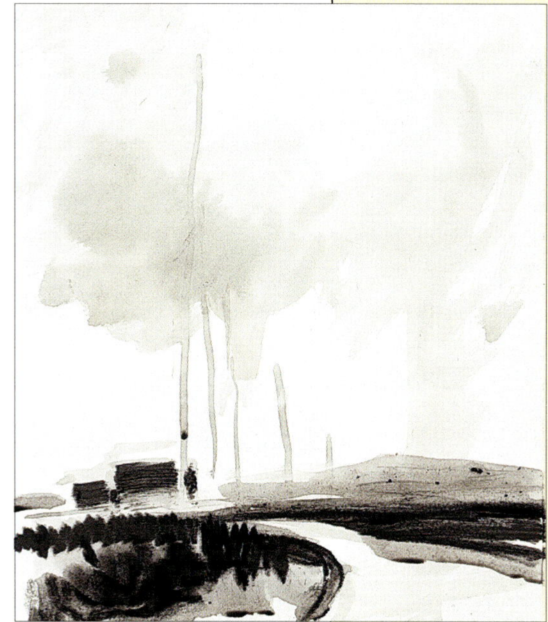

Strokes done on the wet background.

ADD MOISTURE CONSTANTLY

Once the principal zones have been stained and the paper ground is dry, intensifying the darks depends entirely on how much you dampen and wet the ink bar on the stone. Make a deep black by rubbing the reed pen and apply it to the darks on the house walls. Start the stroke at the top, dragging the stick downwards until the limit of the dark area. Every time that you need a new dense dark you have to wet and rub the reed pen. If you only want a line, just wetting the stick is sufficient; you need not rub it on the stone.

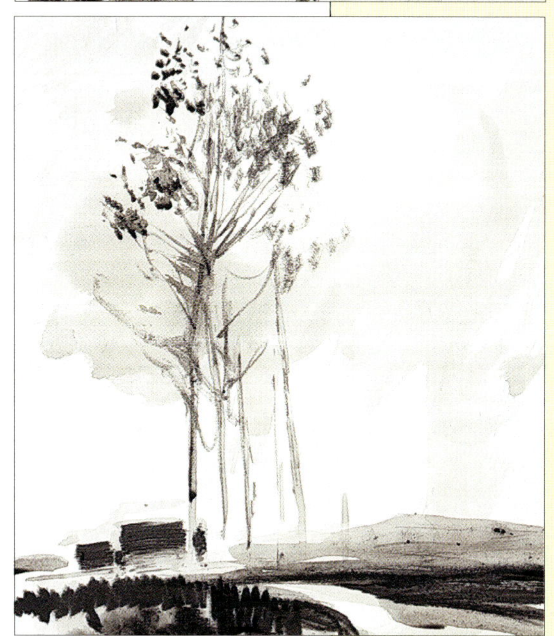

On top of the still wet surface do a few shadings to insinuate the tree top. If you want to draw more intensely, wet the reed pen slightly.

In this close up you can appreciate how the stick is applied on the background house.

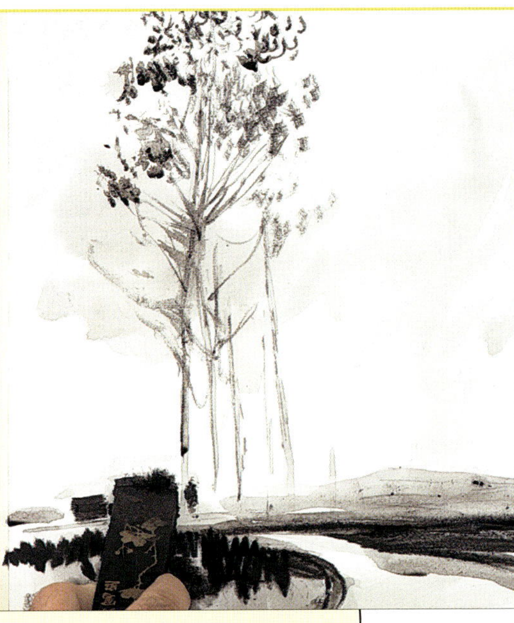

ACCELERATING OR SLOWING UP THE DRYING OF THE WASH

Depending on the season, or where you are drawing, the drying of the stroke can impede the artist working as they would like. Adding a few drops of alcohol to the solution in the stone accelerates the water evaporation, while a few drops of glycerin slow down the process. Do tests before using the ink on the paper.

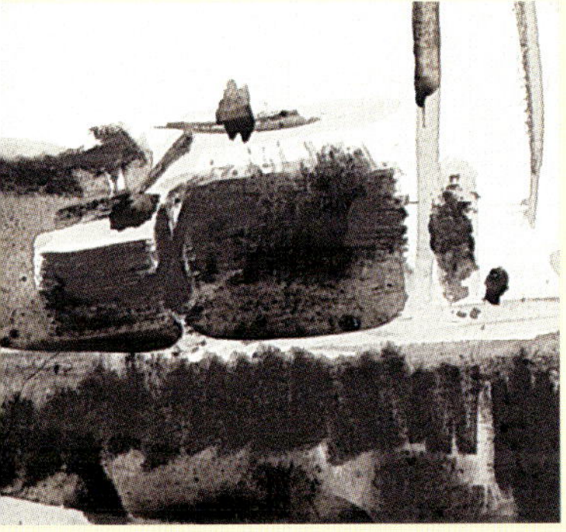

A wet brush allows you to rub and draw, working with the darkness of the paper. However, be careful with the zones that must be completely white, like the house in the background.

A BRUSH FOR THE BACKGROUND

You can get play out of the brush by wetting recently drawn areas, or even where the ink is dry, and then applying more ink to obtain new washes and gray shades. When using the brush respect the zones that must be reserved for whites or luminous tones.

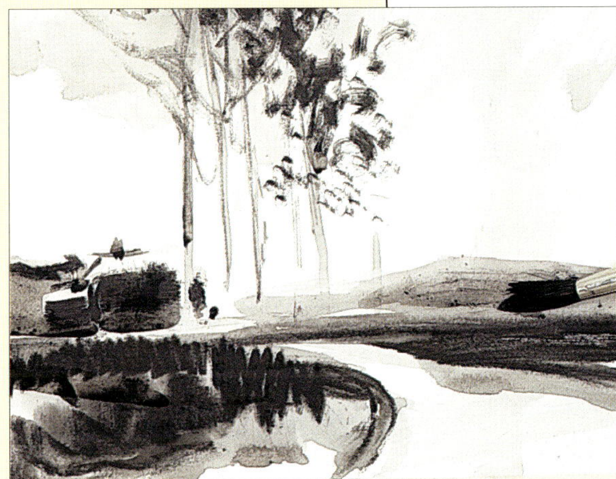

This is how to darken an already dry tone. It now stands out from the mountain horizon line.

DETAILS WITH THE EDGE OF THE STICK

Once the landscape, the base of this drawing, has been constructed, the rest of the details can be done with just the stick. All of the corners offer different strokes regardless of the thickness of the bar. Combine the use of the edge and the narrowest side to draw the upper part of the tree top. Rapidly rub the stick to define the trunks. The background must be moist, and the stick well rubbed, to paint the trees on the right. Finally, the curved lines of the puddles on the path are drawn with a corner of the stick.

An ink stick offers as many possibilities as graphite, sanguine or charcoal crayons.

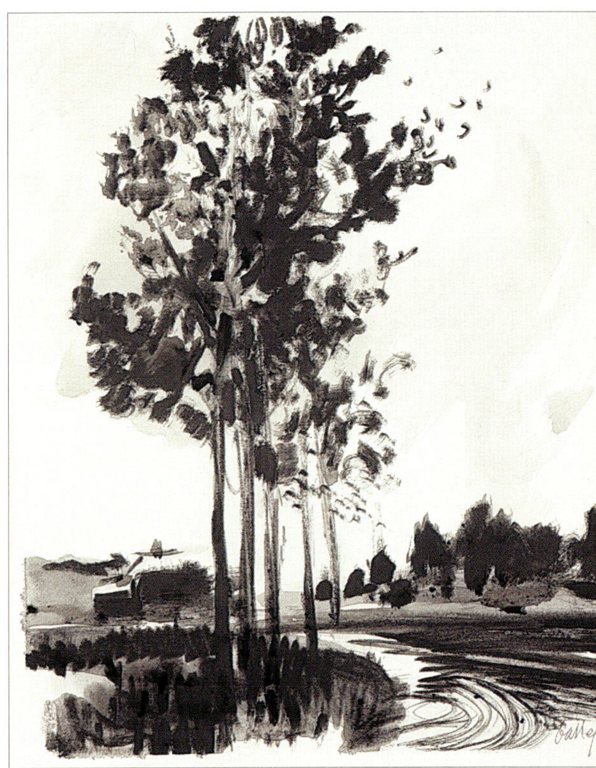

SUMMARY

THE REED PEN AND ITS STROKE
A reed pen correctly wetted and rubbed offers a great variety of drawing strokes.

THE PROCESS
The first strokes must not be too dense. A few soft, gray lines are sufficient.

INTENSIFYING THE TONE AND THE SHADINGS
As the drawing is gradually built up, you can begin to work on the densest darks using the reed pen dipped in the stone or rubbed directly on the paper.

COMBINING THE REED PEN AND BRUSHSTROKES
The brush is a great aid in any ink work because it enables nuances to be added to the wash and soft tones to be created.

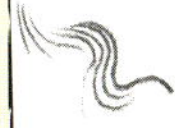

Exercices *Step by step*

Drawing directly with the reed pen is not straightforward. This type of drawings reveal the artist's true abilities because you can go back on no error. We are going to do a standing female figure. Pay attention to how it is constructed initially and take note of how working with the reed pen requires special synthesis skills as the forms have no details.

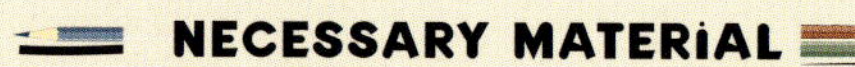

NECESSARY MATERIAL

Chinese ink in stick form, (1)
Black stone to dissolve the ink,(2)
A brush, (3). Paper, (4)

1· THE DRAWING IS STARTED DIRECTLY with the reed pen. The stick is wetted in the stone and rubbed until the ink flows freely. Working patiently you will be able to observe how the tone becomes blacker and more intense. Dip the ink in water to get rid of any excess ink for the first strokes must be grayish. Start with loose, free strokes that gradually combine together to form the figure. A dressed figure is easier to do than a nude because the forms are more synthetic and straighter.

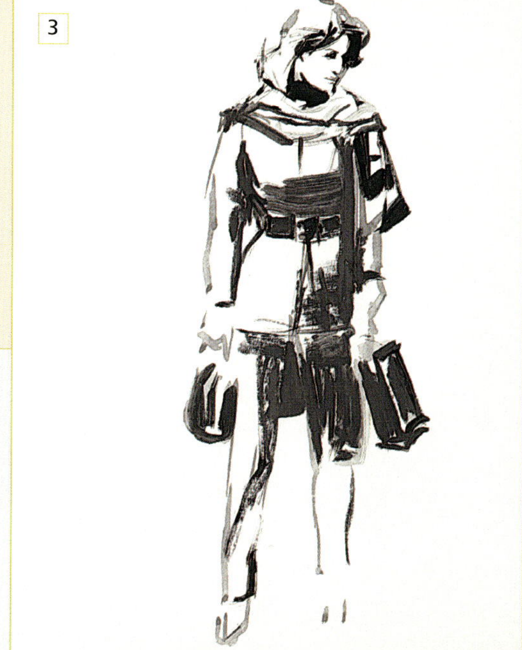

3

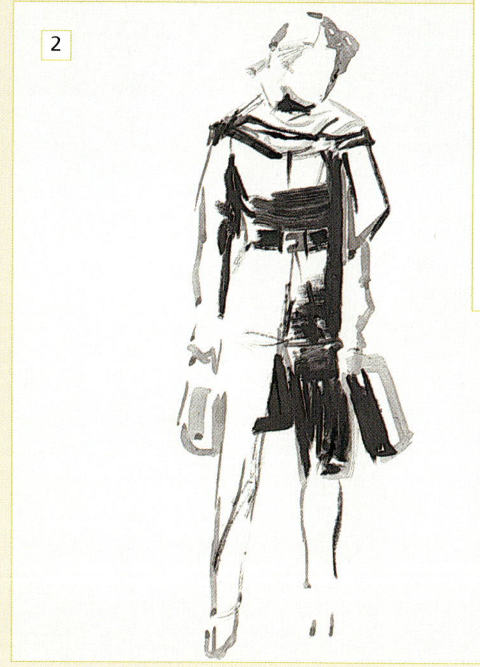

2

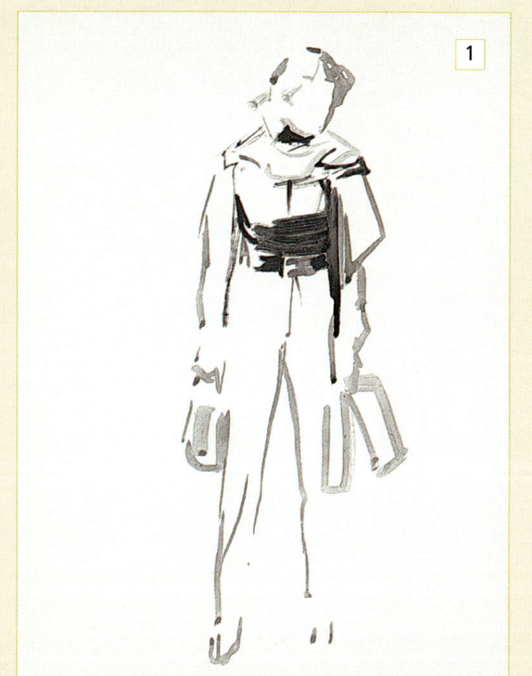

1

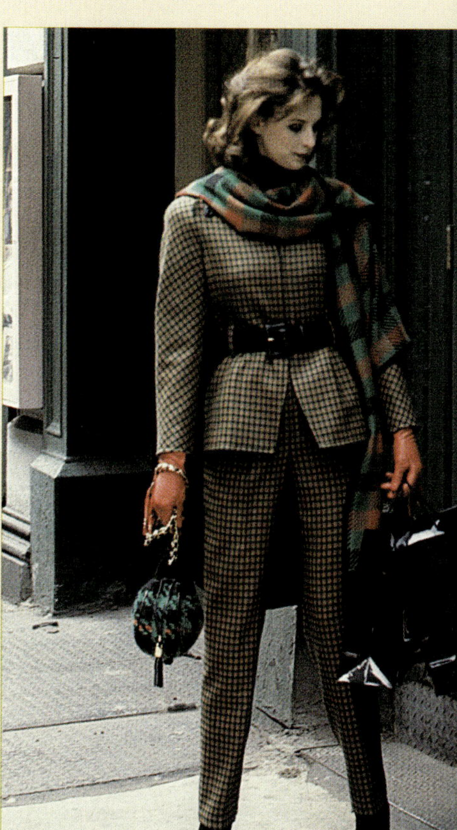

2· ONCE THE ESSENTIAL LINES of the figure have been drawn, you can go over them with a firmer mark. The contrasts are made with a very intense black tone. Do the principal darks of the figure with the flat part of the reed pen; they will be decisive in giving volume. The most illuminated zones will be outlined by these black zones.

Female figure

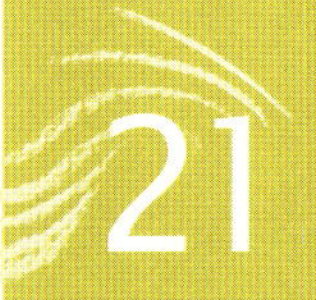

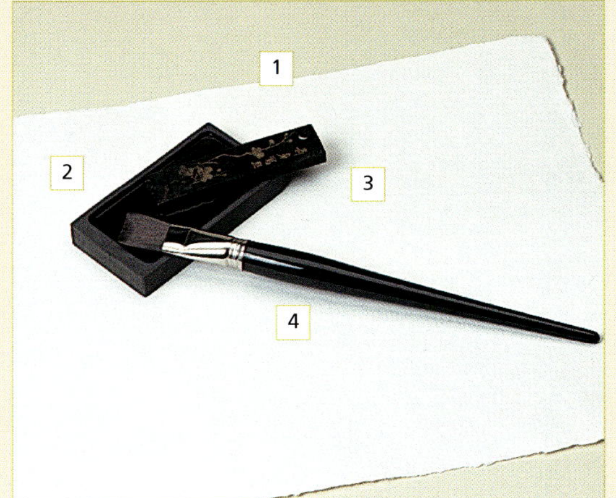

3· IN THIS CLOSE UP YOU CAN APPRECIATE how to do the strokes on the face. The forms have to be as synthetic as possible. Do the work with the edge of the stick, wetted but not dripping. As the ink is hard it produces a delicate stroke, although it is not possible to do too many details.

4· THE NEXT PART OF THE PROCESS is about making the lines of the figure firmer and intensifying the contrasts. The highlights have to remain untouched. Bear in mind that Chinese ink cannot be removed once it is applied: definitive strokes cannot be corrected. Therefore, do approximate strokes and shadings at the beginning and only making definitive strokes when the line is completely decided.

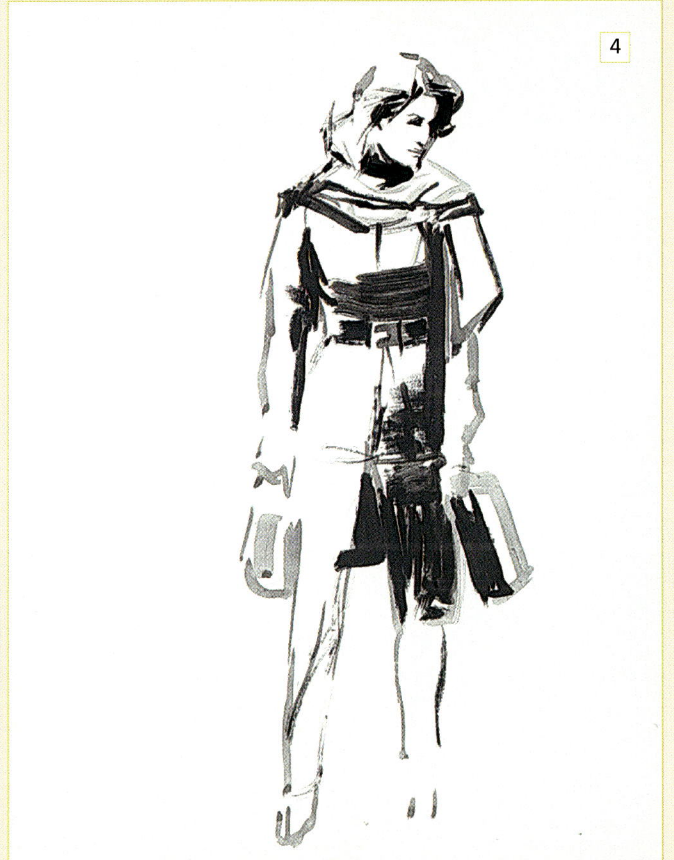

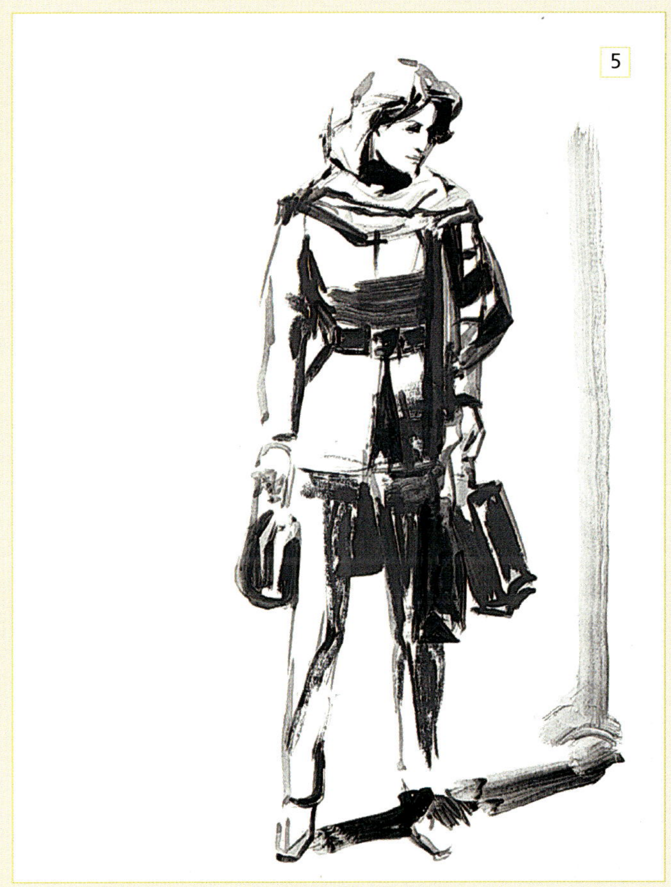

5· THE NEXT PART OF THE WORK PROCESS is done basically with the brush, the first time that this instrument is used. This gray can be obtained by wetting the brush in the ink in the stone. If this tone is too light, rub the ink until it becomes darker. If you need to make the black more transparent, just add water.

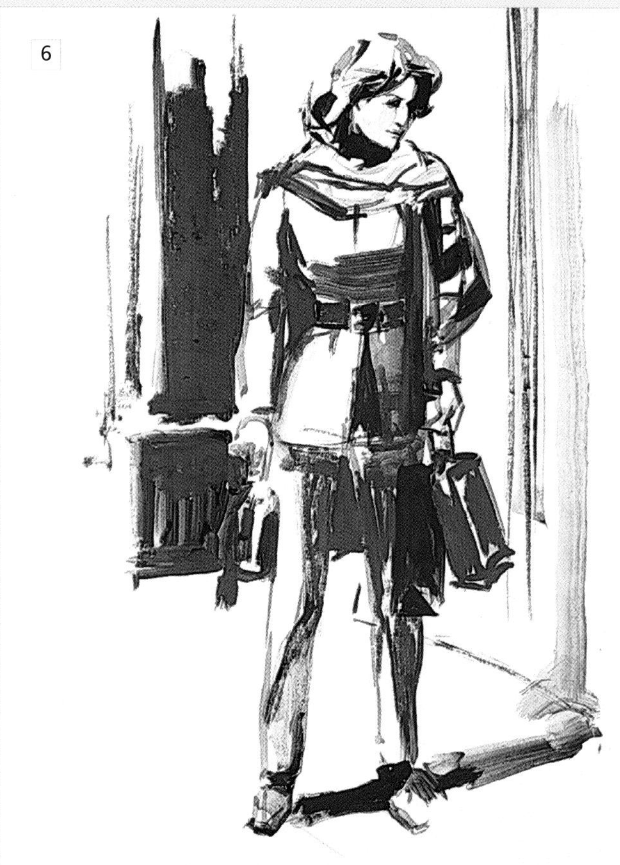
6

6· USE ALL THE WIDTH OF THE WET CHINESE INK stick to do the dark of the column behind the model. The highlights are being left perfectly marked out by the dense form of the pillar. Finally, apply gray shading in the semi-shadow zones of the figure. This gray comes from wetting the brush in water and rubbing part of the ink tone already on the paper.

SUMMARY SCHEME

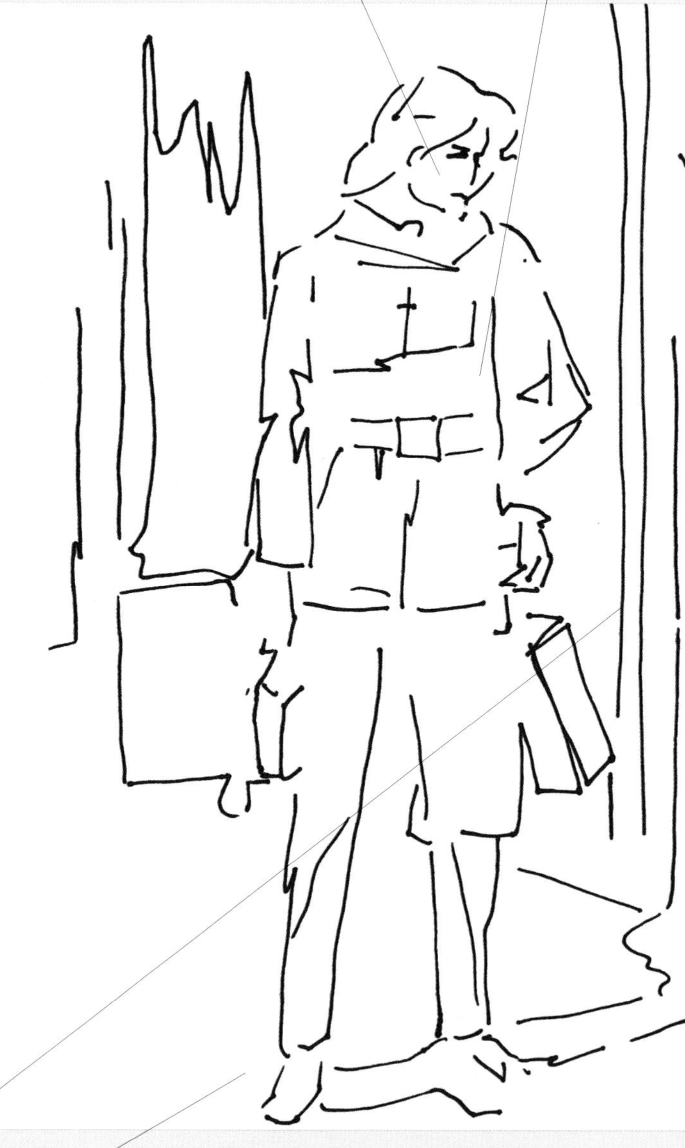

2. The dark parts of the figure are done with the stick flat, outlining the form of the highlights.

3. The features of the face are done with the edge of the stick.

4. Use all the width of the stick for the dark on the column.

1. The first lines are done with a simple stroke, not very black, to outline the form of the image.